CCNP Routing and Switching ROUTE 300-101

Official Cert Guide

Kevin Wallace
CCIE No. 7945

Cisco Press

800 East 96th Street

Indianapolis, IN 46240

CCNP Routing and Switching ROUTE 300-101 Official Cert Guide

Kevin Wallace

Copyright© 2015 Pearson Education, Inc.

Published by:
Cisco Press
800 East 96th Street
Indianapolis, IN 46240 USA

Printed in the United States of America

Second Printing: February 2015

Library of Congress Control Number: 2014951132

ISBN-13: 978-1-58720-559-0
ISBN-10: 1-58720-559-9

Warning and Disclaimer

This book is designed to provide information about the Cisco ROUTE exam (300-101). Every effort has been made to make this book as complete and as accurate as possible, but no warranty or fitness is implied.

The information is provided on an "as is" basis. The authors, Cisco Press, and Cisco Systems, Inc. shall have neither liability nor responsibility to any person or entity with respect to any loss or damages arising from the information contained in this book or from the use of the discs or programs that may accompany it.

The opinions expressed in this book belong to the authors and are not necessarily those of Cisco Systems, Inc.

Trademark Acknowledgments

All terms mentioned in this book that are known to be trademarks or service marks have been appropriately capitalized. Cisco Press or Cisco Systems, Inc., cannot attest to the accuracy of this information. Use of a term in this book should not be regarded as affecting the validity of any trademark or service mark.

Special Sales

For information about buying this title in bulk quantities, or for special sales opportunities (which may include electronic versions; custom cover designs; and content particular to your business, training goals, marketing focus, or branding interests), please contact our corporate sales department at corpsales@pearsoned.com or (800) 382-3419.

For government sales inquiries, please contact governmentsales@pearsoned.com.

For questions about sales outside the U.S., please contact international@pearsoned.com.

Feedback Information

At Cisco Press, our goal is to create in-depth technical books of the highest quality and value. Each book is crafted with care and precision, undergoing rigorous development that involves the unique expertise of members from the professional technical community.

Readers' feedback is a natural continuation of this process. If you have any comments regarding how we could improve the quality of this book, or otherwise alter it to better suit your needs, you can contact us through email at feedback@ciscopress.com. Please make sure to include the book title and ISBN in your message.

We greatly appreciate your assistance.

Publisher: Paul Boger

Associate Publisher: Dave Dusthimer

Business Operation Manager, Cisco Press: Jan Cornelssen

Executive Editor: Brett Bartow

Managing Editor: Sandra Schroeder

Senior Development Editor: Christopher Cleveland

Senior Project Editor: Tonya Simpson

Copy Editor: John Edwards

Technical Editors: Michelle Plumb, Michael J. Shannon

Editorial Assistant: Vanessa Evans

Cover Designer: Mark Shirar

Composition: Bronkella Publishing

Indexer: Tim Wright

Proofreader: Debbie Williams

CISCO

Americas Headquarters	Asia Pacific Headquarters	Europe Headquarters
Cisco Systems, Inc.	Cisco Systems (USA) Pte. Ltd.	Cisco Systems International BV
San Jose, CA	Singapore	Amsterdam, The Netherlands

Cisco has more than 200 offices worldwide. Addresses, phone numbers, and fax numbers are listed on the Cisco Website at www.cisco.com/go/offices.

About the Author

Kevin Wallace, CCIEx2 No. 7945 (Route/Switch and Collaboration), is a Certified Cisco Systems Instructor (CCSI No. 20061) and holds multiple Cisco professional and associate-level certifications in the Route/Switch, Collaboration, Security, Design, and Data Center tracks. With Cisco experience dating back to 1989, Kevin has been a network design specialist for the Walt Disney World Resort, an instructor of Cisco courses for Skillsoft, and a network manager for Eastern Kentucky University.

Currently, Kevin produces video courses and writes books for Cisco Press/Pearson IT Certification (http://kwtrain.com/books). Also, he owns and operates Kevin Wallace Training, LLC (http://kwtrain.com), a provider of self-paced training materials that simplify computer networking. Kevin holds a Bachelor of Science degree in electrical engineering from the University of Kentucky, and he lives in central Kentucky with his wife (Vivian) and two daughters (Sabrina and Stacie).

Kevin can be followed on these social media platforms:

Blog: http://kwtrain.com

Twitter: http://twitter.com/kwallaceccie

Facebook: http://facebook.com/kwallaceccie

YouTube: http://youtube.com/kwallaceccie

LinkedIn: http://linkedin.com/in/kwallaceccie

Google+: http://google.com/+KevinWallace

About the Technical Reviewers

Michelle Plumb is a full-time CCSI (Certified Cisco Systems Instructor) as well as being certified as a Cisco Leading Classroom Virtual Instructor for Skillsoft. Michelle has 25 plus years' experience in the field as an IT professional and telephony specialist. She maintains a high level of Cisco, Microsoft, and CompTIA certifications. Michelle has been a technical reviewer for numerous books related to the Cisco CCNP Routing and Switching, CCNP Voice, and CompTIA course material tracks. She has also written numerous articles around training and implementation of modern technologies. When she is not busy trying out the latest technology gadgets, she spends time at home in Phoenix, Arizona, with her husband and two dogs.

Michael J. Shannon began his career in IT when he transitioned from a studio recording engineer to a network technician for a large telecom in the early 1990s. He soon began to focus on security and was one of the first to attain the Certified HIPAA Security Specialist (CHSS) certification. He has worked as an employee, contractor, and consultant for a number of large companies including Platinum Technologies, MindSharp, IBM, State Farm, Fujitsu, Skillsoft, Pearson PLC, and several others. He has attained the following certifications: CCSI No. 32364, CISSP, CCSP/CCNP Security, ITIL 2011 Intermediate SO/RCV, CWNA, MCSE, Security+, and Network+. He has authored several books and written several articles concerning HealthCare IT Security. He resides with his wife in Corpus Christi, Texas.

Dedication

For the greatest teachers in my life. Career: my role model, Walter Elias Disney. Mentally: authors Zig Ziglar and Anthony Robbins. Spiritually: Pastors Dr. Virgil Grant and Michael Denney. Physically: personal trainers Christopher Poe and Terri Stein (along with all the trainers at Edge Body Boot Camp). Emotionally: the wisest person I know, my best friend and wife, Vivian Wallace.

Acknowledgments

I am very grateful to executive editor Brett Bartow. Over the years, Brett has given me many opportunities to reach people in the Cisco community through books and videos. Also, thanks to the entire team at Cisco Press. Working with each of you is a pleasure.

To my friend Wendell Odom, who made major contributions to this book, thank you for all you've done for the Cisco community. Thanks also go out to technical editors Michelle Plumb and Michael Shannon. I've had the privilege of working with each of you and respect how deeply you care about your students.

What I do would be impossible without support from my wife, Vivian, and my daughters, Stacie and Sabrina. Knowing that you are cheering me on means more to me than you know.

Finally, thanks to Jesus Christ, the source of my strength.

Contents at a Glance

Part VII   Appendixes

CD-Only Appendixes and Glossary

Contents

Icons Used in This Book

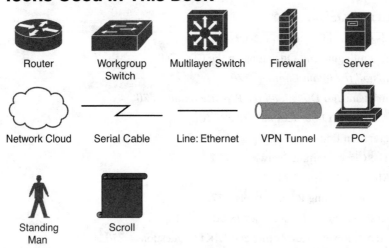

| Router | Workgroup Switch | Multilayer Switch | Firewall | Server |

| Network Cloud | Serial Cable | Line: Ethernet | VPN Tunnel | PC |

| Standing Man | Scroll |

Command Syntax Conventions

The conventions used to present command syntax in this book are the same conventions used in the IOS Command Reference. The Command Reference describes these conventions as follows:

- **Boldface** indicates commands and keywords that are entered literally as shown. In actual configuration examples and output (not general command syntax), boldface indicates commands that are manually input by the user (such as a **show** command).

- *Italics* indicate arguments for which you supply actual values.

- Vertical bars (|) separate alternative, mutually exclusive elements.

- Square brackets ([ ]) indicate an optional element.

- Braces ({ }) indicate a required choice.

- Braces within brackets ([{ }]) indicate a required choice within an optional element.

Introduction

This book focuses on one major goal: to help you prepare to pass the ROUTE exam (300-101). To help you prepare, this book achieves other useful goals as well: It explains a wide range of networking topics, shows how to configure those features on Cisco routers, and explains how to determine whether the feature is working. As a result, you also can use this book as a general reference for IP routing and IP routing protocols. However, the motivation for this book, and the reason it sits within the Cisco Press Official Certification Guide series, is that its primary goal is to help you pass the ROUTE exam.

The rest of this introduction focuses on two topics: the ROUTE exam and a description of this book.

The CCNP ROUTE Exam

Cisco announced the original ROUTE exam (642-902) in January 2010. The term ROUTE does not act as an acronym; instead, the name describes the content of the exam, which focuses on IP routing. Generally, the exam includes detailed coverage of the EIGRP, OSPF, and BGP IP routing protocols; IPv6; and a few other smaller topics related to IP routing.

Cisco first announced its initial professional-level certifications in 1998 with the CCNP Routing and Switching certification. CCNP Routing and Switching certification from its inception has included the same kinds of IP routing topics found in today's ROUTE exam, but the exam names changed over the years. The exam names have tracked the names of the associated Cisco authorized courses for the same topics: *Advanced Cisco Router Configuration (ACRC)* in the early days, followed by *Building Scalable Cisco Internetworks (BSCI)*, and now *ROUTE*, because the current Cisco-authorized course also goes by the name *ROUTE*.

Like its ancestors, the ROUTE exam is a part of the certification requirements for both of the following Cisco certifications:

- Cisco Certified Networking Professional (CCNP)

- Cisco Certified Design Professional (CCDP)

Each of these certifications emphasizes different perspectives on some similar topics. CCNP focuses on the skills needed by a network engineer working for an enterprise— that is, a company that deploys networking gear for its own purposes. CCDP focuses more on design, but good design requires solid knowledge of the technology and con- figuration. So, although this book frequently refers to the most popular certification of these two—CCNP—the ROUTE exam does apply to both certifications.

Contents of the ROUTE Exam

Every student who ever takes an exam wants to know what's on the exam. As with all its exams, Cisco publishes a set of exam topics. These exam topics give general guidance as to what's on the exam.

You can find the exam topics at Cisco.com. The most memorable way to navigate is to go to www.cisco.com/go/ccnp and look for the ROUTE exam. Also, you can go to the Cisco Learning Network website (www.cisco.com/go/learnnetspace)—a less memorable URL but a great Cisco certification site. The Cisco Learning Network site hosts exam information, learning tools, and forums in which you can communicate with others and learn more about this and other Cisco exams.

Interestingly, some of the topics on the ROUTE (300-101) exam are topics that you covered in your CCNA studies (that is, in the CCENT [ICND1] and ICND2 curriculum). Also, several topics on the ROUTE exam are not covered in the Cisco official ROUTE course. A big goal of this book is to make sure that you are prepared for any topic you might encounter on the ROUTE exam. Therefore, in addition to covering topics in the official ROUTE course, this book also covers topics not found in the ROUTE course. Additionally, you might want to review your CCENT (ICND1) and ICND2 materials for exam topics coming from those courses.

Table I-1 lists the topics on the ROUTE exam blueprint, with a reference to the part of this book that covers the topic or a reference to the CCNA course (that is, CCENT [ICND1] or ICND2) that covers the topic.

Table I-1   *ROUTE Exam (300-101) Topics*

Book Part (or CCNA Content)	Exam Topic
Network Principles	
III	Identify Cisco Express Forwarding Concepts
I	Explain General Network Challenges
I	Describe IP Operations
I	Explain TCP Operations
I	Describe UDP Operations
I	Recognize Proposed Changes to a Network
Layer 2 Technologies	
ICND2	WAN Circuit Technologies
ICND2	Explain Frame Relay
Layer 3 Technologies	
CCENT	Identify, Configure, and Verify IPv4 Addressing and Subnetting
III	Identify IPv6 Addressing and Subnetting

Book Part (or CCNA Content)	Exam Topic
CCENT	Configure and Verify Static Routing
II	Configure and Verify Default Routing
I	Evaluate Routing Protocol Types
II	Describe Administrative Distance
II	Troubleshoot Passive Interfaces
III	Configure and Verify VRF-Lite
II	Configure and Verify Filtering with any Routing Protocol
III	Configure and Verify Redistribution Between any Routing Protocol/ Source
II	Configure and Verify Manual and Auto Summarization with any Routing Protocol
III	Configure and Verify Policy-Based Routing
III	Identify Sub-Optimal Routing
III	Explain Route Maps
III	Configure and Verify Loop Prevention Mechanisms
II	Configure and Verify RIPv2
II	Describe RIPng
II	Describe EIGRP Packet Types
II, V	Configure and Verify EIGRP Neighbor Relationship and Authentication
II	Configure and Verify EIGRP Stubs
II	Configure and Verify EIGRP Load-Balancing
II	Describe and Optimize EIGRP Metrics
II	Configure and Verify EIGRP for IPv6
II	Describe OSPF Packet Types
II, V	Configure and Verify OSPF Neighbor Relationships and Authentication
II	Configure and Verify OSPF Network Types, Area Types, and Router Types
II	Configure and Verify OSPF Path Preference
II	Configure and Verify OSPF Operations
II	Configure and Verify OSPF for IPv6 (OSPFv3)

Book Part (or CCNA Content)	Exam Topic
V	Describe, Configure, and Verify BGP Peer Relationships and Authentication
IV	Configure and Verify eBGP
IV	Explain BGP Attributes and Best-Path Selection
Change to VPN Technologies	
I	Configure and Verify GRE
I	Describe DMVPN
I	Describe Easy Virtual Networking (EVN)
Infrastructure Security	
V	Describe Cisco IOS AAA Using Local Database
V	Describe Device Security Using Cisco IOS AAA with TACACS+ and RADIUS
V	Configure and Verify Device Access Control
IV, V	Configure and Verify Router Security Features
Infrastructure Services	
CCENT	Configure and Verify Device Management
ICND2	Configure and Verify SNMP
ICND2	Configure and Verify Logging
V	Configure and Verify Network Time Protocol
CCENT	Configure and Verify IPv4 and IPv6 DHCP
CCENT	Configure and Verify IPv4 Network Address Translation
CCENT	Describe IPv6 Network Address Translation
III	Describe the SLA Architecture
III	Configure and Verify IP SLA
III	Configure and Verify Tracking Objects
ICND2	Configure and Verify NetFlow

Note   Supplemental study materials are available from Cisco Press:

CCNP ROUTE Complete Video Course: http://kwtrain.com/routecourse

CCNA Complete Video Course: http://kwtrain.com/ccnacourse

CCNA Official Certification Library: http://kwtrain.com/ccnabooks

How to Take the ROUTE Exam

As of the publication of this book, Cisco exclusively uses testing vendor Pearson Vue (www.vue.com) for delivery of all Cisco career certification exams. To register, go to www.vue.com, establish a login, and register for the 300-101 ROUTE exam. You also need to choose a testing center near your home.

Who Should Take This Exam and Read This Book

This book has one primary audience, with several secondary audiences. First, this book is intended for anyone wanting to prepare for the ROUTE 300-101 exam. The audience includes self-study readers—people who pass the test by studying 100 percent on their own. It includes Cisco Networking Academy students taking the CCNP curriculum, who use this book to round out their preparation as they get close to the end of the Academy curriculum.

The broader question about the audience might well be why you should take the ROUTE exam. First, the exam is required for the aforementioned CCNP and CCDP certifications from Cisco. These certifications exist at the midpoint of the Cisco certification hierarchy. These certifications have broader and deeper technology requirements as compared to the Cisco Certified Entry Network Technician (CCENT) and Cisco Certified Network Associate (CCNA) certifications.

The real question then about the audience for this book—at least the intended audience—is whether you have motivation to get one of these professional-level Cisco certifications. CCNP in particular happens to be a popular, well-respected certification. Also, CCDP has been a solid certification for a long time, particularly for engineers who spend a lot of time designing networks with customers, rather than troubleshooting.

Format of the CCNP ROUTE Exam

The ROUTE exam follows the same general format as the other Cisco exams. When you get to the testing center and check in, the proctor will give you some general instructions and then take you into a quiet room with a PC. When you're at the PC, you have a few things to do before the timer starts on your exam. For example, you can take a sample quiz, just to get accustomed to the PC and to the testing engine. Anyone who has user-level skills in getting around a PC should have no problems with the testing environment.

When you start the exam, you will be asked a series of questions. You answer the question and then move on to the next question. The exam engine does not let you go back and change your answer.

The exam questions can be in any of the following formats:

- Multiple-choice (MC)

- Testlet

- Drag-and-drop (DND)

- Simulated lab (Sim)

- Simlet

The first three types of questions are relatively common in many testing environments. The multiple-choice format simply requires that you point and click on a circle (that is, a *radio button*) beside the correct answer for a single-answer question or on squares (that is, *check boxes*) beside the correct answers for a multi-answer question. Cisco traditionally tells you how many answers you need to choose, and the testing software prevents you from choosing too many answers. *Testlets* are questions with one general scenario, with a collection of multiple-choice questions about the overall scenario. Drag-and-drop questions require you to left-click and hold a mouse button, move an object (for example, a text box) to another area on the screen, and release the mouse button to place the object somewhere else—typically into a list. For some questions, as an example, to get the question correct, you might need to put a list of five things into the proper order.

The last two types both use a network simulator to ask questions. Interestingly, the two types actually allow Cisco to assess two very different skills. First, *sim* questions generally describe a problem, and your task is to configure one or more routers and/or switches to fix the problem. The exam then grades the question based on the configuration that you changed or added. The *simlet* questions might well be the most difficult style of question on the exams. Simlet questions also use a network simulator, but instead of answering the question by changing the configuration, the question includes one or more MC questions. The questions require that you use the simulator to examine the current behavior of a network, interpreting the output of any **show** commands that you can remember to answer the question. Although sim questions require you to troubleshoot problems related to a configuration, simlets require you to both analyze working networks and networks with problems, correlating **show** command output with your knowledge of networking theory and configuration commands.

The Cisco Learning Network website (http://learningnetwork.cisco.com) has tools that let you experience the environment and see how each of these question types works. The environment should be the same as when you passed CCNA (a prerequisite for CCNP and CCDP).

CCNP ROUTE 300-101 Official Cert Guide

This section lists a general description of the contents of this book. The description includes an overview of each chapter and a list of book features seen throughout the book.

Book Features and Exam Preparation Methods

This book uses several key methodologies to help you discover the exam topics on which you need more review, to help you fully understand and remember those details, and to help you prove to yourself that you have retained your knowledge of those topics. Therefore, this book does not try to help you pass the exams only by memorization but by truly learning and understanding the topics.

The book includes many features that provide different ways to study and be ready for the exam. If you understand a topic when you read it, but do not study it any further, you will probably not be ready to pass the exam with confidence. The features included in this book give you tools that help you determine what you know, review what you know, better learn what you don't know, and be well prepared for the exam. These tools include

- **"Do I Know This Already?" Quizzes:** Each chapter begins with a quiz that helps you determine the amount of time that you need to spend studying that chapter.

- **Foundation Topics:** These are the core sections of each chapter. They explain the protocols, concepts, and configurations for the topics in that chapter.

- **Exam Preparation Tasks:** The "Exam Preparation Tasks" section lists a series of study activities that should be done after reading the "Foundation Topics" section. Each chapter includes the activities that make the most sense for studying the topics in that chapter. The activities include

  - **Planning Tables:** The ROUTE exam topics include some perspectives on how an engineer plans for various tasks. The idea is that the CCNP-level engineer in particular takes the design from another engineer, plans the implementation, and plans the verification steps—handing off the actual tasks to engineers working during change-window hours. Because the engineer plans the tasks, but might not be at the keyboard when implementing a feature, that engineer must master the configuration and verification commands so that the planned commands work for the engineer making the changes off-shift. The planning tables at the end of the chapter give you the chance to take the details in the Foundation Topics core of the chapter and think about them as if you were writing the planning documents.

  - **Key Topics Review:** The Key Topic icon is shown next to the most important items in the "Foundation Topics" section of the chapter. The Key Topics Review activity lists the key topics from the chapter and the page number where each key topic can be found. Although the contents of the entire chapter could be on the exam, you should definitely know the information listed in each key topic. Review these topics carefully.

  - **Memory Tables:** To help you exercise your memory and memorize some lists of facts, many of the more important lists and tables from the chapter are included in a document on the CD. This document lists only partial information, allowing you to complete the table or list. CD-only Appendix D holds the incomplete tables, and Appendix E includes the completed tables from which you can check your work.

  - **Definition of Key Terms:** Although Cisco exams might be unlikely to ask a question such as "Define this term," the ROUTE exam requires that you learn and know a lot of networking terminology. This section lists some of the most important terms from the chapter, asking you to write a short definition and compare your answer to the Glossary on the enclosed CD.

■ **CD-Based Practice Exam:** The companion CD contains an exam engine, including access to a bank of multiple-choice questions. Chapter 18 gives two suggestions on how to use these questions: either as study questions or to simulate the ROUTE exam.

■ **Companion Website:** The website http://kwtrain.com/routebook posts up-to-the-minute materials that further clarify complex exam topics. Check this site regularly for new and updated postings written by the author that provide further insight into the more troublesome topics on the exam.

Book Organization

This book contains 18 chapters, plus appendixes. The topics all focus in some way on IP routing and IP routing protocols, making the topics somewhat focused, but with deep coverage on those topics.

The book organizes the topics into six major parts. The following list outlines the major part organization of this book:

■ **Part I: "Fundamental Routing Concepts":** This part includes two chapters that focus on routing fundamentals within an enterprise network (including connections to remote offices):

   ■ **Chapter 1: "Characteristics of Routing Protocols":** This introductory chapter is theory based and contains minimal Cisco IOS configuration. Specifically, the chapter reviews routing protocol characteristics. The last section of the chapter then introduces a newer routing technology, the ability to run multiple virtual routers inside a single physical router.

   ■ **Chapter 2: "Remote Site Connectivity":** This chapter discusses how Virtual Private Networks (VPN) can be used to connect an enterprise headquarters to remote sites. While a variety of VPN technologies are discussed, the Cisco IOS configuration presented focuses on setting up a GRE tunnel.

■ **Part II: "IGP Routing Protocols":** Because current versions of RIP, EIGRP, and OSPF support IPv6 routing (in addition to IPv4), this seven-chapter part begins with a review of IPv6 addressing and a look at RIPng configuration. Then, this part covers EIGRP and OSPF theory and configuration in detail:

   ■ **Chapter 3: "IPv6 Review and RIPng":** The new version of the ROUTE curriculum dramatically increases the focus on routing IPv6 networks. Therefore, this chapter begins with a CCNA-level review of IPv6 addressing. Then, this chapter shows how to configure RIPng, which supports IPv6 routing (after contrasting RIPng with RIPv2).

   ■ **Chapter 4: "Fundamental EIGRP Concepts":** This chapter reviews the basics of EIGRP, including EIGRP path selection and neighbor formation.

   ■ **Chapter 5: "Advanced EIGRP Concepts":** This chapter discusses the details of how EIGRP builds its topology table, how those EIGRP-learned routes become candidates to be injected into a router's IP routing table, and options for optimizing EIGRP convergence. Then, the chapter explores EIGRP route filtering, route summarization, and the use of default routes with EIGRP.

- **Chapter 6: "EIGRP for IPv6 and Named EIGRP"**: This chapter begins by contrasting EIGRP for IPv4 and EIGRP for IPv6. Then, a hierarchical EIGRP configuration approach, called *Named EIGRP*, is demonstrated.

- **Chapter 7: "Fundamental OSPF Concepts"**: This chapter reviews the basics of OSPF, including configuration, verification, and neighbor formation. The chapter then concludes with a look at virtual links.

- **Chapter 8: "The OSPF Link-State Database"**: This chapter explains the various LSA types that OSPF uses to construct a link-state database. The process involved in exchanging link-state database routers with neighboring routers is also discussed.

- **Chapter 9: "Advanced OSPF Concepts"**: This chapter discusses OSPF route filtering, route summarization, sourcing default route information, and special area types. Then, the chapter concludes with an examination of OSPFv3 and describes how it can be used to route IPv6 networks.

- **Part III: "Route Redistribution and Selection"**: Because many enterprise networks need to simultaneously support multiple IGPs, this part begins by explaining how IGPs can coexist and be redistributed into one another. Then, the discussion delves into how a Cisco router makes its packet-switching decisions and how those decisions can be altered using the Policy-Based Routing (PBR) and IP Service-Level Agreement (IP SLA) features:

  - **Chapter 10: "Route Redistribution"**: This chapter offers an extensive look into route redistribution. Specifically, the chapter begins by explaining route redistribution basics, followed by configuring route redistribution into EIGRP, route redistribution into OSPF, and tuning route redistribution using route maps and distribute lists. Finally, this chapter discusses IPv6 IGP route redistribution.

  - **Chapter 11: "Route Selection"**: This chapter begins with a comparison of packet-switching technologies supported by Cisco IOS routers, with a focus on Cisco Express Forwarding (CEF). Then, this chapter discusses how a router's route selection can be influenced with the use of the Cisco Policy-Based Routing (PBR) and IP Service-Level Agreement (IP SLA) features. Finally, this chapter concludes by examining a basic configuration of VRF-Lite, which can allow a single physical router to run multiple virtual router instances.

- **Part IV: "Internet Connectivity"**: When an enterprise network connects to the Internet, it might do so through a single connection and a default static route. Such a connection often uses Network Address Translation (NAT). However, with multiple Internet connections, the enterprise network might need to run Border Gateway Protocol (BGP). This part of the book examines both approaches to Internet connectivity (along with a discussion of NAT), including how BGP can connect to the Internet through IPv6:

  - **Chapter 12: "Fundamentals of Internet Connectivity"**: This chapter discusses how a network could connect to the Internet using a single connection, using either a statically assigned or a dynamically learned address.

Additionally, this chapter contrasts various approaches to NAT configuration, including a new approach, called *NAT Virtual Interface (NVI)*.

- **Chapter 13: "Fundamental BGP Concepts":** This chapter begins with an overview of Internet routing and addressing, followed by an introduction to BGP. Single-homed and multi-homed Internet connections are contrasted. Then, this chapter discusses a variety of *external BGP (eBGP)* configuration options.

- **Chapter 14: "Advanced BGP Concepts":** While BGP is primarily considered to be an exterior gateway protocol (EGP), *internal BGP (iBGP)* can be used within an autonomous system. This chapter examines the operation, configuration, and verification of iBGP. Then, this chapter discusses approaches for avoiding BGP routing loops, how to filter BGP routes, how BGP makes its route selection decisions, and how to administratively influence those decisions.

- **Chapter 15: "IPv6 Internet Connectivity":** As support for IPv6 continues to grow, enterprise networks have an increasing need to connect to their Internet Service Provider(s) through IPv6. This chapter discusses how an ISP could assign an IPv6 address to a customer router, and how that customer router could use a static, default IPv6 route to point to its ISP. Additionally, this chapter introduces *Multiprotocol BGP (MP-BGP)*, which adds a collection of extensions to BGP version 4 and supports IPv6.

- **Part V: "Router and Routing Security":** Although Cisco has an entire CCNP Security track, the ROUTE curriculum, and this part of the book, does cover general strategies for better securing a Cisco router and authenticating routing protocols used between routers:

  - **Chapter 16: "Fundamental Router Security Concepts":** This chapter introduces the concept of a router security policy, covers time-based ACLs, and offers tips for securing a router's management plane.

  - **Chapter 17: "Routing Protocol Authentication":** This chapter compares various router authentication methods, and then focuses on how to authenticate specific routing protocols, including EIGRP, OSPF, and BGP.

- **Part VI: "Final Preparation":** This part concludes the book with recommendations for exam preparation.

  - **Chapter 18: "Final Preparation":** This nontechnical chapter identifies and explains how to use various exam preparation tools, followed by a step-by-step strategy for using this book to prepare for the ROUTE exam.

In addition to the core chapters of the book, the book has several appendixes. Some appendixes exist in the printed book, whereas others exist in soft-copy form on the CD included with the book.

Appendixes printed in the book include

- **Appendix A, "Answers to the 'Do I Know This Already?' Quizzes"**: Includes the answers to all the questions from Chapters 1 through 17.

- **Appendix B, "ROUTE Exam Updates"**: Covers a variety of short topics that either clarify or expand upon topics covered earlier in the book. This appendix is updated from time to time, and posted at http://kwtrain.com/routebook, with the most recent version available at the time of printing included here as Appendix B. (The first page of the appendix includes instructions on how to check to see whether a later version of Appendix B is available online.)

- **Appendix C, "Conversion Tables"**: Lists a decimal-to-binary conversion table, decimal values 0 through 255, along with the binary equivalents. It also lists a hex-to-decimal conversion table.

The appendixes included on the CD-ROM are

- **Appendix D, "Memory Tables"**: This appendix holds the key tables and lists from each chapter with some of the content removed. You can print this appendix, and as a memory exercise, complete the tables and lists. The goal is to help you memorize facts that can be useful on the exam.

- **Appendix E, "Memory Tables Answer Key"**: This appendix contains the answer key for the exercises in Appendix D.

- **Appendix F, "Completed Planning Practice Tables"**: The ends of Chapters 1 through 17 list planning tables that you can complete to help learn the content more deeply. If you use these tables, refer to this appendix for the suggested answers.

- **Appendix G, "Study Planner"**: A spreadsheet with major study milestones, where you can track your progress through your study.

- **Glossary**: The glossary contains definitions for all the terms listed in the "Define Key Terms" sections at the conclusions of Chapters 1 through 17.

For More Information

If you have any comments about the book, you can submit those through www.ciscopress.com. Just go to the website, select Contact Us, and type in your message.

Cisco might make changes that affect the ROUTE exam from time to time. You should always check www.cisco.com/go/ccnp for the latest details.

This chapter covers the following subjects:

- **Routing Protocol Fundamentals:** This section offers an overview of the role that routing plays in an enterprise network and contrasts various types of routing protocols.

- **Network Technology Fundamentals:** This section distinguishes between different types of network traffic flows and network architectures.

- **TCP/IP Fundamentals:** This section reviews the fundamental characteristics of IP, ICMP, TCP, and UDP.

- **Network Migration Strategies:** This section offers a collection of design considerations for making changes to a network.

CHAPTER 1

Characteristics of Routing Protocols

One of the most fundamental technologies in network is *routing*. Routing, at its essence, is concerned with forwarding packets from their source on one subnet to their destination on another subnet. Of course, a multitude of options and protocols are available for making this happen. In fact, routing is the theme of this entire book, the focus of Cisco's ROUTE course, and the accompanying ROUTE exam (300-101).

This chapter launches the discussion of routing by providing a conceptual introduction. Specifically, this chapter begins with a discussion of routing protocol fundamentals, followed by the basics of network technology and the TCP/IP suite of protocols.

The chapter then concludes with a design discussion revolving around how to accommodate the inevitable changes your network will undergo. For example, you will be given a collection of strategies for changing routing protocols in your network or migrating from IPv4 to IPv6.

"Do I Know This Already?" Quiz

The "Do I Know This Already?" quiz allows you to assess whether you should read the entire chapter. If you miss no more than one of these eight self-assessment questions, you might want to move ahead to the "Exam Preparation Tasks" section. Table 1-1 lists the major headings in this chapter and the "Do I Know This Already?" quiz questions covering the material in those headings so that you can assess your knowledge of these specific areas. The answers to the "Do I Know This Already?" quiz appear in Appendix A.

Table 1-1 *"Do I Know This Already?" Foundation Topics Section-to-Question Mapping*

Foundation Topics Section	Questions
Routing Protocol Fundamentals	1, 2
Network Technology Fundamentals	3, 4
TCP/IP Fundamentals	5, 6
Network Migration Strategies	7, 8

1. Which of the following features prevents a route learned on one interface from being advertised back out of that interface?

   a. Poison Reverse

   b. Summarization

   c. Split Horizon

   d. Convergence

2. Identify the distance-vector routing protocols from the following. (Choose the two best answers.)

   a. IS-IS

   b. EIGRP

   c. RIP

   d. OSPF

   e. BGP

3. Select the type of network communication flow that is best described as "one-to-nearest."

   a. Unicast

   b. Multicast

   c. Broadcast

   d. Anycast

4. An NBMA network has which of the following design issues? (Choose the two best answers.)

   a. Split Horizon issues

   b. Bandwidth issues

   c. Quality of service issues

   d. Designated router issues

5. Which of the following best defines TCP MSS?

   a. The total data in a TCP segment, including only the TCP header

   b. The total data in a TCP segment, not including any headers

   c. The total data in a TCP segment, including only the IP and TCP headers

   d. The total data in a TCP segment, including the Layer 2, IP, and TCP headers

6. A network segment has a bandwidth of 10 Mbps, and packets experience an end-to-end latency of 100 ms. What is the bandwidth-delay product of the network segment?

   a. 100,000,000 bits

   b. 10,000,000 bits

   c. 1,000,000 bits

   d. 100,000 bits

7. When migrating from a PVST+ to Rapid-PVST+, which PVST+ features can be disabled, because similar features are built into Rapid-PVST+? (Choose the two best answers.)

   a. UplinkFast

   b. Loop Guard

   c. BackboneFast

   d. PortFast

8. Cisco EVN uses what type of trunk to carry traffic for all virtual networks between two physical routers?

   a. VNET

   b. ISL

   c. dot1Q

   d. 802.10

Foundation Topics

Routing Protocol Fundamentals

Routing occurs when a router or some other Layer 3 device (for example, a multilayer switch) makes a forwarding decision based on network address information (that is, Layer 3 information). A fundamental question, however, addressed throughout this book, is from where does the routing information originate?

A router could know how to reach a network by simply having one of its interfaces directly connect that network. Perhaps you statically configured a route, telling a router exactly how to reach a certain destination network. However, for large enterprises, the use of static routes does not scale well. Therefore, dynamic routing protocols are typically seen in larger networks (and many small networks, too). A dynamic routing protocol allows routers configured for that protocol to exchange route information and update that information based on changing network conditions.

The first topic in this section explores the role of routing in an enterprise network. Then some of the characteristics of routing protocols are presented, to help you decide which routing protocol to use in a specific environment and to help you better understand the nature of routing protocols you find already deployed in a network.

The Role of Routing in an Enterprise Network

An enterprise network typically interconnects multiple buildings, has connectivity to one or more remote offices, and has one or more connections to the Internet. Figure 1-1 identifies some of the architectural layers often found in an enterprise network design:

- **Building Access:** This layer is part of the Campus network and is used to provide user access to the network. Security (especially authentication) is important at this layer, to verify that a user should have access to the network. Layer 2 switching is typically used at this layer, in conjunction with VLANs.

- **Building Distribution:** This layer is part of the Campus network that aggregates building access switches. Multilayer switches are often used here.

- **Campus Backbone:** This layer is part of the Campus network and is concerned with the high-speed transfer of data through the network. High-end multilayer switches are often used here.

- **Edge Distribution:** This layer is part of the Campus network and serves as the ingress and egress point for all traffic into and out of the Campus network. Routers or multilayer switches are appropriate devices for this layer.

- **Internet Gateways:** This layer contains routers that connect the Campus network out to the Internet. Some enterprise networks have a single connection out to the Internet, while others have multiple connections out to one or more Internet Service Providers (ISP).

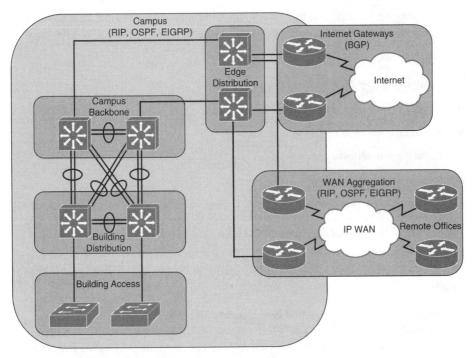

Figure 1-1 *Typical Components of an Enterprise Network*

■ **WAN Aggregation:** This layer contains routers that connect the Campus network out to remote offices. Enterprises use a variety of WAN technologies to connect to remote offices (for example, Multiprotocol Label Switching [MPLS]).

Routing protocols used within the Campus network and within the WAN aggregation layer are often versions of Routing Information Protocol (RIP), Open Shortest Path First (OSPF), or Enhanced Interior Gateway Routing Protocol (EIGRP). However, when connecting out to the Internet, Border Gateway Protocol (BGP) is usually the protocol of choice for enterprises having more than one Internet connection.

An emerging industry trend is to connect a campus to a remote office over the Internet, as opposed to using a traditional WAN technology. Of course, the Internet is considered an untrusted network, and traffic might need to traverse multiple routers on its way from the campus to a remote office. However, a technology called *Virtual Private Networks (VPN)* allows a logical connection to be securely set up across an Internet connection. Chapter 2, "Remote Site Connectivity," examines VPNs in more detail.

Routing Protocol Selection

As you read through this book, you will learn about the RIPv2, RIPng, OSPFv2, OSPFv3, EIGRP, BGP, and MP-BGP routing protocols. With all of these choices (and even more) available, a fundamental network design consideration becomes which routing protocol to use in your network. As you learn more about these routing protocols, keeping the following characteristics in mind can help you do a side-by-side comparison of protocols:

- Scalability

- Vendor interoperability

- IT staff's familiarity with protocol

- Speed of convergence

- Capability to perform summarization

- Interior or exterior routing

- Type of routing protocol

This section of the chapter concludes by taking a closer look at each of these characteristics.

Scalability

How large is your network now, and how large is it likely to become? The answers to those questions can help determine which routing protocols not to use in your network. For example, while you could use statically configured routes in a network with just a couple of routers, such a routing solution does not scale well to dozens of routers.

While all the previously mentioned dynamic routing protocols are capable of supporting most medium-sized enterprise networks, you should be aware of any limitations. For example, all versions of RIP have a maximum *hop count* (that is, the maximum number of routers across which routing information can be exchanged) of 15 routers. BGP, on the other hand, is massively scalable. In fact, BGP is the primary routing protocol used on the Internet.

Vendor Interoperability

Will you be using all Cisco routers in your network, or will your Cisco routers need to interoperate with non-Cisco routers? A few years ago, the answer to this question could be a deal-breaker for using EIGRP, because EIGRP was a Cisco-proprietary routing protocol.

However, in early 2013, Cisco announced that it was releasing EIGRP to the *Internet Engineering Task Force (IETF)* standards body as an Informational RFC. As a result, any networking hardware vendor can use EIGRP on its hardware. If you are working in an environment with routers from multiple vendors, you should ensure that your Cisco router has an appropriate Cisco IOS feature set to support your desired routing protocol and that the third-party router(s) also support that routing protocol.

IT Staff's Familiarity with Protocol

You and the IT staff at your company (or your customer's company) might be much more familiar with one routing protocol than another. Choosing the routing protocol with which the IT staff is more familiar could reduce downtime (because of faster resolutions to troubleshooting issues). Also, if the IT staff is more familiar with the inner workings of one routing protocol, they would be more likely to take advantage of the protocol's non-trivial features and tune the protocol's parameters for better performance.

Speed of Convergence

A benefit of dynamic routing protocols over statically configured routes is the ability of a dynamic routing protocol to reroute around a network failure. For example, consider Figure 1-2. Router R1's routing protocol might have selected the path through Router R3 as the best route to reach the 192.168.1.0 /24 network connected to Router R4. However, imagine that a link failure occurred on the Fast Ethernet link between Routers R3 and R4. Router R1's routing protocol should be able to reroute around the link failure by sending packets destined for the 192.168.1.0 /24 network through Router R2.

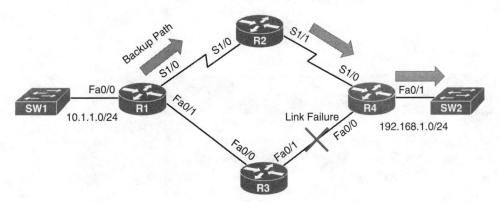

Figure 1-2   *Routing Protocol Convergence*

After this failover occurs, and the network reaches a steady-state condition (that is, the routing protocol is aware of current network conditions and forwards traffic based on those conditions), the network is said to be a *converged network*. The amount of time for the failover to occur is called the *convergence time*.

Some routing protocols have faster convergence times than others. RIP and BGP, for example, might take a few minutes to converge, depending on the network topology. By contrast, OSPF and EIGRP can converge in just a few seconds.

Capability to Perform Summarization

Large enterprise networks can have routing tables with many route entries. The more entries a router maintains in its routing table, the more router CPU resources are required to calculate the best path to a destination network. Fortunately, many routing protocols support the ability to do network summarization, although the summarization options and how summarization is performed do differ.

Network summarization allows multiple routes to be summarized in a single route advertisement. Not only does summarization reduce the number of entries in a router's routing table, but it also reduces the number of network advertisements that need to be sent.

Figure 1-3 shows an example of route summarization. Specifically, Router R1 is summarizing the 10.0.0.0 /24, 10.0.1.0 /24, 10.0.2.0 /24, and 10.0.3.0 /24 networks into a single network advertisement of 10.0.0.0 /22. Notice that the first two octets (and therefore the first 16 bits) of all the networks are the same. Also, as shown in the figure, the first 6 bits in the third octet are the same for all the networks. Therefore, all the networks have the first 22 bits (that is, 16 bits in the first two octets plus 6 bits in the third octet) in common. By using those 22 bits and setting the remaining bits to 0s, you find the network address, 10.0.0.0 /22.

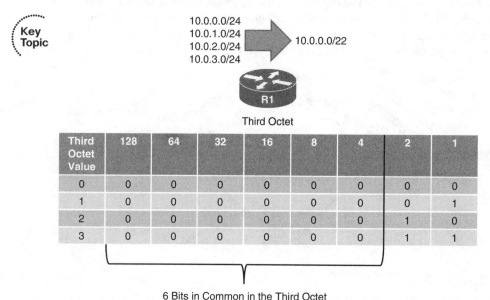

Figure 1-3 *Network Summarization*

Interior or Exterior Routing

An *autonomous system (AS)* is a network under a single administrative control. Your company's network, as an example, might be in a single AS. When your company connects out to two different ISPs, they are each in their own AS. Figure 1-4 shows such a topology.

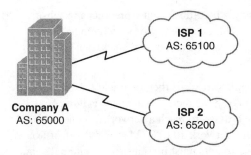

Figure 1-4 *Interconnection of Autonomous Systems*

In Figure 1-4, Company A is represented with an AS number of 65000. ISP 1 is using an AS number of 65100, and ISP 2 has an AS number of 65200.

When selecting a routing protocol, you need to determine where the protocol will run. Will it run within an autonomous system or between autonomous systems? The answer to that question determines whether you need an *interior gateway protocol (IGP)* or an *exterior gateway protocol (EGP)*:

Key Topic

- **IGP:** An IGP exchanges routes between routers in a single AS. Common IGPs include OSPF and EIGRP. Although less popular, RIP and IS-IS are also considered IGPs. Also, be aware that BGP is used as an EGP; however, you can use interior BGP (iBGP) within an AS.

- **EGP:** Today, the only EGP in use is BGP. However, from a historical perspective, be aware that there was once another EGP, which was actually named Exterior Gateway Protocol (EGP).

Routing Protocol Categories

Another way to categorize a routing protocol is based on how it receives, advertises, and stores routing information. The three fundamental approaches are distance-vector, link-state, and path-vector.

Distance-Vector

A distance-vector routing protocol sends a full copy of its routing table to its directly attached neighbors. This is a periodic advertisement, meaning that even if there have been no topological changes, a distance-vector routing protocol will, at regular intervals, re-advertise its full routing table to its neighbors.

Obviously, this periodic advertisement of redundant information is inefficient. Ideally, you want a full exchange of route information to occur only once and subsequent updates to be triggered by topological changes.

Another drawback to distance-vector routing protocols is the time they take to converge, which is the time required for all routers to update their routing table in response to a topological change in a network. Hold-down timers can speed the convergence process.

After a router makes a change to a route entry, a hold-down timer prevents any subsequent updates for a specified period of time. This approach helps stop flapping routes (which are routes that oscillate between being available and unavailable) from preventing convergence.

Yet another issue with distance-vector routing protocols is the potential of a routing loop. To illustrate, consider Figure 1-5. In this topology, the metric being used is *hop count*, which is the number of routers that must be crossed to reach a network. As one example, Router R3's routing table has a route entry for network 10.1.1.0 /24 available off of Router R1. For Router R3 to reach that network, two routers must be transited (Routers R2 and R1). As a result, network 10.1.1.0 /24 appears in Router R3's routing table with a metric (hop count) of 2.

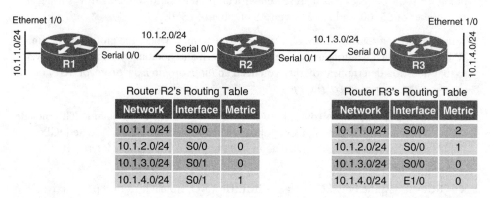

Figure 1-5   *Routing Loop: Before Link Failure*

Continuing with the example, imagine that interface Ethernet 1/0 on Router R3 goes down. As shown in Figure 1-6, Router R3 loses its directly connected route (with a metric of 0) to network 10.1.4.0 /24; however, Router R2 had a route to 10.1.4.0 /24 in its routing table (with a metric of 1), and this route was advertised to Router R3. Router R3 adds this entry for 10.1.4.0 to its routing table and increments the metric by 1.

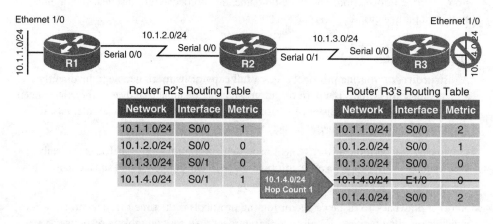

Figure 1-6   *Routing Loop: After Link Failure*

The problem with this scenario is that the 10.1.4.0 /24 entry in Router R2's routing table was because of an advertisement that Router R2 received from Router R3. Now, Router R3 is relying on that route, which is no longer valid. The routing loop continues as Router R3 advertises its newly learned route of 10.1.4.0 /24 with a metric of 2 to its neighbor, Router R2. Because Router R2 originally learned the 10.1.4.0 /24 network from Router R3, when it sees Router R3 advertising that same route with a metric of 2, the network gets updated in Router R2's routing table to have a metric of 3, as shown in Figure 1-7.

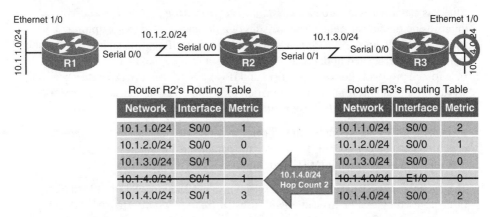

Figure 1-7 *Routing Loop: Routers R2 and R3 Incrementing the Metric for 10.1.4.0 /24*

The metric for the 10.1.4.0 /24 network continues to increment in the routing tables for both Routers R2 and R3, until the metric reaches a value considered to be an unreachable value (for example, 16 in the case of RIP). This process is referred to as a *routing loop*.

Distance-vector routing protocols typically use one of two approaches for preventing routing loops:

Key Topic

- **Split Horizon:** The Split Horizon feature prevents a route learned on one interface from being advertised back out of that same interface.

- **Poison Reverse:** The Poison Reverse feature causes a route received on one interface to be advertised back out of that same interface with a metric considered to be infinite.

Having either approach applied to the previous example would have prevented Router R3 from adding the 10.1.4.0 /24 network into its routing table based on an advertisement from Router R2.

Routing protocols falling under the distance-vector category include

- **Routing Information Protocol (RIP):** A distance-vector routing protocol that uses a metric of hop count. The maximum number of hops between two routers in an RIP-based network is 15. Therefore, a hop count of 16 is considered to be infinite. Also, RIP is an IGP. Three primary versions of RIP exist. RIPv1 periodically broadcasts its entire IP routing table, and it supports only fixed-length subnet masks. RIPv2 supports variable-length subnet masks, and it uses multicasts (to a multicast address of

224.0.0.9) to advertise its IP routing table, as opposed to broadcasts. RIP next generation (RIPng) supports the routing of IPv6 networks, while RIPv1 and RIPv2 support the routing of IPv4 networks.

■ **Enhanced Interior Gateway Routing Protocol (EIGRP):** A Cisco-proprietary protocol until early 2013, EIGRP has been popular in Cisco-only networks; however, other vendors can now implement EIGRP on their routers.

EIGRP is classified as an *advanced distance-vector routing protocol*, because it improves on the fundamental characteristics of a distance-vector routing protocol. For example, EIGRP does not periodically send out its entire IP routing table to its neighbors. Instead it uses triggered updates, and it converges quickly. Also, EIGRP can support multiple routed protocols (for example, IPv4 and IPv6). EIGRP can even advertise network services (for example, route plan information for a unified communications network) using the Cisco *Service Advertisement Framework (SAF)*.

By default, EIGRP uses bandwidth and delay in its metric calculation; however, other parameters can be considered. These optional parameters include reliability, load, and maximum transmission unit (MTU) size.

The algorithm EIGRP uses for its route selection is not Dijkstra's Shortest Path First algorithm (as used by OSPF). Instead, EIGRP uses *Diffusing Update Algorithm (DUAL)*.

Link-State

Rather than having neighboring routers exchange their full routing tables with one another, a link-state routing protocol allows routers to build a topological map of a network. Then, similar to a global positioning system (GPS) in a car, a router can execute an algorithm to calculate an optimal path (or paths) to a destination network.

Routers send link-state advertisements (LSA) to advertise the networks they know how to reach. Routers then use those LSAs to construct the topological map of a network. The algorithm run against this topological map is *Dijkstra's Shortest Path First* algorithm.

Unlike distance-vector routing protocols, link-state routing protocols exchange full routing information only when two routers initially form their adjacency. Then, routing updates are sent in response to changes in the network, as opposed to being sent periodically. Also, link-state routing protocols benefit from shorter convergence times, as compared to distance-vector routing protocols (although convergence times are comparable to EIGRP).

Routing protocols that can be categorized as link-state routing protocols include

■ **Open Shortest Path First (OSPF):** A link-state routing protocol that uses a metric of cost, which is based on the link speed between two routers. OSPF is a popular IGP, because of its scalability, fast convergence, and vendor interoperability.

■ **Intermediate System–to–Intermediate System (IS-IS):** This link-state routing protocol is similar in its operation to OSPF. It uses a configurable, yet dimensionless, metric associated with an interface and runs Dijkstra's Shortest Path First algorithm.

Although using IS-IS as an IGP offers the scalability, fast convergence, and vendor interoperability benefits of OSPF, it has not been as widely deployed as OSPF.

Path-Vector

A path-vector routing protocol includes information about the exact path packets take to reach a specific destination network. This path information typically consists of a series of autonomous systems through which packets travel to reach their destination. *Border Gateway Protocol (BGP)* is the only path-vector protocol you are likely to encounter in a modern network.

Also, BGP is the only EGP in widespread use today. In fact, BGP is considered to be the routing protocol that runs the Internet, which is an interconnection of multiple autonomous systems.

BGP's path selection is not solely based on AS hops, however. BGP has a variety of other parameters that it can consider. Interestingly, none of those parameters are based on link speed. Also, although BGP is incredibly scalable, it does not quickly converge in the event of a topological change. The current version of BGP is BGP version 4 (BGP-4). However, an enhancement to BGP-4, called *Multiprotocol BGP (MP-BGP)*, supports the routing of multiple routed protocols, such as IPv4 and IPv6.

Summary of Categories

As a reference, Table 1-2 categorizes the previously listed routing protocols, based on their type and whether they are primarily an IGP or an EGP.

Key Topic

Table 1-2 *Routing Protocol Characteristics*

Routing Protocol	Type	Primarily IGP or EGP
RIP	Distance-Vector	IGP
EIGRP	(Advanced) Distance-Vector	IGP
OSPF	Link-State	IGP
IS-IS	Link-State	IGP
BGP	Path-Vector	EGP

Note that a network can simultaneously support more than one routing protocol through the process of *route redistribution*. For example, a router could have one of its interfaces participating in an OSPF area of the network and have another interface participating in an EIGRP area of the network. This router could then take routes learned through OSPF and inject those routes into the EIGRP routing process. Similarly, EIGRP-learned routes could be redistributed into the OSPF routing process.

Network Technology Fundamentals

When designing a new network or analyzing an existing network, the ability to determine how traffic flows through that network is a necessary skill. Traffic flow is determined both by the traffic type (for example, unicast, multicast, broadcast, or anycast) and the network architecture type (for example, point-to-point, broadcast, and nonbroadcast multiaccess [NMBA]). This section provides you with the basic characteristics of these network technologies.

Network Traffic Types

Traffic can be sent to a single network host, all hosts on a subnet, or a select grouping of hosts that requested to receive the traffic. These traffic types include unicast, broadcast, multicast, and anycast.

Older routing protocols, such as RIPv1 and IGRP (the now-antiquated predecessor to EIGRP), used broadcasts to advertise routing information; however, most modern IGPs use multicasts for their route advertisements.

Note BGP establishes a TCP session between peers. Therefore, unicast transmissions are used for BGP route advertisement.

Unicast

Most network traffic is unicast in nature, meaning that traffic travels from a single source device to a single destination device. Figure 1-8 illustrates an example of a unicast transmission. In IPv4 networks, unicast addresses are made up of Class A, B, and C addresses. IPv6 networks instead use global unicast addresses, which begin with the 2000::/3 prefix.

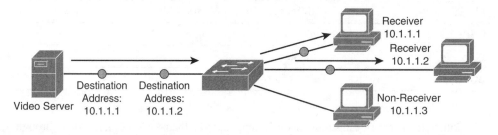

Figure 1-8 *Sample IPv4 Unicast Transmission*

Broadcast

Broadcast traffic travels from a single source to all destinations in a subnet (that is, a broadcast domain). A broadcast address of 255.255.255.255 might seem that it would reach all hosts on an interconnected network. However, 255.255.255.255 targets all devices on a single network, specifically the network local to the device sending a packet destined for 255.255.255.255. Another type of broadcast address is a directed broadcast address, which targets all devices in a remote network. For example, the address 172.16.255.255 /16 is a directed broadcast targeting all devices in the 172.16.0.0 /16 network. Figure 1-9 illustrates an example of a broadcast transmission.

Note   Broadcasts are used in IPv4 networks, but not in IPv6 networks.

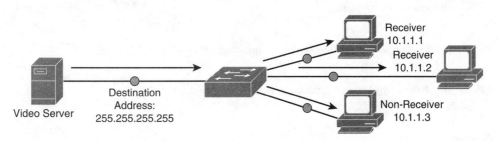

Figure 1-9   *Sample IPv4 Broadcast Transmission*

Multicast

Multicast technology provides an efficient mechanism for a single host to send traffic to multiple, yet specific, destinations. For example, imagine a network with 100 users. Twenty of those users want to receive a video stream from a video server. With a unicast solution, the video server would have to send 20 individual streams, one stream for each recipient. Such a solution could consume a significant amount of network bandwidth and put a heavy processor burden on the video server.

With a broadcast solution, the video server would only have to send the video stream once; however, the stream would be received by every device on the local subnet, even devices not wanting to receive it. Even though those devices do not want to receive the video stream, they still have to pause what they are doing and take time to check each of these unwanted packets.

As shown in Figure 1-10, multicast offers a compromise, allowing the video server to send the video stream only once, and only sending the video stream to devices on the network that want to receive the stream.

What makes this possible in IPv4 networks is the use of a Class D address. A Class D address, such as 239.1.2.3, represents the address of a multicast group. The video server could, in this example, send a single copy of each video stream packet destined for 239.1.2.3. Devices wanting to receive the video stream can join the multicast group. Based on the device request, switches and routers in the topology can then dynamically determine out of which ports the video stream should be forwarded.

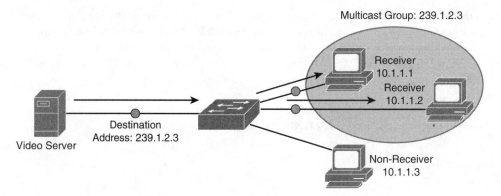

Figure 1-10 *Sample IPv4 Multicast Transmission*

Note   In IPv6 networks, multicast addresses have a prefix of ff00::/8.

Anycast

With anycast, a single IPv6 address is assigned to multiple devices, as depicted in Figure 1-11. The communication flow is one-to-nearest (from the perspective of a router's routing table).

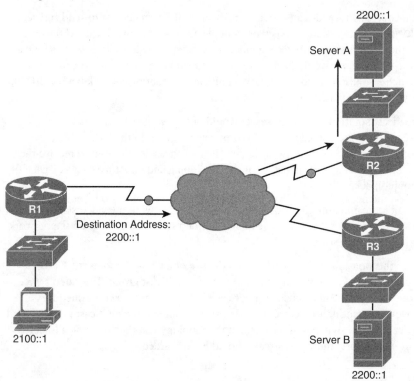

Figure 1-11 *IPv6 Anycast Example*

In Figure 1-11, a client with an IPv6 address of 2100::1 wants to send traffic to a destination IPv6 address of 2200::1. Notice that two servers (Server A and Server B) have an IPv6 address of 2200::1. In the figure, the traffic destined for 2200::1 is sent to Server A through Router R2, because the network on which Server A resides appears to be closer than the network on which Server B resides, from the perspective of Router R1's IPv6 routing table.

Note   Anycast is an IPv6 concept and is not found in IPv4 networks. Also, note that IPv6 anycast addresses are not unique from IPv6 unicast addresses.

Network Architecture Types

Another set of network technologies that impact routing, and determine traffic flow, deal with network architecture types (for example, point-to-point, broadcast, and NBMA). For design and troubleshooting purposes, you should be familiar with the characteristics of each.

Point-to-Point Network

A very basic network architecture type is a *point-to-point* network. As seen in Figure 1-12, a point-to-point network segment consists of a single network link interconnecting two routers. This network type is commonly found on serial links.

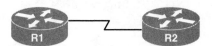

Figure 1-12   *Point-to-Point Network Type*

Broadcast Network

A broadcast network segment uses an architecture in which a broadcast sent from one of the routers on the network segment is propagated to all other routers on that segment. An Ethernet network, as illustrated in Figure 1-13, is a common example of a broadcast network.

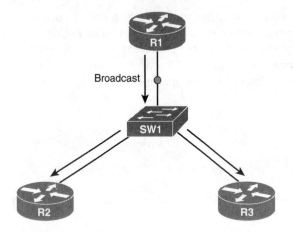

Figure 1-13   *Broadcast Network Type*

NBMA

As its name suggests, a nonbroadcast multiaccess (NBMA) network does not support broadcasts. As a result, if an interface on a router connects to two other routers, as depicted in Figure 1-14, individual messages must be sent to each router.

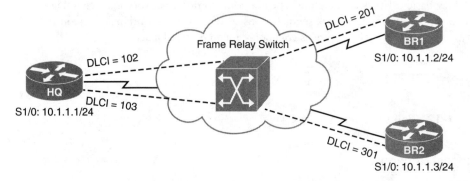

Figure 1-14   *NBMA Network Type*

The absence of broadcast support also implies an absence of multicast support. This can lead to an issue with dynamic routing protocols (such as OSPF and EIGRP) that dynamically form neighborships with neighboring routers discovered through multicasts. Because neighbors cannot be dynamically discovered, neighboring IP addresses must be statically configured. Examples of NBMA networks include ATM and Frame Relay.

The requirement for static neighbor configuration is not the only routing protocol issue stemming from an NBMA network. Consider the following:

Key Topic

- **Split Horizon issues:** Distance-vector routing protocols (RIP and EIGRP, for example) can use the previously mentioned Split Horizon rule, which prevents routes learned on one interface from being advertised back out of that same interface. Consider Figure 1-14 again. Imagine that Router BR2 advertised a route to Router HQ, and Router HQ had Split Horizon enabled for its S 1/0 interface. That condition would prevent Router HQ from advertising that newly learned route to Router BR1, because it would be advertising that route out the same interface on which it was learned. Fortunately, in situations like this, you can administratively disable Split Horizon.

- **Designated router issues:** Recall from your CCNA studies that a broadcast network (for example, an Ethernet network) OSPF elects a designated router (DR), with which all other routers on a network segment form an adjacency. Interestingly, OSPF attempts to elect a DR on an NMBA network, by default. Once again considering Figure 1-14, notice that only Router HQ has a direct connection to the other routers; therefore, Router HQ should be the DR. This election might not happen without administrative intervention, however. Specifically, in such a topology, you would need to set the OSPF Priority to 0 on both Routers BR1 and BR2, which prevents them from participating in a DR election.

TCP/IP Fundamentals

Recall from your CCNA studies that the Internet layer of the TCP/IP stack maps to Layer 3 (that is, the network layer) of the Open Systems Interconnection (OSI) model. While multiple routed protocols (for example, IP, IPX, and AppleTalk) reside at the OSI model's network layer, *Internet Protocol (IP)* has become the de-facto standard for network communication.

Sitting just above IP, at the transport layer (of both the TCP/IP and OSI models) is *Transmission Control Protocol (TCP)* and *User Datagram Protocol (UDP)*. This section reviews the basic operation of the TCP/IP suite of protocols, as their behavior is the foundation of the routing topics in the remainder of this book.

IP Characteristics

Figure 1-15 shows the IP version 4 packet header format.

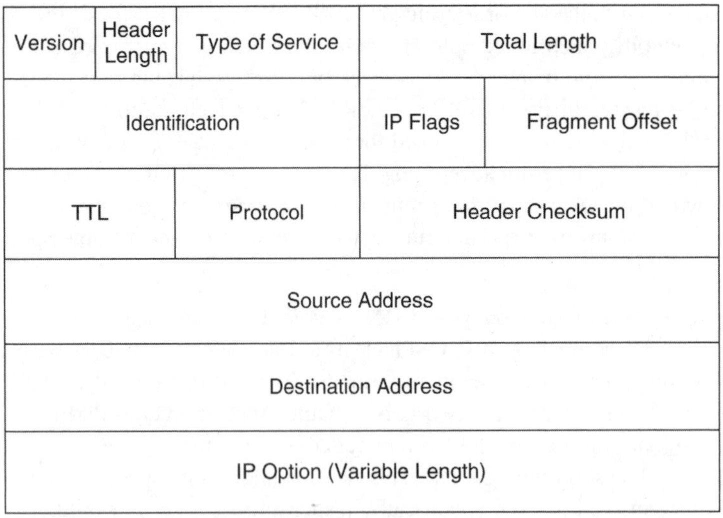

Version	Header Length	Type of Service	Total Length	
Identification			IP Flags	Fragment Offset
TTL		Protocol	Header Checksum	
Source Address				
Destination Address				
IP Option (Variable Length)				

Figure 1-15 *IP Version 4 Packet Header Format*

The functions of the fields in an IPv4 header are as follows:

- **Version field:** The *Version* field indicates IPv4 (with a value of 0100).

- **Header Length field:** The *Header Length* field (commonly referred to as the *Internet Header Length (IHL)* field) is a 4-bit field indicating the number of 4-byte words in the IPv4 header.

- **Type of Service field:** The *Type of Service (ToS)* field (commonly referred to as the *ToS Byte* or *DHCP* field) has 8 bits used to set quality of service (QoS) markings. Specifically, the 6 leftmost bits are used for the *Differentiated Service Code Point (DSCP)* marking, and the 2 rightmost bits are used for *Explicit Congestion Notification* (an extension of Weighted Random Early Detection *(WRED)*, used for flow control).

- **Total Length field:** The *Total Length* field is a 16-bit value indicating the size of the packet (in bytes).

- **Identification field:** The *Identification* field is a 16-bit value used to mark fragments that came from the same packet.

- **IP Flags field:** The *IP Flags* field is a 3-bit field, where the first bit is always set to a 0. The second bit (the *Don't Fragment [DF]* bit) indicates that a packet should not be fragmented. The third bit (the *More Fragments [MF]* bit) is set on all of a packet's fragments, except the last fragment.

- **Fragment Offset field:** The *Fragment Offset* field is a 13-bit field that specifies the offset of a fragment from the beginning of the first fragment in a packet, in 8-byte units.

- **Time to Live (TTL) field:** The *Time to Live (TTL)* field is an 8-bit field that is decremented by 1 every time the packet is routed from one IP network to another (that is, passes through a router). If the TTL value ever reaches 0, the packet is discarded from the network. This behavior helps prevent routing loops.

- **Protocol field:** The *Protocol* field is an 8-bit field that specifies the type of data encapsulated in the packet. TCP and UDP are common protocols identified by this field.

- **Header Checksum field:** The *Header Checksum* field is a 16-bit field that performs error checking for a packet's header. Interestingly, this error checking is performed for UDP segments, in addition to TCP segments, even though UDP is itself an "unreliable" protocol.

- **Source Address field:** The 32-bit *Source Address* field indicates the source of an IPv4 packet.

- **Destination Address field:** The 32-bit *Destination Address* field indicates the destination of an IPv4 packet.

- **IP Option field:** The IP Option field is a seldom-used field that can specify a variety of nondefault packet options. If the IP Option field is used, its length varies based on the options specified.

An IPv6 packet header, as seen in Figure 1-16, is simpler in structure than the IPv4 packet header.

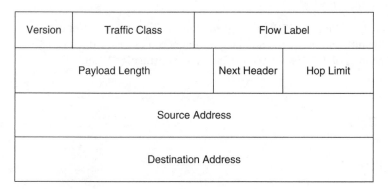

Figure 1-16 *IP Version 6 Packet Header Format*

The purposes of the fields found in an IPv6 header are as follows:

- **Version field:** Like an IPv4 header, an IPv6 header has a *Version* field, indicating IPv6 (with a value of 0110).

- **Traffic Class field:** The *Traffic Class* field is the same size, performs the same functions, and takes on the same values as the *Type of Service* field in an IPv4 header.

- **Flow Label field:** The 20-bit *Flow Label* field can be used to instruct a router to use a specific outbound connection for a traffic flow (if a router has multiple outbound connections). By having all packets in the same flow use the same connection, the probability of packets arriving at their destination out of order is reduced.

- **Payload Length field:** The *Payload Length* field is a 16-bit field indicating the size (in bytes) of the payload being carried by an IPv6 packet.

- **Next Header field:** The *Next Header* field, similar to the Protocol field in an IPv4 header, indicates the type of header encapsulated in the IPv6 header. Typically, this 8-bit header indicates a specific transport layer protocol.

- **Hop Limit field:** The 8-bit *Hop Limit* field replaces, and performs the same function as, the IPv4 header's TTL field. Specifically, it is decremented at each router hop until it reaches 0, at which point the packet is discarded.

- **Source Address field:** Similar to the IPv4 header's 32-bit Source Address field, the IPv6 *Source Address* field is 128 bits in size and indicates the source of an IPv6 packet.

- **Destination Address field:** Similar to the IPv4 header's 32-bit Destination Address field, the IPv6 Destination Address field is 128 bits in size and indicates the destination of an IPv6 packet.

Routing Review

As a review from your CCNA studies, recall how the fields in an IP header are used to route a packet from one network to another. While the process is similar for IPv6, the following example considers IPv4.

In the topology shown in Figure 1-17, PC1 needs to send traffic to Server1. Notice that these devices are on different networks. So, the question becomes, "How does a packet from a source IP address of 192.168.1.2 get forwarded to a destination IP address of 192.168.3.2?"

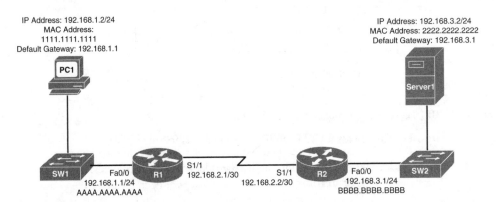

Figure 1-17   *Basic Routing Topology*

The answer is *routing*, as summarized in the following steps:

Step 1.   PC1 compares its IP address and subnet mask of 192.168.1.2 /24 with the destination IP address and subnet mask of 192.168.3.2 /24. PC1 concludes that the destination IP address resides on a remote subnet. Therefore, PC1 needs to send the packet to its default gateway, which could have been manually configured on PC1 or dynamically learned through Dynamic Host Configuration Protocol (DHCP). In this example, PC1 has a default gateway of 192.168.1.1 (Router R1). However, to construct a Layer 2 frame, PC1 also needs the MAC address of its default gateway. PC1 sends an Address Resolution Protocol (ARP) request for Router R1's MAC address. After PC1 receives an ARP reply from Router R1, PC1 adds Router R1's MAC address to its ARP cache. PC1 now sends its data in a frame destined for Server1, as shown in Figure 1-18.

Note   ARP uses broadcasts, which are not supported by IPv6. Therefore, IPv6 exchanges Neighbor Discovery messages with adjacent devices to perform functions similar to ARP.

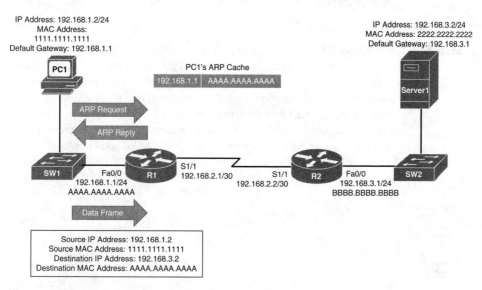

Figure 1-18   *Basic Routing: Step 1*

Step 2.   Router R1 receives the frame sent from PC1 and interrogates the IP header. An IP header contains a Time to Live (TTL) field, which is decremented once for each router hop. Therefore, Router R1 decrements the packet's TTL field. If the value in the TTL field is reduced to 0, the router discards the frame and sends a *time exceeded* Internet Control Message Protocol (ICMP) message back to the source. Assuming that the TTL is not decremented to 0, Router R1 checks its routing table to determine the best path to reach network 192.168.3.0 /24. In this example, Router R1's routing table has an entry stating that network 192.168.3.0 /24 is accessible through interface Serial 1/1. Note that ARPs are not required for serial interfaces, because these interface types do not have MAC addresses. Router R1, therefore, forwards the frame out of its Serial 1/1 interface, as shown in Figure 1-19.

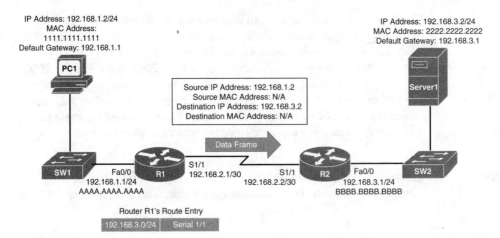

Figure 1-19 *Basic Routing: Step 2*

Step 3.   When Router R2 receives the frame, it decrements the TTL in the IP header,
just as Router R1 did. Again, assuming that the TTL did not get decremented
to 0, Router R2 interrogates the IP header to determine the destination network. In this case, the destination network of 192.168.3.0 /24 is directly
attached to Router R2's Fast Ethernet 0/0 interface. Similar to how PC1 sent
out an ARP request to determine the MAC address of its default gateway,
Router R2 sends an ARP request to determine the MAC address of Server1.
After an ARP Reply is received from Server1, Router R2 forwards the frame
out of its Fast Ethernet 0/0 interface to Server1, as illustrated in Figure 1-20.

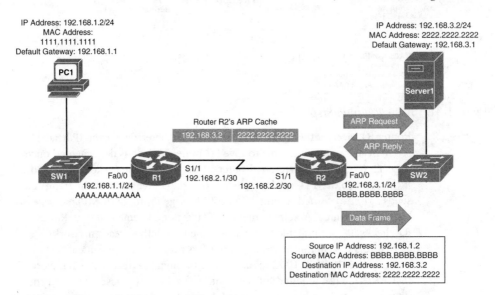

Figure 1-20 *Basic Routing: Step 3*

Asymmetric Routing

Many times, routing operations are impacted by Layer 2 switching in a network. As an example, consider a situation, as depicted in Figure 1-21, where a VLAN is spread across multiple access layer switches, and a *First-Hop Redundancy Protocol (FHRP)* (for example, HSRP, VRRP, or GLBP) is being used on multilayer switches at the distribution layer.

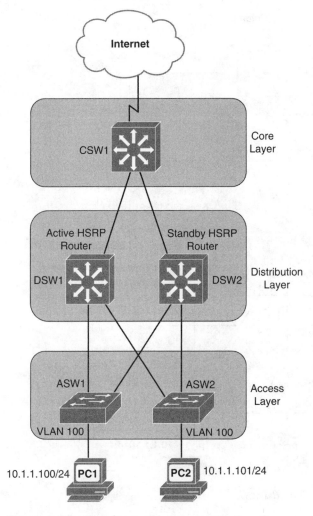

Figure 1-21 *Topology with Asymmetric Routing*

In the figure, notice that VLAN 100 (that is, 10.1.1.0 /24) exists on both switches ASW1 and ASW2 at the access layer. Also, notice that there are two multilayer switches (that is, DSW1 and DSW2) at the distribution layer with an HSRP configuration to provide default gateway redundancy to hosts in VLAN 100. The multilayer switch in the core layer (that is, CSW1) supports equal-cost load balancing between DSW1 and DSW2.

Focusing on the HSRP configuration, imagine that DSW1 is the active HSRP "router" and DSW2 is the standby HSRP "router." Next, imagine that PC1 sends traffic out to the Internet. The traffic flows through ASW1, DSW1 (the active HSRP router), and CSW1, as shown in Figure 1-22.

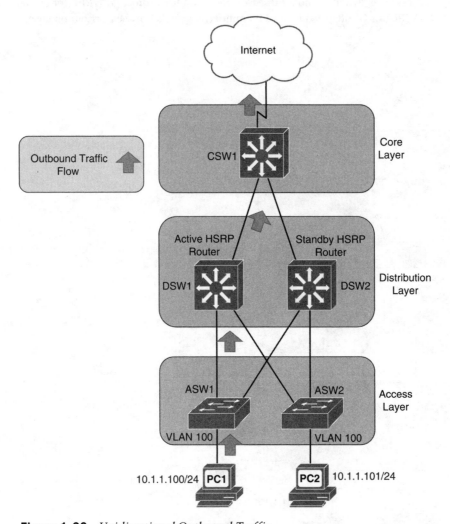

Figure 1-22 *Unidirectional Outbound Traffic*

A challenge with this common scenario can occur with the return traffic, as illustrated in Figure 1-23. The return traffic flows from the Internet and into CSW1, which then load-balances between DSW1 and DSW2. When the path through DSW1 is used, the MAC address of PC1 is known to DSW1's ARP cache (because it just saw PC1's MAC address being used as the source MAC address in a packet going out to the Internet). However, when the path through DSW2 is used, DSW2 might not have PC1's MAC address in its ARP cache (because PC1 isn't normally using DSW2 as its default gateway). As a result, DSW2 floods this unknown unicast traffic out all its other ports. This issue is known as *asymmetric routing*, because traffic might leave through one path (for example, through DSW1) and return through a different path (for example, through DSW2). Another name given to this issue is *unicast flooding*, because of the potential for a backup FHRP router or multilayer switch to flood unknown unicast traffic for returning traffic.

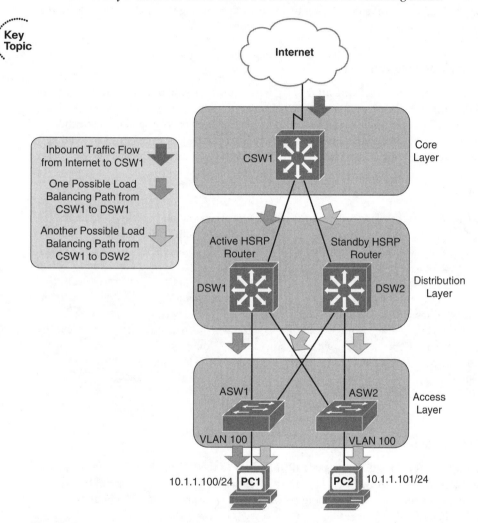

Figure 1-23   *Unidirectional Flooding of Inbound Traffic*

Cisco recommends that you do not span a VLAN across more than one access layer switch to avoid such an issue. However, if a particular design requires the spanning of a VLAN across multiple access layer switches, the best-practice recommendation from Cisco is that you adjust the FHRP device's ARP timer to be equal to or less than the Content Addressable Memory (CAM) aging time. Otherwise, the CAM table entry for the end station will time out before the ARP entry times out, meaning that the FHRP device knows (from its ARP cache) the MAC address corresponding to the destination IP address, and therefore does not need to ARP for the MAC address. However, if the CAM entry has timed out, the FHRP device needs to flood the traffic to make sure that it gets to the intended destination. With an ARP timer equal to or less than the CAM aging time, there will never be an ARP entry for a MAC address not also stored in the CAM table. As a result, if the FHRP device's ARP entry has timed out, it will use ARP to get the MAC address of the destination IP address, thus causing the CAM table to learn the appropriate egress port.

Maximum Transmission Unit

A *Maximum Transmission Unit (MTU)*, in the context of Cisco routers, typically refers to the largest packet size supported on a router interface; 1500 bytes is a common value. Smaller MTU sizes result in more overhead, because more packets (and therefore more headers) are required to transmit the same amount of data. However, if you are sending data over slower link speeds, large MTU values could cause delay for latency-sensitive traffic.

Note *Latency* is the time required for a packet to travel from its source to destination. Some applications, such as Voice over IP (VoIP), are latency sensitive, meaning that they do not perform satisfactorily if the latency of their packets is too high. For example, the G.114 recommendation states that the one-way latency for VoIP traffic should not exceed 150 ms.Latency is a factor in the calculation of the *bandwidth-delay product*. Specifically, the bandwidth-delay product is a measurement of the maximum number of bits that can be on a network segment at any one time, and it is calculated by multiplying the segment's bandwidth (in bits/sec) by the latency packets experience as they cross the segment (in sec). For example, a network segment with a bandwidth of 768 kbps and an end-to-end latency of 100 ms would have a bandwidth-delay product of 76,800 bits (that is 768,000 * 0.1 = 76,800).

ICMP Messages

Another protocol residing alongside IP at Layer 3 of the OSI model is *Internet Control Message Protocol (ICMP)*. ICMP is most often associated with the Ping utility, used to check connectivity with a remote network address (using *ICMP Echo Request* and *ICMP Echo Reply* messages).

Note There is some debate in the industry about where ICMP fits into the OSI model. Although it is generally considered to be a Layer 3 protocol, be aware that ICMP is encapsulated inside of an IP packet, and some of its messages are based on Layer 4 events.

ICMP does have other roles beyond Ping. By using a variety of message types, ICMP can be used by network devices (for example, routers) to provide information to one another. Figure 1-24 shows the structure of an ICMP packet header.

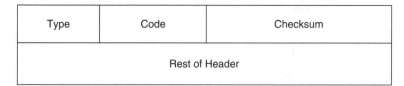

Type	Code	Checksum
Rest of Header		

Figure 1-24   *ICMP Packet Header Format*

The purposes of the fields found in an ICMP packet header are as follows:

- **Type:** The 1-byte *Type* field contains a number indicating the specific type of ICMP message. Here are a few examples: A Type 0 is an *Echo Reply* message, a Type 3 is a *Destination Unreachable* message, a Type 5 is a *Redirect* message, and a Type 8 is an *ICMP Echo Request* message.

- **Code:** The 1-byte *Code* field further defines the ICMP type. For example, there are 16 codes for Destination Unreachable ICMP messages. Here are a couple of examples: A code of 0 means that the destination network is unreachable, while a code of 1 means that the destination host is unreachable.

- **Checksum:** The 2-byte *Checksum* field performs error checking.

- **Rest of Header:** The 4-byte *Rest of Header* field is 4 bytes in length, and its contents are dependent on the specific ICMP type.

While ICMP has multiple messages types and codes, for purposes of the ROUTE exam, you should primarily be familiar with the two following ICMP message types:

- **Destination Unreachable:** If a packet enters a router destined for an address that the router does not know how to reach, the router can let the sender know by sending a Destination Unreachable ICMP message back to the sender.

- **Redirect:** A host might have routing information indicating that to reach a particular destination network, packets should be sent to a certain next-hop IP address. However, if network conditions change and a different next-hop IP address should be used, the original next-hop router can let the host know to use a different path by sending the host a Redirect ICMP message.

TCP Characteristics

TCP is commonly touted as being a reliable transport mechanism, as compared to its unreliable counterpart, UDP. Examination of the TCP segment header format, as shown in Figure 1-25, provides valuable insight into how this reliability happens.

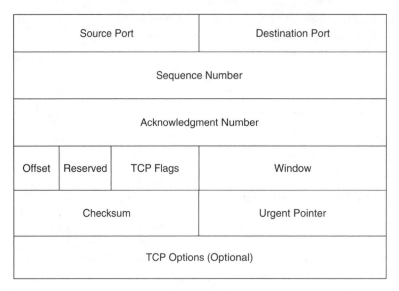

Figure 1-25 *TCP Segment Header Format*

The purposes of the fields found in a TCP segment header are as follows:

■ **Source Port field:** The *Source Port* field is a 16-bit field indicating the sending port number.

■ **Destination Port field:** The *Destination Port* field is a 16-bit field indicating the receiving port number.

■ **Sequence Number field:** The *Sequence Number* field is a 32-bit field indicting the amount of data sent during a TCP session. The sending party can be assured that the receiving party really received the data, because the receiving party uses the sequence number as the basis for the acknowledgment number in the next segment it sends back to the sender. Specifically, the acknowledgment number in that segment equals the received sequence number plus 1. Interestingly, at the beginning of a TCP session, the initial sequence number can be any number in the range 0–4,294,967,295 (that is, the range of numbers that can be represented by 32 bits). However, when you are doing troubleshooting and performing a packet capture of a TCP session, the initial sequence number might appear to be a *relative sequence number* of 0. The use of a relative sequence number can often make data easier to interpret while troubleshooting.

■ **Acknowledgment Number field:** The 32-bit *Acknowledgment Number* field is used by the recipient of a segment to request the next segment in the TCP session. The value of this field is calculated by adding 1 to the previously received sequence number.

■ **Offset field:** The *Offset* field is a 4-bit field that specifies the offset between the data in a TCP segment and the start of the segment, in units of 4-byte words.

- **Reserved field:** The 3-bit *Reserved* field is not used, and each of the 3 bits are set to a value of 0.

- **TCP Flags field:** The *TCP Flags* field is comprised of 9 flag bits (also known as *control bits*), which indicate a variety of segment parameters.

- **Window field:** The 16-bit *Window* field specifies the number of bytes a sender is willing to transmit before receiving an acknowledgment from the receiver.

- **Checksum field:** The *Checksum* field is a 16-bit field that performs error checking for a segment.

- **Urgent Pointer field:** The 16-bit *Urgent Pointer* field indicates that last byte of a segment's data that was considered urgent. The field specifies the number of bytes between the current sequence number and that urgent data byte.

- **TCP Options field:** The optional TCP Options field can range in size from 0 to 320 bits (as long as the number of bits is evenly divisible by 32), and the field can contain a variety of TCP segment parameters.

Three-Way Handshake

The process of setting up a TCP session involves a three-way handshake, as listed in the following steps and as illustrated in Figure 1-26.

Step 1.   The session initiator sends a Synchronization (SYN) message to the target host.

Step 2.   The target host acknowledges receipt of the SYN message with an Acknowledgment (ACK) message and also sends a SYN message of its own.

Step 3.   The session initiator receives the SYN messages from the target host and acknowledges receipt by sending an ACK message.

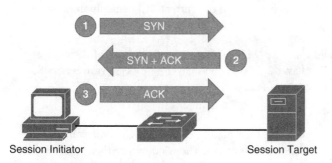

Figure 1-26 *TCP Three-Way Handshake*

TCP Sliding Window

TCP communication uses windowing, meaning that one or more segments are sent at one time, and a receiver can acknowledge the receipt of all the segments in a window with a single acknowledgment. In some cases, as illustrated in Figure 1-27, TCP uses a sliding window, where the window size begins with one segment. If there is a successful acknowledgment of that one segment (that is, the receiver sends an ACK asking for the next segment), the window size doubles to two segments. Upon successful receipt of those two segments, the next window contains four segments. This exponential increase in window size continues until the receiver does not acknowledge successful receipt of all segments within a certain time period (known as the *round-trip time [RTT]*, which is sometimes called *real transfer time*), or until a configured maximum window size is reached.

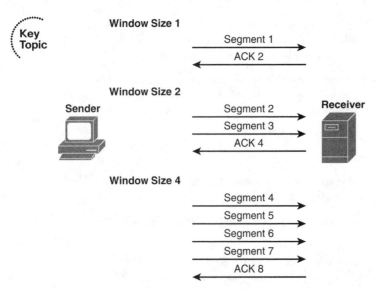

Figure 1-27 *TCP Sliding Window*

The *TCP Maximum Segment Size (MSS)* is the amount of data that can be contained in a single TCP segment. The value is dependent on the current TCP window size.

Note The term *Maximum Segment Size (MSS)* seems to imply the size of the entire Layer 4 segment (that is, including Layer 2, Layer 3, and Layer 4 headers). However, MSS only refers to the amount of data in a segment.

If a single TCP flow drops a packet, that flow might experience *TCP slow start*, meaning that the window size is reduced to one segment. The window size then grows exponentially until it reaches one-half of its congestion window size (that is, the window size when congestion was previously experienced). At that point, the window size begins to grow linearly instead of exponentially.

If a router interface's output queue fills to capacity, all TCP flows can simultaneously start to drop packets, causing all TCP flows to experience slow start. This condition, called *global synchronization* or *TCP synchronization*, results in a very inefficient use of bandwidth, because of all TCP flows having reduced window sizes and therefore spending more time waiting for acknowledgments.

> **Note**   To prevent global synchronization, Cisco IOS supports a feature called *Weighted Random Early Detection (WRED)*, which can pseudo-randomly drop packets from flows based on the number of packets currently in a queue and the quality of service (QoS) markings on the packets. By dropping packets before the queue fills to capacity, the global synchronization issue is avoided.

Out-of-Order Delivery

In many routed environments, a router has more than one egress interface that can reach a destination IP address. If load balancing is enabled in such a scenario, some packets in a traffic flow might go out one interface, while other packets go out of another interface. With traffic flowing out of multiple interfaces, there is a chance that the packets will arrive out of order. Fortunately, TCP can help prevent out-of-order packets by either sequencing them in the correct order or by requesting the retransmission of out-of-order packets.

UDP Characteristics

Figure 1-28 presents the structure of a UDP segment header. Because UDP is considered to be a connectionless, unreliable protocol, it lacks the sequence numbering, window size, and acknowledgment numbering present in the header of a TCP segment. Rather the UDP segment's header contains only source and destination port numbers, a UDP checksum (which is an optional field used to detect transmission errors), and the segment length (measured in bytes).

Source Port	Destination Port
UDP Length	UDP Checksum

Figure 1-28   *UDP Segment Header Format*

Because a UDP segment header is so much smaller than a TCP segment header, UDP becomes a good candidate for the transport layer protocol serving applications that need to maximize bandwidth and do not require acknowledgments (for example, audio or video streams). In fact, the primary protocol used to carry voice and video traffic, *Real-time Transport Protocol (RTP)*, is a Layer 4 protocol that is encapsulated inside of UDP.

If RTP is carrying interactive voice or video streams, the latency between the participants in a voice and/or video call should ideally be no greater than 150 ms. To help ensure that RTP experiences minimal latency, even during times of congestion, Cisco recommends a queuing technology called *Low Latency Queuing (LLQ)*. LLQ allows one or more traffic types to be buffered in a priority queue, which is serviced first (up to a maximum bandwidth limit) during times of congestion. Metaphorically, LLQ works much like a carpool lane found in highway systems in larger cities. With a carpool lane, if you are a special type of traffic (for example, a vehicle with two or more passengers), you get to drive in a separate lane with less congestion. However, the carpool lane is not the autobahn (a German highway without a speed limit). You are still restricted as to how fast you can go.

With LLQ, you can treat special traffic types (for example, voice and video using RTP) in a special way, by placing them in a priority queue. Traffic in the priority queue (much like a carpool lane) gets to go ahead of nonpriority traffic; however, there is a bandwidth limit (much like a speed limit) that traffic in the priority queue cannot exceed. Therefore, priority traffic does not starve out nonpriority traffic.

Network Migration Strategies

As networks undergo expansion or as new technologies are introduced, network engineers need to understand the implications of the changes being made. This section identifies a few key areas where change is likely to occur (if it has not already occurred) in enterprise networks.

Routing Protocol Changes

The primary focus of this book is on routing protocols. As you read through the subsequent chapters covering protocols such as RIPng, OSPF, EIGRP, and BGP, be on the lookout for protocol-specific parameters that need to match between neighboring devices.

As one example, in Chapter 4, "Fundamental EIGRP Concepts," you will read about EIGRP K-values and how they must match between EIGRP neighbors. Therefore, if you make a K-value change on one router, that change needs to be reflected on neighboring routers.

In addition to making adjustments to existing routing protocols, network engineers sometimes need to migrate to an entirely new routing protocol. For example, a network that was running RIP might migrate to OSPF. Two common approaches to routing protocol migration are as follows:

Key Topic

- **Using Administrative Distance (AD):** When migrating from one routing protocol to another, one approach is to configure both routing protocols on all your routers, allowing them to run concurrently. However, when you do your configuration of the new routing protocol, you should make sure that it has a higher AD than the existing routing protocol. This approach allows you to make sure that the new routing protocol has successfully learned all the routes it needs to learn and has appropriate next hops for its route entries. After you are convinced that the new routing protocol is configured appropriately, you can adjust the AD on either the old or the new routing protocol such that the new routing protocol is preferred.

- **Using route redistribution:** Another approach to migrating between routing protocols is to use redistribution, such that you cut over one section of your network at a time, and mutually redistribute routes between portions of your network using the old routing protocol and portions using the new routing protocol. This approach allows you to, at your own pace, roll out and test the new routing protocol in your network locations.

IPv6 Migration

You could argue that there are two kinds of IP networks: those that have already migrated to IPv6 and those that will migrate to IPv6. With the depletion of the IPv4 address space, the adoption of IPv6 for most every IP-based network is an eventuality. Following are a few strategies to consider when migrating your network, or your customers' networks, from IPv4 to IPv6:

Key Topic

- **Check equipment for IPv6 compatibility:** Before rolling out IPv6, you should check your existing network devices (for example, switches, routers, and firewalls) for IPv6 compatibility. In some cases, you might be able to upgrade the Cisco IOS on your existing gear to add IPv6 support for those devices.

- **Run IPv4 and IPv6 concurrently:** Most network devices (including end-user computers) that support IPv6 also support IPv4 and can run both at the same time. This type of configuration is called a *dual-stack* configuration. A dual-stack approach allows you to gradually add IPv6 support to your devices and then cut over to just IPv6 after all devices have their IPv6 configuration in place.

- **Check the ISP's IPv6 support:** Many Internet Service Providers (ISP) allow you to connect with them using IPv6. The connection could be a default static route, or you might be running Multiprotocol BGP (MP-BGP) to peer with multiple ISPs. These options are discussed in Chapter 15, "IPv6 Internet Connectivity."

- **Configure NAT64:** During the transition from a network running IPv4 to a network running IPv6, you might have an IPv6 host that needs to communicate with an IPv4 host. One approach to allow this is to use *NAT64*. You probably recall from your CCNA studies that *Network Address Translation (NAT)* in IPv4 networks is often used to translate private IP addresses used inside of a network (referred to as *inside local addresses*) into publicly routable IP addresses for use on the Internet (referred to as *inside global addresses*). However, NAT64 allows IPv6 addresses to be translated into corresponding IPv4 addresses, thus permitting communication between an IPv4 host and an IPv6 host.

    A router configured for NAT64 maintains a mapping table that specifies which IPv4 address corresponds to an IPv6 address. This mapping table can be manually configured, which is called *stateless translation*. Unfortunately, such a manual configuration is not very scalable. However, a stateless translation can be useful when you have a relatively small number of IPv4 hosts (for example, servers) that need to be reached by IPv6 clients. For more scalability, *stateful translation* can be used. A router configured for stateful translation allows a dynamic IPv6-to-IPv4 address binding to be created.

- **Use NPTv6:** Another type of translation that can benefit IPv6 networks is *Network Prefix Translation version 6* (NPTv6). NPTv6 is sometimes referred to as *IPv6-to-IPv6 Network Prefix Translation*. Unlike NAT, NPTv6 cannot do any sort of NAT address overloading. Instead it simply translates one IPv6 prefix to another. For example, a router configured for NPTv6 might translate a prefix from 2001:1::/64 to 2001:2::/64.

  Many IPv6 networks will have no need for NPTv6. However, as an example of where it can be particularly beneficial, consider a situation where an IPv6 host has more than one global unicast address assigned to a network interface card. Perhaps one of the global unicast addresses has permission (based on network filters in place) to reach a specific destination, while the other global unicast address would be dropped if it attempted to reach that destination. Because the host might not know from which of these IPv6 addresses to source a packet, it might use a source address that gets dropped by the network filter. However, a router configured for NPTv6 can translate the host's unpermitted global unicast IPv6 address into a global unicast IPv6 address that is permitted.

- **Send IPv6 traffic over an IPv6-over-IPv4 tunnel:** Yet another approach to having IPv6 addressing and IPv4 addressing peacefully coexist on the same network is to have an IPv4 tunnel that spans an IPv4-only portion of the network. Routers at each end of this tunnel can run both IPv4 and IPv6 and can encapsulate IPv6 traffic inside of the IPv4 tunnel packets, thus allowing IPv6 traffic to traverse an IPv4-only portion of the network. This type of tunnel is called an *IPv6-over-IPv4 tunnel*.

Spanning Tree Protocol Migration

Spanning Tree Protocol (STP), to which you were introduced in your CCNA studies, supports redundancy in a Layer 2 network, while preserving a loop-free topology. Several variants of STP have been developed since Radia Perlman's first iteration of STP in the mid 1980s.

Typically, the optimal type of STP to run on today's Cisco Catalyst switches is *Rapid Per-VLAN Spanning Tree Protocol Plus (Rapid-PVST+)*. Rapid-PVST+ allows for much faster convergence (commonly, less than one second) as compared to the relatively slow convergence (up to 50 seconds) of IEEE 802.1D (the first industry-standard version of STP). Another benefit of running Rapid-PVST+ is that it allows each VLAN to run its own instance of STP, as opposed to all VLANs using the same spanning-tree topology (which could lead to suboptimal paths for some VLANs).

Fortunately, Rapid-PVST+ is backward compatible with IEEE 802.1D. This backward compatibility allows network engineers to take a phased approach in their migration to Rapid-PVST+.

When converting a Cisco Catalyst switch to Rapid-PVST+, you can remove the following features, because similar features are built into Rapid-PVST+:

- UplinkFast
- BackboneFast

However, the following features still function with Rapid-PVST+ and do not need to be removed from a Cisco Catalyst switch being migrated to Rapid-PVST+:

- PortFast

- BPDU Guard

- BPDU Filter

- Root Guard

- Loop Guard

Migration to Easy Virtual Networking

In recent years, *virtualization* has become a hot topic in the IT industry. Today's data centers commonly use virtualization technologies (for example, VMware and Hyper-V) to allow multiple server instances (possibly running different operating systems) to run on a single physical server. This can make for a much more efficient use of hardware resources.

Interestingly, in addition to virtualizing server instances, you can virtualize networks. Cisco supports a technology called *Virtual Routing and Forwarding (VRF)*, which allows a single router to run multiple virtual router instances. Each virtual router instance can have its own configuration and its own IP routing process.

VRF is therefore able to segment networks and isolate paths as needed. The capability to completely isolate one network from another (even though the networks use the same infrastructure devices) has obvious security benefits.

Additionally, VRF helps network architects meet various industry regulations. For example, the Sarbanes-Oxley Act and the HIPAA Privacy Rule require privacy for customer and patient information. Also, the Payment Card Industry regulations require path segmentation for credit card transactions. Other scenarios for multitenant networks (for example, universities and airports) also have frequent network segmentation and path isolation design requirements.

A traditional way to configure VRF on Cisco routers was to use an approach called *VRF-Lite*. A newer approach to virtualized network configuration, called *Cisco Easy Virtual Network (EVN)*, dramatically simplifies the relatively complex configuration required by VRF-Lite.

An EVN uses a *Virtual Network Trunk (VNET Trunk)* to carry traffic for each virtual network, and eliminates the need to manually configure a subinterface for each virtual network on all routers (which was a requirement with VRF-Lite). Traffic flowing over a VNET Trunk is tagged with a VNET tag, identifying the virtual network to which the traffic belongs. An EVN router connects to a Cisco Catalyst switch through an 802.1Q trunk, with the different VLANs on the 802.1Q trunk carrying traffic for the different virtual networks.

Note Even though VRF is the underlying technology being used, a common practice is to refer to a virtual network as a VRF. For example, an EVN might have three separate virtual networks that you might call VRF A, VRF B, and VRF C.

Figure 1-29 provides a sample EVN topology.

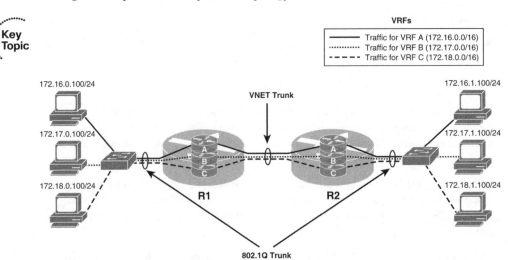

Figure 1-29 *Sample EVN Topology*

Even though an EVN allows a network architect to isolate one virtual network from another (as if they were physically separate networks), there is an occasional need for one of the virtual networks to be accessible by other virtual networks. For example, one virtual network might contain corporate DNS, DHCP, and email servers, which need to be accessed by all the other virtual networks. Cisco EVN makes this possible through a service called *route replication*. The route replication service allows IP routes known to one virtual network to be known to other virtual networks. As an example, consider Figure 1-30.

In Figure 1-30, the 172.16.0.0 /16 virtual network (VRF A) and the 172.17.0.0 /16 virtual network (VRF B) are isolated from one another. However, the 192.168.0.0 /24 network (VRF C) contains servers (for example, DHCP, DNS, and email servers) that need to be accessed by both VRF A and VRF B. Route replication allows networks in VRF C to be added to the routing tables of VRF A and VRF B, while still keeping VRF A and VRF B separate from one another. Also, notice that the routing table for VRF C knows about routes in the other two VRFs.

Note Even though different IP address spaces were used in this example for VRF A and VRF B, in the real world, you could have overlapping address spaces in different VRFs.

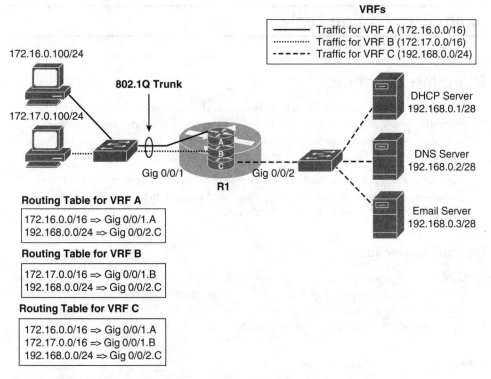

Figure 1-30 *Route Replication*

Exam Preparation Tasks

Planning Practice

The CCNP ROUTE exam expects test takers to review design documents, create implementation plans, and create verification plans. This section provides some exercises that can help you to take a step back from the minute details of the topics in this chapter so that you can think about the same technical topics from the planning perspective.

For each planning practice table, simply complete the table. Note that any numbers in parentheses represent the number of options listed for each item in the solutions in Appendix F, "Completed Planning Practice Tables."

Design Review Table

Table 1-3 lists several design goals related to this chapter. If these design goals were listed in a design document, and you had to take that document and develop an implementation plan, what implementation options come to mind? You should write a general description; specific configuration commands are not required.

Table 1-3 *Design Review*

Design Goal	Possible Implementation Choices Covered in This Chapter
The design requires the number of entries in a router's routing table to be reduced.	
The design calls for the use of a distance-vector routing protocol. Identify the two approaches that a distance-vector routing protocol can use to prevent loops. (2)	
The design calls for the use of a link-state routing protocol. (2)	
The design calls for IPv6 traffic to travel from a source IPv6 address to the nearest device of multiple devices assigned the same destination IPv6 address.	
The design calls for the use of an NBMA network. Identify design issues that might be encountered when using EIGRP or OSPF. (2)	
The design calls for the use of Hot Standby Router Protocol (HSRP). Identify the condition that can be created when return traffic flows through a standby HSRP router.	

Design Goal	Possible Implementation Choices Covered in This Chapter
The design needs to mitigate a global synchronization condition (where all TCP flows simultaneously enter TCP slow start).	
The design requires a network to be migrated to a different routing protocol. (2)	
The design requires that you virtualize multiple routers inside of physical routers and carry traffic for the virtual networks between those physical routers.	

Implementation Plan Peer Review Table

Table 1-4 shows a list of questions that others might ask, or that you might think about, during a peer review of another network engineer's implementation plan. Complete the table by answering the questions.

Table 1-4 *Notable Questions from This Chapter to Consider During an Implementation Plan Peer Review*

Question	Answers
The plan requires that Split Horizon be disabled for the hub router in a hub-and-spoke topology. Describe the purpose of Split Horizon.	
The plan requires the use of EIGRP as the routing protocol. Provide a brief description of EIGRP.	
The plan calls for the use of both IPv4 and IPv6. What network traffic types do IPv4 and IPv6 have in common, and what traffic types are different?	
The plan calls for the use of Hot Standby Router Protocol (HSRP). What can you do to prevent an asymmetric routing issue, where traffic is forwarded from a subnet using the active HSRP router, and some of the return traffic returns using the standby HSRP router (because of load balancing)?	

Question	Answers
The design calls for the transmission of interactive voice and video over a network. What Layer 4 protocols are typically used to transmit voice and data media? (2)	
The plan requires that a network migrate from IPv4 to IPv6. Identify three strategies of a successful IPv6 migration. (3)	
The plan calls for the use of Virtual Routing and Forwarding (VRF). Identify two approaches to configuring VRF. (2)	

Review All the Key Topics

Review the most important topics from inside the chapter, noted with the Key Topic icon in the outer margin of the page. Table 1-5 lists a reference of these key topics and the page numbers on which each is found.

Table 1-5   *Key Topics for Chapter 1*

Key Topic Element	Description	Page Number
Figure 1-3	Network Summarization	10
List	IGP and EGP definitions	11
List	Distance-vector routing protocol approaches to avoid routing loops	13
Table 1-2	Routing Protocol Characteristics	15
List	NBMA design considerations	21
Figure 1-23	Unidirectional Flooding of Inbound Traffic	29
List	Two ICMP message types	31
List	TCP three-way handshake	33
Figure 1-27	TCP Sliding Window	34
List	Approaches to routing protocol migration	36
List	Strategies for IPv6 migration	37
Figure 1-29	Sample EVN Topology	40

Complete the Tables and Lists from Memory

Print a copy of Appendix D, "Memory Tables," (found on the CD) or at least the section for this chapter, and complete the tables and lists from memory. Appendix E, "Memory Tables Answer Key," also on the CD, includes completed tables and lists to check your work.

Definitions of Key Terms

Define the following key terms from this chapter, and check your answers in the glossary.

convergence, route summarization, interior gateway protocol (IGP), exterior gateway protocol (EGP), distance-vector, link-state, path-vector, anycast, nonbroadcast multi-access (NBMA), Split Horizon, Poison Reverse, asymmetric routing, Administrative Distance, Easy Virtual Networking (EVN)

This chapter covers the following subjects:

- **Remote Connectivity Overview:** This section explains why VPNs are often a preferred method of remotely connecting to sites and identifies a collection of available VPN technologies.

- **MPLS VPN:** This section contrasts Layer 2 MPLS VPNs and Layer 3 MPLS VPNs.

- **GRE:** This section describes a GRE tunnel and demonstrates GRE tunnel configuration and verification.

- **DMVPN:** This section discusses how DMVPNs can dynamically bring up connections between specific spokes in a hub-and-spoke VPN topology.

- **Multipoint GRE:** This section explains how a single GRE interface can have connections to multiple GRE peers.

- **NHRP:** This section explains how NHRP can discover next-hop IP addresses in networks using IP tunneling.

- **IPsec:** This section explores how IPsec can be used to secure a VPN connection.

CHAPTER 2

Remote Site Connectivity

Traditional wide-area network (WAN) connections used technologies such as dedicated leased lines and permanent virtual circuits (PVC) defined in frame switching (for example, Frame Relay) and cell switching (for example, ATM) networks. As an example, if a company opened a remote sales office, it might have purchased a Frame Relay connection for that remote office and used a PVC that interconnected that remote office with the corporate headquarters.

However, with the current state of the Internet, high-speed connections are widely accessible. For example, a remote sales office might purchase a DSL or cable modem connection to the Internet, at a relatively low cost as compared to traditional leased lines or frame/cell switching technologies. Over that Internet connection, a *virtual private network (VPN)* could create a logical path between the sales office and the headquarters location.

The theory and configuration of VPNs goes well beyond what is covered in this chapter; however, the ROUTE exam blueprint only requires configuration knowledge for Generic Routing Encapsulation (GRE) tunnels. Therefore, this chapter will help you understand the theory of multiple VPN technologies, while showing the configuration and verification of GRE.

"Do I Know This Already?" Quiz

The "Do I Know This Already?" quiz allows you to assess whether you should read the entire chapter. If you miss no more than one of these seven self-assessment questions, you might want to move ahead to the "Exam Preparation Tasks" section. Table 2-1 lists the major headings in this chapter and the "Do I Know This Already?" quiz questions covering the material in those headings so that you can assess your knowledge of these specific areas. The answers to the "Do I Know This Already?" quiz appear in Appendix A.

Table 2-1   *"Do I Know This Already?" Foundation Topics Section-to-Question Mapping*

Foundation Topics Section	Questions
Remote Connectivity Overview	1
MPLS VPN	2
GRE	3
DMVPN	4
Multipoint GRE	5
NHRP	6
IPsec	7

1. Which of the following is a valid design consideration for a hybrid VPN?

    a. You cannot encapsulate an encrypted packet.

    b. You cannot encrypt an encapsulated packet.

    c. You might need to decrease the MTU size for frames on an interface.

    d. You might need to increase the MTU size for frames on an interface.

2. In a Layer 3 MPLS VPN, with what does a CE router form a neighborship?

    a. A PE in the MPLS network.

    b. A CE at a remote location.

    c. No neighborship is formed, because the MPLS network acts as a logical switch.

    d. No neighborship is formed, because IP multicast traffic cannot be sent across an MPLS network.

3. You want to interconnect two remote sites with a VPN tunnel. The tunnel needs to support IP unicast, multicast, and broadcast traffic. Additionally, you need to encrypt traffic being sent over the tunnel. Which of the following VPN solutions meets the design requirements?

    a. Use a GRE tunnel.

    b. Use an IPsec tunnel.

    c. Use a GRE tunnel inside of an IPsec tunnel.

    d. Use an IPsec tunnel inside of a GRE tunnel.

4. Identify technologies required for a DMVPN network. (Choose three.)

    a. NHRP

    b. IPsec

    c. MPLS

    d. mGRE

5. Which of the following are characteristics of multipoint GRE? (Choose two.)

    a. mGRE supports a wide variety of protocols.

    b. A single mGRE interface can service multiple tunnels.

    c. An mGRE interface is created for each tunnel.

    d. mGRE only transports unicast IP packets.

6. Which of the following are true for NHRP? (Choose two.)

    a. The hub router is configured with the IP addresses of the spoke routers.

    b. The spoke routers are configured with the IP address of the hub router.

    c. Spoke routers query the hub router asking what tunnel interface IP address corresponds to a known physical interface IP address.

    d. Spoke routers query the hub router asking what physical interface IP address corresponds to a known tunnel interface IP address.

7. Which IPsec feature primarily performs encryption?

    a. Integrity

    b. Confidentiality

    c. Antireplay

    d. Authentication

Foundation Topics

Remote Connectivity Overview

The voice, video, and data commonly sent between remote offices and central sites often demand low latency and easy provisioning, all while maintaining a low cost. Traditional WAN solutions (for example, leased lines, Frame Relay, and ATM) typically fail to simultaneously meet all these requirements. Fortunately, a variety of VPN technologies fit nicely into such a design.

This section categorizes various VPN technologies. Then, the remainder of this chapter examines these technologies in a bit more detail.

MPLS-Based Virtual Private Networks

Multiprotocol Label Switching (MPLS) is a technology commonly used by service providers, although many large enterprises also use MPLS for their backbone network. MPLS makes forwarding decisions based on labels rather than IP addresses. Specifically, a 32-bit label is inserted between a frame's Layer 2 and Layer 3 headers. As a result, an MPLS header is often called a *shim header*, because it is stuck in between two existing headers.

MPLS-based VPNs can be grouped into one of two primary categories:

- Layer 2 MPLS VPNs
- Layer 3 MPLS VPNs

These two approaches are discussed further in the section "MPLS VPN," later in this chapter.

Tunnel-Based Virtual Private Networks

A *tunnel* is a virtual connection that can physically span multiple router hops. However, from the perspective of the traffic flowing through the tunnel, the transit from one end of a tunnel to the other appears to be a single router hop.

Multiple VPN technologies make use of virtual tunnels. A few examples discussed in this chapter include

- Generic Routing Encapsulation (GRE)
- Dynamic Multipoint VPN (DMVPN)

- Multipoint GRE

- IPsec

Hybrid Virtual Private Networks

Rather than just using a single MPLS-based VPN technology or a single tunnel-based VPN technology, you can use select VPN technologies in tandem. For example, you might want to extend an MPLS network at one corporate location to MPLS networks at remote corporate locations, while having a requirement that traffic traveling through a service provider's cloud be encrypted.

You could meet the requirements of such a design by having a Layer 3 MPLS VPN set up over a DMVPN. The DMVPN technology carrying the Layer 3 MPLS VPN traffic allows you to efficiently set up direct links between corporate locations, and it also allows you to use IPsec, which can encrypt the traffic flowing through the service provider's cloud.

When it comes to hybrid VPNs, a significant design consideration is *overhead*. Every time you add an encapsulation, you are adding to the total header size of the packet. With more headers, the amount of data you can carry inside a single packet is decreased. As a result, you might have to configure a lower *maximum transmission unit (MTU)* size for frames on an interface.

MPLS VPN

MPLS VPNs extend the capabilities of MPLS, supporting VPNs created across an MPLS network. These VPNs, most commonly found in service provider or large enterprise networks, can be categorized as either Layer 2 MPLS VPNs or Layer 3 MPLS VPNs.

Layer 2 MPLS VPN

With a Layer 2 MPLS VPN, the MPLS network allows *customer edge (CE)* routers at different sites to form routing protocol neighborships with one another as if they were Layer 2 adjacent. Therefore, you can think of a Layer 2 MPLS VPN as a logical Layer 2 switch, as depicted in Figure 2-1.

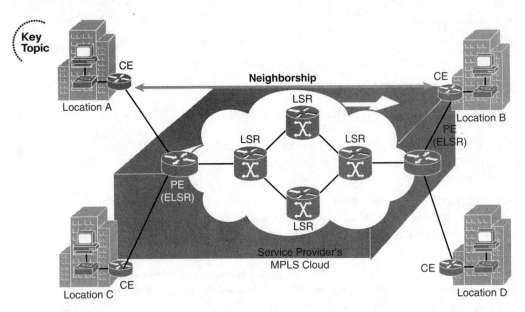

Figure 2-1   *Logical View of a Layer 2 MPLS VPN*

Layer 3 MPLS VPN

With a Layer 3 MPLS VPN, a service provider's *provider edge (PE)* router (also known as an *Edge Label Switch Router [ELSR]*) establishes a peering relationship with a CE router, as seen in Figure 2-2. Routes learned from the CE router are then sent to the remote PE router in the MPLS cloud (typically using *multiprotocol BGP [MP-BGP]*), where they are sent out to the remote CE router.

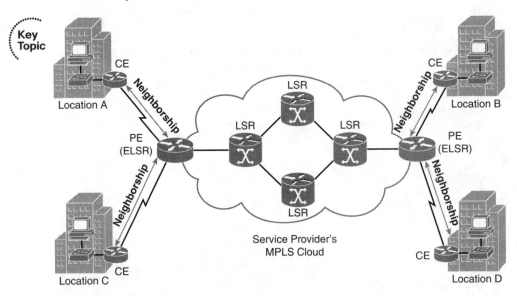

Figure 2-2   *Layer 3 MPLS VPN*

GRE

As its name suggests, a *Generic Routing Encapsulation (GRE)* tunnel can encapsulate nearly every type of data that you could send out of a physical router interface. In fact, GRE can encapsulate any Layer 3 protocol, which makes it very flexible.

GRE by itself does not provide any security for the data it transmits; however, a GRE packet can be sent over an IPsec VPN, causing the GRE packet (and therefore its contents) to be protected. Such a configuration is commonly used, because IPsec can only protect unicast IP packets. This limitation causes issues for routing protocols that use IP multicasts. Fortunately, a GRE tunnel can encapsulate IP multicast packets. The resulting GRE packet is an IP unicast packet, which can then be protected by an IPsec tunnel.

As an example, consider Figure 2-3. Routers R1 and R2 need to form an Open Shortest Path First (OSPF) neighborship across the service provider's cloud. Additionally, traffic between these two routers needs to be protected. While IPsec can protect unicast IP traffic, OSPF communicates through IP multicasts. Therefore, all traffic between Routers R1 and R2 (including the OSPF multicasts) is encapsulated inside of a GRE tunnel. Those GRE packets, which are unicast IP packets, are then sent across, and protected by, an IPsec tunnel.

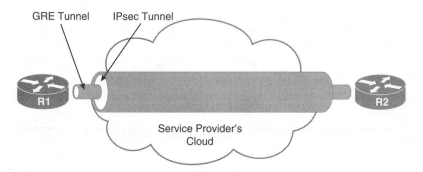

Figure 2-3   *GRE over IPsec Tunnel*

Note   For exam purposes, the only type of tunnel you need to know how to configure, based on the objectives listed in the ROUTE exam blueprint, is a GRE tunnel. Therefore, this chapter only provides a configuration example for a GRE tunnel.

The steps to configure a GRE tunnel are as follows:

Key Topic

Step 1.   Create a virtual tunnel interface in global configuration mode with the **interface tunnel** *id* command.

Step 2.   In interface configuration mode for the tunnel interface, add an IP address with the **ip address** *ip_address subnet_mask* command.

Step 3.   Specify the source of the tunnel with the **tunnel source** {*interface_id* | *ip_address*} command.

Step 4.   Specify the destination of the tunnel with the **tunnel destination** *ip_address* command.

Step 5.   Repeat the previous steps on the router at the far side of the tunnel.

To illustrate this configuration procedure, consider Example 2-1 and the topology shown in Figure 2-4.

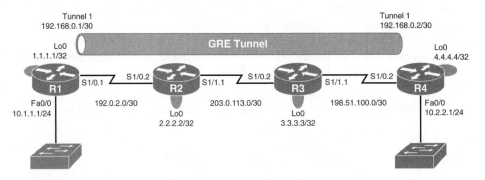

Figure 2-4   *GRE Sample Topology*

Example 2-1   *GRE Sample Configuration*

```
!ROUTER R1
interface Tunnel1
 ip address 192.168.0.1 255.255.255.252
 tunnel source Loopback0
 tunnel destination 4.4.4.4


!ROUTER R4
interface Tunnel1
 ip address 192.168.0.2 255.255.255.252
 tunnel source Loopback0
 tunnel destination 1.1.1.1
```

In Example 2-1, a virtual tunnel interface is created on Router R1 with the **interface Tunnel 1** command. An IP address is then assigned with the **ip address 192.168.0.1 255.255.255.252** command. Next, the **tunnel source Loopback0** command is used to specify Router R1's Lo 0 interface (and therefore its IP address of 1.1.1.1) as one end of the GRE tunnel. The **tunnel destination 4.4.4.4** command is then used to specify the Lo 0 interface on Router R4 as the other end of the tunnel. A mirrored configuration of the tunnel interface is then entered on Router R4.

Example 2-2 shows verification of the GRE tunnel. In the output of the **show interfaces tunnel 1** command, notice that the interface is up at Layer 1 and Layer 2. Also, note that the encapsulation type is TUNNEL. Also, the output of the **traceroute 192.168.0.2** command shows that the IP address of 192.168.0.2 is logically a single hop away from Router R1, even though it is physically three hops away.

Example 2-2 *GRE Tunnel Verification*

```
R1# show interfaces tunnel 1
Tunnel1 is up, line protocol is up
  Hardware is Tunnel
  Internet address is 192.168.0.1/30
  MTU 17916 bytes, BW 100 Kbit/sec, DLY 50000 usec,
     reliability 255/255, txload 1/255, rxload 1/255
  Encapsulation TUNNEL, loopback not set
  Keepalive not set
  Tunnel source 1.1.1.1 (Loopback0), destination 4.4.4.4
   Tunnel Subblocks:
      src-track:
         Tunnel1 source tracking subblock associated with Loopback0
          Set of tunnels with source Loopback0, 1 member (includes iterators), on
             interface <OK>
  Tunnel protocol/transport GRE/IP
    Key disabled, sequencing disabled
    Checksumming of packets disabled
  Tunnel TTL 255, Fast tunneling enabled
  Tunnel transport MTU 1476 bytes
  Tunnel transmit bandwidth 8000 (kbps)
  Tunnel receive bandwidth 8000 (kbps)
  Last input 00:00:01, output 00:00:01, output hang never
  Last clearing of "show interface" counters 00:54:43
  Input queue: 0/75/0/0 (size/max/drops/flushes); Total output drops: 0
  Queueing strategy: fifo
  Output queue: 0/0 (size/max)
  5 minute input rate 0 bits/sec, 0 packets/sec
  5 minute output rate 0 bits/sec, 0 packets/sec
     779 packets input, 67357 bytes, 0 no buffer
     Received 0 broadcasts (0 IP multicasts)
     0 runts, 0 giants, 0 throttles
     0 input errors, 0 CRC, 0 frame, 0 overrun, 0 ignored, 0 abort
     787 packets output, 68037 bytes, 0 underruns
     0 output errors, 0 collisions, 0 interface resets
     0 unknown protocol drops
     0 output buffer failures, 0 output buffers swapped out
R1# traceroute 192.168.0.2
Type escape sequence to abort.
Tracing the route to 192.168.0.2
VRF info: (vrf in name/id, vrf out name/id)
  1 192.168.0.2 108 msec 100 msec 108 msec
```

DMVPN

Consider a hub-and-spoke VPN topology in which multiple remote sites have a site-to-site VPN connection to a headquarters location. In such a topology, if one remote site wanted to communicate securely with another remote site, the traffic would travel between the sites through the headquarters location, rather than directly between the sites. One fix for this suboptimal pathing issue would be to create a full mesh of IPsec site-to-site VPN connections, which would provide a direct IPsec VPN connection between any two remote sites. Such a solution, however, could be complex and expensive to configure and maintain.

A more economical solution to providing optimal pathing without necessitating a full-mesh topology is the *Dynamic Multipoint VPN (DMVPN)* feature. DMVPN allows a VPN tunnel to be dynamically created and torn down between two remote sites on an as-needed basis. Consider Figure 2-5, which shows a hub-and-spoke topology, with the headquarters acting as the hub. Branch B and Branch C want to communicate with one another. Therefore, a DMVPN tunnel is created between these two locations.

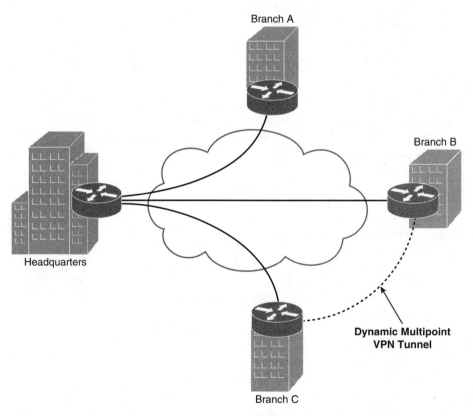

Figure 2-5 *Dynamic Multipoint VPN*

From a troubleshooting perspective, a common issue experienced with DMVPN networks is *flapping* (that is, the DMVPN tunnel is repeatedly torn down and reestablished). When experiencing such an issue, Cisco recommends that you check the routing protocol neighborship between the routers at each end of the DMVPN. If the neighborship is not always up, the DMVPN might flap.

Note   Multipoint GRE, Next Hop Resolution Protocol (NHRP), and IPsec are required to support a DMVPN topology. Each of these technologies is discussed in the remainder of this chapter.

Multipoint GRE

The scalability offered by DMVPN is made possible, in part, by *multipoint GRE (mGRE)*, which allows a router to support multiple GRE tunnels on a single GRE interface.

Some of mGRE's characteristics are as follows:

■   Like traditional GRE, mGRE can transport a wide variety of protocols (for example, IP unicast, multicast, and broadcast).

■   In a hub-and-spoke topology, a hub router can have a single mGRE interface, and multiple tunnels can use that single interface.

■   An interface configured for mGRE is able to dynamically form a GRE tunnel by using *Next Hop Resolution Protocol (NHRP)* to discover the IP address of the device at the far end of the tunnel.

You can deploy mGRE in a hub-and-spoke topology or a spoke-to-spoke topology. Figure 2-6 illustrates a hub-and-spoke topology, where only the hub router is configured with an mGRE interface.

Figure 2-7 shows a spoke-to-spoke mGRE topology. With a spoke-to-spoke mGRE topology, each router has an mGRE interface, which allows the sites in the network to interconnect using a partial mesh or a full mesh collection of tunnels.

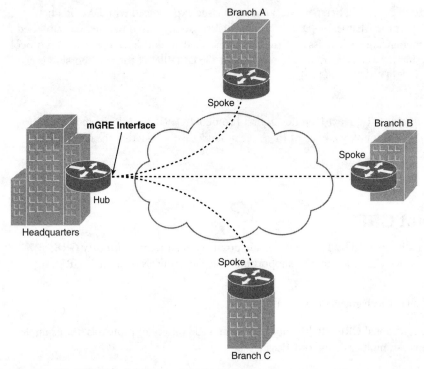

Figure 2-6   *Hub-and-Spoke mGRE Tunnel Topology*

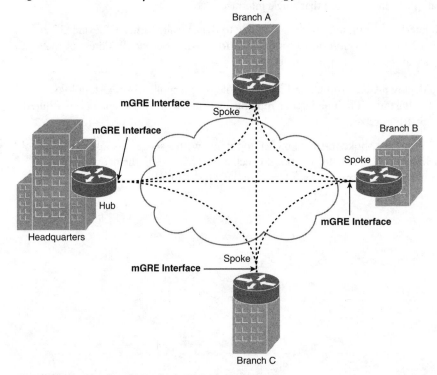

Figure 2-7   *Spoke-to-Spoke mGRE Tunnel Topology*

NHRP

DMVPNs require that routers run *Next Hop Resolution Protocol (NHRP)*, which uses a client-server model. A router designated as a *hub* router acts as a server. The remaining routers, designated as *spokes*, act as clients. NHRP spokes are configured with the IP address of the NHRP hub, and when a spoke comes online, it informs the hub of both a physical IP address (assigned to its physical interface) and a logical IP address (assigned to its virtual tunnel interface) that are going to be used for its tunnels.

As an example, examine Figure 2-8.

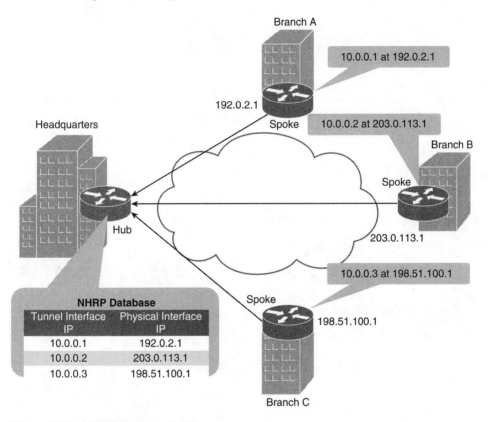

Figure 2-8 *NHRP Registration Process*

In Figure 2-8, the Headquarters router is acting as the hub, and the Branch A, Branch B, and Branch C routers are acting as spokes. When the spokes come online, they each advertise the IP address of their physical interface that is going to be used for tunnel formation, along with the IP address of the virtual tunnel interface. For example, the Branch A router informs the Headquarters router that the IP address of its virtual tunnel interface is 10.0.0.1, and it is available at a physical interface's IP address of 192.0.2.1. The Branch B and Branch C routers send similar advertisements to the Headquarters router. As a result, the Headquarters router populates its NHRP database.

Note The prior description of NHRP used the term *physical interface* to distinguish a nontunnel interface from a tunnel interface. Realize, however, that an interface being referred to here as a physical interface could actually be a loopback interface.

With the hub's database populated, a spoke can query the hub to find out the IP address of a physical interface that corresponds to a specific tunnel interface's IP address. As an example, notice in Figure 2-9 how NHRP helps the Branch C router set up a GRE tunnel with the Branch B router.

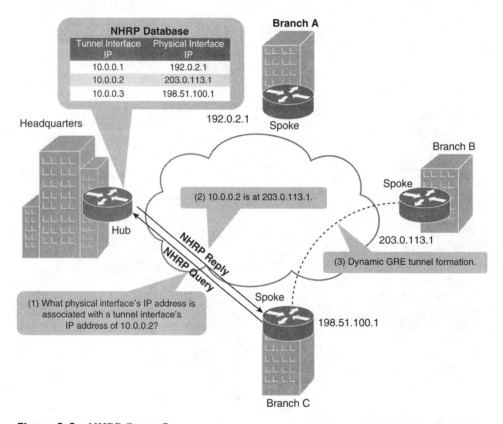

Figure 2-9 *NHRP Query Process*

In Figure 2-9, the Branch C router needs to dynamically form a GRE tunnel with the Branch B router. The Branch C router knows that the other end of the tunnel it wants to form has an IP address of 10.0.0.2. However, the Branch C router does not know the IP address of the physical interface on the Branch B router that corresponds to the virtual tunnel's IP address. The process of discovering the remote physical IP address and the formation of the tunnel is as follows:

Key Topic

Step 1.   The Branch C router sends an NHRP query to the hub router asking what physical interface's IP address is associated with a tunnel interface's IP address of 10.0.0.2.

Step 2.   The hub router (that is, the Headquarters router) checks its NHRP database and responds to the query, telling the Branch C router that the physical interface's IP address corresponding to the tunnel interface IP address of 10.0.0.2 is 203.0.113.1, which is the IP address of the Branch B router.

Step 3.   Having dynamically learned the IP address of the physical interface in the Branch B router, the Branch C router sets up a GRE tunnel with the Branch B router.

While the configuration of NHRP is beyond the scope of the ROUTE curriculum, you should be familiar with the output of the **show ip nhrp** verification command. Example 2-3 shows sample output from this command.

Example 2-3   *Sample Output from the* **show ip nhrp** *Command*

```
Router# show ip nhrp
 192.168.0.2 255.255.255.255, tunnel 100 created 0:00:44 expire 1:59:15
  Type: dynamic Flags: authoritative
  NBMA address: 10.1111.1111.1111.1111.1111.1111.1111.1111.1111.11
 192.168.0.1 255.255.255.255, Tunnel10 created 0:10:04 expire 1:49:56
  Type: static Flags: authoritative
  NBMA address: 192.168.1.2
```

The output in Example 2-3 shows the IP addresses (and corresponding subnet masks) in the IP-to-NBMA address cache. Note that the subnet mask for an IP address is always a /32 mask, because the Cisco implementation of NHRP does not support the aggregation of nonbroadcast multiaccess (NBMA) information. The output also shows the tunnel interface name and how long it has been since the tunnel was created. Finally, notice the **authoritative** flag. This flag indicates that a next-hop server (or router) provided the NHRP information.

IPsec

Security in a DMVPN is provided by IPsec. The following four security features are offered by IPsec:

- **Confidentiality:** Data confidentiality is provided by encrypting data. If a third party intercepts the encrypted data, the party would not be able to interpret the data.

- **Integrity:** Data integrity ensures that data is not modified in transit. For example, routers at each end of a tunnel could calculate a checksum value or a hash value for the data, and if both routers calculate the same value, the data has most likely not been modified in transit.

- **Authentication:** Data authentication allows parties involved in a conversation to verify that the other party is the party it claims to be.

- **Antireplay:** IPsec uses antireplay protection to ensure that packets being sent are not duplicate packets. For example, an attacker might capture packets that make up a valid login to a host and attempt to play those packets back, so that he can gain access to the host. However, IPsec uses sequence numbers to determine whether a packet is to be considered a duplicate packet, and any duplicate packets are not transmitted.

Of these IPsec services, encryption and authentication are particularly helpful in a DMVPN network. For example, encryption can help protect traffic flowing between sites (either over the Internet or through a service provider's cloud). Also, authentication can make sure that GRE tunnels are not dynamically set up with undesired spokes.

IPsec uses a collection of protocols to provide its features. One of the primary protocols used by IPsec is the *Internet Key Exchange (IKE)* protocol. Specifically, IPsec can provide encryption between authenticated peers using encryption keys, which are periodically changed. IKE does, however, allow an administrator to manually configure keys.

There are two phases to establish an IPsec tunnel. During IKE Phase 1, a *secure Internet Security Association and Key Management Protocol (ISAKMP)* session is established. As part of this phase, the IPsec endpoints establish transform sets (that is, a collection of encryption and authentication protocols), hash methods, and other parameters needed to establish a secure ISAKMP session (sometimes called an *ISAKMP tunnel* or an *IKE Phase 1 tunnel*). This collection of parameters is called a *security association (SA)*. With IKE Phase 1, the SA is bidirectional, meaning that the same key exchange is used for data flowing across the tunnel in either direction.

IKE Phase 2 occurs within the protection of an IKE Phase 1 tunnel. A session formed during IKE Phase 2 is sometimes called an *IKE Phase 2 tunnel*, or simply an *IPsec tunnel*. However, unlike IKE Phase 1, IKE Phase 2 performs unidirectional SA negotiations, meaning that each data flow uses a separate key exchange.

In addition to IKE, which establishes the IPsec tunnel, IPsec also relies on either the *Authentication Header (AH)* protocol (IP protocol number 51) or the *Encapsulating Security Payload (ESP)* protocol (IP protocol number 50). Both AH and ESP offer origin authentication and integrity services, which ensure that IPsec peers are who they claim to be and that data was not modified in transit.

The main distinction between AH and ESP, however, is encryption support. ESP encrypts the original packet, while AH does not offer any encryption. As a result, ESP is far more popular on today's networks.

Both AH and ESP can operate in one of two modes, transport mode or tunnel mode. Figure 2-10 illustrates the structure of an ESP transport mode packet versus an ESP tunnel mode packet.

Following is a detailed description of these two modes:

Key Topic

■ **Transport Mode:** Transport mode uses a packet's original IP header, as opposed to adding an additional tunnel header. This approach works well in networks where increasing a packet's size could cause an issue. Also, transport mode is frequently used for client-to-site VPNs, where a PC running VPN client software connects back to a VPN termination device at a headquarters location.

■ **Tunnel Mode:** Tunnel mode, unlike transport mode, encapsulates an entire packet. As a result, the encapsulated packet has a new header (that is, an IPsec header). This new header has source and destination IP address information that reflects the two VPN termination devices at different sites. Therefore, tunnel mode is frequently used in an IPsec site-to-site VPN.

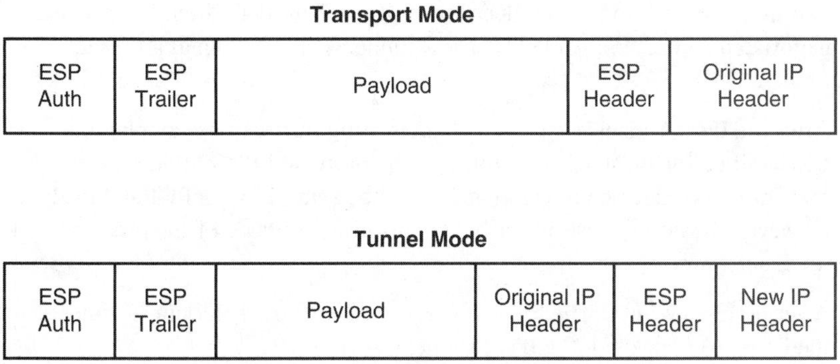

Transport Mode
ESP Auth
ESP Trailer
Payload
ESP Header
Original IP Header
Tunnel Mode
ESP Auth
ESP Trailer
Payload
Original IP Header
ESP Header
New IP Header

Figure 2-10 *Transport Mode Versus Tunnel Mode*

The process of establishing, maintaining, and tearing down an IPsec site-to-site VPN consists of five primary steps, as illustrated in Figure 2-11 and described in the list that follows.

PC1
PC2
R1
R2
Data
Step 1
Step 2
IKE Phase 1 Tunnel
IKE Phase 2 Tunnel
Step 3
IKE Phase 1 Tunnel
Data
Data
Step 4
Step 5

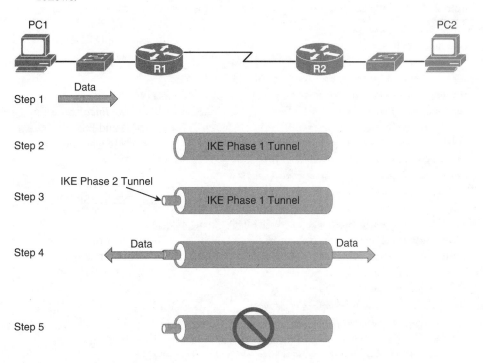

Figure 2-11 *IPsec VPN Steps*

Step 1. PC1 sends traffic destined for PC2. Router1 classifies the traffic as "interesting" traffic, which initiates the creation of an IPsec tunnel.

Step 2. Router1 and Router2 negotiate a security association (SA) used to form an IKE Phase 1 tunnel, which is also known as an ISAKMP tunnel.

Step 3. Within the protection of the IKE Phase 1 tunnel, an IKE Phase 2 tunnel is negotiated and set up. An IKE Phase 2 tunnel is also known as an IPsec tunnel.

Step 4. After the IPsec tunnel is established, interesting traffic (for example, traffic classified by an ACL) flows through the protected IPsec tunnel. Note that traffic not deemed interesting can still be sent between PC1 and PC2. However, the noninteresting traffic is transmitted outside of the protection of the IPsec tunnel.

Step 5. After no interesting traffic has been seen for a specified amount of time, or if the IPsec SA is deleted, the IPsec tunnel is torn down.

Even though the configuration of IPsec is beyond the scope of the ROUTE curriculum, you should be familiar with the output of the **show crypto ipsec sa** command, which lets you see information about the SA negotiated between IPsec peers. Example 2-4 shows sample output from this command.

Example 2-4 *Sample Output from the* **show crypto ipsec sa** *Command*

```
R1# show crypto ipsec sa
  interface: FastEthernet0/0
    Crypto map tag: test, local addr. 30.1.1.1
    local  ident (addr/mask/prot/port): (20.1.1.0/255.255.255.0/0/0)
    remote ident (addr/mask/prot/port): (10.1.1.0/255.255.255.0/0/0)
    current_peer: 30.1.1.2
      PERMIT, flags={origin_is_acl,}
     #pkts encaps: 7647918, #pkts encrypt: 7647918, #pkts digest 7647918
     #pkts decaps: 7640382, #pkts decrypt: 7640382, #pkts verify 7640382
     #pkts compressed: 0, #pkts decompressed: 0
     #pkts not compressed: 0, #pkts compr. failed: 0,
     #pkts decompress failed: 0, #send errors 1, #recv errors 0
      local crypto endpt.: 30.1.1.1, remote crypto endpt.: 30.1.1.2
      path mtu 1500, media mtu 1500
      current outbound spi: 3D3
      inbound esp sas:
       spi: 0x136A010F(325714191)
         transform: esp-3des esp-md5-hmac ,
         in use settings ={Tunnel, }
         slot: 0, conn id: 3442, flow_id: 1443, crypto map: test
         sa timing: remaining key lifetime (k/sec): (4608000/52)
         IV size: 8 bytes
         replay detection support: Y
      inbound ah sas:
      inbound pcp sas:
inbound pcp sas:
outbound esp sas:
   spi: 0x3D3(979)
```

```
    transform: esp-3des esp-md5-hmac ,
    in use settings ={Tunnel, }
    slot: 0, conn id: 3443, flow_id: 1444, crypto map: test
    sa timing: remaining key lifetime (k/sec): (4608000/52)
    IV size: 8 bytes
    replay detection support: Y
outbound ah sas:
outbound pcp sas:
```

In Example 2-4, an IPsec tunnel is formed between 30.1.1.1 and 30.1.1.2. The tunnel goes between networks 10.1.1.0 /24 and 20.1.1.0 /24. An ACL is used to identify (that is, permit) traffic that should be sent over the IPsec tunnel. Encapsulating Security Payload (ESP) or Triple Data Encryption Standard (3DES) is being used for encryption, and Message Digest 5 (MD5) is used for authentication.

Exam Preparation Tasks

Planning Practice

The CCNP ROUTE exam expects test takers to review design documents, create implementation plans, and create verification plans. This section provides some exercises that can help you to take a step back from the minute details of the topics in this chapter so that you can think about the same technical topics from the planning perspective.

For each planning practice table, simply complete the table. Note that any numbers in parentheses represent the number of options listed for each item in the solutions in Appendix F, "Completed Planning Practice Tables."

Design Review Table

Table 2-2 lists several design goals related to this chapter. If these design goals were listed in a design document, and you had to take that document and develop an implementation plan, what implementation options come to mind? For any configuration items, a general description can be used, without concern about the specific parameters.

Table 2-2 *Design Review*

Design Goal	Possible Implementation Choices Covered in This Chapter
The design requires that routers at remote sites appear as adjacent to one another, and they are interconnected over an MPLS network.	
The design requires customer edge (CE) routers at each enterprise site to communicate over an MPLS network and to form neighborships with provider edge (PE) routers to which they connect.	
The design requires that multicast, broadcast, and unicast IP traffic between sites be secured within a VPN.	
The design requires that spokes in a hub-and-spoke VPN topology be able to dynamically form GRE tunnels between themselves.	
The design requires that a single GRE tunnel interface support multiple GRE tunnels.	

Design Goal	Possible Implementation Choices Covered in This Chapter
The design requires that spoke routers in a hub-and-spoke VPN design be able to query the hub to determine the IP address of a physical interface corresponding to the far side of a tunnel.	
The design requires that you provide confidentiality, data integrity, authentication, and antireplay protection for unicast traffic flowing over a VPN.	

Implementation Plan Peer Review Table

Table 2-3 shows a list of questions that others might ask, or that you might think about, during a peer review of another network engineer's implementation plan. Complete the table by answering the questions.

Table 2-3 *Notable Questions from This Chapter to Consider During an Implementation Plan Peer Review*

Question	Answer
The plan requires that an MPLS VPN technology be used to interconnect remote sites. What broad categories of MPLS VPNs could you choose from? (Choose two.)	
The plan mandates the use of a Layer 3 MPLS VPN. What routing protocol will the service provider probably use to propagate route information from a customer edge (CE) router at one site to a CE router at another site?	
The plan calls for the use of a GRE tunnel. What protocols can you send over a GRE tunnel?	
The plan calls for the use of a Dynamic Multipoint VPN (DMVPN). What VPN technologies are required to support a DMVPN? (Choose three.)	
The plan requires a hub router in a hub-and-spoke topology to have four GRE tunnels out to remote sites. If you use mGRE, how many tunnel interfaces need to be configured on the hub router to support the four GRE tunnels?	

Question	Answer
The plan calls for the use of NHRP in a hub-and-spoke VPN topology. What router, or routers, in the topology will hold the NHRP database?	
The plan requires the use of IPsec. What are IPsec's modes of operation? (Choose two.)	

Create an Implementation Plan Table

To practice skills useful when creating your own OSPF implementation plan, list in Table 2-4 configuration commands related to the configuration of the following features. You might want to record your answers outside the book, and set a goal to complete this table (and others like it) from memory during your final reviews before taking the exam.

Table 2-4 *Implementation Plan Configuration Memory Drill*

Feature	Configuration Commands/Notes
Create a GRE virtual tunnel interface (in global configuration mode).	
Assign an IP address to a GRE tunnel (in interface configuration mode).	
Specify the source of a GRE tunnel (in interface configuration mode).	
Specify the destination of a GRE tunnel (in interface configuration mode).	

Choose Commands for a Verification Plan Table

To practice skills useful when creating your own OSPF verification plan, list in Table 2-5 all commands that supply the requested information. You might want to record your answers outside the book, and set a goal to complete this table (and others like it) from memory during your final reviews before taking the exam.

Table 2-5 *Verification Plan Memory Drill*

Information Needed	Command(s)
Verify the interface status and encapsulation of a GRE tunnel.	
Verify that a router sees the far side of a GRE tunnel as a single hop away, even though multiple routers might need to be transited to reach the far side of the tunnel.	

Review All the Key Topics

Review the most important topics from inside the chapter, noted with the Key Topics icon in the outer margin of the page. Table 2-6 lists a reference of these key topics and the page numbers on which each is found.

Table 2-6 *Key Topics for Chapter 2*

Key Topic Element	Description	Page Number
Figure 2-1	Logical View of a Layer 2 MPLS VPN	52
Figure 2-2	A Layer 3 MPLS VPN	52
List	Steps to configure a GRE tunnel	53
Example 2-1	GRE Sample Configuration	54
Example 2-2	GRE Tunnel Verification	55
List	Steps used by NHRP to discover a remote physical IP address and form a tunnel	60
Example 2-3	Sample Output from the **show ip nhrp** Command	61
List	Four security features offered by IPsec	61
List	Two modes of IPsec operation	62
Example 2-4	Sample Output from the **show crypto ipsec sa** Command	64

Complete the Tables and Lists from Memory

Print a copy of Appendix D, "Memory Tables," (found on the CD) or at least the section for this chapter, and complete the tables and lists from memory. Appendix E, "Memory Tables Answer Key," also on the CD, includes completed tables and lists to check your work.

Define Key Terms

Define the following key terms from this chapter, and check your answers in the glossary:

GRE, DMVPN, mGRE, NHRP, IPsec

This chapter covers the following subjects:

■ **Global Unicast Addressing, Routing, and Subnetting:** This section introduces the concepts behind unicast IPv6 addresses, IPv6 routing, and how to subnet using IPv6, all in comparison to IPv4.

■ **IPv6 Global Unicast Address Assignment:** This section examines how global unicast addresses can be assigned to hosts and other devices.

■ **Survey of IPv6 Addressing:** This section examines all types of IPv6 addresses.

■ **Configuring IPv6 Addresses on Cisco Routers:** This section shows how to configure and verify static IPv6 addresses on Cisco routers.

■ **RIP Next Generation (RIPng):** This section compares and contrasts IPv4's RIPv2 and IPv6's RIPng routing protocols and shows how to configure RIPng.

CHAPTER 3

IPv6 Review and RIPng

In your CCNA studies, you were introduced to IP version 6 (IPv6) addressing, and you learned that IPv6 is the replacement protocol for IPv4. IPv6 provides the ultimate solution for the problem of running out of IPv4 addresses in the global Internet by using a 128-bit address, as opposed to IPv4's 32-bit addresses. This gives IPv6 approximately 10^{38} total addresses, versus the mere (approximate) $4*10^9$ total addresses in IPv4. However, many articles over the years have discussed when, if ever, a mass migration to IPv6 would take place. IPv6 has been the ultimate long-term solution for more than ten years, in part because the interim IPv4 solutions, including NAT/PAT, have thankfully delayed the day in which we truly run out of public unicast IP addresses.

With all the promise of IPv6 and its rapid adoption, most networking professionals are still most familiar with IPv4. Therefore, this chapter spends a few pages reviewing the fundamentals of IPv6 to set the stage for a discussion of IPv6 routing protocols.

IPv6 uses an updated version of the three popular interior gateway protocols (IGP) (RIP, EIGRP, and OSPF) to exchange routes inside an enterprise. Additionally, updates to the BGP version 4 standard, called *multiprotocol extensions for BGP-4* (RFC 4760), allow the exchange of IPv6 routing information in the Internet.

This chapter demonstrates how to configure RIPng to support IPv6 routing. Upcoming chapters delve into IPv6 routing using EIGRP and OSPF version 3 (OSPFv3).

"Do I Know This Already?" Quiz

The "Do I Know This Already?" quiz allows you to assess whether you should read the entire chapter. If you miss no more than one of these ten self-assessment questions, you might want to move ahead to the "Exam Preparation Tasks" section. Table 3-1 lists the major headings in this chapter and the "Do I Know This Already?" quiz questions covering the material in those headings so that you can assess your knowledge of these specific areas. The answers to the "Do I Know This Already?" quiz appear in Appendix A.

Table 3-1 *"Do I Know This Already?" Foundation Topics Section-to-Question Mapping*

Foundation Topics Section	Questions
Global Unicast Addressing, Routing, and Subnetting	1, 2
IPv6 Global Unicast Address Assignment	3, 4
Survey of IPv6 Addressing	5, 6

Foundation Topics Section	Questions
Configuring IPv6 Addresses on Cisco Routers	7, 8
RIP Next Generation (RIPng)	9, 10

1. Which of the following is the shortest valid abbreviation for FE80:0000:0000:0000:0 010:0000:0000:0123?

    a. FE80::10::123

    b. FE8::1::123

    c. FE80:0:0:0:10::123

    d. FE80::10:0:0:123

2. An ISP has assigned prefix 3000:1234:5678::/48 to Company1. Which of the following terms would typically be used to describe this type of public IPv6 prefix?

    a. Subnet prefix

    b. ISP prefix

    c. Global routing prefix

    d. Registry prefix

3. Which of the following answers list either a protocol or function that can be used by a host to dynamically learn its own IPv6 address? (Choose two.)

    a. Stateful DHCP

    b. Stateless DHCP

    c. Stateless autoconfiguration

    d. Neighbor Discovery Protocol

4. Which of the following is helpful to allow an IPv6 host to learn the IP address of a default gateway on its subnet?

    a. Stateful DHCP

    b. Stateless RS

    c. Stateless autoconfiguration

    d. Neighbor Discovery Protocol

5. Which of the following answers lists a multicast IPv6 address?

    a. 2000::1:1234:5678:9ABC

    b. FD80::1:1234:5678:9ABC

    c. FE80::1:1234:5678:9ABC

    d. FF80::1:1234:5678:9ABC

6. Router R1 has two LAN interfaces and three serial interfaces enabled for IPv6. All the interfaces use link-local addresses automatically generated by the router. Which of the following could be the link-local address of R1's interface S0/0?

a. FEA0::200:FF:FE11:0

b. FE80::200:FF:FE11:1111

c. FE80::0213:19FF:FE7B:0:1

d. FEB0::211:11FF:FE11:1111

7. Router R1 has the following configuration. Assuming that R1's F0/0 interface has a MAC address of 0200.0011.1111, what IPv6 addresses will R1 list for interface F0/0 in the output of the **show ipv6 interface brief** command? (Choose two.)

```
interface f0/0
  ipv6 address 2345:0:0:8::1/64
```

a. 2345:0:0:8::1

b. 2345:0:0:8:0:FF:FE11:1111

c. FE80::FF:FE11:1111

d. FE80:0:0:8::1

8. Router R1 lists the following output from a **show** command. Which of the following is true about R1?

```
R1# show ipv6 interface f0/0
FastEthernet0/0 is up, line protocol is up
  IPv6 is enabled, link-local address is FE80::213:19FF:FE12:3456
  No Virtual link-local address(es):
  Global unicast address(es):
    2000::4:213:19FF:FE12:3456, subnet is 2000:0:0:4::/64 [EUI]
  Joined group address(es):
    FF02::1
    FF02::2
    FF02::1:FF12:3456
```

a. R1's solicited node multicast address is FF02::1:FF12:3456.

b. R1's 2000::4:213:19FF:FE12:3456 address is a global unicast with all 128 bits statically configured.

c. Address FF02::2 is R1's solicited node multicast.

d. R1's solicited node multicast, not listed in this output, would be FF02::213:19FF:FE12:3456.

9. Which of the following features work the same in both RIPv2 and RIPng? (Choose three.)

   a. Distance Vector Logic

   b. Uses UDP

   c. Uses RIP-specific authentication

   d. Maximum useful metric of 15

   e. Automatic route summarization

10. Router R1 currently has no configuration related to IPv6 or IPv4. The following configuration exists in a planning document, intended to be used to copy/paste into Router R1 to enable RIPng and IPv6 on interfaces Fa0/0 and S0/0/0. No other related configuration exists. Which of the following is true about RIPng on R1 after this configuration has been pasted into R1?

```
ipv6 unicast-routing
interface fa0/0
         ipv6 rip one enable
         ipv6 address 2000::1/64
interface s0/0/0
         ipv6 address 2001::/64 eui-64
         ipv6 rip one enable
```

   a. RIPng will be enabled on no interfaces.

   b. RIPng will be enabled on one interface.

   c. RIPng will be enabled on two interfaces.

   d. RIPng will advertise about prefixes connected to S0/0/0 and Fa0/0, but only send Updates on one interface.

Foundation Topics

The world has changed tremendously over the past 10–20 years as a result of the growth and maturation of the Internet and networking technologies in general. As recently as 1990, a majority of the general public did not know about nor use global networks to communicate, and when businesses needed to communicate, those communications mostly flowed over private networks. During the last few decades, the public Internet grew to the point where people in most parts of the world could connect to the Internet. Many companies connected to the Internet for a variety of applications, with the pre-dominate applications being email and web access. During the first decade of the twenty-first century, the Internet has grown further to billions of addressable devices, with the majority of people on the planet having some form of Internet access. With that perva-sive access came a wide range of applications and uses, including voice, video, collabora-tion, and social networking, with a generation that has grown up with this easily accessed global network.

The eventual migration to IPv6 will likely be driven by the need for more and more IP addresses. Practically every mobile phone supports Internet traffic, requiring the use of an IP address. Most new cars have the capability to acquire and use an IP address, along with wireless communications, allowing a car dealer to contact the customer when the car's diagnostics detect a problem with the car. Some manufacturers have embraced the idea that all their appliances need to be IP-enabled.

Although the two biggest reasons why networks might migrate from IPv4 to IPv6 are the need for more addresses and mandates from government organizations, at least IPv6 includes some attractive features and migration tools. Some of those advantages are as follows:

- **Address assignment features:** IPv6 supports a couple of methods for dynamic address assignment, including DHCP and stateless autoconfiguration.

- **Built-in support for address renumbering:** IPv6 supports the ability to change the public IPv6 prefix used for all addresses in an enterprise, using the capability to advertise the current prefix with a short timeout and the new prefix with a longer lease life.

- **Built-in support for mobility:** IPv6 supports mobility so that IPv6 hosts can move around an internetwork and retain their IPv6 addresses without losing current appli-cation sessions.

- **Provider-independent and -dependent public address space:** Internet Service Providers (ISP) can assign public IPv6 address ranges (dependent), or companies can register their own public address space (independent).

- **Aggregation:** IPv6's huge address space makes for much easier aggregation of blocks of addresses in the Internet, making routing in the Internet more efficient.

- **No need for NAT/PAT:** The huge public IPv6 address space removes the need for NAT/PAT, which avoids some NAT-induced application problems and makes for more efficient routing.

- **IPsec:** Unlike IPv4, IPv6 requires that every IPv6 implementation support IPsec. IPv6 does not require that each device use IPsec, but any device that implements IPv6 must also have the ability to implement IPsec.

- **Header improvements:** Although it might seem like a small issue, the IPv6 header actually improves several things compared to IPv4. In particular, routers do not need to recalculate a header checksum for every packet, reducing per-packet overhead. Additionally, the header includes a flow label that allows easy identification of packets sent over the same single TCP or UDP connection.

- **No broadcasts:** IPv6 does not use Layer 3 broadcast addresses, instead relying on multicasts to reach multiple hosts with a single packet.

- **Transition tools:** As covered later in this chapter, IPv6 has many rich tools to help with the transition from IPv4 to IPv6.

This list includes many legitimate advantages of IPv6 over IPv4, but the core difference is IPv6 addressing. The first two sections of this chapter examine one particular type of IPv6 addresses, global unicast addresses, which have many similarities to IPv4 addresses (particularly public IPv4 addresses). The third section broadens the discussion to include all types of IPv6 addresses, and protocols related to IPv6 address assignment, default router discovery, and neighbor discovery. The fourth section looks at the router configuration commands for IPv6 addressing. The fifth section of this chapter examines RIP Next Generation (RIPng) and shows how it can be used to route traffic for IPv6 networks.

Global Unicast Addressing, Routing, and Subnetting

The original Internet design called for all organizations to register and be assigned one or more public IP networks (Class A, B, or C). By registering to use a particular public network address, the company or organization using that network was assured by the numbering authorities that no other company or organization in the world would be using the same addresses. As a result, all hosts in the world would have globally unique IP addresses.

From the perspective of the Internet infrastructure, in particular the goal of keeping Internet routers' routing tables from getting too large, assigning an entire network to each organization helped to some degree. The Internet routers could ignore all subnets as defined inside an enterprise, instead having a route for each classful network. For example, if a company registered and was assigned Class B network 128.107.0.0/16, the Internet routers just needed one route for that entire network.

Over time, the Internet grew tremendously. It became clear by the early 1990s that something had to be done, or the growth of the Internet would grind to a halt when all the public IP networks were assigned and no more existed. Additionally, the IP routing tables in Internet routers were becoming too large for the router technology of that day. So, the Internet community worked together to come up with both some short-term and long-term solutions to two problems: the shortage of public addresses and the size of the routing tables.

The short-term solutions included a much smarter public address assignment policy in which public addresses were not assigned as only Class A, B, and C networks, but as smaller subdivisions (prefixes), reducing waste. Additionally, the growth of the Internet routing tables was reduced by smarter assignment of the actual address ranges based on geography. For example, assigning the Class C networks that begin with 198 to only a particular ISP in a particular part of the world allowed other ISPs to use one route for 198.0.0.0/8—in other words, all addresses that begin with 198—rather than a route for each of the 65,536 different Class C networks that begin with 198. Finally, Network Address Translation/Port Address Translation (NAT/PAT) achieved amazing results by allowing a typical home or small office to consume only one public IPv4 address, greatly reducing the need for public IPv4 addresses.

IPv6 provides the long-term solution to both problems (address exhaustion and Internet routing table size). The sheer size of IPv6 addresses takes care of the address exhaustion issue. The address assignment policies already used with IPv4 have been refined and applied to IPv6, with good results for keeping the size of IPv6 routing tables smaller in Internet routers. This section provides a general discussion of both issues, in particular how global unicast addresses, along with good administrative choices for how to assign IPv6 address prefixes, aid in routing in the global Internet. This section concludes with a discussion of subnetting in IPv6.

Global Route Aggregation for Efficient Routing

By the time the Internet community started serious work to find a solution to the growth problems in the Internet, many people already agreed that a more thoughtful public address assignment policy for the public IPv4 address space could help keep Internet routing tables much smaller and more manageable. IPv6 public address assignment follows these same well-earned lessons.

Note   The descriptions of IPv6 global address assignment in this section provide a general idea about the process. The process can vary from one Regional Internet Registry (RIR) to another and one Internet Service Provider (ISP) to another, based on many other factors.

The address assignment strategy for IPv6 is elegant, but simple, and can be roughly summarized as follows:

- Public IPv6 addresses are grouped (numerically) by major geographic region.

- Inside each region, the address space is further subdivided by ISPs inside that region.

- Inside each ISP in a region, the address space is further subdivided for each customer.

The same organizations handle this address assignment for IPv6 as for IPv4. The Internet Corporation for Assigned Network Numbers (ICANN, www.icann.org) owns the process, with the Internet Assigned Numbers Authority (IANA) managing the process. IANA assigns one or more IPv6 address ranges to each RIR, of which there are five at the time of this publication, roughly covering North America, Central/South America, Europe, Asia/Pacific, and Africa. These RIRs then subdivide their assigned address space into smaller portions, assigning prefixes to different ISPs and other smaller registries, with the ISPs then assigning even smaller ranges of addresses to their customers.

The IPv6 global address assignment plan results in more efficient routing, as shown in Figure 3-1. The figure shows a fictitious company (Company1), which has been assigned an IPv6 prefix by a fictitious ISP, NA-ISP1 (indicating North American ISP number 1).

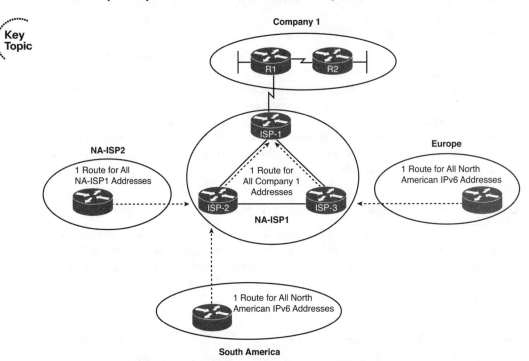

Figure 3-1 *Conceptual View of IPv6 Global Routes*

As shown in the figure, the routers installed by ISPs in other major geographies of the world can have a single route that matches all IPv6 addresses in North America. Although there might be hundreds of ISPs operating in North America, and hundreds of thousands of enterprise customers of those ISPs, and tens of millions of individual customers of those ISPs, all the public IPv6 addresses can be from one (or a few) very large address blocks—requiring only one (or a few) routes on the Internet routers in other parts of the world. Similarly, routers inside other ISPs in North America (for example, NA-ISP2, indicating North American ISP number 2 in the figure) can have one route that matches all address ranges assigned to NA-ISP1. Also, the routers inside NA-ISP1 just need to have one route that matches the entire address range assigned to Company1, rather than needing to know about all the subnets inside Company1.

Besides keeping the routers' routing tables much smaller, this process also results in fewer changes to Internet routing tables. For example, if NA-ISP1 signed a service contract with another enterprise customer, NA-ISP1 could assign another prefix inside the range of addresses already assigned to NA-ISP1 by the American Registry for Internet Numbers (ARIN). The routers outside NA-ISP1's network (that is, the majority of the Internet) do not need to know any new routes, because their existing routes already match the address range assigned to the new customer. The NA-ISP2 routers (another ISP) already have a route that matches the entire address range assigned to NA-ISP1, so they do not need any more routes. Likewise, the routers in ISPs in Europe and South America already have a route that works as well.

Conventions for Representing IPv6 Addresses

IPv6 conventions use 32 hexadecimal numbers, organized into 8 quartets of 4 hex digits separated by a colon, to represent a 128-bit IPv6 address, for example:

2340:1111:AAAA:0001:1234:5678:9ABC:1111

Each hex digit represents 4 bits, so if you want to examine the address in binary, the conversion is relatively easy if you memorize the values shown in Table 3-2.

Table 3-2   *Hexadecimal/Binary Conversion Chart*

Hex	Binary	Hex	Binary
0	0000	8	1000
1	0001	9	1001
2	0010	A	1010
3	0011	B	1011
4	0100	C	1100
5	0101	D	1101
6	0110	E	1110
7	0111	F	1111

Writing or typing 32 hexadecimal digits, although more convenient than writing or typing 128 binary digits, can still be a pain. To make things a little easier, two conventions allow you to shorten what must be typed for an IPv6 address:

- Omit the leading 0s in any given quartet.

- Represent one or more consecutive quartets of all hex 0s with "::" but only for one such occurrence in a given address.

Note   For IPv6, a *quartet* is one set of four hex digits in an IPv6 address. There are eight quartets in each IPv6 address.

For example, consider the following address. The bold digits represent digits in which the address could be abbreviated.

FE00:**0000:0000:000**1:**0000:0000:0000:00**56

This address has two different locations in which one or more quartets have four hex 0s, so two main options exist for abbreviating this address—using the :: abbreviation in one or the other location. The following two options show the two briefest valid abbreviations:

FE00::1:0:0:0:56

FE00:0:0:1::56

In particular, note that the :: abbreviation, meaning "one or more quartets of all 0s," cannot be used twice, because that would be ambiguous. So, the abbreviation FE00::1::56 would not be valid.

Conventions for Writing IPv6 Prefixes

IPv6 prefixes represent a range or block of consecutive IPv6 addresses. Just like routers use IPv4 subnets in IPv4 routing tables to represent ranges of consecutive addresses, routers use IPv6 prefixes to represent ranges of consecutive IPv6 addresses. The concepts mirror those of IPv4 addressing when using a classless view of the IPv4 address. Figure 3-2 reviews both the classful and classless views of IPv4 addresses, compared to the IPv6 view of addressing and prefixes.

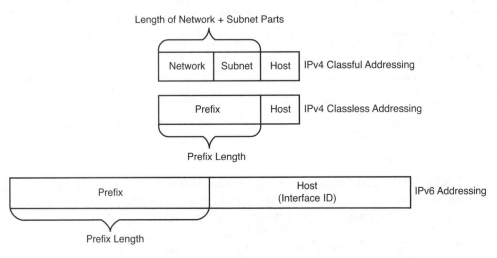

Figure 3-2   *IPv4 Classless and Classful Addressing, IPv6 Addressing*

First, for perspective, compare the classful and classless view of IPv4 addresses. Classful IPv4 addressing means that the class rules always identify part of the address as the network part. For example, the written value 128.107.3.0/24 (or 128.107.3.0 255.255.255.0) means 16 network bits (because the address is in a Class B network), 8 host bits (because the mask has 8 binary 0s), leaving 8 subnet bits. The same value, interpreted with classless rules, means prefix 128.107.3.0, prefix length 24. Classless addressing and classful addressing just give a slightly different meaning to the same numbers.

IPv6 uses a classless view of addressing, with no concept of classful addressing. Like IPv4, IPv6 prefixes list some prefix value, a slash, and then a numeric prefix length. Like IPv4 prefixes, the last part of the number, beyond the length of the prefix, will be represented by binary 0s. And finally, IPv6 prefix numbers can be abbreviated with the same rules as IPv6 addresses.

> **Note**   IPv6 prefixes are often called *IPv6 subnets*. This book uses these terms interchangeably.

For example, consider the following IPv6 address that is assigned to a host on a LAN:

    2000:1234:5678:9ABC:1234:5678:9ABC:1111/64

This value represents the full 128-bit IP address—there are no opportunities to even abbreviate this address. However, the /64 means that the prefix (subnet) in which this address resides is the subnet that includes all addresses that begin with the same first 64 bits as the address. Conceptually, it is the same logic as an IPv4 address. For example, address 128.107.3.1/24 is in the prefix (subnet) whose first 24 bits are the same values as address 128.107.3.1.

As with IPv4, when writing or typing a prefix, the bits past the end of the prefix length are all binary 0s. In the IPv6 address previously shown, the prefix in which the address resides would be

    2000:1234:5678:9ABC:0000:0000:0000:0000/64

Which, when abbreviated, would be

    2000:1234:5678:9ABC::/64

Next, consider one last fact about the rules for writing prefixes before seeing some examples. If the prefix length is not a multiple of 16, the boundary between the prefix and the interface ID (host) part of the address is inside a quartet. In such cases, the prefix value should list all the values in the last quartet in the prefix part of the value. For example, if the address just shown with a /64 prefix length instead had a /56 prefix length, the prefix would include all of the first three quartets (a total of 48 bits), plus the first 8 bits of the fourth quartet. The next 8 bits (last 2 hex digits) of the fourth octet should now be binary 0s, as part of the host portion of the address. So, by convention, the rest of the fourth octet should be written, after being set to binary 0s, as 9A00, which produces the following IPv6 prefix:

    2000:1234:5678:9A00::/56

Key Topic

The following list summarizes some key points about how to write IPv6 prefixes.

■   A prefix has the same value as the IP addresses in the group for the number of bits in the prefix length.

■   Any bits after the prefix length number of bits are binary 0s.

- A prefix can be abbreviated with the same rules as IPv6 addresses.

- If the prefix length is not on a quartet boundary, write down the value for the entire quartet.

Examples can certainly help in this case. Table 3-3 shows several sample prefixes, their format, and a brief explanation.

Table 3-3 *Example IPv6 Prefixes and Their Meanings*

Prefix	Explanation	Incorrect Alternative
2000::/3	All addresses whose first 3 bits are equal to the first 3 bits of hex number 2000 (bits are 001).	2000/3 (omits ::)
2340:1140::/26	All addresses whose first 26 bits match the listed hex number.	2340:114::/26 (omits trailing 0 in the second quartet)
2340:1111::/32	All addresses whose first 32 bits match the listed hex number.	2340:1111:/32 (uses : instead of ::)

Note which options are not allowed. For example, 2::/3 is not allowed instead of 2000::/3, because it omits the rest of the quartet, and a device could not tell whether 2::/3 means "hex 0002" or "hex 2000."

Now that you understand a few of the conventions about how to represent IPv6 addresses and prefixes, a specific example can show how IANA's IPv6 global unicast IP address assignment strategy can allow the easy and efficient routing previously shown in Figure 3-1.

Global Unicast Prefix Assignment Example

IPv6 standards reserve the range of addresses inside the 2000::/3 prefix as global unicast addresses. This address range includes all IPv6 addresses that begin with binary 001, or as more easily recognized, all IPv6 addresses that begin with a 2 or 3. IANA assigns global unicast IPv6 addresses as public and globally unique IPv6 addresses, as discussed using the example previously shown in Figure 3-1, allowing hosts using those addresses to communicate through the Internet without the need for NAT. In other words, these addresses fit the purest design for how to implement IPv6 for the global Internet.

Figure 3-3 shows an example set of prefixes that could result in a company (Company1) being assigned a prefix of 2340:1111:AAAA::/48.

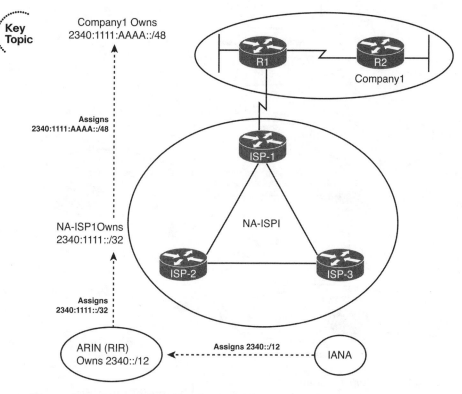

Figure 3-3 *Example IPv6 Prefix Assignment in the Internet*

The process starts with IANA, who owns the entire IPv6 address space and assigns the rights to a registry prefix to one of the RIRs (ARIN in this case, in North America). For the purposes of this chapter, assume that IANA assigns prefix 2340::/12 to ARIN. This assignment means that ARIN has the rights to assign any IPv6 addresses that begin with the first 12 bits of hex 2340 (binary value 0010 0011 0100). For perspective, that's a large group of addresses: 2^{116} to be exact.

Next, NA-ISP1 asks ARIN for a prefix assignment. After ARIN ensures that NA-ISP1 meets some requirements, ARIN might assign ISP prefix 2340:1111::/32 to NA-ISP1. This too is a large group: 2^{96} addresses to be exact. For perspective, this one address block might well be enough public IPv6 addresses for even the largest ISPs, without that ISP ever needing another IPv6 prefix.

Finally, Company1 asks its ISP, NA-ISP1, for the assignment of an IPv6 prefix. NA-ISP1 assigns Company1 the site prefix 2340:1111:AAAA::/48, which is again a large range of addresses: 2^{80} in this case. A little later in this section, the text shows what Company1 could do with that prefix, but first, examine Figure 3-4, which presents the same concepts as in Figure 3-1, but now with the actual prefixes shown.

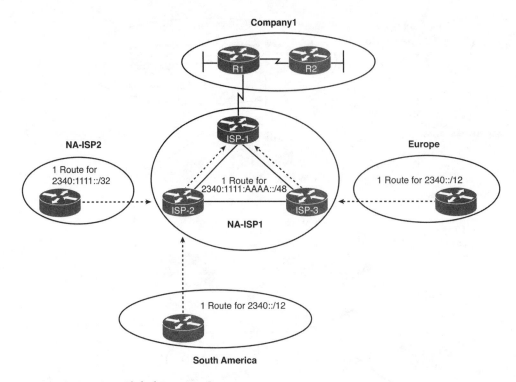

Figure 3-4   *IPv6 Global Routing Concepts*

The figure shows the perspectives of routers outside North America, routers from another ISP in North America, and other routers in the same ISP. Routers outside North America can use a route for prefix 2340::/12, knowing the IANA assigned this prefix to be used only by ARIN. This one route could match all IPv6 addresses assigned in North America. Routers in NA-ISP2, an example alternative ISP in North America, need one route for 2340:1111::/32, the prefix assigned to NA-ISP1. This one route could match all packets destined for all customers of NA-ISP1. Inside NA-ISP1, its routers need to know to which NA-ISP1 router to forward packets for that particular customer (named ISP-1 in this case), so the routes inside NA-ISP1's routers list a prefix of 2340:1111:AAAA::/48.

Note   The /48 prefix assigned to a single company is called either a *global routing prefix* or a *site prefix*.

Subnetting Global Unicast IPv6 Addresses Inside an Enterprise

The original IPv4 Internet design called for each organization to be assigned a classful network number, with the enterprise subdividing the network into smaller address ranges by subnetting the classful network. This same concept of subnetting carries over from IPv4 to IPv6, with the enterprise subnetting its assigned global unicast prefix into smaller prefixes.

To better understand IPv6 subnetting, you can draw on either classful or classless IPv4 addressing concepts, whichever you find most comfortable. From a classless perspective, you can view the IPv6 addresses as follows:

■ The prefix assigned to the enterprise by the ISP (the global routing prefix) acts like the prefix assigned for IPv4.

■ The enterprise engineer extends the prefix length, borrowing host bits, to create a subnet part of the address with which to identify individual subnets.

■ The remaining part of the addresses on the right, called either the interface ID or host part, works just like the IPv4 host part, uniquely identifying a host inside a subnet.

For example, Figure 3-5 shows a more detailed view of the Company1 enterprise network, shown in several of the previous figures in this chapter. The design concepts behind how many subnets are needed with IPv6 are identical to those of IPv4. Specifically, a subnet is needed for each VLAN and for each serial link, with the same Frame Relay subnetting options. In this case, two LANs and two serial links exist. So Company1 needs four subnets.

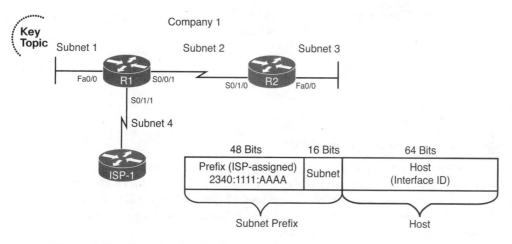

Figure 3-5 *Company1—Needs Four Subnets*

The figure also shows how the enterprise engineer extended the length of the prefix as assigned by the ISP (/48) to /64, thereby creating a 16-bit subnet part of the address structure. To create this extra 16-bit subnet field, the engineer uses the same concept as with IPv4 when choosing a subnet mask, by borrowing bits from the host field of an IPv4 address. In this case, think of the original host field (before subnetting) as having 80 bits, because the site prefix is 48 bits long, leaving 80 bits. The design in Figure 3-5 borrows 16 bits for the subnet field, leaving a measly 64 bits for the host field.

A bit of math about the design choices can help provide some perspective on the scale of IPv6. The 16-bit subnet field allows for 2^{16}, or 65,536, subnets—overkill for all but the very largest organizations or companies. (There are no worries about a zero or broadcast subnet in IPv6!) The host field is seemingly even more overkill: 2^{64} hosts per subnet, which is more than 1,000,000,000,000,000,000 addresses per subnet. However, there is a good reason for this large host or interface ID part of the address. It allows one of the automatic IPv6 address assignment features to work well, as covered later in the "IPv6 Global Unicast Addresses Assignment" section of this chapter.

Figure 3-6 takes the concept to the conclusion, assigning the specific four subnets to be used inside Company1. Note that the figure shows the subnet fields and prefix lengths (64 in this case) in bold.

> **Note**   The subnet numbers in Figure 3-6 could be abbreviated slightly, removing the three leading 0s from the last shown quartets. The figure includes the leading 0s to show the entire subnet part of the prefixes.

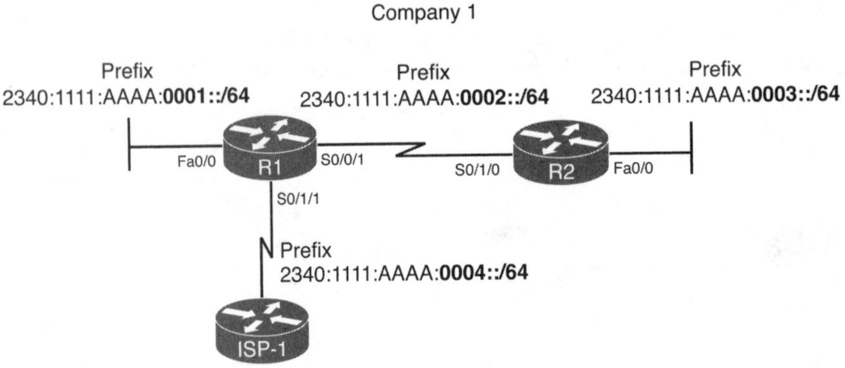

Figure 3-6   *Company1—Four Subnets Assigned*

Figure 3-6 just shows one option for subnetting the prefix assigned to Company1. However, any number of subnet bits could be chosen if the host field retained enough bits to number all hosts in a subnet. For example, a /112 prefix length could be used, extending the /48 prefix by 64 bits (four hex quartets). Then, for the design in Figure 3-6, you could choose the following four subnets:

    2340:1111:AAAA::0001:0000/112

    2340:1111:AAAA::0002:0000/112

    2340:1111:AAAA::0003:0000/112

    2340:1111:AAAA::0004:0000/112

By using global unicast IPv6 addresses, Internet routing can be very efficient. Enterprises can have plenty of IP addresses and plenty of subnets with no requirement for NAT functions to conserve the address space.

Prefix Terminology

Before wrapping up this section, you need to review a few terms. The process of global unicast IPv6 address assignment examines many different prefixes with many different prefix lengths. The text scatters a couple of more specific terms, but for easier study, Table 3-4 summarizes the four key terms with some reminders of what each means.

Table 3-4   *Example IPv6 Prefixes and Their Meanings*

Term	Assignment	Example
Registry prefix	By IANA to an RIR	2340::/12
ISP prefix	By an RIR to an ISP[1]	2340:1111/32
Site prefix or global routing prefix	By an ISP or registry to a customer (site)	2340:1111:AAAA/48
Subnet prefix	By an enterprise engineer for each individual link	2340:1111:AAAA:0001/64

[1] Although an RIR can assign a prefix to an ISP, an RIR can also assign a prefix to other Internet registries, which might subdivide and assign additional prefixes, until eventually an ISP and then its customers are assigned some unique prefix.

IPv6 Global Unicast Addresses Assignment

This section still focuses on global unicast IPv6 addresses but now examines the topic of how a host, router interface, or other device knows what global unicast IPv6 address to use. Also, hosts (and sometimes routers) need to know a few other facts that can be learned at the same time as they learn their IPv6 address. So, this section also discusses how hosts can get all the following relevant information that lets them use their global unicast addresses:

■ IP address

■ IP subnet mask (prefix length)

■ Default router IP address

■ DNS IP address(es)

IPv6 actually has four major options for IPv6 global unicast address assignment. This section looks at these options in the same order as listed in Table 3-5. Each method can use dynamic processes or static configuration, and each method can differ in terms of how a host or router gathers the other pertinent information (such as DNS IP addresses). Table 3-5 summarizes these main methods for easier review.

Table 3-5   *Summary of IPv6 Address Assignment for Global Unicast Addresses*

Method	Dynamic or Static	Prefix and Length Learned from...	Host Learned from...	Default Router Learned from...	DNS Addresses Learned from...
Stateful DHCP	Dynamic	DHCP Server	DHCP Server	Router, using NDP	(Stateful) DHCP Server
Stateless Autoconfig	Dynamic	Router, using NDP	Derived from MAC	Router, using NDP	Stateless DHCP
Static Configuration	Static	Local config	Local config	Router, using NDP	Stateless DHCP
Static Config with EUI-64	Static	Local config	Derived from MAC	Router, using NDP	Stateless DHCP

The rest of this section develops more detail about the topics in the table. Some of the processes work much like IPv4, and some do not. Regardless, as you work through the material, keep in mind one key fact about how IPv6 protocols approach the address assignment process:

> IPv6 address assignment processes can split the IPv6 address assignment into two parts: the prefix/length assignment and the host (interface ID) assignment.

Stateful DHCP for IPv6

IPv6 hosts can use stateful DHCP to learn and lease an IP address and corresponding prefix length (mask) and the DNS IP address(es). The concept works basically like DHCP for IPv4. The host sends a (multicast) packet searching for the DHCP server. When a server replies, the DHCP client sends a message asking for a lease of an IP address, and the server replies, listing an IPv6 address, prefix length, and DNS IP addresses. (Note that Stateful DHCPv6 does not supply the default router information, instead relying on Neighbor Discovery Protocol [NDP] between the client and local routers.) The names and formats of the actual DHCP messages have changed quite a bit from IPv4 to IPv6. So, DHCPv4 and DHCPv6 actually differ in detail, but the basic process remains the same. (The term *DHCPv4* refers to the version of DHCP used for IPv4, and the term *DHCPv6* refers to the version of DHCP used for IPv6.)

DHCPv4 servers retain state information about each client, such as the IP address leased to that client and the length of time for which the lease is valid. In other words, DHCPv4 tracks the current state of DHCP clients. DHCPv6 servers happen to have two operational modes: *stateful*, in which the server does track state information, and *stateless*, in which the server does not track state information. Stateful DHCPv6 servers fill the same role as the older DHCPv4 servers, whereas stateless DHCPv6 servers fill a different purpose as one part of the stateless autoconfiguration process. (Stateless DHCP, and its purpose, is covered in the upcoming section "Finding the DNS IP Addresses Using Stateless DHCP.")

One difference between DHCPv4 and stateful DHCPv6 is that IPv4 hosts send IP broadcasts to find DHCP servers, whereas IPv6 hosts send IPv6 multicasts. IPv6 multicast addresses have a prefix of FF00::/8, meaning that the first 8 bits of an address are binary 11111111, or FF in hex. The multicast address FF02::1:2 (longhand FF02:0000:0000:00 00:0000:0000:0001:0002) has been reserved in IPv6 to be used by hosts to send packets to an unknown DHCP server, with the routers working to forward these packets to the appropriate DHCP server.

Stateless Autoconfiguration

The second of the two options for dynamic IPv6 address assignment uses a built-in IPv6 feature called *stateless autoconfiguration* as the core tool. Stateless autoconfiguration allows a host to automatically learn the key pieces of addressing information—prefix, host, and prefix length—plus the default router IP address and DNS IP addresses. To learn or derive all these pieces of information, stateless autoconfiguration actually uses the following functions:

Step 1.   IPv6 Neighbor Discovery Protocol (NDP), particularly the router solicitation and router advertisement messages, to learn the prefix, prefix length, and default router

Step 2.   Some math to derive the interface ID (host ID) portion of the IPv6 address, using a format called EUI-64

Step 3.   Stateless DHCP to learn the DNS IPv6 addresses

This section examines all three topics in order.

Learning the Prefix/Length and Default Router with NDP Router Advertisements

The IPv6 Neighbor Discovery Protocol (NDP) has many functions. One function allows IPv6 hosts to multicast a message that asks all routers on the link to announce two key pieces of information: the IPv6 addresses of routers willing to act as a default gateway and all known IPv6 prefixes on the link. This process uses ICMPv6 messages called a Router Solicitation (RS) and a Router Advertisement (RA).

For this process to work, before a host sends an RS message on a LAN, some router connected to that same LAN must already be configured for IPv6. The router must have an IPv6 address configured, and it must be configured to route IPv6 traffic. At that point, the router knows it can be useful as a default gateway, and it knows at least one prefix that can be useful to any clients on the LAN.

For example, Figure 3-7 shows a subset of the internetwork seen in Figures 3-5 and 3-6, with the same IPv6 addresses and subnets used. Router R1's Fa0/0 has already been configured with an IPv6 address (2340:1111:AAAA:1:213:19FF:FE7B:5004/64) and has been configured to route IPv6 with the **ipv6 unicast-routing** global command.

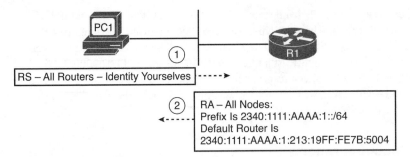

Figure 3-7 *Example NDP RS/RA Process to Find the Default Routers*

In the figure, host PC1, using stateless autoconfig, sends the RS message as an IPv6 multicast message destined to all IPv6 routers on the local link. The RS asks all routers to respond to the questions "What IPv6 prefix(s) is used on this subnet?" and "What is the IPv6 address(s) of any default routers on this subnet?" The figure also shows R1's response (RA), listing the prefix (2340:1111:AAAA:1::/64), and with R1's own IPv6 address as a potential default router.

> **Note**   IPv6 allows multiple prefixes and multiple default routers to be listed in the RA message; Figure 3-7 just shows one of each for simplicity's sake. One router's RA would also include IPv6 addresses and prefixes advertised by other routers on the link.

IPv6 does not use broadcasts. In fact, there is no such thing as a subnet broadcast address, a network-wide broadcast address, or an equivalent of the all-hosts 255.255.255.255 broadcast IPv4 address. Instead, IPv6 makes use of multicast addresses. By defining different multicast IPv6 addresses for different functions, an IPv6 host that has no need to participate in a particular function can simply ignore those particular multicasts, reducing the impact on the host.

For example, the RS message needs to be received and processed only by routers, so the RS message's destination IP address is FF02::2, which IPv6 reserves for use only by IPv6 routers. IPv6 defines that routers send RA messages to a multicast address intended for use by all IPv6 hosts on the link (FF02::1); routers do not forward these messages to other links. As a result, not only does the host that sent the RS message learn the information, but all other hosts on the link also learn the details. Table 3-6 summarizes some of the key details about the RS/RA messages.

Table 3-6 *Details of the RS/RA Process*

Message	RS	RA
Multicast destination	FF02::2	FF02::1
Meaning of multicast address	All routers on this link	All IPv6 nodes on this link

Calculating the Interface ID Using EUI-64

Earlier in the chapter, Figure 3-5 showed the format of an IPv6 global unicast address with the second half of the address called the *host ID* or *interface ID*. The value of the interface ID portion of a global unicast address can be set to any value if no other host in the same subnet attempts to use the same value.

To automatically create a guaranteed-unique interface ID, IPv6 defines a method to calculate a 64-bit interface ID derived from that host's MAC address. Because the burned-in MAC address should be literally globally unique, the derived interface ID should also be globally unique.

The EUI-64 process takes the 6-byte (48-bit) MAC address and expands it into a 64-bit value. To do so, IPv6 fills in 2 more bytes into the middle of the MAC address. IPv6 separates the original MAC address into two 3-byte halves and inserts hex FFFE in between the halves to form the Interface ID field of the IPv6 address. The conversion also requires flipping the seventh bit inside the IPv6 address, resulting in a 64-bit number that conforms to a convention called the *EUI-64 format*. The process is shown in Figure 3-8.

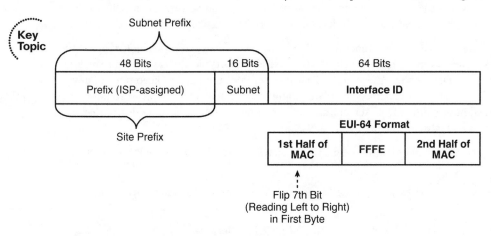

Figure 3-8 *IPv6 Address Format with Interface ID and EUI-64*

Although it might seem a bit convoluted, it works. Also, with a little practice, you can look at an IPv6 address and quickly notice the FFFE late in the address and then easily find the two halves of the corresponding interface's MAC address.

For example, the following two lines list a host's MAC address, and corresponding EUI-64 format Interface ID, assuming the use of an address configuration option that uses the EUI-64 format:

0034:5678:9ABC

0234:56FF:FE78:9ABC

Note To change the seventh bit (left-to-right) in the example, we notice that hex 00 converts to binary 00000000. Then we change the seventh bit to 1 (00000010) and convert back to hex, which gives us hex 02 as the first two hexadecimal digits.

At this point in the stateless autoconfig process, a host knows its full IPv6 address and prefix length, plus a local router to use as the default gateway. The next section discusses how to complete the process using stateless DHCP.

Finding the DNS IP Addresses Using Stateless DHCP

Although the DHCP server function for IPv4 does not explicitly use the word "stateful" in its name, IPv4 DHCP servers keep state information about DHCP clients. The server keeps a record of the leased IP addresses and when the lease expires. The server typically releases the addresses to the same client before the lease expires, and if no response is heard from a DHCP client in time to renew the lease, the server releases that IP address back into the pool of usable IP addresses—again keeping that state information. The server also has configuration of the subnets in use and a pool of addresses in most subnets from which the server can assign IP addresses. It also serves other information, such as the default router IP addresses in each subnet, and the DNS servers' IP addresses.

The IPv6 stateful DHCP server, as previously discussed in the section "Stateful DHCP for IPv6," follows the same general idea. However, for IPv6, this server's name includes the word *stateful*, to contrast it with the *stateless* DHCP server function in IPv6.

The stateless DHCP server function in IPv6 solves one particular problem: It supplies the DNS servers' IPv6 addresses to clients. Because all hosts typically use the same small number of DNS servers, the stateless DHCP server does not need to keep track of any state information. An engineer simply configures the stateless DHCP server to know the IPv6 addresses of the DNS servers, and the server tells any host or other device that asks, keeping no record of the process.

Hosts that use stateless autoconfig also use stateless DHCP to learn the DNS servers' IPv6 addresses.

Table 3-7 summarizes some of the key features of stateful and stateless DHCPv6.

Table 3-7   *Comparing Stateless and Stateful DHCPv6 Services*

Feature	Stateful DHCP	Stateless DHCP
Remembers IPv6 address (state information) of clients that make requests	Yes	No
Assigns IPv6 address to client	Yes	No
Supplies useful information, such as DNS server IP addresses	Yes	Yes
Most useful in conjunction with stateless autoconfiguration	No	Yes

Static IPv6 Address Configuration

Two options exist for static configuration of IPv6 addresses:

■ You configure the entire 128-bit IPv6 address.

■ You configure the 64-bit prefix and tell the device to use an EUI-64 calculation for the interface ID portion of the address.

Both options result in the host or router interface knowing its full 128-bit IPv6 address and prefix length.

When a host uses either form of static IPv6 address configuration, the host does not need to statically configure the other key pieces of information (default router and DNS IP addresses). The host can use the usual NDP process to discover any default routers and stateless DHCP to discover the DNS IPv6 addresses.

When a router uses static IPv6 address configuration, it might still use stateless DHCP to learn the DNS IP addresses. The upcoming section "Configuring IPv6 Addresses on Cisco Routers" shows several examples of this configuration.

Survey of IPv6 Addressing

So far, this chapter has focused on the IPv6 addresses that most closely match the concept of IPv4 addresses: the global unicast IPv6 addresses. This section now takes a broader look at IPv6 addressing, including some concepts that can be tied to older IPv4 concepts, and some that are unique to IPv6.

This section begins with a brief overview of IPv6 addressing. It then looks at unicast IPv6 addresses, along with a brief look at some of the commonly used multicast addresses. This section ends with a discussion of a couple of related protocols, namely, Neighbor Discovery Protocol (NDP) and Duplicate Address Detection (DAD).

Overview of IPv6 Addressing

The entire concept of global unicast addressing with IPv6 does have many similarities to IPv4. If viewing IPv4 addresses from a classless perspective, both IPv4 and IPv6 global unicast addresses have two parts: subnet plus host for IPv4 and prefix plus interface ID for IPv6. The format of the addresses commonly list a slash followed by the prefix length—a convention sometimes referred to as *CIDR notation* and other times as *prefix notation*. Subnetting works much the same, with a public prefix assigned by some numbering authority and the enterprise choosing subnet numbers, extending the length of the prefix to make room to number the subnets.

IPv6 addressing, however, includes several other types of unicast IPv6 addresses in addition to the global unicast address. Additionally, IPv6 defines other general categories of addresses, as summarized in the list that follows:

■ **Unicast:** Like IPv4, hosts and routers assign these IP addresses to a single interface for the purpose of allowing that one host or interface to send and receive IP packets.

- **Multicast:** Like IPv4, these addresses represent a dynamic group of hosts, allowing a host to send one packet that is then delivered to every host in the multicast group. IPv6 defines some special-purpose multicast addresses for overhead functions (such as NDP). IPv6 also defines ranges of multicast addresses for application use.

- **Anycast:** This address type allows the implementation of a nearest server among duplicate servers concept. This design choice allows servers that support the exact same function to use the exact same unicast IP address. The routers then forward a packet destined for such an address to the nearest server that is using the address.

Two big differences exist when comparing general address categories for IPv4 and IPv6:

- IPv6 adds the formal concept of Anycast IPv6 addresses as shown in the preceding list. IPv4 does not formally define an Anycast IP address concept, although a similar concept might be implemented in practice.

- IPv6 simply has no Layer 3 broadcast addresses. For example, all IPv6 routing protocols send Updates either to unicast or multicast IPv6 addresses, and overhead protocols such as NDP make use of multicasts as well. In IPv4, ARP still uses broadcasts, and the RIP version 1 routing protocol also uses broadcasts. With IPv6, there is no need to calculate a subnet broadcast address (hoorah!) and no need to make hosts process overhead broadcast packets meant only for a few devices in a subnet.

Finally, note that IPv6 hosts and router interfaces typically have at least two IPv6 addresses and might well have more. Hosts and routers typically have a link local type of IPv6 address (as described in the upcoming section "Link-local Unicast Addresses"). A router might or might not have a global unicast address, and might well have multiple addresses. IPv6 simply allows the configuration of multiple IPv6 addresses with no need for or concept of secondary IP addressing.

Unicast IPv6 Addresses

IPv6 supports three main types of unicast addresses: unique local, global unicast, and link-local. This section takes a brief look at unique local and link-local addresses.

Unique Local IPv6 Addresses

Unique local unicast IPv6 addresses have the same function as IPv4 RFC 1918 private addresses. RFC 4193 states that these addresses should be used inside a private organization and should not be advertised into the Internet. Unique local unicast addresses begin with hex FC00::/7, with the format shown in Figure 3-9. The L-bit is set to a 1 if the address is locally assigned. This makes FD the first two hex digits in a unique local address that is locally assigned.

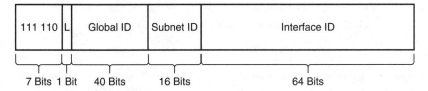

Figure 3-9   *Unique Local Address Format*

To use these addresses, an enterprise engineer would choose a 40-bit global ID in a pseudorandom manner rather than asking for a registered public prefix from an ISP or other registry. To form the complete prefix, the chosen 40 bits would be combined with the initial required 8 bits (hex FD) to form a 48-bit site prefix. The engineer can then use a 16-bit subnet field to create subnets, leaving a 64-bit interface ID. The interface ID could be created by static configuration or by the EUI-64 calculation.

This type of unicast address gives the engineer the ability to create the equivalent of an IPv4 private address structure, but given the huge number of available public IPv6 addresses, it might be more likely that engineers plan to use global unicast IP addresses throughout an enterprise.

Link-local Unicast Addresses

IPv6 uses link-local addresses for sending and receiving IPv6 packets on a single subnet. Many such uses exist; here's just a small sample:

- Used as the source address for RS and RA messages for router discovery (as previously shown in Figure 3-7)

- Used by Neighbor Discovery (the equivalent of ARP for IPv6)

- Used as the next-hop IPv6 address for IP routes

By definition, routers use a link-local scope for packets sent to a link-local IPv6 address. The term *link-local scope* means exactly that—the packet should not leave the local link, or local subnet if you will. When a router receives a packet destined for such a destination address, the router does not forward the packet.

The link-local IPv6 addresses also help solve some chicken-and-egg problems, because each host, router interface, or other device can calculate its own link-local IPv6 address without needing to communicate with any other device. So, before sending the first packets, a host can calculate its own link-local address. Therefore, the host has an IPv6 address to use when doing its first overhead messages. For example, before a host sends an NDP RS (Router Solicitation) message, the host will have already calculated its link-local address, which can be used as the source IPv6 address in the RS message.

Link-local addresses come from the FE80::/10 range, meaning that the first 10 bits must be 1111 1110 10. An easier range to remember is that all hex link-local addresses begin with FE8, FE9, FEA, or FEB. However, practically speaking, for link-local addresses formed automatically by a host (rather than through static configuration), the address always starts with FE80, because the automatic process sets bits 11-64 to binary 0s.

Figure 3-10 shows the format of the link-local address format under the assumption that the host or router is deriving its own link-local address, therefore using 54 binary 0s after the FE80::/10 prefix.

10 Bits	54 Bits	64 Bits
FE80/10 1111111010	All 0s	Interface ID

Figure 3-10 *Link-local Address Format*

IPv6 Unicast Address Summary

You might come across a few other types of IPv6 addresses in other reading. For example, earlier IPv6 RFCs defined the *site local* address type, which was meant to be used like IPv4 private addresses. However, this address type has been deprecated (RFC 3879). Also, IPv6 migration and coexistence tools use some conventions for IPv6 unicast addresses such that IPv4 addresses are embedded in the IPv6 address.

Additionally, it is helpful to know about other special unicast addresses. An address of all hex 0s, written ::/128, represents an unknown address. This can be used as a source IPv6 address in packets when a host has no suitable IPv6 address to use. The address ::1/128, representing an address of all hex 0s except a final hex digit 1, is a loopback address. Packets sent to this address will be looped back up the TCP/IP stack, allowing easier software testing. (This is the equivalent of IPv4's 127.0.0.1 loopback address.)

Table 3-8 summarizes the IPv6 unicast address types for easier study.

Table 3-8 *Common IPv6 Unicast Address Types*

Type of Address	Purpose	Prefix	Easily Seen Hex Prefix(es)
Global unicast	Unicast packets sent through the public Internet	2000::/3	2 or 3
Unique local	Unicast packets inside one organization	FD00::/8	FD
Link-local	Packets sent in the local subnet	FE80::/10	FE8*
Site local	Deprecated; originally meant to be used like private IPv4 addresses	FECO::/10	FEC, FED, FEE, FEF
Unspecified	An address used when a host has no usable IPv6 address	::/128	N/A
Loopback	Used for software testing, like IPv4's 127.0.0.1	::1/128	N/A

*IPv6 RFCs define the FE80::/10 prefix, which technically means that the first three hex digits could be FE8, FE9, FEA, or FEB. However, bit positions 11-64 of link-local addresses should be 0, so in practice, link-local addresses should always begin with FE80.

Multicast and Other Special IPv6 Addresses

IPv6 supports multicasts on behalf of applications and multicasts to support the inner workings of IPv6. To aid this process, IPv6 defines ranges of IPv6 addresses and an associated scope, with the scope defining how far away from the source of the packet the network should forward a multicast.

All IPv6 multicast addresses begin with FF::/8. In other words, they begin with FF as their first two digits. Multicasts with a link-local scope, like most of the multicast addresses referenced in this chapter, begin with FF02::/16; the 2 in the fourth hex digit identifies the scope as link-local. A fourth digit of hex 5 identifies the broadcast as having a site local scope, with those multicasts beginning with FF05::/16.

For reference, Table 3-9 lists some of the more commonly seen IPv6 multicast addresses. Of particular interest are the addresses chosen for use by Routing Information Protocol (RIP), Open Shortest Path First (OSPF), and Enhanced IGRP (EIGRP), which somewhat mirror the multicast addresses that each protocol uses for IPv4. Note also that all but the last two entries have a link-local scope.

Table 3-9   *Common Multicast Addresses*

Purpose	IPv6 Address	IPv4 Equivalent
All IPv6 nodes on the link	FF02::1	Subnet broadcast address
All IPv6 routers on the link	FF02::2	—
OSPF messages	FF02::5, FF02::6	224.0.0.5, 224.0.0.6
RIPv2 messages	FF02::9	224.0.0.9
EIGRP messages	FF02::A	224.0.0.10
DHCP relay agents (routers that forward to the DHCP server)	FF02::1:2	—
DHCP servers (site scope)	FF05::1:3	—
All NTP servers (site scope)	FF05::101	—

Layer 2 Addressing Mapping and Duplicate Address Detection

As with IPv4, any device running IPv6 needs to determine the data link layer address used by devices on the same link. IPv4 uses Address Resolution Protocol (ARP) on LANs and Inverse ARP (InARP) on Frame Relay. IPv6 defines a couple of new protocols that perform the same function. These new functions use ICMPv6 messages and avoid the use of broadcasts, in keeping with IPv6's avoidance of broadcasts. This section gives a brief explanation of each protocol.

Neighbor Discovery Protocol for Layer 2 Mapping

When an IPv6 host or router needs to send a packet to another host or router on the same LAN, the host/router first looks in its neighbor database. This database contains a list of all neighboring IPv6 addresses (addresses on connected links) and their corresponding MAC addresses. If not found, the host or router uses the Neighbor Discovery Protocol (NDP) to dynamically discover the MAC address.

Figure 3-11 shows a sample of such a process, using the same host and router seen earlier in Figure 3-8.

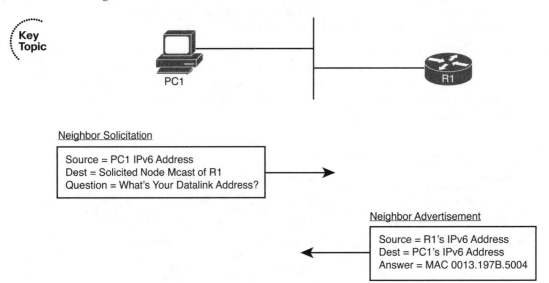

Figure 3-11 *Neighbor Discovery Protocol*

The process acts like the IPv4 ARP process, just with different details. In this case, PC1 sends a multicast message called a Neighbor Solicitation (NS) Internet Control Message Protocol (ICMP) message, asking R1 to reply with R1's MAC address. R1 sends a Neighbor Advertisement (NA) ICMP message, which is unicast back to PC1, listing R1's MAC address. Now PC1 can build a data-link frame with R1's MAC listed as the destination address and send encapsulated packets to R1.

The NS message uses a special multicast destination address called a *solicited node* multicast address. On any given link, the solicited node multicast address represents all hosts with the same last 24 bits of their IPv6 addresses. By sending packets to the solicited node multicast address, the packet reaches the correct host, but it might also reach a few other hosts—which is fine. (Note that packets sent to a solicited node multicast address have a link-local scope.)

The solicited node multicast address begins with FF02::1:FF00:0/104. The final 24 bits (6 hex digits) of the address are formed by adding the last 24 bits of the IPv6 address to which the message is being sent. All IPv6 hosts listen for frames sent to their own solicited node multicast address, so that when a host or router receives such a multicast, the host realizes that it should reply. For example, in this case, based on R1's IPv6 address previously seen in Figure 3-7

■ **R1's IPv6 address:** 2340:1111:AAAA:1:213:19FF:FE7B:5004

■ **R1's solicited node address:** FF02::1:FF7B:5004

> **Note** The corresponding Ethernet multicast MAC address would be 0100.5E7B.5004.

Duplicate Address Detection (DAD)

When an IPv6 interface first learns an IPv6 address, or when the interface begins working after being down for any reason, the interface performs *Duplicate Address Detection (DAD)*. The purpose of this check is to prevent hosts from creating problems by trying to use the same IPv6 address already used by some other host on the link.

To perform such a function, the interface uses the same NS message shown in Figure 3-11 but with small changes. To check its own IPv6 address, a host sends the NS message to the solicited node multicast address based on its own IPv6 address. If some host sends a reply, listing the same IPv6 address as the source address, the original host has found that a duplicate address exists.

Inverse Neighbor Discovery

The ND protocol discussed in this section starts with a known neighbor's IPv6 address and seeks to discover the link-layer address used by that IPv6 address. On Frame Relay networks, and with some other WAN data-link protocols, the order of discovery is reversed. A router begins with knowledge of the neighbor's data link layer address and instead needs to dynamically learn the IPv6 address used by that neighbor.

IPv4 solves this discovery problem on LANs using ARP and the reverse problem over Frame Relay using Inverse ARP (InARP). IPv6 solves the problem on LANs using ND, and now for Frame Relay, IPv6 solves this problem using Inverse Neighbor Discovery (IND). IND, also part of the ICMPv6 protocol suite, defines an Inverse NS (INS) and Inverse NA (INA) message. The INS message lists the known neighbor link-layer address (Data-Link Connection Identifier [DLCI] for Frame Relay), and the INS asks for that neighboring device's IPv6 addresses. The details inside the INS message include the following:

■ **Source IPv6:** IPv6 unicast of sender

■ **Destination IPv6:** FF02::1 (all IPv6 hosts multicast)

■ **Link-layer addresses**

■ **Request:** Please reply with your IPv6 address(es)

The IND reply lists all the IPv6 addresses. As with IPv4, the **show frame-relay map** command lists the mapping learned from this process.

Configuring IPv6 Addresses on Cisco Routers

Most IPv6 implementation plans make use of both static IPv6 address configuration and dynamic configuration options. As is the case with IPv4, the plan assigns infrastructure devices with static addresses, with client hosts using one of the two dynamic methods for address assignment.

IPv6 addressing includes many more options than IPv4, and as a result, many more configuration options exist. A router interface can be configured with a static global unicast IPv6 address, either with or without using the EUI-64 option. Although less likely, a router could be configured to dynamically learn its IPv6 address with either stateful DHCP or stateless autoconfig. The router interface could be configured to either not use a global unicast address, instead relying solely on its link-local address, or to borrow another interface's address using the IPv6 unnumbered feature.

This section summarizes the address configuration commands and shows several examples of configuration and verification commands for IPv6. To that end, Table 3-10 summarizes the IPv6 configuration commands and their meanings.

Table 3-10   *Router IOS IPv6 Configuration Command Reference*

Command	Description
ipv6 unicast-routing	A global configuration mode command that enables the routing of unicast IPv6 traffic.
ipv6 cef	A global configuration mode command that enables Cisco Express Forwarding (CEF) for IPv6.
ipv6 flowset	A global configuration mode command that configures flow-label marking in 1280-byte or larger packets sent from the router.
ipv6 address *address/length*	Static configuration of the entire IPv6 unicast address.
ipv6 address *prefix/length* **eui64**	Static configuration of the first 64 address bits; the router derives the last 64 bits with EUI-64.
ipv6 address autoconfig	Router uses stateless autoconfig to find an address.
ipv6 address dhcp	Router uses stateful DHCP to find an address.
ipv6 unnumbered *interface-type number*	Uses the same IPv6 unicast address as a referenced interface.
ipv6 enable	Enables IPv6 on the interface, but results in only a link-local address.

Command	Description
ipv6 address *address* link-local	Overrides the automatically created link-local address. The configured value must conform to the FE80::/10 prefix.
ipv6 address *address/length* anycast	Designates that the unicast address is an anycast address.

Note All the interface subcommands in Table 3-10 enable IPv6 on an interface, which means that a router derives an IPv6 link-local address for the interface. The description shows what the command does in addition to enabling IPv6.

Configuring Static IPv6 Addresses on Routers

The configuration examples in this section use the internetwork shown in Figure 3-12. The figure shows a diagram that you might see in an implementation plan, with the five IPv6 subnet numbers shown over the five links. The interface ID of each interface is then abbreviated, or shown as EUI-64, as a reminder of whether to configure the entire 128-bit address or to rely on the EUI-64 feature.

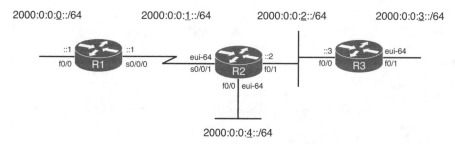

Figure 3-12 *Sample IPv6 Address Planning Diagram*

Example 3-1 shows the configuration process on Router R2, which uses EUI-64 on two interfaces and a complete IPv6 address on another. Also, note that the configuration includes the **ipv6 unicast-routing** global configuration command, which enables the router to route IPv6 traffic. (The addresses can be configured without also configuring **ipv6 unicast-routing**, but without this command, the router acts more like an IPv6 host, and it will not forward IPv6 packets.)

Example 3-1 *R2's IPv6 Configuration*

```
R2# show running-config
! lines omitted for brevity

interface FastEthernet0/0
 ipv6 address 2000:0:0:4::/64 eui-64
```

```
!
interface FastEthernet0/1
 ipv6 address 2000:0:0:2::2/64
!
interface Serial0/0/1
 ipv6 address 2000:0:0:1::/64 eui-64
!
!
R2# show ipv6 interface brief
FastEthernet0/0              [up/up]
    FE80::213:19FF:FE7B:5004
    2000::4:213:19FF:FE7B:5004
FastEthernet0/1              [up/up]
    FE80::213:19FF:FE7B:5005
    2000:0:0:2::2
Serial0/0/0                 [administratively down/down]
    unassigned
Serial0/0/1                 [up/up]
    FE80::213:19FF:FE7B:5004
    2000::1:213:19FF:FE7B:5004
Serial0/1/0                 [administratively down/down]
    unassigned
Serial0/1/1                 [administratively down/down]
    unassigned


R2# show interfaces fa0/0

FastEthernet0/0 is up, line protocol is up
  Hardware is Gt96k FE, address is 0013.197b.5004 (bia 0013.197b.5004)
  MTU 1500 bytes, BW 100000 Kbit/sec, DLY 100 usec,
     reliability 255/255, txload 1/255, rxload 1/255
! lines omitted for brevity
```

The **ipv6 address** commands both enable IPv6 on the associated interfaces and define either the prefix (with the EUI-64 option) or the entire address. The **show** commands listed after the configuration confirm the IPv6 addresses. Of particular note:

- All three interfaces now have link-local addresses that begin with FE80.

- Fa0/1 has the address exactly as configured.

- S0/0/1 and Fa0/0 have the configured prefixes (2000:0:0:1 and 2000:0:0:4, respectively), but with EUI-64-derived interface IDs.

- S0/0/1 uses Fa0/0's MAC address (as shown in the **show interfaces fa0/0** command) when forming its EUI-64.

On this last point, whenever Cisco IOS needs a MAC address for an interface, and that interface does not have a built-in MAC address, the router uses the MAC address of the lowest-numbered LAN interface on the router—in this case, Fa0/0. The following list shows the derivation of the last 64 bits (16 hexadecimal digits) of R2's IPv6 interface IDs for its global unicast IPv6 addresses on Fa0/0 and S0/0/1:

Step 1.   Use Fa0/0's MAC address: 0013.197B.5004.

Step 2.   Split and insert FFFE: 0013:19FF:FE7B:5004.

Step 3.   Invert bit 7: Hex 00 = 00000000 binary, flip for 00000010, and convert back to hex 02, resulting in 0213:19FF:FE7B:5004.

Multicast Groups Joined by IPv6 Router Interfaces

Next, consider the deeper information held in the **show ipv6 interface fa0/0** command output on Router R2, as shown in Example 3-2. Not only does it list the same link-local and global unicast addresses, but it also lists other special addresses as well.

Example 3-2   *All IPv6 Addresses on an Interface*

```
R2# show ipv6 interface fa0/0
FastEthernet0/0 is up, line protocol is up
  IPv6 is enabled, link-local address is FE80::213:19FF:FE7B:5004
  No Virtual link-local address(es):
  Global unicast address(es):
    2000::4:213:19FF:FE7B:5004, subnet is 2000:0:0:4::/64 [EUI]
  Joined group address(es):
    FF02::1
    FF02::2
    FF02::1:FF7B:5004
  MTU is 1500 bytes
  ICMP error messages limited to one every 100 milliseconds
  ICMP redirects are enabled
  ICMP unreachables are sent
  ND DAD is enabled, number of DAD attempts: 1
  ND reachable time is 30000 milliseconds (using 22807)
  ND advertised reachable time is 0 (unspecified)
  ND advertised retransmit interval is 0 (unspecified)
  ND router advertisements are sent every 200 seconds
  ND router advertisements live for 1800 seconds
  ND advertised default router preference is Medium
  Hosts use stateless autoconfig for addresses.
```

The three joined multicast groups should be somewhat familiar after reading this chapter. The first multicast address, FF02::1, represents all IPv6 devices, so router interfaces must listen for packets sent to this address. FF02::2 represents all IPv6 routers, so again, R2 must listen for packets sent to this address. Finally, the FF02::1:FF beginning value is the range for an address's solicited node multicast address, used by several functions, including Duplicate Address Detection (DAD) and Neighbor Discovery (ND).

Connected Routes and Neighbors

The third example shows some new concepts with the IP routing table. Example 3-3 shows R2's current IPv6 routing table that results from the configuration shown in Example 3-1. Note that no IPv6 routing protocols have been configured, and no static routes have been configured.

Example 3-3 *Connected and Local IPv6 Routes*

```
R2# show ipv6 route
IPv6 Routing Table - Default - 7 entries
Codes: C - Connected, L - Local, S - Static, U - Per-user Static route
       B - BGP, M - MIPv6, R - RIP, I1 - ISIS L1
       I2 - ISIS L2, IA - ISIS interarea, IS - ISIS summary, D - EIGRP
       EX - EIGRP external
       O - OSPF Intra, OI - OSPF Inter, OE1 - OSPF ext 1, OE2 - OSPF ext 2
       ON1 - OSPF NSSA ext 1, ON2 - OSPF NSSA ext 2
C   2000:0:0:1::/64 [0/0]
     via Serial0/0/1, directly connected
L   2000::1:213:19FF:FE7B:5004/128 [0/0]
     via Serial0/0/1, receive
C   2000:0:0:2::/64 [0/0]
     via FastEthernet0/1, directly connected
L   2000:0:0:2::2/128 [0/0]
     via FastEthernet0/1, receive
C   2000:0:0:4::/64 [0/0]
     via FastEthernet0/0, directly connected
L   2000::4:213:19FF:FE7B:5004/128 [0/0]
     via FastEthernet0/0, receive
L   FF00::/8 [0/0]
     via Null0, receive
```

First, the IPv6 routing table lists the expected connected and local routes. The connected routes occur for any unicast IPv6 addresses on the interface that happen to have more than link-local scope. So, R2 has routes for subnets 2000:0:0:1::/64, 2000:0:0:2::/64, and 2000:0:0:4::/64, but no connected subnets related to R2's link-local addresses. The local routes, all /128 routes, are essentially host routes for the router's unicast IPv6 addresses. These local routes allow the router to more efficiently process packets directed to the router itself, as compared to packets directed toward connected subnets.

The IPv6 Neighbor Table

The IPv6 neighbor table replaces the IPv4 ARP table, listing the MAC address of other devices that share the same link. Example 3-4 shows a debug that lists messages during the NDP process, a ping to R3's Fa0/0 IPv6 address, and the resulting neighbor table entries on R2.

Example 3-4 *Creating Entries and Displaying the Contents of R2's IPv6 Neighbor Table*

```
R2# debug ipv6 nd
  ICMP Neighbor Discovery events debugging is on
R2# ping 2000:0:0:2::3

Type escape sequence to abort.
Sending 5, 100-byte ICMP Echos to 2000:0:0:2::3, timeout is 2 seconds:
!!!!!
Success rate is 100 percent (5/5), round-trip min/avg/max = 0/0/4 ms
R2#
*Sep  2 17:07:25.807: ICMPv6-ND: DELETE -> INCMP: 2000:0:0:2::3
*Sep  2 17:07:25.807: ICMPv6-ND: Sending NS for 2000:0:0:2::3 on FastEthernet0/1
*Sep  2 17:07:25.807: ICMPv6-ND: Resolving next hop 2000:0:0:2::3 on interface
  FastEthernet0/1
*Sep  2 17:07:25.811: ICMPv6-ND: Received NA for 2000:0:0:2::3 on FastEthernet0/1
  from 2000:0:0:2::3
*Sep  2 17:07:25.811: ICMPv6-ND: Neighbor 2000:0:0:2::3 on FastEthernet0/1 : LLA
  0013.197b.6588

R2# undebug all
All possible debugging has been turned off

R2# show ipv6 neighbors
IPv6 Address                     Age Link-layer Addr State Interface
2000:0:0:2::3                      0 0013.197b.6588  REACH Fa0/1
FE80::213:19FF:FE7B:6588          0 0013.197b.6588  REACH Fa0/1
```

The example shows the entire NDP process by which R2 discovers R3's Fa0/0 MAC address. The example begins with a **debug ipv6 nd** command, which tells R2 to issue messages related to NDP messages. The **ping 2000:0:0:2::3** command that follows tells Cisco IOS to use IPv6 to ping R3's F0/0 address; however, R2 does not know the corresponding MAC address. The debug output that follows shows R2 sending an NS, with R3 replying with an NA message, listing R3's MAC address.

The example ends with the output of the **show ipv6 neighbor** command, which lists the neighbor table entries for both of R3's IPv6 addresses.

Stateless Autoconfiguration

The final example in this section demonstrates stateless autoconfiguration using two routers, R2 and R3. In Example 3-5, R2's Fa0/1 configuration will be changed, using the **ipv6 address autoconfig** subcommand on that interface. This tells R2 to use the stateless autoconfig process, with R2 learning its prefix from Router R3. R2 then builds the rest of its IPv6 address using EUI-64.

Example 3-5 *Using Stateless Autoconfig on Router R2*

```
R2# conf t
Enter configuration commands, one per line.  End with CNTL/Z.
R2(config)# interface fa0/1
R2(config-if)# no ipv6 address
R2(config-if)# ipv6 address autoconfig
R2(config-if)# ^Z

R2# show ipv6 interface brief
FastEthernet0/0            [up/up]
    FE80::213:19FF:FE7B:5004
    2000::4:213:19FF:FE7B:5004
FastEthernet0/1            [up/up]
    FE80::213:19FF:FE7B:5005
    2000::2:213:19FF:FE7B:5005
Serial0/0/0                [administratively down/down]
    unassigned
Serial0/0/1                [up/up]
    FE80::213:19FF:FE7B:5004
    2000::1:213:19FF:FE7B:5004
Serial0/1/0                [administratively down/down]
    unassigned
Serial0/1/1                [administratively down/down]
    unassigned

R2# show ipv6 router
Router FE80::213:19FF:FE7B:6588 on FastEthernet0/1, last update 0 min
  Hops 64, Lifetime 1800 sec, AddrFlag=0, OtherFlag=0, MTU=1500
  HomeAgentFlag=0, Preference=Medium
  Reachable time 0 (unspecified), Retransmit time 0 (unspecified)
  Prefix 2000:0:0:2::/64 onlink autoconfig
    Valid lifetime 2592000, preferred lifetime 604800
```

Starting with the configuration, the **no ipv6 address** command actually removes all configured IPv6 addresses from the interface and also disables IPv6 on interface Fa0/1. Then, the **ipv6 address autoconfig** command again enables IPv6 on Fa0/1 and tells R2 to use stateless autoconfig.

The **show** commands confirm that R2 does indeed learn its IPv6 address: 2000:0:0:2:0213:19FF:FE7B:5005. The **show ipv6 router** command, which lists the cached contents of any received RA messages, lists the information received from R3's RA message, including R3's link-local address (used to identify the routers) and R3's advertised prefix (2000:0:0:2::/64).

RIP Next Generation (RIPng)

To support IPv6, all the IPv4 routing protocols had to go through varying degrees of changes, with the most obvious being that each had to be changed to support longer addresses and prefixes. The actual messages used to send and receive routing information have changed in some cases, using IPv6 headers instead of IPv4 headers, and using IPv6 addresses in those headers. In particular, like their IPv4 versions, each IPv6 IGP uses IPv6 multicast addresses. For example, RIPng sends routing updates to the IPv6 destination address FF02::9 instead of the old RIPv2 IPv4 224.0.0.9 address. Also, the routing protocols typically advertise their link local IP address as the next hop in a route.

Even with these changes, each IPv6 IGP has more similarities than differences compared to its respective IPv4 cousin. For example, RIPng, based on RIPv2, is still a distance vector protocol, with hop count as the metric and 15 hops as the longest valid route (16 is infinity). OSPF version 3 (OSPFv3), created specifically to support IPv6, uses link-state logic like OSPFv2, uses cost as the metric, and retains the link-state advertisement (LSA) types—but there are some changes to how the LSAs work. However, most of the core OSPF operational concepts remain the same. This section examines RIPng. Upcoming chapters examine OSPFv3 and EIGRP for IPv6.

Table 3-11 lists the IPv6 routing protocols and their new RFCs (as appropriate).

Table 3-11 *Updates to Routing Protocols for IPv6*

Routing Protocol	Full Name	RFC
RIPng	RIP next generation	2080
OSPFv3	OSPF version 3	5340
EIGRP for IPv6	EIGRP for IPv6	Proprietary
MP-BGP4	Multiprotocol BGP-4	4760

Routing Information Protocol (RIP) began life as one of the earliest efforts in the field of dynamic IP routing protocols. It eventually became the first dynamic routing protocol for the emerging IP protocol back in the 1970s. Later, in the mid-1990s, the RIP version 2 (RIPv2) specifications enhanced RIP, with the original version becoming known as RIP version 1, or simply RIPv1.

Also in the mid-1990s, the process of defining IPv6 was drawing toward completion, at least for the original IPv6 standards. To support IPv6, the IETF committees defined a new version of RIP to support IPv6. But rather than number this updated flavor of RIP as RIP version 3, the creators chose to number this new protocol as version 1, treating it like a new protocol. However, no one bothered to put "version 1" in the name, simply calling it *RIP next generation (RIPng)*, or even simply *RIP*. To date, no new version of RIPng has been defined, making the original RIPng still the most recent version of the protocol.

Note For you *Star Trek* TV show fans, yes, the name came in part from *Star Trek: The Next Generation.*

RIPng: Theory and Comparisons to RIPv2

The RIPng RFC states that the protocol uses many of the same concepts and conventions as the original RIPv1 specification, also drawing on some RIPv2 concepts. Table 3-12 lists a variety of facts about RIPv2 and RIPng.

Table 3-12 *Comparing RIPv2 to RIPng*

Feature	RIPv2	RIPng
Advertises routes for...	IPv4	IPv6
RIP messages use these Layer 3/4 protocols	IPv4, UDP	IPv6, UDP
UDP port	520	521
Use distance vector	Yes	Yes
Default administrative distance	120	120
Supports VLSM	Yes	Yes
Can perform automatic summarization	Yes	—
Uses Split Horizon	Yes	Yes
Uses Poison Reverse	Yes	Yes
30-second periodic full updates	Yes	Yes
Uses triggered updates	Yes	Yes
Uses Hop Count metric	Yes	Yes
Metric meaning infinity	16	16
Supports route tags	Yes	Yes
Multicast Update destination	224.0.0.9	FF02::9
Authentication	RIP-specific	Uses IPv6 AH/ESP

The overall operation of RIPng closely matches RIPv2. In both, routers send periodic full updates with all routes, except for routes omitted because of Split Horizon rules. No neighbor relationships occur. The continuing periodic Updates, on a slightly variable 30-second period, also serve the purpose of confirming that the neighboring router still works. The metrics work exactly the same. When a router ceases to see a route in received updates, ceases to receive updates, or receives a poisoned (metric 16) route, it reacts to converge, but relatively slowly compared to EIGRP and OSPF.

Some differences relate specifically to IPv6. First, the messages themselves list IPv6 prefixes/lengths, rather than subnet/mask. In RIPv1 and RIPv2, RIP-encapsulated RIP Update messages inside an IPv4 and UDP header; with IPv6, the encapsulation uses IPv6 packets, again with a UDP header. Some small differences in the Update message format exist as well, with the most obvious difference being that the Updates list IPv6 prefixes and prefix lengths.

The last difference of note is that because IPv6 supports authentication using the IPsec Authentication Header (AH), RIPng does not natively support authentication, instead relying on IPsec.

Configuring RIPng

RIPng uses a new command style for the basic configuration, but most of the optional features and verification commands look much like the commands used for RIP for IPv4. This section first takes a look at the basic RIPng configuration, accepting as many defaults as possible.

The big difference between RIPv2 and RIPng configuration is that RIPng discards the age-old RIP **network** command in deference to the **ipv6 rip** *name* **enable** interface sub-command, which enables RIPng on an interface. Another difference relates to the routing of IPv4 and IPv6: Cisco IOS routes IPv4 by default (because of a default global configuration command of **ip routing**), but Cisco IOS does not route IPv6 by default (a default of **no ipv6 unicast-routing**). Finally, RIPng allows multiple RIPng processes on a single router, so Cisco IOS requires that each RIPng process is given a text name that identifies each RIPng process for that one router—another difference compared to RIPv2.

The following list shows the basic configuration steps for RIPng, including steps to enable IPv6 routing and enabling IPv6 on the interfaces:

Key Topic

Step 1.   Enable IPv6 routing with the **ipv6 unicast-routing** global command.

Step 2.   Enable RIPng using the **ipv6 router rip** *name* global configuration command. The name must be unique on a router but does not need to match on neighboring routers.

Step 3.   Enable IPv6 on the interface, typically with one of these two methods:

- Configure an IPv6 unicast address on each interface using the **ipv6 address** *address/prefix-length* [**eui-64**] interface command.

- Configure the **ipv6 enable** command, which enables IPv6 and causes the router to derive its link-local address.

Step 4.   Enable RIP on the interface with the **ipv6 rip** *name* **enable** interface subcommand (where the name matches the **ipv6 router rip** *name* global configuration command).

The list includes just a few straightforward configuration commands, but a few subtle interactions also exist. The list shows steps related directly to RIPng (Steps 2 and 4), plus other steps related to making IPv6 itself work (Steps 1 and 3). The list also pairs two sets of dependent steps with each other, as follows:

■ Step 2 relies on Step 1, because Cisco IOS rejects the command at Step 2 (**ipv6 router rip** *name*) if the command at Step 1 (**ipv6 unicast-routing**) has been omitted.

■ Step 4 relies on Step 3, because Cisco IOS rejects the command at Step 4 if IPv6 has not yet been enabled on the interface.

Finally, note that although the **ipv6 rip** *process-name* **enable** interface subcommand (Step 4) refers to the process name configured at Step 2 (the **ipv6 router rip** *process-name* command), Cisco IOS creates the RIP process in reaction to the **ipv6 rip** *process-name* **enable** interface subcommand if that RIPng process name does not yet exist. In other words, if you followed the previous steps in order, but forgot to do Step 2, the command at Step 4 causes Cisco IOS to automatically create the command at Step 2.

As with RIPv1 and RIPv2, for any interface on which RIPng has been enabled, the RIP process does three main actions:

1. It starts sending RIP updates on that interface.

2. It also starts processing any RIP updates received on that interface.

3. Finally, it advertises the connected routes on that interface. In particular, because IPv6 allows the configuration of multiple IPv6 unicast addresses on an interface, RIP advertises most IPv6 unicast prefixes associated with the interface. The notable exceptions are that RIP does not advertise any link-local addresses, nor does RIP advertise the local host routes—routes with a /128 prefix length—created for each interface IPv6 address. In short, RIP advertises all routable subnets associated with the interface.

Figure 3-13 shows a sample internetwork with IPv6 global unicast IPv6 subnets displayed.

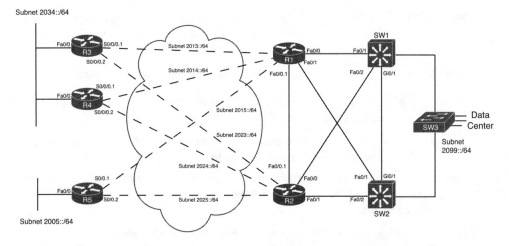

Figure 3-13 *Sample Internetwork for IPv6 Routing Protocol Configuration*

The sample internetwork uses addressing values that are both memorable and make for shorter IPv6 addresses when abbreviated. All the subnets use /64 prefix length, with quartets 2, 3, and 4 composed of all 0 values. The interface ID portion of each address uses all hex 0s in the first three quartets (quartets 5, 6, and 7 in the overall address), with the final digit in the final quartet used to identify each router. This last digit matches the name of each router in most cases.

For example, all of R1's IPv6 addresses' last four octets are 0000:0000:0000:0001. R1's S0/0/0.3 subinterface, which connects with a permanent virtual circuit (PVC) to Router R3, uses a prefix of 2003:0000:0000:0000::/64, making the entire IPv6 address on this interface, when abbreviated, 2003::1/64—a convenient value for sifting through all the output in the upcoming examples.

Example 3-6 shows the RIPng configuration on Router R1 in this design. The RIP process name is **fred**.

Example 3-6 *Configuring IPv6 Routing and Routing Protocols on R1*

```
R1# show running-config
! The output is edited to remove lines not pertinent to this example.
! Next, step 1's task: enable IPv6 routing
ipv6 unicast-routing
!
! Next, on 5 interfaces, steps 3 and 4: configuring an IPv6 address,
! and enable RIPng, process "fred".
interface FastEthernet0/0.1
 ipv6 address 2012::1/64
 ipv6 rip fred enable
!
interface FastEthernet0/0.2
 ipv6 address 2017::1/64
 ipv6 rip fred enable
!
interface FastEthernet0/1.18
 ipv6 address 2018::1/64
 ipv6 rip fred enable
!
interface Serial0/0/0.3
 ipv6 address 2013::1/64
 ipv6 rip fred enable
!
interface Serial0/0/0.4
 ipv6 address 2014::1/64
 ipv6 rip fred enable
!
interface Serial0/0/0.5
 ipv6 address 2015::1/64
 ipv6 rip fred enable
```

```
!
! Next, step 2's task, creating the RIPng process named "fred"
ipv6 router rip fred
```

Verifying RIPng

The **show** commands related to RIPng have the same general kinds of information as seen with RIPv2. However, some of the commands used to get to the same piece of information differ, and of course, some obvious differences exist because of the different IPv6 address structure. Table 3-13 lists a cross-reference comparing all commands related to RIP that begin with either **show ip** or **show ipv6**. It also lists the similar **debug** commands used to display RIP routing information.

Table 3-13   *Comparing Verification Commands:* **show ip** *and* **show ipv6**

Function	IPv4	IPv6
All routes	... **route**	... **route**
All RIP-learned routes	... **route rip**	... **route rip**
Details on the routes for a specific prefix	... **route** *subnet mask*	... **route** *prefix/length*
Interfaces on which RIP is enabled	... **protocols**	... **protocols**
RIP timers	... **protocols**	... **rip**
List of routing information sources	... **protocols**	... **rip next-hops**
Debug that displays sent and received updates	**debug ip rip**	**debug ipv6 rip**

The most notable differences occur with the information seen with IPv4 in the **show ip protocols** command. The **show ip protocols** command displays a wide variety of information for IPv4 RIP, whereas the IPv6 commands spread the information over a couple of different commands, as listed in Table 3-13. Example 3-7 shows a sampling of the commands, taken from Router R3 in Figure 3-13. The explanatory comments are listed within the example in this case. Note that Router R3 used a RIPng process name of **barney**.

Example 3-7   *IPv6 RIPng* **show** *Commands*

```
! On R3, process name "barney" has two current routes to reach the
! datacenter prefix 2099::/64.

R3# show ipv6 route 2099::/64
Routing entry for 2099::/64
  Known via "rip barney", distance 120, metric 3
  Route count is 2/2, share count 0
  Routing paths:
    FE80::22FF:FE22:2222, Serial0/0/0.2
```

```
        Last updated 00:27:12 ago
     FE80::11FF:FE11:1111, Serial0/0/0.1
        Last updated 00:27:10 ago


! Note that the next command lists only RIP-learned routes. It lists
! two next-hops for 2099::64. Note the next-hop information lists
! link-local addresses.
R3# show ipv6 route rip
IPv6 Routing Table - Default - 19 entries
Codes: C - Connected, L - Local, S - Static, U - Per-user Static route
        B - BGP, M - MIPv6, R - RIP, I1 - ISIS L1
        I2 - ISIS L2, IA - ISIS interarea, IS - ISIS summary, D - EIGRP
        EX - EIGRP external
        O - OSPF Intra, OI - OSPF Inter, OE1 - OSPF ext 1, OE2 - OSPF ext 2
        ON1 - OSPF NSSA ext 1, ON2 - OSPF NSSA ext 2
R   2005::/64 [120/3]
     via FE80::11FF:FE11:1111, Serial0/0/0.1
     via FE80::22FF:FE22:2222, Serial0/0/0.2
R   2012::/64 [120/2]
     via FE80::11FF:FE11:1111, Serial0/0/0.1
     via FE80::22FF:FE22:2222, Serial0/0/0.2

! lines omitted for brevity...
R   2099::/64 [120/3]
     via FE80::22FF:FE22:2222, Serial0/0/0.2
     via FE80::11FF:FE11:1111, Serial0/0/0.1


! Unlike show ip protocols, show ipv6 protocols displays little info.
R3# show ipv6 protocols
IPv6 Routing Protocol is "connected"
IPv6 Routing Protocol is "rip barney"
  Interfaces:
    Serial0/0/0.2
    Serial0/0/0.1
    FastEthernet0/0
  Redistribution:
    None


! This command lists the timers displayed for RIPv2 with show ip protocols.
R3# show ipv6 rip
RIP process "barney", port 521, multicast-group FF02::9, pid 258
     Administrative distance is 120. Maximum paths is 16
     Updates every 30 seconds, expire after 180
     Holddown lasts 0 seconds, garbage collect after 120
     Split horizon is on; poison reverse is off
     Default routes are not generated
```

```
       Periodic updates 57, trigger updates 10
 Interfaces:
   Serial0/0/0.2
   Serial0/0/0.1
   FastEthernet0/0
 Redistribution:
   None


! This command lists the equivalent of the information in the
! show ip protocols commands' "Routing Information Sources" heading.
! Note the link-local addresses are listed.
R3# show ipv6 rip next-hops
 RIP process "barney", Next Hops
   FE80::11FF:FE11:1111/Serial0/0/0.1 [9 paths]
   FE80::44FF:FE44:4444/FastEthernet0/0 [3 paths]
   FE80::22FF:FE22:2222/Serial0/0/0.2 [9 paths]
```

Beyond the information emphasized in the comments inside the example, the next-hop IPv6 addresses in the example need to be scrutinized. RIPng uses the link-local IPv6 address as the next-hop IP address. (Reminder: link-local addresses begin with FE80.)

To discover which routers use which link-local addresses, and to make it easier to work with link-local addresses, you have a couple of options. First, you can set the MAC address of each LAN interface to something noticeable. For Example 3-7, the routers each used a recognizable MAC: R1 used 0200.1111.1111, R2 used 0200.2222.2222, and so on. Alternatively, you can just configure the link-local address with the **ipv6 address** command, using the **link-local** keyword at the end, and make each link-local address be more recognizable. Regardless, to find the router whose link-local address is listed in the IPv6 routing table, the **show cdp entry** *name* command can be useful, because it lists both the IPv4 and IPv6 addresses, including the neighbor's link-local address.

Exam Preparation Tasks

Planning Practice

The CCNP ROUTE exam expects test takers to review design documents, create implementation plans, and create verification plans. This section provides some exercises that can help you to take a step back from the minute details of the topics in this chapter so that you can think about the same technical topics from the planning perspective.

For each planning practice table, simply complete the table. Note that any numbers in parentheses represent the number of options listed for each item in the solutions in Appendix F, "Completed Planning Practice Tables."

Design Review Table

Table 3-14 lists several design goals related to this chapter. If these design goals were listed in a design document, and you had to take that document and develop an implementation plan, what implementation options come to mind? You should write a general description; specific configuration commands are not required.

Table 3-14 *Design Review*

Design Goal	Possible Implementation Choices Covered in This Chapter
An IPv6 design suggests that all client hosts should dynamically learn their IPv6 addresses. Which tools can be used? (2)	
A plan shows the use of stateless autoconfiguration. What functions should we expect the IPv6 DHCP server to perform?	

Implementation Plan Peer Review Table

Table 3-15 shows a list of questions that others might ask, or that you might think about, during a peer review of another network engineer's implementation plan. Complete the table by answering the questions.

Table 3-15 *Notable Questions from This Chapter to Consider During an Implementation Plan Peer Review*

Question	Answers
An implementation plan states that router IPv6 addresses should be assigned as obvious values, using the lowest numbers in the range per each assigned prefix. What configuration methods could be used to configure these low address values?	
A plan calls for the use of stateless autoconfig for client hosts. What must be configured on the routers to support this process?	
A RIPng implementation plan lists two neighboring routers with unicast IPv6 addresses 2000::1/64 and 2001::2/64, respectively. Will this cause a neighborship issue?	

Create an Implementation Plan Table

To practice skills useful when creating your own implementation plan, list in Table 3-16 all configuration commands related to the configuration of the following features. You might want to record your answers outside the book, and set a goal to complete this table (and others like it) from memory during your final reviews before taking the exam.

Table 3-16 *Implementation Plan Configuration Memory Drill*

Feature	Configuration Commands/Notes
Globally enable the routing of IPv6 unicast traffic.	
Globally enable Cisco Express Forwarding (CEF) for IPv6.	
Configure flow-label marking in 1280-byte or larger packets sent by the router.	
Configure the full global unicast address on an interface.	
Configure the unicast IPv6 prefix on an interface, and let the router add the interface ID.	
Configure an interface to find its unicast IPv6 address using stateless autoconfig.	

Feature	Configuration Commands/Notes
Configure an interface to enable IPv6 and use another interface's IPv6 address as needed.	
Enable IPv6 on an interface and do not configure a unicast IPv6 address.	
Configure the link-local address of an interface.	
Assuming that IPv6 routing and IPv6 addresses have already been configured, configure RIPng.	

Choose Commands for a Verification Plan Table

To practice skills useful when creating your own verification plan, list in Table 3-17 all commands that supply the requested information. You might want to record your answers outside the book, and set a goal to be able to complete this table (and others like it) from memory during your final reviews before taking the exam.

Note Some of the entries in this table might not have been specifically mentioned in this chapter but are listed in this table for review and reference.

Table 3-17 *Verification Plan Memory Drill*

Information Needed	Commands
All IPv6 routes	
A single line per IPv6 address	
Detailed information about IPv6 on an interface, including multicast addresses	
The MAC address used by an interface	
The MAC addresses of neighboring IPv6 hosts	
The information learned from another router in an RA message	
All RIP-learned IPv6 routes	
All next-hop IPv6 addresses used by RIP routes	
The interfaces on which RIP is enabled	

Review All the Key Topics

Review the most important topics from inside the chapter, noted with the Key Topic icon in the outer margin of the page. Table 3-18 lists a reference of these key topics and the page numbers on which each is found.

Table 3-18 *Key Topics for Chapter 3*

Key Topic Element	Description	Page Number
Figure 3-1	Conceptual View of IPv6 Global Routes	78
List	Rules for abbreviating IPv6 addresses	79
List	Rules about how to write IPv6 prefixes	81
Figure 3-3	Example IPv6 Prefix Assignment in the Internet	83
List	IPv6 subnetting process	85
Figure 3-5	Company1—Needs Four Subnets	85
List	Three steps used by the stateless autoconfig feature	89
Figure 3-8	IPv6 Address Format with Interface ID and EUI-64	91
Table 3-7	Comparing Stateless and Stateful DHCPv6 Services	92
List	IPv6 address types (unicast, multicast, and anycast)	93
Figure 3-10	Link Local Address Format	96
Table 3-8	Common IPv6 Unicast Address Types	96
Figure 3-11	Neighbor Discovery Protocol	98
Table 3-12	Comparing RIPv2 to RIPng	108
List	Configuration steps for RIPng	109

Complete the Tables and Lists from Memory

Print a copy of Appendix D, "Memory Tables," (found on the CD) or at least the section for this chapter, and complete the tables and lists from memory. Appendix E, "Memory Tables Answer Key," also on the CD, includes completed tables and lists to check your work.

Define Key Terms

Define the following key terms from this chapter, and check your answers in the glossary.

global unicast address, link-local address, unique local address, stateful DHCP, stateless DHCP, stateless autoconfig, Neighbor Discovery Protocol (NDP), Neighbor Solicitation (NS), Neighbor Advertisement (NA), Router Solicitation (RS), Router Advertisement (RA), solicited node multicast address, Duplicate Address Detection (DAD), Inverse Neighbor Discovery, RIP next generation (RIPng)

This chapter covers the following topics that you need to master for the CCNP ROUTE exam:

■ **EIGRP Fundamentals:** This section reviews the EIGRP concepts, configuration, and verification commands covered in the CCNA curriculum.

■ **EIGRP Neighborships:** This section discusses a variety of features that impact when a router attempts to form EIGRP neighbor relationships (neighborships), what must be true for those neighborships to work, and what might prevent those neighborships.

■ **Neighborships over WANs:** This section examines the typical usage of EIGRP neighborships over various types of WAN technologies.

CHAPTER 4

Fundamental EIGRP Concepts

Enhanced Interior Gateway Routing Protocol (EIGRP) is configured with a few relatively simple commands. In fact, for most any size network, you could go to every router, enter the **router eigrp 1** command, followed by one or more **network** *net-id* subcommands (one for each classful network to which the router is connected), and EIGRP would likely work, and work very well, with no other configuration.

In spite of that apparent simplicity, here you sit beginning the first of four chapters of EIGRP coverage in this book. Many reasons exist for the amount of EIGRP material included here. First, EIGRP includes many optional configuration features that you need to both understand and master for the CCNP ROUTE exam. Many of these features require a solid understanding of EIGRP internals as well—a topic that can be conveniently ignored if you just do the minimal configuration, but something very important to planning, implementing, and optimizing a medium/large enterprise network.

Another reason for the depth of EIGRP coverage in this book is a fundamental change in the philosophy of the CCNP exams, as compared with earlier CCNP exam versions. Cisco has increased the focus on planning for the implementation and verification of new network designs. The bar has been raised, and in a way that is consistent with typical engineering jobs. Not only do you need to understand all the EIGRP features, but you also need to be able to look at a set of design requirements, and from that decide which EIGRP configuration settings could be useful—and which are not useful. You must also be able to direct others as to what verification steps would tell them if the implementation worked or not, rather than just relying on typing a ? and looking around for that little piece of information you know exists somewhere.

This chapter begins with the "EIGRP Fundamentals" section, which is a review of the core prerequisite facts about EIGRP. Following the review, the chapter examines EIGRP neighbor relationships, including a variety of configuration commands that impact neighbor relationships, and the verification commands that you can use to confirm how well EIGRP neighbors work.

"Do I Know This Already?" Quiz

The "Do I Know This Already?" quiz enables you to assess whether you should read the entire chapter. If you miss no more than one of these seven self-assessment questions, you might want to move ahead to the "Exam Preparation Tasks" section. Table 4-1 lists the major headings in this chapter and the "Do I Know This Already?" quiz questions covering the material in those headings so that you can assess your knowledge of these specific areas. The answers to the "Do I Know This Already?" quiz appear in Appendix A.

Table 4-1   *"Do I Know This Already?" Foundation Topics Section-to-Question Mapping*

Foundation Topics Section	Questions
EIGRP Fundamentals	1, 2
EIGRP Neighborships	3–6
Neighborships over WANs	7

1. A router has been configured with the commands **router eigrp 9** and **network 172.16.1.0 0.0.0.255**. No other EIGRP-related commands have been configured. The answers list the IP addresses that could be assigned to this router's Fa0/0 interface. Which answers list an IP address/prefix length that would cause the router to enable EIGRP on Fa0/0? (Choose two answers.)

   a. 172.16.0.1/23

   b. 172.16.1.1/26

   c. 172.16.1.1/24

   d. 172.16.0.255/23

   e. None of the other answers are correct.

2. Router R1 has working interfaces S0/0, S0/1, and S0/2, with IP address/prefix combinations of 10.10.10.1/24, 10.10.11.2/24, and 10.10.12.3/22. R1's configuration includes the commands **router eigrp 9** and **network 10.0.0.0**. The **show ip eigrp interfaces** command lists S0/0 and S0/1 in the command output, but not S0/2. Which answer gives a possible reason for the omission?

   a. R1 has EIGRP neighbors reachable through S0/0 and S0/1, but not through S0/2, so it is not included.

   b. S0/2 might currently be in a state other than up/up.

   c. The **network 10.0.0.0** command requires the use of mask 255.0.0.0 because of EIGRP being classful by default.

   d. S0/2 might be configured as a passive interface.

3. Routers R1 and R2 are EIGRP neighbors using their Fa0/0 interfaces, respectively. An engineer adds the **ip hello-interval eigrp 9 6** command to R1's Fa0/0 configuration. Which of the following is true regarding the results from this change?

   a. The **show ip eigrp neighbors** command on R1 lists the revised Hello timer.

   b. The **show ip eigrp interfaces** command on R1 lists the revised Hello timer.

   c. The R1-R2 neighborship fails because of a Hello timer mismatch.

   d. The **show ip eigrp interfaces detail** command on R1 lists the revised Hello timer.

4. Router R1 has been configured with the commands **router eigrp 9** and network **172.16.2.0 0.0.0.255**, with no other current EIGRP configuration. R1's (working) Fa0/0 interface has been configured with IP address 172.16.2.2/26. R1 has found three EIGRP neighbors reachable through interface Fa0/0, including the router with IP address 172.16.2.20. When the engineer attempts to add the **neighbor 172.16.2.20 fa0/0** command in EIGRP configuration mode, which of the following occurs?

   a. Fa0/0 fails.

   b. The command is rejected.

   c. The existing three neighbors fail.

   d. The neighborship with 172.16.2.20 fails and then reestablishes.

   e. None of the other answers is correct.

5. Which of the following settings could prevent two potential EIGRP neighbors from becoming neighbors? (Choose two answers.)

   a. The interface used by one router to connect to the other router is passive in the EIGRP process.

   b. Duplicate EIGRP router IDs.

   c. Mismatched Hold Timers.

   d. IP addresses of 10.1.1.1/24 and 10.2.2.2/24, respectively.

6. An engineer has added the following configuration snippet to an implementation planning document. The configuration will be added to Router R1, whose Fa0/0 interface connects to a LAN to which Routers R2 and R3 also connect. R2 and R3 are already EIGRP neighbors with each other. Assuming that the snippet shows all commands on R1 related to EIGRP authentication, which answer lists an appropriate comment to be made during the implementation plan peer review?

```
key chain fred
key 3
key-string whehew
interface fa0/0
ip authentication key-chain eigrp 9 fred
```

   a. The configuration is missing one authentication-related configuration command.

   b. The configuration is missing two authentication-related configuration commands.

   c. Authentication type 9 is not supported; type 5 should be used instead.

   d. The key numbers must begin with key 1, so change the key 3 command to key 1.

7. A company has a Frame Relay WAN with one central-site router and 100 branch office routers. A partial mesh of PVCs exists: one PVC between the central site and each of the 100 branch routers. Which of the following could be true about the number of EIGRP neighborships?

a. A partial mesh totaling 100: one between the central-site router and each of the 100 branches.

b. A full mesh — (101 * 100) / 2 = 5050 — One neighborship between each pair of routers.

c. 101 — One between each router (including the central site) and its nearby PE router.

d. None of the answers is correct.

Foundation Topics

EIGRP Fundamentals

All the CCNP exams consider CCNA materials as prerequisites. So this book also assumes that the reader is already familiar with CCNA topics. However, the CCNP exams do test on features that overlap with CCNA. Additionally, most people forget some details along the way. Therefore, this section reviews the CCNA-level topics as a brief refresher.

To that end, this section begins with a review of EIGRP configuration using only the **router eigrp** and **network** commands. Following that, the next section details the key fields used to verify that EIGRP is working. Finally, the last part of this introduction summarizes the basic EIGRP internals behind this initial simple example.

Configuration Review

Cisco IOS uses the **router eigrp** *asn* command (where *asn* is an autonomous system number [ASN]), plus one or more **network** *net-id wildcard-mask* subcommands, to enable EIGRP on the router and on router interfaces. The rules for these commands are as follows:

Key Topic

1. Neighboring routers' **router eigrp** *asn* commands must be configured with the same ASN parameter to become neighbors.

2. Cisco IOS enables only EIGRP on interfaces matched by an EIGRP **network** command. When enabled, the router does the following:

   a. Attempts to discover EIGRP neighbors on that interface by sending multicast EIGRP Hello messages

   b. Advertises to other neighbors about the subnet connected to the interface

3. If no wildcard mask is configured on the EIGRP **network** command, the command's single parameter should be a classful network number (in other words, a class A, B, or C network number).

4. If no wildcard mask is configured on the EIGRP **network** command, the command enables EIGRP on all of that router's interfaces directly connected to the configured classful network.

5. If the **network** command includes a wildcard mask, the router performs access control list (ACL) logic when comparing the *net-id* configured in the **network** command with each interface's IP address, using the configured wildcard mask as an ACL wildcard mask.

Example 4-1 shows a sample configuration for each router in Figure 4-1, with several variations in the **network** commands to make the details in the preceding list more obvious.

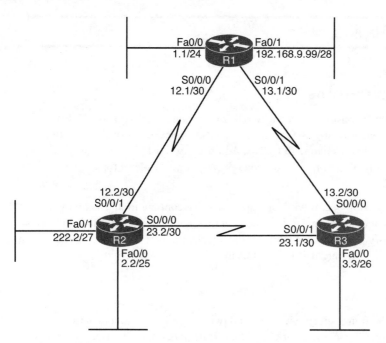

Note: All IP addresses begin with 10.1 unless otherwise noted.

Figure 4-1   *Three-Router Internetwork*

Example 4-1   *EIGRP Configuration on Routers R1, R2, and R3*

```
! On Router R1: !!!!!!!!!!!!!!!!!!!!!!!!!!!!!!!!!!!!!!!!!!!!!
router eigrp 1
 network 10.0.0.0
 network 192.168.9.0


! On Router R2: !!!!!!!!!!!!!!!!!!!!!!!!!!!!!!!!!!!!!!!!!!!!!
router eigrp 1
 network 10.1.0.0 0.0.31.255
 network 10.1.2.2 0.0.0.0


! On Router R3: !!!!!!!!!!!!!!!!!!!!!!!!!!!!!!!!!!!!!!!!!!!!!
router eigrp 1
 network 10.1.0.0 0.0.255.255
```

First, note that all three routers use the **router eigrp 1** command, so all three routers'
ASN values match.

Next, consider the two **network** commands on R1. The **network 10.0.0.0** command,
without a *wildcard-mask* parameter, means that R1 matches all interfaces in class A
network 10.0.0.0—which in this case means R1's Fa0/0, S0/0/0, and S0/0/1 interfaces. The
network 192.168.9.0 command, again without a wildcard mask, matches interface Fa0/1.

On R2, the **network 10.1.0.0 0.0.31.255** command requires a little more thought. The router uses the 0.0.31.255 value—the wildcard (WC) mask—just like an ACL WC mask. Cisco IOS compares the 10.1.0.0 value with each interface IP address, but only for the bit positions for which the WC mask lists a binary 0. For example, 0.0.31.255 represents 19 binary 0s, followed by 13 binary 1s. So, R2 would compare the first 19 bits of 10.1.0.0 with the first 19 bits of each interface's IP address.

Two features of the mechanics of the **network** command require a little extra attention. First, Cisco IOS might convert the address portion of the **network** *address wc-mask* command before putting the command into the running config. Just as Cisco IOS does for the address/WC mask combinations for the **access-list** command, Cisco IOS inverts the WC mask and then performs a Boolean AND of the address and mask. For example, if you type the **network 10.1.1.1 0.0.255.255** command, Cisco IOS inverts the WC mask (to 255.255.0.0) and ANDs this value with 10.1.1.1, resulting in 10.1.0.0. As a result, Cisco IOS stores the command **network 10.1.0.0 0.0.255.255**.

The second feature is that when you know for sure the values in the **network** command, you can easily find the range of interface addresses that match the address/WC mask combination in the **network** command. The low end of the range is the address as listed in the **network** command. To find the high end of the range, just add the address and WC mask together. For example, the **network 10.1.0.0 0.0.31.255** command has a range of 10.1.0.0 through 10.1.31.255.

Finally, on R3, the **network 10.1.0.0 0.0.255.255** command tells R3 to enable EIGRP on all interfaces whose IP addresses begin with 10.1, which includes all three interfaces on R3, as shown in Figure 4-1.

Taking a step back from the details, this config has enabled EIGRP, with ASN 1, on all three routers, and on all interfaces shown in Figure 4-1—except one interface. R2's Fa0/1 interface is not matched by any **network** commands on R2. So, EIGRP is not enabled on that interface. The next section reviews the commands that can be used to confirm that EIGRP is enabled, the interfaces on which it is enabled, the neighbor relationships that have been formed, and which EIGRP routes have been advertised and learned.

Verification Review

Even before starting to configure the routers, an engineer first considers all requirements. Those requirements lead to a design, which in turn leads to a chosen set of configuration commands. Then, the verification process that follows must consider the design requirements. The goal of verification is to determine that the internetwork works as designed, not just that some EIGRP routes have been learned.

For the purposes of this section, assume that the only design goal for the internetwork shown in Figure 4-1 is that EIGRP be used so that all routers have routes to reach all subnets shown in the figure.

To verify such a simple design, an engineer should start by confirming on which interfaces EIGRP has been enabled on each router. The next step should be to determine whether the EIGRP neighbor relationships that should occur are indeed up and working. Then, the EIGRP topology table should be examined to confirm that there is at least one entry for each subnet or network in the design. Finally, the IP routes on each router should be examined, confirming that all routes are known. To that end, Table 4-2 summarizes five key **show** commands that provide the information to answer these questions.

Note   The following table mentions some information that is covered later in this chapter (passive interfaces) or in other chapters (successor/feasible successors).

Example 4-2 shows samples of each command listed in Table 4-2. Note that the output highlights various samples of items that should be verified: the interfaces on which EIGRP is enabled, the known neighbors, the subnets in the topology table, and the EIGRP routes.

Table 4-2   *Key EIGRP Verification Commands*

Command	Key Information
show ip eigrp interfaces	Lists the working interfaces on which EIGRP is enabled (based on the **network** commands); it omits passive interfaces.
show ip protocols	Lists the contents of the **network** configuration commands for each routing process, and a list of neighbor IP addresses.
show ip eigrp neighbors	Lists known neighbors; does not list neighbors for which some mismatched parameter is preventing a valid EIGRP neighbor relationship.
show ip eigrp topology	Lists all successor and feasible successor routes known to this router. It does not list all known topology details. (See Chapter 5, "Advanced EIGRP Concepts," for more detail on successors and feasible successors.)
show ip route	Lists the contents of the IP routing table, listing EIGRP-learned routes with a code of D on the left side of the output.

Example 4-2   *EIGRP Verification on Routers R1, R2, and R3*

```
! On Router R1: !!!!!!!!!!!!!!!!!!!!!!!!!!!!!!!!!!!!!!!!!!!!!
R1# show ip eigrp interfaces
IP-EIGRP interfaces for process 1


                    Xmit Queue      Mean     Pacing Time   Multicast      Pending
Interface    Peers  Un/Reliable     SRTT     Un/Reliable   Flow Timer     Routes
Fa0/0        0      0/0             0        0/1           0              0
Se0/0/0      1      0/0             25       0/15          123            0
```

```
Se0/0/1         1          0/0         23        0/15        111              0
Fa0/1    0         0/0         0          0/1     0         0
```

```
! On Router R2: !!!!!!!!!!!!!!!!!!!!!!!!!!!!!!!!!!!!!!!!!!!!!
R2# show ip protocols
Routing Protocol is "eigrp 1"
  Outgoing update filter list for all interfaces is not set
  Incoming update filter list for all interfaces is not set
  Default networks flagged in outgoing updates
  Default networks accepted from incoming updates
  EIGRP metric weight K1=1, K2=0, K3=1, K4=0, K5=0
  EIGRP maximum hopcount 100
  EIGRP maximum metric variance 1
  Redistributing: eigrp 1
  EIGRP NSF-aware route hold timer is 240s
  Automatic network summarization is in effect
  Maximum path: 4
  Routing for Networks:
     10.1.2.2/32
     10.1.0.0/19
  Routing Information Sources:
     Gateway         Distance      Last Update
     10.1.12.1             90      00:19:36
     10.1.23.1             90      00:19:36
  Distance: internal 90 external 170
```

```
! On Router R3: !!!!!!!!!!!!!!!!!!!!!!!!!!!!!!!!!!!!!!!!!!!!!
R3# show ip eigrp neighbors
IP-EIGRP neighbors for process 1
H   Address               Interface      Hold Uptime   SRTT  RTO  Q    Seq
                                         (sec)         (ms)       Cnt  Num
1   10.1.23.2             Se0/0/1        11 00:19:53   31    200  0    6
0   10.1.13.1             Se0/0/0        10 00:19:53   32    200  0    6
```

```
! On Router R2: !!!!!!!!!!!!!!!!!!!!!!!!!!!!!!!!!!!!!!!!!!!!!
R2# show ip eigrp topology
IP-EIGRP Topology Table for AS(1)/ID(10.1.222.2)

Codes: P - Passive, A - Active, U - Update, Q - Query, R - Reply,
       r - reply Status, s - sia Status

P 10.1.13.0/30, 2 successors, FD is 2681856
        via 10.1.23.1 (2681856/2169856), Serial0/0/0
        via 10.1.12.1 (2681856/2169856), Serial0/0/1
P 10.1.12.0/30, 1 successors, FD is 2169856
        via Connected, Serial0/0/1
```

```
P 10.1.3.0/26, 1 successors, FD is 2172416
        via 10.1.23.1 (2172416/28160), Serial0/0/0
P 10.1.2.0/25, 1 successors, FD is 28160
        via Connected, FastEthernet0/0
P 10.1.1.0/24, 1 successors, FD is 2172416
        via 10.1.12.1 (2172416/28160), Serial0/0/1
```

```
! On Router R3: !!!!!!!!!!!!!!!!!!!!!!!!!!!!!!!!!!!!!!!!!!!!
R3# show ip route
Codes: C - connected, S - static, R - RIP, M - mobile, B - BGP
       D - EIGRP, EX - EIGRP external, O - OSPF, IA - OSPF inter area
       N1 - OSPF NSSA external type 1, N2 - OSPF NSSA external type 2
       E1 - OSPF external type 1, E2 - OSPF external type 2
       i - IS-IS, su - IS-IS summary, L1 - IS-IS level-1, L2 - IS-IS level-2
       ia - IS-IS inter area, * - candidate default, U - per-user static route
       o - ODR, P - periodic downloaded static route


Gateway of last resort is not set


D    192.168.9.0/24 [90/2172416] via 10.1.13.1, 00:19:55, Serial0/0/0
     10.0.0.0/8 is variably subnetted, 6 subnets, 4 masks
C        10.1.13.0/30 is directly connected, Serial0/0/0
D        10.1.12.0/30 [90/2681856] via 10.1.23.2, 00:19:55, Serial0/0/1
                      [90/2681856] via 10.1.13.1, 00:19:55, Serial0/0/0
C        10.1.3.0/26 is directly connected, FastEthernet0/0
D        10.1.2.0/25 [90/2172416] via 10.1.23.2, 00:19:55, Serial0/0/1
D        10.1.1.0/24 [90/2172416] via 10.1.13.1, 00:19:55, Serial0/0/0
C        10.1.23.0/30 is directly connected, Serial0/0/1
```

To verify the interfaces on which EIGRP is enabled, both the **show ip eigrp interfaces** command (shown on R1) and the **show ip protocols** command (shown on R2) list the information. For this example, look at the list of interfaces in R2's **show ip protocols** command output: S0/0/0, S0/0/1, and FA0/0 are listed, but Fa0/1—unmatched by any of R2's network commands—is not.

In this design, each router should form a neighbor relationship with the other two routers, in each case over a point-to-point serial link. The **show ip eigrp neighbors** command (on R3) confirms R3's neighbors.

Finally, one design goal was for all routers to have routes for all subnets/networks. You could move on to the **show ip route** command or first look for all prefixes in the **show ip eigrp topology** command. With relatively general requirements, just looking at the IP routing table is fine. The example highlights R3's topology data and IP route for subnet 10.1.1.0/24. Of more interest might be the fact that the **show ip route** command output on R3 lists all subnet/network numbers except one: subnet 10.1.222.0/27. This subnet exists off R2's Fa0/1 interface (as seen in Figure 4-1), which is the interface on which EIGRP has not yet been enabled.

Internals Review

To complete the review of prerequisite CCNA-level EIGRP knowledge, this section looks at a few of the internals of EIGRP. Some of the facts listed here simply need to be memorized, whereas other topics will be discussed in more detail later.

EIGRP follows three general steps to add routes to the IP routing table, as follows:

Step 1. **Neighbor discovery:** EIGRP routers send Hello messages to discover potential neighboring EIGRP routers and perform basic parameter checks to determine which routers should become neighbors.

Step 2. **Topology exchange:** Neighbors exchange full topology updates when the neighbor relationship comes up, and then only partial updates as needed based on changes to the network topology.

Step 3. **Choosing routes:** Each router analyzes its respective EIGRP topology table, choosing the lowest-metric route to reach each subnet.

Because the majority of the rest of this chapter examines EIGRP neighborships, this review section skips any discussion of EIGRP neighbors, instead focusing on topology exchange and route selection.

Exchanging Topology Information

First, the EIGRP neighbor table lists the neighboring routers. Second, the EIGRP topology table holds all the topology information learned from EIGRP neighbors. Finally, EIGRP chooses the best IP routes, and those routes become candidates to be injected into the IP routing table. (Table 4-2, earlier in this chapter, lists the **show** commands that can be used to examine these tables.) EIGRP routers follow the process shown in Figure 4-2 to build the necessary information in these tables, with the end goal of populating the IP routing table.

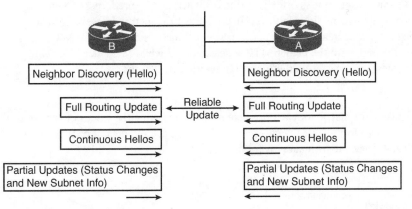

Figure 4-2 *EIGRP Discovery and Update Process*

EIGRP uses Update messages to send topology information to neighbors. These Update messages can be sent to multicast IP address 224.0.0.10 if the sending router needs to update multiple routers on the same subnet. Unlike OSPF, there is no concept of a designated router (DR) or backup designated router (BDR), but the use of multicast packets on LANs allows EIGRP to exchange routing information with all neighbors on the LAN efficiently.

The update messages are sent using the *Reliable Transport Protocol (RTP)*. The significance of RTP is that, like OSPF, EIGRP resends routing updates that are lost in transit. By using RTP to guarantee delivery of the EIGRP messages, EIGRP can better avoid loops.

Note   The acronym RTP also refers to a different protocol, Real-time Transport Protocol (RTP), which is used to transmit voice and video IP packets.

Neighbors use both full routing updates and partial updates, as depicted in Figure 4-2. A full update means that a router sends information about all known routes, whereas a partial update includes only information about recently changed routes. Full updates occur when neighbors first come up. After that, the neighbors send only partial updates in reaction to changes to a route.

Calculating the Best Routes for the Routing Table

EIGRP topology information includes the subnet number and mask, along with the components of the EIGRP composite metric. Each router then calculates an integer metric for each route, using the individual values of the EIGRP metric components listed in the EIGRP topology database. By default, EIGRP only uses the bandwidth and delay settings when calculating the metric. Optionally, the calculation can also include interface load and interface reliability, although Cisco recommends against using either.

Note   Past documents and books often stated that EIGRP, and its predecessor IGRP, also could use Maximum Transmission Unit (MTU) as a part of the metric. However, MTU size is intended to be a tiebreaker if two paths have equal metrics but different MTU sizes. In such a case, the path with the higher MTU is selected. So, while MTU size is listed in EIGRP Update messages, it is not directly used in metric calculations.

EIGRP calculates the metric for each possible route by inserting the values of the composite metric into a formula. If the choice is made to just use the default parameters of bandwidth and delay, the formula is as follows:

$$\text{Metric} = \left(\left(\frac{10^7}{\text{least-bandwidth}} \right) + \text{cumulative-delay} \right) * 256$$

In this formula, the term *least-bandwidth* represents the lowest-bandwidth link in the route, using a unit of kilobits per second. For example, if the slowest link in a route is a 10-Mbps Ethernet link, the first part of the formula is $10^7 / 10^4$, because 10 Mbps equals

10,000 kbps, or 10^4 kbps. The *cumulative-delay* value used by the formula is the sum of all the delay values for all links in the route, with a unit of "tens of microseconds." So, if you add up all the delays (from the output of the **show interfaces** *type number* command) from all egress interfaces, you would take that number (which is in microseconds) and divide by 10 (to give you a unit of *tens of microseconds*) for use in the formula. You can set both bandwidth and delay for each link, using the **bandwidth** and **delay** interface subcommands.

Table 4-3 summarizes some of the key facts about EIGRP.

Key Topic

Table 4-3 *EIGRP Feature Summary*

Feature	Description
Transport	IP, protocol type 88 (does not use UDP or TCP).
Metric	Based on constrained bandwidth and cumulative delay by default, and optionally load and reliability.
Hello interval	Interval at which a router sends EIGRP Hello messages on an interface.
Hold Timer	Timer used to determine when a neighboring router has failed, based on a router not receiving any EIGRP messages, including Hellos, in this timer period.
Update destination address	Normally sent to 224.0.0.10, with retransmissions being sent to each neighbor's unicast IP address. Can also be sent to the neighbor's unicast IP address.
Full or partial updates	Full updates are used when new neighbors are discovered; otherwise, partial updates are used.
Authentication	Supports MD5 authentication only.
VLSM/classless	EIGRP includes the mask with each route, also allowing it to support discontiguous networks and VLSM.
Route tags	Allows EIGRP to tag routes as they are redistributed into EIGRP.
Next-hop field	Supports the advertisement of routes with a different next-hop router than the advertising router.
Manual route summarization	Allows route summarization at any point in the EIGRP network.
Automatic summarization	EIGRP supports, and defaults to use, automatic route summarization at classful network boundaries.
Multiprotocol	Supports the advertisement of IPX, AppleTalk, IP version 4, and IP version 6 routes.

This completes the CCNA-level EIGRP review. The rest of this chapter now examines EIGRP neighbor relationships.

EIGRP Neighborships

Like OSPF, EIGRP uses three major steps to achieve its goal of learning the best available loop-free routes:

Step 1. Establish EIGRP neighbor relationships—*neighborships*—with other routers that share a common subnet.

Step 2. Exchange EIGRP topology data with those neighbors.

Step 3. Calculate the currently best IP route for each subnet, based on the known EIGRP topology data, and add those best routes to the IP routing table.

This three-step process hinges on the first step—the successful creation of neighbor relationships between EIGRP routers. The basic EIGRP configuration described earlier in this chapter, particularly the **network** command, most directly tells EIGRP on which interfaces to dynamically discover neighbors. After EIGRP neighborships have been formed with neighboring routers that are reachable through those interfaces, the final two steps occur without any additional direct configuration.

EIGRP dynamically discovers neighbors by sending EIGRP Hello messages on each EIGRP-enabled interface. When two routers hear EIGRP Hello messages from each other, they check the EIGRP parameters listed in those messages and decide whether the two routers should or should not become neighbors.

The rest of this section focuses on topics related to EIGRP neighborship, specifically:

■ Manipulating EIGRP Hello and Hold Timers

■ Controlling whether routers become neighbors by using either passive interfaces or statically defined neighbors

■ Examining configuration settings that can prevent EIGRP neighborships

Manipulating EIGRP Hello and Hold Timers

The word *convergence* defines the overall process by which routers notice internetwork topology changes, communicate about those changes, and change their routing tables to contain only the best currently working routes. EIGRP converges very quickly, even with all default settings.

One of the slower components of the EIGRP convergence process relates to the timers that EIGRP neighbors use to recognize that a neighborship has failed. If the interface over which the neighbor is reachable fails, and Cisco IOS changes the interface state to anything other than "up/up," a router immediately knows that the neighborship should fail. However, in some cases, an interface state might stay "up/up" during times when the link is not usable. In such cases, EIGRP convergence relies on the Hold Timer to expire, which by default, on LANs, means a 15-second wait. (The default EIGRP Hold time on interfaces/subinterfaces with a bandwidth of T1 or lower, with an encapsulation type of Frame Relay, is 180 seconds.)

The basic operation of these two timers is relatively simple. EIGRP uses the Hello messages in part as a confirmation that the link between the neighbors still works. If a router does not receive a Hello from a neighbor for one entire Hold time, that router considers the neighbor to be unavailable. For example, with a default LAN setting of Hello = 5 and Hold = 15, the local router sends Hellos every 5 seconds. The neighbor resets its downward-counting Hold Timer to 15 upon receiving a Hello from that neighbor. Under normal operation on a LAN, with defaults, the Hold Timer for a neighbor would vary from 15, down to 10, and then be reset to 15. However, if the Hellos were no longer received for 15 seconds, the neighborship would fail, driving convergence.

To optimize convergence, an engineer could simply reduce the Hello and Hold Timers, accepting insignificant additional overhead, in return for shorter convergence times. These settings can be made per interface/subinterface, and per EIGRP process.

Note Although expected to be outside the scope of CCNP, EIGRP can also use the Bi-directional Forwarding Detection (BFD) feature, which provides a means for subsecond detection of a failure in IP connectivity between two neighboring routers.

Configuring the Hello/Hold Timers

Most design engineers would normally choose Hello/Hold Timers that match on all router interfaces on a subnet. However, these settings do not have to match. Interestingly, by setting the Hello and Hold Timers to nondefault values, you can see some oddities with how EIGRP neighbors use these values.

For example, consider four WAN distribution routers, as shown in Figure 4-3. These routers might each have a number of Frame Relay PVCs to remote branches, or multiple MPLS VPN connections to branches. However, to communicate with each other and with data centers at the home office, these four routers connect through a core VLAN/subnet. Note that the design shows routers, rather than Layer 3 switches, but the concept is the same in either case.

A design that hoped to speed EIGRP convergence might call for setting the Hello and Hold Timers to 2 and 6, respectively. (The Hold Timer does not have to be three times the Hello Timer, but the 3:1 ratio is a reasonable guideline.) However, to make an important point about operation of the configuration commands, Example 4-3 sets only R1's Fa0/1 timers to the new values. Note that in this case, EIGRP has already been configured on all four routers, using ASN 9.

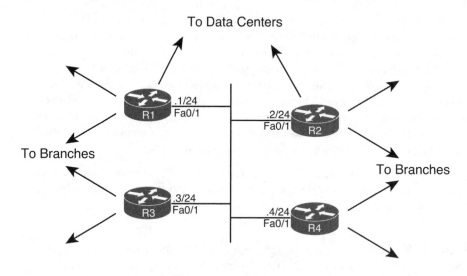

Note: All IP addresses begin with 172.16.1

Figure 4-3 *Four WAN Distribution Routers on the Same VLAN/Subnet*

Example 4-3 *EIGRP Hello and Hold Timer Configuration—R1*

```
interface Fastethernet0/1
 ip hello-interval eigrp 9 2
 ip hold-time eigrp 9 6
```

A couple of interesting points can be made about the operation of these seemingly simple commands. First, these two settings can be made per interface/subinterface, but not per neighbor. In Figure 4-3, the Example 4-3 configuration then applies on R1 for all three neighbors reachable on interface Fa0/1.

The second interesting point about these commands is that one parameter (the Hello Interval) tells R1 what to do, whereas the other (the Hold Timer) actually tells the neighboring routers what to do. As shown in Figure 4-4, the **ip hello-interval eigrp 9 2** interface subcommand tells R1 to send Hellos every 2 seconds. However, the **ip hold-time eigrp 9 6** interface subcommand tells R1, again for the EIGRP process with ASN 9, to tell its neighbors to use a Hold Timer of 6 for their respective neighbor relationships with R1. In short, the EIGRP Hello message sent by R1 announces the Hold Timer that other routers should use in the neighbor relationship with R1. Figure 4-4 shows this idea in graphical form.

Note Cisco IOS does not prevent you from making the unfortunate configuration choice of setting the Hold Timer to a value smaller than the Hello interval. In such a case, the neighborship repeatedly fails and recovers, flapping routes in and out of the routing table.

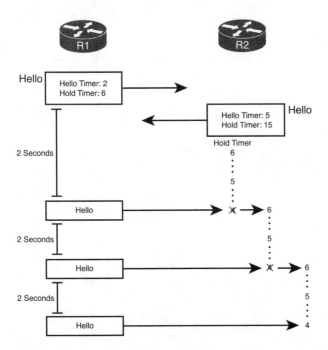

Figure 4-4   *R1 Announcing New Hello and Hold Timers*

Verifying the Hello/Hold Timers

To find the Hello interface and Hold time configured on a router's interface, you could of course look at a router's configuration, but the **show running-config** command might not be available to you on some question types on the ROUTE exam. However, if you have access to only user mode, you can issue the **show ip eigrp interfaces detail** *type number* command. It's important to note, however, that if you use that command on some older versions of Cisco IOS, the Hold time might not displayed.

Example 4-4 shows some sample command output from R1, R2, and R3. Note that the Hello and Hold Timer settings on R1 are all in the range of 10–15 seconds, because the timers on R2, R3, and R4 all still default to 5 and 15 seconds, respectively. R2's neighborship with R1 lists a Hold Timer of 4, which is within the expected range of 4–6 seconds remaining.

Example 4-4   *Demonstration that R2 and R3 Use R1's Configured Hold Timer*

```
! On Router R1: !!!!!!!!!!!!!!!!!!!!!!!!!!!!!!!!!!!!!!!!!!!!!!
R1# show ip eigrp interfaces detail fa0/1


EIGRP-IPv4 Interfaces for AS(9)
                    Xmit Queue    PeerQ        Mean  Pacing Time   Multicast    Pending
Interface Peers  Un/Reliable   Un/Reliable   SRTT  Un/Reliable   Flow Timer   Routes
```

```
Fa0/1       3         0/0       0/0         535       0/1            50              0
  Hello-interval is 2, Hold-time is 6
  Split-horizon is enabled
  Next xmit serial <none>
  Packetized sent/expedited: 0/0
  Hello's sent/expedited: 102/1
  Un/reliable mcasts: 0/1  Un/reliable ucasts: 4/9
  Mcast exceptions: 1  CR packets: 1  ACKs suppressed: 1
  Retransmissions sent: 2  Out-of-sequence rcvd: 0
  Topology-ids on interface - 0
  Authentication mode is not set


R1# show ip eigrp neighbors
IP-EIGRP neighbors for process 9
H   Address             Interface   Hold Uptime        SRTT      RTO     Q    Seq
                                    (sec)              (ms)              Cnt  Num
2   172.16.1.4          Fa0/1       11 00:03:17        1596      5000    0    7
1   172.16.1.3          Fa0/1       11 00:05:21        1         200     0    5
0   172.16.1.2          Fa0/1       13 00:09:04        4         200     0    2
! On Router R2: !!!!!!!!!!!!!!!!!!!!!!!!!!!!!!!!!!!!!!!!!!!
R2# show ip eigrp neighbors
IP-EIGRP neighbors for process 9
H   Address             Interface   Hold Uptime        SRTT      RTO     Q    Seq
                                    (sec)              (ms)              Cnt  Num
2   172.16.1.4          Fa0/1       11 00:03:36        4         200     0    6
1   172.16.1.3          Fa0/1       11 00:05:40        12        200     0    4
0   172.16.1.1          Fa0/1       4 00:09:22         1         200     0    2
! On Router R3: !!!!!!!!!!!!!!!!!!!!!!!!!!!!!!!!!!!!!!!!!!!
R3# show ip eigrp neighbors
IP-EIGRP neighbors for process 9
H   Address             Interface   Hold Uptime        SRTT      RTO     Q    Seq
                                    (sec)              (ms)              Cnt  Num
2   172.16.1.4          Fa0/1       11 00:03:40        4         200     0    5
1   172.16.1.1          Fa0/1       5 00:05:44         1278      5000    0    4
0   172.16.1.2          Fa0/1       13 00:05:44        1277      5000    0    4
```

Preventing Unwanted Neighbors Using Passive Interfaces

When an EIGRP network configuration subcommand matches an interface, EIGRP on that router does two things:

Step 1.   Attempts to find potential EIGRP neighbors by sending Hellos to the 224.0.0.10 multicast address

Step 2.   Advertises the subnet connected to that interface

In some cases, however, no legitimate EIGRP neighbors might exist off an interface. For example, consider the small internetwork shown in Figure 4-5, with three routers, and with only one router connected to each LAN interface. Each router needs to advertise the subnets connected to their various FastEthernet interfaces, but at the same time, there is no benefit to multicast EIGRP Hellos on those interfaces, because only one router connects to each LAN.

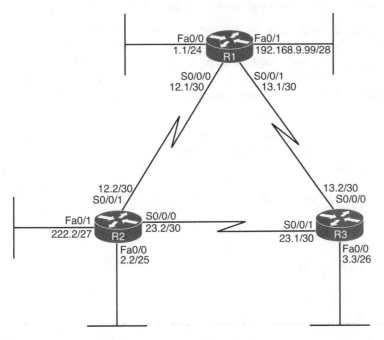

Note: All IP addresses begin with 10.1 unless otherwise noted.

Figure 4-5   *LAN Interfaces That Benefit from the Passive Interface Feature*

The network designer can reasonably choose to limit EIGRP on those interfaces that have no legitimate EIGRP neighbors. However, the subnets connected to those same interfaces also typically need to be advertised by EIGRP. For example, subnet 10.1.1.0/24, off R1's Fa0/0 interface, still needs to be advertised by EIGRP, even though R1 should never find an EIGRP neighbor on that interface.

Given such a requirement—to advertise the subnet while disallowing EIGRP neighborships on the interface—an engineer has two main configuration options to choose from:

- Enable EIGRP on the interface using the EIGRP **network** command, but tell the router to not send any EIGRP messages on the interface by making the interface passive (using the **passive-interface** command).

- Do not enable EIGRP on the interface, and advertise the connected route using route redistribution (and the **redistribute connected** configuration command).

The first option relies on the passive interface feature—a feature specifically created with this design requirement in mind. When an interface is passive, EIGRP does not send any EIGRP messages on the interface—multicasts or EIGRP unicasts—and the router ignores any EIGRP messages received on the interface. However, EIGRP still advertises the connected subnets if matched with an EIGRP **network** command. As a result, the first option in the preceding list directly meets all the design requirements. It has the added advantage of being very secure in that no EIGRP neighborships are possible on the interface.

The second option—redistributing connected subnets—also works, but frankly it is the less preferred option in this case. Specifically, the passive interface option clearly meets the design requirements, while the redistribution option causes the connected route to be advertised as an external EIGRP route. This could cause problems in some cases with multiple redistribution points between routing domains (as discussed in Chapter 10, "Route Redistribution").

The configuration of the passive interface itself is fairly straightforward. To configure the passive interface option, these three routers could be configured as shown in Example 4-5.

Example 4-5 *Configuration of* **passive-interface** *Commands on R1, R2, and R3*

```
! On Router R1: !!!!!!!!!!!!!!!!!!!!!!!!!!!!!!!!!!!!!!!!!!!!!
router eigrp 1
 passive-interface fastethernet0/0
 passive-interface fastethernet0/1
 network 10.0.0.0
 network 192.168.9.0


! On Router R2: !!!!!!!!!!!!!!!!!!!!!!!!!!!!!!!!!!!!!!!!!!!!!
router eigrp 1
 passive-interface default
 no passive-interface serial0/0/0
 no passive-interface serial0/0/1
 network 10.0.0.0


! On Router R3: !!!!!!!!!!!!!!!!!!!!!!!!!!!!!!!!!!!!!!!!!!!!!
router eigrp 1
 passive-interface fastethernet0/0
 network 10.0.0.0
```

R1's configuration lists two **passive-interface** commands, one per LAN interface. As a result, R1 no longer sends EIGRP messages on these two interfaces, including the multicast EIGRP Hellos used to discover neighbors.

R2's configuration uses a slightly different option: the **passive-interface default** command. This command essentially changes the default for an interface from not being passive to instead being passive. Then, to make an interface not passive, you have to use a **no** version of the **passive-interface** command for those interfaces.

Two commands help to verify that the passive interface design is working properly. First, the **show ip eigrp interfaces** command omits passive interfaces, listing the nonpassive interfaces matched by a **network** command. Alternatively, the **show ip protocols** command explicitly lists all passive interfaces. Example 4-6 shows samples of both commands on R2.

Example 4-6   *Verifying the Results of* **passive-interface** *on R2*

```
R2# show ip eigrp interfaces
IP-EIGRP interfaces for process 1


                        Xmit Queue    Mean     Pacing Time    Multicast    Pending
Interface     Peers     Un/Reliable   SRTT     Un/Reliable    Flow Timer   Routes
Se0/0/0         1         0/0          32         0/15           159          0
Se0/0/1         1         0/0         1290        0/15          6443          0
R2# show ip protocols
Routing Protocol is "eigrp 1"
  Outgoing update filter list for all interfaces is not set
  Incoming update filter list for all interfaces is not set
  Default networks flagged in outgoing updates
  Default networks accepted from incoming updates
  EIGRP metric weight K1=1, K2=0, K3=1, K4=0, K5=0
  EIGRP maximum hopcount 100
  EIGRP maximum metric variance 1
  Redistributing: eigrp 1
  EIGRP NSF-aware route hold timer is 240s
  Automatic network summarization is in effect
  Maximum path: 4
  Routing for Networks:
    10.0.0.0
  Passive Interface(s):
    FastEthernet0/0
    FastEthernet0/1
  Routing Information Sources:
    Gateway         Distance      Last Update
    10.1.12.1            90       00:00:39
    10.1.23.1            90       00:00:39
  Distance: internal 90 external 170
```

Controlling Neighborships with Static Configuration

EIGRP supports the ability to statically define neighbors instead of dynamically discovering neighbors.

Although seldom used, you can use this feature to reduce the overhead associated with EIGRP multicast messages. Frame Relay WANs in particular might benefit from the static neighbor definitions, because to support multicasts and broadcasts over Frame Relay, a router must replicate a frame and send a copy over every PVC associated with the interface or subinterface. For example, if a multipoint subinterface has ten PVCs associated with it, but only two of the remote routers used EIGRP, without static neighbors, all ten routers would be sent a copy of the EIGRP multicast Hello packets. With static neighbor definitions for the two routers, EIGRP messages would be sent as unicasts to each of the two neighbors, with no EIGRP messages sent to the eight non-EIGRP routers, reducing overhead.

The configuration seems simple, but it has a few subtle caveats. This section examines the straightforward configuration first and then examines the caveats.

Configuring Static EIGRP Neighbors

To define a neighbor, both routers must configure the **neighbor** *ip-address outgoing-interface* EIGRP router subcommand. The IP address is the interface IP address of the neighboring router. Also, the configured IP address must be from the subnet connected to the interface listed in the **neighbor** command; otherwise, the command is rejected. Also, note that the EIGRP configuration still needs a **network** command that matches the interface referenced by the **neighbor** command.

For example, consider Figure 4-6, which adds a new router (R5) to the internetwork of Figure 4-3. R1 and R5 have a PVC connecting them, with IP addresses and subinterface numbers shown.

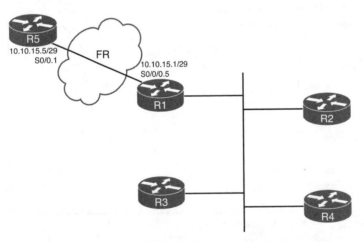

Figure 4-6   *Adding a Branch, with a Static EIGRP Neighbor*

Example 4-7 shows the configuration on both R1 and R5 to use static neighbor definitions. Of note, R1's neighbor command refers to R5's IP address on their common subnet (10.10.15.5), with R1's local interface (S0/0/0.5). R5 lists the reverse, with R1's 10.10.15.1 IP address and R5's local S0/0.1 interface. Also note that both routers have a **network** command that references network 10.0.0.0, and both routers do advertise subnet 10.10.15.0/29.

The **show ip eigrp neighbors** command does not identify a neighbor as static, but the **show ip eigrp neighbors detail** command does. Example 4-7 shows the more detailed output near the end, with the designation of 10.10.15.5 (R5) as a static neighbor.

Example 4-7   *Static EIGRP Neighborship Between R1 and R5*

```
! New configuration on router R1
R1# show running-config
! lines omitted
router eigrp 9
 network 172.16.0.0
 network 10.0.0.0
 no auto-summary
 neighbor 10.10.15.5 Serial0/0/0.5
! Back to R1
R1# show ip eigrp neighbors detail
IP-EIGRP neighbors for process 9
H   Address              Interface    Hold Uptime   SRTT  RTO     Q    Seq
                                          (sec)     (ms)          Cnt  Num
3   10.10.15.5           Se0/0/0.5    10 00:00:51   15    200     0    2
    Static neighbor
    Version 12.4/1.2, Retrans: 0, Retries: 0
2   172.16.1.2           Fa0/1        11 00:02:57   3     200     0    25
    Version 12.4/1.2, Retrans: 1, Retries: 0
1   172.16.1.3           Fa0/1        10 00:03:45   5     200     0    21
    Version 12.4/1.2, Retrans: 0, Retries: 0
0   172.16.1.4           Fa0/1        13 00:03:45   5     200     0    18

! R5's new config added to support the neighbor
R5# show running-config
! lines omitted
router eigrp 9
 network 10.0.0.0
 no auto-summary
 neighbor 10.10.15.1 Serial0/0.1
```

Caveat When Using EIGRP Static Neighbors

Cisco IOS changes how it processes EIGRP packets on any interface referenced by an EIGRP **neighbor** command. Keeping in mind the design goal for this feature—to reduce multicasts—Cisco IOS disables all EIGRP multicast packet processing on an interface when an EIGRP **neighbor** command has been configured. For example, in Example 4-7, R1's S0/0/0.5 subinterface will not process EIGRP multicast packets any more as a result of R1's **neighbor 10.10.15.5 Serial0/0/0.5** EIGRP subcommand.

Because of the operation of the EIGRP **neighbor** command, if at least one EIGRP static neighbor is defined on an interface, no dynamic neighbors can be either discovered or continue to work if already discovered. For example, again in Figure 4-6 and Example 4-7, if R1 added a **neighbor 172.16.1.5 FastEthernet0/1** EIGRP subcommand, R1 would lose its current neighborships with Routers R2, R3, and R4.

Configuration Settings That Could Prevent Neighbor Relationships

Some of the configuration settings already mentioned in this chapter, when configured incorrectly, might prevent EIGRP neighborships. This section summarizes those settings, and introduces a few other configuration settings that can prevent neighbor relationships. The list of items that must match—and that do not have to match—can be a useful place to start troubleshooting neighbor initialization problems in real life, and to troubleshoot neighborship problems for simulation questions on the CCNP ROUTE exam.

Table 4-4 lists the neighbor requirements for both EIGRP and Open Shortest Path First (OSPF). (OSPF is included here just as a frame of reference for those more familiar with OSPF; this information will be repeated in Chapter 7, "Fundamental OSPF Concepts," which discusses OSPF neighborship requirements.) Following the table, the next few pages examine some of these settings for EIGRP.

Table 4-4   *Neighbor Requirements for EIGRP and OSPF*

Requirement	EIGRP	OSPF
The routers must be able to send/receive IP packets to one another.	Yes	Yes
Interfaces' primary IP addresses must be in same subnet.	Yes	Yes
Must not be passive on the connected interface.	Yes	Yes
Must use the same ASN (EIGRP) or process-ID (OSPF) in the router configuration command.	Yes	No
Hello interval/timer, plus either the Hold (EIGRP) or Dead (OSPF) timer, must match.	No	Yes
Must pass neighbor authentication (if configured).	Yes	Yes
Must be in same area.	N/A	Yes
IP MTU must match.	No	Yes
K-values (used in metric calculation) must match.	Yes	—
Router IDs must be unique.	No[1]	Yes

[1] Duplicate EIGRP RIDs do not prevent routers from becoming neighbors, but it can cause problems when adding external EIGRP routes to the IP routing table.

Going through Table 4-4 sequentially, the first two items relate to IP connectivity. Two routers must be able to send and receive IP packets with each other. Additionally, the primary IP address on the interfaces—in other words, the IP address configured without the **secondary** keyword on the **ip address** command—must be in the same subnet.

Note It should not matter for CCNP ROUTE, but possibly for CCIE R/S: EIGRP's rules about neighbor IP addresses being in the same subnet are less exact than OSPF. OSPF requires matching subnet numbers and masks. EIGRP just asks the question of whether the neighbor's IP address is in the range of addresses for the subnet as known to the local router. For example, two routers with addresses of 10.1.1.1/24 (range 10.1.1.1–10.1.1.254) and 10.1.1.2/30 (range 10.1.1.1–10.1.1.2) would actually allow EIGRP neighborship, because each router believes the neighbor's IP address to be in the same subnet as the local router.

The next three items in Table 4-4—passive interfaces, matching the EIGRP ASN number, and allowing mismatching Hello/Hold Timers—have already been covered in this chapter.

The next item, authentication, is discussed in detail in Chapter 17, "Routing Protocol Authentication."

The next two items in the table—matching the IP MTU and matching OSPF areas—do not prevent EIGRP neighborships. These topics, are requirements for OSPF neighborship and will be discussed in Chapter 7.

Finally, the last two items in the table (K-values and router IDs) each require more than a cursory discussion for EIGRP and will be explained in the upcoming pages.

Configuring EIGRP Metric Components (K-values)

EIGRP calculates its integer metric, by default, using a formula that uses constraining bandwidth and cumulative delay. You can change the formula to use link reliability and link load, and even disable the use of bandwidth and/or delay. To change the formula, an engineer can configure five weighting constants, called K-values, which are represented in the metric calculation formula as constants K1, K2, K3, K4, and K5.

From a design perspective, Cisco strongly recommends against using link load and link reliability in the EIGRP metric calculation. Most shops that use EIGRP never touch the K-values at all. However, in labs, it can be useful to disable the use of bandwidth from the metric calculation, because that simplifies the metric math and makes it easier to learn the concepts behind EIGRP.

The **metric weights** command sets five variables (K1 through K5), each of which weights the metric calculation formula more or less heavily for various parts of the formula. Mismatched K-value settings prevent two routers from becoming neighbors. Thankfully, determining whether such a mismatch exists is easy. When a router receives an EIGRP Hello with mismatched K-values (as compared to itself), the router issues a log message stating that a K-value mismatch exists. You can also examine the values either by looking at the running configurations or by looking for the K-values listed in the output of the **show ip protocols** command, as shown in Example 4-8.

> **Note** In the command **metric weights 0 1 0 1 1 0**, the first number (that is, the leftmost 0) represents the Type of Service (ToS) value with which EIGRP packets should be marked. This is a Quality of Service (QoS) setting. It equals 0 and cannot be changed to a different value. The remaining five numbers are the K-values: K1, K2, K3, K4, and K5, respectively.

Example 4-8 *Mismatched K-values*

```
R2(config)# router eigrp 1
R2(config-router)# metric weights 0 1 0 1 1 0
R2(config-router)# end
Feb 23 18:48:21.599: %DUAL-5-NBRCHANGE: IP-EIGRP(0) 1: Neighbor 10.1.12.1
(Serial0/0/1) is down: metric changed
R2#
Feb 23 18:48:24.907: %DUAL-5-NBRCHANGE: IP-EIGRP(0) 1: Neighbor 10.1.12.1
(Serial0/0/1) is down: K-value mismatch
R2# show ip protocols
Routing Protocol is "eigrp 1"
  Outgoing update filter list for all interfaces is not set
  Incoming update filter list for all interfaces is not set
  Default networks flagged in outgoing updates
  Default networks accepted from incoming updates
  EIGRP metric weight K1=1, K2=0, K3=1, K4=1, K5=0
! lines omitted for brevity
```

EIGRP Router ID

EIGRP uses a concept of a representing each router with a router ID (RID). The EIGRP RID is a 32-bit number, represented in dotted decimal. Each router determines its RID when the EIGRP process starts, using the same general rules as does OSPF for determining the OSPF RID, as follows:

Key Topic

Step 1. Use the configured value (using the **eigrp router-id** *a.b.c.d* EIGRP subcommand).

Step 2. Use the highest IPv4 address on an up/up loopback interface.

Step 3. Use the highest IPv4 address on an up/up nonloopback interface.

Although EIGRP does require each router to have an RID, the actual value is of little practical importance. The EIGRP **show** commands seldom list the RID value, and unlike OSPF RIDs, engineers do not need to know each router's EIGRP RID to interpret the EIGRP topology database. Additionally, although it is best to make EIGRP RIDs unique, duplicate RIDs do not prevent routers from becoming neighbors.

The only time the value of EIGRP RIDs matters is when injecting external routes into EIGRP. In that case, the routers injecting the external routes must have unique RIDs to avoid confusion.

Neighborship over WANs

EIGRP configuration and neighborship rules do not differ when comparing typical LAN and typical WAN technologies. However, some design and operational differences exist, particularly regarding which routers become neighbors with which other routers. This short section closes the EIGRP neighbor discussion with a brief look at Frame Relay, MPLS VPNs, and Metro Ethernet as implemented with Virtual Private LAN Service (VPLS).

Neighborship on Frame Relay

Frame Relay provides a Layer 2 WAN service. Each router connects to the service using a physical serial link, called a Frame Relay access link. The provider then creates logical connections, called *permanent virtual circuits (PVC)*, which are logical paths between pairs of routers connected to a Frame Relay service. Any pair of routers that connect to the ends of a Frame Relay PVC can send Frame Relay frames to each other. Therefore, they can send IP packets and become EIGRP neighbors. Figure 4-7 shows a typical case, with R1 as a central-site router, and R2, R3, and R4 acting as branch routers.

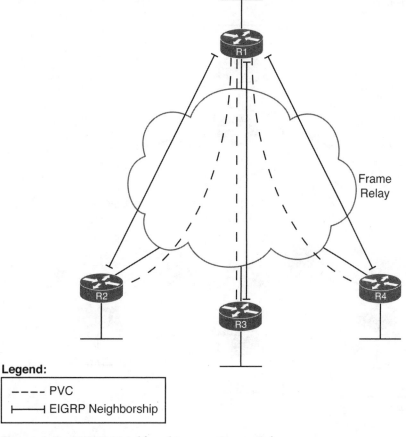

Figure 4-7 *EIGRP Neighborships over Frame Relay*

Figure 4-7 shows EIGRP neighborships, but note that all routers can learn all routes in the internetwork, even though not all routers become neighbors. The neighborships can only form when a PVC exists between the two routers.

Neighborship on MPLS VPN

Multiprotocol Label Switching (MPLS) Virtual Private Networks (VPN) create a WAN service that has some similarities but many differences when compared to Frame Relay. The customer routers connect to the service, often with serial links but at other times with Frame Relay PVCs or with Ethernet. The service itself is a Layer 3 service, forwarding IP packets through a cloud. As a result, no predefined PVCs need to exist between the customer routers. Additionally, the service uses routers at the edge of the service provider cloud—generically called *provider edge (PE)* routers—and these routers are Layer 3 aware.

That Layer 3 awareness means that the *customer edge (CE)* routers form an EIGRP neighborship with the PE router on the other end of their local access link, as shown in Figure 4-8. The PE routers exchange their routes, typically using Multiprotocol BGP (MP-BGP), a topic outside the scope of this book. However, all the CE routers then learn routes from each other, although each CE router has only one EIGRP neighborship for each of its connections into the MPLS VPN cloud.

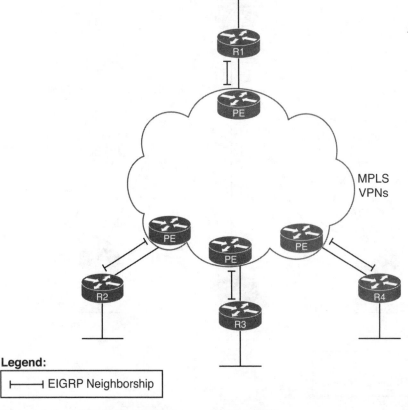

Legend:

├────┤ EIGRP Neighborship

Figure 4-8   *EIGRP Neighborships over MPLS VPN*

Neighborship on Metro Ethernet

The term *Metropolitan Ethernet (MetroE)* represents a range of Layer 2 WAN services in which the CE device connects to the WAN service using some form of Ethernet. Because MetroE provides a Layer 2 Ethernet service, the service delivers an Ethernet frame sent by one customer router to another customer router (for unicast frames), or to many other routers (for multicast or broadcast frames).

MetroE encompasses several underlying technologies to create the service. Of note for the purposes of this book are the Virtual Private Wire Service (VPWS) and the Virtual Private LAN Service (VPLS). Both technical specifications allow for connections using Ethernet links, with the service forwarding Ethernet frames. VPWS focuses on point-to-point topologies, whereas VPLS supports multipoint, approximating the concept of the entire WAN service acting like one large Ethernet switch. Because it is a Layer 2 service, MetroE does not have any Layer 3 awareness, and customer routers (typically referenced with the more general service provider term *customer premises equipment*, or *CPE*) see the MetroE service as a VLAN. Because the customer routers connect to the service as a VLAN, all the routers connected to the service can become EIGRP neighbors, as shown in Figure 4-9.

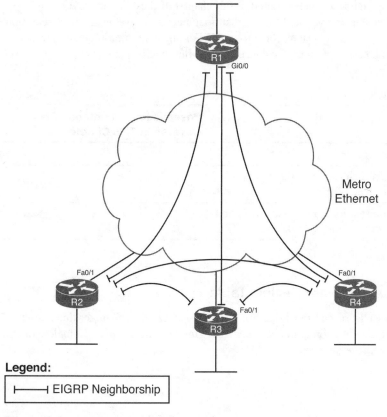

Figure 4-9 *EIGRP Neighborships over Metro Ethernet*

Exam Preparation Tasks

Planning Practice

The CCNP ROUTE exam expects test takers to be able to review design documents, create implementation plans, and create verification plans. This section provides some exercises that can help you to take a step back from the minute details of the topics in this chapter, so that you can think about the same technical topics from the planning perspective.

For each planning practice table, simply complete the table. Note that any numbers in parentheses represent the number of options listed for each item in the solutions in Appendix F, "Completed Planning Practice Tables," which you can find on the CD-ROM accompanying this book.

Design Review Table

Table 4-5 lists several design goals related to this chapter. If these design goals were listed in a design document, and you had to take that document and develop an implementation plan, what implementation options come to mind? For any configuration items, a general description can be used, without any concern about the specific parameters.

Table 4-5   *Design Review*

Design Goal	Possible Implementation Choices Covered in This Chapter
Improve EIGRP convergence.	
Implement EIGRP on each router so that neighborships are formed (2).	
Limit neighborship formation on interfaces matched with an EIGRP **network** command (3).	

Implementation Plan Peer Review Table

Table 4-6 shows a list of questions that others might ask, or that you might think about, during a peer review of another network engineer's implementation plan. Complete the table by answering the questions.

Table 4-6 *Notable Questions from This Chapter to Consider During an Implementation Plan Peer Review*

Question	Answer
What happens on a router interface on which an EIGRP **network** command matches the interface? (2)	
What configuration settings prevent EIGRP neighbor discovery on an EIGRP-enabled interface? (2)	
What configuration settings prevent any neighborships on an EIGRP-enabled interface?	
What settings do potential neighbors check before becoming EIGRP neighbors? (5)	
What settings that you might think would impact EIGRP neighbor relationships actually do not prevent neighborship? (3)	

Create an Implementation Plan Table

To practice skills useful when creating your own EIGRP implementation plan, list in Table 4-7 configuration commands related to the configuration of the following features. You might want to record your answers outside the book, and set a goal to complete this table (and others like it) from memory during your final reviews before taking the exam.

Table 4-7 *Implementation Plan Configuration Memory Drill*

Feature	Configuration Commands/Notes
Enabling EIGRP on interfaces	
Setting Hello and Hold Timers	
Passive interfaces	
Static EIGRP neighbors	
K-values	
EIGRP router ID	

Choose Commands for a Verification Plan Table

To practice skills useful when creating your own EIGRP verification plan, list in Table 4-8 all commands that supply the requested information. You might want to record your answers outside the book, and set a goal to complete this table (and others like it) from memory during your final reviews before taking the exam.

Table 4-8   *Verification Plan Memory Drill*

Information Needed	Command
Routes that have been added to the IP routing table by EIGRP.	
All routes in a router's routing table.	
The specific route for a single destination address or subnet.	
A listing of all (both statically configured and dynamically discovered) EIGRP neighbors.	
Notation as to whether a neighbor was dynamically discovered or statically configured.	
A listing of statistics regarding the numbers of EIGRP messages sent and received by a router.	
A listing of interfaces on which EIGRP has been enabled (by virtue of the EIGRP **network** command).	
A listing of the number of EIGRP peers known through a particular interface.	
The elapsed time since a neighborship was formed.	
The parameters of any EIGRP **network** commands.	
The configured Hello Timer for an interface.	
The configured Hold Timer for an interface.	
The current actual Hold Timer for a neighbor.	
A router's EIGRP ASN.	
A list of EIGRP passive interfaces.	
A list of nonpassive EIGRP interfaces.	
A listing of EIGRP K-values.	
A listing of traffic statistics about EIGRP.	
A router's EIGRP Router ID.	

Review All the Key Topics

Review the most important topics from inside the chapter, noted with the Key Topic icon in the outer margin of the page. Table 4-9 lists a reference of these key topics and the page numbers on which each is found.

Key
Topic

Table 4-9 *Key Topics for Chapter 4*

Key Topic Element	Description	Page Number
List	Configuration step review for basic EIGRP configuration	125
Table 4-2	Key EIGRP verification commands	128
Table 4-3	Summary of EIGRP features and facts	133
List	Methods of disallowing EIGRP neighborships on an interface, while still advertising the connected subnet	139
Table 4-4	List of items that can impact the formation of EIGRP neighborships	144
List	Rules for choosing an EIGRP Router ID	146

Complete the Tables and Lists from Memory

Print a copy of Appendix D, "Memory Tables," (found on the CD), or at least the section for this chapter, and complete the tables and lists from memory. Appendix E, "Memory Tables Answer Key," also on the CD, includes completed tables and lists to check your work.

Define Key Terms

Define the following key terms from this chapter, and check your answers in the glossary:

K-value, neighborship, Hello interval, Hold Timer, passive interface

This chapter covers the following subjects:

- **Building the EIGRP Topology Table:** This section discusses how a router seeds its local EIGRP topology table, and how neighboring EIGRP routers exchange topology information.

- **Building the IP Routing Table:** This section explains how routers use EIGRP topology data to choose the best routes to add to their local routing tables.

- **Optimizing EIGRP Convergence:** This section examines items that have an impact on how fast EIGRP converges for a given route.

- **Route Filtering:** This section examines how to filter prefixes from being sent in EIGRP Updates or filter them from being processed when received in an EIGRP Update.

- **Route Summarization:** This section discusses the concepts and configuration of EIGRP route summarization.

- **Default Routes:** This section examines the benefits of using default routes, and the mechanics of two methods for configuring default routes with EIGRP.

CHAPTER 5

Advanced EIGRP Concepts

Enhanced Interior Gateway Routing Protocol (EIGRP), like Open Shortest Path First (OSPF), uses three major branches of logic, each of which populates a different table. EIGRP begins by forming neighbor relationships and listing those relationships in the EIGRP neighbor table (as described in Chapter 4, "Fundamental EIGRP Concepts"). EIGRP then exchanges topology information with these same neighbors, with newly learned information being added to the router's EIGRP topology table. Finally, each router processes the EIGRP topology table to choose the best IP routes currently available, adding those IP routes to the IP routing table.

This chapter moves from the first major branch (neighborships, as covered in Chapter 4) to the second and third branches: EIGRP topology and EIGRP routes. To that end, the first major section of this chapter describes the protocol used by EIGRP to exchange the topology information and details exactly what information EIGRP puts in its messages sent between routers. The next major section shows how EIGRP examines the topology data to then choose the best route currently available for each prefix. The final section of this chapter examines how to optimize the EIGRP convergence processes so that when the topology does change, the routers in the internetwork quickly converge to the then-best routes. This chapter concludes with three sections covering categories of tools that you can use to limit the number of routes in the routing table: route filtering, route summarization, and default routes.

"Do I Know This Already?" Quiz

The "Do I Know This Already?" quiz allows you to assess whether you should read the entire chapter. If you miss no more than two of these 18 self-assessment questions, you might want to move ahead to the "Exam Preparation Tasks" section. Table 5-1 lists the major headings in this chapter and the "Do I Know This Already?" quiz questions covering the material in those headings, so that you can assess your knowledge of these specific areas. The answers to the "Do I Know This Already?" quiz appear in Appendix A.

Table 5-1 *"Do I Know This Already?" Foundation Topics Section-to-Question Mapping*

Foundation Topics Section	Questions
Building the EIGRP Topology Table	1–3
Building the IP Routing Table	4–8
Optimizing EIGRP Convergence	9
Route Filtering	10–13

Foundation Topics Section	Questions
Route Summarization	14–16
Default Routes	17, 18

1. Which of the following are methods that EIGRP uses to initially populate (seed) its EIGRP topology table, before learning topology data from neighbors? (Choose two.)

   a. By adding all subnets listed by the **show ip route connected** command

   b. By adding the subnets of working interfaces over which static neighbors have been defined

   c. By adding subnets redistributed on the local router from another routing source

   d. By adding all subnets listed by the **show ip route static** command

2. Which of the following are both advertised by EIGRP in the Update message and included in the formula for calculating the integer EIGRP metric? (Choose two.)

   a. Jitter

   b. Delay

   c. MTU

   d. Reliability

3. Router R1 uses S0/0 to connect through a T/1 to the Frame Relay service. Five PVCs terminate on the serial link. Three PVCs (101, 102, and 103) are configured on subinterface S0/0.1, and one each (104 and 105) are on S0/0.2 and S0/0.3. The configuration shows no configuration related to EIGRP WAN bandwidth control, and the **bandwidth** command is not configured. Which of the following is true about how Cisco IOS tries to limit EIGRP's use of bandwidth on S0/0?

   a. R1 limits EIGRP to around 250 kbps on DLCI 102.

   b. R1 limits EIGRP to around 250 kbps on DLCI 104.

   c. R1 limits EIGRP to around 150 kbps on every DLCI.

   d. R1 does not limit EIGRP because no WAN bandwidth control has been configured.

4. The output of **show ip eigrp topology** on Router R1 shows the following output, which is all the output related to subnet 10.11.1.0/24. How many feasible successor routes does R1 have for 10.11.1.0/24?

   ```
   P 10.11.1.0/24, 2 successors, FD is 2172419
           via 10.1.1.2 (2172423/28167), Serial0/0/0.1
           via 10.1.1.6 (2172423/28167), Serial0/0/0.2
   ```

   a. 0

   b. 1

   c. 2

   d. 3

5. A network design shows that R1 has four different possible paths from itself to the data center subnets. Which of the following can influence which of those routes become feasible successor routes, assuming that you follow the Cisco-recommended practice of not changing metric weights? (Choose two.)

   a. The configuration of EIGRP offset lists

   b. Current link loads

   c. Changing interface delay settings

   d. Configuration of variance

6. Router R1 is three router hops away from subnet 10.1.1.0/24. According to various **show interfaces** commands, all three links between R1 and 10.1.1.0/24 use the following settings: bandwidth (in kbps): 1000, 500, 100000 and delay (in microseconds): 12000, 8000, 100. Which of the following answers correctly identify a value that feeds into the EIGRP metric calculation? (Choose two.)

   a. Bandwidth of 101,500 kilobits per second

   b. Bandwidth of about 34,000 kilobits per second

   c. Bandwidth of 500 kilobits per second

   d. Delay of 1200 tens-of-microseconds

   e. Delay of 2010 tens-of-microseconds

   f. Delay of 20100 tens microseconds

7. Routers R1 and R2 are EIGRP neighbors. R1 has been configured with the **eigrp stub connected** command. Which of the following are true as a result? (Choose two.)

   a. R1 can learn EIGRP routes from R2, but R2 cannot learn EIGRP routes from R1.

   b. R1 can send IP packets to R2, but R2 cannot send IP packets to R1.

   c. R2 no longer learns EIGRP routes from R1 for routes not connected to R1.

   d. R1 no longer replies to R2's Query messages.

   e. R2 no longer sends Query messages to R1.

8. Router R1 lists four routes for subnet 10.1.1.0/24 in the output of the **show ip eigrp topology all-links** command. The **variance 100** command is configured, but no other related commands are configured. Which of the following rules is true regarding R1's decision of what routes to add to the IP routing table? Note that RD refers to reported distance and FD to feasible distance.

   a. Adds all routes for which the metric is <= 100 * the best metric among all routes

   b. Adds all routes because of the ridiculously high variance setting

   c. Adds all successor and feasible successor routes

   d. Adds all successor and feasible successor routes for which the metric is <= 100 * the best metric among all routes

9. A network design shows that R1 has four possible paths from itself to the data center subnets. Which of the following commands is most likely to show you all the possible next-hop IP addresses for these four possible routes?

   a. show ip eigrp topology

   b. show ip eigrp topology all-links

   c. show ip route eigrp

   d. show ip route eigrp all-links

   e. show ip eigrp topology all-learned

10. Router R1 has been configured for EIGRP. The configuration also includes an ACL with one line—access-list 1 permit 10.10.32.0 0.0.15.255—and the EIGRP configuration includes the distribute-list 1 in command. Which of the following routes could not be displayed in the output of the show ip eigrp topology command as a result? (Choose two.)

   a. 10.10.32.0 /19

   b. 10.10.44.0 /22

   c. 10.10.40.96 /27

   d. 10.10.48.0 /23

   e. 10.10.60.0 /30

11. The command output that follows was gathered from Router R1. If correctly referenced by an EIGRP distribution list that filters outbound Updates, which of the following statements are true about the filtering of various prefixes by this prefix list? (Choose three.)

```
R1# sh ip prefix-list
ip prefix-list question: 3 entries
    seq 5 deny 10.1.2.0/24 ge 25 le 27
    seq 15 deny 10.2.0.0/16 ge 30 le 30
    seq 20 permit 0.0.0.0/0
```

   a. Prefix 10.1.2.0/24 will be filtered because of clause 5.

   b. Prefix 10.1.2.224/26 will be filtered because of clause 5.

   c. Prefix 10.2.2.4/30 will be filtered because of clause 15.

   d. Prefix 10.0.0.0/8 will be permitted.

   e. Prefix 0.0.0.0/0 will be permitted.

12. R1 has correctly configured EIGRP to filter routes using a route map named question. The configuration that follows shows the entire route map and related configuration. Which of the following is true regarding the filtering action on prefix 10.10.10.0/24 in this case?

```
route-map question deny 10
 match ip address 1
route-map question permit 20
 match ip address prefix-list fred
!
access-list 1 deny 10.10.10.0 0.0.0.255
ip prefix-list fred permit 10.10.10.0/23 le 25
```

    a. It will be filtered because of the deny action in route map clause 10.

    b. It will be allowed because of the double negative (two deny references) in clause 10.

    c. It will be permitted because of matching clause 20's reference to prefix-list **fred**.

    d. It will be filtered because of matching the implied deny all route map clause at the end of the route map.

13. An engineer has typed four different single-line prefix lists in a word processor. The four answers show the four different single-line prefix lists. The engineer then does a copy/paste of the configuration into a router. Which of the lists could match a subnet whose prefix length is 27? (Choose two.)

    a. ip prefix-list fred permit 10.0.0.0/24 ge 16 le 28

    b. ip prefix-list barney permit 10.0.0.0/24 le 28

    c. ip prefix-list wilma permit 10.0.0.0/24 ge 25

    d. ip prefix-list betty permit 10.0.0.0/24 ge 28

14. An engineer plans to configure summary routes with the **ip summary-address eigrp** *asn prefix mask* command. Which of the following, when added to such a command, would create a summary that includes all four of the following subnets: 10.1.100.0/25, 10.1.101.96/27, 10.1.101.224/28, and 10.1.100.128 /25?

    a. 10.1.0.0 255.255.192.0

    b. 10.1.64.0 255.255.192.0

    c. 10.1.100.0 255.255.255.0

    d. 10.1.98.0 255.255.252.0

15. R1 has five working interfaces, with EIGRP neighbors existing off each interface. R1 has routes for subnets 10.1.1.0/24, 10.1.2.0/24, and 10.1.3.0/24, with EIGRP integer metrics of roughly 1 million, 2 million, and 3 million, respectively. An engineer then adds the **ip summary-address eigrp 1 10.1.0.0 255.255.0.0** command to interface Fa0/0. Which of the following is true?

   a. R1 loses and then reestablishes neighborships with all neighbors.

   b. R1 no longer advertises 10.1.1.0/24 to neighbors connected to Fa0/0.

   c. R1 advertises a 10.1.0.0/16 route out Fa0/0, with metric of around 3 million (largest metric of component subnets).

   d. R1 advertises a 10.1.0.0/16 route out Fa0/0, with metric of around 2 million (median metric of component subnets).

16. In a lab, R1 connects to R2, which connects to R3. R1 and R2 each have several working interfaces, all assigned addresses in Class A network 10.0.0.0. Router R3 has some working interfaces in Class A network 10.0.0.0, and others in Class B network 172.16.0.0. The engineer experiments with the **auto-summary** command on R2 and R3, enabling and disabling the command in various combinations. Which of the following combinations will result in R1 seeing a route for 172.16.0.0 /16, instead of the individual subnets of Class B network 172.16.0.0? (Choose two.)

   a. **auto-summary** on R2 and **no auto-summary** on R3

   b. **auto-summary** on R2 and **auto-summary** on R3

   c. **no auto-summary** on R2 and **no auto-summary** on R3

   d. **no auto-summary** on R2 and **auto-summary** on R3

17. Router R1 exists in an enterprise that uses EIGRP as its routing protocol. The **show ip route** command output on Router R1 lists the following phrase: "Gateway of last resort is 1.1.1.1 to network 2.0.0.0." Which of the following is most likely to have caused this output to occur on R1?

   a. R1 has been configured with an **ip default-network 2.0.0.0** command.

   b. R1 has been configured with an **ip route 0.0.0.0 0.0.0.0 1.1.1.1** command.

   c. R1 has been configured with an **ip route 2.0.0.0 255.0.0.0 1.1.1.1** command.

   d. Another router has been configured with an **ip default-network 2.0.0.0** command.

18. Enterprise Router R1 connects an enterprise to the Internet. R1 needs to create and advertise a default route into the enterprise using EIGRP. The engineer creating the implementation plan has chosen to base this default route on the **ip route** command, rather than using **ip default-network**. Which of the following are not useful steps with this style of default route configuration? (Choose two.)

   a. Create the default route on R1 using the **ip route 0.0.0.0 0.0.0.0 outgoing-interface** command.

   b. Redistribute the statically configured default route.

   c. Disable **auto-summary**.

   d. Configure the **network 0.0.0.0** command.

   e. Ensure that R1 has no manually configured summary routes using the **ip summary-address eigrp** command.

Foundation Topics

Building the EIGRP Topology Table

The overall process of building the EIGRP topology table is relatively straightforward. EIGRP defines some basic topology information about each route for each unique prefix/length (subnet). This basic information includes the prefix, prefix length, metric information, and a few other details. EIGRP neighbors exchange topology information, with each router storing the learned topology information in its respective EIGRP topology table. EIGRP on a given router can then analyze the topology table, or topology database, and choose the best route for each unique prefix/length.

EIGRP uses much simpler topology data than does OSPF, which is a link-state protocol that must describe the entire topology of a portion of a network with its topology database. EIGRP, essentially an advanced distance vector protocol, does not need to define nearly as much topology data, nor do EIGRP routers need to run the complex Shortest Path First (SPF) algorithm. This first major section examines the EIGRP topology database, how routers create and flood topology data, and some specific issues related to WAN links.

Seeding the EIGRP Topology Table

Before a router can send EIGRP topology information to a neighbor, that router must have some topology data in its topology table. Routers can, of course, learn about subnets and the associated topology data from neighboring routers. However, to get the process started, each EIGRP router needs to add topology data for some prefixes so that it can then advertise these routes to its EIGRP neighbors. A router's EIGRP process adds subnets to its local topology table, without learning the topology data from an EIGRP neighbor, from three sources:

Key Topic

- Prefixes of connected subnets for interfaces on which EIGRP has been enabled on that router using the **network** command

- Prefixes of connected subnets for interfaces referenced in an EIGRP **neighbor** command

- Prefixes learned by the redistribution of routes into EIGRP from other routing protocols or routing information sources

After a router adds such prefixes to its local EIGRP topology database, that router can then advertise the prefix information, along with other topology information associated with each prefix, to each working EIGRP neighbor. Each router adds any learned prefix information to its topology table, and then that router advertises the new information to other neighbors. Eventually, all routers in the EIGRP domain learn about all prefixes unless some other feature, such as route summarization or route filtering, alters the flow of topology information.

The Content of EIGRP Update Message

EIGRP uses five basic protocol messages to do its work:

- Hello

- Update

- Query

- Reply

- ACK (acknowledgment)

EIGRP uses two messages as part of the topology data exchange process: Update and ACK. The Update message contains the topology information, whereas the ACK acknowledges receipt of the update packet.

The EIGRP Update message contains the following information:

- Prefix

- Prefix length

- Metric components: bandwidth, delay, reliability, and load

- Nonmetric items: MTU and hop count

Note Many courses and books over the years have stated that MTU is part of the EIGRP metric. In practice, the MTU has never been part of the metric calculation, although it is included in the topology data for each prefix.

To examine this entire process in more detail, see Figure 5-1 and Figure 5-2.

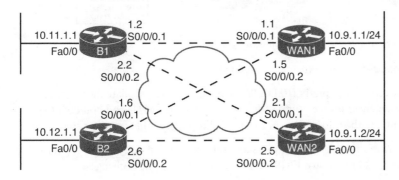

Note: All WAN IP addresses begin with 10.1

Figure 5-1 *Typical WAN Distribution and Branch Office Design*

Figure 5-1 shows a portion of an enterprise network that will be used in several examples in this chapter. Routers B1 and B2 represent typical branch office routers, each with two Frame Relay permanent virtual circuits (PVC) connected back to the main site. WAN1 and WAN2 are WAN distribution routers, each of which could have dozens or hundreds of PVCs.

The routers in Figure 5-1 have been configured and work. For EIGRP, all routers have been configured with as many defaults as possible, with the only configuration related to EIGRP being the **router eigrp 1** and **network 10.0.0.0** commands on each router.

Next, consider what Router B1 does for its connected route for subnet 10.11.1.0/24, which is located on B1's LAN. B1 matches its Fa0/0 interface IP address (10.11.1.1) because of its **network 10.0.0.0** configuration command. So, as mentioned earlier, B1 seeds its own topology table with an entry for this prefix. This topology table entry also lists the interface bandwidth of the associated interface and delay of the associated interface. Using default settings for Fast Ethernet interfaces, B1 uses a bandwidth of 100,000 kbps (the same as 100 Mbps) and a delay of 10, meaning 10 tens-of-microseconds. Router B1 also includes a default setting for the load (1) and reliability (255), even though the router, using the default K-value settings, will not use these values in its metric calculations. Finally, B1 adds to the topology database the MTU of the local interface and a hop count of 0 because the subnet is connected.

Now that B1 has added some topology information to its EIGRP topology database, Figure 5-2 shows how B1 propagates the topology information to router WAN1 and beyond.

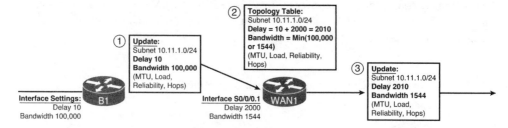

Figure 5-2 *Contents of EIGRP Update Messages*

The steps in Figure 5-2 can be explained as follows:

Step 1.   B1 advertises the prefix (10.11.1.0/24) using an EIGRP Update message. The message includes the four metric components, plus MTU and hop count—essentially the information in B1's EIGRP topology table entry for this prefix.

Step 2.   WAN1 receives the Update message and adds the topology information for 10.11.1.0/24 to its own EIGRP topology table, with these changes:

  ■   WAN1 considers the interface on which it received the Update (S0/0/0.1) to be the outgoing interface of a potential route to reach 10.11.1.0/24.

  ■   WAN1 adds the delay of S0/0/0.1 (2000 tens-of-microseconds per Figure 5-2) to the delay listed in the Update message.

- WAN1 compares the bandwidth of S0/0/0.1 (1544 kbps per Figure 5-2) to the bandwidth listed in the Update message (100,000 kbps) and chooses the lower value (1544) as the bandwidth for this route.

- WAN1 also updates load (highest value), reliability (lowest value), and MTU (lowest value) based on similar comparisons, and adds 1 to the hop count.

Step 3.   WAN1 then sends an Update to its neighbors, with the metric components listed in their own topology table.

This example provides a good backdrop to understand how EIGRP uses cumulative delay and minimum bandwidth in its metric calculation. Note that at Step 2, Router WAN1 adds to the delay value but does not add the bandwidth. For bandwidth, WAN1 simply chooses the lowest bandwidth, comparing the bandwidth of its own interface (S0/0/0.1) with the bandwidth listed in the received EIGRP update.

Next, consider this logic on other routers (not shown in the figure) as WAN1 floods this routing information throughout the enterprise. WAN1 then sends this topology information to another neighbor, and that router sends the topology data to another, and so on. If the bandwidth of those links were 1544 or higher, the bandwidth setting used by those routers would remain the same, because each router would see that the routing update's bandwidth (1544 kbps) was lower than the link's bandwidth. However, each router would add something to the delay.

As a final confirmation of the contents of this Update process, Example 5-1 shows the details of the EIGRP topology database for prefix 10.11.1.0/24 on both B1 and WAN1.

Example 5-1   *Topology Database Contents for 10.11.1.0/24, on B1 and WAN1*

```
! On Router B1: !!!!!!!!!!!!!!!!!!!!!!!!!!!!!!!!!!!!!!!!!!!
B1# show ip eigrp topology 10.11.1.0/24
IP-EIGRP (AS 1): Topology entry for 10.11.1.0/24
  State is Passive, Query origin flag is 1, 1 Successor(s), FD is 28160
  Routing Descriptor Blocks:
  0.0.0.0 (FastEthernet0/0), from Connected, Send flag is 0x0
      Composite metric is (28160/0), Route is Internal
      Vector metric:
        Minimum bandwidth is 100000 Kbit
        Total delay is 100 microseconds
        Reliability is 255/255
        Load is 1/255
        Minimum MTU is 1500
        Hop count is 0

! On Router WAN1: !!!!!!!!!!!!!!!!!!!!!!!!!!!!!!!!!!!!!!!!!!
WAN1# show ip eigrp topology 10.11.1.0/24
IP-EIGRP (AS 1): Topology entry for 10.11.1.0/24
  State is Passive, Query origin flag is 1, 1 Successor(s), FD is 2172416
  Routing Descriptor Blocks:
```

```
10.1.1.2 (Serial0/0/0.1), from 10.1.1.2, Send flag is 0x0
    Composite metric is (2172416/28160), Route is Internal
    Vector metric:
        Minimum bandwidth is 1544 Kbit
        Total delay is 20100 microseconds
        Reliability is 255/255
        Load is 1/255
        Minimum MTU is 1500
        Hop count is 1
```

The highlighted portions of the output match the details shown in Figure 5-2, but with one twist relating to the units on the delay setting. The Cisco IOS **delay** command, which lets you set the delay, along with the data stored in the EIGRP topology database, uses a unit of tens-of-microseconds. However, the **show interfaces** and **show ip eigrp topology** commands list delay in a unit of microseconds. For example, WAN1's listing of "20100 microseconds" matches the "2010 tens-of-microseconds" shown in Figure 5-2.

The EIGRP Update Process

So far, this chapter has focused on the detailed information that EIGRP exchanges with a neighbor about each prefix. This section takes a broader look at the process.

When EIGRP neighbors first become neighbors, they begin exchanging topology information using Update messages using these rules:

- When a neighbor first comes up, the routers exchange full updates, meaning that the routers exchange all topology information.

- After all prefixes have been exchanged with a neighbor, the updates cease with that neighbor if no changes occur in the network. There is no subsequent periodic reflooding of topology data.

- If something changes—for example, one of the metric components changes, links fail, links recover, or new neighbors advertise additional topology information—the routers send partial updates about only the prefixes whose status or metric components have changed.

- If neighbors fail and then recover, or new neighbor adjacencies are formed, full updates occur over these adjacencies.

- EIGRP uses Split Horizon rules on most interfaces by default, which impacts exactly which topology data EIGRP sends during both full and partial updates.

Split Horizon, the last item in the list, needs a little more explanation. Split Horizon limits the prefixes that EIGRP advertises out an interface. Specifically, if the currently best route for a prefix lists a particular outgoing interface, Split Horizon causes EIGRP to not include that prefix in the Update sent out that same interface. For example, router WAN1 uses S0/0/0.1 as its outgoing interface for subnet 10.11.1.0/24. So, WAN1 would not advertise prefix 10.11.1.0/24 in its Update messages sent out S0/0/0.1.

To send the Updates, EIGRP uses the Reliable Transport Protocol (RTP) to send the EIGRP Updates and confirm their receipt. On point-to-point topologies such as serial links, MPLS VPNs, and Frame Relay networks when using point-to-point subinterfaces, the EIGRP Update and ACK messages use a simple process of acknowledging each Update with an ACK. On multiaccess data links, EIGRP typically sends Update messages to multicast address 224.0.0.10 and expects a unicast EIGRP ACK message from each neighbor in reply. RTP manages that process, setting timers so that the sender of an Update waits a reasonable time, but not too long, before deciding whether all neighbors received the Update or whether one or more neighbors did not reply with an ACK.

Interestingly, although EIGRP relies on the RTP process, network engineers cannot manipulate how this works.

WAN Issues for EIGRP Topology Exchange

With all default settings, after you enable EIGRP on all the interfaces in an internetwork, the topology exchange process typically does not pose any problems. However, a few scenarios exist, particularly on Frame Relay, which can cause problems. This section summarizes two issues and shows the solutions.

Split Horizon Default on Frame Relay Multipoint Subinterfaces

Cisco IOS support for Frame Relay allows the configuration of IP addresses on the physical serial interface, multipoint subinterfaces, or point-to-point subinterfaces. Additionally, IP packets can be forwarded over a PVC even when the routers on the opposite ends do not have to use the same interface or subinterface type. As a result, many small intricacies exist in the operation of IP and IP routing protocols over Frame Relay, particularly related to default settings on different interface types.

Frame Relay supports several reasonable configuration options using different interfaces and subinterfaces, each meeting different design goals. For example, if a design includes a few centralized WAN distribution routers, with PVCs connecting each branch router to each distribution router, both distribution and branch routers might use point-to-point subinterfaces. Such a choice makes the Layer 3 topology simple, with all links acting like point-to-point links from a Layer 3 perspective. This choice also removes issues such as Split Horizon.

In some cases, a design might include a small set of routers that have a full mesh of PVCs connecting each. In this case, multipoint subinterfaces might be used, consuming a single subnet and reducing the consumption of the IP address space. This choice also reduces the number of subinterfaces.

Both options—using point-to-point subinterfaces or using multipoint subinterfaces— have legitimate reasons for being used. However, when using the multipoint subinterface option, a particular EIGRP issue can occur when the following are true:

■ Three or more routers, connected over a Frame Relay network, are configured as part of a single subnet.

- The routers use multipoint interfaces.

- Either permanently or for a time, a full mesh of PVCs between the routers does not exist.

For example, consider Router WAN1 shown earlier in Figure 5-1 and referenced again in Figure 5-3. In the earlier configurations, the WAN distribution routers and branch routers all used point-to-point subinterfaces and a single subnet per VC. To see the problem raised in this section, consider that same internetwork, but now the engineer has chosen to configure WAN1 to use a multipoint subinterface and a single subnet for WAN1, B1, and B2, as shown in Figure 5-3.

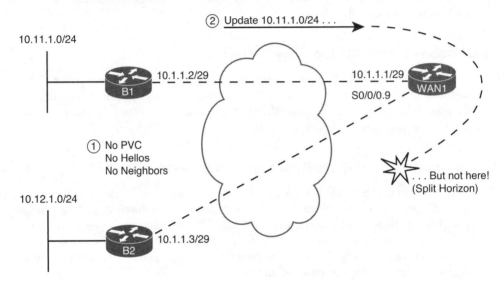

Figure 5-3 *Partial Mesh, Central Sites (WAN1) Uses Multipoint Subinterface*

The first issue to consider in this design is that B1 and B2 will not become EIGRP neighbors with each other, as noted with Step 1 in the figure. EIGRP routers must be reachable using Layer 2 frames before they can exchange EIGRP Hello messages and become EIGRP neighbors. In this case, there is no PVC between B1 and B2. B1 exchanges Hellos with WAN1, and they become neighbors, as will B2 with WAN1. However, routers do not forward received EIGRP Hellos, so WAN1 will not receive a Hello from B1 and forward it to B2 or vice versa. In short, although in the same subnet (10.1.1.0/29), B1 and B2 will not become EIGRP neighbors.

The second problem occurs because of Split Horizon logic on Router WAN1, as noted with Step 2 in the figure. As shown with Step 2, B1 could advertise its routes to WAN1, and WAN1 could advertise those routes to B2—and vice versa. However, with default settings, WAN1 will not advertise those routes because of its default setting of Split Horizon (a default interface subcommand setting of **ip split-horizon eigrp** *asn*). As a result, WAN1 receives the Update from B1 on its S0/0/0.9 subinterface, but Split Horizon prevents WAN1 from advertising that topology data to B2 in Updates sent out interface S0/0/0.9, and vice versa.

The solution is somewhat simple—just configure the **no ip split-horizon eigrp** *asn* command on the multipoint subinterface on WAN1. The remote routers, B1 and B2 in this case, still do not become neighbors, but that does not cause a problem by itself. With Split Horizon disabled on WAN1, B1 and B2 learn routes to the other branch's subnets. Example 5-2 lists the complete configuration and the command to disable Split Horizon. Also shown in Example 5-2 is the output of the **show ip eigrp interfaces detail s0/0/0.9** command, which shows the operational state of Split Horizon on that subinterface.

Note   Frame Relay configuration is considered a prerequisite, because it is part of the CCNA exam and courses. Example 5-2 uses **frame-relay interface-dlci** commands and relies on Inverse ARP. However, if **frame-relay map** commands were used instead, disabling Inverse ARP, the EIGRP details discussed in this example would remain unchanged.

Example 5-2   *Frame Relay Multipoint Configuration on WAN1*

```
! On Router WAN1: !!!!!!!!!!!!!!!!!!!!!!!!!!!!!!!!!!!!!!!!!!!!!!
interface Serial0/0/0
 no ip address
 encapsulation frame-relay

interface Serial0/0/0.9 multipoint
 ip address 10.1.1.1 255.255.255.248
 no ip split-horizon eigrp 1
 frame-relay interface-dlci 103
 frame-relay interface-dlci 104
!
router eigrp 1
 network 10.0.0.0


! Check Split Horizon State: !!!!!!!!!!!!!!!!!!!!!!!!!!!!!!!!!
WAN1# show ip eigrp interfaces detail s0/0/0.9
EIGRP-IPv4 Interfaces for AS(1)
                    Xmit Queue    PeerQ        Mean   Pacing Time  Multicast    Pending
Interface Peers   Un/Reliable   Un/Reliable   SRTT   Un/Reliable  Flow Timer   Routes
Se1/0     1          0/0           0/0          59      0/16         300          0
   Hello-interval is 5, Hold-time is 15
   Split-horizon is disabled
   Next xmit serial <none>
   Packetized sent/expedited: 3/0
   Hello's sent/expedited: 248/2
   Un/reliable mcasts: 0/0  Un/reliable ucasts: 4/4
   Mcast exceptions: 0  CR packets: 0  ACKs suppressed: 0
```

```
Retransmissions sent: 0  Out-of-sequence rcvd: 0
Topology-ids on interface - 0
Authentication mode is not set
```

Note   The [no] **ip split-horizon** command controls Split Horizon behavior for RIP; the [no] **ip split-horizon eigrp** *asn* command controls Split Horizon behavior for EIGRP.

EIGRP WAN Bandwidth Control

In a multiaccess WAN, one physical link passes traffic for multiple data link layer destinations. For example, a WAN distribution router connected to many branches using Frame Relay might literally terminate hundreds, or even thousands, of Frame Relay PVCs.

In a nonbroadcast multiaccess (NBMA) medium such as Frame Relay, when a router needs to send EIGRP updates, the Updates cannot be multicasted at Layer 2. So, the router must send a copy of the Update to each reachable neighbor. For a WAN distribution router with many Frame Relay PVCs, the sheer amount of traffic sent over the Frame Relay access link might overload the link.

The EIGRP WAN bandwidth control allows the engineer to protect a multiaccess Frame Relay interface from being overrun with too much EIGRP message traffic. By default, a router sends EIGRP messages out an interface but only up to 50 percent of the bandwidth defined on the interface with the **bandwidth** command. The engineer can adjust this percentage using the **ip bandwidth-percent eigrp** *asn percent interface/subinterface* subcommand. Regardless of the percentage, Cisco IOS then limits the rate of sending the EIGRP messages so that the rate is not exceeded. To accomplish this, Cisco IOS queues the EIGRP messages in memory, delaying them briefly.

The command to set the bandwidth percentage is simple, but there are a few caveats to keep in mind when trying to limit the bandwidth consumed by EIGRP:

- The Cisco IOS default for bandwidth on serial interfaces and subinterfaces is 1544 (kbps).

- EIGRP limits the consumed bandwidth based on the percentage of interface/subinterface bandwidth.

- This feature keys on the bandwidth of the interface or subinterface through which the neighbor is reachable, so don't set only the physical interface bandwidth and forget the subinterfaces.

- Recommendation: Set the bandwidth of point-to-point links to the speed of the Committed Information Rate (CIR) of the single PVC on the subinterface.

- General recommendation: Set the bandwidth of multipoint subinterfaces to around the total CIR for all VCs assigned to the subinterface.

- Note that for multipoint subinterfaces, Cisco IOS WAN bandwidth control first divides the subinterface bandwidth by the number of configured PVCs and then determines the EIGRP percentage based on that number.

For example, consider Figure 5-4, which shows a router with one multipoint subinterface and one point-to-point subinterface.

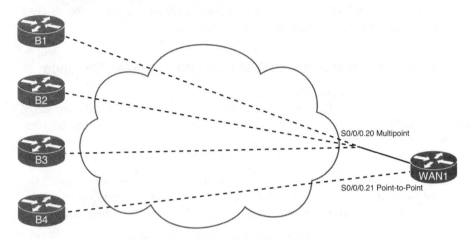

Figure 5-4 *WAN1, One Multipoint, One Point-to-Point*

With the configuration shown in Example 5-3, WAN1 uses the following bandwidth, at most, with each neighbor:

- B1, B2, and B3: 20 kbps (20% of 300 kbps / 3 VCs)

- B4: 30 kbps (30% of 100 kbps)

Example 5-3 *Configuration of WAN1, One Multipoint, One Point-to-Point*

```
! On Router WAN1: !!!!!!!!!!!!!!!!!!!!!!!!!!!!!!!!!!!!!!!!!!!!!!!
interface Serial0/0/0.20 multipoint
 ip address 172.16.1.1 255.255.255.240
 frame-relay interface-dlci 201
 frame-relay interface-dlci 202
 frame-relay interface-dlci 203
 bandwidth 300
 ip bandwidth-percent eigrp 1 20
!
interface Serial0/0/0.21 point-to-point
 ip address 172.16.1.17 255.255.255.252
 frame-relay interface-dlci 221
 bandwidth 100
 ip bandwidth-percent eigrp 1 30
```

Building the IP Routing Table

An EIGRP router builds IP routing table entries by processing the data in the topology table. Unlike OSPF, which uses a computationally complex SPF process, EIGRP uses a computationally simple process to determine which, if any, routes to add to the IP routing table for each unique prefix/length. This part of the chapter examines how EIGRP chooses the best route for each prefix/length and then examines several optional tools that can influence the choice of routes to add to the IP routing table.

Calculating the Metrics: Feasible Distance and Reported Distance

The EIGRP topology table entry, for a single prefix/length, lists one or more possible routes. Each possible route lists the various component metric values—bandwidth, delay, and so on. Additionally, for connected subnets, the database entry lists an outgoing interface. For routes not connected to the local router, in addition to an outgoing interface, the database entry also lists the IP address of the EIGRP neighbor that advertised the route.

EIGRP routers calculate an integer metric based on the metric components. Interestingly, an EIGRP router does this calculation both from its own perspective and from the perspective of the next-hop router of the route. The two calculated values are as follows:

- **Feasible Distance (FD):** Integer metric for the route, from the local router's perspective, used by the local router to choose the best route for that prefix.

- **Reported Distance (RD):** Integer metric for the route, from the neighboring router's perspective (the neighbor that told the local router about the route). Used by the local router when converging to a new route.

> **Note** Some texts use the term *Advertised Distance (AD)* instead of Reported Distance (RD) as used in this book. Be ready for either term on the CCNP ROUTE exam. However, this book uses RD exclusively.

Routers use the FD to determine the best route, based on the lowest metric, and use the RD when falling back to an alternative route when the best route fails (EIGRP's use of the RD is explained in the upcoming section "Successor and Feasible Successor Concepts"). Focusing on the FD, when a router has calculated the integer FD for each possible route to reach a single prefix/length, that router can then consider adding the lowest-metric route to the IP routing table.

As a reminder, the following formula shows how EIGRP calculates the metric, assuming default settings of the EIGRP metric weights (K-values). The metric calculation grows when the slowest bandwidth in the end-to-end route decreases (the slower the bandwidth, the worse the metric), and its metric grows (gets worse) when the cumulative delay grows. Also, note that the unit of measure for *slowest-bandwidth* is *kbps*, and the unit of measure for *cumulative-delay* is *tens-of-microseconds*.

Metric = 256 * [(10^7 / slowest-bandwidth) + cumulative-delay]

An example certainly helps in this case. Figure 5-5 repeats some information about the topology exchange process between Routers B1 and WAN1 (refer to Figure 5-1), essentially showing the metric components as sent by B1 to WAN1 (Step 1) and the metric components from WAN1's perspective (Step 2).

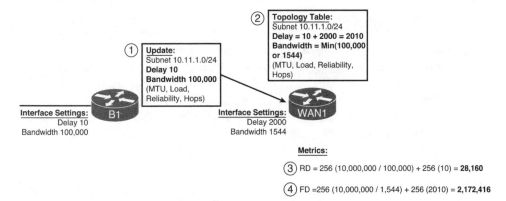

Figure 5-5   *Example Calculation of RD and FD on Router WAN1*

Steps 3 and 4 in Figure 5-5 show WAN1's calculation of the RD and FD for 10.11.1.0/24, respectively. Router WAN1 takes the metric components as received from B1, and plugs them into the formula, to calculate the RD, which is the same integer metric that Router B1 would have calculated as its FD. Step 4 shows the same formula but with the metric components as listed at Step 2—after the adjustments made on WAN1. Step 4 shows WAN1's FD calculation, which is much larger because of the much lower constraining bandwidth plus the much larger cumulative delay.

WAN1 chooses its best route to reach 10.11.1.0/24 based on the lowest FD among all possible routes. Looking back to the much more detailed Figure 5-1, presumably a couple of other routes might have been possible, but WAN1 happens to choose the route shown in Figure 5-5 as its best route. As a result, WAN1's **show ip route** command lists the FD calculated in Figure 5-5 as the metric for this route, as shown in Example 5-4.

Example 5-4   *Router WAN1's EIGRP Topology and IP Route Information for 10.11.1.0/24*

```
! Below, note that WAN1's EIGRP topology table lists two possible next-hop
! routers: 10.1.1.2 (B1) and 10.9.1.2 (WAN2). The metric for each route,
! the first number in parentheses, shows that the lower metric route is the one
! through 10.1.1.2 as next-hop. Also note that the metric components
! match Figure 5-5.
!
WAN1# show ip eigrp topo 10.11.1.0/24
IP-EIGRP (AS 1): Topology entry for 10.11.1.0/24
  State is Passive, Query origin flag is 1, 1 Successor(s), FD is 2172416
  Routing Descriptor Blocks:
  10.1.1.2 (Serial0/0/0.1), from 10.1.1.2, Send flag is 0x0
      Composite metric is (2172416/28160), Route is Internal
```

```
        Vector metric:
            Minimum bandwidth is 1544 Kbit
            Total delay is 20100 microseconds
            Reliability is 255/255
            Load is 1/255
            Minimum MTU is 1500
            Hop count is 1
    10.9.1.2 (FastEthernet0/0), from 10.9.1.2, Send flag is 0x0
        Composite metric is (2174976/2172416), Route is Internal
        Vector metric:
            Minimum bandwidth is 1544 Kbit
            Total delay is 20200 microseconds
            Reliability is 255/255
            Load is 1/255
            Minimum MTU is 1500
            Hop count is 2
!
! The next command not only lists the IP routing table entry for 10.11.1.0/24,
! it also lists the metric (FD), and components of the metric.
!
WAN1# show ip route 10.11.1.0
Routing entry for 10.11.1.0/24
  Known via "eigrp 1", distance 90, metric 2172416, type internal
  Redistributing via eigrp 1
  Last update from 10.1.1.2 on Serial0/0/0.1, 00:02:42 ago
  Routing Descriptor Blocks:
  * 10.1.1.2, from 10.1.1.2, 00:02:42 ago, via Serial0/0/0.1
      Route metric is 2172416, traffic share count is 1
      Total delay is 20100 microseconds, minimum bandwidth is 1544 Kbit
      Reliability 255/255, minimum MTU 1500 bytes
      Loading 1/255, Hops 1
!
! Below, the route for 10.11.1.0/24 is again listed, with the metric (FD), and
! the same next-hop and outgoing interface information.
!
WAN1# show ip route eigrp
     10.0.0.0/8 is variably subnetted, 7 subnets, 2 masks
D       10.11.1.0/24 [90/2172416] via 10.1.1.2, 00:10:40, Serial0/0/0.1
D       10.12.1.0/24 [90/2172416] via 10.1.1.6, 00:10:40, Serial0/0/0.2
D       10.1.2.0/30 [90/2172416] via 10.9.1.2, 00:10:40, FastEthernet0/0
D       10.1.2.4/30 [90/2172416] via 10.9.1.2, 00:10:40, FastEthernet0/0
```

EIGRP Metric Tuning

EIGRP metrics can be changed using several methods: setting interface bandwidth, setting interface delay, changing the metric calculation formula by configuring K-values, and even by adding to the calculated metric using offset lists. In practice, the most reasonable and commonly used methods are to set the interface delay and the interface bandwidth. This section examines all the methods, in part so that you will know which useful tools exist and in part to make you aware of some other design issues that then might impact the routes chosen by EIGRP.

Configuring Bandwidth and Delay

The **bandwidth** and **delay** interface subcommands set the bandwidth and delay associated with the interface. The commands themselves require little thought, other than keeping the units straight. The unit for the **bandwidth** command is kilobits/second, and the **delay** command uses a unit of tens-of-microseconds.

If a design requires that you influence the choice of route by changing bandwidth or delay, setting the delay value is typically the better choice. Cisco IOS uses the bandwidth setting of an interface for many other reasons: calculating interface utilization, as the basis for several QoS parameters, and for Simple Network Management Protocol (SNMP) statistics reporting. However, the delay setting has little influence on other Cisco IOS features besides EIGRP, so the better choice when influencing EIGRP metrics is to tune the delay.

Table 5-2 lists some of the common default values for both bandwidth and delay. As a reminder, **show** commands list the bandwidth in kbps, which matches the **bandwidth** command, but lists the delay in microseconds, which does not match the tens-of-microseconds unit of the **delay** command.

Table 5-2 *Common Defaults for Bandwidth and Delay*

Interface Type	Bandwidth (kbps)	Delay (Microseconds)
Serial	1544	20,000
GigE	1,000,000	10
FastE	100,000	100
Ethernet	10,000	1000

Note that on LAN interfaces that can run at different speeds, the bandwidth and delay settings default based on the current actual speed of the interface.

Choosing Bandwidth Settings on WAN Subinterfaces

Frame Relay and Metro Ethernet installations often use an access link with a particular physical sending rate (clock rate if you will) but with the contracted speed, over time, being more or less than the speed of the link. For example, with Frame Relay, the provider might supply a full T1 access link, so configuring **bandwidth 1544** for such an interface is reasonable. However, the subinterfaces have one or more PVCs associated with them, and those PVCs each have Committed Information Rates (CIR) that are typically less than the access link's clock speed. However, the cumulative CIRs for all PVCs often exceed the clock rate of a physical interface. Conversely, MetroE designs use Ethernet access links of 10-Mbps, 100-Mbps, or 1-Gbps actual link speed, but often the business contract limits the amount of traffic to some number below that link speed.

Choosing a useful interface **bandwidth** setting on the subinterfaces in a Frame Relay or MetroE design requires some thought, with most of the motivations for choosing one number or another being unrelated to EIGRP. For example, imagine the network shown in Figure 5-6. Router WAN1 has a single T1 (1.544-Mbps) access link. That interface has one multipoint subinterface, with three PVCs assigned to it. It also has nine other point-to-point subinterfaces, each with a single PVC assigned.

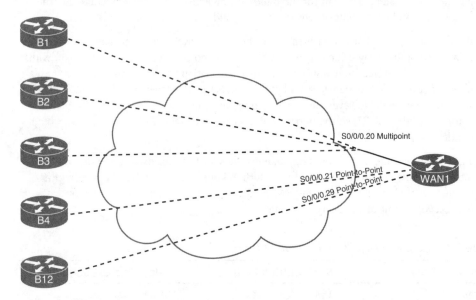

Figure 5-6   *One Multipoint and Nine Point-to-Point Subinterfaces*

For the sake of discussion, the design in Figure 5-6 oversubscribes the T1 access link off Router WAN1 by a 2:1 factor. Assume that all 12 PVCs have a CIR of 256 kbps, making the total bandwidth for the 12 PVCs roughly 3 Mbps. The design choice to oversubscribe the access link might be reasonable given the statistical chance of all sites sending at the same time.

Now imagine that Router WAN1 has been configured with subinterfaces as shown in the figure:

- S0/0/0.20: Multipoint, 3 PVCs

- S0/0/0.21 through S0/0/0.29: Point-to-point, 1 PVC each

Next, consider the options for setting the **bandwidth** command's value on these ten sub-interfaces. The point-to-point subinterfaces could be set to match the CIR of each PVC (256 kbps, in this example). You could choose to set the bandwidth based on the CIR of all combined PVCs on the multipoint subinterface—in this case, setting **bandwidth 768** on multipoint subinterface s0/0/0.20. However, these bandwidths would total about

3 Mbps—twice the actual speed of WAN1's access link. Alternatively, you could set the various bandwidths so that the total matches the 1.5 Mbps of the access link. Or you could split the difference, knowing that during times of low activity to most sites, that the sites with active traffic get more than their CIR's worth of capacity anyway.

As mentioned earlier, these bandwidth settings impact much more than EIGRP. The settings impact interface statistics, both in **show** commands and in SNMP reporting. They impact QoS features to some extent as well. Given that the better option for setting EIGRP metrics is to set the interface delay, EIGRP metric tuning might not be the driving force behind the decision as to what bandwidth values to use. However, some installations might change these values over time while trying to find the right compromise numbers for features other than EIGRP. So, you need to be aware that changing those values might result in different EIGRP metrics and impact the choices of best routes.

Similar issues exist on the more modern Layer 2 WAN services like MetroE, particularly with the multipoint design of Virtual Private LAN Service (VPLS). Figure 5-7 shows a design that might exist after migrating the internetwork of Figure 5-6 to VPLS. Router WAN1 has been replaced by a Layer 3 switch, using a Gigabit interface to connect to the VPLS service. The remote sites might use the same routers as before, using a Fast Ethernet interface, and might be replaced with Layer 3 switch hardware as well.

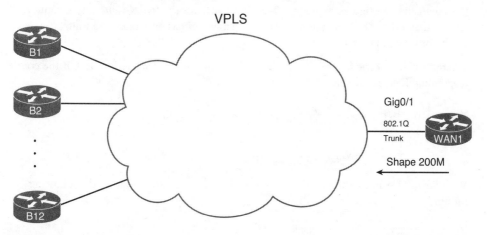

Figure 5-7 *VPLS Service—Issues in Choosing Bandwidth*

Concentrating on the mechanics of what happens at the central site, WAN1 might use 802.1Q trunking. With 12 remote sites, WAN1 configures 12 VLAN interfaces, one per VLAN, with a different subnet used for the connection to each remote branch. Such a design, from a Layer 3 perspective, looks like the age-old Frame Relay design with a point-to-point link from the main site to each remote branch.

Additionally, the VPLS business contract might specify that WAN1 cannot send more than 200 Mbps of traffic into the VPLS cloud, with the excess being discarded by the VPLS service. To prevent unnecessary discards, the engineer likely configures a feature called *shaping*, which reduces the average rate of traffic leaving the Gi0/1 interface of WAN1 (regardless of VLAN). To meet the goal of 200 Mbps, WAN1 would send only part of the time—in this case averaging a sending rate of 1/5th of the time—so that the average rate is 1/5th of 1 Gbps, or 200 Mbps.

Of note with the shaping function, the shaping feature typically limits the cumulative traffic on the interface, not per VLAN (branch). As a result, if the only traffic waiting to be sent by WAN1 happens to be destined for branch B1, WAN1 sends 200 Mbps of traffic to just branch B1.

Pulling the discussion back around to EIGRP, as with Frame Relay, other design and implementation needs can drive the decision to set or change the bandwidth on the associated interfaces. In this case, Layer 3 switch WAN1 probably has 12 VLAN interfaces. Each VLAN interface can be set with a bandwidth that influences EIGRP route choices. Should this setting be 1/12th of 1 Gbps, what is the speed at which the bits are actually sent? Should the setting be 1/12th of 200 Mbps, what is the shaping rate? Or knowing that a site might get most or all of that 200 Mbps for some short period of time, should the bandwidth be set somewhere in between? As with Frame Relay, there is no set answer. For the sake of EIGRP, be aware that changes to the bandwidth settings impact the EIGRP metrics.

Metric Weights (K-values)

Engineers can change the EIGRP metric calculation by configuring the weightings (also called K-values) applied to the EIGRP metric calculation. To configure new values, use the **metric weights** *tos k1 k2 k3 k4 k5* command in EIGRP configuration mode. To configure this command, configure any integer 0–255 inclusive for the five K-values. By default, K1 = K3 = 1, and the others default to 0. The *tos* parameter has only one valid value, 0, and can be otherwise ignored.

The full EIGRP metric formula is as follows. Note that some items reduce to 0 if the corresponding K-values are also set to 0.

$$\text{Metric} = \left[\left(K1 * BW_{min} + \frac{K2 * BW_{min}}{256 - load} + K3 * delay \right) * \frac{K5}{K4 + reliability} \right] * 256$$

$$BW_{min} = \frac{10^7}{\text{least-bandwidth}}$$

With default K-values, the EIGRP metric calculation can be simplified to the following formula:

$$\text{Metric} = \left(\left(\frac{10^7}{\text{least-bandwidth}} \right) + cumulative\text{-}delay \right) * 256$$

EIGRP requires that two routers' K-values match before those routers can become neighbors. Also note that Cisco recommends against using K-values K2, K4, and K5, because a nonzero value for these parameters causes the metric calculation to include interface load and reliability. The load and reliability change over time, which causes EIGRP to reflood topology data, and might cause routers to repeatedly choose different routes (route flapping).

Offset Lists

EIGRP offset lists, the final tool for manipulating the EIGRP metrics listed in this chapter, allow an engineer to simply add a value—an offset, if you will—to the calculated integer metric for a given prefix. To do so, an engineer can create and enable an EIGRP offset list that defines the value to add to the metric, plus some rules regarding which routes should be matched and therefore have the value added to their computed FD.

An offset list can perform the following functions:

■ Match prefixes/prefix lengths using an IP ACL, so that the offset is applied only to routes matched by the ACL with a **permit** clause.

■ Match the direction of the Update message, either sent (out) or received (in).

■ Match the interface on which the Update is sent or received.

■ Set the integer metric added to the calculation for both the FD and RD calculations for the route.

The configuration itself uses the following command in EIGRP configuration mode, in addition to any referenced IP ACLs:

offset-list {*access-list-number* | *access-list-name*} {**in** | **out**} **offset** [*interface-type interface-number*]

For example, consider again branch office Router B1 in Figure 5-1, with its connection to both WAN1 and WAN2 over a Frame Relay network. Formerly, WAN1 calculated a metric of 2,172,416 for its route, through B1, to subnet 10.11.1.0/24. (Refer to Figure 5-5 for the math behind WAN1's calculation of its route to 10.11.1.0/24.) Router B1 also calculated a value of 28,160 for the RD of that same direct route. Example 5-5 shows the addition of an offset on WAN1, for received updates from Router B1.

Example 5-5   *Inbound Offset of 3 on WAN1, for Updates Received on S0/0/0.1*

```
WAN1(config)# access-list 11 permit 10.11.1.0
WAN1(config)# router eigrp 1
WAN1(config-router)# offset-list 11 in 3 Serial0/0/0.1
WAN1(config-router)# end


Mar  2 11:34:36.667: %DUAL-5-NBRCHANGE: IP-EIGRP(0) 1: Neighbor 10.1.1.2
(Serial0/0/0.1) is resync: peer graceful-restart
WAN1# show ip eigrp topo 10.11.1.0/24
IP-EIGRP (AS 1): Topology entry for 10.11.1.0/24
  State is Passive, Query origin flag is 1, 1 Successor(s), FD is 2172416
  Routing Descriptor Blocks:
  10.1.1.2 (Serial0/0/0.1), from 10.1.1.2, Send flag is 0x0
      Composite metric is (2172419/28163), Route is Internal
      Vector metric:
        Minimum bandwidth is 1544 Kbit
        Total delay is 20100 microseconds
        Reliability is 255/255
        Load is 1/255
        Minimum MTU is 1500
        Hop count is 1
! output omitted for brevity
```

The configuration has two key elements: ACL 11 and the **offset-list** command. ACL 11 matches prefix 10.11.1.0, and that prefix only, with a **permit** clause. The **offset-list 11 in 3 s0/0/0.1** command tells Router WAN1 to examine all EIGRP Updates received on S0/0/0.1, and if prefix 10.11.1.0 is found, add 3 to the computed FD and RD for that prefix.

The **show ip eigrp topology 10.11.1.0/24** command in Example 5-5 shows that the FD and RD, highlighted in parentheses, are now each three larger as compared with the earlier metrics.

Next, continuing this same example, Router B1 has now been configured to add an offset (4) in its sent updates to all routers, but for prefix 10.11.1.0/24 only, as demonstrated in Example 5-6.

Example 5-6   *Outbound Offset of 4 on B1, for Updates Sent to All Neighbors, 10.11.1.0/24*

```
B1(config)# access-list 12 permit 10.11.1.0
B1(config)# router eigrp 1
B1(config-router)# offset-list 12 out 4
B1(config-router)# end
B1#

! Back to router WAN1
WAN1# show ip eigrp topology
IP-EIGRP Topology Table for AS(1)/ID(10.9.1.1)

Codes: P - Passive, A - Active, U - Update, Q - Query, R - Reply,
       r - reply Status, s - sia Status

P 10.11.1.0/24, 1 successors, FD is 2172419
        via 10.1.1.2 (2172423/28167), Serial0/0/0.1
! lines omitted for brevity
```

Note that the metrics, both FD and RD, are now four larger than in Example 5-5.

Unequal Metric Route Load Sharing

Convergence to a feasible successor route should happen within a second after a router realizes the successor route has failed. Even in large well-designed networks, particularly with features like stub routers and route summarization in use, convergence can still happen in a reasonable amount of time even when going active. The next feature, load sharing, takes convergence to another level, giving instantaneous convergence, while reaching other goals as well.

Cisco IOS allows routing protocols to place multiple routes into the routing table for an individual prefix/length. Cisco IOS then balances traffic across those routes, by default balancing traffic on a per-destination IP address basis.

Load balancing, sometimes called *load sharing*, provides a primary benefit of making use of the available bandwidth, rather than using some links as simply backup links. For example, with the two-PVC design shown previously in Figure 5-1, without load sharing, a branch router would send traffic over one PVC, but not both. With load sharing, some traffic would flow over each PVC.

A useful secondary benefit—faster convergence—occurs when using load balancing. By placing multiple routes into the routing table for a single prefix, convergence happens essentially instantly. For example, if a branch router has two routes for each data center subnet—one using each PVC that connects the branch to the core—and one of the routes fails, the other route is already in the routing table. In this case, the router does not need to look for FS routes nor go active on the route. The router uses the usual EIGRP convergence tools only when all such routes are removed from the routing table.

The load-balancing configuration requires two commands, one of which already defaults to a reasonable setting. First, you need to define the number of allowed routes for each prefix/prefix length using the **maximum-paths** *number* EIGRP subcommand. The default setting of 4 is often high enough, because most internetworks do not have enough redundancy to have more than four possible routes.

Note The maximum number of paths varies based on Cisco IOS version and router platform. However, for the much older Cisco IOS versions, the maximum was 6 routes, with later versions typically supporting 16 or more.

The second part of the load-balancing configuration overcomes a challenge introduced by EIGRP's metric calculation. The EIGRP integer metric calculation often results in 8- to 10-digit integer metrics, so the metrics of competing routes are seldom the exact same value. Calculating the exact same metric for different routes for the same prefix is statistically unlikely.

Cisco IOS includes the concept of EIGRP *variance* to overcome this problem. Variance lets you tell Cisco IOS that the EIGRP metrics can be close in value and still be considered worthy of being added to the routing table—and you can define how close.

The **variance** *multiplier* EIGRP router subcommand defines an integer in the range of 1 through 128. The router then multiplies the variance by the successor route's FD—the metric of the best route to reach that subnet. Any FS routes whose metric is less than or equal to the product of the variance by the FD are considered to be equal routes and can be placed into the routing table, up to and including the number of routes defined by the **maximum-paths** command.

For example, consider the example as shown in Figure 5-8 and Table 5-3. In this example, to keep the focus on the concepts, the metrics are small easy-to-compare numbers, rather than the usual large EIGRP metrics. The example focuses on R4's three possible routes to reach Subnet 1. The figure shows the RD of each route next to Routers R1, R2, and R3, respectively.

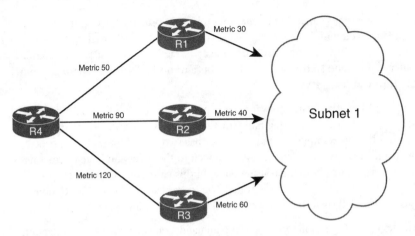

Figure 5-8 *Example of the Use of Variance*

Table 5-3 *Example of Routes Chosen as Equal Because of Variance*

Next-hop	Metric	RD	Added to Routing Table at Variance 1?	Added to Routing Table at Variance 2?	Added to Routing Table at Variance 3?
R1	50	30	Yes	Yes	Yes
R2	90	40	No	Yes	Yes
R3	120	60	No	No	No

Before considering the variance, note that in this case the route through R1 is the successor route, because it has the lowest metric. This also means that the FD is 50. The route through R2 is an FS route, because its RD of 40 is less than the FD of 50. The route through R3 is not an FS route, because R3's RD of 60 is more than the FD of 50.

At a default variance setting of 1, the metrics must be exactly equal to be considered equal, so only the successor route is added to the routing table (the route through R1). With variance 2, the FD (50) is multiplied by the variance (2) for a product of 100. The route through R2, with FD 90, is less than 100, so R4 will add the route through R2 to the routing table as well. The router can then load-balance traffic across these two routes.

In the third case, with variance 3, the product of the FD (50) times 3 equals 150. All three routes' calculated metrics (their FD values) are less than 150. However, the route through R3 is not an FS route, so it cannot be added to the routing table for fear of causing a routing loop. So, R4 adds only the routes through R1 and R2 to its IP routing table. (Note that the **variance** and **maximum-paths** settings can be verified by using the **show ip protocols** command.)

The following list summarizes the key points to know about variance:

- The variance is multiplied by the current FD (the metric of the best route to reach a subnet).

- Any FS routes whose calculated metric is less than or equal to the product of variance and FD are added to the IP routing table, assuming that the **maximum-paths** setting allows more routes.

- Routes that are neither successor nor feasible successor routes can never be added to the IP routing table, regardless of the variance setting.

When the routes have been added to the routing table, the router supports a couple of methods for how to load-balance traffic across the routes. The router can load-balance the traffic proportionally with the metrics, meaning that lower metric routes send more packets. Alternately, the router can send all traffic over the lowest-metric route, with the other routes just being in the routing table for faster convergence in case the best route fails.

Optimizing EIGRP Convergence

The previous major section of this chapter focused on how EIGRP calculates metrics and how to change that metric calculation. However, that section discussed only one motivation for changing the metric: to make a router pick one route instead of another. This section, which focuses on optimizing the EIGRP convergence process, discusses another reason for choosing to manipulate the EIGRP metric calculations: faster convergence.

EIGRP converges very quickly, but EIGRP does not achieve the most optimal fast convergence times in all conditions. One design goal might be to tune EIGRP configuration settings so that EIGRP uses faster convergence methods for as many routes as possible, and when not possible, that EIGRP converge as quickly as it can without introducing routing loops. As a result, routers might converge in some cases in a second instead of tens of seconds (from the point of a router realizing that a route has failed).

For those of you who have not thought about EIGRP convergence before now, you must first get a comfortable understanding of the concept of EIGRP feasible successors—the first topic in this section. Following that, the text examines the EIGRP query process and route summarization. This section ends with EIGRP load balancing, which allows both spreading the load across multiple routes in addition to improving EIGRP convergence.

Fast Convergence to Feasible Successors

Earlier in this chapter, in the section "Calculating the Metrics: Feasible Distance and Reported Distance," the text explains how a router, for each possible route, calculates two metric values. One value is the *feasible distance (FD)*, which is the metric from that router's perspective. The other metric is the *reported distance (RD)*, which is the integer metric from the perspective of a next-hop router.

EIGRP routers use the RD value when determining whether a possible route can be considered to be a loop-free backup route called a *feasible successor*. This section explains the concepts and shows how to confirm the existence or nonexistence of such routes.

Successor and Feasible Successor Concepts

For each prefix/prefix length, when multiple possible routes exist, the router chooses the route with the smallest integer metric (smallest FD). EIGRP defines each such route as the *successor route* for that prefix, and EIGRP defines the next-hop router in such a route as the *successor*. EIGRP then creates an IP route for this prefix, with the successor as the next-hop router, and places that route into the IP routing table.

If more than one possible route exists for a given prefix/prefix length, the router examines these other (nonsuccessor) routes and asks this question: Can any of these routes be used immediately if the currently best route fails, without causing a routing loop? EIGRP runs a simple algorithm to identify which routes could be used without causing a routing loop, and EIGRP keeps these loop-free backup routes in its topology table. Then, if the successor route (the best route) fails, EIGRP immediately uses the best of these alternate loop-free routes for that prefix.

EIGRP calls these alternative, immediately usable, loop-free routes *feasible successor routes*, because they can feasibly be used as a new successor route when the current successor route fails. The next-hop router of such a route is called the *feasible successor*.

> **Note** In general conversation, the term *successor* might refer to the route or specifically to the next-hop router. Likewise, the term *feasible successor* might refer to the route, or the next-hop router, of an alternative route.

A router determines whether a route is a feasible successor based on the feasibility condition, defined as follows:

Key Topic

> If a nonsuccessor route's RD is less than the FD, the route is a feasible successor route.

Although technically correct, the preceding definition is much more understandable with an example as shown in Figure 5-9. The figure illustrates how EIGRP figures out which routes are feasible successors for Subnet 1.

In Figure 5-9, Router E learns three routes to Subnet 1, from Routers B, C, and D. After calculating each route's metric, Router E finds that the route through Router D has the lowest metric. Router E adds this successor route for Subnet 1 to its routing table, as shown. The FD in this case for this successor route is 14,000.

EIGRP decides whether a route can be a feasible successor by determining whether the reported distance for that route (the metric as calculated on that neighbor) is less than its own best computed metric (the FD). If that neighbor has a lower metric for its route to the subnet in question, that route is said to have met the feasibility condition.

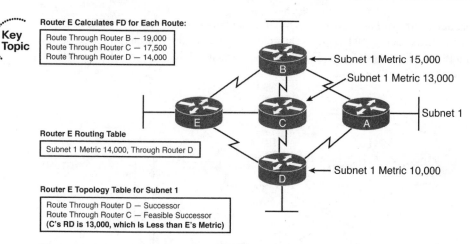

Router E Calculates FD for Each Route:

Route Through Router B — 19,000
Route Through Router C — 17,500
Route Through Router D — 14,000

← Subnet 1 Metric 15,000

Subnet 1 Metric 13,000

Subnet 1

Router E Routing Table

Subnet 1 Metric 14,000, Through Router D

← Subnet 1 Metric 10,000

Router E Topology Table for Subnet 1

Route Through Router D — Successor
Route Through Router C — Feasible Successor
(C's RD is 13,000, which Is Less than E's Metric)

Figure 5-9 *Successors and Feasible Successors with EIGRP*

For example, Router E computes a metric (FD) of 14,000 on its successor route (through Router D). Router C's computed metric—E's RD for this alternate router through Router C—is 13,000, which is lower than E's FD (14,000). As a result, E knows that C's best route for this subnet could not possibly point toward Router E, so Router E believes that its route, to Subnet 1 through Router C, would not cause a loop. As a result, Router E marks its topology table entry for the route through Router C as a feasible successor route.

Conversely, E's RD for the route through Router B to Subnet 1 is 15,000, which is larger than Router E's FD of 14,000. So, this alternative route does not meet the feasibility condition, so Router E does not consider the route through Router B a feasible successor route.

If the route to Subnet 1 through Router D fails, Router E can immediately put the route through Router C into the routing table without fear of creating a loop. Convergence occurs almost instantly in this case. However, if both C and D fail, E would not have a feasible successor route, and would have to do additional work, as described later in the section "Converging by Going Active," before using the route through Router B.

By tuning EIGRP metrics, an engineer can create feasible successor routes in cases where none existed, improving convergence.

Verification of Feasible Successors

Determining which prefixes have both successor and feasible successor routes is somewhat simple if you keep the following in mind:

■ The **show ip eigrp topology** command does not list all known EIGRP routes, but instead lists only successor and feasible successor routes.

■ The **show ip eigrp topology all-links** command lists all possible routes, including those that are neither successor nor feasible successor routes.

For example, consider Figure 5-10, which again focuses on Router WAN1's route to Router B1's LAN subnet, 10.11.1.0/24. The configuration on all routers has reverted back to defaults for all settings that impact the metric: default bandwidth and delay, no offset lists, and all interfaces are up.

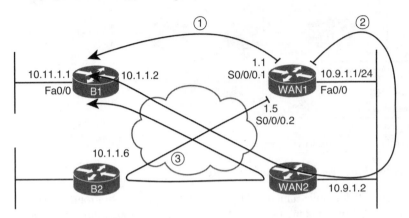

Note: All WAN IP addresses begin with 10.1

Figure 5-10 *Three Possible Routes from WAN1 to 10.11.1.0/24*

Figure 5-10 shows the three topologically possible routes to reach 10.11.1.0/24, labeled 1, 2, and 3. Route 1, direct to Router B1, is the current successor. Route 3, which goes to another branch router, back to the main site, and then to Router B1, is probably a route you would not want to use anyway. However, route 2, through WAN2, would be a reasonable backup route.

If the PVC between WAN1 and B1 failed, WAN1 would converge to route 2 from the figure. However, with all default settings, route 2 is not an FS route, as demonstrated in Example 5-7.

Example 5-7 *Only a Successor Route on WAN1 for 10.11.1.0/24*

```
WAN1# show ip eigrp topology
IP-EIGRP Topology Table for AS(1)/ID(10.9.1.1)


Codes: P - Passive, A - Active, U - Update, Q - Query, R - Reply,
       r - reply Status, s - sia Status


P 10.11.1.0/24, 1 successors, FD is 2172416
        via 10.1.1.2 (2172416/28160), Serial0/0/0.1
! lines omitted for brevity; no other lines of output pertain to 10.11.1.0/24.


WAN1# show ip eigrp topology all-links
```

```
IP-EIGRP Topology Table for AS(1)/ID(10.9.1.1)


Codes: P - Passive, A - Active, U - Update, Q - Query, R - Reply,
       r - reply Status, s - sia Status


P 10.11.1.0/24, 1 successors, FD is 2172416, serno 45
        via 10.1.1.2 (2172416/28160), Serial0/0/0.1
        via 10.9.1.2 (2174976/2172416), FastEthernet0/0
! lines omitted for brevity; no other lines of output pertain to 10.11.1.0/24.
```

A quick comparison of the two commands shows that the **show ip eigrp topology** command shows only one next-hop address (10.1.1.2), whereas the **show ip eigrp topology all-links** command shows two (10.1.1.2 and 10.9.1.2). The first command lists only successor and feasible successor routes. So in this case, only one such route for 10.11.1.0/24 exists—the successor route, direct to B1 (10.1.1.2).

The output of the **show ip eigrp topology all-links** command is particularly interesting in this case. It lists two possible next-hop routers: 10.1.1.2 (B1) and 10.9.1.2 (WAN2). It does not list the route through Router B2 (10.1.1.6), because B2's current successor route for 10.11.1.0/24 is through WAN1. EIGRP's Split Horizon rules tell B2 to not advertise 10.11.1.0/24 to WAN1.

Next, focus on the route labeled as option 2 in Figure 5-9, the route from WAN1, to WAN2, then to B1. Per the **show ip eigrp topology all-links** command, this route has an RD of 2,172,416—the second number in parentheses as highlighted toward the end of Example 5-7. WAN1's successor route has an FD of that exact same value. So, this one possible alternate route for 10.11.1.0/24, through WAN2, does not meet the feasibility condition—but just barely. To be an FS route, a route's RD must be less than the FD, and in this example, the two are equal.

To meet the design requirement for quickest convergence, you could use any method to manipulate the metrics such that either WAN2's metric for 10.11.1.0 is lower or WAN1's metric for its successor route is higher. Example 5-8 shows the results of simply adding back the offset list on WAN1, as seen in Example 5-5, which increases WAN1's metric by 3.

Example 5-8 *Increasing WAN1's Metric for 10.11.1.0/24, Creating an FS Route*

```
WAN1# configure terminal
Enter configuration commands, one per line.  End with CNTL/Z.
WAN1(config)# access-list 11 permit 10.11.1.0
WAN1(config)# router eigrp 1
WAN1(config-router)# offset-list 11 in 3 s0/0/0.1
WAN1(config-router)# ^Z
WAN1# show ip eigrp topology
IP-EIGRP Topology Table for AS(1)/ID(10.9.1.1)


Codes: P - Passive, A - Active, U - Update, Q - Query, R - Reply,
       r - reply Status, s - sia Status
```

```
P 10.11.1.0/24, 1 successors, FD is 2172419
        via 10.1.1.2 (2172419/28163), Serial0/0/0.1
        via 10.9.1.2 (2174976/2172416), FastEthernet0/0
! lines omitted for brevity; no other lines of output pertain to 10.11.1.0/24.
```

Note that now WAN1's successor route FD is 2,172,419, which is higher than WAN2's (10.9.1.2's) RD of 2,172,416. As a result, WAN1's route through WAN2 (10.9.1.2) now meets the feasibility condition. Also, the **show ip eigrp topology** command, which lists only successor and feasible successor routes, now lists this new feasible successor route. Also note that the output still states "1 successor." So, this counter only counts successor routes and does not include FS routes.

When EIGRP on a router notices that a successor route has been lost, if a feasible successor exists in the EIGRP topology database, EIGRP places that feasible successor route into the routing table. The elapsed time from noticing that the route failed, until the route is replaced, is typically less than 1 second. (A Cisco Live conference presentation asserts that this convergence approaches 200 milliseconds.) With well-tuned EIGRP Hold Timers and with feasible successor routes, convergence time can be held low.

Converging by Going Active

When EIGRP removes a successor route and no FS route exists, the router begins a process by which the router discovers whether any loop-free alternative routes exist to reach that prefix. This process is called *going active* on a route. Routes for which the router has a successor route, and no failure has yet occurred, remain in a passive state. Routes for which the successor route fails, and no feasible successor routes exist, move to an active state, as follows:

- Change the state, as listed in the **show ip eigrp topology** command, from passive (p) to active (a).

- Send EIGRP Query messages to every neighbor except the neighbor in the failed route. The Query asks a neighbor whether that neighbor has a loop-free route for the listed prefix/length.

- The neighbor considers itself to have a loop-free route if that neighbor is passive for that prefix/length. If so, the neighbor 1) sends an EIGRP Reply message, telling the original router that it does indeed have a loop-free route and 2) does not forward the Query.

- If the neighbor itself is active on this route, that neighbor 1) floods EIGRP Query messages to its neighbors and 2) does not immediately send an EIGRP Reply back to the original router—instead waiting on replies to its own set of Query messages.

- When a router has received Reply messages from all neighbors to which it sent any Query messages, that router can then send a Reply message to any of its neighbors as necessary.

- When a router has received a Reply for all its Query messages, that router can safely use the best of the routes confirmed to be loop-free.

Note   The EIGRP convergence process when going active on a route is sometimes also referenced by the name of the underlying algorithm, named *Diffusing Update Algorithm (DUAL)*.

The process can and does work well in many cases, often converging to a new route in less than 10 seconds. However, in internetworks with many remote sites, with much redundancy, and with a large number of routers in a single end-to-end route, convergence when going active can be inefficient. For example, consider the internetwork in Figure 5-11. The figure shows five branch routers as an example, but the internetwork has 300 branch routers, each with a PVC connected to two WAN routers, WAN1 and WAN2. When Router WAN1 loses its route for the LAN subnet at branch B1, without an FS route, the Query process can get out of hand.

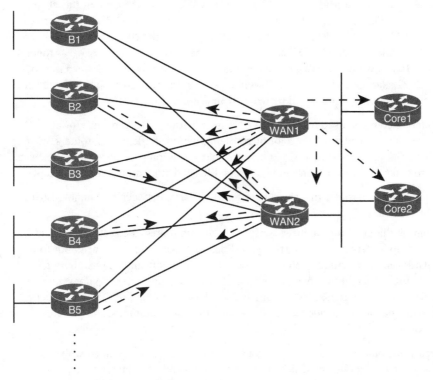

Figure 5-11   *Issues with Query Scope*

The arrowed lines show WAN1's Query messages and the reaction by several other routers to forward the Query messages. Although only five branch routers are shown, WAN1 would forward Query messages to 299 branch routers. WAN2 would do the same, assuming that its route to B1's LAN also failed. These branch routers would then send Query messages back to the WAN routers. The network would converge, but more slowly than if an FS route existed.

Note   EIGRP sends every Query and Reply message using RTP, so every message is acknowledged using an EIGRP ACK message.

By configuring EIGRP so that a router has FS routes for most routes, the entire Query process can be avoided. However, in some cases, creating FS routes for all routes on all routers is impossible. So, engineers should take action to limit the scope of queries. The next two sections discuss two tools—stub routers and route summarization—that help reduce the work performed by the DUAL and the scope of Query messages.

The Impact of Stub Routers on Query Scope

Some routers, by design, should not be responsible for forwarding traffic between different sites. For example, consider the familiar internetwork shown throughout this chapter, most recently in Figure 5-11, and focus on the branch routers. If WAN2's LAN interface failed, and WAN1's PVC to B1 failed, a route still exists from the core to branch B1's 10.11.1.0/24 subnet: WAN1–B2–WAN2–B1. (This is the same long route shown as route 3 in Figure 5-10.) However, this long route consumes the link bandwidth between the core and branch B2, and the traffic to/from B1 will be slower. Users at both branches will suffer, and these conditions might well be worse than just not using this long route.

Route filtering could be used to prevent WAN1 from learning such a route. However, using route filtering would require a lot of configuration on all the branch routers, with specifics for the subnets—and it would have to change over time. A better solution exists, which is to make the branch routers stub routers. EIGRP defines stub routers as follows:

Key Topic

> A stub router is a router that should not forward traffic between two remote EIGRP-learned subnets.

To accomplish this goal, the engineer configures the stub routers using the **eigrp stub** command. Stub routers do not advertise EIGRP-learned routes from one neighbor to other EIGRP neighbors. Additionally, and possibly more significantly, nonstub routers note which EIGRP neighbors are stub routers, and the nonstub routers do not send Query messages to the stub routers. This action greatly reduces the scope of Query messages when a route goes active, in addition to preventing the long, circuitous, and possibly harmful route.

The **eigrp stub** command has several options. When issued simply as **eigrp stub**, the router uses default parameters, which are the **connected** and **summary** options. (Note that Cisco IOS adds these two parameters onto the command as added to the running config.) Table 5-4 lists the **eigrp stub** command options and explains some of the logic behind using them.

Key Topic

Table 5-4 *Parameters on the* eigrp stub *Command*

Option	This Router Is Allowed to...
connected	Advertise connected routes but only for interfaces matched with a **network** command.
summary	Advertise auto-summarized or statically configured summary routes.
static	Advertise static routes, assuming that the **redistribute static** command is configured.
leak-map *name*	Advertise routes (that would otherwise be part of a summary route) specified by a leak map.
redistributed	Advertise redistributed routes, assuming that redistribution is configured.
receive-only	Does not advertise any routes. This option cannot be used with any other option.

Note that stub routers still form neighborships, even in receive-only mode. The stub router simply performs less work and reduces the Query scope because neighbors will not send these routers any Query messages.

For example, Example 5-9 shows the **eigrp stub connected** command on Router B2, with the results being noticeable on WAN1 (**show ip eigrp neighbors detail**).

Example 5-9 *Evidence of Router B2 as an EIGRP Stub Router*

```
B2# configure terminal
B2(config)# router eigrp 1
B2(config-router)# eigrp stub connected
B2(config-router)#
Mar  2 21:21:52.361: %DUAL-5-NBRCHANGE: IP-EIGRP(0) 1: Neighbor 10.9.1.14
  (FastEthernet0/0.12) is down: peer info changed
! A message like the above occurs for each neighbor.


! Moving to router WAN1 next
WAN1# show ip eigrp neighbors detail
IP-EIGRP neighbors for process 1
H   Address      Interface       Hold Uptime    SRTT    RTO   Q     Seq
                                 (sec)          (ms)          Cnt   Num
1   10.9.1.2     Fa0/0            11 00:00:04     7     200   0     588
    Version 12.4/1.2, Retrans: 0, Retries: 0, Prefixes: 8
2   10.1.1.6     Se0/0/0.2        13 00:21:23     1     200   0     408
    Version 12.4/1.2, Retrans: 2, Retries: 0, Prefixes: 2
    Stub Peer Advertising ( CONNECTED ) Routes
    Suppressing queries
0   10.9.1.6     Fa0/0.4          12 00:21:28     1     200   0     175
    Version 12.2/1.2, Retrans: 3, Retries: 0, Prefixes: 6
```

The Impact of Summary Routes on Query Scope

In addition to EIGRP stub routers, route summarization also limits EIGRP Query scope and therefore improves convergence time. The reduction in Query scope occurs because of the following rule:

If a router receives an EIGRP Query for a prefix/prefix length, does not have an exactly matching (both prefix and prefix length) route, but does have a summary route that includes the prefix/prefix length, that router immediately sends an EIGRP Reply and does not flood the Query to its own neighbors.

For example, consider Figure 5-12.

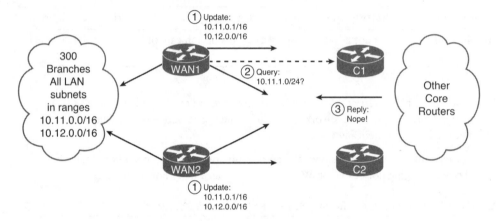

Figure 5-12 *Route Summaries Limiting Query Scope*

Multilayer switches C1 and C2 sit in the core of the network shown in various other figures in this chapter, and both C1 and C2 run EIGRP. The IP subnetting design assigns all branch office LAN subnets from the range 10.11.0.0/16 and 10.12.0.0/16. As such, Routers WAN1 and WAN2 advertise summary routes for these ranges, rather than for individual subnets. So, under normal operation, ignoring the entire Query scope issue, C1 and C2 would never have routes for individual branch subnets like 10.11.1.0/24 but would have routes for 10.11.0.0/16 and 10.12.0.0/16.

The figure highlights three steps:

Step 1. WAN1 and WAN2 advertise summary routes, so that C1, C2, and all other routers in the core have a route for 10.11.0.0/16 but not a route for 10.11.1.0/24.

Step 2. Some time in the future, WAN1 loses its route for 10.11.1.0/24, so WAN1 sends a Query for 10.11.1.0/24 to C1 and C2.

Step 3. C1 and C2 send an EIGRP Reply immediately afterward, because both do not have a route for that specific prefix/length (10.11.1.0/24), but both do have a summary route (10.11.0.0/16) that includes that range of addresses.

Stuck in Active

When a router notices a route failure and moves a route from the passive to active state, that router sends Query messages to its neighbors. With a sufficiently large network, particularly when routers exist several router hops away, the number of Queries might not only be large, but there also might be a string of routers that all must wait on multiple Reply messages before they can, in turn, issue a Reply. For example, in Figure 5-13, Router R1 must wait on Routers R11, R12, and R13 to send a Reply. R11 must wait on Routers R21, R22, and R23. R21 must wait on three other routers, and so on—meaning that R1 might have to wait quite a while before getting a response.

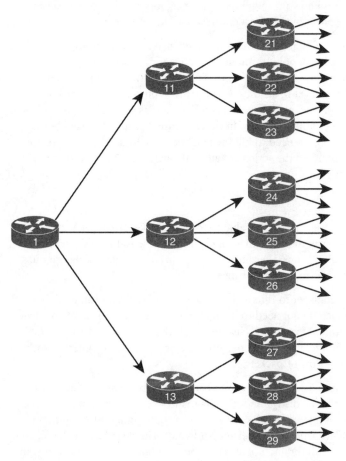

Figure 5-13 *Network Design That Causes Unreasonably Long Convergence*

Although the design shown in Figure 5-13 is admittedly contrived, the point is that a router might wait a while before getting a Reply message in response to each Query message for an active route. A router cannot use any alternative paths for that route until all such Reply messages have been received.

To deal with this potentially long time, Cisco IOS first sets a limit on how long it should take to receive all such replies. That timer, called the *active timer*, is set to 3 minutes by default. (The timer can be configured for an entire EIGRP process using the **timers active-time** *time* EIGRP subcommand, where *time* is represented in minutes.) Routes for which a router does not receive a Reply within the active timer are considered to be *Stuck-in-Active (SIA)* routes.

Cisco IOS has two major branches of logic when reacting to SIA routes. Earlier versions of Cisco IOS took a rather drastic action, bringing down the uncooperative neighbors that had yet to send back an EIGRP Reply for that route. For example, in Figure 5-12, if R1 received Reply messages from R11 and R12, but not R13, and the active timer expired, R1 would bring down the neighborship with R13. The active route would be considered to have failed, and all routes known through the failed neighbor would also be considered to have failed—possibly generating more Query messages for other routes.

Later Cisco IOS versions (beginning in the 12.2 mainline) make an attempt to avoid failing the neighborship. At the halfway point through the Active timer—a seemingly long 90 seconds by default—a router sends an SIA-Query (Stuck-in-Active Query) EIGRP message to each neighbor that has yet to send back a Reply. The purpose of the message is to either get an SIA-Reply back, meaning that the neighbor really is still waiting for replies to its own queries, or to get nothing in reply. In the first case, because the neighbor is alive and still working, there is no need to kill the neighborship. In the second case, the neighbor was not able to reply, so the action of failing the neighborship is reasonable.

Route Filtering

Does a router in a branch office need to be able to forward packets to hosts in another branch office? Does a router in the sales division need to be able to forward packets to hosts in the manufacturing division? These questions are just a sampling of design questions for which route filtering can be part of the solution.

Route filtering allows the engineer to filter which routes are advertised in an EIGRP update. If routers in a branch do not need to learn routes about subnets in other branches, routers can filter that routing information. This filtering reduces the size of routing tables, saving memory, possibly improving routing performance, and making the internetwork more secure by limiting the flow of packets.

EIGRP enables route filtering using the **distribute-list** router subcommand. The concept is relatively straightforward: The distribute list refers to an access control list (ACL), prefix list, or route map. These three tools classify whether a route should be permitted to be sent/received in an EIGRP Update or be denied (filtered). The **distribute-list** command also specifies the direction—outbound updates or inbound updates—and optionally, the specific interface on which to filter updates.

For example, Figure 5-14 shows an expanded version of an internetwork used previously. The figure adds several links between the WAN routers and some core Layer 3 switches. It also notes the address ranges for all data centers (10.16.0.0/16) and the range of addresses used for subnets in the manufacturing division (10.17.32.0/19).

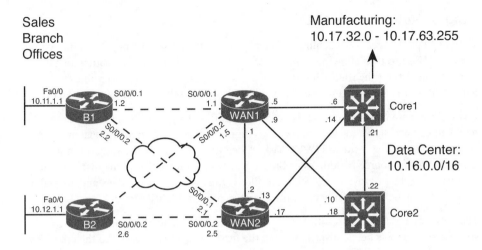

Figure 5-14   *Expanded Design with a Range of Addresses in Manufacturing*

The design engineer could make many choices about what routes to filter, for example

- Filter routes to WAN subnets so that the core and manufacturing do not learn those routes, because these subnets should not be the destination of any user traffic.

- Filter manufacturing routes from being advertised to the branches, because the branches are in the sales division.

- Filter routes for the subnets sitting between the Layer 3 switches in the core, preventing them from being advertised to either manufacturing or the sales branches, because no users in these divisions should be sending packets to these subnets.

The examples in this section focus on the second of these design options.

Filtering the subnets that exist between Layer 3 devices, as is suggested in the second and third items in the list, have both pros and cons. For example, the first design goal filters the WAN subnets, because no end users need to be able to send packets to those subnets. This meets the goal of having smaller routing tables. However, operations personnel might have a larger challenge when monitoring and troubleshooting, because when a ping or traceroute fails, they also need to figure out whether the command failed by design because of the purposefully filtered routes or whether a problem has occurred.

This section next examines how to filter EIGRP routes using ACLs, prefix lists, and then route maps. All three of these tools will be used throughout this book, so this chapter lays the foundation for understanding these tools, in addition to showing how to use these tools when filtering EIGRP routes.

Filtering by Referencing ACLs

To filter EIGRP routes by matching them using ACLs, the ACL must match a route with a permit clause to then allow the route to be advertised, and match the route with a deny clause to filter the route. Before getting into how an ACL matches a route, first it is important to review what can be examined based on the configuration of an IP ACL.

EIGRP distribute lists support the use of standard IP ACLs. The syntax of both numbered and named standard ACLs allows a configuration of one dotted-decimal number and its corresponding wildcard (WC) mask. When used for packet filtering, this number is compared to the source IP address of the packet. When referenced by the **distribute-list** command for the purpose of EIGRP route filtering, EIGRP compares the standard ACL source address field to the subnet number (prefix) of each EIGRP route.

The best way to learn the specifics is to consider several examples. Figure 5-15 shows the specific size subnets being advertised from the manufacturing division into the core. The design calls for the WAN routers to filter these routes from being advertised toward the Sales division's branch offices.

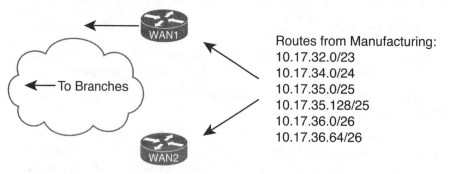

Figure 5-15 *Specific Manufacturing Routes to Be Filtered*

Figure 5-15 shows the **distribute-list 2 out s0/0/0.1** command on Router WAN1 as one sample of the syntax. A command like this would need to be included in WAN1's configuration for each interface connected to a branch. ACL number 2 would then be configured to match the manufacturing routes with a **deny** clause, and all other routes with a **permit** clause, filtering the routes.

If WAN1 has hundreds of serial subinterfaces for its WAN connections, following the sample in the previous paragraph, WAN1 would have hundreds of **distribute-list 2 out serial** *number* commands, one per WAN interface/subinterface. Alternatively, the engineer could configure a single **distribute-list 2 out** command on Router WAN1, not specifying an interface. In this case, Router WAN1 would not advertise these routes to any neighbors, greatly reducing WAN1's configuration.

Consider the following **access-list** commands. Imagine that each command in this list is the first of two commands in a single access list. The second and only other command is a command that permits all other routes—for example, **access-list 2 permit any**. Then, ask yourself: If used by a distribute list on WAN1 to filter the manufacturing routes (as seen in Figure 15-15), and you want that ACL to filter only manufacturing routes, which of these two-line ACLs meet the requirements?

```
access-list 3 deny 10.17.32.0
access-list 4 deny 10.17.32.0 0.0.0.255
access-list 5 deny 10.17.32.0 0.0.3.255
access-list 6 deny 10.16.0.0 0.1.255.255
```

Table 5-5 supplies the answers and explanation.

Table 5-5 *Analysis of the Sample ACLs Used with the* **distribute-list** *Command*

ACL	Routes Filtered	Explanation
3	10.17.32.0 /23	The ACL matches exactly prefix 10.17.32.0, so it matches a single manufacturing route.
4	10.17.32.0 /23	The ACL matches all prefixes that begin with 10.17.32 because of the WC mask, again matching a single route.
5	10.17.32.0 /23 10.17.34.0 /24 10.17.35.0 /25 10.17.35.128 /25	The ACL matches all prefixes in the range 10.17.32.0–10.17.35.255, which includes four manufacturing routes.
6	All manufacturing and data center routes	The ACL matches all prefixes in the range 10.16.0.0–10.17.255.255, which includes the data center routes.

Note To find the range of numbers matched by an ACL's address and wildcard mask values, use the address field as the low end of the range and simply add the address and wildcard mask to find the high end of the range.

Example 5-10 shows the configuration on Router WAN1 to filter the manufacturing routes, with distribute lists enabled on its two WAN subinterfaces. The ACL matches (with a deny action) all manufacturing routes and matches all other routes with a permit clause.

Example 5-10 *WAN1's* **distribute-list** *to Filter Manufacturing Routes*

```
! On Router B1, before the filtering is applied:
B1# show ip route | include 10.17
D       10.17.35.0/25 [90/2300416] via 10.1.1.1, 00:00:18, Serial0/0/0.1
D       10.17.34.0/24 [90/2300416] via 10.1.1.1, 00:00:18, Serial0/0/0.1
D       10.17.32.0/23 [90/2300416] via 10.1.1.1, 00:00:18, Serial0/0/0.1
D       10.17.36.0/26 [90/2300416] via 10.1.1.1, 00:00:18, Serial0/0/0.1
```

```
D        10.17.36.64/26 [90/2300416] via 10.1.1.1, 00:00:18, Serial0/0/0.1
D        10.17.35.128/25 [90/2300416] via 10.1.1.1, 00:00:18, Serial0/0/0.1
```

```
! On Router WAN1:
WAN1# configure terminal
Enter configuration commands, one per line.  End with CNTL/Z.
WAN1(config)# access-list 2 deny 10.17.32.0 0.0.31.255
WAN1(config)# access-list 2 permit any
WAN1(config)# router eigrp 1
WAN1(config-router)# distribute-list 2 out
WAN1(config-router)# ^Z
WAN1#
```

```
! On Router B1, after the filtering is applied
B1# show ip route | include 10.17
B1#
```

Note   The same configuration added to Router WAN1 was also added to Router WAN2; however, the commands were not repeated in Example 5-10.

The ACL in this case, ACL 2, matches all subnets with a value between 10.17.32.0 and 10.17.63.255 inclusive, based on the IP address value of 10.17.32.0 and WC mask of 0.0.31.255. By matching these routes with a **deny** clause, the ACL, used as a distribute list, filters the routes. The **access-list 2 permit any** command matches all other routes, allowing them to be advertised.

Filtering by Referencing IP Prefix Lists

The Cisco IOS IP **prefix-list** feature gives the network engineer another tool for matching routes when performing route filtering. IP prefix lists can examine both the prefix and the prefix length, and a range of prefixes or a range of prefix lengths. The command then sets either a **deny** or **permit** action for each matched prefix/length. To use the prefix list, the configuration simply refers to the **prefix-list** with the same **distribute-list** command seen earlier.

Using IP prefix lists for route filtering has several advantages. First, IP prefix lists allow matching of the prefix length, whereas the ACLs used by the EIGRP **distribute-list** command cannot. (Some other route filtering configurations can match both the prefix and prefix length using extended ACLs.) Many people find IP prefix lists more intuitive for configuring route filtering. Finally, the internal processing of the IP prefix lists uses an internal tree structure that results in faster matching of routes as compared with ACLs.

This section begins by examining IP prefix lists as an end to itself, followed by an example of filtering EIGRP routes using a prefix list.

IP Prefix List Concepts

IP prefix lists provide mechanisms to match two components of an IP route:

- The route prefix (the subnet number)

- The prefix length (the subnet mask)

Each single IP prefix list has similar characteristics to a single ACL, with subtle similarities to both numbered and named ACLs. The IP prefix list consists of one or more global configuration commands (like numbered ACLs), with commands using the same name being in the same list (like named ACLs). As with named ACLs, each **ip prefix-list** command has a sequence number to allow later deletion of individual commands and insertion of commands into a particular sequence position. Each command has a **permit** or **deny** action, but because it is used only for matching routes, and not for packet filtering, the **permit** or **deny** keyword just implies whether a route is matched (**permit**) or not (**deny**).

The generic command syntax is as follows:

```
ip prefix-list list-name [seq seq-value] {deny | permit prefix/prefix-length} [ge
   ge-value] [le le-value]
```

The following steps summarize the logic:

Key Topic

Step 1.   The route's prefix must be within the range of addresses implied by the **prefix-list** command's *prefix/prefix-length* parameters.

Step 2.   The route's prefix length must match the range of prefixes implied by the **prefix-list** command's *prefix-length*, *ge*, and *le* parameters.

The matching of the prefix works much like the ACL matching logic. The configured prefix/prefix length implies a range of IP addresses. For example, an **ip prefix-list barney deny 10.0.0.0/8**... implies any number whose first 8 bits (per the /8) match 10.0.0.0—in other words, all IPv4 addresses that begin with 10. Any route whose prefix is in this range—for example, 10.0.0.0, 10.1.1.0, and 10.5.255.128—would be considered to match this part of the logic.

However, IP prefix lists always examine the prefix length as well. To perform the logic of matching a route's prefix length, Cisco IOS considers the following parts of the **ip prefix-list** command:

- The required *prefix-length* parameter

- The optional *ge-value*, which stand for *greater-than-or-equal-to*

- The optional *le-value*, which stand for *less-than-or-equal-to*

For a given **ip prefix-list** command, one of four configuration combinations affect the logic of matching prefix lengths, as listed in Table 5-6. The text following the table provides a more detailed explanation as compared with the summarized information in the table.

Table 5-6 *LE and GE Parameters on IP Prefix List, and the Implied Range of Prefix Lengths*

Prefix List Parameter	Range of Prefix Length
Neither	*conf length must = route*
Both ge and le	*ge-value <= route-length <= le-value*
Only le	*conf length <= route*
Only ge	*ge-value <= route-length <= 32*

The first case in the table occurs when neither **ge** nor **le** is configured. In that case, an exact match of prefix length must occur between the configured prefix length and a route's prefix length. For example, the **ip prefix-list fred deny 10.0.0.0/8** command matches route 10.0.0.0/8, but not 10.0.0.0/20.

The second case in the table occurs when both **ge** and **le** are configured. In that case, the route's prefix length must be between the configured ge and le values, inclusive. For example, **ip prefix-list fred deny 10.0.0.0/8 ge 20 le 22** matches route 10.0.0.0/20, but not 10.0.0.0/8, because the prefix length must either be 20, 21, or 22.

The cases in which either ge or le is configured, but not both, require a little more thought. A visual representation can help, as shown in Figure 5-16.

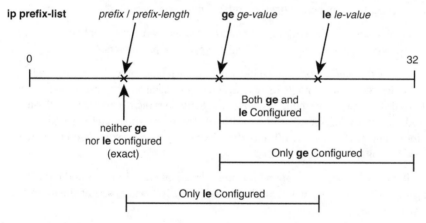

Figure 5-16 *Representation of Prefix Length Ranges for* **ip prefix-list** *Command*

In short, with only **ge** configured, the command matches prefix length ranges from the *ge-value* up to 32 (the longest IPv4 prefix length), inclusive. With only le configured, the command matches prefix length ranges between the *prefix-length* parameter and the *le-value*, inclusive.

> **Note**   Cisco IOS requires that the configured *prefix-length*, *ge-value*, and *le-value* meet the following requirement: *prefix-length* <= *ge-value* <= *le-value*. Otherwise, Cisco IOS rejects the **ip prefix-list** command.

Samples of Prefix List Matching

Several examples can really help nail down prefix list logic. The following routes will be examined by a variety of prefix lists, with the routes numbered for easier reference:

1. 10.0.0.0/8

2. 10.128.0.0/9

3. 10.1.1.0/24

4. 10.1.2.0/24

5. 10.128.10.4/30

6. 10.128.10.8/30

Next, Table 5-7 shows the results of seven different one-line prefix lists applied to these six example routes. The table lists the matching parameters in the **prefix-list** commands, omitting the first part of the commands. The table explains which of the six routes would match the listed prefix list, and why.

Table 5-7   *Example Prefix Lists Applied to the List of Routes*

prefix-list Command Parameter	Routes Matched from Previous List of Prefixes	Result
10.0.0.0/8	1	Without **ge** or **le** configured, both the prefix (10.0.0.0) and length (8) must be an exact match.
10.128.0.0/9	2	Without **ge** or **le** configured, the prefix (10.128.0.0) and length (9) must be an exact match.
10.0.0.0/8 ge 9	2–6	The 10.0.0.0/8 means "all routes whose first octet is 10." The prefix length must be between 9 and 32, inclusive.
10.0.0.0/8 ge 24 le 24	3, 4	The 10.0.0.0/8 means "all routes whose first octet is 10," and the prefix range is 24 to 24—meaning only routes with prefix length 24.
10.0.0.0/8 le 28	1–4	The prefix length needs to be between 8 and 28, inclusive.

prefix-list Command Parameter	Routes Matched from Previous List of Prefixes	Result
0.0.0.0/0	None	0.0.0.0/0 means "match all prefixes." However, because no **le** nor **ge** parameter is configured, the /0 also means that the prefix length must be 0. So, it would match all routes' prefixes but none of their prefix lengths. Only a default route would match this prefix list.
0.0.0.0/0 le 32	All	The range implied by 0.0.0.0/0 is all IPv4 addresses. The **le 32** combined with prefix length 0 implies any prefix length between 0 and 32, inclusive. This is the syntax for "match all" prefix list logic.

Note Pay particular attention to the match all logic of the final entry in the table.

Using IP Prefix Lists to Filter EIGRP Routes

After you master the logic behind IP prefix lists, using them with the **distribute-list** command requires minimal extra effort. For example, to refer to a prefix list name Fred, you could configure the **distribute-list prefix Fred...** command, instead of **distribute-list 2...** to refer to ACL 2. (Note that the prefix list names are case sensitive.)

For example, using the internetwork of Figure 5-14 and Figure 5-15 again, consider the following revised design requirements for route filtering:

■ Of the routes from manufacturing, filter only those routes that begin with 10.17.35 and 10.17.36.

■ Of the routes for subnets on the WAN links, filter routes to prevent the core routers and branch routers from learning routes whose prefix length is /30.

Although the first of the preceding two requirements mainly exists to demonstrate the **ip prefix-list** command, the second goal might be more useful for real networks. Often, routes with a /30 prefix length are routes used between two routers, either on WAN links or over LANs between Layer 3–enabled devices. Users should not need to send packets to addresses in these subnets. So, the only need to have routes to these subnets is for network management (ping tests, for example).

Example 5-11 shows the configuration on WAN1; the equivalent configuration has been added on WAN2 as well.

Example 5-11 *Filtering All Routes with a /30 Prefix Length*

```
! On Router WAN1: !!!!!!!!!!!!!!!!!!!!!!!!!!!!!!!!!!!!!!!!!!!!!!!
WAN1# show running-config
! lines omitted for brevity
router eigrp 1
 network 10.0.0.0
 distribute-list prefix fred out
 auto-summary
!
ip prefix-list fred seq 5 deny 10.17.35.0/24 ge 25 le 25
ip prefix-list fred seq 10 deny 10.17.36.0/24 ge 26 le 26
ip prefix-list fred seq 15 deny 0.0.0.0/0 ge 30 le 30
ip prefix-list fred seq 20 permit 0.0.0.0/0 le 32
```

```
! On Router B1:
B1# show ip route
Codes: C - connected, S - static, R - RIP, M - mobile, B - BGP
       D - EIGRP, EX - EIGRP external, O - OSPF, IA - OSPF inter area
       N1 - OSPF NSSA external type 1, N2 - OSPF NSSA external type 2
       E1 - OSPF external type 1, E2 - OSPF external type 2
       i - IS-IS, su - IS-IS summary, L1 - IS-IS level-1, L2 - IS-IS level-2
       ia - IS-IS inter area, * - candidate default, U - per-user static route
       o - ODR, P - periodic downloaded static route

Gateway of last resort is not set

     10.0.0.0/8 is variably subnetted, 7 subnets, 3 masks
C       10.11.1.0/24 is directly connected, FastEthernet0/0
D       10.12.1.0/24 [90/2684416] via 10.1.2.1, 00:06:15, Serial0/0/0.2
                     [90/2684416] via 10.1.1.1, 00:06:15, Serial0/0/0.1
C       10.1.2.0/30 is directly connected, Serial0/0/0.2
C       10.1.1.0/30 is directly connected, Serial0/0/0.1
D       10.16.1.0/24 [90/2172672] via 10.1.2.1, 00:00:32, Serial0/0/0.2
                     [90/2172672] via 10.1.1.1, 00:00:32, Serial0/0/0.1
D       10.17.34.0/24 [90/2300416] via 10.1.2.1, 00:06:15, Serial0/0/0.2
                      [90/2300416] via 10.1.1.1, 00:06:15, Serial0/0/0.1
D       10.17.32.0/23 [90/2300416] via 10.1.2.1, 00:06:15, Serial0/0/0.2
                      [90/2300416] via 10.1.1.1, 00:06:15, Serial0/0/0.1

B1# show ip route 10.17.32.0 255.255.248.0 longer-prefixes
! The legend is normally displayed; omitted here for brevity

     10.0.0.0/8 is variably subnetted, 7 subnets, 3 masks
D       10.17.34.0/24 [90/2300416] via 10.1.2.1, 00:04:12, Serial0/0/0.2
                      [90/2300416] via 10.1.1.1, 00:04:12, Serial0/0/0.1
D       10.17.32.0/23 [90/2300416] via 10.1.2.1, 00:04:12, Serial0/0/0.2
                       [90/2300416] via 10.1.1.1, 00:04:12, Serial0/0/0.1
```

The configuration on WAN1 includes a four-line prefix list. The first line (sequence number 5) matches 10.17.35.0 /25 and 10.17.35.128 /25, in part because it asks for a range of prefix lengths from 25 to 25—meaning an exact length of 25. Similarly, the second statement (sequence number 10) matches routes 10.17.36.0 /26 and 10.17.36.64 /26. The third statement (sequence number 15) uses wildcard logic (**0.0.0.0/0**) to match all prefixes, but only those with prefix length 30 (**ge 30 le 30**). The last command matches all prefixes, with prefix lengths from 0 to 32 (all prefix lengths).

The resulting IP routing table on branch Router B1 shows only a small number of routes. B1 has a route to the other example branch's subnet (10.12.1.0) and another in the range of addresses for the data centers (10.16.1.0 /24). It has the two routes leaked from manufacturing. Note that the only two /30 routes known on B1 are two connected routes, so the distribute list is filtering all the /30 routes.

Filtering by Using Route Maps

Route maps, the third EIGRP route-filtering tool that can be referenced with the **distribute-list** command, provide programming logic similar to the If/Then/Else logic seen in programming languages. A single route map has one or more **route-map** commands in it, and routers process **route-map** commands in sequential order based on sequence numbers. Each **route-map** command has underlying matching parameters, configured with the aptly named **match** command. (To match all packets, the **route-map** clause simply omits the **match** command.)

Route maps can be used for many functions besides being used to filter routes for a single routing protocol like EIGRP. Route maps can be used to filter routes during the route redistribution process, and to set Border Gateway Protocol (BGP) Path Attributes (PA) for the purpose of influencing the choice of the best routes in an internetwork.

When used for filtering EIGRP routes, route maps do provide a few additional features beyond what can be configured using ACLs and prefix lists. However, route maps can be tricky to understand and sometimes counterintuitive. This subsection begins with an examination of the concepts behind Cisco IOS route maps, followed by some examples of their use for filtering EIGRP routes.

Route Map Concepts

Route maps have many similarities when compared to ACLs and prefix lists. A single route map has several **route-map** commands, with the commands in the same route map all having the same text name. When referenced by the **distribute-list** command, Cisco IOS processes the commands in the route map sequentially, based on the sequence numbers in the commands. Like ACLs and prefix lists, Cisco IOS adds the sequence numbers automatically if omitted when configuring the **route-map** commands. And after a particular route has been matched and determined to be either filtered (**deny**) or allowed to pass (**permit**), even if more **route-map** commands exist later in the list, Cisco IOS stops processing the route map for that route.

Each **route-map** command includes the name of the route map, an action (**permit** or **deny**), and possibly a sequence number (optional). After typing this command, the CLI user is in route-map configuration mode for that **route-map** clause. Any **match** commands configured in that mode apply to that single **route-map** command. For example, Example 5-12 shows the configuration of a sample route map on Router WAN1.

Example 5-12   *Pseudocode for Route Map Used as EIGRP Route Filter*

```
route-map sample-rm deny 8
 match (1st set of criteria)
route-map sample-rm permit 17
 match (2nd set of criteria)
route-map sample-rm deny 30
 match (3rd set of criteria)
route-map sample-rm permit 35
!
router eigrp 1
 distribute-list route-map sample-rm out
```

Example 5-12 shows pseudocode, ignoring the specifics of what is matched with the **match** commands. Focus on the actions in the **route-map** command (**permit** or **deny**) and the overall logic, as listed here:

■ **Seq #8:** The action is **deny**, so discard or filter all routes matched by the **match** command (first set of criteria).

■ **Seq #17:** The action is **permit**, so allow through all routes matched by the **match** command (second set of criteria).

■ **Seq #30:** The action is **deny**, so discard or filter all routes matched by the **match** command (third set of criteria).

■ **Seq #35:** The action is **permit**. The absence of a **match** command means "match all," so allow through all remaining routes.

The **match** command can reference an ACL or prefix list, but doing so does introduce the possibility of confusion. The confusing part is that the decision to filter a route or allow the route through is based on the **deny** or **permit** in the **route-map** command, and not the **deny** or **permit** in the ACL or prefix list. When referencing an ACL or prefix list from a route map, the ACL or prefix list simply matches all routes permitted by the ACL or prefix list. Routes that are denied by the ACL or prefix list simply do not match that **match** command's logic, making Cisco IOS then consider the next **route-map** command.

The following list summarizes the key points about route map logic when used for redistribution:

**Key
Topic**

■ **route-map** commands with the **permit** option either cause a route to be allowed through (if matched by the **match** command) or remain in the list of routes to be examined by the next **route-map** clause.

■ **route-map** commands with the **deny** option either filter the route (if matched by the **match** command) or leave the route in the list of routes to be examined by the next **route-map** clause.

■ If a clause's **match** commands refer to an ACL or prefix list, and the ACL or prefix list matches a route with the **deny** action, the route is not necessarily filtered. Instead, it just means that route does not match that particular **match** command and can then be considered by the next **route-map** clause.

■ The **route-map** command includes an implied deny all clause at the end; to configure a permit all, use the **route-map** command, with a **permit** action but without a **match** command.

Route maps have several more options on the **match** command as compared to what can be examined by ACLs and IP prefix lists. However, for the purposes of EIGRP route filtering, the items that might be matched do not provide significant help in filtering routes. However, when redistributing routes from other routing protocols, as is covered in Chapter 10, "Route Redistribution," some of the **match** command's other options can be very helpful.

Using Route Maps to Filter EIGRP Routes

The mechanics of the configuration work much like the other two filtering features. The **distribute-list** command refers to the feature that matches the packets, in this case a **route-map** command option. The **distribute-list** command again lists a direction (in or out) and optionally an interface.

Example 5-13 shows the configuration results in an excerpt from the **show running-config** command, along with the output of the **show route-map** command. The configuration implements the same logic as used in Example 5-11 earlier in this chapter, in the section "Using IP Prefix Lists to Filter EIGRP Routes." The design criteria are the same as with that earlier example:

■ Of the routes from manufacturing, filter only those routes that begin with 10.17.35 and 10.17.36.

■ Filter WAN routers from advertising any /30 routes in the Layer 3 core.

Example 5-13 *Filtering All Routes with a /30 Prefix Length, Plus Some Routes from Manufacturing*

```
! On Router WAN2: !!!!!!!!!!!!!!!!!!!!!!!!!!!!!!!!!!!!!!!!!!!!!!!!
WAN2# show running-config
! lines omitted for brevity
router eigrp 1
 network 10.0.0.0
 distribute-list route-map filter-man-slash30 out
 auto-summary
!
ip prefix-list manufacturing seq 5 permit 10.17.35.0/24 ge 25 le 25
ip prefix-list manufacturing seq 10 permit 10.17.36.0/24 ge 26 le 26
!
ip prefix-list slash30 seq 5 permit 0.0.0.0/0 ge 30 le 30
```

```
 !
route-map filter-man-slash30 deny 8
 match ip address prefix-list manufacturing
 !
route-map filter-man-slash30 deny 15
 match ip address prefix-list slash30
 !
route-map filter-man-slash30 permit 23

! Notice - no match commands, so the above clause matches all remaining routes
 !
! lines omitted for brevity
WAN2# show route-map
route-map filter-man-slash30, deny, sequence 8
  Match clauses:
    ip address prefix-lists: manufacturing
  Set clauses:
  Policy routing matches: 0 packets, 0 bytes
route-map filter-man-slash30, deny, sequence 15
  Match clauses:
    ip address prefix-lists: slash30
  Set clauses:
  Policy routing matches: 0 packets, 0 bytes
route-map filter-man-slash30, permit, sequence 23
  Match clauses:
  Set clauses:
  Policy routing matches: 0 packets, 0 bytes
```

In particular, note that the first two **route-map** commands list a **deny** action, meaning that all routes matched in these two clauses will be filtered. The IP prefix lists referenced in the **match** commands, called **manufacturing** and **slash30**, respectively, each match (permit) the routes listed in one of the two design goals. Note that the logic of both prefix lists could have easily been configured into a single prefix list, reducing the length of the **route-map** command as well. Finally, note that the last **route-map** command has a permit action, with no **match** command, meaning that the default action is to allow the route to be advertised.

Also, it can be useful to take a moment and review Example 5-11 as a point of comparison for the use of the IP prefix lists in each case. In the route map of Example 5-13, the prefix list needs to match the routes with a **permit** clause so that the route-map **deny** action causes the routes to be filtered. Earlier, Example 5-11 shows the same basic logic in the prefix list, but with an action of **deny**. The reasoning is that when the **distribute-list prefix-list...** command refers directly to an IP prefix list, Cisco IOS then filters routes denied by the prefix list.

Route Summarization

Keeping routing tables small helps conserve memory and can improve the time required by a router to forward packets. Route summarization allows an engineer to keep the routing tables more manageable, without limiting reachability. Instead of advertising routes for every subnet, a router advertises a single route that encompasses multiple subnets. Each router can forward packets to the same set of destinations, but the routing table is smaller. For example, instead of advertising routes 10.11.0.0/24, 10.11.1.0/24, 10.11.2.0/24, and so on—all subnets up through 10.11.255.0/24—a router could advertise a single route for 10.11.0.0/16, which includes the exact same range of addresses.

Route summarization works best when the subnet planning process considers route summarization. To accommodate summarization, the engineer assigning subnets can assign larger address blocks to one part of the topology. The engineers working with that part of the internetwork can break the address blocks into individual subnets as needed. At the edge of that part of the network, the engineers can configure route summaries to be advertised to the other parts of the internetwork. In short, when possible, plan the route summaries before deploying the new parts of an internetwork, and then assign addresses to different parts of the internetwork within their assigned address blocks.

For example, consider Figure 5-17, which shows a variation on the same internetwork shown earlier in this chapter, with the address blocks planned before deployment.

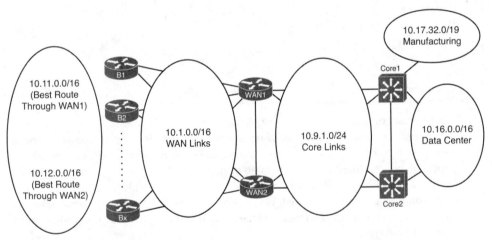

Figure 5-17 *Address Blocks Planned for Example Enterprise Internetwork*

Figure 5-17 shows the address blocks planned for various parts of the internetwork, as follows:

- Assign branch subnets from two consecutive ranges—10.11.0.0/16 and 10.12.0.0/16.

- Assign WAN router-to-router subnets from the range 10.1.0.0/16.

- Assign core LAN router-to-router subnets from the range 10.9.1.0/24.

- Assign data center subnets from the range 10.16.0.0/16.

■ Give the manufacturing division, which has a separate IT staff, address block 10.17.32.0/19.

Inside each of the circles in Figure 5-17, the engineering staff can assign subnets as the need arises. As long as addresses are not taken from one range and used in another part of the internetwork, the routers at the boundary between the regions (circles) in Figure 5-17 can configure EIGRP route summarization to both create one large summary route and prevent the advertisement of the smaller individual routes.

Calculating Summary Routes

The math to analyze a subnet/mask pair, or prefix/length pair, is identical to the math included as part of the CCNA certification. As such, this book does not attempt to explain those same concepts, other than this brief review of one useful shortcut when working with potential summary routes.

If you can trust that the subnet/mask or prefix/length is a valid subnet or summary, the following method can tell you the range of numbers represented. For example, consider 10.11.0.0/16. Written in subnet/mask form, it is 10.11.0.0/255.255.0.0. Then, invert the mask by subtracting the mask from 255.255.255.255, yielding 0.0.255.255 in this case. Add this inverted mask to the subnet number (10.11.0.0 in this case), and you have the high end of the range (10.11.255.255). So, summary 10.11.0.0/16 represents all numbers from 10.11.0.0 to 10.11.255.255.

When using less obvious masks, the process works the same. For example, consider 10.10.16.0/20. Converting to mask format, you have 10.10.16.0/255.255.240.0. Inverting the mask gives you 0.0.15.255. Adding the inverted mask to the subnet number gives you 10.10.31.255 and a range of 10.10.16.0–10.10.31.255.

Note that the process of adding the inverted subnet mask assumes that the prefix/length or subnet/mask is a valid subnet number or valid summary route. If it is not, you can still do the math, but neither the low end nor high end of the range is valid. For example, 10.10.16.0/19, similar to the previous example, is not actually a subnet number. 10.10.16.0 would be an IP address in subnet 10.10.0.0/19, with range of addresses 10.10.0.0–10.10.31.255.

Choosing Where to Summarize Routes

EIGRP supports route summarization at any router, unlike OSPF, which requires that summarization be performed only at area border routers (ABR) or autonomous system border routers (ASBR). EIGRP's flexibility helps when designing the internetwork, but it also poses some questions as to where to summarize EIGRP routes.

In some cases, the options are relatively obvious. For example, consider the 10.17.32.0/19 address block in manufacturing in Figure 5-17. The manufacturing division's router could summarize all its routes as a single 10.17.32.0/19 route when advertising to Core1. Alternately, Core1 could summarize all those same routes, advertising a summary for 10.17.32.0/19. In either case, packets from the rest of the internetwork will flow toward Core1 and then to the Manufacturing division.

Next, consider the 10.16.0.0/16 address block in the data center. Because all these subnets reside to the right of Layer 3 switches Core1 and Core2, these two devices could summarize 10.16.0.0/16. However, these routes could also be summarized on WAN1/WAN2 for advertisement to the branches on the left. Summarizing on Core1/Core2 helps reduce the size of the routing tables on WAN1 and WAN2. However, the sheer number of subnets in a data center is typically small compared to the number of small remote sites, so the savings of routing table space might be small. One advantage of summarizing 10.16.0.0/16 on WAN1/WAN2 instead of Core1/Core2 in this case is to avoid routing inefficiencies in the core of the internetwork.

Influencing the Choice of Best Route for Summary Routes

Often, engineers plan route summarization for the same address block on multiple routers. Such a design takes advantage of redundancy and can be used to perform basic load balancing of traffic across the various paths through the internetwork. Figure 5-18 shows one such example, with Routers WAN1 and WAN2 summarizing routes for the two address blocks located on the branch office LANs: 10.11.0.0/16 and 10.12.0.0/16.

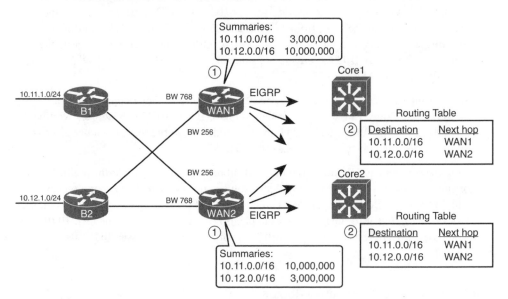

Figure 5-18   *Choosing Locations for Route Summarization*

The figure shows the advertisements of the summary routes. WAN1 and WAN2 both advertise the same summaries: 10.11.0.0/16 for some branches and 10.12.0.0/16 for the others. Note that by advertising the WAN routes, instead of filtering, the operations staff might have an easier time monitoring and troubleshooting the internetwork, while still meeting the design goal of reducing the size of the routing table. (Also, note that Router WAN1 summarizes Manufacturing's routes of 10.17.32.0/19.)

In some cases, the network designer has no preference for which of the two or more routers should be used to reach hosts within the summary route range. For example, for most data center designs, as shown earlier in Figure 5-13, the routes from the left of the figure toward the data center, through Core1 and Core2, would typically be considered equal.

However, in some cases, as in the design shown in Figure 5-18, the network designer wants to improve the metric of one of the summary routes for a single address block to make that route the preferred route. Using 10.11.0.0/16 as an example, consider this more detailed description of the design:

- Use two PVCs to each branch—one faster PVC with 768-kbps CIR and one slower PVC (either 128-kbps or 256-kbps CIR).

- Roughly half the branches should have a faster PVC connecting to Router WAN1, and the other half of the branches should have a faster PVC connecting to Router WAN2.

- Assign user subnets from the range 10.11.0.0/16 for branches that use WAN1 as the primary WAN access point, and from 10.12.0.0/16 for the branches that use WAN2 as primary.

- Routing should be influenced such that packets flow in both directions over the faster WAN link, assuming that link is working.

This design requires that both directions of packets flow over the faster PVC to each branch. Focusing on the outbound (core-toward-branch) direction for now, by following the design and setting the interface bandwidth settings to match the PVC speeds, the outbound routes will send packets over the faster PVCs. The main reason for the route choices is the following fact about summary routes with Cisco IOS:

Set the summary route's metric components based on the lowest metric route upon which the summary route is based.

By setting the interface bandwidth settings to match the design, the two WAN routers should summarize and advertise routes for 10.11.0.0/16 and 10.12.0.0/16, advertising these routes toward the core—but with different metrics.

WAN1 advertises its 10.11.0.0/16 route with a lower metric than WAN2's summary for 10.11.0.0/16, because all of WAN1's routes for subnets that begin with 10.11 are reachable over links set to use 768 kbps of bandwidth. All WAN1's links to branches whose subnets begin with 10.12 are reachable over links of speed 128 kbps or 256 kbps, so WAN1's metric is higher than WAN2's metric for the 10.12.0.0/16 summary. WAN2 follows the same logic but with the lower metric route for 10.12.0.0/16.

As a result of the advertisements on WAN1 and WAN2, the core routers both have routing table entries that drive traffic meant for the faster-through-WAN1 branches to WAN1, and traffic for the faster-through-WAN2 branches to WAN2.

Suboptimal Forwarding with Summarization

An important concept to consider when summarizing routes is that the packets might take a longer path than if summarization is not used. The idea works a little like this story. Say that you were traveling to Europe from the United States. You knew nothing of European geography, other than that you wanted to go to Paris. So, you look around and find hundreds of flights to Europe and just pick the cheapest one. When you get to

Europe, you worry about how to get the rest of the way to Paris—be it a taxi ride from the Paris airport or whether it takes a day of train travel. Although you do eventually get to Paris, if you had chosen to know more about European geography before you left, you could have saved yourself some travel time in Europe.

Similarly, routers that learn a summary route do not know about the details of the subnets inside the summary. Instead, like the person who just picked the cheapest flight to Europe, the routers pick the lowest metric summary route for a prefix. That router forwards packets based on the summary route. Later, when these packets arrive at routers that do know all the subnets inside the summary, those routers can then use the best route—be it a short route or long route.

For example, Figure 5-19 shows the less efficient routing of packets to host 10.11.1.1, a host off Router B1, assuming that the route summarization shown in Figure 5-14 still exists. When WAN1's 768-kbps CIR PVC to Router B1 fails, WAN1 does not change its route advertisement for its 10.11.0.0/16 summary route. When EIGRP advertises a summary route, the advertising router considers the summary route to be up and working unless all subordinate routes fail. Unless all of WAN1's specific routes in the 10.11.0.0/16 range failed, R1 would not notify routers on the right about any problem. So, when the example shown in Figure 5-19 begins, the 10.11.0.0/16 summary advertised by WAN1, as seen earlier in Figure 5-18, is still working, and both Core1 and Core2 use WAN1 as their next-hop router for their routes to 10.11.0.0/16.

10.11.1.0/24   10.11.1.0/24 - WAN2   10.11.0.0/16 - WAN1

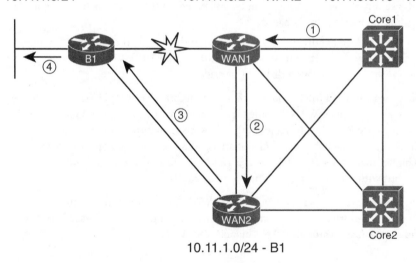

10.11.1.0/24 - B1

Figure 5-19 *Suboptimal Forwarding Path When Primary PVC Fails*

Following the steps in the figure:

Step 1. Core 1 sends a packet to 10.11.1.1, using its route for 10.16.0.0/16, to WAN1.

Step 2. WAN1, which has routes for all the subnets that begin with 10.11, has a route for 10.11.1.0/24 with WAN2 as the next hop (because WAN1's link to B1 has failed).

Step 3.   WAN2 has a route for 10.11.1.0/24, with B1 as the next hop, so WAN2 forwards the packet.

Step 4.   B1 forwards the packet to host 10.11.1.1.

Route Summarization Benefits and Trade-offs

The previous section showed details of a classic trade-off with route summarization: the benefits of the summary route versus the possibility of inefficient routing. For easier study, the benefits and trade-offs for route summarization are listed here:

Benefits:

- Smaller routing tables, while all destinations are still reachable.
- Reduces Query scope: EIGRP Query stops at a router that has a summary route that includes the subnet listed in the Query but not the specific route listed in the Query.
- EIGRP supports summarization at any location in the internetwork.
- The summary has the metric of the best of the subnets being summarized.

Trade-offs:

- Can cause suboptimal routing.
- Packets destined for inaccessible destinations will flow to the summarizing router before being discarded.

Configuring EIGRP Route Summarization

The more difficult part of EIGRP route summarization relates to the planning, design, and analysis of trade-offs, as covered in the preceding section. After you have made those design choices, configuring route summarization requires the addition of a few instances of the following interface subcommand:

```
ip summary-address eigrp asn prefix subnet-mask
```

When configured on an interface, the router changes its logic for the EIGRP Update messages sent out the interface, as follows:

- The router brings down, and then back up, all EIGRP neighbors reachable on that interface, effectively causing neighbors to forget previous topology information and to listen to new information (when the neighborships recover).
- When the neighborships recover, the router advertises the summary route, per the **ip summary-address** command, assuming that the router has at least one route whose address range is inside the range of the summary route.
- The router does not advertise the subordinate routes. (The term *subordinate route* refers to the routes whose address ranges are inside the range of addresses defined by the summary route.)

■ The router adds a route to its own routing table, for the summary prefix/prefix
  length, with an outgoing interface of null0.

In Figure 5-20, WAN1 and WAN2 summarize the routes for the data center in the range
10.16.0.0/16, instead of sending individual routes for this range to the branch offices.
Example 5-14 shows the results of summarization on both routers.

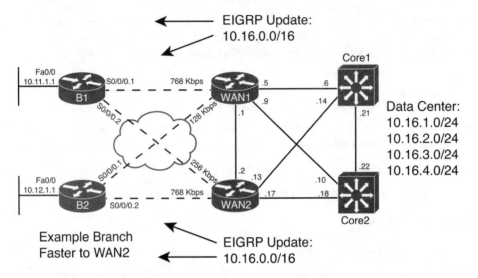

Figure 5-20   *Summary for 10.16.0.0/16 on WAN1, WAN2*

Example 5-14   *Summarizing Routes for Data Center (10.16.0.0/16) on WAN1/WAN2*

```
! On Router WAN2: !!!!!!!!!!!!!!!!!!!!!!!!!!!!!!!!!!!!!!!!!!!!!
WAN2# show running-config
! lines omitted for brevity
!
interface Serial0/0/0.1 point-to-point
 bandwidth 256
 ip address 10.1.2.1 255.255.255.252
 ip summary-address eigrp 1 10.16.0.0 255.255.0.0 5
 frame-relay interface-dlci 103
!
interface Serial0/0/0.2 point-to-point
 bandwidth 768
 ip address 10.1.2.5 255.255.255.252
 ip summary-address eigrp 1 10.16.0.0 255.255.0.0 5
 frame-relay interface-dlci 104
!
WAN2# show ip eigrp topology 10.16.0.0/16
IP-EIGRP (AS 1): Topology entry for 10.16.0.0/16
  State is Passive, Query origin flag is 1, 1 Successor(s), FD is 28416
  Routing Descriptor Blocks:
```

```
0.0.0.0 (Null0), from 0.0.0.0, Send flag is 0x0
    Composite metric is (28416/0), Route is Internal
    Vector metric:
      Minimum bandwidth is 100000 Kbit
      Total delay is 110 microseconds
      Reliability is 255/255
      Load is 1/255
      Minimum MTU is 1500
      Hop count is 1
10.1.2.2 (Serial0/0/0.1), from 10.1.2.2, Send flag is 0x0
    Composite metric is (11026688/3847936), Route is Internal
    Vector metric:
      Minimum bandwidth is 256 Kbit
      Total delay is 40110 microseconds
      Reliability is 255/255
      Load is 1/255
      Minimum MTU is 1500
      Hop count is 3

! Note that the following command lists only routes in the range
! of the summary - 10.16.0.0 - 10.16.255.255.
WAN2# show ip route 10.16.0.0 255.255.0.0 longer-prefixes
Codes: C - connected, S - static, R - RIP, M - mobile, B - BGP
       D - EIGRP, EX - EIGRP external, O - OSPF, IA - OSPF inter area
       N1 - OSPF NSSA external type 1, N2 - OSPF NSSA external type 2
       E1 - OSPF external type 1, E2 - OSPF external type 2
       i - IS-IS, su - IS-IS summary, L1 - IS-IS level-1, L2 - IS-IS level-2
       ia - IS-IS inter area, * - candidate default, U - per-user static route
       o - ODR, P - periodic downloaded static route


Gateway of last resort is not set


     10.0.0.0/8 is variably subnetted, 23 subnets, 6 masks
D       10.16.2.0/24 [90/156160] via 10.9.1.14, 00:19:06, FastEthernet0/0.12
D       10.16.3.0/24 [90/156160] via 10.9.1.14, 00:19:06, FastEthernet0/0.12
D       10.16.0.0/16 is a summary, 00:14:07, Null0
D       10.16.1.0/24 [90/28416] via 10.9.1.18, 00:19:06, FastEthernet0/1.16
                     [90/28416] via 10.9.1.14, 00:19:06, FastEthernet0/0.12
D       10.16.4.0/24 [90/156160] via 10.9.1.14, 00:19:06, FastEthernet0/0.12
WAN2# show ip route 10.16.0.0 255.255.0.0
Routing entry for 10.16.0.0/16
  Known via "eigrp 1", distance 5, metric 28416, type internal
  Redistributing via eigrp 1
  Routing Descriptor Blocks:
  * directly connected, via Null0
      Route metric is 28416, traffic share count is 1
```

```
Total delay is 110 microseconds, minimum bandwidth is 100000 Kbit
Reliability 255/255, minimum MTU 1500 bytes
Loading 1/255, Hops 0
```

Example 5-14 shows the results only on Router WAN2, but WAN1 will be identically configured with the **ip summary-address** command. With only two branch office routers actually implemented in my lab, WAN2 needs only two **ip summary-address** commands: one for the subinterface connected to Router B1 and another for the subinterface connected to B2. With a full implementation, this same command would be needed on each subinterface connected to a branch router.

The example also shows how a router like WAN2 uses a summary route to null0. This route—10.16.0.0/16 with an outgoing interface of null0—causes the router (WAN2) to discard packets matched by this route. However, as you can see from the end of Example 5-14, WAN2 also has routes for all the known specific subnets. Pulling all these thoughts together, when the summarizing router receives a packet within the summary route's range:

■ If the packet matches a more specific route than the summary route, the packet is forwarded based on that route.

■ When the packet does not match a more specific route, it matches the summary route and is discarded.

To ensure that the router adds this local summary route, the router uses the administrative distance (AD) setting of 5. The user might have typed the **ip summary-address eigrp 1 10.16.0.0 255.255.0.0** command, without the **5** at the end. Even so, Cisco IOS will add this default AD value as seen in Example 5-10. With an AD of 5, WAN2 will ignore any EIGRP-advertised summary routes for 10.16.0.0/16—for example, the summary created by neighbor WAN1—because EIGRP's default AD for internal routes is 90. In fact, the output of WAN2's **show ip eigrp topology 10.16.0.0/16** command lists two known routes for 10.16.0.0/16: one to null0 and the other to branch Router WAN1 (outgoing interface S0/0/0.1). WAN2 uses the lower-AD route to null0, which prevents a routing loop. (Note that this summary route with outgoing interface null0 is often called a *discard route*.)

Next, consider the results on the branch routers. The following might be reasonable design requirements that should be verified on the branch routers:

■ Each branch router's route for 10.16.0.0/16 should use the primary (faster) PVC (see Figure 5-20).

■ Each branch router should be able to converge quickly to the other 10.16.0.0/16 summary route without using EIGRP Queries (in other words, there should be an FS route).

Example 5-15 confirms that both requirements are met.

Example 5-15 *Results of the 10.16.0.0/16 Summary on Routers B1, B2*

```
! Router B1 first !!!!!!!!!!!!!!!!!!!!!
B1# show ip route 10.16.0.0 255.255.0.0 longer-prefixes
! lines omitted for brevity


     10.0.0.0/8 is variably subnetted, 5 subnets, 3 masks
D        10.16.0.0/16 [90/3847936] via 10.1.1.1, 00:16:53, Serial0/0/0.1

B1# show ip eigrp topology
! lines omitted for brevity
P 10.16.0.0/16, 1 successors, FD is 3847936
        via 10.1.1.1 (3847936/28416), Serial0/0/0.1
        via 10.1.2.1 (10514688/28416), Serial0/0/0.2


! Router B2 Next !!!!!!!!!!!!!!!!!!!!!
B2# show ip route 10.16.0.0 255.255.0.0 longer-prefixes
! lines omitted for brevity


     10.0.0.0/8 is variably subnetted, 5 subnets, 3 masks
D        10.16.0.0/16 [90/3847936] via 10.1.2.5, 00:16:44, Serial0/0/0.2
```

First, on Router B1, the router has an IP route for 10.16.0.0/16, with outgoing interface S0/0/0.1. Per Figure 5-20, this subinterface indeed connects to the primary PVC. Per the **show ip eigrp topology** command, two possible routes for 10.16.0.0/16 are listed; this command only lists successor and feasible successor routes. Also, note that the FS route's RD (28,416) is less than the successor route's FD (3,847,936), which means that the secondary route indeed meets the feasibility condition.

The reverse is true on Router B2. B2's best route for 10.16.0.0/16 uses its S0/0/0.2, which connects to B2's primary (faster) PVC through WAN2. Although not shown, it also lists its backup route over the slower PVC as a feasible successor.

The route summarization feature discussed in this section is sometimes referred to as *manual route summarization* to contrast it with the term *auto-summarization*. EIGRP auto-summarization is explained next.

Auto-summary

Automatic summarization, also called *auto-summary*, causes a router to automatically advertise a summary route under certain conditions, without the use of the **ip summary-address** command. When using auto-summary, if a router has interfaces in more than one Class A, B, or C network, that router will advertise a single summary route for an entire Class A, B, or C network into the other classful network, rather than advertise routes for the individual subnets. The following is a more formal definition:

Key Topic

> When a router has multiple working interfaces, and those interfaces use IP addresses in different classful networks, the router advertises a summary route for each classful network on interfaces attached to a different classful network.

The auto-summary feature first existed as a required feature of classful routing protocols. By definition, classful routing protocols (RIPv1 and IGRP) do not advertise subnet mask information. The omission of the subnet mask in routing updates causes several design problems—in particular, these protocols cannot support variable-length subnet masks (VLSM), route summarization, or discontiguous network designs.

The newer IGPs (for example, EIGRP, OSPF, and RIPv2) are classless routing protocols, because they advertise the subnet mask and support VLSM. However, with auto-summary enabled, EIGRP acts like classful routing protocols in one specific way: They do not support discontiguous networks. To support discontiguous networks with EIGRP, simply disable auto-summary.

To better understand discontiguous networks, consider this analogy. U.S. residents can appreciate the concept of a discontiguous network based on the common term *contiguous 48*, referring to the 48 U.S. states other than Alaska and Hawaii. To drive to Alaska from the contiguous 48 U.S. states, for example, you must drive through another country (Canada), so Alaska is not contiguous with the 48 states. In other words, it is discontiguous.

More formally:

- **Contiguous network:** A single classful network in which packets sent between every pair of subnets will pass only through subnets of that same classful network, without having to pass through subnets of any other classful network.

- **Discontiguous network:** A single classful network in which packets sent between at least one pair of subnets must pass through subnets of a different classful network.

Figure 5-21 shows a classic example of a discontiguous network 10.0.0.0. Subnets of Class A network 10.0.0.0 exist on the left and the right, with subnets of Class B network 172.16.0.0 in the middle of the internetwork. Following the figure, the problem created by the auto-summary feature is described.

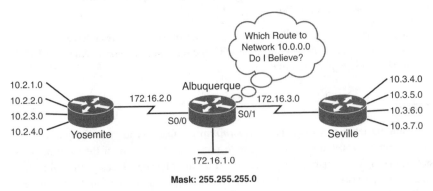

Figure 5-21 *Discontiguous Network 10.0.0.0*

The problem is that when EIGRP auto-summarizes routes at the boundary between classful networks, routers in other classful networks cannot route packets to all the destinations. For example, because both Yosemite and Seville use auto-summary, they both advertise a route for 10.0.0.0/8 to Albuquerque. Albuquerque might choose one of the two as the better route—for example, it might choose the route to the left, through Yosemite. However, in that case, Albuquerque cannot forward packets to the network 10.0.0.0 hosts on the right. Even if Albuquerque decided to add both routes to its routing table, the load sharing typically occurs per destination IP address, not per subnet. So, some packets might be delivered to the correct host and others not.

For EIGRP, two solutions exist. First, you could design the network to not use a discontiguous network. Alternatively, you can just disable auto-summary using the **no auto-summary** subcommand inside EIGRP configuration mode. This command affects the behavior of the router on which it is configured only and tells that router to not advertise a summary route for the entire classful network. Instead, that router advertises all the subnets, as if the auto-summary feature did not exist.

Note   The **auto-summary** and **no auto-summary** commands have no effect on routers that connect to a single classful network.

Default Routes

A router's default route matches the destination of all packets that are not matched by any other route in the IP routing table. In fact, a default route can be thought of as the ultimate summary route—a route for the prefix that includes all IPv4 addresses, as represented by prefix/length 0.0.0.0/0.

This section first examines the most common use of default routes inside an enterprise: to draw Internet traffic toward the Internet-connected routers without having to put routes for all Internet destinations into the enterprise routers' routing tables. Following that, this section examines two methods for EIGRP to advertise the default route.

Default Routing to the Internet Router

Consider an enterprise network and its connection to the Internet, as shown in Figure 5-22. For now, the design shows a single Internet-facing router (I1). As is often the case, the entire enterprise in this figure uses private IP addresses. In this case, all enterprise subnets are part of private Class A network 10.0.0.0.

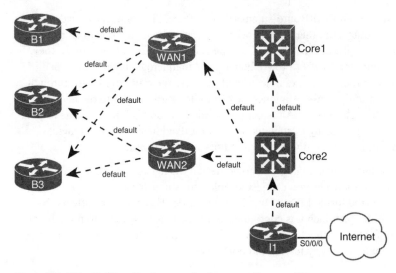

Figure 5-22   *Pulling Packets to the Internet Router (I1)*

From a design perspective, the entire enterprise can use a default route to forward packets to the Internet. To accomplish this design, the Internet-facing router advertises a default route. All routers flood this default prefix throughout the EIGRP domain, building their own default routes.

When converged, all routers have a default route, plus the usual enterprise routes. Packets destined for addresses inside the enterprise use the same old routes, ignoring the default route. Packets destined outside the enterprise use each router's respective default route because no other routes match the destination. Eventually, these packets arrive at Router I1. When I1 receives these packets, it can forward toward the Internet, either based on a default route or on routes learned using BGP.

Figure 5-22 shows a case with just one Internet-facing router, but with multiple routers, the same concepts can be used. The multiple Internet-facing routers can each advertise a default route, and each enterprise router will think that one of the available defaults is best—causing the packets to arrive at the nearest Internet access point.

Default Routing Configuration with EIGRP

This section examines the two main options for EIGRP to advertise default routes: to define a static default route and advertise it with EIGRP and to flag an existing route to be used also as a default route.

Advertising Static Default Routes with EIGRP

To cause the advertisement of the default routes shown in Figure 5-22, Router I1 can follow these steps:

Step 1.   Create a static route default route using the **ip route 0.0.0.0 0.0.0.0 S0/0/0** command.

Step 2. Inject this route into the EIGRP topology database, either using the **network 0.0.0.0** command or by redistributing the static route.

First, examine the command listed for Step 1: **ip route 0.0.0.0 0.0.0.0 S0/0/0**. The prefix and mask together represent all IPv4 addresses. The reasoning is that if a mask of 255.255.0.0 means "the last two octets can be any value," and 255.0.0.0 means "the last three octets can be any value," a subnet mask of 0.0.0.0 means that all four octets can be any value. The outgoing interface, S0/0/0 in this case, tells I1 to send packets for otherwise unknown destinations over the link to the Internet, as intended.

After Step 1, Router I1 has a route in its routing table, but EIGRP does not yet advertise the route. I1 could be configured to perform route redistribution for this static route. (Refer to Chapter 10 for more information on route redistribution.) The other option is to use the **network 0.0.0.0** EIGRP subcommand. Oddly enough, this is a special case in which Cisco IOS thinks "if my routing table has a default route in it, put a default route (0.0.0.0/0) into the EIGRP table." (If the route leaves the routing table, the router will notify neighbors that the route has failed.)

Configuring a Default Network

The second option for creating a default route is to flag a route for a classful network—for a prefix that will be advertised into the EIGRP domain—as a route that can be used as a default route. Then each router can use the forwarding details in that route—the outgoing interface and next-hop router—as its default route.

Configuring this feature requires a couple of steps. The concepts require the most thought, with the configuration commands that follow being relatively simple:

Key Topic

Step 1. On the router to which all traffic should be directed, identify a classful network that can be advertised into the EIGRP domain, and ensure that network is being advertised into EIGRP (typically using the EIGRP **network** command).

Step 2. Configure that network as a default network using the global command **ip default-network** *network-number*.

Step 1 requires a Class A, B, or C network, known in the routing table of the router that will generate the default route (Router I1 in Figure 5-23). Most often, that route is either created off a loopback interface for the purpose of making this process work, or an existing route on the Internet side of the router is used.

Figure 5-23 shows two examples. First, Class C network 198.133.219.0/24 exists off I1's S0/0/0 interface, so I1 has a connected route for this Class C network in its routing table. Alternatively, the engineer could configure a loopback interface, such as loopback 8, so that I1 would have a connected route for 192.31.7.0/24. In both cases, the routes would need to be advertised into EIGRP, by matching the address using the **network** command.

If the configuration stopped at Step 1, the enterprise routers simply know yet another route. By adding the **ip default-network** command to refer to one of these networks, EIGRP then flags this route as a candidate default route. As a result, each EIGRP router treats its route for this particular network also as if it were a default route.

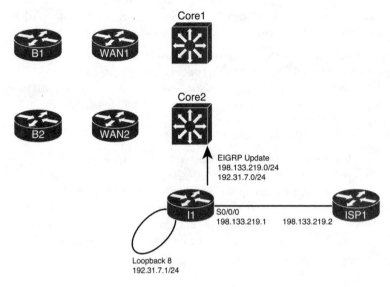

Figure 5-23 *Example Default Networks*

Example 5-16 shows an example of the configuration on Router I1, along with some of the **show** commands on Router I1.

Example 5-16 *Configuring a Default Network on Router I1*

```
I1# configure terminal
Enter configuration commands, one per line.  End with CNTL/Z.
I1(config)# interface loopback 8
I1(config-if)# ip address 192.31.7.1 255.255.255.0
I1(config-if)# router eigrp 1
I1(config-router)# network 192.31.7.0
I1(config-router)# exit
I1(config)# ip default-network 192.31.7.0
I1(config-router)# ^Z


I1# show ip route
Codes: C - connected, S - static, R - RIP, M - mobile, B - BGP
       D - EIGRP, EX - EIGRP external, O - OSPF, IA - OSPF inter area
       N1 - OSPF NSSA external type 1, N2 - OSPF NSSA external type 2
       E1 - OSPF external type 1, E2 - OSPF external type 2
       i - IS-IS, su - IS-IS summary, L1 - IS-IS level-1, L2 - IS-IS level-2
       ia - IS-IS inter area, * - candidate default, U - per-user static route
       o - ODR, P - periodic downloaded static route

Gateway of last resort is not set

     10.0.0.0/8 is variably subnetted, 15 subnets, 3 masks
! lines omitted for brevity
```

```
C*    192.31.7.0/24 is directly connected, Loopback8

I1# show ip eigrp topology 192.31.7.0/24
IP-EIGRP (AS 1): Topology entry for 192.31.7.0/24
  State is Passive, Query origin flag is 1, 1 Successor(s), FD is 128256
  Routing Descriptor Blocks:
  0.0.0.0 (Loopback8), from Connected, Send flag is 0x0
    Composite metric is (128256/0), Route is Internal
    Vector metric:
      Minimum bandwidth is 10000000 Kbit
      Total delay is 5000 microseconds
      Reliability is 255/255
      Load is 1/255
      Minimum MTU is 1514
      Hop count is 0
      Exterior flag is set
```

The configuration has several results, as seen in the example:

- A connected route for 192.31.7.0/24, a Class C network

- The advertisement of that network into EIGRP because of the **network 192.31.7.0**
  command

- The setting of the exterior flag on the route

Because of the **ip default-network 192.31.7.0** command, the routing table lists the route
as a candidate default route, as denoted by an asterisk.

Interestingly, the router with the **ip default-network** command configured (I1 in this
case) does not use that route as a default route, as indicated by the highlighted phrase
"Gateway of last resort is not set." (*Gateway of last resort* refers to the next-hop router
of a router's current default route.) Although I1 flags the route as a candidate default
route, I1 itself does not use that route as its default, because I1 is actually the original
advertiser of the default.

Moving on to another enterprise router, in this case B1, you can see in Example 5-17 that
not only does the remote router learn the candidate default route, but that B1 also uses
this same information as B1's default route.

Example 5-17 *Gateway of Last Resort on Router B1*

```
B1# show ip route
Codes: C - connected, S - static, R - RIP, M - mobile, B - BGP
       D - EIGRP, EX - EIGRP external, O - OSPF, IA - OSPF inter area
       N1 - OSPF NSSA external type 1, N2 - OSPF NSSA external type 2
       E1 - OSPF external type 1, E2 - OSPF external type 2
       i - IS-IS, su - IS-IS summary, L1 - IS-IS level-1, L2 - IS-IS level-2
       ia - IS-IS inter area, * - candidate default, U - per-user static route
```

```
        o - ODR, P - periodic downloaded static route

Gateway of last resort is 10.1.1.1 to network 192.31.7.0

     10.0.0.0/8 is variably subnetted, 15 subnets, 3 masks
Lines omitted for brevity
D*    192.31.7.0/24 [90/2297856] via 10.1.1.1, 00:05:10, Serial0/0/0.1
```

In this case, B1 has indeed learned an EIGRP route for 192.31.7.0/24, a route flagged as exterior. Because this happens to be the only candidate default route learned by B1 at this point, it is the best default route. So, B1 sets its gateway of last resort to 10.1.1.1— the next-hop IP address of B1's route to 192.31.7.0/24. If B1 knew of multiple candidate default routes, it would have chosen the best route based on administrative distance and then metric, and used that route as the basis for the gateway of last resort.

Exam Preparation Tasks

Planning Practice

The CCNP ROUTE exam expects test takers to review design documents, create implementation plans, and create verification plans. This section provides exercises that can help you to take a step back from the minute details of the topics in this chapter so that you can think about the same technical topics from the planning perspective.

For each planning practice table, simply complete the table. Note that any numbers in parentheses represent the number of options listed for each item in the solutions in Appendix F, "Completed Planning Practice Tables."

Design Review Table

Table 5-8 lists several design goals related to this chapter. If these design goals were listed in a design document, and you had to take that document and develop an implementation plan, what implementation options come to mind? For any configuration items, a general description can be used, without concern about the specific parameters.

Table 5-8 *Design Review*

Design Goal	Possible Implementation Choices Covered in This Chapter
Limit consumption of IP subnets in Frame Relay WAN design.	
In a relatively slow Frame Relay WAN, protect against consuming too much bandwidth with overhead EIGRP traffic.	
Plan to change bandwidth from 1X CIR to 2X CIR on all Frame Relay subinterfaces.	
Plan to set bandwidth to values other than actual interface speeds to manipulate EIGRP metrics.	
A goal of ensuring all remote routers' secondary EIGRP routes do not require Queries for convergence.	
What tools can we use to meet the design goal of fast convergence? (four items)	
R1 and R2 will advertise the same summary route; ensure that R1 is the preferred EIGRP path for that summary.	

Design Goal	Possible Implementation Choices Covered in This Chapter
Prevent the edge routers in sites for one division of the company from knowing routes for subnets in another division.	
Always ensure that the shortest path is taken with each route.	

Implementation Plan Peer Review Table

Table 5-9 shows a list of questions that others might ask, or that you might think about, during a peer review of another network engineer's implementation plan. Complete the table by answering the questions.

Table 5-9 *Notable Questions from This Chapter to Consider During an Implementation Plan Peer Review*

Question	Answer
A Frame Relay multipoint interface, with 20 PVCs attached, has a configuration for 10 percent of the bandwidth to be used for EIGRP. How much is allocated per PVC?	
A configuration lists the **no ip split-horizon** command. When would that matter?	
The plan calls for setting all EIGRP K-values to 1. What negative effect could this have on routes in the IP routing table?	
The configuration uses offset lists. Will that impact the calculation of FD and/or RD?	
The plan lists a sample configuration migrating an interface from delay 20 to delay 200. How much will the metric go up?	
The plan shows extensive use of Class C private networks inside a large enterprise. What effect might EIGRP auto-summary have?	
The plan shows a sample configuration of the **ip summary-address eigrp 1 10.10.0.0 255.255.252.0** command on Router R1. What routes should I see on R1? What will their administrative distance be?	

Question	Answer
The plan shows the use of the **variance 4** command. What must be configured to add other routes to a routing table? (two items)	
The plan calls for filtering 10.10.10.0/26 and 10.10.12.0/26, but not 10.10.11.0/24. What tools can be used?	

Create an Implementation Plan Table

To practice skills useful when creating your own EIGRP implementation plan, list in Table 5-10 configuration commands related to the configuration of the following features. You might want to record your answers outside the book and set a goal to complete this table (and others like it) from memory during your final reviews before taking the exam.

Table 5-10 *Implementation Plan Configuration Memory Drill*

Feature	Configuration Commands/Notes
Enabling EIGRP on interfaces	
Enabling or disabling Split Horizon for EIGRP	
Setting the bandwidth consumed by EIGRP on an interface	
Setting an interface's logical bandwidth	
Setting an interface's logical delay	
K-values	
Configuring an EIGRP offset list that matches a prefix	
Configuring an EIGRP offset list that matches a prefix and prefix length	
Configuring a summary route	
Enabling or disabling auto-summary	
Configuring unequal-cost load balancing	
Configuring an EIGRP stub router	
Filtering EIGRP routes using numbered	
ACLs	
Filtering EIGRP routes using prefix lists	

Feature	Configuration Commands/Notes
Enabling filtering EIGRP routes using route maps	
Configure a default route using **ip default-network**	
Configure a default route using static routes	

Choose Commands for a Verification Plan Table

To practice skills useful when creating your own EIGRP verification plan, list in Table 5-11 all commands that supply the requested information. You might want to record your answers outside the book, and set a goal to complete this table (and others like it) from memory during your final reviews before taking the exam.

Key
Topic

Table 5-11 *Verification Plan Memory Drill*

Information Needed	Command
The composite metric values for all EIGRP prefixes.	
Display EIGRP Split Horizon settings.	
Calculate the maximum bandwidth EIGRP will consume on a physical or point-to-point subinterface.	
Calculate the maximum bandwidth EIGRP will consume per PVC on a multipoint Frame Relay subinterface.	
Display the increase in RD after implementing an EIGRP offset list.	
Display interface bandwidth and delay settings.	
List EIGRP K-values.	
Find the number of successor and feasible successor routes.	
Find all routes, including nonsuccessors.	
Determine whether the local router is a stub router.	
Determine whether a neighboring router is a stub router.	
Display a summary IP route.	

Information Needed	Command
On summarizing router, display EIGRP topology info on a summary route.	
On summarizing router, display IP routes for a summary route and its subordinate routes.	
On summarizing router, display the administrative distance of the null route.	
Display the current auto-summary setting.	
Find the current settings of variance and maximum-paths.	
Display messages each time EIGRP suppresses a prefix advertisement because of Split Horizon.	
Display prefix lists.	
Display route maps.	
Determine whether a prefix in the EIGRP topology table has been flagged as a candidate default route.	
Determine whether an IP route has been flagged as a candidate default route.	
Display a router's preferred default route.	

Review All the Key Topics

Review the most important topics from the chapter, noted with the Key Topic icon in the outer margin of the page. Table 5-12 lists a reference of these key topics and the page numbers on which each is found.

Key
Topic

Table 5-12   *Key Topics for Chapter 5*

Key Topic Element	Description	Page Number
List	Three sources for seeding a local router's EIGRP topology table	162
List	EIGRP message types (5)	163
List	Rules for EIGRP topology exchange	166
Definitions	Feasible Distance, Reported Distance	172
List	Key points about variance	183

Key Topic Element	Description	Page Number
Definition	Feasibility condition	184
Figure 5-9	Successors and Feasible Successors with EIGRP	185
List	Two commands to find all EIGRP routes versus all successor/feasible successor routes	185
List	EIGRP process of finding routes when going active	188
Definition	EIGRP stub router	190
Table 5-4	Parameters on the **eigrp stub** Command	191
Definition	Rule by which summary routes reduce Query scope	192
List	Prefix list logic	199
Table 5-6	LE and GE Parameters on IP Prefix List, and the Implied Range of Prefix Lengths	200
List	Key points of route map logic	205
List	Benefits and trade-offs regarding the use of route summarization	213
List	A summary of what occurs when configuring an EIGRP summary route	213
Definition	Auto-summary	217
List	Steps to advertise static routes with EIGRP	220
List	Steps to configure a default network	221

Complete the Tables and Lists from Memory

Print a copy of Appendix D, "Memory Tables," (found on the CD) or at least the section for this chapter, and complete the tables and lists from memory. Appendix E, "Memory Tables Answer Key," also on the CD, includes completed tables and lists to check your work.

Define Key Terms

Define the following key terms from this chapter, and check your answers in the glossary.

feasibility condition, feasible distance, feasible successor, full update, partial update, reported distance, advertised distance, successor, Split Horizon, bandwidth, delay, K-value, offset list, going active, DUAL, Query scope, EIGRP stub router, variance, prefix list, route map, distribute list, address block, subordinate route, auto-summary, default network, static default route, gateway of last resort

This chapter covers the following subjects:

- **EIGRP for IPv6:** This section compares and contrasts EIGRP for IPv4 and for IPv6, and shows how to configure EIGRP for IPv6. Verification commands are also covered in this section.

- **Named EIGRP:** This section examines an alternate approach to configuring EIGRP. While traditional EIGRP configuration necessitates that some commands be entered under interface configuration mode and other commands be entered under router configuration mode, *Named EIGRP* allows those commands to be entered collectively, under a single EIGRP virtual instance.

CHAPTER 6

EIGRP for IPv6 and Named EIGRP

EIGRP's original architecture allowed it to support the routing of multiple protocols, including IPv4, IPX, and AppleTalk. As a result, it was not difficult for Cisco to allow IPv6 support with Enhanced Interior Gateway Routing Protocol (EIGRP). One of the primary configuration differences between EIGRP for IPv4 and EIGRP for IPv6 is how an interface is told to participate in an EIGRP autonomous system (AS). As you'll see in this chapter, you enter interface configuration mode and directly tell the interface to route IPv6 traffic as part of a specific EIGRP AS, as opposed to using a **network** command in router configuration mode for EIGRP.

Another fairly recent enhancement to EIGRP is a new hierarchical approach to configuration, specifically *Named EIGRP* configuration. While the configuration of Named EIGRP might seem more complex at first, it allows you to enter all your EIGRP configuration commands under a single configuration section, rather than going back and forth between interface configuration mode and router configuration mode, which introduces the possibility of mistyping the EIGRP AS every time you go back into router configuration mode. Also, for many complex EIGRP configurations, a Named EIGRP configuration requires fewer commands than classic EIGRP configuration.

"Do I Know This Already?" Quiz

The "Do I Know This Already?" quiz allows you to assess whether you should read the entire chapter. If you miss no more than one of these six self-assessment questions, you might want to move ahead to the "Exam Preparation Tasks" section. Table 6-1 lists the major headings in this chapter and the "Do I Know This Already?" quiz questions covering the material in those headings, so that you can assess your knowledge of these specific areas. The answers to the "Do I Know This Already?" quiz appear in Appendix A.

Table 6-1 *"Do I Know This Already?" Foundation Topics Section-to-Question Mapping*

Foundation Topics Section	Questions
EIGRP for IPv6	1, 2
Named EIGRP	3–6

1. You are attempting to configure EIGRP for IPv6 on a router. However, Cisco IOS presents you with a message indicating that routing is not enabled for IPv6. What command would you issue to enable IPv6 routing?

    a. Router(config)# **ipv6 unicast-routing**

    b. Router(config-rtr)# **ipv6 unicast-routing**

    c. Router(config-rtr)# **ipv6 cef**

    d. Router(config)# **ipv6 eigrp**

2. Router R1 connects to Router R2 over an Ethernet LAN with both routers using their Fa0/0 interfaces. R1 learns a route from R2 using EIGRP for IPv6. That route lists Fa0/0 as the outgoing interface with R2 as the next hop. The configuration excerpt shows all relevant configuration on R2's Fa0/0 interface. Which of the following is true about R1's route?

```
interface f0/0
mac-address 1111.1111.1111
ipv6 address 2000::/64 eui-64
ipv6 address 2001::1/64
```

    a. The next hop is 2000::1311:11FF:FE11:1111

    b. The next hop is FE80::1311:11FF:FE11:1111

    c. The next hop is FE80::5111:11FF:FE11:1111

    d. The next hop is 2001::1

3. Under what configuration mode for Named EIGRP would you configure a passive interface?

    a. Address-Family configuration mode

    b. Address-Family-Interface configuration mode

    c. Address-Family-Global configuration mode

    d. Address-Family-Topology configuration mode

4. Under what configuration mode for Named EIGRP would you configure variance?

    a. Address-Family configuration mode

    b. Address-Family-interface configuration mode

    c. Address-Family-Global configuration mode

    d. Address-Family-Topology configuration mode

5. When configuring Named EIGRP, you want to specify the Hello interval for all interfaces. You could go into address-family-interface configuration mode for each interface and enter the **hello-interval** command. However, what command could you give from address-family configuration mode to go into a configuration mode that allowed you to configure the Hello Interval for all interfaces with a single **hello-interval** command?

    a. address-family global

    b. af-interface default

    c. af-interface-all

    d. address-family *

6. You configured a router with a Named EIGRP configuration. What command would you use to view the EIGRP for IPv4 topology table?

    a. show address-family ipv4 topology

    b. show ip eigrp topology

    c. show address-family-topology

    d. show ip address-family

Foundation Topics

IPv6 is no longer a curiosity that we know we will need to migrate to someday. IPv6 is happening all around us right now. So, we have to be able to support it on our networks. What IGP routing protocol options do we have for IPv6? Well, the common ones we might think of are RIP next generation (RIPng), EIGRP, and Open Shortest Path First version 3 (OSPFv3). The choice of which routing protocol to use will probably be based on what we are currently using to route IPv4 traffic.

However, if you are currently running EIGRP for your IPv4 networks, you might want to stay with EIGRP as your interior gateway protocol (IGP) of choice to support IPv6 traffic. That is the focus of the first section in this chapter.

The second major section of this chapter introduces you to a new paradigm for EIGRP configuration, called *named mode* configuration, which we will also refer to as *Named EIGRP*. This hierarchical approach to configuration can help reduce configuration errors, while being more efficient for complex EIGRP configurations.

EIGRP for IPv6

Cisco originally created EIGRP to advertise routes for IPv4, IPX, and AppleTalk. This original EIGRP architecture easily allowed for yet another Layer 3 protocol, IPv6, to be added. As a result, Cisco did not have to change EIGRP significantly to support IPv6, so many similarities exist between the IPv4 and IPv6 versions of EIGRP.

Note   Many documents, including this chapter, refer to the IPv6 version of EIGRP as *EIGRP for IPv6*. However, some documents at www.cisco.com also refer to this protocol as *EIGRPv6*, not because it is the sixth version of the protocol, but because it implies a relationship with IPv6.

This section begins with a discussion of the similarities and differences between the IPv4 and IPv6 versions of EIGRP. The remaining coverage of EIGRP in this section focuses on the changes to EIGRP configuration and verification in support of IPv6.

EIGRP for IPv4 and IPv6: Theory and Comparisons

For the most part, EIGRP for IPv4 and for IPv6 have many similarities. The following list outlines some of the key differences:

■ EIGRP for IPv6 advertises IPv6 prefixes/lengths, rather than IPv4 subnet/mask information.

■ EIGRP for IPv6 uses the neighbor's link-local address as the next-hop IP address; EIGRP for IPv4 has no equivalent concept.

- EIGRP for IPv6 encapsulates its messages in IPv6 packets, rather than IPv4 packets.

- EIGRP for IPv4 defaults to use automatic route summarization at the boundaries of classful IPv4 networks. IPv6 has no concept of classful networks, so EIGRP for IPv6 cannot perform any automatic summarization.

- EIGRP for IPv6 does not require neighbors to be in the same IPv6 subnet as a requirement to become neighbors.

Other than these differences, most of the details of EIGRP for IPv6 work like EIGRP for IPv4. For reference, Table 6-2 compares the features of each.

Table 6-2   *Comparing EIGRP for IPv4 and IPv6*

Feature	EIGRP for IPv4	EIGRP for IPv6
Advertises routes for...	IPv4	IPv6
Layer 3 protocol for EIGRP messages	IPv4	IPv6
Layer 3 header protocol type	88	88
UDP port	—	—
Uses Successor, Feasible Successor logic	Yes	Yes
Uses DUAL	Yes	Yes
Supports VLSM	Yes	Yes
Can perform automatic summarization	Yes	—
Uses triggered updates	Yes	Yes
Uses composite metric, default using bandwidth and delay	Yes	Yes
Metric meaning infinity	$2^{32} - 1$	$2^{32} - 1$
Supports route tags	Yes	Yes
Multicast Update destination	224.0.0.10	FF02::A

Configuring EIGRP for IPv6

EIGRP for IPv6 follows the same basic configuration style as for RIPng. The specific EIGRP for IPv6 configuration steps are as follows:

Step 1.   Enable IPv6 routing with the **ipv6 unicast-routing** global command.

Step 2.   Enable EIGRP using the **ipv6 router eigrp** {*1 – 65535*} global configuration command.

Step 3. Enable IPv6 on the interface, typically with one of these two methods:

- Configure an IPv6 unicast address on each interface, using the **ipv6 address** *address/prefix-length* [**eui-64**] interface command.

- Configure the **ipv6 enable** command, which enables IPv6 and causes the router to derive its link-local address.

Step 4. Enable EIGRP on the interface with the **ipv6 eigrp** *asn* interface subcommand (where the *asn* matches the **ipv6 router eigrp** *asn* global configuration command).

Step 5. Enable EIGRP for IPv6 with a **no shutdown** command while in EIGRP configuration mode, if EIGRP is currently disabled.

Step 6. If no EIGRP router ID has been automatically chosen, because of not having at least one working interface with an IPv4 address, configure an EIGRP router ID with the **router-id** *rid* command in EIGRP configuration mode.

The first four steps essentially mirror the four steps in the RIPng configuration process discussed in Chapter 3, "IPv6 Review and RIPng." The same interdependencies exist for EIGRP for IPv6 as well. Specifically, the command at Step 2 works only if Step 1's command has been configured, and the command at Step 4 fails if the command at Step 3 has not yet been completed.

EIGRP for IPv6 might also require Steps 5 and 6, whereas RIPng does not need equivalent steps. First, at Step 5, Cisco IOS supports the ability to stop and start the EIGRP process with the **shutdown** and **no shutdown** router mode subcommands.

Step 6 shows the other difference as compared to RIPng configuration, but this step might or might not be needed. The EIGRP for IPv6 process must have a router ID (RID) before the process works. EIGRP for IPv6 uses the same process as EIGRP for IPv4 for choosing the RID. The EIGRP for IPv6 RID is indeed a 32-bit number. The following list defines how EIGRP for IPv6 picks its RID, listed in the order of preference:

Step 1. Use the configured value (using the **router-id** *a.b.c.d* EIGRP subcommand under the **ipv6 router eigrp** configuration mode).

Step 2. Use the highest IPv4 address on an up/up loopback interface.

Step 3. Use the highest IPv4 address on an up/up nonloopback interface.

Note that although most installations already have IPv4 addresses configured, it is possible that the EIGRP for IPv6 process cannot derive an RID value. If the router has no working interfaces that have IPv4 addresses, and the EIGRP for IPv6 RID is not explicitly configured, the EIGRP for IPv6 process simply does not work. So, the six-step configuration process includes a mention of the EIGRP RID. More generally, it might be prudent to configure an RID explicitly as a matter of habit.

After being enabled on an interface, EIGRP for IPv6 performs the same two basic tasks as it does with EIGRP for IPv4: It discovers neighbors and advertises connected subnets. EIGRP for IPv6 uses the same set of neighbor checks as do routers using EIGRP for IPv4, except that EIGRP for IPv6 does not require that neighboring IPv6 routers have IPv6

addresses in the same subnet. Also, as with EIGRP for IPv4, EIGRP for IPv6 advertises any and all connected subnets on an interface, with the exception of the link-
local addresses and the local routes (the host routes for a router's own interface IPv6
addresses).

Example 6-1 shows a sample configuration on Router R1 from Figure 6-1. All neighboring
routers must use the same ASN; ASN 9 will be used in this case.

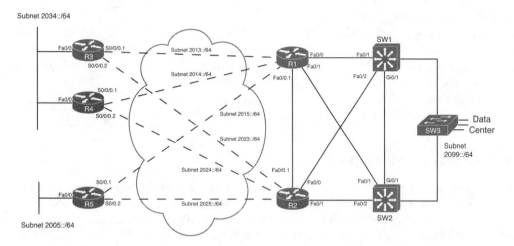

Subnet 2034::/64

Subnet 2005::/64

Figure 6-1 *Sample Internetwork for IPv6 Routing Protocol Configuration*

Example 6-1 *Configuring EIGRP for IPv6 Routing on R1*

Key
Topic

```
R1# show running-config
! output is edited to remove lines not pertinent to this example
! Configuration step 1: enabling IPv6 routing
ipv6 unicast-routing

! Next, configuration steps 3 and 4, on 5 different interfaces
interface FastEthernet0/0.1
 ipv6 address 2012::1/64
 ipv6 eigrp 9
!
interface FastEthernet0/0.2
 ipv6 address 2017::1/64
 ipv6 eigrp 9
!
interface FastEthernet0/1.18
 ipv6 address 2018::1/64
 ipv6 eigrp 9
!
interface Serial0/0/0.3
 ipv6 address 2013::1/64
```

```
 ipv6 eigrp 9
!
interface Serial0/0/0.4
 ipv6 address 2014::1/64
 ipv6 eigrp 9
!
interface Serial0/0/0.5
 ipv6 address 2015::1/64
 ipv6 eigrp 9
!
! Configuration steps 2, 5, and 6
ipv6 router eigrp 9
 no shutdown
 router-id 10.10.34.3
```

Verifying EIGRP for IPv6

The EIGRP for IPv6 **show** commands generally list the same kinds of information as the equivalent commands for EIGRP for IPv4, even more so than RIPng. In most cases, simply use the same **show ip...** commands applicable with IPv4 and EIGRP, and substitute **ipv6** for **ip**. Table 6-3 lists a cross-reference comparing popular EIGRP-related commands for both versions. Note that the table assumes that the commands begin with either **show ip** or **show ipv6** in all but the last row of the table.

Key Topic

Table 6-3 *Comparing EIGRP Verification Commands:* **show ip...** *and* **show ipv6...**

Function	show ip...	show ipv6...
All routes	... **route**	... **route**
All EIGRP-learned routes	... **route eigrp**	... **route eigrp**
Details on the routes for a specific prefix	... **route** *subnet mask*	... **route** *prefix/length*
Interfaces on which EIGRP is enabled, plus metric weights, variance, redistribution, maxpaths, admin distance	... **protocols**	... **protocols**
List of routing information sources	... **protocols** ... **eigrp neighbors**	... **eigrp neighbors**
Hello interval	... **eigrp interfaces detail**	... **eigrp interfaces detail**
EIGRP database	... **eigrp topology [all-links]**	... **eigrp topology [all-links]**
Debug that displays sent and received Updates	**debug ip eigrp notifications**	**debug ipv6 eigrp notifications**

Example 6-2 shows a few sample **show** commands taken from Router R3 in the internetwork shown in Figure 6-1. The explanatory comments are listed within the example.

Example 6-2   *IPv6 EIGRP* show *Commands*

```
! On R3, as when using RIPng, the next-hop address is the
! link-local address of the next router.

R3# show ipv6 route 2099::/64
Routing entry for 2099::/64
  Known via "eigrp 9", distance 90, metric 2174976, type internal
  Route count is 2/2, share count 0
  Routing paths:
    FE80::22FF:FE22:2222, Serial0/0/0.2
      Last updated 00:24:32 ago
    FE80::11FF:FE11:1111, Serial0/0/0.1
      Last updated 00:07:51 ago


! Note that the next command lists only EIGRP-learned routes. It lists
! two next-hops for 2099::64. Note the next-hop information lists
! link-local addresses.
R3# show ipv6 route eigrp
IPv6 Routing Table - Default - 19 entries
Codes: C - Connected, L - Local, S - Static, U - Per-user Static route
       B - BGP, M - MIPv6, R - RIP, I1 - ISIS L1
       I2 - ISIS L2, IA - ISIS interarea, IS - ISIS summary, D - EIGRP
       EX - EIGRP external
       O - OSPF Intra, OI - OSPF Inter, OE1 - OSPF ext 1, OE2 - OSPF ext 2
       ON1 - OSPF NSSA ext 1, ON2 - OSPF NSSA ext 2
D   2005::/64 [90/2684416]
     via FE80::11FF:FE11:1111, Serial0/0/0.1
     via FE80::22FF:FE22:2222, Serial0/0/0.2
D   2012::/64 [90/2172416]
     via FE80::22FF:FE22:2222, Serial0/0/0.2
     via FE80::11FF:FE11:1111, Serial0/0/0.1
D   2014::/64 [90/2681856]
     via FE80::11FF:FE11:1111, Serial0/0/0.1
D   2015::/64 [90/2681856]
     via FE80::11FF:FE11:1111, Serial0/0/0.1

! lines omitted for brevity...
D   2099::/64 [90/2174976]
     via FE80::22FF:FE22:2222, Serial0/0/0.2
     via FE80::11FF:FE11:1111, Serial0/0/0.1
! show ipv6 protocols displays less info than its IPv4 cousin.
R3# show ipv6 protocols
IPv6 Routing Protocol is "eigrp 9"
```

```
    EIGRP metric weight K1=1, K2=0, K3=1, K4=0, K5=0
    EIGRP maximum hopcount 100
    EIGRP maximum metric variance 1
    Interfaces:
      FastEthernet0/0
      Serial0/0/0.1
      Serial0/0/0.2
    Redistribution:
      None
    Maximum path: 16
    Distance: internal 90 external 170


 ! This command lists the equivalent of the information in the
 ! show ip protocols commands' "Routing Information Sources" heading.
 ! Note the link-local addresses are listed.
 R3# show ipv6 eigrp neighbors
 IPv6-EIGRP neighbors for process 9
 H   Address               Interface       Hold Uptime    SRTT   RTO  Q   Seq
                                           (sec)          (ms)        Cnt Num
 1   Link-local address:   Se0/0/0.2       14 01:50:51    3      200  0   82
     FE80::22FF:FE22:2222
 0   Link-local address:   Se0/0/0.1       13 01:50:52    14     200  0   90
     FE80::11FF:FE11:1111


 ! The next command lists the EIGRP topology database, including
 ! feasible distance calculations, reported distance, and listing
 ! all successor and feasible successor routes.
 R3# show ipv6 eigrp topology
 IPv6-EIGRP Topology Table for AS(9)/ID(10.10.34.3)


 Codes: P - Passive, A - Active, U - Update, Q - Query, R - Reply,
        r - reply Status, s - sia Status


 P 2005::/64, 2 successors, FD is 2684416
         via FE80::11FF:FE11:1111 (2684416/2172416), Serial0/0/0.1
         via FE80::22FF:FE22:2222 (2684416/2172416), Serial0/0/0.2
 P 2012::/64, 2 successors, FD is 2172416
         via FE80::11FF:FE11:1111 (2172416/28160), Serial0/0/0.1
         via FE80::22FF:FE22:2222 (2172416/28160), Serial0/0/0.2
 P 2013::/64, 1 successors, FD is 2169856
         via Connected, Serial0/0/0.1
```

```
! lines omitted for brevity
P 2099::/64, 2 successors, FD is 2174976
        via FE80::11FF:FE11:1111 (2174976/30720), Serial0/0/0.1
        via FE80::22FF:FE22:2222 (2174976/30720), Serial0/0/0.2


! Finally, the link-local address of neighbor R1 is identified.
R3# show cdp entry R1
-------------

Device ID: R1
Entry address(es):
  IP address: 10.10.13.1
  IPv6 address: 2013::1  (global unicast)
  IPv6 address: FE80::11FF:FE11:1111  (link-local)
Platform: Cisco 1841,  Capabilities: Router Switch IGMP
Interface: Serial0/0/0.1,  Port ID (outgoing port): Serial0/0/0.3
! lines omitted for brevity
```

The most notable fact listed in the example is that the output confirms that little difference exists with the **show** commands for EIGRP for IPv4 versus IPv6. The main differences relate to the **show ip protocols/show ipv6 protocols** commands and that EIGRP for IPv6 uses a link-local IP address for the next hop of each route.

Named EIGRP

Configuring EIGRP for a simple topology that needs few if any parameters changed from their default settings is a fairly simple task. However, consider a router that needs one EIGRP instance to support IPv4 networks and another EIGRP instance to support IPv6 networks. Also, imagine that you want to adjust the default timers, configure the variance option, summarize addresses, and specify a router ID. Suddenly, EIGRP configuration becomes much more challenging, and you are required to jump back and forth between different configuration modes (that is, interface configuration mode, EIGRP for IPv4 configuration mode, and EIGRP for IPv6 configuration mode).

Fortunately, Named EIGRP consolidates all of these disparate commands under a single hierarchical structure, as depicted in Figure 6-2. By having all EIGRP-related commands in one place, not only is configuration simplified, but troubleshooting is also more efficient.

This section describes Named EIGRP's hierarchical structure. Also, to illustrate the difference in the traditional and Named EIGRP configuration approaches, an example of each approach is provided, both of which accomplish the same objectives.

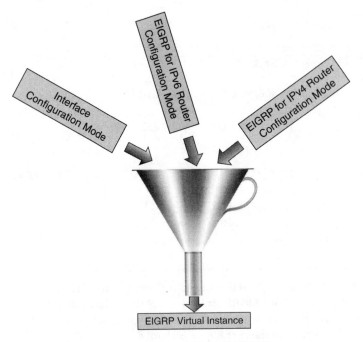

Figure 6-2   *Conceptual View of Named EIGRP*

The Named EIGRP Hierarchical Structure

Although Named EIGRP is configured very differently from traditional EIGRP, the configurations are compatible, meaning that an EIGRP-speaking router configured with the traditional approach can form a neighborship with an EIGRP-speaking router configured with the Named approach. Named EIGRP's hierarchical structure consists of three primary configuration modes. Table 6-4 identifies and describes these modes.

Key
Topic

Table 6-4   *Configuration Modes of Named EIGRP*

Configuration Mode	Description
Address-Family	General EIGRP configuration commands are issued under this configuration mode. For example, router ID, network, and EIGRP stub router configurations are performed here. Multiple address families (for example, IPv4 and IPv6) can be configured under the same EIGRP virtual instance.
Address-Family-Interface	Commands entered under interface configuration mode with a traditional EIGRP configuration are entered here for Named EIGRP configuration. For example, timer and passive interface configurations are performed here.
Address-Family-Topology	Commands that have a direct impact on a router's EIGRP topology table are given in this configuration mode. For example, variance and redistribution are configured in this mode.

Note   Named EIGRP also has *Service-Family* and *Service-Family-Interface* configuration modes, similar to the Address-Family and Address-Family-Interface configuration modes. The service family modes are used when EIGRP is advertising a service, using the *Service Advertisement Framework (SAF)* feature. For example, the *Call Control Discovery (CCD)* service uses SAF to advertise dial plan information (as opposed to IP route information) for unified communications networks. However, the ROUTE course only focuses on address families.

The following steps can be used to configure Named EIGRP:

Step 1.   Configure a Named EIGRP virtual instance using the **router eigrp** *virtual-instance-name* command in global configuration mode. It is under this single virtual instance that all address families are configured.

Step 2.   Specify an address family along with an autonomous system number using the **address-family** {**ipv4** | **ipv6**} **autonomous-system** *asn* command.

Step 3.   Configure general EIGRP settings under Address-Family configuration mode. Examples of commands issued in this configuration mode include **metric**, **network**, **eigrp stub**, and **eigrp router-id**.

Step 4.   (Optional) Enter Address-Family-Interface configuration mode, with the command **af-interface** {**default** | *interface-id*}. If you specify the **default** option, commands entered in this configuration mode apply to all interfaces (unless overridden by a command applied to a specific interface). Examples of commands issued in this configuration mode include **authentication**, **bandwidth-percent**, **hello-interval**, **hold-time**, **passive-interface**, and **split-horizon**.

Step 5.   (Optional) Exit Address-Family-Interface configuration mode (if currently in that mode) with the **exit** command, and enter Address-Family-Topology configuration mode with the **topology base** command. Examples of commands issued in the Address-Family-Topology configuration mode include **auto-summary**, **maximum-paths**, **redistribute**, and **variance**.

To better understand the structure of a Named EIGRP configuration, the next part of this section contrasts a couple of traditional EIGRP configurations with Named EIGRP configurations.

Traditional EIGRP and Named EIGRP Configurations Compared

If a network does not have any special EIGRP requirements (for example, load balancing or summarization), many network administrators configure EIGRP by simply starting an EIGRP routing process and instructing all interfaces to participate in EIGRP. For example, using the topology seen in Figure 6-3, Example 6-3 shows a basic EIGRP for IPv4 configuration using the traditional configuration approach.

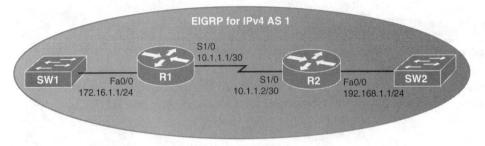

Figure 6-3   *EIGRP for IPv4 Sample Topology*

Example 6-3   *Basic EIGRP Configuration Using the Traditional Configuration Approach*

```
!Router R1 Configuration
R1# conf term
R1(config)# router eigrp 1
R1(config-router)# network 0.0.0.0

!Router R2 Configuration
R2# conf term
R2(config)# router eigrp 1
R2(config-router)# network 0.0.0.0
```

The configuration in Example 6-3 is very straightforward. It enters router configuration mode with the **router eigrp** *asn* command and instructs all router interfaces to partici-pate in that EIGRP autonomous system with the command **network 0.0.0.0**. Example 6-4, still using the topology in Figure 6-3, accomplishes the same result using the Named EIGRP configuration approach.

Example 6-4   *Basic EIGRP Configuration Using the Named Configuration Approach*

```
!R1 Router Configuration
R1# conf term
R1(config)# router eigrp R1DEMO
R1(config-router)# address-family ipv4 autonomous-system 1
R1(config-router-af)# network 0.0.0.0

!R2 Router Configuration
R2# conf term
R2(config)# router eigrp R2DEMO
R2(config-router)# address-family ipv4 autonomous-system 1
R2(config-router-af)# network 0.0.0.0
```

Although still very straightforward, the configuration seen in Example 6-4 is just a bit longer than the configuration seen in Example 6-3. However, the benefit of the Named EIGRP configuration approach becomes more evident when EIGRP has more complex requirements.

For example, consider Example 6-5. It uses the traditional EIGRP configuration approach to meet the following requirements for both Routers R1 and R2 in Figure 6-4:

- All interfaces should participate in EIGRP for IPv4 AS 1.

- All interfaces should participate in EIGRP for IPv6 AS 2.

- The variance option should be set to 2 for both autonomous systems.

- The Hello Interval should be set to 2 seconds for EIGRP for IPv4 AS1.

- The Hold Time should be set to 10 seconds for EIGRP for IPv4 AS1.

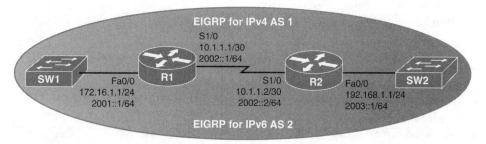

Figure 6-4 *EIGRP for IPv4 and EIGRP for IPv6 Sample Topology*

Example 6-5 *Advanced EIGRP Configuration Using the Traditional Configuration Approach*

```
!Router R1 Configuration
interface FastEthernet0/0
 ip address 172.16.1.1 255.255.255.0
 ipv6 address 2001::1/64
 ipv6 eigrp 2
!
interface Serial1/0
 ip address 10.1.1.1 255.255.255.252
 ip hello-interval eigrp 1 2
 ip hold-time eigrp 1 10
 ipv6 address 2002::1/64
 ipv6 eigrp 2
!
router eigrp 1
 variance 2
 network 0.0.0.0
 passive-interface default
 no passive-interface Serial1/0
!
ipv6 router eigrp 2
 variance 2
```

```
!Router R2 Configuration
interface FastEthernet0/0
 ip address 192.168.1.1 255.255.255.0
 ipv6 address 2003::1/64
 ipv6 eigrp 2
!
interface Serial1/0
 ip address 10.1.1.2 255.255.255.252
 ip hello-interval eigrp 1 2
 ip hold-time eigrp 1 10
 ipv6 address 2002::2/64
 ipv6 eigrp 2
!

router eigrp 1
 variance 2
 network 0.0.0.0
 passive-interface default
 no passive-interface Serial1/0
!
ipv6 router eigrp 2
 variance 2
```

Using the same topology, Example 6-6 meets the previously stated goals; however, Example 6-6 uses the Named EIGRP configuration approach.

Example 6-6 *Advanced EIGRP Configuration Using the Named Configuration Approach*

```
!Router R1 Configuration
router eigrp R1DEMO
 !
 address-family ipv4 unicast autonomous-system 1
  !
  af-interface default
   hello-interval 2
   hold-time 10
   passive-interface
  exit-af-interface
  !
  af-interface Serial1/0
   no passive-interface
  exit-af-interface
  !
  topology base
   variance 2
  exit-af-topology
```

```
  network 0.0.0.0
 exit-address-family
 !
 address-family ipv6 unicast autonomous-system 2
  !
  topology base
   variance 2
  exit-af-topology
 exit-address-family
```

```
!Router R2 Configuration
interface FastEthernet0/0
 ip address 192.168.1.1 255.255.255.0
 ipv6 address 2003::1/64
!
interface Serial1/0
 ip address 10.1.1.2 255.255.255.252
 ipv6 address 2002::2/64
!
router eigrp R2DEMO
 !
 address-family ipv4 unicast autonomous-system 1
  !
  af-interface default
   hello-interval 2
   hold-time 10
    passive-interface
  exit-af-interface
  !
  af-interface Serial1/0
   no passive-interface
  exit-af-interface
  !
  topology base
   variance 2
  exit-af-topology
  network 0.0.0.0
 exit-address-family
 !
 address-family ipv6 unicast autonomous-system 2
  !
  topology base
   variance 2
  exit-af-topology
 exit-address-family
```

In the Named EIGRP configuration, notice that each router has a single EIGRP virtual instance, and the EIGRP virtual instance on each router includes two address families, one for IPv4 and one for IPv6. Also notice that each of the configuration commands required to meet the objectives is logically organized under an appropriate configuration mode of the Named EIGRP hierarchy.

Verifying Named EIGRP

Even though Named EIGRP is configured differently than traditional EIGRP, the verification commands remain the same. To illustrate, consider Example 6-7, which shows the output (on Router R1) from a collection of common EIGRP troubleshooting commands.

Example 6-7 *Verifying a Named EIGRP Configuration*

```
R1# show ip protocols
*** IP Routing is NSF aware ***


Routing Protocol is "eigrp 1"
  Outgoing update filter list for all interfaces is not set
  Incoming update filter list for all interfaces is not set
  Default networks flagged in outgoing updates
  Default networks accepted from incoming updates
  EIGRP-IPv4 VR(R1DEMO) Address-Family Protocol for AS(1)
    Metric weight K1=1, K2=0, K3=1, K4=0, K5=0 K6=0
    Metric rib-scale 128
    Metric version 64bit
    NSF-aware route hold timer is 240
    Router-ID: 172.16.1.1
    Topology : 0 (base)
      Active Timer: 3 min
      Distance: internal 90 external 170
      Maximum path: 4
      Maximum hopcount 100
      Maximum metric variance 2
      Total Prefix Count: 3
      Total Redist Count: 0

  Automatic Summarization: disabled
  Maximum path: 4
  Routing for Networks:
    0.0.0.0
  Passive Interface(s):
    FastEthernet0/0
  Routing Information Sources:
    Gateway         Distance      Last Update
    10.1.1.2             90        01:18:03
```

```
       Distance: internal 90 external 170


R1# show ip eigrp interfaces
EIGRP-IPv4 VR(R1DEMO) Address-Family Interfaces for AS(1)

                      Xmit Queue    PeerQ        Mean   Pacing Time   Multicast    Pending
Interface Peers   Un/Reliable   Un/Reliable   SRTT   Un/Reliable   Flow Timer   Routes
Se1/0      1         0/0           0/0          81       0/16         352          0


R1# show ip eigrp interfaces detail s1/0
EIGRP-IPv4 VR(R1DEMO) Address-Family Interfaces for AS(1)

                      Xmit Queue    PeerQ        Mean   Pacing Time   Multicast    Pending
Interface Peers   Un/Reliable   Un/Reliable   SRTT   Un/Reliable   Flow Timer   Routes
Se1/0      1         0/0           0/0          81       0/16         352          0
  Hello-interval is 2, Hold-time is 10
   Split-horizon is enabled
   Next xmit serial <none>
   Packetized sent/expedited: 2/0
   Hello's sent/expedited: 2980/2
   Un/reliable mcasts: 0/0  Un/reliable ucasts: 3/3
   Mcast exceptions: 0  CR packets: 0  ACKs suppressed: 0
   Retransmissions sent: 0  Out-of-sequence rcvd: 0
   Topology-ids on interface - 0
   Authentication mode is not set


R1# show ipv6 protocols
IPv6 Routing Protocol is "connected"
IPv6 Routing Protocol is "ND"
IPv6 Routing Protocol is "eigrp 2"
EIGRP-IPv6 VR(R1DEMO) Address-Family Protocol for AS(2)
  Metric weight K1=1, K2=0, K3=1, K4=0, K5=0 K6=0
  Metric rib-scale 128
  Metric version 64bit
  NSF-aware route hold timer is 240
  Router-ID: 172.16.1.1
  Topology : 0 (base)
    Active Timer: 3 min
    Distance: internal 90 external 170
    Maximum path: 16
    Maximum hopcount 100
    Maximum metric variance 2
    Total Prefix Count: 3
    Total Redist Count: 0
```

```
Interfaces:
  FastEthernet0/0
  Serial1/0
Redistribution:
  None
```

The verification commands demonstrated in Example 6-7 confirm that the previously stated design goals have all been satisfied by the Named EIGRP configuration presented in Example 6-6.

Exam Preparation Tasks

Planning Practice

The CCNP ROUTE exam expects test takers to review design documents, create implementation plans, and create verification plans. This section provides some exercises that can help you to take a step back from the minute details of the topics in this chapter so that you can think about the same technical topics from the planning perspective.

For each planning practice table, simply complete the table. Note that any numbers in parentheses represent the number of options listed for each item in the solutions in Appendix F, "Completed Planning Practice Tables."

Design Review Table

Table 6-5 lists several design goals related to this chapter. If these design goals were listed in a design document, and you had to take that document and develop an implementation plan, what implementation options come to mind? For any configuration items, a general description can be used, without concern about the specific parameters.

Table 6-5 *Design Review*

Design Goal	Possible Implementation Choices Covered in This Chapter
Support the routing of IPv6 routes on a network currently using EIGRP for IPv4.	
A router currently has a complex EIGRP configuration, with multiple EIGRP-related commands under various interfaces, in addition to multiple EIGRP commands under router configuration mode. This configuration needs to be simplified so that it becomes easier to understand and troubleshoot.	

Implementation Plan Peer Review Table

Table 6-6 shows a list of questions that others might ask, or that you might think about, during a peer review of another network engineer's implementation plan. Complete the table by answering the questions.

Table 6-6   *Notable Questions from This Chapter to Consider During an Implementation Plan Peer Review*

Question	Answer
Some documentation refers to EIGRP for IPv4 as EIGRPv4 and to EIGRP for IPv6 as EIGRPv6. Does this mean there is a "version 5" of EIGRP?	
If the EIGRP configuration on corporate routers is migrated from a traditional EIGRP configuration to a Named EIGRP configuration, will network technicians and help desk staff need to learn a new set of verification and troubleshooting commands?	

Create an Implementation Plan Table

To practice skills useful when creating your own OSPF implementation plan, list in Table 6-7 configuration commands related to the configuration of the following features. You might want to record your answers outside the book, and set a goal to complete this table (and others like it) from memory during your final reviews before taking the exam.

Table 6-7   *Implementation Plan Configuration Memory Drill*

Feature	Configuration Commands/Notes
Enable IPv6 routing.	
Enable EIGRP for IPv6.	
Enable IPv6 on an interface, causing a router to derive a link-local address for the interface.	
Configure an IPv6 address on an interface.	
Enable EIGRP for IPv6 on an interface.	
Configure a router ID for EIGRP for IPv6.	
Create a Named EIGRP virtual instance.	
Specify an address family along with an autonomous system number.	
Enter Address-Family-Interface configuration mode.	
Enter Address-Family-Topology configuration mode for the base topology.	

Choose Commands for a Verification Plan Table

To practice skills useful when creating your own OSPF verification plan, list in Table 6-8 all commands that supply the requested information. You might want to record your answers outside the book, and set a goal to complete this table (and others like it) from memory during your final reviews before taking the exam.

Table 6-8 *Verification Plan Memory Drill*

Information Needed	Command(s)
Show all EIGRP-learned IPv4 routes.	
Show all EIGRP-learned IPv6 routes.	
Show the variance configured for an EIGRP for IPv4 autonomous system.	
Show the variance configured for an EIGRP for IPv6 autonomous system.	
Show the Hello Interval for an EIGRP for IPv4 autonomous system.	
Show the Hello Interval for an EIGRP for IPv6 autonomous system.	
Display the EIGRP topology table for an EIGRP for IPv4 autonomous system.	
Display the EIGRP topology table for an EIGRP for IPv6 autonomous system.	
Display sent and received updates for an EIGRP for IPv4 autonomous system.	
Display sent and received updates for an EIGRP for IPv6 autonomous system.	

Note   Some of the entries in this table may not have been specifically mentioned in this chapter but are listed in this table for review and reference.

Review All the Key Topics

Review the most important topics from inside the chapter, noted with the Key Topic icon in the outer margin of the page. Table 6-9 lists a reference of these key topics and the page numbers on which each is found.

Table 6-9   *Key Topics for Chapter 6*

Key Topic Element	Description	Page Number
Table 6-2	Comparing EIGRP for IPv4 and IPv6	237
List	EIGRP for IPv6 configuration steps	237
Example 6-1	Configuring EIGRP for IPv6 Routing on R1	239
Table 6-3	Comparing EIGRP Verification Commands: **show ip...** and **show ipv6...**	240
Table 6-4	Configuration Modes of Named EIGRP	244
List	Named EIGRP configuration steps	245
Example 6-6	Advanced EIGRP Configuration Using the Named Configuration Approach	248

Complete the Tables and Lists from Memory

Print a copy of Appendix D, "Memory Tables," (found on the CD) or at least the section for this chapter, and complete the tables and lists from memory. Appendix E, "Memory Tables Answer Key," also on the CD, includes completed tables and lists to check your work.

Define Key Terms

Define the following key terms from this chapter, and check your answers in the glossary.

EIGRP for IPv6, Named EIGRP

This chapter covers the following subjects:

- **OSPF Review:** This section reviews the OSPF concepts, configuration, and verification commands assumed as prerequisites, specifically those details included in the CCNA Exam's coverage of OSPF.

- **OSPF Neighbors and Adjacencies on LANs:** This section discusses a variety of features that impact when a router attempts to form OSPF neighbor relationships (neighborships), what must be true for those neighborships to work, and what might prevent those neighborships.

- **OSPF Neighbors and Adjacencies on WANs:** This short section examines the typical usage of OSPF neighborships over various types of WAN technologies.

- **Virtual Links:** This section examines how engineers can use virtual links to connect separate parts of an area through another area to maintain the requirement that OSPF areas be contiguous.

CHAPTER 7

Fundamental OSPF Concepts

Open Shortest Path First (OSPF) requires only a few relatively simple commands when using it in a small- to medium-sized internetwork. However, behind those commands resides a fairly complex routing protocol, with internals that can intimidate those new to OSPF. When compared to the less-complex Enhanced Interior Gateway Routing Protocol (EIGRP), OSPF requires more thought when planning and a few more configuration commands. Additionally, the underlying complexity of OSPF makes operating and verifying an OSPF internetwork more challenging.

This chapter begins with a review of OSPF concepts covered in your CCNA studies. Next, the chapter turns its attention to the formation of OSPF neighborships and adjacencies, followed by the establishment of OSPF neighbors and adjacencies over various WAN technologies. Finally, this chapter examines how a virtual link can be used to make discontiguous areas appear to be contiguous, or how an area not adjacent to an OSPF backbone area can appear to be adjacent.

"Do I Know This Already?" Quiz

The "Do I Know This Already?" quiz allows you to assess whether you should read the entire chapter. If you miss no more than one of these nine self-assessment questions, you might want to move ahead to the "Exam Preparation Tasks" section. Table 7-1 lists the major headings in this chapter and the "Do I Know This Already?" quiz questions covering the material in those headings so that you can assess your knowledge of those specific areas. The answers to the "Do I Know This Already?" quiz appear in Appendix A.

Table 7-1 *"Do I Know This Already?" Foundation Topics Section-to-Question Mapping*

Foundation Topics Section	Question
OSPF Review	1–3
OSPF Neighbors and Adjacencies on LANs	4–6
OSPF Neighbors and Adjacencies on WANs	7
Virtual Links	8, 9

1. A router has been configured with the commands **router ospf 9**, **network 172.16.1.0 0.0.0.255 area 8** and **network 172.16.0.0 0.0.255.255 area 9**, in that order. No other OSPF-related commands have been configured. The answers list the IP addresses that could be assigned to this router's Fa0/0 interface. Which answers list an IP address/prefix length that would cause the router to put Fa0/0 into area 9? (Choose two.)

   a. 172.16.0.1/23

   b. 172.16.1.1/26

   c. 172.16.1.1/24

   d. 172.16.0.255/23

   e. None of the other answers is correct.

2. Which of the following is true about an OSPF area border router (ABR)?

   a. The ABR must have multiple interfaces connected to the backbone area.

   b. An ABR is a router with two interfaces, each connected to a different nonbackbone area.

   c. The only requirement to be considered an ABR is at least one interface connected to the backbone area.

   d. An ABR must have at least one interface in the backbone area plus at least one other interface in a nonbackbone area.

3. Which of the following can either directly or indirectly identify all the interfaces for which 1) OSPF has been enabled and 2) OSPF is not passive? (Choose two.)

   a. show ip ospf database

   b. show ip ospf interface brief

   c. show ip protocols

   d. show ip route ospf

   e. show ip ospf neighbors

4. Router R1 directly connects to subnet 10.1.1.0/24 with its Fa0/0 interface. R1 can ping four other working OSPF routers in that subnet. R1 is neither the designated router (DR) nor backup DR (BDR). OSPF is working correctly on all five routers. Which of the following are true on R1? (Choose two.)

   a. The **show ip ospf neighbors** command lists two neighbors off Fa0/0.

   b. The **show ip ospf neighbors** command lists four neighbors off Fa0/0.

   c. The **show ip ospf neighbors** command lists two neighbors off Fa0/0 in the FULL state.

   d. The **show ip ospf neighbors** command lists two neighbors off Fa0/0 in the DISCO state.

5. Routers R1 and R2 are OSPF neighbors using their Fa0/0 interfaces, respectively, using default settings for all timers. An engineer adds the **ip ospf hello-interval 6** command to R1's Fa0/0 configuration. Which of the following are true regarding the results from this change? (Choose two.)

  a. The **show ip ospf neighbor** command on R1 lists the revised Hello timer.

  b. The **show ip ospf interface brief** command on R1 lists the revised Hello timer.

  c. The R1-R2 neighborship fails because of Hello timer mismatch.

  d. The **show ip ospf interface** command on R1 lists the revised Hello timer.

6. Which of the following settings do not prevent two potential OSPF neighbors from becoming neighbors?

  a. The interface used to connect to that neighbor being passive in the OSPF process

  b. Duplicate OSPF router IDs

  c. Mismatched Dead timers

  d. IP addresses of 10.1.1.1/24 and 10.2.2.2/24

  e. Mismatched OSPF process IDs

7. A company has a Frame Relay WAN with one central-site router and 100 branch office routers. A partial mesh of PVCs exists: one PVC between the central site and each of the 100 branch routers. All routers use point-to-point subinterfaces and one subnet per PVC. Which of the following is true about OSPF in this design?

  a. The central-site router has 100 fully adjacent neighborships with the 100 branches.

  b. The central-site router has neighborships with all branch routers, but fully adjacent neighborships with only two branches.

  c. The central-site router has a neighborship with the Frame Relay switch.

  d. None of the other answers is correct.

8. Which of the following answers can be verified as true based on the following command output from Router R1?

```
R1# show ip ospf virtual-links
Virtual Link OSPF_VL0 to router 4.4.4.4 is up
  Run as demand circuit
  DoNotAge LSA allowed.
  Transit area 1, via interface FastEthernet0/1, Cost of using 3?
```

  a. R1 is configured with an **area 0 virtual-link 4.4.4.4 cost 3** command.

  b. The **ping 4.4.4.4** command on R1 must currently be successful.

  c. R1's Fa0/1 OSPF cost is 3.

  d. 4.4.4.4 is known to R1 based on a Type 1 LSA in area 1.

9. Several links have been broken so that for the next day or two, what was formerly a contiguous area 0 has been broken into two parts. However, both parts of area 0 have working links into area 1 using routers with RID 1.1.1.1 and 2.2.2.2. Which answer lists the command on the router with RID 1.1.1.1 to create a virtual link to help solve this temporary problem?

a. area 0 virtual-link 2.2.2.2

b. area 1 virtual-link 2.2.2.2

c. area 0 source-rid 1.1.1.1 dest-rid 2.2.2.2

d. virtual-link transit-area 1 RID 2.2.2.2

Foundation Topics

OSPF Review

All the CCNP exams consider CCNA materials as prerequisite. Similarly, this book also assumes that the reader is already familiar with CCNA topics. However, the CCNP exams do include features that overlap with CCNA. Additionally, most people forget some details about CCNA topics along the way. This section is intended as a quick reminder of the basics from your earlier CCNA studies related to OSPF, with the addition of a few related details you might not have seen during your CCNA study.

Note that this section does not cover every detail of CCNA-level OSPF topics—the main goal is a quick refamiliarization. To that end, this section begins with a review of OSPF terminology and link-state theory, followed by a configuration and verification sample.

OSPF Link-State Concepts

OSPF uses *link-state (LS)* logic, which can be broken into three major branches. The first step, neighbor discovery, has the same overall goal as EIGRP's neighbor discovery process: to find the neighboring routers and exchange enough information so that the two routers know whether they should exchange topology data. (Like EIGRP, OSPF keeps a list of neighbors in its neighbor table.)

The second step, topology database exchange, requires each OSPF router to cooperate by sending messages so that all routers learn topology information—information that is the equivalent of the kinds of information a human would draw and write in a diagram of the internetwork. Each router stores this topology information in its topology database, sometimes called its *link-state database (LSDB)*. The information communicated by OSPF routers and held in their LSDBs includes

- The existence of, and an identifier for, each router (router ID)

- Each router interface, IP address, mask, and subnet

- The list of routers reachable by each router on each interface

During the third major step, route computation, each router independently analyzes the topology data to choose the best routes from its perspective. In particular, LS algorithms such as OSPF use a *Shortest Path First (SPF)* algorithm to analyze the data, choose the shortest (best) route for each reachable subnet, and add the correct next-hop/outgoing interface information for those routes to the IP routing table.

OSPF requires more planning than does EIGRP, particularly with regard to the necessity for a hierarchical design using OSPF areas. Each router interface exists in a single area, with some special routers, called *area border routers (ABR)*, being the boundary between areas. Inside an area, routers exchange detailed topology information. However, the detailed topology information does not flow between areas. Instead, the ABRs advertise briefer information between areas, including information about subnets/masks, but the information advertised into one area does not include details about the topology of the other area. For perspective on the OSPF design issues, consider Figure 7-1, which shows a typical hierarchical design.

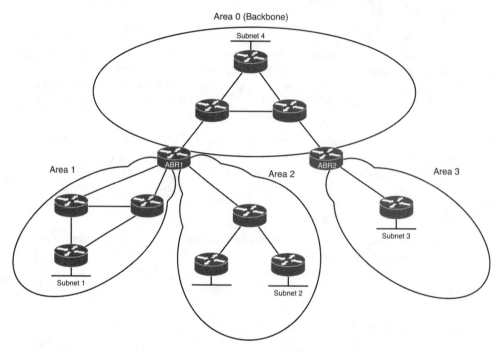

Figure 7-1 *Typical Hierarchical OSPF Design*

One area, called the *backbone area*, must connect to all other areas. Packets that need to pass between two nonbackbone areas must pass through (at least) one backbone router. The ABRs must keep a copy of the LSDB for each area to which they attach. For example, ABR1 has LSDBs for area 0, area 1, and area 2. However, the ABRs do not forward all the topology details between areas. Instead, they simply advertise the subnets (prefix/length) between the areas.

Because of the sparse information advertised into one area about another area, topologically, routers inside one area know only about the subnets in another area. They do not know about the details of the topology in the other area; instead, from a topology perspective, it appears as if the subnets from another area connect to the ABR. Figure 7-2 shows the concept with the two routers in area 3 from Figure 7-1.

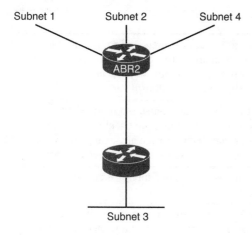

Figure 7-2 *Area 3 LSDB Concept*

Figure 7-2 essentially shows the contents of area 3's LSDB in graphical form. Two routers exist, with a link between them, and one LAN subnet (Subnet 3) internal to the area. However, the other three sample subnets shown in Figure 7-1 (Subnets 1, 2, and 4) appear connected to ABR2. (Other subnets exist outside area 3 as well; the figure just shows a few as examples.) The routers inside area 3 can calculate and add routes to their routing tables, but without needing all the topology information shown in Figure 7-1. By using an area design similar to the one illustrated in Figure 7-1, network engineers can group routers and interfaces into areas, which results in smaller topology databases on those routers, as shown in Figure 7-2. As a result, each router reduces the processing time, memory consumption, and effort to calculate the best routes.

OSPF uses a fairly large number of terms. Table 7-2 lists some of the more common OSPF terms as an early reference as you read through the chapter.

Key Topic

Table 7-2 *Commonly Used OSPF Terms*

Term	Definition
Link-state database (LSDB)	The data structure held by an OSPF router for the purpose of storing topology data
Shortest Path First (SPF)	The name of the algorithm OSPF uses to analyze the LSDB (Note: The analysis determines the best [lowest-cost] route for each prefix/length.)
Link-State Update (LSU)	The name of the OSPF packet that holds the detailed topology information, specifically LSAs
Link-State Advertisement (LSA)	The name of a class of OSPF data structures that hold topology information (Note: LSAs are held in memory in an LSDB and communicate over a network in LSU messages.)

Term	Definition
Area	A contiguous grouping of routers and router interfaces (Note: Routers in an area strive to learn all topology information about the area, but they do not learn topology information about all other areas.)
Area border router (ABR)	A router that has interfaces connected to at least two different OSPF areas, including the backbone area (Note: ABRs hold topology data for each area, calculate routes for each area, and advertise those routes between areas.)
Backbone router	Any router that has at least one interface connected to the backbone area
Internal routers	A router that has interfaces connected to only one area, making the router completely internal to that one area
Designated router (DR)	On multiaccess data links like LANs, an OSPF router elected by the routers on that data link to perform special functions (Note: These functions include generating LSAs representing the subnet and playing a key role in the database exchange process.)
Backup designated router (BDR)	A router on a multiaccess data link that monitors the DR and becomes prepared to take over for the DR, should the DR fail

OSPF Configuration Review

Other than the configuration of the OSPF areas, a basic configuration of OSPF basics looks similar to a simple EIGRP configuration. Cisco IOS uses the **router ospf** *process-id* command, plus one or more **network** *net-id wildcard-mask* **area** *area-id* subcommands, to enable OSPF on the router and on router interfaces. The rules for these commands are as follows:

Step 1. Neighboring routers' **router ospf** *process-id* commands do not have to be configured with the same *process-id* parameter to become neighbors.

Step 2. Cisco IOS only enables OSPF on interfaces matched by an OSPF **network** command. When enabled, the router does the following:

    a. Attempts to discover OSPF neighbors on that interface by sending multicast OSPF Hello messages

    b. Includes the connected subnet in future topology database exchanges

Step 3. To match an interface with the **network** command, Cisco IOS compares the *net-id* configured in the **network** command with each interface's IP address, while using the configured wildcard mask as an ACL wildcard mask.

Step 4.   Regardless of the order in which the **network** commands are added to the configuration, Cisco IOS puts these commands into the configuration file with the most specific (most binary 0s) wildcard mask first, for overlapping network ranges. Cisco IOS lists the **network** commands in this sorted order in the configuration.

Step 5.   The first **network** command that matches an interface, per the order shown in the output of the **show running-config** command, determines the OSPF area number associated with the interface.

Example 7-1 shows a sample configuration for each router in Figure 7-3.

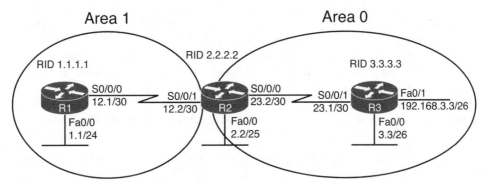

Note: All IP addresses begin with 10.1 unless otherwise noted.

Figure 7-3   *Three-Router Internetwork with Two OSPF Areas*

Example 7-1   *OSPF Configuration on Routers R1, R2, and R3*

```
! On Router R1: !!!!!!!!!!!!!!!!!!!!!!!!!!!!!!!!!!!!!!!!!!!!!!!!
interface loopback 1
 ip address 1.1.1.1 255.255.255.255
router ospf 1
 network 10.0.0.0 0.255.255.255 area 1

! On Router R2: !!!!!!!!!!!!!!!!!!!!!!!!!!!!!!!!!!!!!!!!!!!!!!!!
interface loopback 1
 ip address 2.2.2.2 255.255.255.255

router ospf 2
 network 10.1.12.2 0.0.0.0 area 1
 network 10.1.0.0 0.0.255.255 area 0

! On Router R3: !!!!!!!!!!!!!!!!!!!!!!!!!!!!!!!!!!!!!!!!!!!!!!!!
interface loopback 1
 ip address 3.3.3.3 255.255.255.255

router ospf 3
```

```
network 10.1.0.0 0.0.255.255 area 0
network 192.168.3.3 0.0.0.0 area 0
```

First, note that all three routers use a different process ID on their respective **router ospf** *process-id* commands. These mismatches do not prevent neighborships from forming.

Next, consider the requirement that R1's S0/0/0 and R2's S0/0/1 must be in the same area. Typically, all routers on the same subnet need to be in the same area; the routers themselves are the boundary between areas. In this case, R1's **network 10.0.0.0 0.255.255.255 area 1** command matches all interfaces whose addresses begin with 10 in the first octet and assigns those interfaces (Fa0/0 and S0/0/0) to area 1. Similarly, R2's **network 10.1.12.2 0.0.0.0 area 1** command matches only one IP address—R2's S0/0/1 IP address—and places it in area 1. Looking further at R2's OSPF configuration, note that both **network** commands actually match the 10.1.12.2 S0/0/1 IP address: one with area 0 and one with area 1. However, R2 orders these two **network** commands with the most-specific wildcard mask first, placing the command with wildcard mask 0.0.0.0 first and the one with wildcard mask 0.0.255.255 second. Then, R2 compares the commands to the interface IP addresses in order, so R2 places S0/0/1 into area 1. (Note that in real internetworks, choosing wildcard masks such that it is clear which **network** command should match each interface is the better choice.)

On R3, the **network 10.1.0.0 0.0.255.255 area 0** command matches interfaces Fa0/0 and S0/0/0, adding them to area 0. R3 then needs an additional **network** command to enable OSPF on R3's Fa0/1 interface with all three interfaces in area 0.

Finally, note that the addition of the loopback interfaces causes each router to choose an obvious OSPF *router ID (RID)*. OSPF uses the same logic as does EIGRP to choose a router ID on each router, at the time the OSPF process is initialized, as follows, in the listed order of precedence:

Step 1.   Use the router ID defined in the **router-id** *x.x.x.x* OSPF router subcommand.

Step 2.   Use the highest IP address of any up loopback interface.

Step 3.   Use the highest IP address of any up nonloopback interface.

Note that for the second and third choices, the interface does not need to have OSPF enabled.

OSPF Verification Review

The verification process, whether it uses a formal verification plan or not, requires some knowledge of the intended design and function of the network. The design and implementation documents dictate what the network should do, and the verification plan should confirm whether the network is meeting those goals.

For the purposes of this OSPF review section, assume that the only design goal for the internetwork in Figure 7-3 is that OSPF be used so that all routers have routes to reach all subnets shown in the figure, within the constraints of the area design.

To verify such a simple design, an engineer should start by confirming on which interfaces OSPF has been enabled on each router. The next step should be to determine whether the OSPF neighbor relationships that should occur are indeed up and working. Then, the OSPF topology table should be examined to confirm that non-ABRs have only topology information for their respective areas. Finally, the IP routes on each router should be examined, confirming that all routes are known. To that end, Table 7-3 summarizes five key **show** commands that provide the information to answer these questions:

Table 7-3 *Commonly Used OSPF* **show** *Commands*

Command	Key Information
show ip ospf interface brief	Lists the interfaces on which OSPF is enabled (based on the **network** commands), omitting passive interfaces
show ip protocols	Lists the contents of the network configuration commands for each routing process and a list of enabled but passive interfaces
show ip ospf neighbors	Lists known neighbors, including neighbor state; does not list neighbors for which some mismatched parameter is preventing a valid OSPF neighbor relationship
show ip ospf database	Lists all LSAs for all connected areas
show ip route	Lists the contents of the IP routing table, listing OSPF-learned routes with a code of O on the left side of the output

Example 7-2 shows samples of each command listed in Table 7-3. Note that the output highlights various samples of items that should be verified, including the interfaces on which OSPF is enabled, the known neighbors, the neighbors' states, the LSAs in the topology table, and the OSPF routes.

Example 7-2 *OSPF Verification on Routers R1, R2, and R3*

```
! On Router R2: !!!!!!!!!!!!!!!!!!!!!!!!!!!!!!!!!!!!!!!!!!!!!!!
! Note that S0/0/1 is shown as in area 1, while the other 2 interfaces are all in
! Area 0.

R2# show ip ospf interface brief
Interface   PID  Area        IP Address/Mask    Cost  State Nbrs F/C
Se0/0/0     2    0           10.1.23.2/30       64    P2P   1/1
Fa0/0       2    0           10.1.2.2/25        1     DR    0/0
Se0/0/1     2    1           10.1.12.2/30       64    P2P   1/1

! Next, note that R2 lists two "Routing Information Sources", 1.1.1.1 (R1) and
! 3.3.3.3 (R3).
! These routers, listed by RID, should mirror those listed in the output of the show
! ip ospf neighbors command that follows.
```

```
R2# show ip protocols
Routing Protocol is "ospf 2"
  Outgoing update filter list for all interfaces is not set
  Incoming update filter list for all interfaces is not set
  Router ID 2.2.2.2
  It is an area border router
  Number of areas in this router is 2. 2 normal 0 stub 0 nssa
  Maximum path: 4
  Routing for Networks:
    10.1.12.2 0.0.0.0 area 1
    10.1.0.0 0.0.255.255 area 0
  Reference bandwidth unit is 100 mbps
  Routing Information Sources:
    Gateway         Distance      Last Update
    3.3.3.3              110      00:01:08
    1.1.1.1              110      00:01:08
  Distance: (default is 110)


! Note that the Full state means that the database exchange process is fully
! completed
! between these two neighbors.
R2# show ip ospf neighbors

Neighbor ID    Pri   State        Dead Time   Address       Interface
3.3.3.3          0   FULL/  -     00:00:34    10.1.23.1     Serial0/0/0
1.1.1.1          0   FULL/  -     00:00:34    10.1.12.1     Serial0/0/1


! On Router R1: !!!!!!!!!!!!!!!!!!!!!!!!!!!!!!!!!!!!!!!!!!!!!!
! Note that R1's LSDB includes a "Router Link State" for RID 1.1.1.1 (R1) ,2.2.2.2
! (R2), but not 3.3.3.3 (R3), because R3 is not attached to area 1.


R1# show ip ospf database

              OSPF Router with ID (1.1.1.1) (Process ID 1)


              Router Link States (Area 1)


Link ID        ADV Router      Age       Seq#        Checksum Link count
1.1.1.1        1.1.1.1         210       0x80000004  0x001533 3
2.2.2.2        2.2.2.2         195       0x80000002  0x0085DB 2


              Summary Net Link States (Area 1)


Link ID        ADV Router      Age       Seq#        Checksum
10.1.2.0       2.2.2.2         190       0x80000001  0x00B5F0
```

```
10.1.3.0         2.2.2.2          190      0x80000001 0x00AE76
10.1.23.0        2.2.2.2          190      0x80000001 0x0031A4
192.168.3.0      2.2.2.2          191      0x80000001 0x008B3B


! Below, note that R1 has routes for all remote subnets, including R3's
! LAN subnets, even though R1 does not list R3 in its LSDB.


R1# show ip route ospf
     10.0.0.0/8 is variably subnetted, 5 subnets, 4 masks
O IA    10.1.3.0/26 [110/129] via 10.1.12.2, 00:04:13, Serial0/0/0
O IA    10.1.2.0/25 [110/65] via 10.1.12.2, 00:04:13, Serial0/0/0
O IA    10.1.23.0/30 [110/128] via 10.1.12.2, 00:04:13, Serial0/0/0
     192.168.3.0/26 is subnetted, 1 subnets
O IA    192.168.3.0 [110/129] via 10.1.12.2, 00:04:13, Serial0/0/0
```

OSPF Feature Summary

Table 7-4 summarizes some key OSPF facts. The table includes some review items from
CCNA-level OSPF topics, plus some topics that will be developed in this and upcoming
chapters. The items that are not CCNA topics are included just for convenience when
reviewing for final preparation before taking the exam.

Table 7-4 *OSPF Feature Summary*

Feature	Description
Transport	IP, protocol type 89 (does not use UDP or TCP).
Metric	Based on cumulative cost of all outgoing interfaces in a route. The interface cost defaults to a function of interface bandwidth but can be set explicitly.
Hello interval	Interval at which a router sends OSPF Hello messages out of an interface.
Dead interval	Timer used to determine when a neighboring router has failed, based on a router not receiving any OSPF messages, including Hellos, in this timer period.
Update destination address	Normally sent to 224.0.0.5 (All SPF Routers) and 224.0.0.6 (All Designated Routers).
Full or partial updates	Full updates used when new neighbors are discovered; partial updates used otherwise.
Authentication	Supports MD5 and clear-text authentication.
VLSM/classless	Includes the mask with each route, also allowing OSPF to support discontiguous networks and VLSM.

Feature	Description
Route tags	Allows OSPF to tag routes as they are redistributed into OSPF.
Next-hop field	Supports the advertisement of routes with a different next-hop router than the advertising router.
Manual route summarization	Allows route summarization at ABR routers only.

This concludes the review of OSPF topics. The rest of this chapter focuses on OSPF topics related to the formation of OSPF neighbor relationships.

OSPF Neighbors and Adjacencies on LANs

With EIGRP, neighborship is relatively simple, if two EIGRP routers discover each other (using Hellos) and meet several requirements (like being in the same subnet). After becoming neighbors, the two EIGRP routers exchange topology information.

Comparing OSPF and EIGRP, OSPF neighborship is more complex. First, with EIGRP, two routers either become neighbors or they do not. With OSPF, even after all the neighbor parameter checks pass, two classes of neighborships exist: *neighbors* and *fully adjacent neighbors*. The OSPF neighbor discovery process has many pitfalls when the internetwork uses Frame Relay, with a class of issues that simply do not exist with EIGRP. Finally, OSPF uses an underlying *Finite State Machine (FSM)* with eight neighbor states used to describe the current state of each OSPF neighbor, adding another layer of complexity compared to EIGRP.

This section breaks down the OSPF neighbor relationship, the logic, and the OSPF configuration settings—anything that impacts OSPF neighborship on LAN interfaces. This section examines the following questions:

- On what interfaces will this router attempt to discover neighbors by sending multicast OSPF Hello messages?

- Does a potential neighbor meet all requirements to become a neighbor?

This section examines these topics, in sequence.

Enabling OSPF Neighbor Discovery on LANs

OSPF sends multicast OSPF Hello messages on LAN interfaces, attempting to discover OSPF neighbors, when two requirements are met:

- OSPF has been enabled on the interface, either through the **network** router subcommand or the **ip ospf area** interface subcommand.

- The interface has not been made passive by the **passive-interface** router subcommand.

When both requirements are met, OSPF sends Hellos to the 224.0.0.5 multicast address, an address reserved for all OSPF-speaking routers. The Hello itself contains several parameters that must be checked, including the OSPF RID of the router sending the Hello and the OSPF area that router has assigned to that LAN subnet.

Of the three configuration commands that might impact whether a router attempts to discover potential neighbors on an interface, one is commonly understood (**network**) and was already covered in this chapter's "OSPF Configuration Review" section. The second configuration command that impacts whether potential neighbors discover each other, **passive-interface**, works just like it does with EIGRP. In short, when a router configures an interface as passive to OSPF, OSPF quits sending OSPF Hellos, so the router will not discover neighbors. The router will still advertise the interface's connected subnet if OSPF is enabled on the interface, but all other OSPF processing on the interface is stopped.

The third configuration command that impacts whether a router discovers potential neighbors using Hellos is the **ip ospf** *process-id* **area** *area-id* interface subcommand. This command acts as a replacement for the OSPF **network** command. Simply put, this command enables OSPF directly on the interface and assigns the area number.

To demonstrate the **ip ospf area** and **passive-interface** commands, Example 7-3 shows a revised configuration on Router R3, as seen originally in Example 7-1. In this new example configuration, R3 has made two interfaces passive, because no other OSPF routers exist on its LAN subnets. Additionally, R3 has migrated its configuration away from the older **network** commands, instead using the **ip ospf area** interface subcommand.

Example 7-3 *Configuring* **passive-interface** *and* **ip ospf area**

```
interface loopback 1
 Ip address 3.3.3.3 255.255.255.255

router ospf 3
 passive-interface FastEthernet0/0
 passive-interface FastEthernet0/1

interface FastEthernet0/0
 ip ospf 3 area 0
interface FastEthernet0/1
 ip ospf 3 area 0
interface Serial0/0/1
 ip ospf 3 area 0

R3# show ip protocols
Routing Protocol is "ospf 3"
  Outgoing update filter list for all interfaces is not set
  Incoming update filter list for all interfaces is not set
  Router ID 3.3.3.3
  Number of areas in this router is 1. 1 normal 0 stub 0 nssa
  Maximum path: 4
```

```
Routing for Networks:
Routing on Interfaces Configured Explicitly (Area 0):
  Serial0/0/1
  FastEthernet0/1
  FastEthernet0/0
Reference bandwidth unit is 100 mbps
Passive Interface(s):
  FastEthernet0/0
  FastEthernet0/1
Routing Information Sources:
  Gateway         Distance      Last Update
Distance: (default is 110)
```

Note that in the second half of Example 7-3, the **show ip protocols** command now lists the interfaces as matched with the **ip ospf area** commands, and it lists the passive interfaces. You can take the list of explicitly configured interfaces, remove the passive interfaces, and know which interfaces on which R3 will attempt to discover OSPF neighbors. Also, take a moment to compare this output with the same command's output in Example 7-2, with the earlier example listing the parameters of the configured network commands.

Settings That Must Match for OSPF Neighborship

After an OSPF router has discovered a potential neighbor by receiving a Hello from the other router, the local router considers the router that sent the Hello as a potential neighbor. The local router must examine the contents of the received Hello, plus a few other factors, compare those settings to its own, and check for agreement, and only then can that other router be considered an OSPF neighbor.

For reference, the following list details the items seen in OSPF Hello messages. Note that some fields might not be present in a Hello, depending on the conditions in the network.

- OSPF router ID

- Stub area flag

- Hello interval

- Dead interval

- Subnet mask

- List of neighbors reachable on the interface

- Area ID

- Router priority

- Designated router (DR) IP address

- Backup DR (BDR) IP address

- Authentication digest

Table 7-5 summarizes the items that two routers will compare when deciding whether they can become OSPF neighbors. For study purposes, the table also lists some items that one might think prevent OSPF neighborship but do not, with comparisons to EIGRP.

Key Topic

Table 7-5 *Neighbor Requirements for EIGRP and OSPF*

Requirement	OSPF	EIGRP
Interfaces' primary IP addresses must be in same subnet.	Yes	Yes
Must not be passive on the connected interface.	Yes	Yes
Must be in same area.	Yes	N/A
Hello interval/timer, plus either the Hold (EIGRP) or Dead (OSPF) timer, must match.	Yes	No
Router IDs must be unique.	Yes	No
IP MTU must match.	Yes[1]	No
Must pass neighbor authentication (if configured).	Yes	Yes
K-values (used in metric calculation) must match.	N/A	Yes
Must use the same ASN (EIGRP) or process ID (OSPF) on the **router** configuration command.	No	Yes

[1] Might allow the other router to be listed in the output of the **show ip ospf neighbor** command, but the MTU mismatch will prevent proper operation of the topology exchange.

The first few items in Table 7-5 require only a minor amount of discussion. First, OSPF checks the IP address (found as the source address of the Hello message) and mask (listed in the Hello message) of the potential neighbor, calculates the subnet address, and compares the subnet address and mask to its own interface IP address. Both the subnet address and mask must match. Additionally, the OSPF Hello messages include the area number of the subnet, as defined by that router. The receiving router compares the received Hello with its own configuration and rejects the potential neighbor if the area numbers do not match.

The next several sections examine other settings that can prevent OSPF neighborship.

Optimizing Convergence Using Hello and Dead Timers

Using the same concept as EIGRP, but with different terminology, OSPF uses two timers to monitor the reachability of neighbors. With OSPF, the Hello interval defines how often the router sends a Hello on the interface. The Dead interval defines how long a router should wait, without hearing any Hello messages from a neighbor, before deciding that the neighbor failed. For example, with a default LAN interface Hello timer of 10 seconds, and a Dead interval of 40 seconds, the local router sends Hello messages every 10 seconds. The neighbor resets its downward-counting Hold timer to 40 upon receiving a Hello from that neighbor. Under normal operation on a LAN, with defaults, the Dead timer for a neighbor would vary from 40 down to 30, and then be reset to 40 upon receipt of the next Hello. However, if Hello messages were not received for 40 seconds, the neighborship would fail, driving convergence.

To tune for faster convergence, you can configure OSPF to set a lower Hello and Dead timer. It speeds convergence in some cases. Note that if the interface fails, OSPF will immediately realize that all neighbors reached through that interface have also failed and will not wait on the Dead timer to count down to 0. For example, consider the internetwork in Figure 7-4. This internetwork has four routers connected to the same VLAN, with interfaces, IP addresses, masks, and OSPF areas as shown.

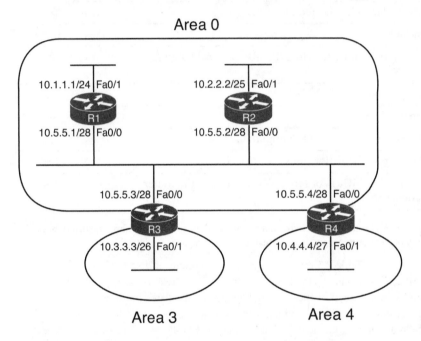

Figure 7-4 *Four OSPF Routers on the Same Subnet, with Two OSPF Areas*

Example 7-4 verifies some of the facts about the routers in Figure 7-4, showing the changes to the Hello interval and the resulting failed neighborships. Each router has been assigned an obvious RID: 1.1.1.1 for R1, 2.2.2.2 for R2, and so on.

Example 7-4 *Effect of Configuring a Different OSPF Hello Interval*

```
R4# show ip ospf neighbors
Neighbor ID     Pri   State          Dead Time   Address     Interface
1.1.1.1           1   2WAY/DROTHER   00:00:35    10.5.5.1    FastEthernet0/0
2.2.2.2           1   FULL/BDR       00:00:39    10.5.5.2    FastEthernet0/0
3.3.3.3           1   FULL/DR        00:00:38    10.5.5.3    FastEthernet0/0
R4# conf t
Enter configuration commands, one per line.  End with CNTL/Z.
R4(config)# interface fastethernet0/0
R4(config-if)# ip ospf hello-interval 9
R4(config-if)# ^Z
```

```
*Apr 28 00:06:20.271: %SYS-5-CONFIG_I: Configured from console by console
R4# show ip ospf interface fa0/0
FastEthernet0/0 is up, line protocol is up
  Internet Address 10.5.5.4/28, Area 0
  Process ID 4, Router ID 4.4.4.4, Network Type BROADCAST, Cost: 1
  Enabled by interface config, including secondary ip addresses
  Transmit Delay is 1 sec, State DROTHER, Priority 1
  Designated Router (ID) 3.3.3.3, Interface address 10.5.5.3
  Backup Designated router (ID) 2.2.2.2, Interface address 10.5.5.2
  Timer intervals configured, Hello 9, Dead 36, Wait 36, Retransmit 5
    oob-resync timeout 40
    Hello due in 00:00:01
  Supports Link-local Signaling (LLS)
  Index 1/1, flood queue length 0
  Next 0x0(0)/0x0(0)
  Last flood scan length is 0, maximum is 3
  Last flood scan time is 0 msec, maximum is 4 msec
  Neighbor Count is 3, Adjacent neighbor count is 2
    Adjacent with neighbor 2.2.2.2  (Backup Designated Router)
    Adjacent with neighbor 3.3.3.3  (Designated Router)
  Suppress hello for 0 neighbor(s)
R4#
*Apr 28 00:06:51.559: %OSPF-5-ADJCHG: Process 4, Nbr 1.1.1.1 on FastEthernet0/0
from 2WAY to DOWN, Neighbor Down: Dead timer expired
*Apr 28 00:06:57.183: %OSPF-5-ADJCHG: Process 4, Nbr 3.3.3.3 on FastEthernet0/0 from
FULL to DOWN,
Neighbor Down: Dead timer expired
*Apr 28 00:06:58.495: %OSPF-5-ADJCHG: Process 4, Nbr 2.2.2.2 on FastEthernet0/0 from
FULL to DOWN,
Neighbor Down: Dead timer expired
```

This example demonstrates several interesting facts. First, note that upon configuring the **ip ospf hello-interval 9** command under Fa0/0, the **show ip ospf interface fa0/0** command shows that not only did the Hello interval change, but the Dead timer was also set to 4X the Hello interval, or 36. To directly set the Dead timer on the interface, use the **ip ospf dead-interval** *value* interface subcommand. Then, at the end of the example, note that all three of R4's neighbor relationships failed, because those routers now have mismatched Hello and Dead timers. However, the neighbor relationships failed only after the Dead timers expired, as noted in the messages and as confirmed by the timestamps on the messages.

Example 7-4 also shows the two normal, stable, and working neighbor states. Look to the heading "state" in the output of the **show ip ospf neighbors** command at the top of the example. The first word (before the /) lists the state or status of each neighbor. FULL refers to a fully adjacent neighbor, meaning that the OSPF topology has been fully exchanged with that neighbor. The other state listed there, 2WAY, is a normal, stable, working state for neighbors with which topology data was not exchanged directly. In some cases, OSPF routers exchange their topology information to one specific router on a LAN, called the *designated router (DR)*, but they do not exchange their database directly with other routers. In the preceding example, taken from R4, R4 lists its relationship with R1 as 2WAY, which happens to be the status for a working neighbor that does not become fully adjacent.

> **Note**   OSPF has two methods to tune the Hello and Dead intervals to subsecond values. Like EIGRP, OSPF supports *Bidirectional Forwarding Detection (BFD)*. Additionally, OSPF supports the command **ip ospf dead-interval minimal hello-multiplier** *multiplier*, which sets the Dead interval to one second, and the Hello interval to a fraction of a second based on the multiplier. For example, the command **ip ospf dead-interval minimal hello-multiplier 4** sets the Dead interval to one second, with Hellos occurring four times (the multiple) per second, for an effective Hello interval of 1/4 seconds.

Using a Unique OSPF Router ID

As mentioned earlier in the "OSPF Review" section, each OSPF router assigns itself a router ID, based on the same rules as EIGRP. In OSPF's case, that means a router first looks for the OSPF **router-id** *rid-value* OSPF subcommand; next, to the highest IP address of any up loopback interface; and finally, to the highest IP address of any up non-loopback interface.

An OSPF RID mismatch makes for unpredictable results, because OSPF routers base their view of the topology on the topology database, and the database identifies routers based on their RIDs. By design, all OSPF RIDs in a domain should be unique. To avoid such issues, OSPF prevents neighborships between routers with duplicate RIDs.

The next example shows what happens when two routers discover each other as potential neighbors but notice a duplicate RID. Using the same network as in Figure 7-4, each router has been assigned an obvious RID: 1.1.1.1 for R1, 2.2.2.2 for R2, and so on. Unfortunately, R4 has been mistakenly configured with RID 1.1.1.1, duplicating R1's RID. R4 is powered on after all three other routers have established neighbor relationships. Example 7-5 shows some of the results.

Example 7-5   *OSPF RID Mismatch—R1 and R4, R4 Connects After R1*

```
! On R1... the following output occurs AFTER R4 powers on. R1, RID 1.1.1.1,
! does not form a neighbor relationship with R4.
R1# show ip ospf neighbors

Neighbor ID     Pri   State        Dead Time   Address     Interface
2.2.2.2           1   FULL/BDR     00:00:35    10.5.5.2    FastEthernet0/0
3.3.3.3           1   FULL/DR      00:00:33    10.5.5.3    FastEthernet0/0

! On R3
```

```
! R3 does form a neighbor relationship, but does not learn routes from
! R4. Note that R3 does not have a route for R4's 10.4.4.0/27 subnet.
R3# show ip ospf neighbors


Neighbor ID     Pri   State          Dead Time   Address      Interface
1.1.1.1         1     FULL/DROTHER   00:00:38    10.5.5.1     FastEthernet0/0
1.1.1.1         1     FULL/DROTHER   00:00:37    10.5.5.4     FastEthernet0/0
2.2.2.2         1     FULL/BDR       00:00:35    10.5.5.2     FastEthernet0/0
R3# show ip route ospf
    10.0.0.0/8 is variably subnetted, 4 subnets, 4 masks
O      10.2.2.0/25 [110/2] via 10.5.5.2, 00:06:56, FastEthernet0/0
O      10.1.1.0/24 [110/2] via 10.5.5.1, 00:01:34, FastEthernet0/0
```

As you can see from the output on R1, whose RID is duplicated with R4, the routers with duplicate RIDs do not form a neighbor relationship. Additionally, other routers, such as R3, do form neighbor relationships with the two routers, but the duplication confuses the topology flooding process. Because R3 formed its neighborship with R1 before R4, R3 does learn a route for R1's 10.1.1.0/24 subnet, but does not for R4's 10.4.4.0/27 subnet. However, with the same configuration, but a different sequence and timing of neighbors coming up, R3 might learn about 10.4.4.0/27 instead of 10.1.1.0/24.

Note The OSPF process will not start without an RID.

Using the Same IP MTU

The *maximum transmission unit (MTU)* of an interface tells Cisco IOS the largest IP packet that can be forwarded out an interface. This setting protects the packet from being discarded on data links whose Layer 2 features will not pass a frame over a certain size. For example, routers typically default to an IP MTU of 1500 bytes.

From a data plane perspective, when a router needs to forward a packet larger than the outgoing interface's MTU, the router either fragments the packet or discards it. If the IP header's *Do Not Fragment (DF)* bit is set, the router discards the packet. If the DF bit is not set, the router can perform Layer 3 fragmentation on the packet, creating two (or more) IP packets with mostly identical IP headers, spreading the data that follows the original IP packet header out among the fragments. The fragments can then be forwarded, with the reassembly process being performed by the receiving host.

From a design perspective, the MTU used by all devices attached to the same data link ought to be the same value. However, routers have no dynamic mechanism to prevent the misconfiguration of MTU on neighboring routers.

When an MTU mismatch occurs between two OSPF neighbors, one router will attempt to become neighbors with the other router whose MTU differs. The other router will be listed in the list of neighbors (**show ip ospf neighbor**). However, the two routers will not exchange topology information, and the two routers will not calculate routes that use this neighbor as a next-hop router.

The IP MTU can be set on an interface using the **ip mtu** *value* interface subcommand and for all Layer 3 protocols with the **mtu** *value* interface subcommand. Example 7-6 shows an example, with R4 again configured so that it has problems.

Example 7-6 *Setting IP MTU and Failing the OSPF Database Exchange Process*

```
R4# configure terminal
Enter configuration commands, one per line.  End with CNTL/Z.
R4(config)# int fastethernet0/0
R4(config-if)# ip mtu 1498
R4(config-if)# ^Z
R4#
R4# show ip interface fa0/0
FastEthernet0/0 is up, line protocol is up
  Internet address is 10.5.5.4/28
  Broadcast address is 255.255.255.255
  Address determined by non-volatile memory
  MTU is 1498 bytes
! lines omitted for brevity
R4# show ip ospf neighbors

Neighbor ID     Pri   State           Dead Time   Address         Interface
1.1.1.1           1   EXSTART/DROTHER 00:00:39    10.5.5.1        FastEthernet0/0
2.2.2.2           1   EXSTART/DROTHER 00:00:37    10.5.5.2        FastEthernet0/0
3.3.3.3           1   EXSTART/BDR     00:00:39    10.5.5.3        FastEthernet0/0


*Apr 28 12:36:00.231: %OSPF-5-ADJCHG: Process 4, Nbr 2.2.2.2 on FastEthernet0/0
from EXSTART to DOWN, Neighbor Down: Too many retransmissions
R4# show ip ospf neighbors

Neighbor ID     Pri   State           Dead Time   Address         Interface
1.1.1.1           1   INIT/DROTHER    00:00:39    10.5.5.1        FastEthernet0/0
2.2.2.2           1   DOWN/DROTHER        -       10.5.5.2        FastEthernet0/0
3.3.3.3           1   INIT/DROTHER    00:00:39    10.5.5.3        FastEthernet0/0
```

Note that you could argue that the mismatched MTU does not prevent routers from becoming neighbors, but it does prevent them from successfully exchanging topology data. When the mismatch occurs, a pair of routers tries to become neighbors, and they list each other in the output of the **show ip ospf neighbors** command, as seen in Example 7-6. However, the neighbor state (listed before the /, under the heading "State") moves from EXSTART (which means that the database exchange process is starting), but it fails as implied by the highlighted message in the example. Then, the state changes to DOWN, and later one router tries again, moving to the INIT (initializing) state. So, the neighbor is listed in the output of the **show ip ospf neighbors** command, but it never succeeds at exchanging topology data.

OSPF Neighbors and Adjacencies on WANs

To form OSPF neighbor relationships on WAN connections, OSPF still must meet the same requirements as on LANs. The area number must match with each neighbor; the IP subnet address and mask of each router must match; authentication must pass; and so on. In short, the items in Table 7-5 earlier in this chapter must be true.

However, the operation of OSPF on WAN links of various types requires some additional thought, particularly when developing an implementation and verification plan. In particular, depending on the WAN technology and configuration, the following additional questions might matter for proper OSPF operation over WAN connections:

■ Will the routers discover each other using multicast OSPF Hello messages, or do the neighbors require predefinition?

■ Will the routers try to elect a DR, and if so, which router should be the DR?

■ With which other routers should each router become an OSPF neighbor?

The first two of these items depend in part on the setting of the OSPF network type, and the third question depends on the WAN service. This section first examines the concept of OSPF network types and then examines the use of OSPF over common WAN technologies.

OSPF Network Types

The OSPF network type (a per-interface setting) directs OSPF in regard to three important facts:

■ Whether the router can expect to discover neighbors using multicast Hello messages

■ Whether only two or more than two OSPF routers can exist in the subnet attached to the interface

■ Whether the router should attempt to elect an OSPF DR on that interface

For example, LAN interfaces require a DR because of the default OSPF network type of broadcast. An OSPF network type of broadcast dynamically discovers neighbors using multicast Hello messages. Also, the broadcast OSPF network type supports more than two routers on the same subnet, and it elects a DR. Conversely, point-to-point links and point-to-point WAN subinterfaces default to use a network type of point-to-point, meaning that only two OSPF routers can exist in the subnet, neighbors can be dynamically discovered through Hellos, and the routers do not elect a DR.

In production networks, the network type is often ignored, because there is no motivation to change this setting—you pick a combination that works, and most everyone ignores it. However, for the sake of CCNP ROUTE, you need to be able to distinguish between these different OSPF network types.

Table 7-6 summarizes the OSPF network types and their meanings. Note that this per-interface or per-subinterface setting is configured with the **ip ospf network** *type* interface subcommand.

Table 7-6 *OSPF Network Types*

Interface Type	Uses DR/BDR?	Default Hello Interval	Dynamic Discovery of Neighbors?	More Than Two Routers Allowed in the Subnet?
Broadcast	Yes	10	Yes	Yes
Point-to-point[1]	No	10	Yes	No
Loopback	No	—	—	No
Nonbroadcast[2] (NBMA)	Yes	30	No	Yes
Point-to-multipoint	No	30	Yes	Yes
Point-to-multipoint nonbroadcast	No	30	No	Yes

[1] Default on Frame Relay point-to-point subinterfaces.

[2] Default on Frame Relay physical and multipoint subinterfaces.

OSPF Neighborship over Point-to-Point Links

Point-to-point serial links can be a bit boring. You configure IP addresses on either end, configure the clock rate if using a back-to-back serial cable in a lab, and configure **no shutdown** on the interfaces. When enabling OSPF on the interfaces, no extra effort is required compared to LANs—just enable OSPF on the interface, and rely on the default OSPF network type of point-to-point.

However, serial links can provide a convenient and uncluttered place to experiment with OSPF network types. As such, Figure 7-5 shows a small network with two routers, with Example 7-7 that follows showing several examples of the OSPF network type. (This small network matches a portion of the network shown in Figure 7-1 earlier in this chapter.)

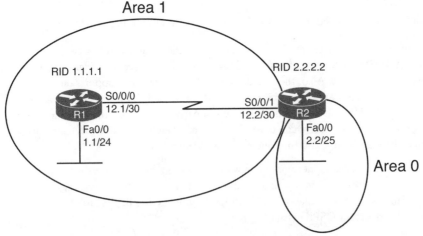

Note: All IP addresses begin with 10.1 unless otherwise noted.

Figure 7-5 *Simple Two-Router Internetwork*

Example 7-7 demonstrates OSPF network types with all defaults on the High-Level Data Link Control (HDLC) link between R1 and R2.

Example 7-7   *OSPF Network Types, Default, on an HDLC Link*

```
R1# show run int s0/0/0
Building configuration...

Current configuration : 102 bytes
!
interface Serial0/0/0
 ip address 10.1.12.1 255.255.255.252
 no fair-queue
 clock rate 1536000
!
router ospf 1
 network 10.0.0.0 0.255.255.255 area 1
!
end


R1# show ip ospf interface s0/0/0
Serial0/0/0 is up, line protocol is up
  Internet Address 10.1.12.1/30, Area 1
  Process ID 1, Router ID 1.1.1.1, Network Type POINT_TO_POINT, Cost: 64
! lines omitted for brevity


R1# show ip ospf neighbor

Neighbor ID     Pri   State           Dead Time   Address         Interface
2.2.2.2           0   FULL/   -       00:00:31    10.1.12.2       Serial0/0/0
```

Example 7-7 begins listing R1's configuration on the serial link, mainly to make the point that the OSPF network type has not been explicitly configured. The **show ip ospf interface** command then lists the network type (point-to-point). Based on Table 7-7, this type should dynamically discover neighbors, and it does, with neighbor 2.2.2.2 (R2) being listed at the end of the example. In particular, note that under the state heading in the **show ip ospf neighbor** command output, after the /, only a dash is listed. This notation means that no attempt was made to elect a DR. If the network type had implied that a DR should be elected, some text would be listed after the /, for example, "/DR" meaning that the neighbor was the DR. (Refer back to the end of Example 7-4 for an example of the output of **show ip ospf neighbor** in which a DR has been elected.)

Example 7-8 shows an alternative where both routers change their OSPF network type on the serial link to nonbroadcast. This change is nonsensical in real designs and is only done for the purposes of showing the results: that the neighbors are not discovered dynamically, but after being defined, a DR is elected.

> **Note** R2 has been preconfigured to match the configuration on R1 in Example 7-8. Specifically, the OSPF network type has been changed (**ip ospf network non-broadcast**), and R2 has been configured with a **neighbor 10.1.12.1** OSPF router subcommand.

Example 7-8 *Configuring OSPF Network Type Nonbroadcast on an HDLC Link*

```
R1# configure terminal
Enter configuration commands, one per line.  End with CNTL/Z.
R1(config)# interface s0/0/0
R1(config-if)# ip ospf network ?
  broadcast            Specify OSPF broadcast multi-access network
  non-broadcast        Specify OSPF NBMA network
  point-to-multipoint  Specify OSPF point-to-multipoint network
  point-to-point       Specify OSPF point-to-point network
R1(config-if)# ip ospf network non-broadcast
R1(config-if)# ^Z


R1# show ip ospf neighbor


R1# configure terminal
Enter configuration commands, one per line.  End with CNTL/Z.
R1(config)# router ospf 1
R1(config-router)# neighbor 10.1.12.2
R1(config-router)# ^Z
R1#


*Apr 28 20:10:15.755: %OSPF-5-ADJCHG: Process 1, Nbr 2.2.2.2 on Serial0/0/0 from
LOADING to FULL, Loading Done
R1# show ip ospf neighbor


Neighbor ID    Pri   State        Dead Time   Address       Interface
2.2.2.2          1   FULL/DR      00:01:58    10.1.12.2     Serial0/0/0
```

The example begins with R2 already configured, so the neighbor relationship has already failed. When the OSPF network type changes on R1's S0/0/0, the routers do not dynamically discover each other, based on the network type (nonbroadcast). However, by completing the configuration in the example by adding R1's **neighbor 10.1.12.2** command, the neighbor relationship is formed. Also, note that the final **show ip ospf neighbor** command lists a state of FULL, then a /, and then DR, meaning that a DR was indeed elected, as required by this OSPF network type.

Neighborship over Frame Relay Point-to-Point Subinterfaces

Frame Relay design allows several options for IP addressing and subnetting. One option treats each pair of routers on the ends of each PVC as a point-to-point topology, with one subnet assigned to each pair of routers. Another option treats more than two routers as a group, whether connected with a full mesh or partial mesh of PVCs, with a single subnet assigned to that group.

Many Frame Relay designs use the first option, treating each pair of routers on the ends of a PVC as a single subnet, as shown in Figure 7-6. In such cases, it makes sense to treat each PVC as a separate point-to-point connection, assigning a single subnet (at Layer 3) to each Layer 2 PVC.

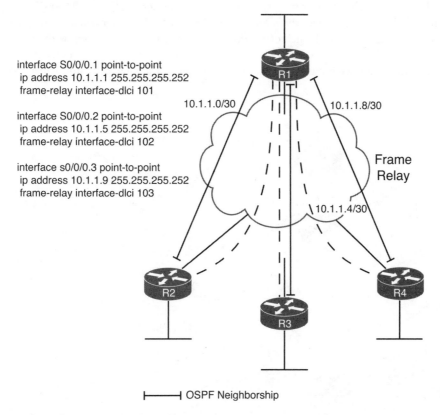

interface S0/0/0.1 point-to-point
ip address 10.1.1.1 255.255.255.252
frame-relay interface-dlci 101

interface S0/0/0.2 point-to-point
ip address 10.1.1.5 255.255.255.252
frame-relay interface-dlci 102

interface s0/0/0.3 point-to-point
ip address 10.1.1.9 255.255.255.252
frame-relay interface-dlci 103

10.1.1.0/30   10.1.1.8/30

Frame Relay

10.1.1.4/30

├────────┤ OSPF Neighborship

Figure 7-6 *Hub-and-Spoke Frame Relay Network*

With this design, if all the routers use point-to-point subinterfaces as shown in R1's configuration in the figure, you can ignore the OSPF network (interface) type and OSPF works fine. Cisco IOS point-to-point subinterfaces unsurprisingly default to use an OSPF network type of point-to-point. The two routers discover each other using multicast OSPF Hellos. They do not bother to elect a DR, and everything works well.

Neighborship on MPLS VPN

Multiprotocol Label Switching (MPLS) virtual private networks (VPN) create a WAN service that has some similarities but many differences when compared to Frame Relay. The customer routers connect to the service, often with serial links but at other times with Frame Relay PVCs or with Ethernet. The service itself is a Layer 3 service, forwarding IP packets through a cloud. As a result, no predefined PVCs need to exist between the customer routers. Additionally, the service uses routers at the edge of the service provider cloud—generically called provider edge (PE) routers—and these routers are Layer 3 aware.

That Layer 3 awareness means that the customer edge (CE) routers form an OSPF neighborship with the PE router on the other end of their local access link, as shown in Figure 7-7. The PE routers exchange their routes, typically using Multiprotocol BGP (MP-BGP). So, unlike the design seen previously in Figure 7-6, the central-site router will not have an OSPF neighborship with each branch office router but will have a neighborship with the MPLS VPN provider's PE router. MPLS VPN characteristics do impact the data seen in the LSDB in the enterprise routers and require some different thinking in regard to area design.

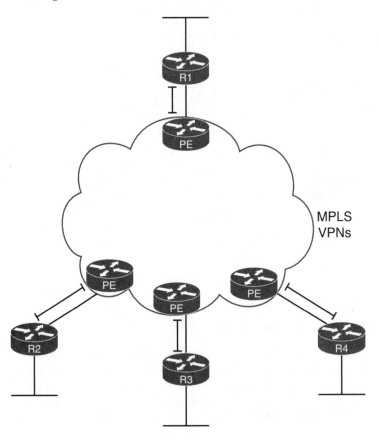

Figure 7-7   *OSPF Neighborships over MPLS VPN*

Neighborship on Metro Ethernet

In the like-named section "Neighborship on Metro Ethernet" in Chapter 4, "Fundamental EIGRP Concepts," you were introduced to some basic terminology for Metro Ethernet, including Virtual Private Wire Service (VPWS), a point-to-point service, and Virtual Private LAN Service (VPLS), a multipoint service. In both cases, however, if a customer connects to the service using a router, the configuration typically uses VLAN trunking with subinterfaces off a Fast Ethernet or Gigabit Ethernet interface. If connecting with a Layer 3 switch, the configuration again often uses VLAN trunking, with the Layer 3 configuration being made on various VLAN interfaces inside the switch configuration.

Because MetroE services provide Layer 2 connectivity, customer routers do not form OSPF neighborships with routers inside the service provider's network. Instead, OSPF neighborships form between customer routers, essentially as if the service were a large WAN. Figure 7-8 shows the basic idea, with four routers connected to the service.

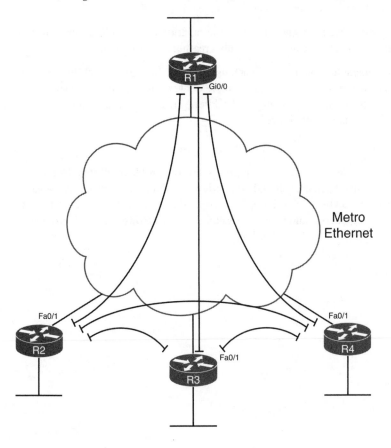

Figure 7-8 *OSPF Neighborships over Metro Ethernet*

Figure 7-8 shows four routers with any-to-any connectivity, typical of a VPWS service. However, from an OSPF design perspective, each pair of routers could communicate over a different VLAN, using a different Layer 3 subnet. Each Layer 3 subnet could be in a different area.

Virtual Links

OSPF area design requires the use of a backbone area, area 0, with each area connecting to area 0 through an ABR. However, in some cases, two backbone areas exist. In other cases, a nonbackbone area might not have a convenient point of connection to the backbone area, for example:

- **Case 1:** An existing internetwork needs to add a new area, with a convenient, low-cost connection point with another nonbackbone area; however, that connection does not give the new area any connection to area 0.

- **Case 2:** Even with a well-designed area 0, a combination of link failures might result in a discontiguous backbone area, essentially creating two backbone areas.

- **Case 3:** Two companies could merge, each using OSPF. To merge the OSPF domains, one backbone area must exist. It might be more convenient to connect the two networks using links through an existing nonbackbone area, but that design means two backbone areas, which is not allowed.

Figure 7-9 shows an example of each of the first two cases.

The problems in each case have different symptoms, but the problems all stem from the area design requirements: Each area should be contiguous, and each nonbackbone area should connect to the backbone area through an ABR. When the network does not meet these requirements, engineers could simply redesign the areas. However, OSPF provides an alternative tool called an OSPF *virtual link*.

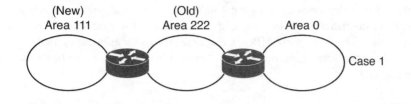

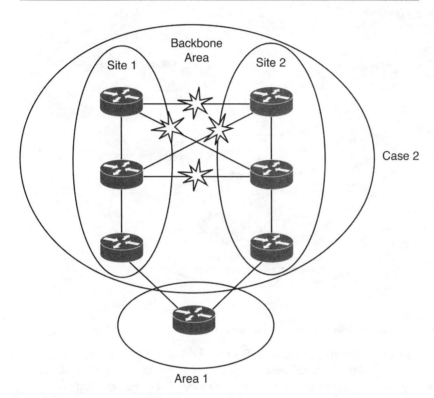

Figure 7-9   *Examples of Area Design Issues*

Understanding OSPF Virtual Link Concepts

An OSPF virtual link allows two ABRs that connect to the same nonbackbone area to form a neighbor relationship through that nonbackbone area, even when separated by many other routers and subnets. This virtual link acts like a virtual point-to-point connection between the two routers, with that link inside area 0. The routers form a neighbor relationship, inside area 0, and flood LSAs over that link.

For example, consider the topology in Figure 7-10, which shows an example of the third of the three cases described in the beginning of this section. In this case, two companies merged. Both companies had a small office in the same city, so for expediency's sake, they connected the two former enterprise internetworks through a newly combined local sales office in area 1.

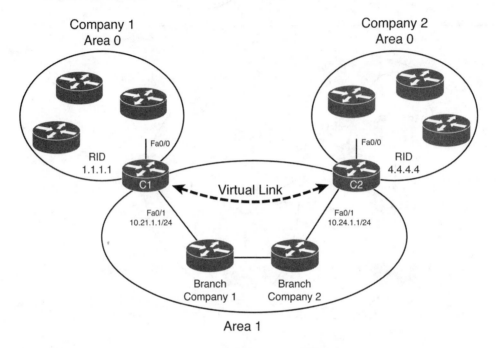

Figure 7-10   *Connecting Two Area 0s with a Virtual Link*

Although adding the link between branch offices can be a cost-effective temporary choice, it creates a design problem: Two backbone areas now exist, and OSPF requires that the backbone area be contiguous. To solve this problem, the engineer configures a virtual link between ABRs C1 and C2. The virtual link exists inside area 0, making area 0 contiguous.

To define the virtual link, each router configures the other router's RID and a reference to the area through which the virtual link passes (area 1 in this case). The two routers send the usual OSPF message types, encapsulated inside unicast IP packets, with a destination IP address of the router on the other end of the virtual link. Any routers between the two routers that create the virtual link—for example, the two branch routers in Figure 7-10—just forward these OSPF packets like any other packet. The neighbors on the ends of the virtual link flood their LSDBs to each other so that all routers in both parts of area 0 learn the routes from the other area 0.

The ABRs connected over a virtual link act mostly like any other ABR, with a couple of differences. The first difference is that ABRs send all OSPF messages as unicasts to the IP address of the router on the other end of the link. Second, the routers also mark the Do Not Age (DNA) bit in the LSAs, meaning that all routers on the other side of the virtual link will not expect the LSAs to be reflooded over the virtual link on the usual 30-minute refresh interval. This helps reduce overhead over the virtual link, which often runs over slower links and less-powerful routers. The router also assigns an OSPF cost to the virtual link, just as it would for an interface.

After the virtual link is up, the ABRs' SPF processes can calculate their best routes just like before, using the virtual link as another point-to-point link in area 0. For packets destined to pass from one part of the backbone over the virtual link to the other part of the backbone, the chosen best routes eventually lead the packets to the router with the virtual link. That router, connected to the transit nonbackbone area, has already calculated its next hop based on the LSDB in the transit area (Router C1 and transit area 1 in the example of Figure 7-10). The routers in the transit area choose routes that eventually deliver the packet to the router on the other end of the virtual link (Router C2 in Figure 7-10).

Configuring OSPF Virtual Links

Configuring an OSPF virtual link requires a minor amount of configuration just to get the link working, with several optional configuration items. Most of the optional configuration settings relate to features that would normally be configured on the interface connecting two neighboring routers, but with a virtual link, there is no such interface, so the parameters must be added to the **area virtual-link** command. The following list summarizes the key configuration options on the **area virtual-link** router subcommand:

- The *remote-RID* in the **area** *area-num* **virtual-link** *remote-RID* command refers to the other router's RID.

- The *area-num* in the **area** *area-num* **virtual-link** *remote-RID* command refers to the transit area over which the packets flow between the two routers.

- The transit area over which the two routers communicate must not be a stubby area.

- The optional configuration of OSPF neighbor authentication parameters, normally configured as interface subcommands, must be configured as additional parameters on the **area virtual-link** command.

- The optional configuration of Hello and Dead intervals, normally configured as interface subcommands, must be configured as additional parameters on the **area virtual-link** command.

- The router assigns the virtual link an OSPF cost as if it were a point-to-point link. The router calculates the cost as the cost to reach the router on the other end of the link, as calculated using the transit area's LSDB.

Example 7-9 shows the configuration of a virtual link on Router C1 and Router C2 shown in Figure 7-10. The configuration shows the virtual link, referencing area 1 as the transit area, with each router referring to the other router's RIDs. The configuration also shows the loopback IP addresses on which the ABR's RIDs are based being advertised into OSPF.

Example 7-9 *OSPF Virtual Link Configuration on Routers C1 and C2*

```
! On Router C1:
router ospf 1
 area 1 virtual-link 4.4.4.4
!
interface fastethernet0/0
 ip address 10.1.1.1 255.255.255.0
 ip ospf 1 area 0
!
interface fastethernet0/1
 ip address 10.21.1.1 255.255.255.0
 ip ospf 1 area 1
!
interface loopback 1
 ip address 1.1.1.1 255.255.255.0
 ip ospf 1 area 1

! On Router C2:
router ospf 4
 area 1 virtual-link 1.1.1.1
!
interface fastethernet0/0
 ip address 10.4.4.4 255.255.255.0
 ip ospf 4 area 0
!
interface fastethernet0/1
 ip address 10.24.1.1 255.255.255.0
 ip ospf 4 area 1
!
interface loopback 1
 ip address 4.4.4.4 255.255.255.0
 ip ospf 4 area 1
```

Verifying the OSPF Virtual Link

To prove whether the virtual link works, a neighbor relationship between C1 and C2 must reach the FULL state, resulting in all routers in both parts of area 0 having the same area 0 LSDB. Example 7-10 shows the working neighbor relationship, plus status information for the virtual link with the **show ip ospf virtual-links** command.

Example 7-10 *OSPF Virtual Link Configuration on Routers C1 and C2*

```
C1# show ip ospf virtual-links
Virtual Link OSPF_VL0 to router 4.4.4.4 is up
  Run as demand circuit
  DoNotAge LSA allowed.
```

```
Transit area 1, via interface FastEthernet0/1, Cost of using 3
Transmit Delay is 1 sec, State POINT_TO_POINT,
Timer intervals configured, Hello 10, Dead 40, Wait 40, Retransmit 5
  Hello due in 00:00:02
  Adjacency State FULL (Hello suppressed)
  Index 1/2, retransmission queue length 0, number of retransmission 0
  First 0x0(0)/0x0(0) Next 0x0(0)/0x0(0)
  Last retransmission scan length is 0, maximum is 0
  Last retransmission scan time is 0 msec, maximum is 0 msec
!
! next, note that the neighbor reaches FULL state, with no DR elected.

C1# show ip ospf neighbor

Neighbor ID     Pri   State          Dead Time   Address        Interface
4.4.4.4           0   FULL/  -           -        10.24.1.1      OSPF_VL0
2.2.2.2           1   FULL/DR       00:00:35     10.21.1.2      FastEthernet0/1


C1# show ip ospf neighbor detail 4.4.4.4
 Neighbor 4.4.4.4, interface address 10.24.1.1
    In the area 0 via interface OSPF_VL0
    Neighbor priority is 0, State is FULL, 6 state changes
    DR is 0.0.0.0 BDR is 0.0.0.0
    Options is 0x32 in Hello (E-bit, L-bit, DC-bit)
    Options is 0x72 in DBD (E-bit, L-bit, DC-bit, O-bit)
    LLS Options is 0x1 (LR)
    Neighbor is up for 00:00:21
    Index 1/2, retransmission queue length 0, number of retransmission 0
    First 0x0(0)/0x0(0) Next 0x0(0)/0x0(0)
    Last retransmission scan length is 0, maximum is 0
    Last retransmission scan time is 0 msec, maximum is 0 msec
```

The only new command in the example, **show ip ospf virtual-links,** details some items unique to virtual links. In particular, the first highlighted portion shows the assignment of a name to the link (VL0); if multiple virtual links were configured, each would have a different number. This virtual link name/number is then referenced inside the LSDB. It also shows that the routers both allow the use of the Do Not Age (DNA) bit, so periodic reflooding will not occur over this virtual link. It lists a cost of 3. As it turns out, each of the three interfaces between Router C1 and C2 have an OSPF cost of 1, so C1's area 1 cost to reach C2 is 3. The output also confirms that the routers have reached a fully adjacent state and are suppressing the periodic Hello messages.

The familiar **show ip ospf neighbor** command lists a few new items as well. Note that the interface refers to the virtual link "OSPF VL0" instead of the interface, because there is no interface between the neighbors. It also lists no Dead timer, because the neighbors choose to not use the usual Hello/Dead interval process over a virtual link. (Instead, if all the transit area's routes to reach the router on the other router of the link fail, the virtual link fails.) Finally, the **show ip ospf neighbor detail 4.4.4.4** command shows the interesting phrase "In the area 0 via interface OSPF VL0," confirming that the neighborship does indeed exist in area 0.

Note   OSPF does not require that the RID IP address range be advertised as a route in OSPF. As a result, the RID listed in the **area virtual-link** command might not be pingable, but the virtual link still works.

Exam Preparation Tasks

Planning Practice

The CCNP ROUTE exam expects test takers to review design documents, create implementation plans, and create verification plans. This section provides some exercises that can help you to take a step back from the minute details of the topics in this chapter, so that you can think about the same technical topics from the planning perspective.

For each planning practice table, simply complete the table. Note that any numbers in parentheses represent the number of options listed for each item in the solutions in Appendix F, "Completed Planning Practice Tables."

Design Review Table

Table 7-7 lists several design goals related to this chapter. If these design goals were listed in a design document, and you had to take that document and develop an implementation plan, what implementation options come to mind? For any configuration items, a general description can be used, without concern about specific parameters.

Table 7-7 *Design Review*

Design Goal	Possible Implementation Choices Covered in This Chapter
Improve OSPF convergence.	
Implement OSPF on each router so that neighborships are formed (2).	
Limit neighborship formation on OSPF-enabled interfaces (2).	
The design shows branch routers with WAN interfaces in area 0 and LAN interfaces in different areas for each branch. What LSDB information do you expect to see in the branch routers?	
A merger design plan shows two companies with OSPF backbone areas. How can the two area 0s be connected? (2)	

Implementation Plan Peer Review Table

Table 7-8 shows a list of questions that others might ask, or that you might think about, during a peer review of another network engineer's implementation plan. Complete the table by answering the questions.

Table 7-8 *Notable Questions from This Chapter to Consider During an Implementation Plan Peer Review*

Question	Answers
What happens on a router interface on which an OSPF **network** command matches the interface? (2)	
What configuration settings prevent OSPF neighbor discovery on an OSPF-enabled interface?	
What settings do potential neighbors check before becoming OSPF neighbors? (7)	
What settings that many CCNP candidates might think would impact OSPF neighbor relationships actually do not prevent a neighborship from forming?	
A design shows one main site and 100 branches, with OSPF and MPLS VPNs. How many OSPF neighborships over the WAN do you expect to see on the central-site router?	
A design shows one main site and 100 branches, with one Frame Relay PVC between the main site and each branch. How many OSPF neighborships over the WAN do you expect to see on the central-site router?	
A design shows six routers connected to the same VLAN and subnet. How many OSPF fully adjacent neighborships over this subnet do you expect each router to have?	
A design shows one main site and 100 branches, each connected with a VPWS service. The configuration shows that the central-site router uses a separate VLAN subinterface to connect to each branch, but the branch routers do not have a VLAN connecting to other branches. How many OSPF fully adjacent neighborships over the WAN do you expect to see on the central site router?	

Create an Implementation Plan Table

To practice skills useful when creating your own OSPF implementation plan, list in Table 7-9 configuration commands related to the configuration of the following features. You might want to record your answers outside the book and set a goal to complete this table (and others like it) from memory during your final reviews before taking the exam.

Table 7-9 *Implementation Plan Configuration Memory Drill*

Feature	Configuration Commands/Notes
Enabling OSPF on interfaces—traditional method	
Enabling OSPF on interfaces—using interface subcommands	
Setting Hello and Dead intervals	
Passive interfaces, with router subcommands	
OSPF router ID	
Create a virtual link through transit area X	

Choose Commands for a Verification Plan Table

To practice skills useful when creating your own OSPF verification plan, list in Table 7-10 all commands that supply the requested information. You might want to record your answers outside the book and set a goal to complete this table (and others like it) from memory during your final reviews before taking the exam.

Table 7-10 *Verification Plan Memory Drill*

Information Needed	Command
Which routes have been added to the IP routing table by OSPF?	
All routes in a router's routing table	
The specific route for a single destination address or subnet	
A list of all (both static and dynamically discovered) OSPF neighbors	
List interfaces on which OSPF has been enabled	
List the number of OSPF neighbors and fully adjacent neighbors known through a particular interface	
The elapsed time since a neighborship was formed	
The configured Hello timer for an interface	
The configured Dead interval timer for an interface	

Information Needed	Command
The current actual Dead timer for a neighbor	
A router's RID	
A list of OSPF passive interfaces	
List traffic statistics about OSPF	
Display the name and status of a virtual link	

Note Some of the entries in this table may not have been specifically mentioned in this chapter but are listed in this table for review and reference.

Review All the Key Topics

Review the most important topics from inside the chapter, noted with the Key Topic icon in the outer margin of the page. Table 7-11 lists a reference of these key topics and the page numbers on which each is found.

Table 7-11 *Key Topics for Chapter 7*

Key Topic Element	Description	Page Number
Table 7-2	Commonly Used OSPF Terms	265
List	Base OSPF configuration steps	266
List	Rules for choosing an OSPF router ID	268
Table 7-3	Commonly Used OSPF **show** Commands	269
Table 7-4	OSPF Feature Summary	271
List	Requirements before OSPF will attempt to dynamically discover neighbors	272
Table 7-5	Neighbor Requirements for EIGRP and OSPF	275
Table 7-6	OSPF Network Types	282
List	Configuration options for the **area virtual-link** command	291

Complete the Tables and Lists from Memory

Print a copy of Appendix D, "Memory Tables," (found on the CD) or at least the section for this chapter, and complete the tables and lists from memory. Appendix E, "Memory Tables Answer Key," also on the CD, includes completed tables and lists to check your work.

Define Key Terms

Define the following key terms from this chapter, and check your answers in the glossary:

area, area border router (ABR), backbone router, router ID, Hello interval, Dead interval, fully adjacent, OSPF network type, virtual link

This chapter covers the following topics:

- **LSAs and the OSPF Link-State Database:**
  This section examines LSA Types 1, 2, and 3 and
  describes how they allow OSPF routers to model a
  topology and choose the best routes for each known
  subnet.

- **The Database Exchange Process:** This section
  details how neighboring routers use OSPF messages
  to exchange their LSAs.

- **Choosing the Best Internal OSPF Routes:** This
  section examines how OSPF routers calculate the
  cost for each possible route to each subnet.

CHAPTER 8

The OSPF Link-State Database

Open Shortest Path First (OSPF) and Enhanced Interior Gateway Routing Protocol (EIGRP) both use three major branches of logic, each of which populates a different table: the neighbor table, the topology table, or the IP routing table. This chapter examines topics related to the OSPF topology table—the contents and the processes by which routers exchange this information—and describes how OSPF routers choose the best routes in the topology table to be added to the IP routing table.

In particular, this chapter begins by looking at the building blocks of an OSPF topology table, namely, the OSPF *link-state advertisement (LSA)*. Following that, the chapter examines the process by which OSPF routers exchange LSAs with each other. Finally, the last major section of the chapter discusses how OSPF chooses the best route among many when running the *Shortest Path First (SPF)* algorithm.

Note that this chapter focuses on OSPF version 2, the long-available version of OSPF that supports IPv4 routes. Chapter 9, "Advanced OSPF Concepts," discusses OSPF version 3, which applies to IPv6.

"Do I Know This Already?" Quiz

The "Do I Know This Already?" quiz allows you to assess whether you should read the entire chapter. If you miss no more than one of these nine self-assessment questions, you might want to move ahead to the "Exam Preparation Tasks" section. Table 8-1 lists the major headings in this chapter and the "Do I Know This Already?" quiz questions covering the material in those headings so that you can assess your knowledge of those specific areas. The answers to the "Do I Know This Already?" quiz appear in Appendix A.

Table 8-1 *"Do I Know This Already?" Foundation Topics Section-to-Question Mapping*

Foundation Topics Section	Questions
LSAs and the OSPF Link-State Database	1–3
The Database Exchange Process	4, 5
Choosing the Best OSPF Routes	6–9

1. A network design shows area 1 with three internal routers, area 0 with four internal routers, and area 2 with five internal routers. Additionally, one ABR (ABR1) connects areas 0 and 1, plus a different ABR (ABR2) connects areas 0 and 2. How many Type 1 LSAs would be listed in ABR2's LSDB?

   a. 6

   b. 7

   c. 15

   d. 12

   e. None of the other answers are correct.

2. A network planning diagram shows a large internetwork with many routers. The configurations show that OSPF has been enabled on all interfaces, IP addresses correctly configured, and OSPF working. For which of the following cases would you expect a router to create and flood a Type 2 LSA?

   a. When OSPF is enabled on a LAN interface, and the router is the only router connected to the subnet

   b. When OSPF is enabled on a point-to-point serial link, and that router has both the higher router ID and higher interface IP address on the link

   c. When OSPF is enabled on a Frame Relay point-to-point subinterface, has the lower RID and lower subinterface IP address, and otherwise uses default OSPF configuration on the interface

   d. When OSPF is enabled on a working LAN interface on a router, and the router has been elected as a BDR

   e. None of the other answers are correct.

3. A verification plan shows a network diagram with branch office Routers B1 through B100, plus two ABRs, ABR1 and ABR2, all in area 100. The branches connect to the ABRs using Frame Relay point-to-point subinterfaces. The verification plan lists the output of the **show ip ospf database summary 10.100.0.0** command on a Router B1, one of the branches. Which of the following is true regarding the output that could be listed for this command?

   a. The output lists nothing unless 10.100.0.0 has been configured as a summary route using the **area range** command.

   b. If 10.100.0.0 is a subnet in area 0, the output lists one Type 3 LSA, specifically the LSA with the lower metric when comparing ABR1's and ABR2's LSA for 10.100.0.0.

   c. If 10.100.0.0 is a subnet in area 0, the output lists two Type 3 LSAs, one each created by ABR1 and ABR2.

   d. None, because the Type 3 LSAs would exist only in the ABR's LSDBs.

4. Which of the following OSPF messages contains complete LSAs used during the database exchange process?

   a. LSR

   b. LSAck

   c. LSU

   d. DD

   e. Hello

5. Routers R1, R2, R3, and R4 connect to the same 10.10.10.0/24 LAN-based subnet. OSPF is fully working in the subnet. Later, R5, whose OSPF priority is higher than the other four routers, joins the subnet. Which of the following are true about the OSPF database exchange process over this subnet at this point? (Choose two.)

   a. R5 will send its DD, LSR, and LSU packets to the 224.0.0.5 all-DR-routers multicast address.

   b. R5 will send its DD, LSR, and LSU packets to the 224.0.0.6 all-DR-routers multicast address.

   c. The DR will inform R5 about LSAs by sending its DD, LSR, and LSU packets to the 224.0.0.6 all-SPF-routers multicast address.

   d. The DR will inform R5 about LSAs by sending its DD, LSR, and LSU packets to the 224.0.0.5 all-SPF-routers multicast address.

6. R1 is internal to area 1, and R2 is internal to area 2. Subnet 10.1.1.0/24 exists in area 2 as a connected subnet off R2. ABR1 connects area 1 to backbone area 0, and ABR2 connects area 0 to area 2. Which of the following LSAs must R1 use when calculating R1's best route for 10.1.1.0/24?

   a. R2's Type 1 LSA

   b. Subnet 10.1.1.0/24's Type 2 LSA

   c. ABR1's Type 1 LSA in area 0

   d. Subnet 10.1.1.0/24's Type 3 LSA in Area 0

   e. Subnet 10.1.1.0/24's Type 3 LSA in Area 1

7. Which of the following LSA types describe topology information that, when changed, requires a router in the same area to perform an SPF calculation? (Choose two.)

   a. 1

   b. 2

   c. 3

   d. 4

   e. 5

   f. 7

8. The following output was taken from Router R3. A scan of R3's configuration shows that no **bandwidth** commands have been configured in this router. Which of the following answers list configuration settings that could be a part of a configuration that results in the following output? Note that only two of the three interface's costs have been set directly. (Choose two.)

```
R3# show ip ospf interface brief
Interface      PID   Area          IP Address/Mask      Cost   State Nbrs F/C
Se0/0/0.2      3     34            10.10.23.3/29        647    P2P   1/1
Se0/0/0.1      3     34            10.10.13.3/29        1000   P2P   1/1
Fa0/0          3     34            10.10.34.3/24        20     BDR   1/1
```

a. An **auto-cost reference-bandwidth 1000** command in router ospf mode

b. An **auto-cost reference-bandwidth 2000** command in router ospf mode

c. An **ip ospf cost 1000 interface S0/0/0.1** command in router ospf mode

d. An **auto-cost reference-bandwidth 64700** command in router ospf mode

9. Which of the following LSA types describe information related to topology or subnets useful for calculating routes for subnets inside the OSPF domain? (Choose three.)

a. 1

b. 2

c. 3

d. 4

e. 5

f. 7

Foundation Topics

LSAs and the OSPF Link-State Database

Every router that connects to a given OSPF area should learn the exact same topology data. Each router stores the data, composed of individual *link-state advertisements (LSA)*, in its own copy of the *link-state database (LSDB)*. Then, the router applies the *Shortest Path First (SPF)* algorithm to the LSDB to determine the best (lowest-cost) route for each reachable subnet (prefix/length).

When a router uses SPF to analyze the LSDB, the SPF process has some similarities to how humans put a jigsaw puzzle together—but without a picture of what the puzzle looks like. Humans faced with such a challenge might first look for the obvious puzzle pieces, such as the corner and edge pieces, because they are easily recognized. You might then group puzzle pieces together if they have the same color or look for straight lines that might span multiple puzzle pieces. And of course, you would be looking at the shapes of the puzzle pieces to see which ones fit together.

Similarly, a router's SPF process must examine the individual LSAs and see how they fit together, based on their characteristics. To better appreciate the SPF process, the first section of this chapter examines the three LSA types that OSPF uses to describe an enterprise OSPF topology inside an OSPF domain. By understanding the types of LSAs, you can get a better understanding of what a router might look for to take the LSAs—the pieces of a network topology puzzle, if you will—and build the equivalent of a network diagram.

Table 8-2 lists the various OSPF LSA types. Not all of these LSA types are discussed in this chapter but are provided in the table as a convenience when studying.

Key Topic

Table 8-2 *OSPF LSA Types*

LSA Type	Common Name	Description
1	Router	Each router creates its own Type 1 LSA to represent itself for each area to which it connects. The LSDB for one area contains one Type 1 LSA per router per area, listing the RID and all interface IP addresses on that router that are in that area. Represents stub networks as well.
2	Network	One per transit network. Created by the DR on the subnet, and represents the subnet and the router interfaces connected to the subnet.
3	Net Summary	Created by ABRs to represent subnets listed in one area's Type 1 and 2 LSAs when being advertised into another area. Defines the links (subnets) in the origin area, and cost, but no topology data.

LSA Type	Common Name	Description
4	ASBR Summary	Like a Type 3 LSA, except it advertises a host route used to reach an ASBR.
5	AS External	Created by ASBRs for external routes injected into OSPF.
6	Group Membership	Defined for MOSPF; not supported by Cisco IOS.
7	NSSA External	Created by ASBRs inside an NSSA area, instead of a Type 5 LSA.
8	Link LSAs	Type 8 LSAs only exist on a local link, where they are used by a router to advertise the router's link-local address to all other routers on the same link. Additionally, the Type 8 LSA provides to routers on that link a listing of all IPv6 addresses associated with the link.
9	Intra-Area Prefix LSAs	Can send information about IPv6 networks (including stub networks) attached to a router (similar to the Type 1 LSA for IPv4 networks). Additionally, a Type 9 LSA can send information about transit IPv6 network segments within an area (similar to the Type 2 LSA for IPv4 networks).
10, 11	Opaque	Used as generic LSAs to allow easy future extension of OSPF. For example, Type 10 has been adapted for MPLS traffic engineering.

LSA Type 1: Router LSA

An LSA type 1, called a *Router LSA*, identifies an OSPF router based on its OSPF router ID (RID). Each router creates a Type 1 LSA for itself and floods the LSA throughout the same area. To flood the LSA, the originating router sends the Type 1 LSA to its neighbors inside the same area, who in turn send it to their other neighbors inside the same area, until all routers in the area have a copy of the LSA.

Besides the RID of the router, this LSA also lists information about the attached links. In particular, the Type 1 LSA lists

- For each interface on which no designated router (DR) has been elected, it lists the router's interface subnet number/mask and interface OSPF cost. (OSPF refers to these subnets as *stub networks*.)

- For each interface on which a DR has been elected, it lists the IP address of the DR and a notation that the link attaches to a transit network (meaning that a Type 2 LSA exists for that network).

- For each interface with no DR, but for which a neighbor is reachable, it lists the neighbor's RID.

As with all OSPF LSAs, OSPF identifies a Type 1 LSA using a 32-bit link-state identifier (LSID). When creating its own Type 1 LSA, each router uses its own OSPF RID value as the LSID.

Internal routers each create a single Type 1 LSA for themselves, but area border routers (ABR) create multiple Type 1 LSAs for themselves: one per area. The Type 1 LSA in one area will list only interfaces in that area and only neighbors in that area. However, the router still has only a single RID, so all its Type 1 LSAs for a single router list the same RID. The ABR then floods each of its Type 1 LSAs into the appropriate area.

To provide a better backdrop for the upcoming LSA discussions, Figure 8-1 shows a sample internetwork, which will be used in most of the examples in this chapter.

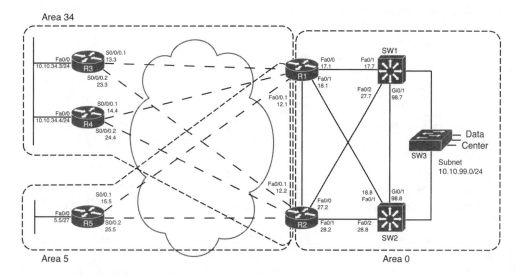

Figure 8-1 *Sample OSPF Multiarea Design*

Note Unless otherwise noted, the first two octets of all networks in Figure 8-1 are 10.10, which are not shown to make the figure more readable.

All routers that participate in an area, be they internal routers or ABRs, create and flood a Type 1 LSA inside the area. For example, in Figure 8-1, area 5 has one internal router (R5, RID 5.5.5.5) and two ABRs: R1 with RID 1.1.1.1 and R2 with RID 2.2.2.2. Each of these three routers creates and floods its own Type 1 LSA inside area 5 so that all three routers know the same three Type 1 LSAs.

Next, to further understand the details inside a Type 1 LSA, first consider the OSPF configuration of R5 as an example. R5 has three IP-enabled interfaces: Fa0/0, S0/0.1, and S0/0.2. R5 uses point-to-point subinterfaces, so R5 should form neighbor relationships with both R1 and R2 with no extra configuration beyond enabling OSPF, in area 5, on all three interfaces. Example 8-1 shows this baseline configuration on R5.

Example 8-1   *R5 Configuration—IP Addresses and OSPF*

```
interface Fastethernet0/0
 ip address 10.10.5.5 255.255.255.224
 ip ospf 5 area 5
!
interface s0/0.1 point-to-point
 ip address 10.10.15.5 255.255.255.248
 frame-relay interface-dlci 101
 ip ospf 5 area 5
!
interface s0/0.2 point-to-point
 ip address 10.10.25.5 255.255.255.248
 frame-relay interface-dlci 102
 ip ospf 5 area 5
!
router ospf 5
 router-id 5.5.5.5
!
R5# show ip ospf interface brief
Interface   PID   Area        IP Address/Mask   Cost  State Nbrs F/C
se0/0.2     5     5           10.10.25.5/29     64    P2P   1/1
se0/0.1     5     5           10.10.15.5/29     64    P2P   1/1
fa0/0       5     5           10.10.5.5/27      1     DR    0/0
R5# show ip ospf neighbor

Neighbor ID   Pri   State       Dead Time   Address       Interface
2.2.2.2       0     FULL/  -    00:00:30    10.10.25.2    Serial0/0.2
1.1.1.1       0     FULL/  -    00:00:38    10.10.15.1    Serial0/0.1
```

R5's OSPF configuration enables OSPF, for process ID 5, placing three interfaces in area 5. As a result, R5's Type 1 LSA will list at least these three interfaces as links, plus it will refer to the two working neighbors. Example 8-2 displays the contents of R5's area 5 LSDB, including the detailed information in R5's Type 1 LSA, including the following:

- The LSID of R5's Type 1 LSA (5.5.5.5)

- Three links that connect to a stub network, each listing the subnet/mask

- Two links that state a connection to another router, one listing R1 (RID 1.1.1.1) and one listing R2 (RID 2.2.2.2)

Example 8-2   *R5 Configuration—IP Addresses and OSPF*

```
R5# show ip ospf database


            OSPF Router with ID (5.5.5.5) (Process ID 5)


            Router Link States (Area 5)
```

```
Link ID         ADV Router      Age         Seq#        Checksum  Link count
1.1.1.1         1.1.1.1         835         0x80000002  0x006BDA  2
2.2.2.2         2.2.2.2         788         0x80000002  0x0082A6  2
5.5.5.5         5.5.5.5         787         0x80000004  0x0063C3  5


                Summary Net Link States (Area 5)


Link ID         ADV Router      Age         Seq#        Checksum
10.10.12.0      1.1.1.1         835         0x80000001 0x00F522
10.10.12.0      2.2.2.2         787         0x80000001 0x00D73C
! lines omitted for brevity


R5# show ip ospf database router 5.5.5.5


                OSPF Router with ID (5.5.5.5) (Process ID 5)


                Router Link States (Area 5)


  LS age: 796
  Options: (No TOS-capability, DC)
  LS Type: Router Links
  Link State ID: 5.5.5.5
  Advertising Router: 5.5.5.5
  LS Seq Number: 80000004
  Checksum: 0x63C3
  Length: 84
  Number of Links: 5


    Link connected to: another Router (point-to-point)
     (Link ID) Neighboring Router ID: 2.2.2.2
     (Link Data) Router Interface address: 10.10.25.5
     Number of TOS metrics: 0
       TOS 0 Metrics: 64


    Link connected to: a Stub Network
     (Link ID) Network/subnet number: 10.10.25.0
     (Link Data) Network Mask: 255.255.255.248
     Number of TOS metrics: 0
       TOS 0 Metrics: 64


    Link connected to: another Router (point-to-point)
     (Link ID) Neighboring Router ID: 1.1.1.1
     (Link Data) Router Interface address: 10.10.15.5
     Number of TOS metrics: 0
       TOS 0 Metrics: 64


    Link connected to: a Stub Network
```

```
(Link ID) Network/subnet number: 10.10.15.0
(Link Data) Network Mask: 255.255.255.248
  Number of TOS metrics: 0
    TOS 0 Metrics: 64


Link connected to: a Stub Network
  (Link ID) Network/subnet number: 10.10.5.0
  (Link Data) Network Mask: 255.255.255.224
    Number of TOS metrics: 0
      TOS 0 Metrics: 1
```

The first command, **show ip ospf database**, displays a summary of the LSAs known to R5. The output mainly consists of a single line per LSA, listed by LSA ID. The three high-lighted lines of this output, in Example 8-2, highlight the RID of the three router (Type 1) LSAs, namely, 1.1.1.1 (R1), 2.2.2.2 (R2), and 5.5.5.5 (R5).

The output of the **show ip ospf database router 5.5.5.5** command displays the detailed information in R5's Router LSA. Looking at the highlighted portions, you see three stub networks—three interfaces on which no DR has been elected—and the associated subnet numbers. The LSA also lists the neighbor IDs of two neighbors (1.1.1.1 and 2.2.2.2) and the interfaces on which these neighbors can be reached.

Armed with the same kind of information in R1's and R2's Type 1 LSAs, a router has enough information to determine which routers connect, over which stub links, and then use the interface IP address configuration to figure out the interfaces that connect to the other routers. Figure 8-2 shows a diagram of area 5 that could be built just based on the detailed information held in the Router LSAs for R1, R2, and R5.

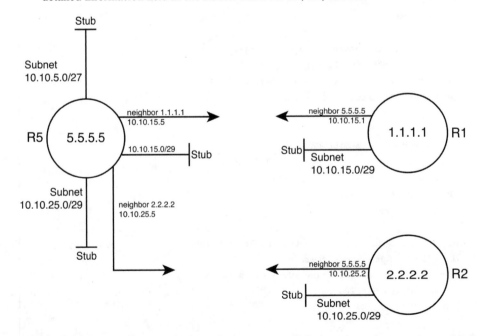

Figure 8-2   *Three Type 1 LSAs in Area 5*

Note that Figure 8-2 displays only information that could be learned from the Type 1 Router LSAs inside area 5. Each Type 1 Router LSA lists information about a router, but only the details related to a specific area. As a result, Figure 8-2 shows R1's interface in area 5 but none of the interfaces in area 34 nor in area 0. To complete the explanation surrounding Figure 8-2, Example 8-3 lists R1's Type 1 Router LSA for area 5.

Example 8-3   *R1's Type 1 LSA in Area 5*

```
R5# show ip ospf database router 1.1.1.1


           OSPF Router with ID (5.5.5.5) (Process ID 5)


                 Router Link States (Area 5)


Routing Bit Set on this LSA
LS age: 1306
Options: (No TOS-capability, DC)
LS Type: Router Links
Link State ID: 1.1.1.1
Advertising Router: 1.1.1.1
LS Seq Number: 80000002
Checksum: 0x6BDA
Length: 48
Area Border Router
Number of Links: 2

  Link connected to: another Router (point-to-point)
   (Link ID) Neighboring Router ID: 5.5.5.5
   (Link Data) Router Interface address: 10.10.15.1
   Number of TOS metrics: 0
    TOS 0 Metrics: 64


  Link connected to: a Stub Network
   (Link ID) Network/subnet number: 10.10.15.0
   (Link Data) Network Mask: 255.255.255.248
   Number of TOS metrics: 0
    TOS 0 Metrics: 64
```

Note   Because OSPF uses the RID for many purposes inside different LSAs—for example, as the LSID of a Type 1 LSA—Cisco recommends setting the RID to a stable, predictable value. To do this, use the OSPF **router-id** *value* OSPF subcommand or define a loopback interface with an IP address.

LSA Type 2: Network LSA

SPF requires that the LSDB model the topology with nodes (routers) and connections between nodes (links). In particular, each link must be between a pair of nodes. When a multiaccess data link exists—for example, a LAN—OSPF must somehow model that LAN so that the topology represents nodes and links between only a pair of nodes. To do so, OSPF uses the concept of a Type 2 *Network LSA*.

OSPF routers actually choose whether to use a Type 2 LSA for a multiaccess network based on whether a designated router (DR) has or has not been elected on an interface. So, before discussing the details of the Type 2 Network LSA, a few more facts about the concept of a DR need to be discussed.

Background on Designated Routers

As discussed in Chapter 7's section "OSPF Network Types," the OSPF network type assigned to a router interface tells that router whether to attempt to elect a DR on that interface. Then, when a router has heard a Hello from at least one other router, the routers elect a DR and BDR.

OSPF uses a DR in a particular subnet for two main purposes:

- To create and flood a Type 2 Network LSA for that subnet

- To aid in the detailed process of database exchange over that subnet

Routers elect a DR, and a backup DR (BDR), based on information in the OSPF Hello. The Hello message lists each router's RID and a priority value. When no DR exists at the time, routers use the following election rules when neither a DR nor BDR yet exists:

- Choose the router with the highest priority (default 1, max 255, set with the **ip ospf priority** *value* interface subcommand).

- If tied on priority, choose the router with highest RID.

- Choose a BDR, based on next-best priority, or if a tie, next-best (highest) RID.

The preceding describes the election when no DR currently exists. However, the rules differ a bit when a DR and BDR already exist. After a DR and BDR are elected, no election is held until either the DR or BDR fails. If the DR fails, the BDR becomes the DR—regardless of whether a higher-priority router has joined the subnet—and a new election is held to choose a new BDR. If the BDR fails, a new election is held for the BDR, and the DR remains unchanged.

On LANs, the choice of DR matters little from a design perspective, but it does matter from an operational perspective. Throughout this chapter, note the cases in which the output of **show** commands identifies the DR and its role. Now, back to the topic of Type 2 LSAs.

Type 2 Network LSA Concepts

OSPF uses the concept of a Type 2 LSA to model a multiaccess network—a network with more than two routers connected to the same subnet—while still conforming to the "a link connects only two nodes" rule for the topology. For example, consider the network in Figure 8-3 (also shown as Figure 7-4 in the previous chapter). As seen in Chapter 7, "Fundamental OSPF Concepts," all four routers form neighbor relationships inside area 0, with the DR and BDR becoming fully adjacent with the other routers.

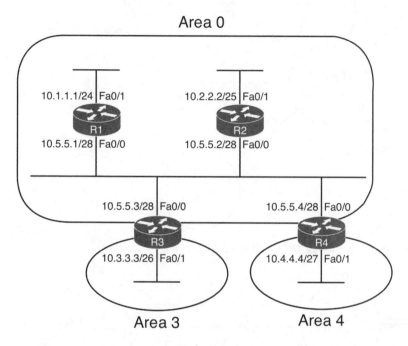

Figure 8-3   *Small Network, Four Routers, on a LAN*

OSPF cannot represent the idea of four routers connected through a single subnet by using a link connected to all four routers. Instead, OSPF defines the Type 2 Network LSA, used as a pseudonode. Each router's Type 1 Router LSA lists a connection to this pseudonode, often called a transit network, which is then modeled by a Type 2 Network LSA. The Type 2 Network LSA itself then lists references back to each Type 1 Router LSA connected to it—four in this example, as shown in Figure 8-4.

The elected DR in a subnet creates the Type 2 LSA for that subnet. The DR identifies the LSA by assigning an LSID of the DR's interface IP address in that subnet. The Type 2 LSA also lists the DR's RID as the router advertising the LSA.

Type 2 LSA show Commands

To see these concepts in the form of OSPF **show** commands, next consider area 34 back in Figure 8-1. This design shows that R3 and R4 connect to the same LAN, which means that a DR will be elected. (OSPF elects a DR on LANs when at least two routers pass the neighbor requirements and can become neighbors.) If both R3 and R4 default to use priority 1, R4 wins the election, because of its 4.4.4.4 RID (versus R3's 3.3.3.3 RID). So, R4 creates the Type 2 LSA for that subnet and floods the LSA. Figure 8-5 depicts the area 34 topology, and Example 8-4 shows the related LSDB entries.

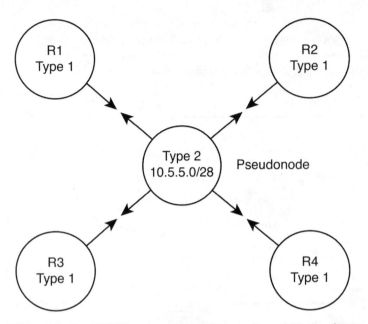

Figure 8-4   *OSPF Topology When Using a Type 2 Network LSA*

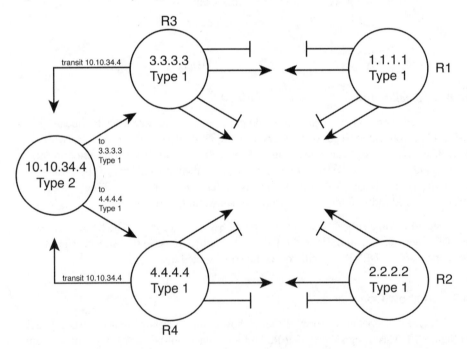

Figure 8-5   *Area 34 Topology with Four Type 1 LSAs and One Type 2 LSA*

Example 8-4   *Area 34 LSAs for R3, Network 10.10.34.0 /24*

```
R3# show ip ospf database

           OSPF Router with ID (3.3.3.3) (Process ID 3)

              Router Link States (Area 34)

Link ID         ADV Router      Age        Seq#        Checksum Link count
1.1.1.1         1.1.1.1         1061       0x80000002 0x00EA7A 4
2.2.2.2         2.2.2.2         1067       0x80000001 0x0061D2 4
3.3.3.3         3.3.3.3         1066       0x80000003 0x00E2E8 5
4.4.4.4         4.4.4.4         1067       0x80000003 0x007D3F 5

              Net Link States (Area 34)

Link ID         ADV Router      Age        Seq#        Checksum
10.10.34.4      4.4.4.4         1104       0x80000001 0x00AB28

              Summary Net Link States (Area 34)

Link ID         ADV Router      Age        Seq#        Checksum
10.10.5.0       1.1.1.1         1023       0x80000001 0x000BF2
10.10.5.0       2.2.2.2         1022       0x80000001 0x00EC0D
! lines omitted for brevity
R3# show ip ospf database router 4.4.4.4

           OSPF Router with ID (3.3.3.3) (Process ID 3)

              Router Link States (Area 34)

  LS age: 1078
  Options: (No TOS-capability, DC)
  LS Type: Router Links
  Link State ID: 4.4.4.4
  Advertising Router: 4.4.4.4
  LS Seq Number: 80000003
  Checksum: 0x7D3F
  Length: 84
  Number of Links: 5

    Link connected to: another Router (point-to-point)
     (Link ID) Neighboring Router ID: 2.2.2.2
     (Link Data) Router Interface address: 10.10.24.4
     Number of TOS metrics: 0
      TOS 0 Metrics: 64
```

```
     Link connected to: a Stub Network
       (Link ID) Network/subnet number: 10.10.24.0
       (Link Data) Network Mask: 255.255.255.248
       Number of TOS metrics: 0
         TOS 0 Metrics: 64

     Link connected to: another Router (point-to-point)
       (Link ID) Neighboring Router ID: 1.1.1.1
       (Link Data) Router Interface address: 10.10.14.4
       Number of TOS metrics: 0
         TOS 0 Metrics: 64

     Link connected to: a Stub Network
       (Link ID) Network/subnet number: 10.10.14.0
       (Link Data) Network Mask: 255.255.255.248
       Number of TOS metrics: 0
         TOS 0 Metrics: 64


     Link connected to: a Transit Network
       (Link ID) Designated Router address: 10.10.34.4
       (Link Data) Router Interface address: 10.10.34.4
       Number of TOS metrics: 0
         TOS 0 Metrics: 1
R3# show ip ospf database network 10.10.34.4


            OSPF Router with ID (3.3.3.3) (Process ID 3)


               Net Link States (Area 34)


  Routing Bit Set on this LSA
  LS age: 1161
  Options: (No TOS-capability, DC)
  LS Type: Network Links
  Link State ID: 10.10.34.4 (address of Designated Router)
  Advertising Router: 4.4.4.4
  LS Seq Number: 80000001
  Checksum: 0xAB28
  Length: 32
  Network Mask: /24
        Attached Router: 4.4.4.4
        Attached Router: 3.3.3.3
```

The **show ip ospf database** command lists a single line for each LSA. Note that the (high-lighted) heading for Network LSAs lists one entry, with LSID 10.10.34.4, which is R4's Fa0/0 IP address. The LSID for Type 2 Network LSAs is the interface IP address of the DR that creates the LSA.

The **show ip ospf database router 4.4.4.4** command shows the new style of entry for the reference to a transit network, which again refers to a connection to a Type 2 LSA. The output lists an LSID of 10.10.34.4, which again is the LSID of the Type 2 LSA.

Finally, the **show ip ospf database network 10.10.34.4** command shows the details of the Type 2 LSA, based on its LSID of 10.10.34.4. Near the bottom, the output lists the attached routers, based on RID. The SPF process can then use the cross-referenced information, as shown in Figure 8-5, to determine which routers connect to this transit network (pseudonode). The SPF process has information in both the Type 1 LSAs that refer to the transit network link to a Type 2 LSA, and the Type 2 LSA has a list of RIDs of Type 1 LSAs that connect to the Type 2 LSA, making the process of modeling the network possible.

OSPF can model all the topology inside a single area using Type 1 and 2 LSAs. When a router uses its SPF process to build a model of the topology, it can then calculate the best (lowest-cost) route for each subnet in the area. The next topic completes the LSA picture for internal OSPF routes by looking at Type 3 LSAs, which are used to model interarea routes.

LSA Type 3: Summary LSA

OSPF areas exist in part so that engineers can reduce the consumption of memory and compute resources in routers. Instead of having all routers, regardless of area, know all Type 1 and Type 2 LSAs inside an OSPF domain, ABRs do not forward Type 1 and Type 2 LSAs from one area into another area, and vice versa. This convention results in smaller per-area LSDBs, saving memory and reducing complexity for each run of the SPF algorithm, which saves CPU resources and improves convergence time.

However, even though ABRs do not flood Type 1 and Type 2 LSAs into other areas, routers still need to learn about subnets in other areas. OSPF advertises these interarea routes using the Type 3 *Summary LSA*. ABRs generate a Type 3 LSA for each subnet in one area, and advertise each Type 3 LSA into the other areas.

For example, if subnet A exists in area 3, the routers in area 3 learn of that subnet as part of Type 1 and Type 2 LSAs. However, an ABR connected to area 3 will not forward the Type 1 and Type 2 LSAs into other areas, instead creating a Type 3 LSA for each subnet (including subnet A). The routers inside the other areas can then calculate a route for the subnets (like subnet A) that exist inside another area.

Type 3 Summary LSAs do not contain all the detailed topology information, so in comparison to Types 1 and 2, these LSAs summarize the information—hence the name *Summary LSA*. Conceptually, a Type 3 LSA appears to be another subnet connected to the ABR that created and advertised the Type 3 LSA. The routers inside that area can calculate their best route to reach the ABR, which gives the router a good loop-free route to reach the subnet listed in a Type 3 LSA.

An example can certainly help in this case. First, consider the comparison shown in the top and bottom of Figure 8-6. The top depicts the topology shown back in Figure 8-1 if that design had used a single area. In that case, every router would have a copy of each

Type 1 LSA (shown as a router name in the figure) and each Type 2 LSA (abbreviated as T2 in the figure). The bottom of Figure 8-6 shows the area 5 topology, when holding to the three-area design shown in Figure 8-1.

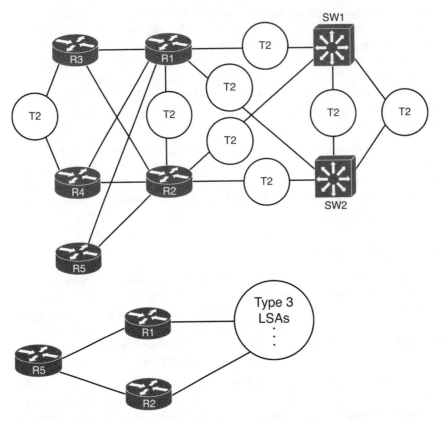

Figure 8-6   *Comparing a Single-Area LSDB to a Three-Area LSDB*

The ABR creates and floods each Type 3 LSA into the next area. The ABR assigns an LSID of the subnet address being advertised. It also adds its own RID to the LSA as well, so that routers know which ABR advertised the route. It also includes the subnet mask. The correlation between the advertising router's RID and the LSID (subnet address) allows the OSPF processes to create the part of the topology as shown with Type 3 LSAs at the bottom of Figure 8-6.

Example 8-5 focuses on the Type 3 LSAs in area 34 of the network shown in Figure 8-1. Ten subnets exist outside area 34. As ABRs, both R1 and R2 create and flood a Type 3 LSA for each of these ten subnets, resulting in 20 Type 3 LSAs listed in the output of the **show ip ospf database** command inside area 34. Then, the example focuses specifically on the Type 3 LSA for subnet 10.10.99.0/24.

Example 8-5   *Type 3 LSAs in Area 34*

```
R3# show ip ospf database

              OSPF Router with ID (3.3.3.3) (Process ID 3)

                    Router Link States (Area 34)

Link ID          ADV Router       Age        Seq#        Checksum Link count
1.1.1.1          1.1.1.1          943        0x80000003  0x00E87B 4
2.2.2.2          2.2.2.2          991        0x80000002  0x005FD3 4
3.3.3.3          3.3.3.3          966        0x80000004  0x00E0E9 5
4.4.4.4          4.4.4.4          977        0x80000004  0x007B40 5


                    Net Link States (Area 34)

Link ID          ADV Router       Age        Seq#        Checksum
10.10.34.4       4.4.4.4          977        0x80000002  0x00A929


                Summary Net Link States (Area 34)

Link ID          ADV Router       Age        Seq#        Checksum
10.10.5.0        1.1.1.1          943        0x80000002   0x0009F3
10.10.5.0        2.2.2.2          991        0x80000002  0x00EA0E
10.10.12.0       1.1.1.1          943        0x80000002  0x00F323
10.10.12.0       2.2.2.2          991        0x80000002  0x00D53D
10.10.15.0       1.1.1.1          943        0x80000002  0x0021BA
10.10.15.0       2.2.2.2          993        0x80000003  0x008313
10.10.17.0       1.1.1.1          946        0x80000002  0x00BC55
10.10.17.0       2.2.2.2          993        0x80000002  0x00A864
10.10.18.0       1.1.1.1          946        0x80000002  0x00B15F
10.10.18.0       2.2.2.2          994        0x80000002  0x009D6E
10.10.25.0       1.1.1.1          946        0x80000002  0x00355C
10.10.25.0       2.2.2.2          993        0x80000002  0x009439
10.10.27.0       1.1.1.1          946        0x80000002  0x0058AE
10.10.27.0       2.2.2.2          993        0x80000002  0x0030D3
10.10.28.0       1.1.1.1          947        0x80000002  0x004DB8
10.10.28.0       2.2.2.2          993        0x80000002  0x0025DD
10.10.98.0       1.1.1.1          946        0x80000002  0x004877
10.10.98.0       2.2.2.2          993        0x80000002  0x002A91
10.10.99.0       1.1.1.1          946        0x80000002  0x003D81
10.10.99.0       2.2.2.2          993        0x80000002  0x001F9B

R3# show ip ospf database summary 10.10.99.0
```

```
              OSPF Router with ID (3.3.3.3) (Process ID 3)


                Summary Net Link States (Area 34)


  Routing Bit Set on this LSA
  LS age: 1062
  Options: (No TOS-capability, DC, Upward)
  LS Type: Summary Links(Network)
  Link State ID: 10.10.99.0 (summary Network Number)
  Advertising Router: 1.1.1.1
  LS Seq Number: 80000002
  Checksum: 0x3D81
  Length: 28
  Network Mask: /24
        TOS: 0  Metric: 2


  Routing Bit Set on this LSA
  LS age: 1109
  Options: (No TOS-capability, DC, Upward)
  LS Type: Summary Links(Network)
  Link State ID: 10.10.99.0 (summary Network Number)
  Advertising Router: 2.2.2.2
  LS Seq Number: 80000002
  Checksum: 0x1F9B
  Length: 28
  Network Mask: /24
        TOS: 0  Metric: 2
```

Note   The Type 3 Summary LSA is not used for the purpose of route summarization. OSPF does support route summarization, and Type 3 LSAs might indeed advertise such a summary, but the Type 3 LSA does not inherently represent a summary route. The term *Summary* reflects the idea that the information is sparse compared to the detail inside Type 1 and Type 2 LSAs.

The upcoming section "Calculating the Cost of Interarea Routes" discusses how a router determines the available routes to reach subnets listed in a Type 3 LSA and how a router chooses which route is best.

Limiting the Number of LSAs

By default, Cisco IOS does not limit the number of LSAs that a router can learn. However, it might be useful to protect a router from learning too many LSAs to protect router memory. Also, with a large number of LSAs, the router might be unable to process the LSDB with SPF well enough to converge in a reasonable amount of time.

The maximum number of LSAs learned from other routers can be limited by a router using the **max-lsa** *number* OSPF subcommand. When configured, if the router learns more than the configured number of LSAs from other routers (ignoring those created by the router itself), the router reacts. The first reaction is to issue log messages. The router ignores the event for a time period, after which the router repeats the warning message. This ignore-and-wait strategy can proceed through several iterations, ending when the router closes all neighborships, discards its LSDB, and then starts adding neighbors again. (The ignore time, and the number of times to ignore the event, can be configured with the **max-lsa** command.)

Summary of Internal LSA Types

OSPF uses Type 1, 2, and 3 LSAs to calculate the best routes for all routes inside an OSPF routing domain. In a later chapter, we will explore Types 4, 5, and 7, which OSPF uses to calculate routes for external routes—routes redistributed into OSPF.

Table 8-3 summarizes some of the key points regarding OSPF Type 1, 2, and 3 LSAs. In particular for the ROUTE exam, the ability to sift through the output of various **show ip ospf database** commands can be important. Knowing what the OSPF LSID represents can help you interpret the output, and knowing the keywords used with the **show ip ospf database** *lsa-type lsid* commands can also be very useful. Table 8-3 summarizes these details.

Key Topic

Table 8-3   *Facts About LSA Types 1, 2, and 3*

LSA Type (Number)	LSA Type (Name)	This Type Represents	Display Using show ip ospf database keyword...	LSID Is Equal to	Created by
1	Router	A router	**router**	RID of router	Each router creates its own
2	Network	A subnet in which a DR exists	**network**	DR's IP address in the subnet	The DR in that subnet
3	Summary	A subnet in another area	**summary**	Subnet number	An ABR

The Database Exchange Process

Every router in an area, when OSPF stabilizes after topology changes occur, should have an identical LSDB for that area. Internal routers (routers inside a single area) have only that area's LSAs, but an ABR's LSDB will contain LSAs for each area to which it connects. The ABR does, however, know which LSAs exist in each area.

OSPF routers flood both the LSAs they create, and the LSAs they learn from their neighbors, until all routers in the area have a copy of each of the most recent LSAs for that area. To manage and control this process, OSPF defines several messages, processes, and neighbor states that indicate the progress when flooding LSAs to each neighbor. This section begins by listing reference information for the OSPF messages and neighbor states. Next, the text describes the flooding process between two neighbors when a DR does not exist, followed by a description of the similar process used when a DR does exist. This section ends with a few items related to how routers avoid looping the LSA advertisements and how they periodically reflood the information.

OSPF Message and Neighbor State Reference

For reference, Table 8-4 lists the OSPF message types that will be mentioned in the next few pages. Additionally, Table 8-5 lists the various neighbor states. Although useful for study, when you are first learning this topic, feel free to skip these tables for now.

Table 8-4　*OSPF Message Types and Functions*

Message Name/Number	Description
Hello	Used to discover neighbors and supply information used to confirm that two routers should be allowed to become neighbors, to bring a neighbor relationship to a 2-Way state, and to monitor a neighbor's responsiveness in case it fails
Database Description (DD or DBD)	Used to exchange brief versions of each LSA, typically on initial topology exchange, so that a router knows a list of that neighbor's known LSAs
Link-State Request (LSR)	A packet that lists the LSIDs of LSAs that the sender of the LSR would like the receiver of the LSR to supply during database exchange
Link-State Update (LSU)	A packet that contains fully detailed LSAs, typically sent in response to an LSR message
Link-State Acknowledgment (LSAck)	Sent to confirm receipt of an LSU message

Table 8-5　*OSPF Neighbor State Reference*

State	Meaning
Down	No Hellos have been received from this neighbor for more than the Dead interval.
Attempt	Used when the neighbor is defined with the **neighbor** command, after sending a Hello, but before receiving a Hello from that neighbor.
Init	A Hello has been received from the neighbor, but it did not have the local router's RID in it or list parameters that do not pass the neighbor verification checks. This is a permanent state when Hello parameters do not match.

State	Meaning
2-Way	A Hello has been received from the neighbor; it has the router's RID in it, and all neighbor verification checks passed.
ExStart	Currently negotiating the DD sequence numbers and master/slave logic used for DD packets.
Exchange	Finished negotiating the DD process particulars, and currently exchanging DD packets.
Loading	All DD packets are exchanged, and the routers are currently sending LSR, LSU, and LSAck packets to exchange full LSAs.
Full	Neighbors are fully adjacent, meaning that they believe that their LSDBs for that area are identical. Routing table (re)calculations can begin.

Exchange Without a Designated Router

As discussed in Chapter 7, an OSPF interface's network type tells a router whether to attempt to elect a DR on that interface. The most common case for which routers do not elect a DR occur on point-to-point topologies, such as true point-to-point serial links and point-to-point subinterfaces. This section examines the database exchange process on such interfaces, in preparation for the slightly more complex process when using a DR on an OSPF broadcast network type, like a LAN.

Each OSPF neighborship begins by exchanging Hellos until the neighbors (hopefully) reach the 2-Way state. During these early stages, the routers discover each other by sending multicast Hellos and then check each other's parameters to make sure that all required items match (as listed in Chapter 7's Table 7-5). Figure 8-7 shows the details, with the various neighbor states listed on the outside of the figure and the messages listed in the middle.

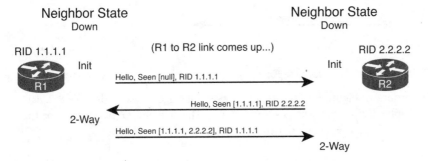

Figure 8-7 *Neighbor Initialization—Early Stages*

Figure 8-7 shows an example that begins with a failed neighborship, so the neighborship is in a down state. When a router tries to reestablish the neighborship, each router sends a multicast Hello and moves to an INIT state. After a router has both received a Hello and verified that all the required parameters agree, the router lists the other router's RID in the

Hello as being seen, as shown in the bottom two Hello messages in the figure. When a router receives a Hello that lists its own RID as having been seen by the other router, the router can transition to the 2-Way state.

When a router has reached the 2-Way state with a neighbor, as shown at the bottom of Figure 8-7, the router then decides whether it should exchange its LSDB entries. When no DR exists, the answer is always "yes." Each router next follows this general process:

Step 1. Discover the LSAs known to the neighbor but unknown to me.

Step 2. Discover the LSAs known by both routers, but the neighbor's LSA is more up to date.

Step 3. Ask the neighbor for a copy of all the LSAs identified in the first two steps.

Figure 8-8 details the messages and neighbor states used to exchange the LSAs between two neighbors. As with Figure 8-7, Figure 8-8 shows neighbor states on the outer edges of the flows (refer to Table 8-5 for reference). Routers display these neighbor states (with variants of the **show ip ospf neighbor** command), so a particular state can be useful in determining how far two neighbors have gotten in the database exchange process. The more important neighbor states will be mentioned throughout the chapter.

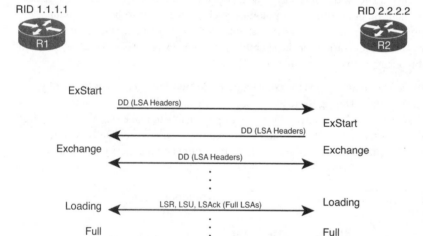

Figure 8-8 *Overview of the Database Exchange Process Between Two Neighbors*

The inner portions of Figure 8-8 represent the OSPF message flows, with Table 8-2, earlier in the chapter, listing the messages for reference. The next several pages examine the process shown in Figure 8-8 in more detail.

Discovering a Description of the Neighbor's LSDB

After a router has decided to move forward from a 2-Way state and exchange its LSDB with a neighbor, the routers use the sequence shown in Figure 8-8. The next step in that process requires both routers to tell each other the LSIDs of all their known LSAs in that area. The primary goal is for each neighbor to realize which LSAs it does not know, so it can then ask for those full LSAs to be sent. To learn the list of LSAs known by a neighbor, the neighboring routers follow these steps:

Step 1.   Multicast database description packets (abbreviated as both DD and DBD, depending on the reference) to 224.0.0.5, which is the all-SPF-routers multicast address.

Step 2.   When sending the first DD message, transition to the ExStart state until one router, the one with the higher RID, becomes the master in a master/slave relationship.

Step 3.   After electing a master, transition the neighbor to the Exchange state.

Step 4.   Continue multicasting DD messages to each other until both routers have the same shared view of the LSIDs known collectively by both routers, in that area.

Note that the DD messages themselves do not list the entire LSAs, but rather just the LSA headers. These headers include the LSIDs of the LSAs and the LSA sequence number. The LS sequence number for an LSA begins at value 0x80000001 (hex) when initially created. The router creating the LSA increments the sequence number, and refloods the LSA, whenever the LSA changes. For example, if an interface moves from the up to down state, that router changes its Type 1 LSA to list that interface state as down, increments the LSA sequence number, and refloods the LSA.

The master router for each exchange controls the flow of DD messages, with the slave responding to the master's DD messages. The master keeps sending DD messages until it lists all its known LSIDs in that area. The slave responds by placing LSA headers in its DD messages. Some of those LSA headers simply repeat what the slave heard from the master, for the purpose of acknowledging to the master that the slave learned that LSA header from the master. Additionally, the slave includes the LSA headers for any LSAs that the master did not list.

This exchange of DD messages ends with each router knowing a list of LSAs that it does not have in its LSDB, but the other router does have those LSAs. Additionally, each router also ends this process with a list of LSAs that the local router already knows, but for which the other router has a more recent copy (based on sequence numbers).

Exchanging the LSAs

When the two neighbors realize that they have a shared view of the list of LSIDs, they transition to the Loading state and start exchanging the full LSAs—but only those that they do not yet know about or those that have changed.

For example, when the two routers in Figure 8-8 first become neighbors, neither router will have a copy of the Type 1 LSA for the other router. So, R1 will request that R2 send its LSA with LSID 2.2.2.2. R2 will send its Type 1 LSA, and R1 will acknowledge receipt. The mechanics work like this:

Step 1.   Transition the neighbor state to Loading.

Step 2.   For any missing LSAs, send a Link-State Request (LSR) message, listing the LSID of the requested LSA.

Step 3. Respond to any LSR messages with a Link-State Update (LSU), listing one or more LSAs in each message.

Step 4. Acknowledge receipt by either sending a Link-State Acknowledgment (LSAck) message (called *explicit acknowledgment*) or by sending the same LSA that was received back to the other router in an LSU message (*implicit acknowledgment*).

Step 5. When all LSAs have been sent, received, and acknowledged, transition the neighborship to the FULL state (fully adjacent).

> **Note**   Because this section examines the case without a DR, all these messages flow as multicasts to 224.0.0.5, the all SPF routers multicast address, unless the neighbors have been defined with an OSPF **neighbor** command.

By the end of this process, both routers should have an identical LSDB for the area to which the link has been assigned. At that point, the two routers can run the SPF algorithm to choose the currently best routes for each subnet.

Exchange with a Designated Router

Database exchange with a DR differs slightly than database exchange when no DR exists. The majority of the process is similar, with the same messages, meanings, and neighbor states. The big difference is the overriding choice of with whom each router chooses to perform database exchange.

Non-DR routers do not exchange their databases directly with all neighbors on a subnet. Instead, they exchange their database with the DR. Then, the DR exchanges any new/ changed LSAs with the rest of the OSPF routers in the subnet.

The concept actually follows along with the idea of a Type 2 LSA as seen earlier in Figure 8-4. Figure 8-9 represents four Type 1 LSAs, for four real routers on the same LAN, plus a single Type 2 LSA that represents the multiaccess subnet. The DR created the Type 2 LSA as part of its role in life.

Figure 8-9 shows two conceptual steps for database exchange. The non-DR router (R3) first exchanges its database with the pseudonode, and then the Type 2 pseudonode exchanges its database with the other routers. However, the pseudonode is a concept, not a router. To make the process depicted in Figure 8-9 work, the DR takes on the role of the Type 2 pseudonode. The messages differ slightly as well, as follows:

Key Topic

- The non-DR performs database exchange with the same messages, as shown in Figure 8-9, but sends these messages to the 224.0.0.6 all-DR-routers multicast address.

- The DR performs database exchange with the same messages but sends the messages to the 224.0.0.5 all-SPF-routers multicast address.

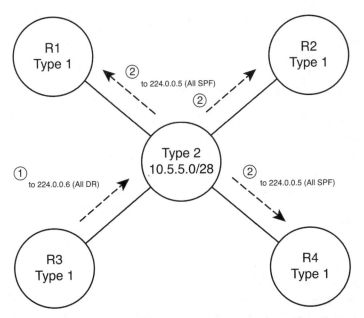

Figure 8-9   *Conceptual View—Exchanging the Database with a Pseudonode*

Consider these two conventions one at a time. First, the messages sent to 224.0.0.6 are processed by the DR and the BDR only. The DR actively participates, replying to the messages, with the BDR acting as a silent bystander. In effect, this allows the non-DR router to exchange its database directly with the DR and BDR, but with none of the other routers in the subnet.

Next, consider the multicast messages from the DR to the 224.0.0.5 all-SPF-router multicast address. All OSPF routers process these messages, so the rest of the routers—the DROthers to use the Cisco IOS term—also learn the newly exchanged LSAs. This process completes the second step shown in the conceptual Figure 8-9, where the DR, acting like the pseudonode, floods the LSAs to the other OSPF routers in the subnet.

The process occurs in the background and can be generally ignored. However, for operating an OSPF network, an important distinction must be made. With a DR in existence, a DROther router performs the database exchange process (as seen in Figure 8-9) with the DR/BDR only and not any other DROther routers in the subnet. For example, in Figure 8-9, R1 acts as DR, R2 acts as BDR, and R3/R4 act as DROther routers. Because the underlying process does not make R3 and R4 perform database exchange with each other, the routers do not reach the FULL neighbor state, remaining in a 2-Way state.

Example 8-6 shows the resulting output for the LAN shown in Figure 8-9, with four routers. The output, taken from DROther R3, shows a 2-Way state with R4, the other DROther. It also shows on interface Fa0/0 that its own priority is 2. This output also shows a neighbor count (all neighbors) of 3 and an adjacent neighbor count (all fully adjacent neighbors) of 2, again because the neighborship between DROthers R3 and R4 is not a full adjacency.

Example 8-6 *Demonstrating OSPF FULL and 2-Way Adjacencies*

```
R3# show ip ospf interface fa0/0
FastEthernet0/0 is up, line protocol is up
  Internet Address 172.16.1.3/24, Area 0
  Process ID 75, Router ID 3.3.3.3, Network Type BROADCAST, Cost: 1
  Transmit Delay is 1 sec, State DROTHER, Priority 2
  Designated Router (ID) 1.1.1.1, Interface address 172.16.1.1
  Backup Designated router (ID) 2.2.2.2, Interface address 172.16.1.2
  Timer intervals configured, Hello 10, Dead 40, Wait 40, Retransmit 5
    oob-resync timeout 40
    Hello due in 00:00:02
  Supports Link-local Signaling (LLS)
  Cisco NSF helper support enabled
  IETF NSF helper support enabled
  Index 1/1, flood queue length 0
  Next 0x0(0)/0x0(0)
  Last flood scan length is 0, maximum is 4
  Last flood scan time is 0 msec, maximum is 0 msec
  Neighbor Count is 3, Adjacent neighbor count is 2
    Adjacent with neighbor 1.1.1.1   (Designated Router)
    Adjacent with neighbor 2.2.2.2   (Backup Designated Router)
  Suppress hello for 0 neighbor(s)


R3# show ip ospf neighbor fa0/0


Neighbor ID     Pri   State         Dead Time    Address       Interface
1.1.1.1           4   FULL/DR       00:00:37     172.16.1.1    FastEthernet0/0
2.2.2.2           3   FULL/BDR      00:00:37     172.16.1.2    FastEthernet0/0
44.44.44.44       1   2WAY/DROTHER  00:00:36     172.16.1.4    FastEthernet0/0
```

Flooding Throughout the Area

So far in this section, the database exchange process has focused on exchanging the database between neighbors. However, LSAs need to be flooded throughout an area. To do so, when a router learns new LSAs from one neighbor, that router then knows that its other neighbors in that same area might not know of that LSA. Similarly, when an LSA changes—for example, when an interface changes state—a router might learn the same old LSA but with a new sequence number, and again need to flood the changed LSA to other neighbors in that area.

Figure 8-10 shows a basic example of the process. In this case, R2, R3, and R4 have established neighbor relationships, with four LSAs in their LSDB in this area. R1 is again the new router added to the internetwork.

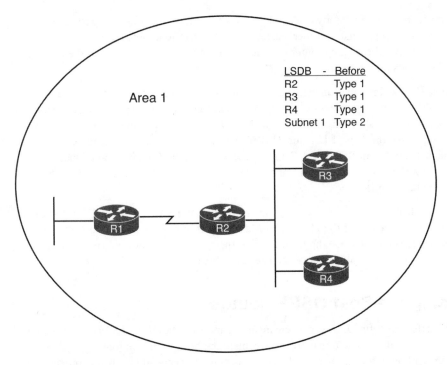

Figure 8-10 *Flooding Throughout an Area*

First, consider what happens as the new R1-R2 neighborship comes up and goes through database exchange. When R1 loads and the link comes up, R1 and R2 reach a full state and have a shared view of the area 1 LSDB. R2 has learned all R1's new LSAs (should only be R1's Type 1 Router LSA), and R1 has learned all the area 1 LSAs known to R2, including the Type 1 LSAs for R3 and R4.

Next, think about the LSDBs of R3 and R4 at this point. The database exchange between R1-R2 did not inform R3 or R4 about any of the new LSAs known by R1. So, R2, when it learns of R1's Type 1 LSA, sends DD packets to the DR on the R2/R3/R4 LAN. LSR/LSU packets follow, resulting in R3 and R4 learning about the new LSA for R1. If more routers existed in area 1, the flooding process would continue throughout the entire area, until all routers know of the best (highest sequence number) copy of each LSA.

The flooding process prevents the looping of LSAs as a side effect of the database exchange process. Neighbors use DD messages to learn the LSA headers known by the neighbor, and then only request the LSAs known by the neighbor but not known by the local router. By requesting only unknown LSAs or new versions of old LSAs, routers prevent the LSA advertisements from looping.

Periodic Flooding

Although OSPF does not send routing updates on a periodic interval, as do distance vector protocols, OSPF does reflood each LSA every 30 minutes based on each LSA's age variable. The router that creates the LSA sets this age to 0 (seconds). Each router then increments the age of its copy of each LSA over time. If 30 minutes pass with no changes to an LSA—meaning that no other reason existed in that 30 minutes to cause a reflooding of the LSA—the owning router increments the sequence number, resets the timer to 0, and refloods the LSA.

Because the owning router increments the sequence number and resets the LSAge every 1800 seconds (30 minutes), the output of various **show ip ospf database** commands should also show an age of less than 1800 seconds. For example, referring back to Example 8-5, the Type 1 LSA for R1 (RID 1.1.1.1) shows an age of 943 seconds and a sequence number of 0x80000003. Over time, the sequence number should increment once every 30 minutes, with the LSAge cycle upward toward 1800 and then back to 0 when the LSA is reflooded.

Note also that when a router realizes it needs to flush an LSA from the LSDB for an area, it actually sets the age of the LSA to the MaxAge setting (3600) and refloods the LSA. All the other routers receive the LSA, see that the age is already at the maximum, and cause those routers to also remove the LSA from their LSDBs.

Choosing the Best OSPF Routes

All this effort to define LSA types, create areas, and fully flood the LSAs has one goal in mind: to allow all routers in that area to calculate the best, loop-free routes for all known subnets. Although the database exchange process might seem laborious, the process by which SPF calculates the best routes requires a little less thought, at least to the level required for the CCNP ROUTE exam. In fact, the choice of the best route for a given subnet, and calculated by a particular router, can be summarized as follows:

Key
Topic

- Analyze the LSDB to find all possible routes to reach the subnet.

- For each possible route, add the OSPF interface cost for all outgoing interfaces in that route.

- Pick the route with the lowest total cost.

For humans, if you build a network diagram and note the OSPF cost for each interface (as shown with **show ip ospf interface**), you can easily add up the costs for each router's possible routes to each subnet and tell which route OSPF will choose. The routers must use a more complex SPF algorithm to derive a mathematical model of the topology based on the LSAs. This section examines both the simpler human view of metric calculation and folds in some of the basics of what SPF must do on a router to calculate the best routes. It also goes through the options for tuning the metric calculation to influence the choice of routes.

OSPF Metric Calculation for Internal OSPF Routes

The process of calculating the cost from a router to each subnet might be intuitive to most people. However, spending a few minutes considering the details is worthwhile, in part to link the concepts with the LSAs, and to be better prepared for questions on the

ROUTE exam. This section breaks the discussion into four sections: intra-area routes, interarea routes, a short discussion about cases when both intra-area and interarea routes exist for the same subnet, and an explanation of SPF calculations.

Calculating the Cost of Intra-Area Routes

When a router analyzes the LSDB to calculate the best route to each subnet, it does the following:

Key Topic

Step 1. Finds all subnets inside the area, based on the stub interfaces listed in the Type 1 LSAs and based on any Type 2 Network LSAs

Step 2. Runs SPF to find all possible paths through the area's topology, from itself to each subnet

Step 3. Calculates the OSPF interface costs for all outgoing interfaces in each route, picking the lowest-total-cost route for each subnet as the best route

For example, Figure 8-11 shows the routers and links inside area 34, as a subset of the internetwork also shown in Figure 8-1. Figure 8-11 shows the interface numbers and OSPF costs.

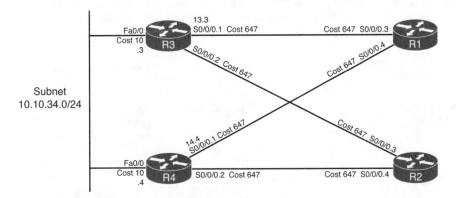

Figure 8-11 *Area 34 Portion of Figure 8-1*

Following the basic three-step process, at Step 1, R1 can determine that subnet 10.10.34.0/24 exists in area 34 because of the Type 2 LSA created by the DR in that subnet. For Step 2, R1 can then run SPF and determine four possible routes, two of which are clearly more reasonable to humans: R1-R3 and R1-R4. (The two other possible routes, R1-R3-R2-R4 and R1-R4-R2-R3, are possible and would be considered by OSPF but would clearly be higher cost.) For Step 3, R1 does the simple math of adding the costs of the outgoing interfaces in each route, as follows:

- **R1-R3:** Add R1's S0/0/0.3 cost (647) and R3's Fa0/0 cost (10), total 657

- **R1-R4:** Add R1's S0/0/0.4 cost (647) and R4's Fa0/0 cost (10), total 657

The metrics tie, so with a default setting of **maximum-paths 4**, R1 adds both routes to its routing table. Specifically, the routes list the metric of 657 and the next-hop IP address on the other end of the respective links: 10.10.13.3 (R3's S0/0/0.1) and 10.10.14.4 (R4's S0/0/0.1).

Note that OSPF supports equal-cost load balancing, but it does not support unequal-cost load balancing. The **maximum-paths** OSPF subcommand can be set as low as 1, with the maximum being dependent on router platform and Cisco IOS version. Modern Cisco IOS versions typically support 16 or 32 concurrent routes to one destination (maximum).

Calculating the Cost of Interarea Routes

From a human perspective, the cost for interarea routes can be calculated just like for intra-area routes if we have the full network diagram, subnet addresses, and OSPF interface costs. To do so, just find all possible routes from a router to the destination subnet, add up the costs of the outgoing interfaces, and choose the router with the lowest total cost.

However, OSPF routers cannot do the equivalent for interarea routes, because routers internal to one area do not have topological data—LSA Types 1 and 2—for other areas. Instead, ABRs create and flood Type 3 Summary LSAs into an area, listing the subnet address and mask, but not listing details about routers and links in the other areas. For example, Figure 8-12 shows both areas 34 and 0 from Figure 8-1, including interface costs. Then consider how OSPF determines the lowest-cost route from Router R3 for subnet 10.10.99.0/24, the data center subnet on the right.

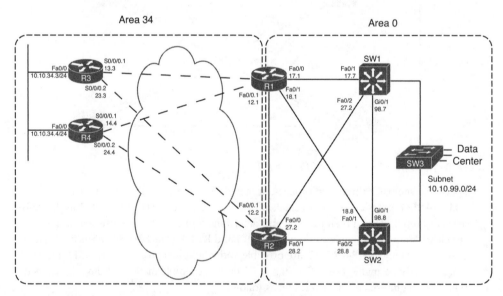

Figure 8-12 *Area 34 and Area 0 Portion of Figure 8-1*

R3 has a large number of possible routes to reach subnet 10.10.99.0/24. For example, just to get from R3 to R1, there are several possibilities: R3-R1, R3-R4-R1, and R3-R2-R1. From R1 the rest of the way to subnet 10.10.99.0/24, many more possibilities exist. The SPF algorithm has to calculate all possible routes inside an area to the ABR, so with more redundancy, SPF's run time goes up. And SPF has to consider all the options, whereas we humans can rule out some routes quickly, because they appear to be somewhat ridiculous.

Because of the area design, with R1 and R2 acting as ABRs, R3 does not process all the topology shown in Figure 8-12. Instead, R3 relies on the Type 3 Summary LSAs created by the ABRs, which have the following information:

- The subnet number/mask represented by the LSA

- The cost of the ABR's lowest-cost route to reach the subnet

- The RID of the ABR

Example 8-7 begins to examine the information that R3 will use to calculate its best route for subnet 10.10.99.0/24, on the right side of Figure 8-12. To see these details, Example 8-7 lists several commands taken from R1. It lists R1's best route (actually two that tie) for subnet 10.10.99.0/24, with cost 11. It also lists the Type 3 LSA R1 generated by R1 for 10.10.99.0/24, again listing cost 11, and listing the Type 3 LSA created by ABR R2 and flooded into area 34.

Example 8-7 *Route and Type 3 LSA on R1 for 10.10.99.0/24*

```
R1# show ip route ospf
     10.0.0.0/8 is variably subnetted, 15 subnets, 3 masks
O       10.10.5.0/27 [110/648] via 10.10.15.5, 00:04:19, Serial0/0/0.5
O       10.10.23.0/29 [110/711] via 10.10.13.3, 00:04:19, Serial0/0/0.3
O       10.10.24.0/29 [110/711] via 10.10.14.4, 00:04:19, Serial0/0/0.4
O       10.10.25.0/29 [110/711] via 10.10.15.5, 00:04:19, Serial0/0/0.5
O       10.10.27.0/24 [110/11] via 10.10.17.7, 00:04:19, FastEthernet0/0
                      [110/11] via 10.10.12.2, 00:04:19, FastEthernet0/0.1
O       10.10.28.0/24 [110/11] via 10.10.18.8, 00:04:19, FastEthernet0/1
                      [110/11] via 10.10.12.2, 00:04:19, FastEthernet0/0.1
O       10.10.34.0/24 [110/648] via 10.10.14.4, 00:04:19, Serial0/0/0.4
                      [110/648] via 10.10.13.3, 00:04:19, Serial0/0/0.3
O       10.10.98.0/24 [110/11] via 10.10.18.8, 00:04:19, FastEthernet0/1
                      [110/11] via 10.10.17.7, 00:04:19, FastEthernet0/0
O       10.10.99.0/24 [110/11] via 10.10.18.8, 00:04:19, FastEthernet0/1
                      [110/11] via 10.10.17.7, 00:04:19, FastEthernet0/0

R1# show ip ospf database summary 10.10.99.0

            OSPF Router with ID (1.1.1.1) (Process ID 1)

! omitting output for area 5...
            Summary Net Link States (Area 34)

  LS age: 216
  Options: (No TOS-capability, DC, Upward)
```

```
LS Type: Summary Links(Network)
Link State ID: 10.10.99.0 (summary Network Number)
Advertising Router: 1.1.1.1
LS Seq Number: 80000003
Checksum: 0x951F
Length: 28
Network Mask: /24
      TOS: 0  Metric: 11


LS age: 87
Options: (No TOS-capability, DC, Upward)
LS Type: Summary Links(Network)
Link State ID: 10.10.99.0 (summary Network Number)
Advertising Router: 2.2.2.2
LS Seq Number: 80000002
Checksum: 0x7938
Length: 28
Network Mask: /24
      TOS: 0  Metric: 11
```

Note   The examples use default bandwidth settings, but with all routers configured with the **auto-cost reference-bandwidth 1000** command. This command is explained in the upcoming section "Changing the Reference Bandwidth."

For routers in one area to calculate the cost of an interarea route, the process is simple when you realize that the Type 3 LSA lists the ABR's best cost to reach that interarea subnet. To calculate the cost

Step 1.   Calculate the intra-area cost from that router to the ABR listed in the Type 3 LSA.

Step 2.   Add the cost value listed in the Type 3 LSA. (This cost represents the cost from the ABR to the destination subnet.)

A router applies these two steps for each possible route to reach the ABR. Following the example of Router R3 and subnet 10.10.99.0/24, Figure 8-13 shows the components of the calculation.

Figure 8-13 shows the calculation of both routes, with the intra-area cost to reach R1 either 647 or 657 in this case. For both routes, the cost listed in the Type 3 LSA sourced by R1, cost 11, is added.

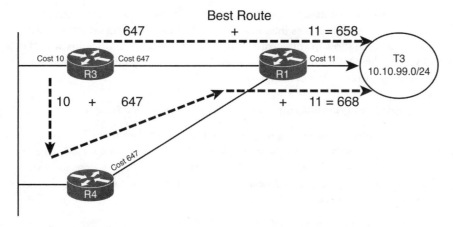

Figure 8-13 *R3's Calculation of Cost for 10.10.99.0/24*

When more than one ABR exists, as is the case as shown in Figure 8-12, each ABR should have created a Type 3 LSA for the subnet. In fact, the output in Example 8-7 showed the Type 3 LSA for 10.10.99.0/24 created by both R1 and another created by R2. For example, in the internetwork used throughout this chapter, ABRs R1 and R2 would create a Type 3 LSA for 10.10.99.0/24. So, in this particular example, R3 would also have to calculate the best route to reach 10.10.99.0/24 through ABR R2. Then, R3 would choose the best route among all routes for 10.10.99.0/24.

Each router repeats this process for all known routes to reach the ABR, considering the Type 3 LSAs from each ABR. In this case, R3 ties on metrics for one route through R1 and one through R2, so R3 adds both routes to its routing table, as shown in Example 8-8.

Example 8-8 *Route and Type 3 LSA on R3 for 10.10.99.0/24*

```
R3# show ip route 10.10.99.0 255.255.255.0
Routing entry for 10.10.99.0/24
  Known via "ospf 3", distance 110, metric 658, type inter area
  Last update from 10.10.13.1 on Serial0/0/0.1, 00:08:06 ago
  Routing Descriptor Blocks:
  * 10.10.23.2, from 2.2.2.2, 00:08:06 ago, via Serial0/0/0.2
      Route metric is 658, traffic share count is 1
    10.10.13.1, from 1.1.1.1, 00:08:06 ago, via Serial0/0/0.1
      Route metric is 658, traffic share count is 1


R3# show ip route ospf
      10.0.0.0/8 is variably subnetted, 15 subnets, 3 masks
O IA    10.10.5.0/27 [110/1304] via 10.10.23.2, 00:07:57, Serial0/0/0.2
                     [110/1304] via 10.10.13.1, 00:07:57, Serial0/0/0.1
O IA    10.10.12.0/24 [110/657] via 10.10.23.2, 00:08:17, Serial0/0/0.2
                      [110/657] via 10.10.13.1, 00:08:17, Serial0/0/0.1
! lines omitted for brevity
O IA    10.10.99.0/24 [110/658] via 10.10.23.2, 00:08:17, Serial0/0/0.2
                      [110/658] via 10.10.13.1, 00:08:17, Serial0/0/0.1
```

Besides the information that matches the expected outgoing interfaces per the figures, the output also flags these routes as interarea routes. The first command lists "type inter area" explicitly, and the **show ip route ospf** command lists the same information with the code "O IA," meaning OSPF, interarea. Simply put, interarea routes are routes for which the subnet is known from a Type 3 Summary LSA.

Special Rules Concerning Intra-Area and Interarea Routes on ABRs

OSPF has a couple of rules concerning intra-area and interarea routes that take precedence over the simple comparison of the cost calculated for the various routes. The issue exists when more than one ABR connects to the same two areas. Many designs use two routers between the backbone and each nonbackbone area for redundancy, so this design occurs in many OSPF networks.

The issue relates to the fact that with two or more ABRs, the ABRs themselves, when calculating their own routing tables, can calculate both an intra-area route and interarea route for subnets in the backbone area. For example, consider the perspective of Router R1 from the last several examples, as depicted in Figure 8-14.

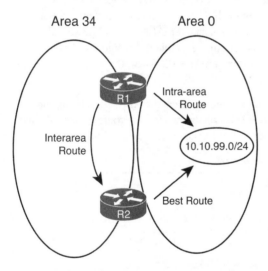

Figure 8-14 *R1's Choice: Intra-Area or Interarea Route to 10.10.99.0/24*

Conceptually, R1 could calculate both the intra-area route and interarea route to 10.10.99.0/24. However, the OSPF cost settings could be set so that the lower-cost route for R1 actually goes through area 34, to ABR R2, and then on through area 0 to 10.10.99.0/24. However, two OSPF rules prevent such a choice by R1:

Step 1. When choosing the best route, an intra-area route is always better than a competing interarea route, regardless of metric.

Step 2. If an ABR learns a Type 3 LSA inside a nonbackbone area, the ABR ignores that LSA when calculating its own routes.

Because of the first rule, R1 would never choose the interarea route if the intra-area route were available. The second rule goes further, stating that R1 could never choose the interarea route—R1 simply ignores that LSA for the purposes of choosing its own best IP routes.

Metric and SPF Calculations

Before moving on to discuss how to influence route choices by changing the OSPF interface costs, first take a moment to consider the CPU-intensive SPF work done by a router. SPF does the work to piece together topology information to find all possible routes to a destination. As a result, SPF must execute when the intra-area topology changes, because changes in topology impact the choice of best route. However, changes to Type 3 LSAs do not drive a recalculation of the SPF algorithm, because the Type 3 LSAs do not actually describe the topology.

To take the analysis a little deeper, remember that an internal router, when finding the best interarea route for a subnet, uses the intra-area topology to calculate the cost to reach the ABR. When each route is identified, the internal router adds the intra-area cost to the ABR, plus the corresponding Type 3 LSA's cost. A change to the Type 3 LSA—it fails, comes back up, or the metric changes—does impact the choice of best route, so the changed Type 3 LSA must be flooded. However, no matter the change, the change does not affect the topology between a router and the ABR—and SPF focuses on processing that topology data. So, only changes to Type 1 and 2 LSAs require an SPF calculation.

You can see the number of SPF runs, and the elapsed time since the last SPF run, using several variations of the **show ip ospf** command. Each time a Type 3 LSA changes and is flooded, SPF does not run, and the counter does not increment. However, each time a Type 1 or 2 LSA changes, SPF runs and the counter increments. Example 8-9 highlights the counter that shows the number of SPF runs on that router, in that area, and the time since the last run. Note that ABRs list a group of messages per area, showing the number of runs per area.

Example 8-9 *Example with New Route Choices but No SPF Run*

```
R3# show ip ospf  | begin Area 34
   Area 34
       Number of interfaces in this area is 3
       Area has no authentication
       SPF algorithm last executed 00:41:02.812 ago
       SPF algorithm executed 15 times
       Area ranges are
       Number of LSA 25. Checksum Sum 0x0BAC6B
       Number of opaque link LSA 0. Checksum Sum 0x000000
       Number of DCbitless LSA 0
       Number of indication LSA 0
       Number of DoNotAge LSA 0
        Flood list length 0
```

Metric Tuning

Engineers have a couple of commands available that allow them to tune the values of the OSPF interface cost, thereby influencing the choice of best OSPF route. This section discusses the three methods: changing the reference bandwidth, setting the interface bandwidth, and setting the OSPF cost directly.

Changing the Reference Bandwidth

OSPF calculates the default OSPF cost for an interface based on the following formula:

Cost = Reference-Bandwidth / Interface-Bandwidth

The reference-bandwidth, which you can set using the **auto-cost reference-bandwidth** *bandwidth* router subcommand, sets the numerator of the formula for that one router, with a unit of Mbps. This setting can be different on different routers, but Cisco recommends using the same setting on all routers in an OSPF routing domain.

For example, serial interfaces default to a bandwidth setting of 1544, meaning 1544 kbps. The reference bandwidth defaults to 100, meaning 100 Mbps. After converting the reference bandwidth units to kbps (by multiplying by 1000) to match the bandwidth unit of measure, the cost, calculated per the defaults, for serial links would be

Cost = 100,000 / 1544 = 64

Note   OSPF always rounds down when the calculation results in a decimal value.

The primary motivation for changing the reference bandwidth is to accommodate good defaults for higher-speed links. With a default of 100 Mbps, the cost of Fast Ethernet interfaces is a cost value of 1. However, the minimum OSPF cost is 1, so Gigabit Ethernet and 10 Gigabit interfaces also then default to OSPF cost 1. By setting the OSPF reference bandwidth so that there is some difference in cost between the higher-speed links, OSPF can then choose routes that use those higher-speed interfaces.

Note   Although Cisco recommends that all routers use the same reference bandwidth, the setting is local to each router.

Note that in the examples earlier in this chapter, the bandwidth settings used default settings, but the **auto-cost reference-bandwidth 1000** command was used on each router to allow different costs for Fast Ethernet and Gigabit interfaces.

Setting Bandwidth

You can indirectly set the OSPF cost by configuring the **bandwidth** *speed* interface subcommand (where *speed* is in kbps). In such cases, the formula shown in the previous section is used, just with the configured bandwidth value.

While on the topic of the interface **bandwidth** subcommand, a couple of seemingly trivial facts might matter to your choice of how to tune the OSPF cost. First, on serial links, the bandwidth defaults to 1544. On subinterfaces of those serial interfaces, the same bandwidth default is used.

On Ethernet interfaces, if not configured with the **bandwidth** command, the interface bandwidth matches the actual speed. For example, on an interface that supports autonegotiation for 10/100, the bandwidth is either 100,000 kbps (or 100 Mbps) or 10,000 kbps (or 10 Mbps), depending on whether the link currently runs at 100 or 10 Mbps, respectively.

Configuring Cost Directly

The most controllable method of configuring OSPF costs, but the most laborious, is to configure the interface cost directly. To do so, use the **ip ospf cost** *value* interface sub-command, substituting your chosen value as the last parameter.

Verifying OSPF Cost Settings

Several commands can be used to display the OSPF cost settings of various interfaces. Example 8-10 shows several, along with the configuration of all three methods for changing the OSPF cost. In this example, the following have been configured:

- The reference bandwidth is set to 1000.

- Interface S0/0/0.1 has its bandwidth set to 1000 kbps.

- Interface Fa0/0 has its cost set directly to 17.

Example 8-10 *R3 with OSPF Cost Values Set*

```
router ospf 3
 auto-cost reference-bandwidth 1000
interface S0/0/0.1
 bandwidth 1000
interface fa0/0
 ip ospf cost 17


R3# show ip ospf interface brief
Interface    PID   Area        IP Address/Mask    Cost   State  Nbrs F/C
Se0/0/0.2    3     34          10.10.23.3/29      647    P2P    1/1
Se0/0/0.1    3     34          10.10.13.3/29      1000   P2P    1/1
Fa0/0        3     34          10.10.34.3/24      17     BDR    1/1


R3# show ip ospf interface fa0/0
FastEthernet0/0 is up, line protocol is up
  Internet Address 10.10.34.3/24, Area 34
  Process ID 3, Router ID 3.3.3.3, Network Type BROADCAST, Cost: 17
  Enabled by interface config, including secondary ip addresses
  Transmit Delay is 1 sec, State BDR, Priority 1
  Designated Router (ID) 4.4.4.4, Interface address 10.10.34.4
  Backup Designated router (ID) 3.3.3.3, Interface address 10.10.34.3
! lines omitted for brevity
```

Exam Preparation Tasks

Planning Practice

The CCNP ROUTE exam expects test takers to review design documents, create implementation plans, and create verification plans. This section provides some exercises that can help you to take a step back from the minute details of the topics in this chapter so that you can think about the same technical topics from the planning perspective.

For each planning practice table, simply complete the table. Note that any numbers in parentheses represent the number of options listed for each item in the solutions in Appendix F, "Completed Planning Practice Tables."

Design Review Table

Table 8-6 lists several design goals related to this chapter. If these design goals were listed in a design document, and you had to take that document and develop an implementation plan, what implementation options come to mind? For any configuration items, a general description can be used, without concern about the specific parameters.

Table 8-6   *Design Review*

Design Goal	Possible Implementation Choices Covered in This Chapter
The design sets specific limits to the number of Type 1 and 2 LSAs in each area. Describe how to predict the number of each type of LSA.	
How could you tune OSPF metrics to favor 10-Gbps links over 1-Gbps and 1-Gig over 100-Mbps? (2)	
The design shows one physical path from ABR1 to core subnet 1 inside area 0, and one longer area 1 path to the same subnet. What can be done to ensure that both paths can be used?	

Implementation Plan Peer Review Table

Table 8-7 shows a list of questions that others might ask, or that you might think about, during a peer review of another network engineer's implementation plan. Complete the table by answering the questions.

Table 8-7   *Notable Questions from This Chapter to Consider During an Implementation Plan Peer Review*

Question	Answer
What conditions must be true for a router to create/flood a Type 2 LSA? (2)	
The plan shows Frame Relay with all point-to-point subinterfaces. By default, will a DR/BDR be elected?	
The plan shows a reference bandwidth change planned for all routers with high-speed links, but not all other routers. What is the impact? (2)	
The plan shows many different WAN links speeds but with the interface bandwidths not matching the actual speed. All OSPF cost changes are made explicitly with the **ip ospf cost** interface subcommand. Do the incorrect bandwidths cause any OSPF problems?	

Create an Implementation Plan Table

To practice skills useful when creating your own OSPF implementation plan, list in Table 8-8 configuration commands related to the configuration of the following features. You might want to record your answers outside the book and set a goal to complete this table (and others like it) from memory during your final reviews before taking the exam.

Table 8-8   *Implementation Plan Configuration Memory Drill*

Feature	Configuration Commands/Notes
Tune metrics by changing the formula for calculating OSPF cost based on interface bandwidth.	
Tune metrics by changing interface bandwidth.	
Change metrics by setting cost directly.	
Set the number of equal-cost OSPF routes allowed in a router's routing table.	
Influence the choice of DR on a LAN. (2)	

Choose Commands for a Verification Plan Table

To practice skills useful when creating your own OSPF verification plan, list in Table 8-9 all commands that supply the requested information. You might want to record your answers outside the book and set a goal to complete this table (and others like it) from memory during your final reviews before taking the exam.

Table 8-9 *Verification Plan Memory Drill*

Information Needed	Command(s)
Display a summary of the OSPF database.	
Display all Type 1 Router LSAs known to a router.	
Display the details of a particular Type 1 Router LSA.	
Display all Type 2 Network LSAs known to a router.	
Display the details of a particular Type 2 Router LSA.	
Display all Type 3 Summary LSAs known to a router.	
Display the details of a particular Type 3 Router LSA.	
Display a list of OSPF-enabled interfaces on a router.	
Determine on which interfaces a router has formed at least one OSPF neighborship.	
Determine the number of fully adjacent neighbors on an interface.	
Determine which transit networks connect to a Type 1 LSA.	
Determine the router that created and flooded a Type 3 LSA.	
Determine the router that created and flooded a Type 2 LSA.	
Determine the router that created and flooded a Type 1 LSA.	
Display the IP address of the current DR and BDR on a LAN.	
Display the OSPF interface cost (metric).	
Display all OSPF-learned routes.	
Display statistics about the number of SPF algorithm runs.	

Note Some of the entries in this table might not have been specifically mentioned in this chapter but are listed in this table for review and reference.

Review All the Key Topics

Review the most important topics from inside the chapter, noted with the Key Topic icon in the outer margin of the page. Table 8-10 lists a reference of these key topics and the page numbers on which each is found.

Table 8-10 *Key Topics for Chapter 8*

Key Topic Element	Description	Page Number
Table 8-2	OSPF LSA Types	305
List	Two main functions of a DR	312
Table 8-3	Facts About LSA Types 1, 2, and 3	321
Table 8-4	OSPF Message Types and Functions	322
Table 8-5	OSPF Neighbor State Reference	322
List	Key differences between database exchange with and without a DR	326
List	Three considerations a router makes when choosing the best OSPF IP routes	330
List	Three steps to calculate OSPF costs for intra-area routes	331
List	Two steps for calculating OSPF costs for interarea routes	334

Complete the Tables and Lists from Memory

Print a copy of Appendix D, "Memory Tables," (found on the CD) or at least the section for this chapter, and complete the tables and lists from memory. Appendix E, "Memory Tables Answer Key," also on the CD, includes completed tables and lists to check your work.

Define Key Terms

Define the following key terms from this chapter, and check your answers in the glossary.

link-state identifier (LSID), designated router (DR), backup designated router (BDR), internal router, area border router (ABR), all-SPF-routers multicast, all-DR-routers multicast, link-state advertisement, Database Description (DD) packet, Link-State Request (LSR) packet, Link-State Acknowledgment (LSA) packet, Link-State Update (LSU) packet, Router LSA, Network LSA, Summary LSA, Type 1 LSA, Type 2 LSA, Type 3 LSA, reference bandwidth, SPF calculation

This chapter covers the following subjects:

- **Route Filtering:** This section introduces three separate methods of route filtering with OSPF and discusses the commands to configure two of these methods.

- **Route Summarization:** This section examines how OSPF can summarize routes at ABRs and at ASBRs.

- **Default Routes and Stub Areas:** This section examines the two main reasons that an enterprise might use default routes and then shows OSPF's solution to each need: flooding a domain-wide default route and using OSPF stub areas.

- **OSPF version 3:** This section introduces the newest version of OSPF, OSPF version 3 (commonly written as *OSPFv3*). OSPFv3 adds support for the routing of IPv6 traffic. The theory and commands for OSPFv3 Address Family configuration are also covered.

CHAPTER 9

Advanced OSPF Concepts

This chapter discusses several features that optimize Open Shortest Path First (OSPF) operations: route filtering, route summarization, default routing, and OSPF stub areas, in addition to the features available in OSPFv3.

Route filtering can be used to purposefully prevent hosts in one part of an internetwork from sending packets to another part. It can also reduce the size of a topology table and IP routing table, reducing both OSPF memory and CPU consumption, plus make the packet-forwarding process run slightly better. Route summarization can also reduce routing protocol and packet forwarding overhead, but with a potential negative effect of creating less-efficient paths through an internetwork.

Additionally, this chapter briefly covers default routing, followed by a discussion of OSPF stub routers. These stub routers can be used to limit the amount of topology data in an area, again reducing overhead.

Finally, this chapter concludes with a look at OSPFv3, including configuration examples. This discussion also introduces the concept of OSPFv3 Address Families and includes configuration and verification examples.

"Do I Know This Already?" Quiz

The "Do I Know This Already?" quiz allows you to assess whether you should read the entire chapter. If you miss no more than two of these 11 self-assessment questions, you might want to move ahead to the "Exam Preparation Tasks" section. Table 9-1 lists the major headings in this chapter and the "Do I Know This Already?" quiz questions covering the material in those headings so that you can assess your knowledge of these specific areas. The answers to the "Do I Know This Already?" quiz appear in Appendix A.

Table 9-1 *"Do I Know This Already?" Foundation Topics Section-to-Question Mapping*

Foundation Topics Section	Questions
Route Filtering	1–3
Route Summarization	4, 5
Default Routing and Stub Areas	6–8
OSPF version 3	9–11

1. Router B1, an internal router in area 1, displays the following output. The only two ABRs connected to area 1 are performing Type 3 LSA filtering. Which of the following answers is true based on the information in the output from B1?

```
R1# show ip route 10.1.0.0 255.255.0.0 longer-prefixes
! Legend lines omitted for brevity

      10.0.0.0/8 is variably subnetted, 17 subnets, 3 masks
O        10.1.2.0/24 [110/658] via 10.10.13.1, 00:00:32, Serial0/0/0.1
O IA     10.1.1.0/24 [110/658] via 10.10.23.2, 00:41:39, Serial0/0/0.2
O IA     10.1.3.0/24 [110/658] via 10.10.23.2, 00:41:39, Serial0/0/0.2
```

   a. A Type 3 LSA for 10.2.2.0/24 was filtered by both ABRs.

   b. A Type 3 LSA for 10.1.2.0/24 was not filtered by both ABRs.

   c. A Type 3 LSA for 10.1.3.0/24 was not filtered by at least one ABR.

   d. A Type 3 LSA for 10.1.1.0/24 was filtered by both ABRs.

2. The following command output was gathered from Router R1, an ABR between area 0 (backbone) and area 1. In this internetwork, area 0 contains all the subnets of Class A network 10.0.0.0. R1's OSPF process has a distribute list configured. Assuming that the subnets listed in the answers actually exist in area 0, which of the following occurs on Router R1?

```
R1# sh ip prefix-list
ip prefix-list question: 3 entries
   seq 5 deny 10.1.2.0/24 ge 25 le 27
   seq 15 deny 10.2.0.0/16 ge 30 le 30
   seq 20 permit 0.0.0.0/0 le 32
```

   a. R1 will not create/flood a Type 3 LSA for subnet 10.1.2.0/26 into area 1.

   b. R1 will not create/flood a Type 3 LSA for subnet 10.1.2.0/24 into area 1.

   c. R1 will not have an OSPF route for subnet 10.1.2.0/26 in its IP routing table.

   d. R1 will not have an OSPF route for subnet 10.1.2.0/24 in its IP routing table.

3. Use the same scenario as the previous question, with one change. Instead of the distribute list configured on R1, R1's OSPF process has an area 1 filter list configured. Again assuming that the subnets listed in the answers actually exist in area 0, which of the following occurs on Router R1?

```
R1# sh ip prefix-list
ip prefix-list question: 3 entries
    seq 5 deny 10.1.2.0/24 ge 25 le 27
    seq 15 deny 10.2.0.0/16 ge 30 le 30
    seq 20 permit 0.0.0.0/0 le 32
```

   a. R1 will not create/flood a Type 3 LSA for subnet 10.1.2.0/26 into area 1.

   b. R1 will not create/flood a Type 3 LSA for subnet 10.1.2.0/24 into area 1.

   c. R1 will not have an OSPF route for subnet 10.1.2.0/26 in its IP routing table.

   d. R1 will not have an OSPF route for subnet 10.1.2.0/24 in its IP routing table.

4. R1, an ABR between backbone area 0 and area 1, has intra-area routes in area 0 for 10.1.1.0/24, 10.1.2.0/24, and 10.1.3.0/24. These routes have metrics of 21, 22, and 23, respectively. An engineer then adds the **area 0 range 10.1.0.0 255.255.0.0** command under the OSPF process of R1. Which of the following are true? (Choose two.)

   a. R1 loses and then reestablishes neighborships with all neighbors.

   b. R1 no longer advertises 10.1.1.0/24 to neighbors into area 1.

   c. R1 advertises a 10.1.0.0/16 route into area 1 with a metric of 23 (largest metric).

   d. R1 advertises a 10.1.0.0/16 route into area 1 with a metric of 21 (lowest metric).

5. The following output exists on Router R1, a router internal to area 1. What can you determine as true from the output of the **show ip ospf database summary** command?

```
Routing Bit Set on this LSA
LS age: 124
Options: (No TOS-capability, DC, Upward)
LS Type: Summary Links (Network)
Link State ID: 10.1.0.0 (summary Network Number)
Advertising Router: 1.1.1.1
LS Seq Number: 80000001
Checksum: 0x878F
Length: 28
Network Mask: /22
      TOS: 0  Metric: 11
```

   a. The LSA was created by an ABR because of an **area range** command.

   b. The LSA was created by an ASBR because of a **summary-address** command.

   c. If created by an **area range** command, the best metric for a subordinate subnet on that ABR must have been 11.

   d. None of the other answers are correct.

6. Router R1, an ASBR connected to the Internet and to backbone area 0, has been configured with a **default-information originate** command. Which of the following is true about the effects of this configuration command?

   a. R1 will always create and flood a default route into the OSPF domain.

   b. R1 will create and flood an LSA for prefix/length 0.0.0.0/0 into the OSPF domain if R1's IP routing table has a route to 0.0.0.0/0.

   c. R1 will set a flag on the LSA for the subnet between itself and one of the ISPs, noting this subnet as a default network, regardless of whether R1 has a default route.

   d. R1 will set a flag on the LSA for the subnet between itself and one of the ISPs, noting this subnet as a default network, but only if R1 has a route to 0.0.0.0/0.

7. Which of the following are true about routers internal to a totally NSSA area? (Choose two.)

   a. Routers cannot redistribute external routes into the area.

   b. Routers should have zero Type 3 LSAs in their LSDBs.

   c. Routers should have zero Type 5 LSAs in their LSDBs.

   d. Routers should learn default routes from the ABRs attached to the area.

8. ABR R1 has been configured with an **area 1 stub no-summary** command. Which stubby area type is area 1?

   a. Stub

   b. Totally stubby

   c. NSSA

   d. Totally NSSA

9. With an OSPFv3 Address Family configuration supporting both IPv4 and IPv6 routing, which of the following is true regarding OSPFv3's link-state database?

   a. IPv4 LSAs populate one database, while IPv6 LSAs populate a second database.

   b. Information received from all LSAs is aggregated in a single link-state database.

   c. OSPFv3 does not use a link-state database. Rather, it represents link-state information in a lookup table similar to Cisco Express Forwarding (CEF).

   d. A virtual Address Family is created, and it contains information from both IPv4 and IPv6 LSAs.

10. In an OSPFv3 Address Family configuration, how do you tell an interface to participate in the OSPFv3 process for IPv6 routes?

    a. Router(config-router)# **ospfv3** *process_id* **ipv6 area** *area_number*

    b. Router(config-router-af)# **ospfv3** *process_id* **ipv6 area** *area_number*

    c. Router(config-router-af-if)# **ospfv3** *process_id* **ipv6 area** *area_number*

    d. Router(config-if)# **ospfv3** *process_id* **ipv6 area** *area_number*

11. Which LSA used in IPv6 networks carries information similar to the information carried by Type 1 and Type 2 LSAs in IPv4 networks?

    a. Type 6 LSA

    b. Type 8 LSA

    c. Type 9 LSA

    d. Type 10 LSA

Foundation Topics

Route Filtering

OSPF supports several methods to filter routes. However, the OSPF's internal logic restricts most filtering, requiring that the filtering be done either on an area border router (ABR) or autonomous system boundary router (ASBR). This same internal logic dictates what each type of filtering can do and what it cannot do. So, when thinking about OSPF route filtering, you need to go beyond the concept of matching IP prefix/length information and consider OSPF internals as well. This first major section begins with a discussion of the OSPF internals that impact OSPF route filtering, followed by information about two of OSPF's route-filtering tools.

First, consider the difference in how OSPF chooses intra-area versus interarea routes. For intra-area routes, OSPF uses pure link-state logic, with full topology information about an area, piecing together the topology map from the Type 1 and Type 2 LSAs. This logic relies on all routers inside the area having an identical copy of the link-state database (LSDB) for that area. With the full topology, the shortest path first (SPF) algorithm can be run, finding all possible routes to each subnet.

For interarea routes, OSPF uses distance vector logic. The intra-area SPF calculation includes the calculation of the metric of the best route to reach each ABR in the area. To choose the best interarea route, a router uses distance vector logic of taking its known metric to reach the ABR and adds the metric for that subnet as advertised by the ABR. This means that no additional SPF calculation is required to find all interarea routes for a given prefix/length, making this logic more like distance vector logic.

Keeping these thoughts in mind, next consider the concept of route filtering inside one area. First, OSPF routers do not advertise routes; instead, they advertise LSAs. Any filtering applied to OSPF messages would need to filter the transmission of LSAs. However, inside one area, all routers must know all LSAs, or the entire SPF concept fails, and routing loops could occur. As a result, OSPF cannot and does not allow the filtering of LSAs inside an area, specifically the Type 1 and Type 2 LSAs that describe the intra-area topology.

OSPF does allow some route filtering, however, taking advantage of the fact that OSPF uses distance vector logic with Type 3 LSAs (and Type 5 LSAs used for external routes). Because of the underlying distance vector logic, an OSPF ABR can be configured to filter Type 3 LSAs, with no risk of creating routing loops. (The same applies for ASBRs filtering Type 5 LSAs created for external routes.) As a result of these related concepts, Cisco IOS limits OSPF route filtering to the following:

- Filtering Type 3 LSAs on ABRs

- Filtering Type 5 LSAs on ASBRs

- Filtering the routes that OSPF would normally add to the IP routing table on a single router

Of these, the second option occurs as an option of the route redistribution process as explained in Chapter 10, "Route Redistribution." So, it will not be covered in this chapter. The other two topics will be examined next.

Type 3 LSA Filtering

ABRs, by definition, connect to the backbone area and at least one other area. ABRs, as a fundamental part of their role, create and flood Type 3 Summary LSAs into one area to represent the subnets in the other areas connected to that ABR. Type 3 LSA filtering tells the ABR to filter the advertisement of these Type 3 LSAs.

For example, consider Figure 9-1, which shows a generalized design with two ABR routers. The figure focuses on three subnets in area 0 for which each ABR would normally create and flood a Type 3 Summary LSA into area 1. However, in this case, the engineer has made the following choices:

- On ABR1, filter subnet 3 from being advertised.

- On ABR2, filter both subnets 2 and 3 from being advertised.

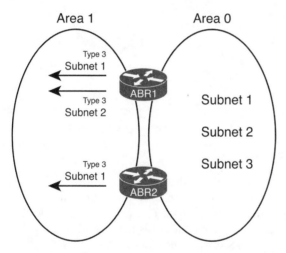

Figure 9-1 *Generic View of Type 3 LSA Filtering*

The goal of such a filtering plan could be to prevent all area 1 users from reaching subnet 3 and to allow access to subnet 2—but only through ABR1. If ABR1 were to fail, none of the area 1 routers could calculate a route for subnet 2 through ABR2, because ABR2 has not created and flooded a Type 3 LSA for that subnet. The goal for subnet 1 would be to allow each area 1 router to choose the best route through either ABR, while having a redundant route in case one route failed.

To configure Type 3 LSA filtering, you use the **area** *number* **filter-list prefix** *name* {**in** | **out**} command under **router ospf** configuration mode. The referenced prefix list matches subnets, with subnets matched by a deny action being filtered, and subnets matched with a permit action allowed through as normal. OSPF then performs the filtering by not flooding the Type 3 LSAs into the appropriate areas.

The trickiest part of the configuration relates to the in and out parameters at the end of the **area filter-list** router subcommand. These parameters define the direction relative to the area listed in the command, as follows:

- When **in** is configured, Cisco IOS filters prefixes being created and flooded into the configured area.

- When **out** is configured, Cisco IOS filters prefixes coming out of the configured area.

The need for the **in** and **out** parameters makes more sense when you consider an ABR connected to at least three areas. Figure 9-2 shows just such a sample, with both the in and out directions represented.

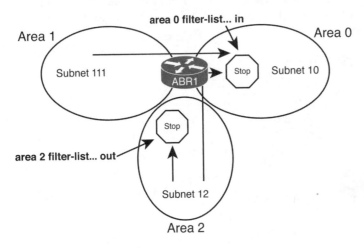

Figure 9-2   *Generic View of Type 3 LSA Filtering*

The **area 0 filter-list... in** command in the figure shows that the ABR considers filtering routes from all other areas (areas 1 and 2, in this case) when creating and flooding Type 3 LSAs into area 0. The **area 2 filter-list... out** command in the figure shows how the ABR only considers prefixes that exist in area 2. However, in this case, the ABR filters LSAs regardless of the area into which the Type 3 LSAs would be advertised.

For example, consider the case of subnet 111, in area 1. Assume that all prefix lists happen to match subnet 111, so that subnet 111 should be filtered. The following list summarizes what happens on ABR1 regarding the potential advertisement of a Type 3 LSA for this subnet being flooded into areas 0 and 2:

- ABR1 filters the subnet 111 LSA from being sent into area 0 because of the **area 0 filter-list... in** command.

- ABR1 does not filter the subnet 111 LSA from being sent into area 2, because there is no **area 1 filter-list... out** command nor **area 2 filter-list... in** command.

As another example, Figure 9-3 shows an example internetwork with three candidate routes to be filtered by ABRs R1 and R2. ABRs R1 and R2 will play the roles of ABR1 and ABR2 in Figure 9-1, with R1 filtering one of the three subnets and R2 filtering two of the subnets. Note that R1 and R2 will each use different **in** and **out** keywords as well.

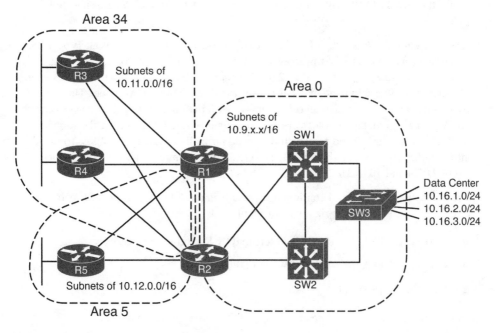

Figure 9-3   *Type 3 LSA Filtering Example*

Example 9-1 shows the configuration on both R1 and R2.

Example 9-1   *R1's and R2's **distribute-list** to Filter Manufacturing Routes*

```
! On Router R1:
ip prefix-list filter-into-area-34 seq 5 deny 10.16.3.0/24
ip prefix-list filter-into-area-34 seq 10 permit 0.0.0.0/0 le 32
!
router ospf 1
 area 34 filter-list prefix filter-into-area-34 in
```

```
! On Router R2:
ip prefix-list filter-out-of-area-0 seq 5 deny 10.16.2.0/23 ge 24 le 24
ip prefix-list filter-out-of-area-0 seq 10 permit 0.0.0.0/0 le 32
!
router ospf 2
 area 0 filter-list prefix filter-out-of-area-0 out
```

First, take a closer look at the specifics of the R1 configuration commands. The prefix list on R1 exactly matches route 10.16.3.0/24, with a deny action. The second **prefix-list** command matches all subnets, because the **0.0.0.0/0** parameter matches all subnet numbers, and the **le 32** parameter, combined with the original /0 prefix length, matches all prefix lengths from /0 through /32. The **area 34... in** command tells R1 to apply this filtering to all Type 3 LSAs that R1 creates and would otherwise flood into area 34. As a result, the area 34 LSDB will not contain a Type 3 LSA for 10.16.3.0/24, as injected by R1.

R2's configuration uses a slightly different prefix list. The filter examines all Type 3 LSAs for subnets in area 0. The first **prefix-list** command matches all prefixes in the range 10.16.2.0–10.16.3.255 (per the **10.16.2.0/23** parameter) but specifically for a prefix length of exactly 24. This command matches two of the three data center subnets. The second **prefix-list** command matches all other subnets with the same match-all logic seen earlier on R1, using a permit action. R2's **area 0... out** command tells R2 to filter the subnets that R2 learns in area 0 and for which R2 would normally create Type 3 LSAs to flood into all other areas. So, neither area 34 nor area 5 will learn these two filtered subnets (10.16.2.0/24 and 10.16.3.0/24) in Type 3 LSAs from R2.

The end result of this added configuration results in the following Type 3 LSAs for the three subnets shown on the right side of Figure 9-3:

- Two Type 3 LSAs for 10.16.1.0/24 (created by R1 and R2, respectively)

- One Type 3 LSA for 10.16.2.0/24 (created by R1)

- None for 10.16.3.0/24

Example 9-2 confirms the contents of the LSDB in area 34, on Router R3.

Example 9-2   *Area 34 LSDB, as Seen on R3*

```
R3# show ip route 10.16.0.0 255.255.0.0 longer-prefixes
! Legend lines omitted for brevity


     10.0.0.0/8 is variably subnetted, 17 subnets, 3 masks
O IA    10.16.2.0/24 [110/658] via 10.10.13.1, 00:00:32, Serial0/0/0.1
O IA    10.16.1.0/24 [110/658] via 10.10.23.2, 00:41:39, Serial0/0/0.2
                     [110/658] via 10.10.13.1, 00:00:32, Serial0/0/0.1


R3# show ip ospf database | include 10.16
10.16.1.0       1.1.1.1         759         0x80000002 0x008988
10.16.1.0       2.2.2.2         745         0x80000002 0x006BA2
10.16.2.0       1.1.1.1         759         0x80000002 0x007E92
```

The first command in the example lists R3's routes for all subnets whose first two octets are 10.16. Note that R3 has no route to 10.16.3.0/24, because both R1 and R2 filtered the Type 3 LSA. R3 happens to have equal-cost routes for 10.16.1.0/24, which is possible, because both R1 and R2 permitted the advertisement of the Type 3 LSA for that subnet. R3 has only one route for 10.16.2.0/24, through R1, because R2 filtered its Type 3 LSA for that prefix.

The second command in Example 9-2 lists all LSAs that include "10.16," which includes the two Type 3 LSAs for 10.16.1.0/24 and the single Type 3 LSA for 10.16.2.0/24.

Finally, note that although the configuration in Example 9-1 showed **area filter-list** commands with both **in** and **out** parameters for variety, the result of R2's **area filter-list... out** command is that R2 does not flood the filtered LSAs to either area 34 or area 5. If the design goals specifically meant to filter only LSAs from being advertised from area 0 into area 34, the **area 34 filter-list... in** command should have been used on both routers.

Filtering OSPF Routes Added to the Routing Table

In some cases, an engineer might need to filter a route, but the area design does not lend itself well to his filtering goals. For example, if an area has 20 routers and the engineer wants to filter a route so that five of the routers do not learn the route, Type 3 LSA filtering cannot be used. Type 3 LSA filtering can only filter the LSAs from being flooded throughout the entire area.

The next feature discussed in this section, referenced as *filtering with distribute lists* (based on the configuration command it uses), allows individual routers to filter OSPF routes from getting into their respective IP routing tables. This type of filtering injects logic between the SPF algorithm on a router and that same router's IP routing table. This feature does not change the LSDB flooding process, does not change the LSAs added by ABRs or ASBRs, and does not change the SPF algorithm's choice of best route. However, when SPF chooses routes to add to the IP routing table, if a router has been configured with a **distribute-list in** router subcommand, enabling this feature, that router then filters the routes before adding them to that router's IP routing table. Figure 9-4 shows the general idea.

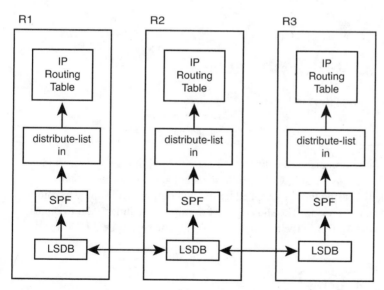

Figure 9-4 *OSPF Filtering with Distribute Lists*

In effect, you could prevent an OSPF route from being added to one or more routers' routing tables, but without risking causing routing loops, because the intra-area LSDB topology remains intact. By filtering routes from being added to the IP routing table, you prevent the routers from forwarding packets to the filtered subnets, but presumably that's the intended goal of route filtering.

The mechanics of the **distribute-list** router subcommand have a few surprises, which are summarized in this list:

■   The command requires either an **in** or **out** direction. Only the in direction works for filtering routes as described in this section.

■   The command must refer to either a numbered access control list (ACL), named ACL, prefix list, or route map. Regardless, routes matched with a permit action are allowed into the IP routing table, and routes matched with a deny action are filtered.

■   Optionally, the command can include the **interface** *interface-name-and-number* parameters. The router compares these parameters to the route's outgoing interface.

Example 9-3 shows a sample configuration on Router R3 from Figure 9-3. In this case, all filtering listed in Examples 9-1 and 9-2 has been removed, so no routes or LSAs have been filtered. Then, the engineer adds the **distribute-list** command on R3 to filter the route for 10.16.1.0/24, based on prefix-list filter-1.

Example 9-3 *R3's **distribute-list** to Filter 10.16.1.0/24*

```
! On Router R3:
ip prefix-list filter-1 seq 5 deny 10.16.1.0/24
ip prefix-list filter-1 seq 10 permit 0.0.0.0/0 le 32
!
router ospf 3
 distribute-list prefix filter-1 in
!
R3# show ip route ospf | include 10.16.1
R3#
R3# show ip ospf database | include 10.16.1.0
10.16.1.0       1.1.1.1         1143       0x80000007 0x007F8D
10.16.1.0       2.2.2.2         1538        0x80000007 0x0061A7
```

Note that the configuration matches only prefix 10.16.1.0/24 with a deny clause and permits all other routes. As a result, OSPF on R3 does not add a route for subnet 10.16.1.0/24 to the IP routing table, as implied by the null output of the **show ip route ospf | include 10.16.1** command. The **show ip ospf database | include 10.16.1** command lists all LSAs that have 10.16.1 in the text output, showing the two Type 3 LSAs for the subnet.

Route Summarization

OSPF allows summarization at both ABRs and ASBRs but not on other OSPF routers. The main reason is again that the LSDB must be the same for all routers in a single area. So, if summarization is needed, the summary prefixes should be created at the edge of an area (ABR or ASBR) and flooded throughout that area. However, the idea of summarizing on a router internal to an area, hoping that some routers in the area use the summary route and others in the same area do not, cannot be done with OSPF.

Good planning of route summaries can overcome the restriction of performing the summarization only on ABRs and ASBRs. A good OSPF area design includes consideration of future address summaries, and a good OSPF route summarization design considers the ABR locations. Although it is rare to design a large internetwork from scratch, an addressing plan that assigns all or most subnets in an area from one large address block does make address summarization easier.

OSPF summarization differs slightly on ABRs versus ASBRs. This section first examines route summarizations on ABRs and then considers ASBRs.

Manual Summarization at ABRs

The more difficult task with OSPF route summarization occurs when planning the design of IP address blocks and OSPF areas. When the IP addressing plan and OSPF design have been completed, if the subnet numbers inside an area happen to be from the same general range, and none of the subnets in that range exist in other OSPF areas, a reasonable summary route can be created at the ABRs connected to that area. Without first having such a reasonable block of addresses, route summarization might not be a useful option.

After a range of subnets has been chosen for summarization, the parameters in the **area range** command must be planned. This command defines the parameters for the summary route, most notably the origin area from which the subnets exist and the subnet number/mask that defines the summary route that should be advertised. The generic version of the command is listed next, followed by some notes about the various parameters:

area *area-id* **range** *ip-address mask* [**cost** *cost*]

Key Topic

- The configured area number refers to the area where the subnets exist; the summary will be advertised into all other areas connected to the ABR.

- The ABR compares the summary route's range of addresses with all intra-area OSPF routes, in the origin area, for which the ABR is creating Type 3 LSAs. If at least one subordinate subnet exists (subnets that sit inside the range), the ABR advertises the summary route as a Type 3 LSA.

- The ABR does not advertise the subordinate subnet's Type 3 LSAs.

- The ABR assigns a metric for the summary route's Type 3 LSA, by default, to match the best metric among all subordinate subnets.

- The **area range** command can also explicitly set the cost of the summary.

- If no subordinate subnets exist, the ABR does not advertise the summary.

For example, Figure 9-3 (shown earlier in this chapter) lists three subnets on the right side of the figure, noted as data center subnets 10.16.1.0/24, 10.16.2.0/24, and 10.16.3.0/24. ABR R1 could be configured to summarize these routes as 10.16.0.0/22, which includes all three subnets. (10.16.0.0/22 implies a range from 10.16.0.0 to 10.16.3.255.) The ABRs (R1 and R2) could be configured to advertise a summary route using the **area 0 range 10.16.0.0 255.255.252.0** router subcommand.

Behind the scenes, ABR route summarization causes the ABR to no longer advertise the subordinate routes' Type 3 LSAs, but to instead advertise one Type 3 LSA for the summary prefix. Figure 9-5 shows this concept on ABR R1, assuming that the **area 0 range 10.16.0.0 255.255.252.0** router subcommand has been configured. The three Type 3 LSAs that would normally have been advertised are shown above the ABR, and the one Type 3 LSA for the summary route, which replaces the upper LSAs, is shown under the ABR.

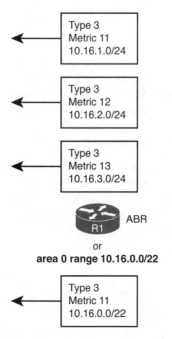

Figure 9-5 *OSPF Area Summarization—Consolidating Type 3 LSAs*

Example 9-4 shows some **show** command output related to this example. All route filtering in earlier examples has been removed, and both R1 and R2 have configured OSPF to summarize 10.16.0.0/22 with the **area 0 range 10.16.0.0 255.255.252.0** router OSPF subcommand. However, in R2's case, the **metric 12** parameter was used.

Example 9-4 *R1/R2/R3's Area Summarization on 10.16.0.0/16*

```
! On Router R1, before the summarization:
R1# sh ip route ospf | incl 10.16
O        10.16.2.0/24 [110/12] via 10.10.17.7, 00:00:24, FastEthernet0/0
O        10.16.3.0/24 [110/13] via 10.10.17.7, 00:00:24, FastEthernet0/0
O        10.16.1.0/24 [110/11] via 10.10.17.7, 00:00:34, FastEthernet0/0


! Next, configuring the summarization:
```

```
router ospf 1
 area 0 range 10.16.0.0 255.255.252.0


! Next, on R2, configuring the same summary
router ospf 2
 area 0 range 10.16.0.0 255.255.252.0 cost 12


! Next, from R3
R3# show ip ospf database summary 10.16.0.0


                OSPF Router with ID (3.3.3.3) (Process ID 3)


                   Summary Net Link States (Area 34)


   Routing Bit Set on this LSA
   LS age: 124
   Options: (No TOS-capability, DC, Upward)
   LS Type: Summary Links(Network)
   Link State ID: 10.16.0.0 (summary Network Number)
   Advertising Router: 1.1.1.1
   LS Seq Number: 80000001
   Checksum: 0x878F
   Length: 28
   Network Mask: /22
         TOS: 0  Metric: 11


   LS age: 103
   Options: (No TOS-capability, DC, Upward)
   LS Type: Summary Links(Network)
   Link State ID: 10.16.0.0 (summary Network Number)
   Advertising Router: 2.2.2.2
   LS Seq Number: 80000001
   Checksum: 0x739E
   Length: 28
   Network Mask: /22
         TOS: 0  Metric: 12


R3# show ip route 10.16.0.0 255.255.0.0 longer-prefixes
! legend omitted for brevity


     10.0.0.0/8 is variably subnetted, 16 subnets, 4 masks
O IA    10.16.0.0/22 [110/658] via 10.10.13.1, 00:03:46, Serial0/0/0.1
```

The example demonstrates the theory of what happens behind the scenes. R3 lists only two Type 3 LSAs related to the 10.16.1.0/24, 10.16.2.0/24, and 10.16.3.0/24 subnets: the Type 3 LSAs created by R1 and R2 for 10.16.0.0/22. However, the output does not denote that this LSA represents a summarized route. It simply looks like yet another Type 3 LSA. (Any mention of the word "summary" in the output refers to the fact that Type 3 LSAs are called *Summary LSAs*.) In this case, R3's path to reach both R1 and R2 ties, but the LSA for R1's 10.16.0.0/22 summary was injected with metric 11, based on the lowest metric subordinate route on R1, whereas R2's uses the explicitly configured metric 12. As a result, R3's best route for 10.16.0.0/22 uses R1, as shown in the route at the end of the example.

The first **show** command in the example shows R1's metrics for the three subordinate subnets, specifically metrics 11, 12, and 13. As such, R1's summary for 10.16.0.0/22, as shown in R3's **show ip ospf database summary 10.16.0.0** command, confirms that, by default, R1 gave the summary route's Type 3 LSA the best metric among the component subnets.

> **Note**   Although not discussed in depth here, the optional **not-advertise** option on the **area range** command tells the ABR to not advertise the Type 3 LSA for the summary route, making it possible to do the equivalent of Type 3 LSA filtering with the **area range** command.

Manual Summarization at ASBRs

OSPF defines an ASBR as a router that redistributes routes into OSPF from some other routing sources. When redistributing the routes, the ASBR creates a Type 5 External LSA for each redistributed subnet, listing the subnet number as the LSID and listing the mask as one of the fields in the LSA. The LSA also lists the ASBR's RID as the advertising router and a cost metric for the route. For the purposes of route summarization, you can think of a Type 5 LSA as working much like a Type 3 LSA, except for routes learned externally.

This section describes ASBR route summarization, which has many similarities to summarization by an ABR. If you add the **summary-address** *prefix mask* OSPF subcommand, OSPF will then attempt to summarize the external routes by creating a Type 5 LSA for the summary route, and by no longer advertising the Type 5 LSAs for the subordinate subnets. When looking for potential subordinate subnets inside the summary, the ASBR looks at all routes being redistributed into OSPF from all outside route sources, and if any subordinate subnets exist, the ASBR performs the route summarization.

Notably, this command works very much like the **area range** command on ABRs, with the main exception being that the **summary-address** command cannot explicitly set the metric of the summary route. The list of features is as follows:

Key Topic

- The ASBR compares the summary route's range of addresses with all routes redistributed into OSPF on that ASBR to find any subordinate subnets (subnets that sit inside the summary route range). If at least one subordinate subnet exists, the ASBR advertises the summary route.

- The ASBR does not advertise the subordinate subnets.

- To create the summary, the ASBR actually creates a Type 5 LSA for the summary route.

- The ASBR assigns the summary route the same metric as the lowest metric route among all subordinate subnets.

- If no subordinate subnets exist, the ASBR does not advertise the summary.

- Unlike the **area range** command, the **summary-address** command cannot be used to directly set the metric of the summary route.

The **summary-address** subcommand defines the summary route on the ASBR, with similar syntax and parameters as compared to the **area range** command seen on ABRs. Table 9-2 lists the two commands for comparison and study.

Table 9-2   *OSPF Route Summarization Commands*

Where Used	Command
ASBR	**summary-address** {{*ip-address mask*}	{*prefix mask*}} [**not-advertise**]
ABR	**area** *area-id* **range** *ip-address mask* [**advertise**	**not-advertise**] [**cost** *cost*]

Default Routes and Stub Areas

Enterprises typically use default routes in two different cases:

- To direct remote-site routers at the edge of the enterprise network to send all packets toward the core of the enterprise, with the core routers knowing all the more-specific routes to enterprise destination addresses

- To direct traffic on all enterprise routers toward an Internet-facing router so that all traffic destined for the Internet eventually arrives at the enterprise's Internet-connected routers

Engineers could achieve both of these goals by using route summarization with the **area range** and **summary-address** commands. For example, consider a case in which the goal is to drive all packets destined for Internet hosts to one of two equal Internet routers for an enterprise, as shown in Figure 9-6. The design shows two ASBRs connected to the Internet. Both ASBRs could learn routes with Border Gateway Protocol (BGP). Rather than redistribute all BGP routes into the enterprise, the ASBRs summarize to the ultimate summary, 0.0.0.0/0. The two OSPF ASBRs flood the Type 5 LSA for a summary route— one from ASBR1 and one from ASBR2—throughout the enterprise. As a result, all OSPF routers choose a default route, with the packets destined for locations in the Internet eventually reaching one of the two ASBRs, which then forwards the packets into the Internet.

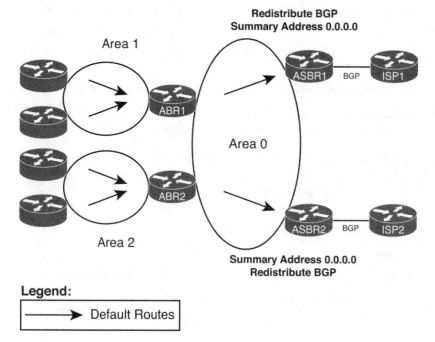

Figure 9-6 *Using ASBR Route Summarization to Advertise Summary Routes*

To meet the other design goal for using defaults—to get the routers in an area to use default routing to deliver packets to an ABR—the ABR could use the **area range** command to flood a default route into a single area. Again in Figure 9-6, if the design called for the routers in area 1 to use a default route to reach other destinations in the enterprise, the ABRs connected to area 1, like ABR1, could use the **area 0 range 0.0.0.0 0.0.0.0** command. ABR1 would then advertise a default route into the area, as an LSA Type 3, and not advertise any of the other Type 3 LSAs known from area 0. The routers internal to area 1 would use their default route for packets destined to unknown destination addresses, but the ABRs would have full knowledge of the routes inside the enterprise and know how to forward the packets at that point.

Even though you can use the **summary-address** and **area range** commands, most engineers use other methods to introduce and control default routes inside an OSPF domain. The first tool, the **default-information originate** OSPF subcommand, introduces a default route to be flooded throughout the OSPF domain. As a result, it is most useful for default routing to draw packets toward ASBRs connected to external networks. The other tool, *stub areas*, focuses on the other common use of default routes, controlling when ABRs flood default routes into a given area. This section examines both topics.

Domain-Wide Defaults Using the default-information originate Command

The OSPF subcommand **default-information originate** tells OSPF to create a Type 5 LSA (used for external routes) for a default route—0.0.0.0/0—and flood it like any other Type

5 LSA. In other words, it tells the router to create and flood information about a default route throughout the OSPF domain.

For example, consider a typical single multihomed Internet design, as shown in Figure 9-7. In this case, the enterprise has two Internet-connected routers, and the engineer wants to use default routing inside the enterprise to cause all the enterprise routers to send packets toward either ASBR1 or ASBR2.

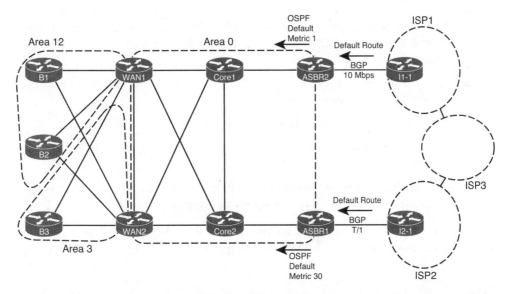

Figure 9-7 *Single Multihomed Internet Design Using Default Routes*

The **default-information originate** command tells the ASBRs to flood a default route into OSPF, but only if the ASBR itself has a default route in its IP routing table. This logic relies on the fact that the ASBRs typically either have a static default route pointing to the connected ISP router, or they learn a default route from the ISP using BGP. (In Figure 9-7, each ISP is advertising a default route.) All the routers then learn a default route, based on the Type 5 LSAs for 0.0.0.0/0 as flooded by the ASBRs.

Because a router withdraws its OSPF default route when its own IP route to 0.0.0.0/0 fails, OSPF allows the design in Figure 9-7 to fail over to the other default route. When all is well, both ISP1 and ISP2 advertise a default route to the enterprise using BGP, so both ASBR1 and ASBR2 have a route to 0.0.0.0/0. As shown in the figure, ASBR2 has been configured to advertise its OSPF default with a lower metric (1) than does ASBR1 (metric 30). Therefore, the enterprise routers will forward traffic to the Internet through ASBR2. However, if ISP1 quits advertising that default with BGP, or if BGP fails between ASBR2 and ISP1's I1-1 router, ASBR2 will withdraw its OSPF default route. The only remaining OSPF default route will be the one that leads to ASBR1, making use of the backup default route.

The full command syntax, as shown here, provides several optional parameters that impact its operation:

```
default-information originate [always] [metric metric-value] [metric-type type-
   value] [route-map map-name]
```

The following list summarizes the features of the **default-information originate** OSPF subcommand:

■ With all default parameters, it injects a default route into OSPF, as an External Type 2 route, using a Type 5 LSA, with metric 1, but only if a default route exists in that router's routing table.

■ With the **always** parameter, the default route is advertised even if there is no default route in the router's routing table.

■ The **metric** keyword defines the metric listed for the default route (default 1).

■ The **metric-type** keyword defines whether the LSA is listed as external Type 1 or external Type 2 (default).

■ The decision of when to advertise, and when to withdraw, the default route is based on matching the referenced **route-map** with a permit action.

When configured, OSPF will flood the default route throughout the OSPF routing domain, drawing traffic to each ASBR, as shown earlier in Figure 9-6.

Note The type of external OSPF route (Type 1 or Type 2) is explained more fully in Chapter 10.

Stubby Areas

As mentioned earlier, the two most common reasons to consider using default routes are to drive all Internet-destined traffic toward Internet-connected routers in an enterprise and to drive traffic inside an area toward an ABR in that area. This second design choice allows the routers in an area to use default routes for forwarding packets to ABRs, rather than more specific routes. Using default routes inside an area reduces memory consumption and CPU processing time on routers inside the area, because the routers in that area can have fewer LSAs in their LSDBs.

The OSPF stub router feature provides engineers with a very simple way to enable the function of flooding default routes inside an area, with those default routes driving IP packets back toward the ABRs attached to that area. ABRs in stub areas advertise a default route into the stub area. At the same time, the ABR chooses to not advertise external routes (Type 5 LSAs) into the area. Similarly, the ABR chooses to not advertise interarea routes (in Type 3 LSAs) into the area. As a result, all routers in the stub area can still route to the destinations (based on default route information), and the routers require less memory and processing.

The following list summarizes these features of stub areas for easier study and review:

- ABRs create a default route, using a Type 3 LSA, listing subnet 0.0.0.0 and mask 0.0.0.0, and flood that into the stub area.

- ABRs do not flood Type 5 LSAs into the stub area.

- ABRs might not flood other Type 3 LSAs into the area.

- The default route has a metric of 1 unless otherwise configured using the router sub-command **area** *area-num* **default-cost** *cost*.

- Routers inside stub areas cannot redistribute external routes into the stubby area, because that would require a Type 5 LSA in the area.

- All routers in the area must be configured to be stubby; if not, neighbor relationships cannot form between potential neighbors based on this mismatched configuration.

Figure 9-8 shows a familiar design in which area 34 will become a stub area. The design shows three external routes and lists three of many internal routes inside area 0. The figure shows ABRs R1 and R2 advertising defaults into area 34.

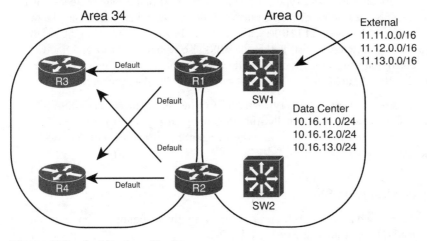

Figure 9-8 *Stubby Area Design*

Figure 9-8 demonstrates the core feature common to all types of stub areas: The ABRs flood a default route into the area. The routers inside the area can then calculate their best default route. Next, the text examines the different types of OSPF areas, before moving on to the details of configuration and verification.

Introducing Stubby Area Types

Even within the realm of stubby areas, four types of stubby areas exist: stub, totally stubby, not-so-stubby areas (NSSA), and totally NSSA.

Two types of stubby areas have the word "totally" as part of the name, and two do not. The differences between those with the word "totally" and those without have to do with whether Type 3 LSAs are flooded into the area. The rules are

■   For all types of stubby areas, the ABR always filters Type 5 (external) LSAs.

■   For totally stubby and totally NSSA areas, the ABR also filters Type 3 LSAs.

■   For stubby and NSSA areas—those without the word "totally" in the name—the ABRs do not filter Type 3 LSAs, advertising Type 3 LSAs as normal.

For example, consider the diagram shown in Figure 9-8, with area 34 as simply a stub area. As for all types, the ABRs each advertise a default route into area 34. As for all stubby area types, the ABRs filter all Type 5 LSAs, which means that the three Type 5 LSAs for 11.11.0.0/16, 11.12.0.0/16, and 11.13.0.0/16 would not exist in the LSDBs for area 34. Finally, because the area is not a totally stubby area, the ABRs do create and flood Type 3 LSAs for interarea routes as usual. So, they flood LSAs for the 10.16.11.0/24, 10.16.12.0/24, and 10.16.13.0/24 subnets listed in the figure.

Next, consider a similar scenario but with a totally stubby area for area 5, as seen back in Figure 9-3. As for all stubby area types, the ABRs each advertise a default route into area 5. As for all stubby area types, the ABRs filter all Type 5 LSAs, which means that the three Type 5 LSAs for 11.11.0.0/16, 11.12.0.0/16, and 11.13.0.0/16 would not exist in the LSDBs for area 5. The key difference exists in that the ABRs also would not create and flood Type 3 LSAs for interarea routes as usual, so they would not advertise Type 3 LSAs for the 10.16.11.0/24, 10.16.12.0/24, and 10.16.13.0/24 subnets listed in the figure into area 5.

The other difference in stubby area types relates to whether the name uses NSSA (NSSA or totally NSSA) or not (stubby, totally stubby). Stubby area types that use the NSSA name can redistribute external routes into the area; stubby area types without NSSA in the name cannot.

Configuring and Verifying Stubby Areas

Configuring stub and totally stubby areas requires only three commands, but with at least one command on each router, as listed in Table 9-3.

Key Topic

Table 9-3   *Stub Area Configuration Options*

Action	Configuration Steps
Stubby	Configure **area** *area-id* **stub** on each router in the area.
Totally stubby	Configure the **area** *area-id* **stub no-summary** command on the ABRs.
	Configure **area** *area-id* **stub**, without the **no-summary** keyword, on all other routers in the area.
Set the metric of the default route	Configure **area** *area-id* **default-cost** *metric* on an ABR (can differ from ABR to ABR). Default value is 1.

Note   For totally stubby areas, only the ABRs must have the **no-summary** keyword on the **area** *area-id* **stub no-summary** command. However, including this keyword on internal routers does not cause a problem.

Figure 9-9 shows a more detailed view of area 34 from Figure 9-8. By making area 34 a stub area, ABRs R1 and R2 will not flood Type 3 LSAs into area 34—other than the Type 3 LSAs for the default routes. Example 9-5 shows the configuration on Routers R1, R2, and R3 from Figure 9-9.

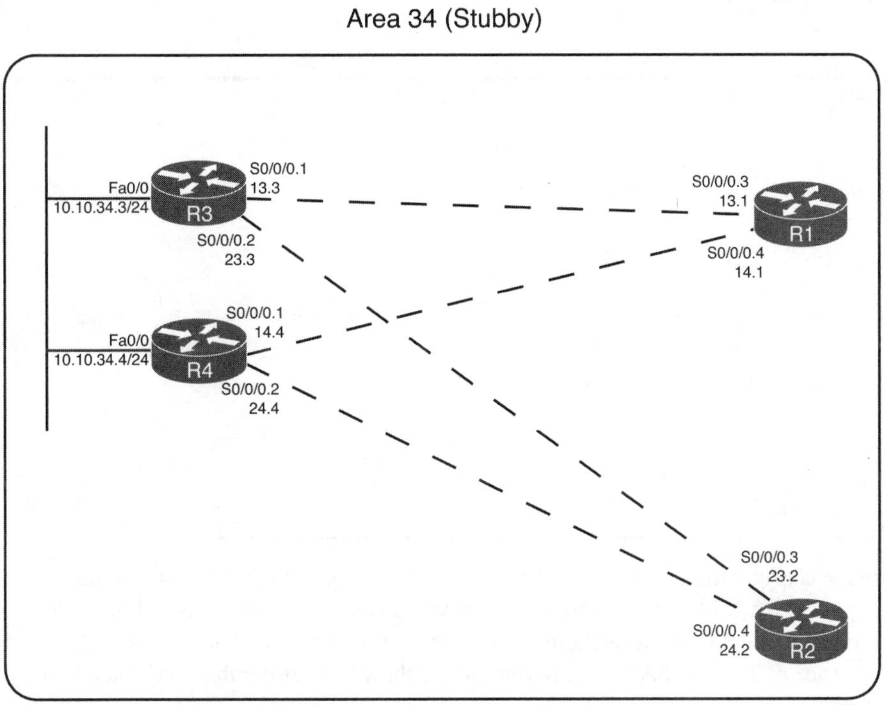

Area 34 (Stubby)

Figure 9-9   *Detailed View of Area 34*

Example 9-5   *Stub Area Configuration*

```
! On Router R1:
router ospf 1
 area 34 stub
 auto-cost reference-bandwidth 1000
!
interface s0/0/0.3 point-to-point
 ip ospf 1 area 34
!
interface s0/0/0.4 point-to-point
```

```
 ip ospf 1 area 34

! On Router R2:
router ospf 2
 area 34 stub
 auto-cost reference-bandwidth 1000
!
interface s0/0/0.3 point-to-point
 ip ospf 2 area 34
!
interface s0/0/0.4 point-to-point
 ip ospf 2 area 34

! On Router R3:
router ospf 3
 area 34 stub
 auto-cost reference-bandwidth 1000
!
interface s0/0/0.1 point-to-point
 ip ospf 3 area 34
 ip ospf 3 cost 500
!
interface s0/0/0.2 point-to-point
 ip ospf 3 area 34
!
interface fa0/0
 ip ospf 3 area 34
```

With the configuration as shown, both R1 and R2 will inject a default route, represented as a Type 3 LSA, with default metric 1. They will also not flood the Type 5 LSAs into area 34. Example 9-6 confirms these facts, showing the Type 3 LSA for the summary, and the absence of Type 5 LSAs in the output of the **show ip ospf database** command on Router R3.

Example 9-6 *Evidence of Type 5 LSAs Existing, Disappearing, and Defaults Appearing*

```
! Before making Area 34 stubby:

R3# show ip ospf database | begin AS External
                Type-5 AS External Link States

Link ID         ADV Router      Age        Seq#        Checksum Tag
11.11.0.0       7.7.7.7         929        0x80000001  0x00016D 0
12.12.0.0       7.7.7.7         845        0x80000001  0x00E784 0
13.13.0.0       7.7.7.7         835        0x80000001  0x00CE9B 0
```

```
! After making area 34 stubby - no output from the next command.


R3# show ip ospf database | begin AS External
R3#


! The database for area 34 now has two Type 3 LSAs for default routes.
R3# show ip ospf database

            OSPF Router with ID (3.3.3.3) (Process ID 3)


            Router Link States (Area 34)


! Lines omitted for brevity - skipped to "Summary Net" (Type 3) section

            Summary Net Link States (Area 34)


Link ID         ADV Router      Age         Seq#        Checksum
0.0.0.0         1.1.1.1         692         0x80000001 0x0093A6
0.0.0.0         2.2.2.2         686         0x80000001 0x0075C0
10.10.5.0       1.1.1.1         692         0x8000000E 0x00445C
10.10.5.0       2.2.2.2         686         0x8000000F 0x002477
10.10.12.0      1.1.1.1         692         0x8000000E 0x0054AF
10.10.12.0      2.2.2.2         686         0x8000000E 0x0036C9
! Many Type 3 LSAs omitted for brevity's sake
```

Example 9-6 shows the existence of the Type 5 external LSAs before area 34 became a stubby area, and the disappearance of those same LSAs after it was made a stubby area. The **show ip ospf database** command then shows two LSAs that list default routes, one learned from RID 1.1.1.1 (R1) and one learned from RID 2.2.2.2 (R2).

Example 9-7 continues the verification of how stub areas work with three more commands.

Example 9-7 *Three External Routes Before and None After Changing to Stubby*

```
! Next, R3 confirms it thinks area 34 is a stub area
R3# show ip ospf
 Routing Process "ospf 3" with ID 3.3.3.3
 Start time: 00:00:38.756, Time elapsed: 07:51:19.720
! lines omitted for brevity
    Area 34
        Number of interfaces in this area is 3
        It is a stub area
        Area has no authentication
        SPF algorithm last executed 00:11:21.640 ago
        SPF algorithm executed 18 times
        Area ranges are
```

```
        Number of LSA 29. Checksum Sum 0x0D3E01
        Number of opaque link LSA 0. Checksum Sum 0x000000
        Number of DCbitless LSA 0
        Number of indication LSA 0
        Number of DoNotAge LSA 0
        Flood list length 0


! The next command shows all Type 3 (summary) LSAs of prefix 0.0.0.0


R3# show ip ospf database summary 0.0.0.0

            OSPF Router with ID (3.3.3.3) (Process ID 3)


                Summary Net Link States (Area 34)


   Routing Bit Set on this LSA
   LS age: 879
   Options: (No TOS-capability, DC, Upward)
   LS Type: Summary Links(Network)
   Link State ID: 0.0.0.0 (summary Network Number)
   Advertising Router: 1.1.1.1
   LS Seq Number: 80000001
   Checksum: 0x93A6
   Length: 28
   Network Mask: /0
        TOS: 0  Metric: 1


   LS age: 873
   Options: (No TOS-capability, DC, Upward)
   LS Type: Summary Links(Network)
   Link State ID: 0.0.0.0 (summary Network Number)
   Advertising Router: 2.2.2.2
   LS Seq Number: 80000001
   Checksum: 0x75C0
   Length: 28
   Network Mask: /0
        TOS: 0  Metric: 1
! The next command lists statistics of the number of LSAs of each type -
! note a total of 0 Type 5 LSAs, but many Type 3 LSAs


R3# show ip ospf database database-summary

            OSPF Router with ID (3.3.3.3) (Process ID 3)


Area 34 database summary
  LSA Type      Count    Delete    Maxage
```

```
Router           4          0         0
Network          1          0         0
Summary Net     24          0         0
Summary ASBR     0          0         0
Type-7 Ext       0          0         0
   Prefixes redistributed in Type-7  0
Opaque Link      0          0         0
Opaque Area      0          0         0
Subtotal        29          0         0


Process 3 database summary
  LSA Type       Count    Delete    Maxage
  Router           4          0         0
  Network          1          0         0
  Summary Net     24          0         0
  Summary ASBR     0          0         0
  Type-7 Ext       0          0         0
  Opaque Link      0          0         0
  Opaque Area      0          0         0
  Type-5 Ext       0          0         0
      Prefixes redistributed in Type-5  0
  Opaque AS        0          0         0
  Non-self        28
  Total           29          0         0
```

Following are the three commands in Example 9-7, in order:

- **show ip ospf:** Confirms with one (highlighted) line that the router believes the area is a stub area.

- **show ip ospf database summary 0.0.0.0:** By definition, this command lists all summary (Type 3) LSAs with a prefix of 0.0.0.0. It lists two such LSAs, created by R1 and R2 (RIDs 1.1.1.1 and 2.2.2.2, respectively), both with metric 1 (the default setting).

- **show ip ospf database database-summary:** This command lists statistics about the numbers of and types of LSAs in the database. The counters show 0 Type 5 LSAs, and several Type 3 LSAs—confirming that the area, while stubby, is not totally stubby.

Configuring and Verifying Totally Stubby Areas

Configuring totally stubby areas requires almost no additional effort as compared with stubby areas. As listed earlier in Table 9-3, the only difference for totally stubby configuration versus stubby configuration is that the ABRs include the **no-summary** keyword on the **area stub** command. (**no-summary** refers to the fact that ABRs in totally stubby areas do not create/flood Type 3 summary LSAs.)

Example 9-7 shows another example configuration, this time with area 34 as a totally stubby area. Additionally, the default routes' metrics have been set so that both R3 and R4 will use R1 as their preferred ABR, by setting R2's advertised summary to a relatively high metric (500). Example 9-8 just shows the changes to the configuration shown in Example 9-4.

Example 9-8 *Totally Stubby Area Configuration*

```
! On Router R1:
router ospf 1
 area 34 stub no-summary
 auto-cost reference-bandwidth 1000


! On Router R2:
router ospf 2
 area 34 stub no-summary
 area 34 default-cost 500
 auto-cost reference-bandwidth 1000
```

The configuration of a totally stubby area reduces the size of the LSDB in area 34, because the ABRs no longer flood Type 3 LSAs into area 34, as shown in Example 9-9. R3 displays its LSDB, listing only two Summary (Type 3) LSAs—the two default routes advertised by the two ABRs, respectively. No other Type 3 LSAs exist, nor do any external (Type 5) or ASBR summary (Type 4) LSAs.

Also, note that the example lists the OSPF routes known to R3. Interestingly, in the topology shown for area 34, R3 learns only three OSPF routes: the two intra-area routes for the subnets between R4 and the two ABRs plus the best default route. The default route has a metric of 501, based on R3's S0/0/0.1 interface cost plus the cost 1 listed for R1's Type 3 LSA for the default route.

Example 9-9 *Confirmation of the Effects of a Totally Stubby Area*

```
R3# show ip route
Codes: C - connected, S - static, R - RIP, M - mobile, B - BGP
       D - EIGRP, EX - EIGRP external, O - OSPF, IA - OSPF inter area
       N1 - OSPF NSSA external type 1, N2 - OSPF NSSA external type 2
       E1 - OSPF external type 1, E2 - OSPF external type 2
       i - IS-IS, su - IS-IS summary, L1 - IS-IS level-1, L2 - IS-IS level-2
       ia - IS-IS inter area, * - candidate default, U - per-user static route
       o - ODR, P - periodic downloaded static route


Gateway of last resort is 10.10.13.1 to network 0.0.0.0

     10.0.0.0/8 is variably subnetted, 5 subnets, 2 masks
C       10.10.13.0/29 is directly connected, Serial0/0/0.1
O       10.10.14.0/29 [110/657] via 10.10.34.4, 00:57:37, FastEthernet0/0
C       10.10.23.0/29 is directly connected, Serial0/0/0.2
```

```
O        10.10.24.0/29 [110/657] via 10.10.34.4, 00:57:37, FastEthernet0/0
C        10.10.34.0/24 is directly connected, FastEthernet0/0
O*IA     0.0.0.0/0 [110/501] via 10.10.13.1, 00:24:35, Serial0/0/0.1


R3# show ip ospf database database-summary


          OSPF Router with ID (3.3.3.3) (Process ID 3)
! lines omitted for brevity


Process 3 database summary
   LSA Type        Count    Delete    Maxage
   Router          4        0         0
   Network         1        0         0
   Summary Net     2        0         0
   Summary ASBR    0        0         0
   Type-7 Ext      0        0         0
   Opaque Link     0        0         0
   Opaque Area     0        0         0
   Type-5 Ext      0        0         0
      Prefixes redistributed in Type-5   0
   Opaque AS       0        0         0
   Non-self        6
   Total           7        0         0


R3# show ip ospf database | begin Summary
               Summary Net Link States (Area 34)


Link ID         ADV Router      Age      Seq#        Checksum
0.0.0.0         1.1.1.1         1407     0x80000003 0x008FA8
0.0.0.0         2.2.2.2         1506     0x80000004 0x00FF3E
```

Following are the three commands in Example 9-9, in order:

- **show ip route:** It lists a single interarea route—a default route, with destination 0.0.0.0/0. The output also lists this same next-hop information as the gateway of last resort.

- **show ip ospf database database-summary:** The statistics still show no external Type 5 LSAs, just as when the area was stubby, but now show only two Type 3 LSAs, whereas before, several existed.

- **show ip ospf database | begin Summary:** This command shows the output beginning with the Type 3 Summary LSAs. It lists two default route LSAs: one from R1 and one from R2.

Examples 9-7 and 9-9 demonstrate the key differences between stub areas (they do see Type 3 LSAs) and totally stubby areas (which do not see Type 3 LSAs). Next, this section looks at the different types of not-so-stubby areas.

The Not-So-Stubby Area (NSSA)

Stub and totally stubby areas do not allow external routes to be injected into a stubby area—a feature that originally caused some problems. The problem is based on the fact that stub areas by definition should never learn a Type 5 LSA, and OSPF injects external routes into OSPF as Type 5 LSAs. These two facts together mean that a stubby area could not normally have an ASBR that was injecting external routes into the stub area.

The not-so-stubby area (NSSA) option for stubby areas overcomes the restriction on external routes. The solution itself is simple: Because stubby areas can have no Type 5 LSAs, later OSPF RFCs defined a newer LSA type (Type 7) that serves the same purpose as the Type 5 LSA, but only for external routes in stubby areas. So, an NSSA area can act just like a stub area, except that routers can inject external routes into the area.

Figure 9-10 shows an example, with four steps. The same stubby area 34 from the last few figures still exists; it does not matter at this point whether area 34 is totally stubby or simply stubby.

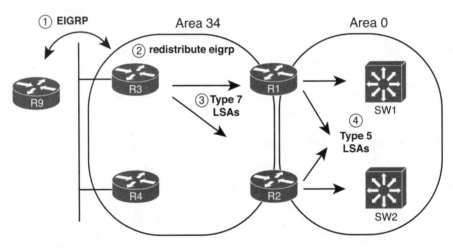

Figure 9-10   *External Routes in an NSSA (34)*

The steps labeled in the figure are as follows:

Step 1.   ASBR R3 learns routes from some external source of routing information, in this case, EIGRP from R9.

Step 2.   An engineer configures route redistribution using the **redistribute** command, taking the routes learned with EIGRP and injecting them into OSPF.

Step 3.   R3 floods Type 7 LSAs throughout stub area 34.

Step 4.   ABRs R1 and R2 then create Type 5 LSAs for the subnets listed in the Type 7 LSAs, and flood these Type 5 LSAs into other areas, like area 0.

Configuring NSSA works much like the configuration of stubby areas. For totally NSSAs, configure **area** *area-number* **nssa no-summary** instead of **area** *area-number* **stub no-summary**. For normal NSSAs, as with stub areas, omit the **no-summary** keyword.

Additionally, normal NSSAs require that ABRs have the **default-information-originate** keyword specified, making the command on ABRs **area** *area-number* **nssa default-information-originate**.

Example 9-10 shows a sample with the configuration of a totally NSSA 34 from the network represented in the last four figures. Note that as with the **area stub** command, the **area nssa** command's **no-summary** option is required only on the ABRs.

Example 9-10 *Totally NSSA Configuration and Verification*

```
! On Router R1:
router ospf 1
 area 34 nssa no-summary

! On Router R2:
router ospf 2
 area 34 nssa no-summary
 area 34 default-cost 500

! On Router R3:
router ospf 3
 area 34 nssa

! On Router R4:
router ospf 4
 area 34 nssa
```

The same verification steps and commands can be used for NSSAs as were shown in the earlier examples for stub areas. In particular, the **show ip ospf** command states that the area is an NSSA. You can also see Type 7 LSAs in the OSPF LSDB after redistribution has been configured.

Table 9-4 summarizes the key points regarding stubby areas.

Key Topic

Table 9-4 *OSPF Stubby Area Types*

Area Type	ABRs Flood Type 5 External LSAs into the Area?	ABRs Flood Type 3 Summary LSAs into the Area?	Allows Redistribution of External LSAs into the Stubby Area?
Stub	No	Yes	No
Totally stubby	No	No	No
NSSA	No	Yes	Yes
Totally NSSA	No	No	Yes

> **Note**   Both types of totally stubby areas (totally stubby, totally NSSA) are Cisco proprietary.

OSPF Version 3

The OSPF discussions thus far in this book focused on OSPF version 2 (OSPFv2). While OSPFv2 is feature-rich and widely deployed, it does have one major limitation in that it does not support the routing of IPv6 networks. Fortunately, OSPF version 3 (OSPFv3) does support IPv6 routing, and it can be configured to also support IPv4 routing.

This section discusses two OSPFv3 configuration options:

- The traditional approach
- The OSPF Address Family approach

The *OSPF Address Family* configuration approach is somewhat similar to Named EIGRP configuration, where you can have an IPv4 Address Family and an IPv6 Address Family hierarchically configured under the same routing protocol instance.

This section begins by discussing some of the similarities and differences between OSPFv2 and OSPFv3. Then, the traditional OSPFv3 configuration is presented, followed by an explanation of the OSPF Address Family approach.

OSPFv2 and OSPFv3 Comparison

OSPFv3 bears many similarities to OSPFv2. For example, they both use interface cost as their metric; the same network types exist (that is, broadcast, point-to-point nonbroadcast, multiaccess, and virtual links); the same packet types are used; and LSAs behave in much the same way.

However, a couple of OSPFv2 LSA types are renamed, and a couple of new LSAs are introduced. The LSA changes are as follows:

- **Renamed LSAs:**

    - **Type 3:** The Type 3 LSA is renamed as *Interarea prefix LSA for ABRs*. As with OSPFv2, this Type 3 LSA advertises one area's internal networks with another area. This LSA is generated by an area border router (ABR).

    - **Type 4:** The Type 4 LSA is renamed *Interarea prefix LSA for ASBRs*. As with OSPFv2, this Type 4 LSA advertises information about how to reach an autonomous system boundary router (ASBR) to routers in a different area than the ASBR. Then, those routers wanting to reach an external network (that is, outside the OSPF autonomous system) use the Type 4 LSAs to determine the best path to reach the ASBR that will get them to a desired external network.

- **New LSAs:**

  - **Type 8:** The Type 8 LSAs, called *Link LSAs*, only exist on a local link, where they are used by a router to advertise the router's link-local address to all other routers on the same link. Additionally, the Type 8 LSA provides to routers on that link a listing of all IPv6 addresses associated with the link. OSPFv3 also uses the Type 8 LSA to set option bits for a specific network's LSA. These bits give OSPFv3 more information about the nature of a network advertisement. As just one example, the NU (no unicast) bit indicates that a network should not be used in OSPF calculations. See RFC 5340 for a complete discussion of the option bits.

  - **Type 9:** Type 9 LSAs, called *Intra-Area Prefix LSAs*, can send information about IPv6 networks (including stub networks) attached to a router (similar to the Type 1 LSA for IPv4 networks). Additionally, a Type 9 LSA can send information about transit IPv6 network segments within an area (similar to the Type 2 LSA for IPv6 networks).

OSPFv3 Traditional Configuration

The traditional approach to OSPFv3 configuration involves creating an OSPF routing process, going into the interfaces that you want to participate in the OSPF process, and instructing those interfaces to be part of that process.

The steps required to configure OSPFv3 using the traditional approach are as follows:

Key Topic

Step 1.   Enable IPv6 unicast routing on the router (if it is not already enabled). This can be accomplished with the **ipv6 unicast-routing** global configuration mode command. Although not required, a best practice is to also enable Cisco Express Forwarding (CEF) for IPv6, using the **ipv6 cef** command, because CEF enables the router to make more efficient route lookups.

Step 2.   Start the OSPF process with the **ipv6 router ospf** *process-id* command, issued in global configuration mode.

Step 3.   (Optional) Configure a router ID for the OSPF process with the **router-id** *rid* command, where the *rid* is a 32-bit value, in router configuration mode. This router ID is commonly an IPv4 address of one of the router's interfaces. If you do not statically configure a router ID, the router attempts to dynamically determine a router ID to use based on currently active IPv4 addresses on the router. However, if you do not set a router ID, and no active IPv4 addresses exist on the router, the OSPF process will fail to start.

Step 4.   Instruct one or more interfaces to participate in the OSPF routing process by entering the **ipv6 ospf** *process-id* **area** *area_number* command in interface configuration mode.

To illustrate the traditional approach to OSPFv3 configuration, Examples 9-11, 9-12, 9-13, and 9-14 show a sample OSPFv3 configuration for the topology illustrated in Figure 9-11.

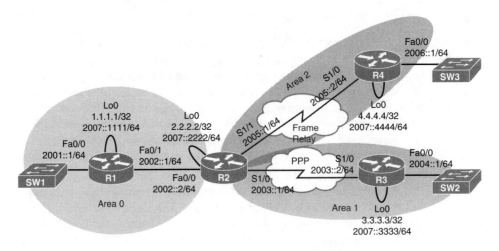

Figure 9-11 *Sample IPv6 OSPFv3 Topology with Multiple Areas*

Example 9-11 *Traditional OSPFv3 Configuration—Router R1*

```
! Configuration on Router R1
ipv6 unicast-routing
ipv6 cef
!
interface Loopback0
 ip address 1.1.1.1 255.255.255.255
 ipv6 address 2007::1111/64
 ipv6 ospf 1 area 0
!
interface FastEthernet0/0
 ip address 10.1.1.1 255.255.255.0
 ipv6 address 2001::1/64
 ipv6 ospf 1 area 0
!
interface FastEthernet0/1
 ip address 10.1.2.1 255.255.255.252
 ipv6 address 2002::1/64
 ipv6 ospf 1 area 0
!
ipv6 router ospf 1
 router-id 1.1.1.1
 passive-interface FastEthernet0/0
 passive-interface Loopback0
```

Example 9-12 *Traditional OSPFv3 Configuration—Router R2*

```
!Configuration on Router R2
ipv6 unicast-routing
ipv6 cef
!
interface Loopback0
 ip address 2.2.2.2 255.255.255.255
 ipv6 address 2007::2222/64
 ipv6 ospf 1 area 0
!
interface FastEthernet0/0
 ip address 10.1.2.2 255.255.255.252
 ipv6 address 2002::2/64
 ipv6 ospf 1 area 0
!
interface Serial1/0
 ip address 10.1.2.5 255.255.255.252
 encapsulation ppp
 ipv6 address 2003::1/64
 ipv6 ospf 1 area 1
!
interface Serial1/1
 ip address 10.1.2.9 255.255.255.252
 encapsulation frame-relay IETF
 ipv6 address 2005::1/64
 ipv6 ospf 1 area 2
 frame-relay map ipv6 2005::2 204 broadcast
 frame-relay map ipv6 FE80::C804:DFF:FE24:0 204 broadcast
 frame-relay map ip 10.1.2.10 204 broadcast
!
ipv6 router ospf 1
 router-id 2.2.2.2
 passive-interface Loopback0
```

Example 9-13 *Traditional OSPFv3 Configuration—Router R3*

```
!Configuration on Router R3
ipv6 unicast-routing
ipv6 cef
!
interface Loopback0
 ip address 3.3.3.3 255.255.255.255
 ipv6 address 2007::3333/64
 ipv6 ospf 1 area 1
!
interface FastEthernet0/0
```

```
 ip address 10.1.3.1 255.255.255.0
 ipv6 address 2004::1/64
 ipv6 ospf 1 area 1
!
interface Serial1/0
 ip address 10.1.2.6 255.255.255.252
 encapsulation ppp
 ipv6 address 2003::2/64
 ipv6 ospf 1 area 1
!
ipv6 router ospf 1
 router-id 3.3.3.3
 passive-interface FastEthernet0/0
 passive-interface Loopback0
```

Example 9-14 *Traditional OSPFv3 Configuration—Router R4*

```
!Configuration on Router R4
ipv6 unicast-routing
ipv6 cef
!
interface Loopback0
 ip address 4.4.4.4 255.255.255.255
 ipv6 address 2007::4444/64
 ipv6 ospf 1 area 2
!
interface FastEthernet0/0
 ip address 10.1.4.1 255.255.255.0
 ipv6 address 2006::1/64
 ipv6 ospf 1 area 2
!
interface Serial1/0
 ip address 10.1.2.10 255.255.255.252
 encapsulation frame-relay IETF
 ipv6 address 2005::2/64
 ipv6 ospf 1 area 2
 frame-relay map ipv6 2005::1 402 broadcast
 frame-relay map ipv6 FE80::C802:1FF:FEC0:0 402 broadcast
 frame-relay map ip 10.1.2.9 402 broadcast
!
ipv6 router ospf 1
 router-id 4.4.4.4
 passive-interface FastEthernet0/0
 passive-interface Loopback0
```

In each of the four preceding examples, notice that an OSPF routing process was started with the **ipv6 router ospf** *process-id* command, and a router ID was associated with each routing process using the **router-id** *rid* command. Additionally, under router configuration mode, a **passive-interface** *interface-id* command was issued for each interface not connecting to another OSPF-speaking router. This prevents unnecessarily sending OSPF messages out of those interfaces.

These examples illustrate how an interface is made to participate in an OSPFv3 routing process. Specifically, you enter interface configuration mode and enter the **ipv6 ospf** *process-id* **area** *area_number* command.

Note   Routers R2 and R4 have a series of **frame-relay map** commands. This is because these configurations are for IPv6 over Frame Relay, an NBMA network. Interestingly, on some NBMA networks, you need to statically configure the mapping of IPv6 addresses to Layer 2 circuit identifiers (for example, Data-Link Connection Identifiers [DLCI] in Frame Relay networks).

Verification can be performed using the same commands you used to verify OSPFv2 configurations, except **ip** is replaced with **ipv6**. For example, instead of issuing the **show ip ospf interface brief** command, as you would with OSPFv2 to get a brief listing of OSPF-speaking interfaces, you would issue the **show ipv6 ospf interface brief** command for OSPFv3. The following examples provide sample output from a collection of verification commands.

Example 9-15 shows sample output from the **show ipv6 ospf interface brief** command, issued on Router R2. The output from this command indicates that four interfaces on Router R2 are participating in the OSPFv3 routing process, along with the area membership for each interface. Additionally, the interface costs are listed and the number of neighbors (if any) residing off of each interface is listed.

Example 9-15   *Viewing Interfaces Participating in an OSPFv3 Process*

```
R2# show ipv6 ospf interface brief
Interface    PID   Area          Intf ID   Cost   State  Nbrs F/C
Lo0          1     0             8         1      LOOP   0/0
Fa0/0        1     0             2         1      BDR    1/1
Se1/0        1     1             3         64     P2P    1/1
Se1/1        1     2             4         64     DR     0/0
```

In Example 9-16, the **show ipv6 ospf neighbor** command is used to create a listing of OSPFv3 neighbors. Interestingly, while Routers R1 (1.1.1.1) and R3 (3.3.3.3) are neighbors, Router R2 is not a neighbor.

Example 9-16 *Viewing OSPFv3 Neighbors*

```
R2# show ipv6 ospf neighbor


            OSPFv3 Router with ID (2.2.2.2) (Process ID 1)


Neighbor ID     Pri    State           Dead Time    Interface ID    Interface
1.1.1.1           1    FULL/DR         00:00:36     3               FastEthernet0/0
3.3.3.3           0    FULL/  -        00:00:30     3               Serial1/0
```

Before reading on, pause for a moment and consider what might be happening to prevent this neighborship from forming. Recall that a nonbroadcast multiaccess (NBMA) network, as the name suggests, does not support broadcasts (or multicasts). Therefore, routers belonging to an NBMA network do not dynamically discover one another. Instead, you need to statically configure a neighbor on at least one of the routers on the NBMA network.

To resolve the specific issue seen in Example 9-16, an **ipv6 ospf neighbor** *neighbor_ipv6_address* command is given on Router R2, pointing to Router R4's link-local address for the Frame Relay link interconnecting Routers R2 and R4. This command is shown in Example 9-17, along with a verification that Router R4 then appears as Router R2's neighbor.

Example 9-17 *Statically Configuring a Neighbor on an NBMA Network*

```
R2# conf term
R2(config)# interface s 1/1
R2(config-if)# ipv6 ospf neighbor FE80::C804:DFF:FE24:0
R2(config-if)# end
R2# show ipv6 ospf neigh


            OSPFv3 Router with ID (2.2.2.2) (Process ID 1)


Neighbor ID     Pri    State           Dead Time    Interface ID    Interface
1.1.1.1           1    FULL/DR         00:00:35     3               FastEthernet0/0
3.3.3.3           0    FULL/  -        00:00:32     3               Serial1/0
4.4.4.4           1    FULL/DR         00:01:42     3               Serial1/1
```

As a final OSPFv3 verification command, consider the output of the **show ipv6 ospf database** command issued on Router R1, as seen in Example 9-18.

Example 9-18 *Viewing the Contents of the OSPFv3 Link-State Database*

```
R1# show ipv6 ospf database


            OSPFv3 Router with ID (1.1.1.1) (Process ID 1)


                Router Link States (Area 0)
```

ADV Router	Age	Seq#	Fragment ID	Link count	Bits
1.1.1.1	1490	0x80000002	0	1	None
2.2.2.2	1491	0x80000001	0	1	B

Net Link States (Area 0)

ADV Router	Age	Seq#	Link ID	Rtr count
1.1.1.1	1490	0x80000001	3	2

Inter Area Prefix Link States (Area 0)

ADV Router	Age	Seq#	Prefix
2.2.2.2	1482	0x80000001	2003::/64
2.2.2.2	1482	0x80000001	2005::/64
2.2.2.2	1342	0x80000001	2007::3333/128
2.2.2.2	1259	0x80000001	2004::/64
2.2.2.2	147	0x80000001	2007::4444/128
2.2.2.2	147	0x80000001	2006::/64

Link (Type-8) Link States (Area 0)

ADV Router	Age	Seq#	Link ID	Interface
1.1.1.1	1855	0x80000001	3	Fa0/1
2.2.2.2	1491	0x80000001	2	Fa0/1
1.1.1.1	1876	0x80000001	2	Fa0/0

Intra Area Prefix Link States (Area 0)

ADV Router	Age	Seq#	Link ID	Ref-lstype	Ref-LSID
1.1.1.1	1490	0x80000004	0	0x2001	0
1.1.1.1	1490	0x80000001	3072	0x2002	3
2.2.2.2	1224	0x80000001	0	0x2001	0

In the output shown in Example 9-18, Type 1 LSAs show up as *Router Link States*, just as they did with OSPFv2. Also like OSPFv3, Type 2 LSAs show up as *Net Link States*. However, the Type 3 LSAs have been renamed from Summary Net Link States to *Inter-Area Prefix Link States*.

Also, as described earlier in this chapter, OSPFv3 introduces a couple of new LSA types, both of which are visible in this output. Specifically, OSPFv3 introduced Type 8 LSAs (which appear as *Link (Type-8) Link States* in the output) and Type 9 LSAs (which appear as *Intra-Area Prefix Link States*). For details about what these new LSA types do, refer to the "OSPFv2 and OSPFv3 Comparison" section, earlier in this chapter.

OSPFv3 Address Family Configuration

Somewhat similar to Named EIGRP, the *OSPFv3 Address Family* configuration approach lets you support the routing of both IPv4 and IPv6 under a single OSPF process. With such a configuration, there is a single link-state database containing information for both IPv4 and IPv6 networks. The steps to configure OSPFv3 using the Address Family approach are as follows:

Key Topic

Step 1. Start the OSPFv3 routing process with the **router ospfv3** *process-id* command.

Step 2. (Optional) Configure a router ID with the **router-id** *rid* command.

Step 3. Create an Address Family for IPv4 and/or IPv6 with the **address-family {ipv4 | ipv6} unicast** command.

Step 4. Enter interface configuration mode for the interface(s) that you want to participate in the OSPF process, and enter the **ospfv3** *process-id* {**ipv4 | ipv6**} **area** *area_number* command.

Note Even though the OSPFv3 Address Family configuration approach supports both IPv4 and/or IPv6 networks, it will not peer with a router using an OSPFv2 configuration.

Notice that the topology in Figure 9-12 is configured with both IPv4 and IPv6 addresses, and it is configured with OSPFv3. Examples 9-19, 9-20, 9-21, and 9-22 show the OSPFv3 configuration for each router, to support the routing of both IPv4 and IPv6 networks.

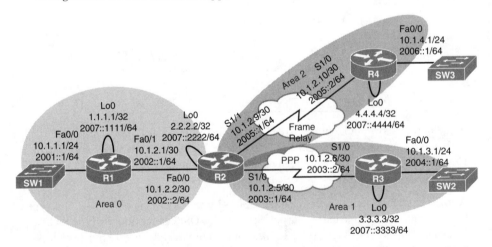

Figure 9-12 *Sample IPv4 and IPv6 OSPFv3 Address Family Topology with Multiple Areas*

Example 9-19 *OSPFv3 Address Family Configuration on Router R1*

```
ipv6 unicast-routing
ipv6 cef
!
interface Loopback0
 ip address 1.1.1.1 255.255.255.255
 ipv6 address 2007::1111/64
 ospfv3 1 ipv6 area 0
 ospfv3 1 ipv4 area 0
!
interface FastEthernet0/0
 ip address 10.1.1.1 255.255.255.0
 ipv6 address 2001::1/64
 ospfv3 1 ipv6 area 0
 ospfv3 1 ipv4 area 0
!
interface FastEthernet0/1
 ip address 10.1.2.1 255.255.255.252
 ipv6 address 2002::1/64
 ospfv3 1 ipv6 area 0
 ospfv3 1 ipv4 area 0
!
router ospfv3 1
 router-id 1.1.1.1
 !
 address-family ipv4 unicast
  passive-interface FastEthernet0/0
  passive-interface Loopback0
 exit-address-family
 !
 address-family ipv6 unicast
  passive-interface FastEthernet0/0
  passive-interface Loopback0
  maximum-paths 32
```

Example 9-20 *OSPFv3 Address Family Configuration on Router R2*

```
ipv6 unicast-routing
ipv6 cef
!
interface Loopback0
 ip address 2.2.2.2 255.255.255.255
 ipv6 address 2007::2222/64
 ospfv3 1 ipv6 area 0
 ospfv3 1 ipv4 area 0
!
```

```
interface FastEthernet0/0
 ip address 10.1.2.2 255.255.255.252
 ipv6 address 2002::2/64
 ospfv3 1 ipv6 area 0
 ospfv3 1 ipv4 area 0
!
interface Serial1/0
 ip address 10.1.2.5 255.255.255.252
 encapsulation ppp
 ipv6 address 2003::1/64
 ospfv3 1 ipv6 area 1
 ospfv3 1 ipv4 area 1
!
interface Serial1/1
 ip address 10.1.2.9 255.255.255.252
 encapsulation frame-relay IETF
 ipv6 address 2005::1/64
 ospfv3 neighbor FE80::C800:AFF:FE20:0
 ospfv3 1 neighbor FE80::C800:AFF:FE20:0
 ospfv3 1 ipv4 area 2
 ospfv3 1 ipv6 area 2
 frame-relay map ipv6 FE80::C800:AFF:FE20:0 204 broadcast
 frame-relay map ip 10.1.2.10 204 broadcast
 frame-relay map ipv6 2005::2 204 broadcast
!
router ospfv3 1
 router-id 2.2.2.2
 !
 address-family ipv4 unicast
  passive-interface Loopback0
 exit-address-family
 !
 address-family ipv6 unicast
  passive-interface Loopback0
  maximum-paths 32
  area 2 stub no-summary
 exit-address-family
```

Example 9-21   *OSPFv3 Address Family Configuration on Router R3*

```
ipv6 unicast-routing
ipv6 cef
!
interface Loopback0
 ip address 4.4.4.4 255.255.255.255
 ipv6 address 2007::4444/64
```

```
 ospfv3 1 ipv6 area 2
 ospfv3 1 ipv4 area 2
!
interface FastEthernet0/0
 ip address 10.1.4.1 255.255.255.0
 ipv6 address 2006::1/64
 ospfv3 1 ipv4 area 2
 ospfv3 1 ipv6 area 2
!
interface Serial1/0
 ip address 10.1.2.10 255.255.255.252
 encapsulation frame-relay IETF
 ipv6 address 2005::2/64
 ospfv3 1 neighbor FE80::C803:AFF:FEB8:0
 ospfv3 1 ipv4 area 2
 ospfv3 1 ipv6 area 2
 frame-relay map ipv6 FE80::C803:AFF:FEB8:0 402 broadcast
 frame-relay map ip 10.1.2.9 402 broadcast
 frame-relay map ipv6 2005::1 402 broadcast
!
router ospfv3 1
 router-id 4.4.4.4
 !
 address-family ipv4 unicast
  passive-interface FastEthernet0/0
  passive-interface Loopback0
 exit-address-family
 !
 address-family ipv6 unicast
  passive-interface FastEthernet0/0
  passive-interface Loopback0
  area 2 stub no-summary
 exit-address-family
```

Example 9-22   *OSPFv3 Address Family Configuration on Router R4*

```
ipv6 unicast-routing
ipv6 cef
!
interface Loopback0
 ip address 3.3.3.3 255.255.255.255
 ipv6 address 2007::3333/64
 ospfv3 1 ipv4 area 1
 ospfv3 1 ipv6 area 1
!
interface FastEthernet0/0
```

```
 ip address 10.1.3.1 255.255.255.0
 ipv6 address 2004::1/64
 ospfv3 1 ipv6 area 1
 ospfv3 1 ipv4 area 1
!
interface Serial1/0
 ip address 10.1.2.6 255.255.255.252
 encapsulation ppp
 ipv6 address 2003::2/64
 ospfv3 1 ipv6 area 1
 ospfv3 1 ipv4 area 1
!
router ospfv3 1
 router-id 3.3.3.3
 !
 address-family ipv4 unicast
  passive-interface FastEthernet0/0
  passive-interface Loopback0
 exit-address-family
 !
 address-family ipv6 unicast
  passive-interface FastEthernet0/0
  passive-interface Loopback0
  area 2 stub no-summary
 exit-address-family
```

In addition to the OSPFv3 configuration steps given earlier, these examples have a few optional features configured. For example, each router has one or more passive interfaces specified. Interestingly, even though the **passive-interface** *interface_identifier* command appears under Address Family configuration mode for both IPv4 and IPv6, those commands were entered under router configuration mode. The commands were then automatically copied down to the various Address Families configured under the router process.

Also, the **maximum-paths 32** command is entered under the IPv6 Address Family on Routers R1 and R2, illustrating that OSPFv3 allows you to load-balance across as many as 32 equal-cost paths.

Additionally, notice that Routers R2 and R4 have area 2 configured as a totally stubby area, with the **area 2 stub no-summary** command. This option dramatically reduces the number of OSPFv3 routes that appear on Router R4, as illustrated in Example 9-23. This example contrasts the multiple OSPFv3 routes on Router R1 (which has all its interfaces residing in area 0) and the single summary OSPFv3 route on Router R4 (which has all its interfaces residing in area 2).

Example 9-23 *Verifying the Effect of a Totally Stubby Area Configuration*

```
!OSPFv3 Routes on R1
R1# show ip route ospfv3
Codes: L - local, C - connected, S - static, R - RIP, M - mobile, B - BGP
       D - EIGRP, EX - EIGRP external, O - OSPF, IA - OSPF inter area
       N1 - OSPF NSSA external type 1, N2 - OSPF NSSA external type 2
       E1 - OSPF external type 1, E2 - OSPF external type 2
       i - IS-IS, su - IS-IS summary, L1 - IS-IS level-1, L2 - IS-IS level-2
       ia - IS-IS inter area, * - candidate default, U - per-user static route
       o - ODR, P - periodic downloaded static route, H - NHRP, l - LISP
       + - replicated route, % - next hop override


Gateway of last resort is not set

      2.0.0.0/32 is subnetted, 1 subnets
O        2.2.2.2 [110/1] via 10.1.2.2, 01:20:19, FastEthernet0/1
      3.0.0.0/32 is subnetted, 1 subnets
O IA     3.3.3.3 [110/65] via 10.1.2.2, 01:14:36, FastEthernet0/1
      4.0.0.0/32 is subnetted, 1 subnets
O IA     4.4.4.4 [110/65] via 10.1.2.2, 00:33:00, FastEthernet0/1
      10.0.0.0/8 is variably subnetted, 8 subnets, 3 masks
O IA     10.1.2.4/30 [110/65] via 10.1.2.2, 01:20:19, FastEthernet0/1
O IA     10.1.2.8/30 [110/65] via 10.1.2.2, 01:20:19, FastEthernet0/1
O IA     10.1.3.0/24 [110/66] via 10.1.2.2, 01:14:26, FastEthernet0/1
O IA     10.1.4.0/24 [110/66] via 10.1.2.2, 00:33:00, FastEthernet0/1


!OSPFv3 Routes on R4
R4# show ipv6 route ospf
IPv6 Routing Table - default - 8 entries
Codes: C - Connected, L - Local, S - Static, U - Per-user Static route
       B - BGP, R - RIP, H - NHRP, I1 - ISIS L1
       I2 - ISIS L2, IA - ISIS interarea, IS - ISIS summary, D - EIGRP
       EX - EIGRP external, ND - ND Default, NDp - ND Prefix, DCE - Destination
       NDr - Redirect, O - OSPF Intra, OI - OSPF Inter, OE1 - OSPF ext 1
       OE2 - OSPF ext 2, ON1 - OSPF NSSA ext 1, ON2 - OSPF NSSA ext 2, l - LISP
OI  ::/0 [110/65]
     via FE80::C803:AFF:FEB8:0, Serial1/0
```

Next, consider a few OSPFv3 verification commands. Example 9-24 shows output from the **show ospfv3 neighbor** command. Notice that one section of the output is for the IPv4 Address Family, and the other section is for the IPv6 Address Family.

Example 9-24 *Sample Output from the* **show ospfv3 neighbor** *Command*

```
R1# show ospfv3 neighbor


           OSPFv3 1 address-family ipv4 (router-id 1.1.1.1)


Neighbor ID     Pri    State          Dead Time    Interface ID    Interface
2.2.2.2           1    FULL/BDR       00:00:35     2               FastEthernet0/1


           OSPFv3 1 address-family ipv6 (router-id 1.1.1.1)


Neighbor ID     Pri    State          Dead Time    Interface ID    Interface
2.2.2.2           1    FULL/BDR       00:00:38     2               FastEthernet0/1
```

Example 9-25 shows output from the **show ospfv3 interface brief** command. Again, a portion of the output is for the IPv4 Address Family, and another portion is for the IPv6 Address Family.

Example 9-25 *Sample Output from the* **show ospfv3 interface brief** *Command*

```
R1# show ospfv3 interface brief
Interface    PID    Area          AF       Cost   State Nbrs F/C
Lo0          1      0             ipv4     1      LOOP  0/0
Fa0/0        1      0             ipv4     1      DR    0/0
Fa0/1        1      0             ipv4     1      DR    1/1
Lo0          1      0             ipv6     1      LOOP  0/0
Fa0/0        1      0             ipv6     1      DR    0/0
Fa0/1        1      0             ipv6     1      DR    1/1
```

Example 9-26 provides sample output from the **show ospfv3 database** command. Note that OSPFv3's single link-state database contains information for both IPv4 and IPv6 networks.

Example 9-26 *Sample Output from the* **show ospfv3 database** *Command*

```
R1# show ospfv3 database


           OSPFv3 1 address-family ipv4 (router-id 1.1.1.1)


               Router Link States (Area 0)


ADV Router      Age        Seq#          Fragment ID  Link count  Bits
 1.1.1.1        677        0x80000010    0            1           None
 2.2.2.2        917        0x8000000E    0            1           B


               Net Link States (Area 0)


ADV Router      Age        Seq#          Link ID    Rtr count
```

```
 1.1.1.1           677         0x8000000D  3              2


               Inter Area Prefix Link States (Area 0)


ADV Router        Age         Seq#        Prefix
  2.2.2.2         917         0x8000000D  10.1.2.4/30
  2.2.2.2         917         0x8000000D  10.1.2.8/30
  2.2.2.2         408         0x8000000D  3.3.3.3/32
  2.2.2.2         408         0x8000000D  10.1.3.0/24
  2.2.2.2         1920        0x8000000B  4.4.4.4/32
  2.2.2.2         1920        0x8000000B  10.1.4.0/24


...OUTPUT OMITTED...



       OSPFv3 1 address-family ipv6 (router-id 1.1.1.1)


           Router Link States (Area 0)


ADV Router        Age         Seq#        Fragment ID Link count  Bits
  1.1.1.1         853         0x80000010  0              1        None
  2.2.2.2         792         0x8000000E  0              1        B


           Net Link States (Area 0)


ADV Router        Age         Seq#        Link ID    Rtr count
  1.1.1.1         853         0x8000000D  3              2


               Inter Area Prefix Link States (Area 0)


ADV Router        Age         Seq#        Prefix
  2.2.2.2         545         0x8000000D  2003::/64
  2.2.2.2         282         0x8000000D  2007::3333/128
  2.2.2.2         282         0x8000000D  2004::/64
  2.2.2.2         1048        0x8000000B  2007::4444/128
  2.2.2.2         1048        0x8000000B  2006::/64
  2.2.2.2         1048        0x8000000B  2005::/64


...OUTPUT OMITTED...
```

Note   Even though the preceding commands used a series of **show ospfv3** commands, you can still use the more traditional **show ipv6 ospf** commands to verify your OSPFv3 Address Family configuration.

Exam Preparation Tasks

Planning Practice

The CCNP ROUTE exam expects test takers to review design documents, create implementation plans, and create verification plans. This section provides some exercises that can help you to take a step back from the minute details of the topics in this chapter so that you can think about the same technical topics from the planning perspective.

For each planning practice table, simply complete the table. Note that any numbers in parentheses represent the number of options listed for each item in the solutions in Appendix F, "Completed Planning Practice Tables."

Design Review Table

Table 9-5 lists several design goals related to this chapter. If these design goals were listed in a design document, and you had to take that document and develop an implementation plan, what implementation options come to mind? For any configuration items, a general description can be used, without concern about the specific parameters.

Table 9-5 *Design Review*

Design Goal	Possible Implementation Choices Covered in This Chapter
When using OSPF, prevent the routers in sites for one division of the company from knowing IP routes for subnets in another division. (3)	
The design shows an enterprise that uses only OSPF. It lists a goal of keeping the LSDBs and routing tables in each area small. (3)	
The design lists a goal of extremely small LSDBs and IP routing tables on branch office routers. Which stub area types work best? (2)	
The design calls for the flooding of a domain-wide default route to draw traffic toward Internet-connected routers.	
The design requires the routing of both IPv4 and IPv6 networks. (2)	

Implementation Plan Peer Review Table

Table 9-6 shows a list of questions that others might ask, or that you might think about, during a peer review of another network engineer's implementation plan. Complete the table by answering the questions.

Table 9-6 *Notable Questions from This Chapter to Consider During an Implementation Plan Peer Review*

Question	Answer
The plan shows a design with area 0, with different ABRs connecting area 0 to areas 1, 2, and 3. The configurations show Type 3 LSA filtering into the nonbackbone areas but not in the opposite direction. Could this configuration filter subnets in area 1 from being seen in area 2?	
The design shows the configuration of Type 3 LSA filtering on an internal router in area 1. Could the filter have any effect?	
The plan shows the configuration of the **area range** command on an ABR. What is the metric for the summary route, and in what conditions will the ABR advertise the summary?	
The plan shows the configuration of the **area 1 stub** command for an area mostly located on the west coast of the United States. The company just bought another company whose sites are also on the west coast. What issues exist if you add links from the acquired company into area 1?	
The plan shows the configuration of the **default-information originate always** command on the one router to which Internet links connect. What happens to the default route when the Internet link fails, and what happens to packets destined for the Internet during this time?	
The plan calls for the routing of both IPv4 and IPv6 networks. What new, or renamed, LSA types might appear in an area's link-state database?	

Create an Implementation Plan Table

To practice skills useful when creating your own OSPF implementation plan, list in Table 9-7 configuration commands related to the configuration of the following features. You might want to record your answers outside the book, and set a goal to complete this table (and others like it) from memory during your final reviews before taking the exam.

Table 9-7 *Implementation Plan Configuration Memory Drill*

Feature	Configuration Commands/Notes
Filter Type 3 LSAs from being sent into an area.	
Filter the OSPF routes calculated on one router from being added to that one router's routing table.	
Configure route summarization on ABRs.	
Configure route summarization on ASBRs.	
Configure the OSPF domain-wide advertisement of a default route.	
Configure stubby or totally stubby areas.	
Configure NSSAs or totally NSSAs.	
Start an OSPFv3 process, using the traditional configuration approach.	
Instruct an interface to participate in an OSPFv3 area, using the traditional configuration approach.	
Start an OSPFv3 process, using the Address Family configuration approach.	
Instruct an interface to participate in an OSPFv3 area, using the Address Family configuration approach.	

Choose Commands for a Verification Plan Table

To practice skills useful when creating your own OSPF verification plan, list in Table 9-8 all commands that supply the requested information. You might want to record your answers outside the book, and set a goal to complete this table (and others like it) from memory during your final reviews before taking the exam.

Table 9-8 *Verification Plan Memory Drill*

Information Needed	Command(s)
Display all IP routes for subnets in a range, regardless of prefix length.	
Display the contents of an IP prefix list.	
Display details of all Type 3 LSAs known to a router.	
Display details of all Type 5 external LSAs known to a router.	
Display the metric advertised in a summary route created by the **area range** command.	
Display the metric advertised in a summary route created by the **summary-address** command.	
Discover whether a router resides in a stubby area, and if so, which kind.	
Confirm stubby area concepts by looking at the numbers of Type 3 and Type 5 LSAs known to a router.	
List the interfaces participating in a traditional OSPFv3 configuration.	
Display neighbors in a traditional OSPFv3 configuration.	
Display the contents of a router's link-state database using a traditional OSPFv3 configuration.	
List the interfaces participating in an IPv4 and/or IPv6 OSPFv3 routing process configured with the OSPFv3 Address Family configuration approach.	
Display IPv4 and/or IPv6 neighbors configured with the OSPFv3 Address Family configuration approach.	
Display the contents of a router's link-state database, containing entries for IPv4 and/or IPv6 networks, using the OSPFv3 Address Family configuration approach.	

Note Some of the entries in this table may not have been specifically mentioned in this chapter but are listed in this table for review and reference.

Review All the Key Topics

Review the most important topics from inside the chapter, noted with the Key Topic icon in the outer margin of the page. Table 9-9 lists a reference of these key topics and the page numbers on which each is found.

Table 9-9 *Key Topics for Chapter 9*

Key Topic Element	Description	Page Number
List	Explanations of the features of the **area range** command	357
List	Explanations of the features of the **summary-address** command	360
Table 9-2	OSPF Route Summarization Commands	361
Table 9-3	Stub Area Configuration Options	366
Table 9-4	OSPF Stubby Area Types	375
List	Renamed and new LSAs for OSPFv3	376
List	Steps to configure OSPFv3 using the traditional approach	377
Example 9-11	Traditional OSPFv3 Configuration—Router R1	378
List	Steps to configure OSPFv3 using the Address Family configuration approach	384
Example 9-19	OSPFv3 Address Family Configuration on Router R1	385

Complete the Tables and Lists from Memory

Print a copy of Appendix D, "Memory Tables," (found on the CD) or at least the section for this chapter, and complete the tables and lists from memory. Appendix E, "Memory Tables Answer Key," also on the CD, includes completed tables and lists to check your work.

Define Key Terms

Define the following key terms from this chapter, and check your answers in the glossary.

Type 3 LSA filtering, stub area, totally stubby area, not-so-stubby area, Type 5 external LSA, OSPFv3, OSPFv3 Address Family

This chapter covers the following subjects:

- **Route Redistribution Basics:** This section discusses the reasons why designers might choose to use route redistribution, and how routing protocols redistribute routes from the IP routing table.

- **Redistribution in EIGRP:** This section discusses the mechanics of how Cisco IOS redistributes routes from other sources into EIGRP.

- **Redistribution in OSPF:** This section discusses the mechanics of how Cisco IOS redistributes routes from other sources into OSPF.

- **Redistribution with Route Maps and Distribution Lists:** This section focuses on the functions available using route maps and distribute lists on the same router that performs redistribution into either EIGRP or OSPF.

- **Issues with Multiple Redistribution Points:** This section examines the domain loop problem that can occur when multiple routers redistribute routes between the same two routing domains. This section also examines various solutions, including the setting of large metrics, setting the administrative distance, and using route tags.

CHAPTER 10

Route Redistribution

This chapter examines how routers can exchange routes between routing protocols through route redistribution. Specifically, this chapter begins by discussing the mechanics of what happens when the routes are redistributed. Then the discussion shifts to filtering and summarizing routes when redistributing, along with typical issues and solutions when multiple routers redistribute the same routes.

This chapter examines how routers can exchange routes between routing protocols through route redistribution. Specifically, this chapter begins by discussing the mechanics of what happens when the routes are redistributed. Then the discussion shifts to filtering and summarizing routes when redistributing, along with typical issues and solutions when multiple routers redistribute the same routes.

This chapter then looks at the methods by which a router can manipulate the routes being redistributed, beyond the settings of the metrics. This manipulation includes the filtering of routes and the setting of other values that can be associated with a route during the redistribution process.

Next, this chapter examines a variety of design issues that occur when multiple redistribution points exist between routing domains. Many designs use multiple redistribution points for redundancy and even for load sharing. This redundancy creates some additional complexity. (This complexity has long been a favorite topic for the CCIE R/S Lab.) This chapter also shows methods of dealing with the design issues, including the manipulation of metrics, administrative distance, and route tags.

"Do I Know This Already?" Quiz

The "Do I Know This Already?" quiz allows you to assess whether you should read the entire chapter. If you miss no more than two of these 16 self-assessment questions, you might want to move ahead to the "Exam Preparation Tasks" section. Table 10-1 lists the major headings in this chapter and the "Do I Know This Already?" quiz questions covering the material in those headings so that you can assess your knowledge of these specific areas. The answers to the "Do I Know This Already?" quiz appear in Appendix A.

Table 10-1   *"Do I Know This Already?" Foundation Topics Section-to-Question Mapping*

Foundation Topics Section	Questions
Route Redistribution Basics	1–2
Redistribution into EIGRP	3–5
Redistribution into OSPF	6–8
Redistribution with route maps and distribute lists	9–12
Issues with multiple redistribution points	13–16

1. Which of the following answers is the least likely reason for an engineer to choose to use route redistribution?

   a. To exchange routes between merged companies

   b. To give separate control over routing to different parts of one company

   c. To support multiple router vendors

   d. To knit together an OSPF area if the area becomes discontiguous

2. For a router to successfully redistribute routes between OSPF and EIGRP, which of the following are true? (Choose two.)

   a. The router must have one routing protocol configured, but configuration for both routing protocols is not necessary.

   b. The router must have at least one working link connected to each routing domain.

   c. The **redistribute** command must be configured under EIGRP to send the routes to OSPF.

   d. The **redistribute** command should be configured under OSPF to take routes from EIGRP into OSPF.

3. Process EIGRP 1 is redistributing routes from process OSPF 2. Which of the following methods can be used to set the metrics of the redistributed routes? (Choose two.)

   a. Let the metrics default.

   b. Set the metric components using the **redistribute** command's **metric** keyword.

   c. Set the metric components using the **default-metric** subcommand under router configuration mode.

   d. Set the integer (composite) metric using the **redistribute** command's **metric** keyword.

4. Examine the following excerpt from the **show ip eigrp topology 10.2.2.0/24** command on Router R1. Which answer can be verified as definitely true based on this output?

```
External data:
  Originating router is 10.1.1.1
  AS number of route is 1
  External protocol is OSPF, external metric is 64
  Administrator tag is 0 (0x00000000)
```

   a. R1 is the router that redistributed the route.

   b. R1's metric to reach subnet 10.2.2.0/24 is 64.

   c. The route was redistributed on a router that has a **router ospf 1** command configured.

   d. R1 is redistributing a route to prefix 10.2.2.0/24 into OSPF.

5. Router R1 has a connected route for 10.1.1.0/24 off interface Fa0/0. Interface Fa0/0 has been enabled for OSPF because of a **router ospf 1** and **network 10.1.1.0 0.0.0.255 area 0** command. R1 also has EIGRP configured, with the **redistribute ospf 1 metric 1000 100 10 1 1500** command configured under EIGRP. Which of the following is true?

   a. R1 will not redistribute 10.1.1.0/24 into EIGRP, because R1 knows it as a connected route and not as an OSPF route.

   b. For any OSPF routes redistributed into EIGRP, the metric components include a value equivalent to 1 Mbps of bandwidth.

   c. For any OSPF routes redistributed into EIGRP, the metric components include a value equivalent to 100 microseconds of delay.

   d. No subnets of network 10.1.1.0 will be redistributed because of the omission of the **subnets** parameter.

6. Process OSPF 1 is redistributing routes from process OSPF 2. Which of the following methods can be used to set the metrics of the redistributed routes? (Choose two.)

   a. Let the metrics default.

   b. Use each redistributed route's OSPF metric using the **redistribute** command's **metric transparent** keywords.

   c. Set the metric using the **default-metric** subcommand under router configuration mode.

   d. Redistribution is not allowed between two OSPF processes.

7. Examine the following excerpt from the **show ip ospf database asbr-summary** command on Router R1 (RID 1.1.1.1). Which answer can be verified as definitely true based on this output?

```
LS Type: Summary Links (AS Boundary Router)
Link State ID: 9.9.9.9 (AS Boundary Router address)
Advertising Router: 3.3.3.3
LS Seq Number: 8000000D
Checksum: 0xE43A
Length: 28
Network Mask: /0
        TOS: 0  Metric: 100
```

   a. The output describes the contents of a Type 5 LSA.

   b. 3.3.3.3 identifies a router as being the router performing redistribution.

   c. R1's metric for its best route to reach the router with RID 9.9.9.9 is 100.

   d. The router with RID 3.3.3.3's metric for its best route to reach the router with RID 9.9.9.9 is 100.

8. Router R1 sits inside OSPF area 1. Router R2 redistributes an E1 route into OSPF for prefix 2.2.2.0/24, with external metric 20. Router R22 redistributes an E2 route for the same prefix/length, external metric 10. Under what conditions will R1 choose as its best route the route through R22?

   a. R1 will always choose the route through R22.

   b. As long as R1's best internal OSPF cost to reach R22 is less than 10.

   c. As long as R1's best internal OSPF cost to reach R22 is less than 20.

   d. R1 will never choose the route through R22 if the E1 route through R2 is available.

9. Router R1 has been configured with the **redistribute ospf 1 route-map fred** command under **router eigrp 1**. The route map named fred needs to be configured to match routes to determine which routes are redistributed into EIGRP. Which of the following answers lists an item that cannot be matched by route map fred?

   a. Subnet number

   b. Next-hop router IP address of the route

   c. Whether the route is an E1 or E2 route

   d. The route's tag

   e. The number of router hops between the router and the subnet

10. Router R1 refers to route map fred when redistributing from EIGRP into OSPF. The entire route map is listed next. Which of the following answers must be true based on the configuration as shown?

```
route-map fred deny 10
 match ip address one
route-map fred deny 20
 match ip address two
route-map fred permit 100
```

    a. The third route map clause will allow any routes not already filtered by the first two clauses.

    b. Routes permitted by ACL "two" will be redistributed.

    c. Routes denied by ACL "one" will be redistributed.

    d. All routes will be filtered.

11. On Router R1, process EIGRP 1 is redistributing routes from process OSPF 2, calling route map fred with the **redistribute ospf 2 route-map fred** command. R1 has learned intra-area routes for 10.1.1.0/24 and 10.1.2.0/24 in part because of the Type 2 LSAs known for each subnet. The route map filters route 10.1.1.0/24 and allows 10.1.2.0/24 through. Which of the following commands on Router R1 list subnet 10.1.1.0/24? (Choose two.)

    a. show ip route

    b. show ip eigrp topology

    c. show ip ospf database

    d. show ip eigrp topology 10.1.1.0/24

12. Router R1 is redistributing between two OSPF processes. Given the configuration shown, which includes all commands in the route map named fred, which of the following answers is true regarding the redistribution into OSPF process 1?

```
router ospf 1
 redistribute ospf 2 match external 2 route-map fred
 !
route-map fred permit 10
 match ip address 1
 set metric-type type-1
```

    a. No routes are redistributed because a route cannot be both E1 and E2.

    b. Only OSPF E2 routes in the OSPF 2 domain will be considered for redistribution.

    c. Inside the OSPF 2 domain, any formerly E2 routes will become E1 routes.

    d. Routes permitted by ACL 1 will be redistributed, regardless of whether the routes are E1 or E2 routes.

13. Which of the following is not true regarding Cisco IOS default settings for administrative distance?

   a. EIGRP internal: 90

   b. OSPF external: 110

   c. EIGRP external: 90

   d. RIP: 120

   e. OSPF internal: 110

14. A network includes a RIPv2 domain, an EIGRP domain, and an OSPF domain. Each pair of routing domains has multiple routers redistributing routes between the pair of domains. The design requires that the redistribution configuration avoid matching based on prefix/length because of the trouble in maintaining such configurations. Which of the following tools can be used in all three routing domains to attempt to prevent domain loops? (This book uses the term *domain loop* to refer to the long routes that might be chosen for routes when redistribution exists—for example, a route might forward packets from the EIGRP domain, to the OSPF domain, back to EIGRP, and then to subnet *X* in the RIP domain.)

   a. Setting route tags

   b. Setting the default administrative distance differently for internal and external routes

   c. Setting administrative distance differently per route

   d. Setting metrics much higher for all external routes than for all internal routes

15. A coworker is developing an implementation plan for a design that uses OSPF 2 and RIPv2 routing domains, with two routers redistributing between the two domains. The coworker asks your help in choosing how to prevent domain loops by setting administrative distance. Assuming that all other related settings use defaults, which of the following would solve the domain loop problem?

   a. The **distance ospf intra-area 80 inter-area 80** OSPF subcommand

   b. The **distance ospf external 80** OSPF subcommand

   c. The **distance ospf intra-area 180 inter-area 180** OSPF subcommand

   d. The **distance ospf external 180** OSPF subcommand

16. Router R1 sets a route tag for subnet 10.1.1.0/24 when redistributing from OSPF into EIGRP. Which of the following units is assigned to the route tag?

   a. Kilobits/second

   b. Tens-of-microseconds

   c. Cost

   d. Hop count

   e. No units assigned

Foundation Topics

Route Redistribution Basics

Most internetworks use a single interior gateway protocol (IGP) to advertise and learn IP routes. However, in some cases, more than one routing protocol exists inside a single enterprise. Also, in some cases, the routes learned with an IGP must then be advertised with Border Gateway Protocol (BGP), and vice versa. In such cases, engineers often need to take routing information learned by one routing protocol and advertise those routes into the other routing protocol—a function provided by the Cisco IOS route redistribution feature.

This section examines the basics of route redistribution.

The Need for Route Redistribution

The potential need for route redistribution exists when a route learned through one source of routing information, most typically one routing protocol, needs to be distributed into a second routing protocol domain. For example, two companies might merge, with one company using Enhanced Interior Gateway Routing Protocol (EIGRP) and the other using Open Shortest Path First (OSPF). The engineers could choose to immediately migrate away from OSPF to instead use EIGRP exclusively, but that migration would take time and potentially cause outages. Route redistribution allows those engineers to connect a couple of routers to both routing domains, and exchange routes between the two routing domains, with a minimal amount of configuration and with little disruption to the existing networks.

Figure 10-1 shows just such a case, with R1 performing redistribution by using its knowledge of subnet 1 from the EIGRP domain and advertising a route for subnet 1 into the OSPF domain. Note that the opposite should also occur, with the OSPF domain's subnet 2 being redistributed into the EIGRP domain.

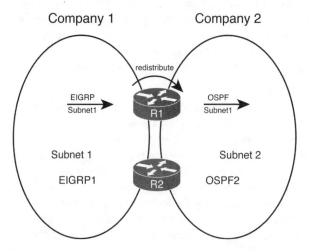

Figure 10-1 *Typical Use of Redistribution*

The main technical reason for needing redistribution is straightforward: An internetwork uses more than one routing protocol, and the routes need to be exchanged between those routing domains, at least temporarily. The business reasons vary widely but include the following:

- Mergers when different IGPs are used.

- Mergers when the same IGP is used.

- Momentum (The enterprise has been using multiple routing protocols for a long time.)

- Different company divisions are under separate control for business or political reasons.

- Connections between partners.

- Between IGPs and BGP when BGP is used between large segments of a multinational company.

- Layer 3 WAN (Multiprotocol Label Switching [MPLS]).

The list begins with two entries for mergers just to make the point that even if both merging companies use the same IGP, redistribution can still be useful. Even if both companies use EIGRP, they probably use a different autonomous system number (ASN) in their EIGRP configuration (with the **router eigrp** *asn* command). In such a case, to have all routers exchange routing information with EIGRP, all the former company's routers would need to migrate to use the same ASN as the first company. Such a migration might be simple, but it still requires disruptive configuration changes in a potentially large number of routers. Redistribution could be used until a migration could be completed.

Although useful as an interim solution, many permanent designs use redistribution as well. For example, it could be that a company has used different routing protocols (or different instances of the same routing protocol) in different divisions of a company. The network engineering groups can remain autonomous, and manage their own routing protocol domains, using redistribution to exchange routes at a few key connecting points between the divisions. Similarly, partner companies have separate engineering staffs, and want autonomy for managing routing, but also need to exchange routes for key subnets to allow the partnership's key applications to function. Figure 10-2 depicts both of these cases.

The last two cases in the previous list each relate to BGP in some way. First, some large corporations actually use BGP internal to the company's internetwork, redistributing routes from IGPs. Each large autonomous division of the company can design and configure its respective routing protocol instance, redistribute into BGP, and then redistribute out of BGP into other divisions. Also, when an enterprise uses an MPLS Virtual Private Network (VPN) service, the MPLS provider's provider edge (PE) router typically redistributes customer routes with BGP inside the MPLS provider's MPLS network. Figure 10-3 shows samples of both these cases. In each of these cases, a given prefix/length (subnet/mask) is typically distributed into BGP at one location, advertised over a BGP domain, and redistributed back into some IGP.

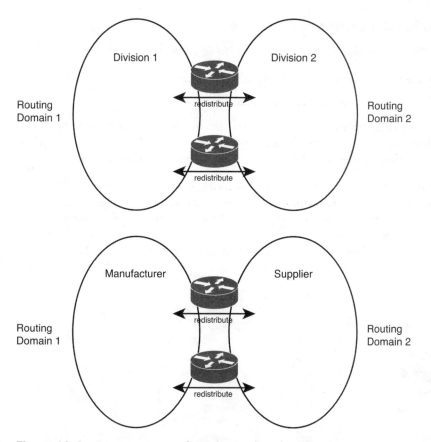

Figure 10-2 *Permanent Uses for Route Redistribution*

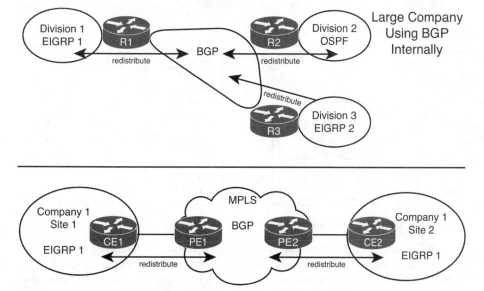

Figure 10-3 *Using Redistribution to Pass Routes Using BGP*

Redistribution Concepts and Processes

Route redistribution requires at least one router to do the following:

■ Use at least one working physical link with each routing domain.

■ A working routing protocol configuration for each routing domain.

■ Additional redistribution configuration for each routing protocol, specifically the **redistribute** command, which tells the routing protocol to take the routes learned by another source of routing information and to then advertise those routes.

The first two steps do not require any new knowledge or commands, but the third step represents the core of the redistribution logic and requires some additional background information. To appreciate the third step, Figure 10-4 shows an example router, RD1, which has met the first two requirements. RD1 uses EIGRP on the left and OSPF on the right, and has learned some routes with each routing protocol (Steps 1 and 2). However, no redistribution has yet been configured.

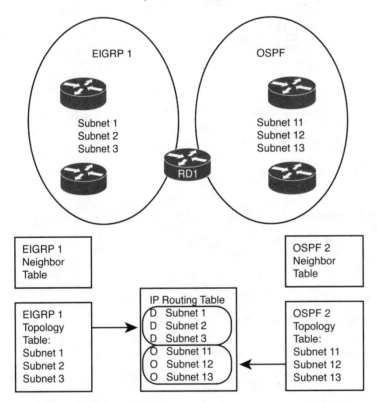

Figure 10-4 *Routing Protocol Tables on a Router Doing Redistribution*

The goal for redistribution in this case is to have EIGRP advertise subnets 11, 12, and 13, which exist inside the OSPF domain, and have OSPF advertise subnets 1, 2, and 3, which exist inside the EIGRP domain. To do that, EIGRP must put topology information about subnets 11, 12, and 13 into its EIGRP topology table, and OSPF must put topology information about subnets 1, 2, and 3 into its topology table. However, OSPF's topology table has a lot of different information in it compared to EIGRP's topology table. OSPF has link-state advertisements (LSA) and EIGRP does not. EIGRP lists the components of the composite metric and the neighbor's reported distance (RD)—but OSPF does not. In short, EIGRP and OSPF differ significantly in the contents of their topology tables.

Because the details of various routing protocols' topology tables differ, the redistribution process does not use the topology tables when redistributing routes. Instead, redistribution uses the one table that both routing protocols understand: the IP routing table. Specifically, the Cisco IOS **redistribute** command takes routes from the IP routing table and passes those routes to a routing protocol for redistribution. The **redistribute** command, configured inside a routing protocol configuration mode, redistributes routes into that routing protocol from some other source. Figure 10-5 spells it out with an example, which focuses on the internal logic of Router RD1 as shown in Figure 10-4.

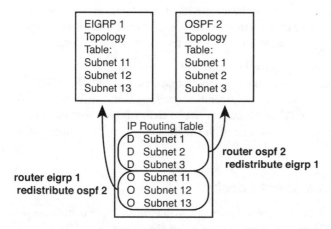

Figure 10-5 *Mutual Redistribution Between OSPF and EIGRP on Router RD1*

Starting on the left of the figure, RD1's EIGRP 1 process configuration lists the **redistribute ospf 2** command. This command tells RD1 to look in the IP routing table, take all OSPF routes added to the IP routing table by the OSPF 2 process on RD1, and put those routes into EIGRP's topology table. Conversely, the **redistribute eigrp 1** command configured on the OSPF process tells RD1 to take IP routes from the IP routing table, if learned by EIGRP process 1, and add those routes to OSPF 2's topology table.

The process works as shown in Figure 10-5, but the figure leaves out some important details regarding the type of routes and the metrics used. For EIGRP, the EIGRP topology table needs more than the integer metric value held by the IP routing table—it needs values for the components of the EIGRP composite metric. EIGRP can use default settings that define the metric components for all routes redistributed into EIGRP, or the engineer can set the metric components in a variety of ways, as covered in several locations later in this chapter.

Like EIGRP, OSPF treats the redistributed routes as external routes. OSPF creates an LSA to represent each redistributed subnet—normally a Type 5 LSA, but when redistributed into a not-so-stubby area (NSSA), the router instead creates a Type 7 LSA. In both cases, OSPF needs an integer metric to assign to the external route's LSA. The redistribution configuration should include the OSPF cost setting, which might or might not match the metric listed for the route in the redistributing router's IP routing table.

The last concept, before moving on to the configuration options, is that the **redistribute** command tells the router to take not only routes learned by the source routing protocol but also connected routes on interfaces enabled with that routing protocol—including passive interfaces. Example 10-1, later in this chapter, demonstrates this concept.

Redistribution into EIGRP

This section looks at the specifics of how EIGRP performs redistribution—that is, how EIGRP takes routes from other routing sources, such as OSPF, and advertises them into EIGRP. In real life, engineers often use both route filtering and route summarization at the redistribution point on a router. However, for the sake of making the underlying concepts clear, this portion of the chapter focuses on the mechanics of redistribution, without filtering, or summarization, or any other changes to the redistributed routes. This chapter later looks at the interesting options for manipulating routes at the redistribution point.

This section begins with a couple of short discussions of reference information. The first topic summarizes the parameters of the main configuration command, the EIGRP **redistribute** command. Next, the baseline configuration used in the upcoming samples is listed, including all EIGRP and OSPF configuration, but no redistribution configuration. With those details listed for reference, the rest of this section examines the configuration of redistribution into EIGRP.

EIGRP redistribute Command Reference

First, for reference, the following lines show the generic syntax of the **redistribute** command when used as a **router eigrp** subcommand. Note that the syntax differs slightly depending on the routing protocol into which routes will be redistributed. Following that, Table 10-2 lists the options on the command with a brief description.

```
redistribute protocol [process-id | as-number] [metric bw delay reliability load
   mtu ] [match {internal | nssa-external | external 1 | external 2}] [tag tag-value]
   [route-map name]
```

Table 10-2 *Parameters of the EIGRP* redistribute *Command*

Option	Description
protocol	The source of routing information. Includes **bgp, connected, eigrp, isis, mobile, ospf, static** and **rip**.
process-id, as-number	If redistributing a routing protocol that uses a process ID or ASN on the **router** global config command, use this parameter to refer to that process or ASN value.
metric	A keyword after which follows the four metric components (bandwidth, delay, reliability, link load), plus the MTU associated with the route.

Option	Description
match	If redistributing from OSPF, this keyword lets you match internal OSPF routes, external (by type), and NSSA external routes, essentially filtering which routes are redistributed.
tag	Assigns a unitless integer value to the routes redistributed by this command—tags that can be later matched by other routers using a route map.
route-map	Applies the logic in the referenced route map to filter routes, set metrics, and set route tags.

Baseline Configuration for EIGRP Redistribution Examples

The best method to see the results of redistribution is to use examples, so this section explains the sample internetwork used in the upcoming EIGRP redistribution examples. Figure 10-6 shows the sample internetwork. In this case, the EIGRP domain on the left uses subnets of Class B network 172.30.0.0, and the OSPF domain on the right uses subnets of Class B network 172.16.0.0. Note that all OSPF subnets reside in area 0 in this example internetwork, although that is not a requirement.

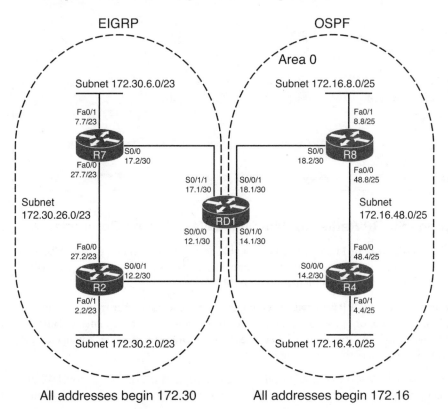

Figure 10-6 *Sample Internetwork Used for Redistribution Examples*

The internetwork uses a single router (RD1) to perform redistribution, just to avoid some interesting issues that occur when multiple routers redistribute the same routes (issues that are discussed later in this chapter). Example 10-1 shows the configuration on RD1, listing the IP addresses of the four active serial interfaces shown in Figure 10-6, plus the complete but basic EIGRP and OSPF configuration—but without any redistribution configured yet.

Example 10-1 *Configuration on Router RD1 Before Adding Redistribution Configuration*

```
interface Serial0/0/0
 ip address 172.30.12.1 255.255.255.252
 clock rate 1536000
!
interface Serial0/0/1
 ip address 172.16.18.1 255.255.255.252
 clock rate 1536000
!
interface Serial0/1/0
 ip address 172.16.14.1 255.255.255.252
 clock rate 1536000
!
interface Serial0/1/1
 ip address 172.30.17.1 255.255.255.252
 clock rate 1536000
!
router eigrp 1
 network 172.30.0.0
 no auto-summary
!
router ospf 2
 router-id 1.1.1.1
 network 172.16.0.0 0.0.255.255 area 0
```

Configuring EIGRP Redistribution with Default Metric Components

For the internetwork of Figure 10-6, a reasonable design goal would be to redistribute EIGRP routes into OSPF, and OSPF routes into EIGRP. This section examines the case of redistributing the routes into EIGRP from OSPF.

First, consider the EIGRP **redistribute** command. For those unfamiliar with the command, the direction of redistribution might not be obvious. A better command name might have been "take-routes-from," because the first parameter after the command tells Cisco IOS from where to get the routes.

For example, consider the configuration in Example 10-2, which was added to RD1's existing configuration in Example 10-1. The configuration uses only required parameters;

namely, a reference to the source from which routes should be redistributed. Because the configuration places this command in EIGRP configuration mode, the command tells Cisco IOS to redistribute the routes into EIGRP 1, from OSPF 2 in this case.

Example 10-2 *Minimal Configuration for Redistribution from OSPF into EIGRP*

```
RD1# configure terminal
Enter configuration commands, one per line.  End with CNTL/Z.
RD1(config)# router eigrp 1
RD1(config-router)# redistribute ospf 2
RD1(config-router)# end
```

Cisco IOS does accept the configuration. Unfortunately, Cisco IOS does not actually redistribute routes from OSPF into EIGRP in this case. EIGRP does not have a default setting for the metric components to use when redistributing into EIGRP from OSPF. To confirm these results, examine the output shown in Example 10-3, which lists **show** command output from RD1 when configured as shown in the previous example. Note that RD1's EIGRP topology table lists only routes for Class B network 172.30.0.0, which all sit inside the EIGRP domain. None of the routes from Class B network 172.16.0.0, which exist inside the OSPF domain, have been added to RD1's EIGRP topology table.

Example 10-3 *Redistribution Did Not Work on RD1*

```
RD1# show ip eigrp topology
IP-EIGRP Topology Table for AS(1)/ID(172.30.17.1)


Codes: P - Passive, A - Active, U - Update, Q - Query, R - Reply,
       r - reply Status, s - sia Status


P 172.30.17.0/30, 1 successors, FD is 2169856
        via Connected, Serial0/1/1
P 172.30.26.0/23, 2 successors, FD is 2172416
        via 172.30.12.2 (2172416/28160), Serial0/0/0
        via 172.30.17.2 (2172416/28160), Serial0/1/1
P 172.30.2.0/23, 1 successors, FD is 2172416
        via 172.30.12.2 (2172416/28160), Serial0/0/0
        via 172.30.17.2 (2174976/30720), Serial0/1/1
P 172.30.6.0/23, 1 successors, FD is 2172416
        via 172.30.17.2 (2172416/28160), Serial0/1/1
        via 172.30.12.2 (2174976/30720), Serial0/0/0
P 172.30.12.0/30, 1 successors, FD is 2169856
         via Connected, Serial0/0/0
```

To complete the configuration of redistribution into EIGRP, Router RD1 needs to set the metric values. EIGRP can set the metrics for redistributed routes in three ways, as summarized in Table 10-3.

Table 10-3 *Methods of Setting EIGRP Metrics When Redistributing into EIGRP*

Function	Command
Setting the default for all **redistribute** commands	The **default-metric** *bw delay reliability load mtu* EIGRP subcommand.
Setting the component metrics applied to all routes redistributed by a single **redistribute** command	The **metric** *bw delay reliability load mtu* parameters on the **redistribute** command.
Setting different component metrics to different routes from a single route source	Use the **route-map** parameter on the **redistribute** command, matching routes and setting metric components.

Note EIGRP does have a default metric when redistributing from another EIGRP process, in which case it takes the metric from the source of the routing information. In all other cases, the metric must be set using one of the methods in Table 10-3.

If the metrics do not matter to the design, which is likely when only a single redistribution point exists as in Figure 10-6, either of the first two methods listed in Table 10-3 is reasonable. The first method, using the **default-metric** command in EIGRP configuration mode, sets the metric for all routes redistributed into EIGRP, unless set by one of the other methods. Alternatively, the second method, which uses additional parameters on the **redistribute** command, sets the metric for all routes redistributed because of that one **redistribute** command. Finally, if the **redistribute** command also refers to a route map, the route map can use the **set metric** command to set the metric components for routes matched by the route map clause, overriding the metric settings in the **default-metric** command or with the **metric** keyword on the **redistribute** command.

Example 10-4 shows the addition of the **default-metric 1000 33 255 1 1500** command to RD1's configuration. This command sets the bandwidth to 1000 (kbps), the delay to 33 (tens-of-microseconds, or 330 microseconds), the reliability to 255 (a value in the range 1–255, where 255 is best), the load to 1 (a value in the range 1–255, where 1 is best), and the maximum transmission unit (MTU) to 1500. Note that even though EIGRP ignores the last three parameters by default when calculating integer metrics, you still must configure these settings for the commands to be accepted.

Example 10-4 *Redistributed Routes in RD1*

```
RD1# configure terminal
Enter configuration commands, one per line.  End with CNTL/Z.
RD1(config)# router eigrp 1
RD1(config-router)# default-metric 1000 33 255 1 1500
RD1(config-router)# end
```

Because this example uses a single **redistribute** command for the EIGRP 1 process, you could have used the **redistribute ospf 2 metric 1000 33 255 1 1500** command and ignored the **default-metric** command to achieve the same goal.

Verifying EIGRP Redistribution

As shown earlier in Figure 10-5, redistribution takes routes from the routing table and places the correct information for those subnets into the redistributing router's topology table. The redistributing router then advertises the routes from its topology table as it would for other routes. To verify that redistribution works, Example 10-5 shows the proof that RD1 indeed created entries in its EIGRP topology table for the five subnets in the OSPF domain.

Example 10-5 *Verifying That RD1 Added EIGRP Topology Data for Five OSPF Subnets*

```
RD1# show ip eigrp topology
IP-EIGRP Topology Table for AS(1)/ID(172.30.17.1)


Codes: P - Passive, A - Active, U - Update, Q - Query, R - Reply,
       r - reply Status, s - sia Status


! Note - all lines for class B network 172.30.0.0 have been omitted for brevity
P 172.16.48.0/25, 1 successors, FD is 2568448
       via Redistributed (2568448/0)
P 172.16.18.0/30, 1 successors, FD is 2568448
       via Redistributed (2568448/0)
P 172.16.14.0/30, 1 successors, FD is 2568448
       via Redistributed (2568448/0)
P 172.16.8.0/25, 1 successors, FD is 2568448
       via Redistributed (2568448/0)
P 172.16.4.0/25, 1 successors, FD is 2568448
       via Redistributed (2568448/0)
RD1# show ip eigrp topology 172.16.48.0/25
IP-EIGRP (AS 1): Topology entry for 172.16.48.0/25
  State is Passive, Query origin flag is 1, 1 Successor(s), FD is 2568448
  Routing Descriptor Blocks:
  172.16.18.2, from Redistributed, Send flag is 0x0
      Composite metric is (2568448/0), Route is External
      Vector metric:
          Minimum bandwidth is 1000 Kbit
          Total delay is 330 microseconds
          Reliability is 255/255
          Load is 1/255
          Minimum MTU is 1500
          Hop count is 0
      External data:
          Originating router is 172.30.17.1 (this system)
          AS number of route is 2
          External protocol is OSPF, external metric is 65
          Administrator tag is 0 (0x00000000)
```

The **show** command output lists several interesting facts:

- On Router RD1, which performed the redistribution, the EIGRP topology table lists the outgoing interface as "via redistributed."

- All the redistributed routes have the same feasible distance (FD) calculation (2568448), because all use the same component metrics per the configured **default-metric** command.

- RD1's two connected subnets in the OSPF 2 domain—subnets 172.16.14.0/30 and 172.16.18.0/30—were also redistributed, even though these routes are connected routes in RD1's routing table.

- The output of the **show ip eigrp topology 172.16.48.0/25** command confirms that the component metrics match the values configured on the **default-metric** command.

- The bottom of the output of the **show ip eigrp topology 172.16.48.0/25** command lists information about the external source of the route, including the routing source (OSPF) and that source's metric for the route (65). It also lists the phrase "(this system)," meaning that the router on which the command was issued (RD1 in this case) redistributed the route.

The third item in the list—the fact that RD1 redistributed some connected routes—bears further consideration. The **redistribute ospf 2** command tells EIGRP to redistribute routes learned by the OSPF 2 process. However, it also tells the router to redistribute connected routes for interfaces on which process OSPF 2 has been enabled. Back in Example 10-1, the configuration on RD1 lists a **network 172.16.0.0 0.0.255.255 area 0** command, enabling OSPF 2 on RD1's S0/0/1 and S0/1/0 interfaces. As such, the redistribution process also redistributed those routes.

Stated more generally, when the **redistribute** command refers to another IGP as the routing source, it tells the router to redistribute the following:

- All routes in the routing table learned by that routing protocol

- All connected routes of interfaces on which that routing protocol is enabled

Although Example 10-5 shows the evidence that Router RD1 added the topology data to its EIGRP topology database, it did not show any routes. Example 10-6 shows the IP routing tables on both RD1 and Router R2, a router internal to the EIGRP domain. R2's routes forward the packets toward the redistributing router, which in turn has routes from the OSPF domain with which to forward the packet to the destination subnet.

Example 10-6 *Verification of IP Routes on RD1 and R2*

```
! First, on RD1
RD1# show ip route 172.16.0.0
Routing entry for 172.16.0.0/16, 5 known subnets
  Attached (2 connections)
  Variably subnetted with 2 masks
```

```
   Redistributing via eigrp 1

O        172.16.48.0/25 [110/65] via 172.16.18.2, 00:36:25, Serial0/0/1
                        [110/65] via 172.16.14.2, 00:36:25, Serial0/1/0
C        172.16.18.0/30 is directly connected, Serial0/0/1
C        172.16.14.0/30 is directly connected, Serial0/1/0
O        172.16.8.0/25 [110/65] via 172.16.18.2, 00:36:25, Serial0/0/1
O        172.16.4.0/25 [110/65] via 172.16.14.2, 00:36:25, Serial0/1/0
```

```
! Next, on Router R2
R2# show ip route
Codes: C - connected, S - static, R - RIP, M - mobile, B - BGP
       D - EIGRP, EX - EIGRP external, O - OSPF, IA - OSPF inter area
       N1 - OSPF NSSA external type 1, N2 - OSPF NSSA external type 2
       E1 - OSPF external type 1, E2 - OSPF external type 2
       i - IS-IS, su - IS-IS summary, L1 - IS-IS level-1, L2 - IS-IS level-2
       ia - IS-IS inter area, * - candidate default, U - per-user static route
       o - ODR, P - periodic downloaded static route


Gateway of last resort is not set


     172.16.0.0/16 is variably subnetted, 5 subnets, 2 masks
D EX    172.16.48.0/25 [170/3080448] via 172.30.12.1, 00:25:15, Serial0/0/1
D EX    172.16.18.0/30 [170/3080448] via 172.30.12.1, 00:25:15, Serial0/0/1
D EX    172.16.14.0/30 [170/3080448] via 172.30.12.1, 00:25:15, Serial0/0/1
D EX    172.16.8.0/25 [170/3080448] via 172.30.12.1, 00:25:15, Serial0/0/1
D EX    172.16.4.0/25 [170/3080448] via 172.30.12.1, 00:25:15, Serial0/0/1
     172.30.0.0/16 is variably subnetted, 5 subnets, 2 masks
D        172.30.17.0/30 [90/2172416] via 172.30.27.7, 00:25:15, FastEthernet0/0
C        172.30.26.0/23 is directly connected, FastEthernet0/0
C        172.30.2.0/23 is directly connected, FastEthernet0/1
D        172.30.6.0/23 [90/30720] via 172.30.27.7, 00:25:15, FastEthernet0/0
C         172.30.12.0/30 is directly connected, Serial0/0/1
```

Beginning with the output for R2, in the second half of the example, R2 knows routes
for all five subnets in Class B network 172.16.0.0, listing all as external EIGRP routes. The
routes all use R2's link connected to RD1. Also, note that the administrative distance
(AD) is set to 170, rather than the usual 90 for EIGRP routes. EIGRP defaults to use AD
90 for internal routes and AD 170 for external routes.

RD1 has routes for all routes in the OSPF domain as well, but as either connected or
OSPF-learned routes.

Redistribution into OSPF

As you might expect, OSPF redistribution has several similarities and differences as compared to redistribution into EIGRP. Unlike EIGRP, OSPF does have useful default metrics

for redistributed routes, but OSPF does use the same general methods to configure metrics for redistributed routes. Like EIGRP, OSPF flags redistributed routes as being external. Unlike EIGRP, OSPF creates LSAs to represent each external route, and OSPF must then apply some much different logic than EIGRP to calculate the best route to each external subnet.

This section examines the OSPF redistribution process and configuration. It also discusses background on three OSPF LSA Types—Types 4, 5, and 7—all created to help OSPF distribute information so that routers can calculate the best route to each external subnet.

OSPF redistribute Command Reference

First, for reference, the following lines show the generic syntax of the **redistribute** command when used as a **router ospf** subcommand. Note that the syntax differs slightly depending on the routing protocol into which routes will be redistributed. Following that, Table 10-4 lists the options on the command with a brief description.

```
redistribute protocol [process-id | as-number] [metric metric-value] [metric-type
  type-value] [match {internal | external 1 | external 2 | nssa-external}] [tag tag-
  value] [route-map map-tag] [subnets]
```

Table 10-4 *Parameters on the OSPF* redistribute *Command*

Option	Description
protocol	The source of routing information. Includes **bgp, connected, eigrp, isis, mobile, ospf, static,** and **rip.**
process-id, as-number	If redistributing a routing protocol that uses a process ID or AS number on the **router** global config command, use this parameter to refer to that process ID or ASN value.
metric	Defines the cost metric assigned to routes redistributed by this command, unless overridden by a referenced route map.
metric-type {1	2}	Defines the external metric type for the routes redistributed by this command: 1 (E1 routes) or 2 (E2 routes).
match	If redistributing from another OSPF process, this keyword lets you match internal OSPF routes, external OSPF routes (either E1 or E2), and NSSA external routes, essentially filtering which routes are redistributed.
tag	Assigns a unitless integer value to the routes redistributed by this command—a tag that can be later matched by other routers using a route map.
route-map	Applies the logic in the referenced route map to filter routes, set metrics, and set route tags.
subnets	Redistribute subnets of classful networks. Without this parameter, only routes for classful networks are redistributed. (This behavior is unique to the OSPF **redistribute** command.)

Configuring OSPF Redistribution with Minimal Parameters

The **redistribute** subcommand under **router ospf** has many optional settings. To better appreciate some of these settings, this section first examines the results when using all defaults, using as few parameters as possible. Following the discussion of the behavior with defaults, the next examples add the parameters that complete the redistribution configuration.

Redistribution into OSPF uses the following defaults:

Key Topic

- When taking from BGP, use a default metric of 1.

- When taking from another OSPF process, take the source route's metric.

- When taking from all other sources, use a default metric of 20.

- Create a Type 5 LSA for each redistributed route (external) if not inside an NSSA; create a Type 7 LSA if inside an NSSA.

- Use external metric type 2.

- Redistribute only routes of classful (Class A, B, and C) networks, and not routes for subnets.

To demonstrate OSPF redistribution, this section uses an example that uses the same internetwork shown in Figure 10-6, including the baseline configuration shown in Example 10-1, and the EIGRP redistribution configuration shown in Examples 10-2 and 10-4. Essentially, the upcoming OSPF examples begin with Router RD1 including all the configurations seen in all the earlier examples in this chapter. According to those examples, OSPF has been correctly configured on the routers on the right side of Figure 10-6, EIGRP has been configured on the left, and the configuration of redistribution of OSPF routes into EIGRP has been completed. However, no redistribution into OSPF has yet been configured.

For perspective, before showing the redistribution into OSPF, Example 10-7 reviews the OSPF configuration, along with **show** commands listing RD1's IP routing table entries and its OSPF LSDB.

Example 10-7 *Router RD1 Routing Protocol Configuration, Before Redistribution into OSPF*

```
RD1# show run
! lines omitted for brevity
router eigrp 1
 redistribute ospf 2
 network 172.30.0.0
 default-metric 1000 33 255 1 1500
 no auto-summary
!
router ospf 2
 router-id 1.1.1.1
```

```
   log-adjacency-changes
   network 172.16.0.0 0.0.255.255 area 0


RD1# show ip route 172.30.0.0
Routing entry for 172.30.0.0/16, 5 known subnets
  Attached (2 connections)
  Variably subnetted with 2 masks
  Redistributing via eigrp 1


C       172.30.17.0/30 is directly connected, Serial0/1/1
D       172.30.26.0/23 [90/2172416] via 172.30.17.2, 01:08:50, Serial0/1/1
                       [90/2172416] via 172.30.12.2, 01:08:50, Serial0/0/0
D       172.30.2.0/23 [90/2172416] via 172.30.12.2, 01:08:50, Serial0/0/0
D       172.30.6.0/23 [90/2172416] via 172.30.17.2, 01:08:50, Serial0/1/1
C       172.30.12.0/30 is directly connected, Serial0/0/0
RD1# show ip ospf database


        OSPF Router with ID (1.1.1.1) (Process ID 2)


            Router Link States (Area 0)


Link ID         ADV Router      Age         Seq#        Checksum Link count
1.1.1.1         1.1.1.1         1425        0x80000007 0x007622 4
4.4.4.4         4.4.4.4         1442        0x8000000D 0x00B1E9 4
8.8.8.8         8.8.8.8         1466        0x80000006 0x00640E 4


            Net Link States (Area 0)


Link ID         ADV Router      Age         Seq#        Checksum
172.16.48.4     4.4.4.4         1442        0x80000004 0x007E07


! The following occurs on OSPF internal router R4
R4# show ip route 172.30.0.0
% Network not in table
```

The output in Example 10-7 shows several important points relative to the upcoming redistribution configuration. First, by design, the EIGRP domain contains subnets of network 172.30.0.0. Router RD1 knows routes for five subnets in this range. RD1 has four LSAs: three Type 1 Router LSAs (one each for Routers RD1, R4, and R8) plus one Type 2 network LSA (because only one subnet, 172.16.48.0/25, has elected a DR). Because the design for this internetwork puts all OSPF routers in area 0, no Type 3 summary LSAs exist in RD1's LSDB. Also, because no routers have redistributed external routes into OSPF yet, no Type 5 external nor Type 7 NSSA external routes are listed.

By adding the **redistribute eigrp 1** command in OSPF configuration mode, OSPF tries to redistribute routes from EIGRP—but with no success. The reason is that by omitting the

subnets parameter, OSPF will only redistribute routes for entire classful subnets, and only if such a route is listed in the IP routing table. Example 10-8 shows the results.

Example 10-8 *Redistributing into OSPF from EIGRP 1, All Default Settings*

```
RD1# configure terminal
Enter configuration commands, one per line.  End with CNTL/Z.
RD1(config)# router ospf 2
RD1(config-router)# redistribute eigrp 1
% Only classful networks will be redistributed
RD1(config-router)# end
RD1#
RD1# show ip ospf database

            OSPF Router with ID (1.1.1.1) (Process ID 2)

              Router Link States (Area 0)

Link ID         ADV Router      Age         Seq#        Checksum Link count
1.1.1.1         1.1.1.1         6           0x80000008  0x007A1B 4
4.4.4.4         4.4.4.4         1782        0x8000000D 0x00B1E9 4
8.8.8.8         8.8.8.8         1806        0x80000006 0x00640E 4

              Net Link States (Area 0)

Link ID         ADV Router      Age         Seq#        Checksum
172.16.48.4      4.4.4.4         1782        0x80000004  0x007E07
```

Cisco IOS even mentions that only classful routes will be redistributed. As seen in Example 10-7, no route exists for the exact Class B network prefix of 172.30.0.0/16, and by default, OSPF does not redistribute any subnets inside that range, as noted in the informational message in Example 10-8. So, the OSPF database on Router RD1 remains unchanged.

By changing the configuration to use the **redistribute eigrp 1 subnets** command, OSPF indeed redistributes the routes, as shown in Example 10-9.

Example 10-9 *Redistributing from EIGRP into OSPF, with Subnets*

```
RD1# configure terminal
Enter configuration commands, one per line.  End with CNTL/Z.
RD1(config)# router ospf 2
RD1(config-router)# redistribute eigrp 1 subnets
RD1(config-router)# end
RD1#
May 12 12:49:48.735: %SYS-5-CONFIG_I: Configured from console by console
RD1# show ip ospf database
```

```
! omitting the Type 1 and 2 LSA output for brevity


              Type-5 AS External Link States


Link ID         ADV Router       Age        Seq#        Checksum Tag
172.30.2.0      1.1.1.1          3          0x80000001 0x008050 0
172.30.6.0      1.1.1.1          3          0x80000001 0x005478 0
172.30.12.0     1.1.1.1          3          0x80000001 0x0005C3 0
172.30.17.0     1.1.1.1          3          0x80000001 0x00CDF5 0
172.30.26.0     1.1.1.1          3          0x80000001 0x007741 0
```

```
! The following occurs on router R4
R4# show ip route 172.30.0.0
Routing entry for 172.30.0.0/16, 5 known subnets
  Variably subnetted with 2 masks


O E2    172.30.17.0/30 [110/20] via 172.16.14.1, 00:01:10, Serial0/0/0
O E2    172.30.26.0/23 [110/20] via 172.16.14.1, 00:01:11, Serial0/0/0
O E2    172.30.2.0/23 [110/20] via 172.16.14.1, 00:01:11, Serial0/0/0
O E2    172.30.6.0/23 [110/20] via 172.16.14.1, 00:01:11, Serial0/0/0
O E2    172.30.12.0/30 [110/20] via 172.16.14.1, 00:01:11, Serial0/0/0
```

After adding the **subnets** option, Router RD1 redistributes the five routes from the EIGRP domain. Of particular interest:

■ If you look back to Example 10-7's **show ip route** command output from Router RD1, you see three EIGRP-learned routes, plus two connected routes, inside the EIGRP domain. Example 10-9's two **show** commands confirm that OSPF redistributes the three EIGRP-learned routes, plus the two connected subnets on which EIGRP is enabled (172.30.12.0/30 and 172.30.17.0/30).

■ The **show ip ospf database** command in Example 10-9 lists R1 (RID 1.1.1.1) as the advertising router of the five new Type 5 LSAs, because RD1 (with RID 1.1.1.1) created each Type 5 LSA.

■ Per OSPF internal Router R4's **show ip route 172.30.0.0** command at the end of Example 10-9, the external metric type is indeed E2, meaning external Type 2.

■ Per that same command on Router R4, the metric for each route is 20. The reasoning is that the default metric is 20 when redistributing from EIGRP into OSPF, and with an E2 route, internal OSPF costs are not added to the cost of the route.

That last point regarding the external route type requires a little more discussion. OSPF defines external routes as either an external Type 1 (E1) or external Type 2 (E2) route. By default, the OSPF **redistribute** command creates Type 2 routes, noting this external route type in the Type 5 LSA. The difference between the two lies in how OSPF calculates the metrics for E1 and E2 routes.

The next section completes the discussion of how OSPF can set the metrics when redistributing routes—or more specifically, the metric as listed in the Type 5 LSA created for that subnet. Following that, the text takes a detailed look at how OSPF calculates the best route for E2 routes. Later, the section "Redistributing into OSPF as E1 Routes" discusses the same subject, but for E1 routes.

Setting OSPF Metrics on Redistributed Routes

As mentioned earlier, no matter the source of the redistributed route, OSPF has a default metric to use. However, OSPF can set the metrics for redistributed routes using the same options used for EIGRP. Table 10-5 summarizes the defaults and metric setting options for redistribution into OSPF.

Key
Topic

Table 10-5 *Summary of Metric Values When Redistributing into OSPF*

Function	Command or Metric Values
Default if no metric configuration exists	Cost 1 for routes learned from BGP.
	If redistributed from another OSPF process, use the source route's OSPF cost.
	Cost 20 for all other route sources.
Setting the default for all **redistribute** commands	The **default-metric** *cost* OSPF subcommand.
Setting the metric for one route source	The **metric** *cost* parameters on the **redistribute** command.
Setting different metrics for routes learned from a single source	Use the **route-map** parameter on the **redistribute** command.

LSAs and Metrics for External Type 2 Routes

To appreciate how OSPF calculates the possible routes for each E2 route, you need to take a moment to think about the Type 5 LSA in more detail. First, by definition, the router that performs the redistribution into OSPF becomes an *autonomous system border router (ASBR)*, because it injects external routes into OSPF. For each such route, that ASBR creates a Type 5 LSA for that subnet. The Type 5 LSA includes the following fields:

- **LSID (Link-state ID):** The subnet number
- **Mask:** The subnet mask
- **Advertising Router:** The RID of the ASBR injecting the route
- **Metric:** The metric as set by the ASBR
- **External Metric Type:** The external metric type, either 1 or 2

When created, the ASBR floods the Type 5 LSA throughout the area. Then, if any area border routers (ABR) exist, the ABRs flood the Type 5 LSAs into any normal (nonstubby) areas (note that ABRs cannot forward Type 5 LSAs into any type of stubby area, instead relying on default routes). Figure 10-7 shows a sample flooding of the Type 5 LSA for EIGRP subnet 172.30.27.0/23 as an E2 route.

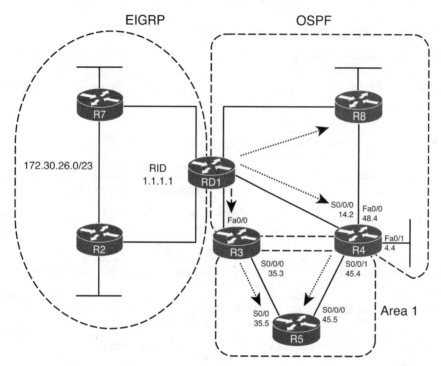

Figure 10-7 *Flooding of Type 5 LSAs*

When flooded, OSPF has little work to do to calculate the metric for an E2 route, because by definition, the E2 route's metric is simply the metric listed in the Type 5 LSA. In other words, the OSPF routers do not add any internal OSPF cost to the metric for an E2 route.

Because routers ignore internal cost when calculating E2 external route metrics, whenever an alternative route can be calculated, the metrics tie. For example, in Figure 10-7, Router R4 has two possible physical routes to ASBR RD1—one directly to RD1 and one through R8. The cost for both routes to external subnet 172.30.26.0/23 will be 20, because that is the cost that RD1 assigned to the route (actually, the Type 5 LSA) when redistributing the route.

To avoid loops, OSPF routers use a tiebreaker system to allow a router to choose a best external route. The logic differs slightly depending on whether the router in question resides in the same area as the ASBR (intra-area) or in a different area (interarea), as discussed in the next two sections.

Determining the Next Hop for Type 2 External Routes—Intra-area

When a router finds multiple routes for the same E2 destination subnet, it chooses the best route based on the lowest cost to reach any ASBR(s) that advertised the lowest E2 metric. For example, if five ASBRs all advertised the same subnet as an E2 route, and two ASBRs advertised a metric of 10, and the other three advertised a metric of 20, either of the first two ASBRs could be used. Then, the router calculates its lowest-cost route to reach the ASBR and uses the next-hop IP address and outgoing interface listed in that route.

The following list spells out the mechanics of the calculation used to break the tie when multiple equal-cost E2 routes exist for a particular subnet:

Key Topic

Step 1.   Find the advertising ASBR(s) as listed in the Type 5 LSA(s) for Type 5 LSAs.

Step 2.   Calculate the lowest-cost route to reach any of the ASBR(s) based on the intra-area LSDB topology.

Step 3.   Use the outgoing interface and next hop based on the best route to reach the ASBR (as chosen at Step 2).

Step 4.   The route's metric is unchanged—it is still simply the value listed in the Type 5 LSA.

For example, use Router R4 in Figure 10-7 as an example and the E2 route for 172.30.26.0/23. Before using these four steps, R4 calculated two possible routes for 172.16.26.0/23: an E2 route directly to RD1 and another route through R8. Both routes use metric 20 in this case so the routes tie. Because of the tie, R4 proceeds with the following steps:

Step 1.   R4 looks in the Type 5 LSA and sees RID 1.1.1.1 (RD1) is the advertising ASBR.

Step 2.   R4 then looks at its area 0 LSDB entries, including the Type 1 LSA for RID 1.1.1.1, and calculates all possible area 0 routes to reach 1.1.1.1.

Step 3.   R4's best route to reach RID 1.1.1.1 happens to be through its S0/0/0 interface, to next-hop RD1 (172.16.14.1), so R4's route to 172.16.26.0/23 uses these details.

Step 4.   The route lists metric 20, as listed in the Type 5 LSA.

Figure 10-8 shows the interface costs that Router R4 will use, based on its LSDB, to calculate the cost for two possible routes to reach ASBR RD1. Again using subnet 172.30.26.0/23 as an example, RD1 first looks at the Type 5 external LSA and sees RID 1.1.1.1 as the advertising ASBR. R4 then calculates the costs based on its intra-area LSDB—but we can perform the equivalent by adding the interface costs seen in Figure 10-8. Example 10-10 lists the external Type 5 LSAs, highlighting subnet 172.30.26.0/23 and the interface costs on both R4 and R8, as seen in the figure.

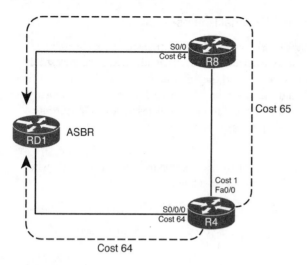

Figure 10-8 *R4's Cost to Reach ASBR RD1*

Example 10-10 *Verifying OSPF External Routes—Intra-area*

```
R4# show ip ospf database | begin Ext
                Type-5 AS External Link States


Link ID         ADV Router      Age       Seq#        Checksum Tag
172.30.2.0      1.1.1.1         189       0x80000002 0x007E51 0
172.30.6.0      1.1.1.1         189       0x80000002 0x005279 0
172.30.12.0     1.1.1.1         189       0x80000002 0x0003C4 0
172.30.17.0     1.1.1.1         189       0x80000002 0x00CBF6 0
172.30.26.0     1.1.1.1         189       0x80000002 0x007542 0

R4# show ip ospf database external 172.30.26.0

            OSPF Router with ID (4.4.4.4) (Process ID 4)


            Type-5 AS External Link States


  Routing Bit Set on this LSA
  LS age: 175
  Options: (No TOS-capability, DC)
  LS Type: AS External Link
  Link State ID: 172.30.26.0 (External Network Number )
  Advertising Router: 1.1.1.1
  LS Seq Number: 80000001
  Checksum: 0x7741
  Length: 36
  Network Mask: /23
        Metric Type: 2 (Larger than any link state path)
```

```
        TOS: 0
            Metric: 20
        Forward Address: 0.0.0.0
        External Route Tag: 0


R4# show ip ospf interface brief
Interface    PID    Area        IP Address/Mask    Cost   State Nbrs F/C
Se0/0/0      4      0           172.16.14.2/30     64     P2P   1/1
Fa0/1        4      0           172.16.4.4/25      1      DR    0/0
Fa0/0        4      0           172.16.48.4/25     1      DR    1/1
Se0/0/1      4      1           172.16.45.4/25     64     P2P   1/1


! Next output occurs on R8
R8# show ip ospf interface brief
Interface    PID    Area        IP Address/Mask    Cost   State Nbrs F/C
Fa0/1        8      0           172.16.8.8/25      1      DR    0/0
Se0/0        8      0           172.16.18.2/30     64     P2P   1/1
Fa0/0        8      0           172.16.48.8/25     1      BDR   1/1
```

Determining the Next Hop for Type 2 External Routes—Interarea

When a router exists in a different area than the ASBR, the issues remain the same, but the tiebreaker calculation of choosing the least-cost route to reach the ASBR changes. If a router finds multiple routes to reach a single E2 subnet, some or all might tie based on metric, because the metric is based solely on the external cost as defined by the ASBR. (If multiple ASBRs redistribute routes for the same prefix, each ASBR can assign a different metric.) A router then chooses the best route based on the least-cost route to reach an ASBR that has advertised the lowest E2 cost for the subnet.

When the ASBR is in a different area, the calculation of the cost to reach the ASBR requires more information, and even an additional LSA type, as compared with the intra-area calculation. To calculate its best route to reach the ASBR, a router in another area adds the cost to reach an ABR between the areas, plus that ABR's cost to reach the ASBR. To make more sense of that concept, Figure 10-9 shows a portion of Figure 10-7, with costs highlighted, assuming that the OSPF reference bandwidth is also using default settings.

R5 has two possible routes shown in Figure 10-9 to reach ASBR RD1. On the left, the path through R3 has a total cost of 65. To the right, the router through ABR R4 has a total cost of 128. R5 then chooses the route through R3 as the best route based on the least cost to reach the ASBR.

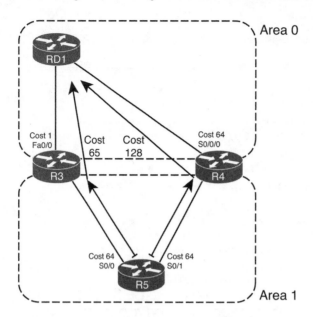

Figure 10-9 *R5's Cost to Reach ASBR RD1*

For humans, when you have a figure and know all costs, the calculation of the costs of the two routes is simple. However, for routers, the calculation occurs in two parts:

Step 1. Calculate the cost to reach the ABR, based on the local area's topology database.

Step 2. Add the cost from the ABR to the ASBR, as listed in a Type 4 LSA.

ABRs create this new type of LSA—the Type 4 Summary ASBR LSA—to support the logic mentioned at Step 2. The Type 4 ASBR LSA lists the RID of the ASBR, and the RID of the ABR that created and flooded the Type 4 LSA. Most importantly, the Type 4 LSA lists that ABR's cost to reach the ASBR. In effect, the LSA makes an announcement like this: "I am ABR X. I can reach ASBR Y, and my cost to reach that ASBR is Z." In short, it allows the second part of the computation.

ABRs create Type 4 LSAs in reaction to receiving an external LSA from some ASBR. When an ABR forwards a Type 5 LSA into an area, the ABR looks at the RID of the ASBR that created the Type 5 LSA. The ABR then creates a Type 4 LSA listing that ASBR, and the cost to reach that ASBR, flooding that Type 4 LSA into the neighboring areas.

For example, using Figure 10-9 again, R3 would create and flood a Type 4 Summary ASBR LSA into area 1. R3's Type 4 LSA lists ASBR 1.1.1.1 (RD1), ABR 3.3.3.3 (itself), and cost 1 (R3's cost to reach 1.1.1.1). Similarly, in that same example, ABR R4 would create another Type 4 ASBR Summary LSA. This LSA also lists ASBR 1.1.1.1 (RD1), but with advertising ABR 4.4.4.4 (R4), and lists cost 64 (R4's cost to reach 1.1.1.1).

R5, internal to area 1, then calculates the cost for each competing route by adding R5's intra-area cost to reach the respective ABRs (Step 1 in the previous list) to the cost listed in the corresponding Type 4 LSAs (Step 2 in the previous list). When R5 calculates two possible routes to reach external subnet 172.30.26.0/23, R5 finds routes both have a metric of 20, so R5 tries to break the tie by looking at the cost to reach the ASBR over each route. To do so, R5 examines each route, adding its intra-area cost to reach the ABR to the ABR's cost to reach the ASBR (as listed in the Type 4 LSA). In this case, R5 finds that the route through R3 has the lower cost (65), so R5 uses outgoing interface S0/0 for its route to 172.30.26.0/23.

Example 10-11 lists the **show** command output that demonstrates the same example. Again focusing on R5's route for 172.30.26.0/23, the example first shows R5's LSDB, beginning with the Summary ASBR LSAs. More discussion follows the example.

Example 10-11   *Redistributing from EIGRP into OSPF, with Subnets*

```
R5# show ip ospf database | begin ASB
            Summary ASB Link States (Area 1)


Link ID          ADV Router      Age        Seq#        Checksum
1.1.1.1          3.3.3.3         956        0x8000000D 0x00E43A
1.1.1.1          4.4.4.4         1044       0x8000000B 0x00439A


            Type-5 AS External Link States


Link ID          ADV Router      Age        Seq#        Checksum Tag
172.30.2.0       1.1.1.1         1185       0x8000000B 0x006C5A 0
172.30.6.0       1.1.1.1         1185       0x8000000B 0x004082 0
172.30.12.0      1.1.1.1         1185       0x8000000B 0x00F0CD 0
172.30.17.0      1.1.1.1         1185       0x8000000B 0x00B9FF 0
172.30.26.0      1.1.1.1         1185       0x8000000B 0x00634B 0


R5# show ip ospf database asbr-summary


            OSPF Router with ID (5.5.5.5) (Process ID 5)


            Summary ASB Link States (Area 1)


  Routing Bit Set on this LSA
  LS age: 984
  Options: (No TOS-capability, DC, Upward)
  LS Type: Summary Links(AS Boundary Router)
  Link State ID: 1.1.1.1 (AS Boundary Router address)
  Advertising Router: 3.3.3.3
  LS Seq Number: 8000000D
  Checksum: 0xE43A
  Length: 28
```

```
       Network Mask: /0
             TOS: 0  Metric: 1


       LS age: 1072
       Options: (No TOS-capability, DC, Upward)
       LS Type: Summary Links(AS Boundary Router)
       Link State ID: 1.1.1.1 (AS Boundary Router address)
       Advertising Router: 4.4.4.4
       LS Seq Number: 8000000B
       Checksum: 0x439A
       Length: 28
       Network Mask: /0
             TOS: 0  Metric: 64


R5# show ip ospf border-routers
OSPF Process 5 internal Routing Table
Codes: i - Intra-area route, I - Inter-area route


i 4.4.4.4 [64] via 172.16.45.4, Serial0/1, ABR, Area 1, SPF 6
I 1.1.1.1 [65] via 172.16.35.3, Serial0/0, ASBR, Area 1, SPF 6
i 3.3.3.3 [64] via 172.16.35.3, Serial0/0, ABR, Area 1, SPF 6


R5# show ip route 172.30.0.0
Routing entry for 172.30.0.0/16, 5 known subnets
  Variably subnetted with 2 masks


O E2    172.30.17.0/30 [110/20] via 172.16.35.3, 05:48:42, Serial0/0
O E2    172.30.26.0/23 [110/20] via 172.16.35.3, 05:48:42, Serial0/0
O E2    172.30.2.0/23  [110/20] via 172.16.35.3, 05:48:42, Serial0/0
O E2    172.30.6.0/23  [110/20] via 172.16.35.3, 05:48:42, Serial0/0
O E2    172.30.12.0/30 [110/20] via 172.16.35.3, 05:48:42, Serial0/0
```

The **show ip ospf database | begin ASB** command's output lists two Type 4 LSAs. (The command itself lists the summary of R5's OSPF LSDB, beginning with the section that lists Type 4 LSAs.) Both Type 4 LSAs list ASBR RD1's RID of 1.1.1.1 as the LSID, but they each list different advertising routers: 3.3.3.3 (R3) and 4.4.4.4 (R4). In that same command, the output lists five Type 5 LSAs for the five subnets in the EIGRP domain, each with advertising Router 1.1.1.1 (RD1).

The next command, **show ip ospf database asbr-summary**, lists the same two Type 4 LSAs seen in the previous command, but in detail. The first lists ASBR 1.1.1.1 (RD1), with ABR 3.3.3.3 (R3) and a cost of 1. The second lists ASBR 1.1.1.1, but with ABR 4.4.4.4 (R4) and a cost of 64. The costs list the respective ABR's cost to reach ASBR 1.1.1.1.

The third command, **show ip ospf border-routers**, lists a line for every ABR and ASBR known to the local router. It lists whether the router is inside the same area or in another area, the RID of the ABR or ASBR, and this router's best route to reach each ABR and

ASBR. This command essentially shows the answer to the question "Which route to ASBR 1.1.1.1 is best?" Finally, the last command lists R5's IP route for 172.30.26.0, with the same next-hop and outgoing interface information as seen in the entry for RID 1.1.1.1 in the output of the **show ip ospf border-routers** command.

Redistributing into OSPF as E1 Routes

OSPF's external metric type feature gives engineers a design tool for influencing the choice of best route. E2 routes work well when the design needs to choose the best route based on the external metric—in other words, the metric as perceived outside the OSPF domain. E2 routes ignore the internal OSPF cost (except when breaking ties for best route). Therefore, when OSPF compares two E2 routes for the same subnet, that first choice to pick the lowest-metric route is based on the external metric only.

OSPF routers calculate the metrics of E1 routes by adding the internal cost to reach the ASBR to the external cost defined on the redistributing ASBR. As a result, an engineer can influence the choice of routes based on the combination of the external and internal OSPF cost simply by redistributing a route as an E1 route instead of as an E2 route. To take advantage of this feature, the **redistribute** command simply needs to set the metric type.

Example 10-12 shows the simple change to the redistribution configuration on RD1 (as shown earlier in Example 10-9) to make all routes redistributed from EIGRP into OSPF be E1 routes. The example also lists output from R4 demonstrating the metric, which is based on the (default) external metric (20) plus R4's best internal metric to reach ASBR 1.1.1.1 (64).

Example 10-12 *Redistributing from EIGRP into OSPF, with Subnets*

```
RD1# conf t
Enter configuration commands, one per line.  End with CNTL/Z.
RD1(config)# router ospf 2
RD1(config-router)# redistribute eigrp 1 subnets metric-type 1
RD1(config-router)# end
RD1#


! Moving to router R4
R4# show ip route 172.30.0.0
Routing entry for 172.30.0.0/16, 5 known subnets
  Variably subnetted with 2 masks

O E1    172.30.17.0/30 [110/84] via 172.16.14.1, 00:00:06, Serial0/0/0
O E1    172.30.26.0/23 [110/84] via 172.16.14.1, 00:00:06, Serial0/0/0
O E1    172.30.2.0/23 [110/84] via 172.16.14.1, 00:00:06, Serial0/0/0
O E1    172.30.6.0/23 [110/84] via 172.16.14.1, 00:00:06, Serial0/0/0
O E1    172.30.12.0/30 [110/84] via 172.16.14.1, 00:00:06, Serial0/0/0
```

```
R4# show ip ospf border-routers

OSPF Process 4 internal Routing Table
Codes: i - Intra-area route, I - Inter-area route

i 1.1.1.1 [64] via 172.16.14.1, Serial0/0/0, ASBR, Area 0, SPF 16
i 3.3.3.3 [65] via 172.16.14.1, Serial0/0/0, ABR, Area 0, SPF 16
i 3.3.3.3 [128] via 172.16.45.5, Serial0/0/1, ABR, Area 1, SPF 8
```

Note that for routers in a different area than the ASBR, the calculation of metric follows the same general logic used when breaking ties for E2 routes. Generally, the computation adds three items:

- The best intra-area cost to reach the ABR (per that area's LSDB)

- The cost from that ABR to the ASBR (per Type 4 LSA)

- The external cost for the route (per Type 5 LSA)

For example, Figure 10-9 shows that R5's best cost to reach ASBR RD1 was out S0/0, to R3 next, with a cost of 65. Adding the external cost of 20, R5's best route will have a metric of 85. R5 calculates that cost by adding the following:

- The intra-area cost to ABR R3 (64), by analyzing the area 1 LSDB entries

- R3's cost to reach ASBR 1.1.1.1, as listed in its Type 4 LSA (1)

- The external cost as listed in the Type 5 LSA (20)

A Brief Comparison of E1 and E2 Routes

OSPF defines two types of external routes to give network designers two slightly different tools with which to calculate the best route to reach a destination external to OSPF. For E1 routes, both the external cost and internal OSPF cost matter to the choice of best route. For E2 routes, only the external cost matters to the choice of best route (unless a tie needs to be broken).

The benefits of the different external route types apply mostly to when multiple ASBRs advertise the same subnet. For example, imagine two ASBRs, ASBR1 and ASBR2, between OSPF and another routing domain. If the goal is to always send traffic through ASBR1, you could use E2 routes and set the metric for ASBR1's redistributed routes to a lower metric than ASBR2. Because routers ignore the internal metrics when calculating the E2 metrics, every router chooses ASBR1 as the better ASBR. Conversely, if the goal were to load-balance the traffic, and make each router pick the closest ASBR, both ASBRs could set the same metric on their redistributed routes, but make the routes Type E1. As a result, routers closer to each ASBR choose best routes based on the lower OSPF internal costs.

Also, note that for a given prefix/length, OSPF always prefers an E1 route over an E2 route.

External Routes in NSSAs

Routes can be redistributed into OSPF on any OSPF router, with a few exceptions. The router can be internal to area 0, like Router RD1 in the many examples earlier in this chapter. It can also be an ABR connected to several areas. It can be a router internal to a nonbackbone area as well.

Of the four types of stubby areas, two do not allow redistribution into the area, and two do allow redistribution—even though none of the stubby area types allow Type 5 LSAs. OSPF does not allow routers in stubby and totally stubby areas to inject external routes. However, routers in not-so-stubby areas—NSSAs—can redistribute routes, while still holding to the restriction of having no Type 5 LSAs.

OSPF supports the injection of external routes into NSSAs by defining the Type 7 AS External LSA. This LSA type essentially replaces the Type 5 LSA's role, but only inside the NSSA. Figure 10-10 shows a conceptual view.

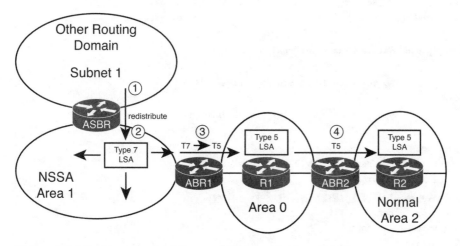

Figure 10-10   *Process of Adding and Converting Type 7 LSAs*

Following the steps in the figure:

Step 1.   The ASBR attached to NSSA area 1 redistributes a route for subnet 1, creating a Type 7 LSA.

Step 2.   The ASBR floods the Type 7 LSA throughout NSSA area 1.

Step 3.   ABR1 converts the Type 7 LSA to a Type 5 LSA when forwarding into other areas (area 0 in this case).

Step 4.   ABR2, connected to another normal area, forwards the Type 5 LSA for subnet 1 into normal area 2.

Example 10-13 demonstrates the concept using area 1 from Figures 10-7 and 10-9. Area 1 has been converted to be an NSSA. R5 has been configured to redistribute connected routes. This feature allows a router to inject connected routes into a routing domain without having to enable the routing protocol on the corresponding interfaces. In this case,

R5 will redistribute subnet 10.1.1.0/24, a connected route added by R5 using interface Loopback0.

Example 10-13 *Redistributing from EIGRP into OSPF, with Subnets*

```
! R5's new configuration here:
interface loopback0
 ip address 10.1.1.1 255.255.255.0
router ospf 5
 area 1 nssa
 redistribute connected subnets

R5# show ip ospf database | begin Type-7
              Type-7 AS External Link States (Area 1)


Link ID         ADV Router      Age         Seq#        Checksum Tag
10.1.1.0        5.5.5.5         26          0x80000001 0x00E0A6 0


R5# show ip ospf database nssa-external

            OSPF Router with ID (5.5.5.5) (Process ID 5)


            Type-7 AS External Link States (Area 1)


  LS age: 69
  Options: (No TOS-capability, Type 7/5 translation, DC)
  LS Type: AS External Link
  Link State ID: 10.1.1.0 (External Network Number )
  Advertising Router: 5.5.5.5
  LS Seq Number: 80000001
  Checksum: 0xE0A6
  Length: 36
  Network Mask: /24
        Metric Type: 2 (Larger than any link state path)
        TOS: 0
        Metric: 20
        Forward Address: 172.16.45.5
        External Route Tag: 0


! Moving to router R8
R8# show ip ospf database | begin Type-7

R8# show ip ospf database | begin External
              Type-5 AS External Link States


Link ID         ADV Router   Age    Seq#       Checksum  Tag
10.1.1.0        4.4.4.4      263    0x80000001 0x009302   0
```

```
172.30.2.0    1.1.1.1    1655    0x8000000E   0x00665D   0
172.30.6.0    1.1.1.1    1655    0x8000000E   0x003A85   0
172.30.12.0   1.1.1.1    1655    0x8000000E   0x00EAD0   0
172.30.17.0   1.1.1.1    1655    0x8000000E   0x00B303   0
172.30.26.0   1.1.1.1    1655    0x8000000E   0x005D4E   0
```

The example begins with configuration on R5, followed by **show** commands on both
Router R5 and R8. In particular, the **show ip ospf database | begin Type-7** command on
R5 skips output until the heading for Type 7 LSAs, listing one such LSA. The LSA lists
the subnet number (10.1.1.0) as the LSID and the ASBR's RID (5.5.5.5, or R5). The next
command provides output from the **show ip ospf database nssa-external** command on
R5, which shows the details in the Type 7 LSA, including the LSA cost of 20—the same
default used when injecting routes as Type 5 LSAs.

The second half of the output, on Router R8, starts with another **show ip ospf database
| begin Type-7** command—the same command seen earlier in the example on R5. The
null output in this command confirms that R8 has no Type 7 LSAs. However, the final
command in the example confirms that R8 does have a Type 5 external LSA for subnet
10.1.1.0, with a listing of R4 (4.4.4.4) as the advertising router. This LSA does not list
R5's RID of 5.5.5.5 as the advertising router, because R5 did not create this Type 5 LSA.
Instead, R4 created this Type 5 LSA when R4 reacted to learning the Type 7 LSA inside
area 1.

Finally, Example 10-14 shows a few interesting items about the IP routing table with
NSSAs. Routers inside the NSSA use a different code in the output of **show ip route**
to denote NSSA external routes as compared with normal external routes. The example
shows R4's IP routing table, which lists an N2 route. This means that it is external Type 2,
but inside an NSSA, and using a Type 7 AS external LSA. The second part of the example shows R8's route for the same subnet. Because R8 is inside a non-NSSA, R8 knows of
subnet 10.1.1.0/24 because of a Type 5 LSA, so R8 lists the route as an E2 route.

Example 10-14 *Redistributing from EIGRP into OSPF, with Subnets*

```
! R4's output here:
R4# show ip route
Codes: C - connected, S - static, R - RIP, M - mobile, B - BGP
       D - EIGRP, EX - EIGRP external, O - OSPF, IA - OSPF inter area
       N1 - OSPF NSSA external type 1, N2 - OSPF NSSA external type 2
       E1 - OSPF external type 1, E2 - OSPF external type 2
       i - IS-IS, su - IS-IS summary, L1 - IS-IS level-1, L2 - IS-IS level-2
       ia - IS-IS inter area, * - candidate default, U - per-user static route
       o - ODR, P - periodic downloaded static route

Gateway of last resort is not set

! lines omitted for brevity

     10.0.0.0/24 is subnetted, 1 subnets
```

```
O N2    10.1.1.0 [110/20] via 172.16.45.5, 00:10:54, Serial0/0/1
```

```
! R8, in area 0, next
R8# show ip route | begin 10.0.0.0
     10.0.0.0/24 is subnetted, 1 subnets
O E2    10.1.1.0 [110/20] via 172.16.48.4, 00:10:24, FastEthernet0/0
```

Redistribution with Route Maps and Distribute Lists

In some cases, a redistribution design calls for all routes to be redistributed, all with the same metric and all with the same external route type (if applicable). However, in other cases, the metrics might need to be set differently for different routes. Additionally, some designs require that only a subset of the routes should be redistributed, for example, when only a few key subnets need to be exposed for connections from a partner. And with routing protocols that have different types of external routes, such as OSPF and IS-IS, the design might or might not allow all redistributed routes to be of the same external route type.

All these features require a tool by which Cisco IOS can identify the routes that need to be treated differently, whether given different metrics, filtered, or assigned a different external route type. Cisco IOS provides such a feature by allowing a reference to a route map from the **redistribute** command. Specifically, the route map can perform the following:

Key
Topic

- Identify the subset of the routes to filter or change based on the route's prefix/ length, plus many other factors.

- Make filtering choices about which routes are redistributed and which are not.

- Set the metric to different values based on information matchable by the route map.

- Set the type of external route for different redistributed routes, for example, OSPF Type 1 for some routes and Type 2 for others.

- Set a route tag, a unitless integer value that can later be matched with a route map at another redistribution point.

This section examines the mechanics of using the **route-map** option of the **redistribute** command to filter routes and set the metrics, along with a few other small features.

Overview of Using Route Maps with Redistribution

The **redistribute** command has two mechanisms that allow filtering of routes:

- The **match {internal | external 1 | external 2 | nssa-external}** parameters

- The **route-map** *map-name* option

Of these two options, the first applies only when redistributing from OSPF, and matches routes solely based on the types of routes listed here. However, the route map referenced by the **redistribute** command has many options for identifying routes by matching various facts about the route.

To identify the routes, route maps use the **match** subcommand. The match command can refer to ACLs and prefix lists to match anything matchable by those tools, plus match other facts more directly. Table 10-6 lists the **match** command options that matter when using route maps for IGP redistribution.

Key Topic

Table 10-6   match *Command Options for Redistribution*

match Command	Description
match interface *interface-type interface-number* [*... interface-type interface-number*]	Looks at outgoing interface of routes
* **match ip address** {[*access-list-number* | *access-list-name*] | **prefix-list** *prefix-list-name*}	Examines route destination prefix and prefix length
* **match ip next-hop** {*access-list-number* | *access-list-name*}	Examines route's next-hop address
* **match ip route-source** {*access-list-number* | *access-list-name*}	Matches advertising router's IP address
match metric *metric-value* [*+- deviation*]	Matches route's metric, or a range (plus/minus the configured deviation)
match route-type {**internal** | **external** [**type–1** | **type–2**] | **level–1** | **level–2**}	Matches route type
match tag *tag-value* [*...tag-value*]	Matches the route tag, which requires that another router has earlier set the tag

* Can reference multiple numbered and named ACLs with a single **match** command.

A route map referenced by the **redistribute** command always attempts to filter routes. If the route map matches a particular route with a particular **route-map** clause, and the action in that clause is permit, the route is redistributed. However, if the first **route-map** clause matched by a route has a **deny** action, the route is filtered—in other words, not redistributed.

Additionally, for routes not filtered by the route map, the route map can set other values (like the route's metric) using the aptly named **set** command. Table 10-7 lists the various route map **set** subcommands that can be used to set the values used for routes redistributed into IGPs.

Table 10-7 set *Command Options for Redistribution into IGPs*

set Command	Description
set metric *metric-value*	Sets the route's metric for OSPF, RIP, and IS-IS
set metric *bandwidth delay reliability loading mtu*	Sets an EIGRP route's metric values
set metric-type {type–1 | type–2}	Sets type of route for OSPF
set tag *tag-value*	Sets the unitless tag value in a route

Filtering Redistributed Routes with Route Maps

As usual, the best way to understand the configuration, and the methods to verify the results, is to use an example. In this case, the same internetwork seen earlier in this chapter is used, but with some more routes added. Figure 10-11 shows some of the details of the internetwork.

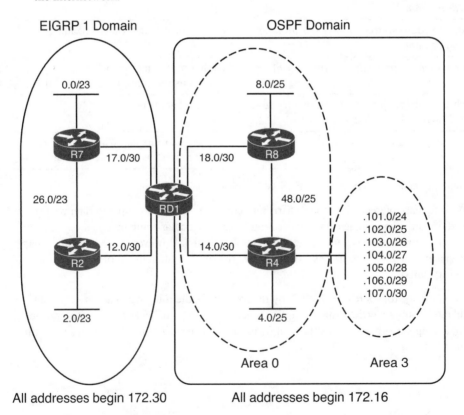

Figure 10-11 *Sample Internetwork Used for Redistribution Route Map Examples*

The internetwork has been preconfigured with mainly defaults, as follows:

- EIGRP works on the left side of Figure 10-11.

- OSPF works on the right side.

- Mutual redistribution has been configured on Router RD1, with no filtering.

- All routes use these metric settings: EIGRP (1500 10 255 1 1500), OSPF (20).

Example 10-15 shows the routing protocol configuration on Router RD1 at the beginning of the example.

Example 10-15 *Initial Configuration—Mutual Redistribution, No Filtering*

```
RD1# show run
! lines omitted for brevity
router eigrp 1
 redistribute ospf 2
 network 172.30.0.0
 default-metric 1500 10 255 1 1500
 auto-summary
!
router ospf 2
 router-id 1.1.1.1
 log-adjacency-changes
 redistribute eigrp 1 subnets
 network 172.16.0.0 0.0.255.255 area 0
```

Configuring Route Filtering with Redistribution

The configuration shown in Example 10-15 shows mutual redistribution with no filtering. The next example extends that same configuration to now use a route map that should filter routes being redistributed from OSPF process 2 into EIGRP AS 1. Any routes not mentioned in Table 10-8, but shown in Figure 10-11, should be redistributed.

Table 10-8 *Parameters Used in Route-Filtering Example*

Prefixes	Action
172.16.101.0/24	deny
172.16.102.0/25	
172.16.103.0/26	permit
172.16.104.0/27	
172.16.105.0/28	deny
172.16.106.0/29	
172.16.107.0/30	permit

The route map simply needs to match the routes to be filtered with a **route-map** clause that has a deny action and match the routes to not be filtered with a clause that has a permit action. Example 10-16 shows two such potential solutions, with route map names **option1** and **option2**. The general style of the two options, both of which work, is as follows:

- **option1:** Begin with a match of the routes to be filtered, using extended IP ACLs, with a deny action so that the routes are filtered. Then use a **permit** clause with no **match** command, matching and allowing through all remaining routes.

- **option2:** Begin with a match of the routes to be allowed, matching with prefix lists, with a **permit** action. Then use the implicit **deny** all at the end of the route map to filter unwanted routes.

Example 10-16   *Redistribution Filtering Configuration Example*

```
! This ACL matches subnet 172.16.101.0, with mask 255.255.255.0
ip access-list extended match-101
 permit ip host 172.16.101.0 host 255.255.255.0


! This ACL matches subnets 172.16.104.0 and 172.16.105.0, with masks
! 255.255.255.224 and 255.255.255.240, respectively.
ip access-list extended match-104-105
 permit ip host 172.16.104.0 host 255.255.255.224
 permit ip host 172.16.105.0 host 255.255.255.240
!
! This prefix list matches the five subnets in area 0
ip prefix-list match-area0-permit seq 5 permit 172.16.14.0/30
ip prefix-list match-area0-permit seq 10 permit 172.16.18.0/30
ip prefix-list match-area0-permit seq 15 permit 172.16.8.0/25
ip prefix-list match-area0-permit seq 20 permit 172.16.4.0/25
ip prefix-list match-area0-permit seq 25 permit 172.16.48.0/25
!
! This prefix list matches the two sets of two area 3 subnets that will
! be permitted to be redistributed
ip prefix-list match-area3-permit seq 5 permit 172.16.102.0/23 ge 25 le 26
ip prefix-list match-area3-permit seq 10 permit 172.16.106.0/23 ge 29 le 30


! The first alternative route-map:
route-map option1 deny 10
 match ip address match-101
!
route-map option1 deny 20
 match ip address match-104-105
!
route-map option1 permit 100
```

```
! The second alternative route-map:
route-map option2 permit 10
 match ip address prefix-list match-area3-permit
!
route-map option2 permit 20
 match ip address prefix-list match-area0-permit


! Finally, the configuration shows the enablement of option 1.
router eigrp 1
 redistribute ospf 2 route-map option1
```

Route map **option1** takes the approach of denying the redistribution of some routes and then allowing the rest through. The last clause in this route map, with sequence number 100, does not have a **match** command, meaning that it will match any and all routes. The permit action on this last clause overrides the implied deny all at the end of the route map.

The ACLs referenced by route map **option1** show some particularly interesting features for matching routes. With an extended ACL, Cisco IOS compares the source IP address parameter to the subnet address of the route and the destination IP address to the subnet mask of the route. For example, the **permit ip host 172.16.101.0 host 255.255.255.0** command matches the specific route for subnet 172.16.101.0, specifically with mask 255.255.255.0.

Route map **option2** takes the opposite approach compared to **option1**, for no other reason than to just show an alternative. It uses two different prefix lists to match the routes—one for subnets in area 0, all of which are redistributed, and another for subnets in area 3 that should be allowed through the redistribution process. Alternatively, all routes could have been matched with a single prefix list, with a single permit clause in the **option2** route map.

Finally, the very end of the example shows the syntax of the **redistribute** command, with route map **option1** enabled.

Verifying Redistribution Filtering Operations

The redistribution process takes routes from the IP routing table of a router and adds the appropriate entries to the destination routing protocol's topology table. The filtering process prevents some of the routes from being added to the topology table, so an examination of the destination routing protocol's topology table shows whether the filtering worked correctly. Additionally, the routing tables of other routers in the destination routing domain can be checked.

A good redistribution verification plan should check that the correct routes are filtered and confirm that no extra routes are filtered. In a production environment, that work might be laborious. With the example shown in Figure 10-11 and Example 10-16, verification takes a little less time because of the relatively small number of routes and the fact that the subnets in the OSPF domain all begin with 172.16.

Example 10-17 shows an abbreviated version of the EIGRP topology table on Router RD1. The **show ip route 172.16.0.0** command lists the 12 OSPF subnets that currently exist in the OSPF domain (as shown in Figure 10-11). The **show ip eigrp topology | include 172[.]16** command lists only routes that include text "172.16," listing only nine subnets—and omitting the three subnets that should have been filtered, which confirms that the filtering worked.

Note   The brackets in the **show ip eigrp topology | include 172[.]16** command tell Cisco IOS to treat the period as a literal, searching for the text "172.16" in the command output, instead of treating the period as a wildcard in a Cisco IOS regular expression.

Example 10-17   *Verifying Redistribution Filtering*

```
RD1# show ip route 172.16.0.0
Routing entry for 172.16.0.0/16, 12 known subnets
  Attached (2 connections)
  Variably subnetted with 7 masks
  Redistributing via eigrp 1

O       172.16.48.0/25 [110/65] via 172.16.18.2, 03:25:56, Serial0/0/1
                        [110/65] via 172.16.14.2, 03:24:09, Serial0/1/0
C       172.16.18.0/30 is directly connected, Serial0/0/1
C       172.16.14.0/30 is directly connected, Serial0/1/0
O       172.16.8.0/25 [110/65] via 172.16.18.2, 03:25:56, Serial0/0/1
O       172.16.4.0/25 [110/65] via 172.16.14.2, 03:24:49, Serial0/1/0
O IA    172.16.104.0/27 [110/65] via 172.16.14.2, 03:24:44, Serial0/1/0
O IA    172.16.105.0/28 [110/65] via 172.16.14.2, 03:24:44, Serial0/1/0
O IA    172.16.106.0/29 [110/65] via 172.16.14.2, 03:24:44, Serial0/1/0
O IA    172.16.107.0/30 [110/65] via 172.16.14.2, 03:24:44, Serial0/1/0
O IA    172.16.101.0/24 [110/65] via 172.16.14.2, 03:24:44, Serial0/1/0
O IA    172.16.102.0/25 [110/65] via 172.16.14.2, 03:24:44, Serial0/1/0
O IA    172.16.103.0/26 [110/65] via 172.16.14.2, 03:24:44, Serial0/1/0


RD1# show ip eigrp topology | include 172[.]16
P 172.16.48.0/25, 1 successors, FD is 1709056
P 172.16.18.0/30, 1 successors, FD is 1709056
P 172.16.14.0/30, 1 successors, FD is 1709056
P 172.16.8.0/25, 1 successors, FD is 1709056
P 172.16.4.0/25, 1 successors, FD is 1709056
P 172.16.106.0/29, 1 successors, FD is 1709056
P 172.16.107.0/30, 1 successors, FD is 1709056
P 172.16.102.0/25, 1 successors, FD is 1709056
P 172.16.103.0/26, 1 successors, FD is 1709056
```

Besides examining the topology tables on the router doing the redistribution, a **show ip route** command on other routers inside the EIGRP domain, like R2, could be used to confirm the presence and absence of the routes according to the plan. However, the routing table on the redistributing router will list the routes as learned from the original routing domain.

Any ACLs or prefix lists used to match packets can also be used as a gauge to tell whether the correct statements matched routes. The **show ip access-list** [*number | name*] and **show ip prefix-list detail** [*name*] commands list counters that increment each time Cisco IOS matches a route for redistribution. Particularly when first using the ACL or prefix list, these commands can confirm which statements have been matched. The counters do increment each time the router considers whether to redistribute a route. Specifically, when a route fails, and the redistributing router removes the route from the routing table and then later adds the route to the routing table again, the counters for matching the ACL or prefix list will increment. Example 10-18 shows an example of each command and the appropriate counters.

Example 10-18   *Verifying Redistribution Filtering*

```
RD1# show access-list
Extended IP access list match-101
    10 permit ip host 172.16.101.0 host 255.255.255.0 (1 match)
Extended IP access list match-104-105
    10 permit ip host 172.16.104.0 host 255.255.255.224 (1 match)
    20 permit ip host 172.16.105.0 host 255.255.255.240 (1 match)
RD1# show ip prefix-list detail match-area0-permit
ip prefix-list match-area0-permit:
   count: 5, range entries: 0, sequences: 5 - 25, refcount: 3
   seq 5 permit 172.16.14.0/30 (hit count: 6, refcount: 1)
   seq 10 permit 172.16.18.0/30 (hit count: 5, refcount: 1)
   seq 15 permit 172.16.8.0/25 (hit count: 4, refcount: 2)
   seq 20 permit 172.16.4.0/25 (hit count: 3, refcount: 3)
   seq 25 permit 172.16.48.0/25 (hit count: 2, refcount: 2)
```

Setting Metrics When Redistributing

Setting a different metric for different redistributed routes requires only a minor amount of additional configuration. The redistributing router still needs a route map and still needs to match the routes. Additionally, to set the metric for routes matched by a particular clause, the route map needs the **set metric** route map subcommand. When redistributing into EIGRP, this command has five parameters (bandwidth, delay, reliability, load, and MTU). When redistributing into OSPF or Routing Information Protocol (RIP), a single integer metric is used.

Configuring the Metric Settings

Continuing with the same internetwork shown in Figure 10-11, and with the same filtering goals summarized earlier in Table 10-8, Table 10-9 further defines the goals from redistribution from OSPF into EIGRP in this internetwork. The same routes will be filtered, but now the metrics of the allowed routes will be set differently as listed in the table.

Table 10-9 *Parameters Used in Metric and Tag Setting Example*

Prefix	Action	Metric (Bandwidth, Delay, Reliability, Load, MTU)
172.16.101.0	deny	—
172.16.102.0		
172.16.103.0	permit	1000 44 255 1 1500
172.16.104.0		
172.16.105.0	deny	—
172.16.106.0		
172.16.107.0	permit	100 4444 255 1 1500
All others	permit	1500 10 255 1 1500

The requirements in Table 10-9 list three different sets of metrics for the redistributed routes. To implement this design, the route map needs at least three clauses: one for each set of routes for which the metric should differ. The example route maps listed earlier in Example 10-16 do not happen to separate the three groups of allowed routes into different **route-map** clauses, so a new route map will be used. Example 10-19 shows the new configuration. Note that it does make use of one of the old IP prefix lists; namely, **match-area0-permit**.

Example 10-19 *Route Map to Set Metrics According to Table 10-9*

```
! First, two new prefix lists are added - one to match subnets 102 and 103,
! and another to match subnets 106 and 107.

ip prefix-list match-102-103 seq 5 permit 172.16.102.0/23 ge 25 le 26
!
ip prefix-list match-106-107 seq 5 permit 172.16.106.0/23 ge 29 le 30

! The following is a repeat of the prefix list that matches the five routes
! in area 0
ip prefix-list match-area0-permit seq 5 permit 172.16.14.0/30
ip prefix-list match-area0-permit seq 10 permit 172.16.18.0/30
ip prefix-list match-area0-permit seq 15 permit 172.16.8.0/25
ip prefix-list match-area0-permit seq 20 permit 172.16.4.0/25
ip prefix-list match-area0-permit seq 25 permit 172.16.48.0/25

! A new route map to filter and set metrics, with three clauses
```

```
route-map set-metric permit 10
 match ip address prefix-list match-area0-permit
!
route-map set-metric permit 20
 match ip address prefix-list match-102-103
 set metric 1000 44 255 1 1500
!
route-map set-metric permit 30
 match ip address prefix-list match-106-107
 set metric 100 4444 255 1 1500


!
router eigrp 1
 default-metric 1500 10 255 1 1500
 redistribute ospf 2 route-map set-metric
```

The new route map has three explicitly configured clauses, two of which explicitly set
the metric values using the **set metric** command. However, the first clause (sequence
number 10), which matches routes for the five subnets inside area 0, does not use a **set
metric** command to set the metric. Instead, because this route map clause omits the **set
metric** command, routes that match this clause use the **metric** keyword on the **redistribute** command, or if not listed, the metrics as defined by the **default-metric** EIGRP
subcommand. In this case, because the **redistribute** command does not list a **metric** keyword, routes matched by this clause (sequence number 10) use the metric values listed in
the **default-metric** command.

Verifying the Metric Settings

Verifying the metrics again requires an examination of the EIGRP topology table. In this
case, Example 10-20 displays a couple of views of RD1's EIGRP topology table, focusing on routes to 172.16.102.0/25 and 172.16.106.0/29. The configuration in the previous
Example 10-19 set the metrics to different values, and next the output in Example 10-20
shows the differences.

Example 10-20   *Verifying Metrics as Set During Redistribution*

```
RD1# show ip eigrp topology 172.16.102.0/25
IP-EIGRP (AS 1): Topology entry for 172.16.102.0/25
  State is Passive, Query origin flag is 1, 1 Successor(s), FD is 1709056
  Routing Descriptor Blocks:
  172.16.14.2, from Redistributed, Send flag is 0x0
      Composite metric is (2571264/0), Route is External
      Vector metric:
        Minimum bandwidth is 1000 Kbit
        Total delay is 440 microseconds
        Reliability is 255/255
        Load is 1/255
```

```
       Minimum MTU is 1500
       Hop count is 0
    External data:
       Originating router is 172.30.17.1 (this system)
       AS number of route is 2
       External protocol is OSPF, external metric is 65
       Administrator tag is 0 (0x00000000)

RD1# show ip eigrp topology 172.16.104.0/25
% IP-EIGRP (AS 1): Route not in topology table

RD1# show ip eigrp topo 172.16.106.0/29
IP-EIGRP (AS 1): Topology entry for 172.16.106.0/29
  State is Passive, Query origin flag is 1, 1 Successor(s), FD is 1709056
  Routing Descriptor Blocks:
  172.16.14.2, from Redistributed, Send flag is 0x0
     Composite metric is (26737664/0), Route is External
     Vector metric:
       Minimum bandwidth is 100 Kbit
       Total delay is 44440 microseconds
       Reliability is 255/255
       Load is 1/255
       Minimum MTU is 1500
       Hop count is 0
    External data:
       Originating router is 172.30.17.1 (this system)
       AS number of route is 2
       External protocol is OSPF, external metric is 65
       Administrator tag is 0 (0x00000000)
!
RD1# show ip prefix-list detail match-102-103
ip prefix-list match-102-103:
   count: 1, range entries: 1, sequences: 5 - 5, refcount: 2
   seq 5 permit 172.16.102.0/23 ge 25 le 26 (hit count: 14, refcount: 1)
```

Although you could use variations of the **show ip route** command to verify the new metrics, because the redistribution process sets the EIGRP component metrics, the **show ip eigrp topology** command displays much more useful verification information.

Setting the External Route Type

When redistributing into OSPF, Cisco IOS automatically sets the external route type to external Type 2 (E2). However, the type can be configured as E1 or E2 by using the **set metric-type {type-1 | type-2}** route map subcommand. When a **redistribute** OSPF subcommand references such a route map, the routes matched by the route map clause with the **set metric-type** command will be designated as that external type in the Type 5 LSA created for that subnet.

Note that the **redistribute** command also allows the **match** {**internal** | **external 1** | **external 2** | **nssa-external**} parameters, but these parameters do not set the type or route. Instead, these parameters match existing routes as part of the process of deciding which routes to redistribute.

Redistribution Filtering with the distribute-list Command

Using a route map as referenced on the **redistribute** command provides many features. You can filter routes, assign different metrics for different routes, and assign external route types. You can even assign route tags as discussed later in the section "Preventing Domain Loops by Filtering on Route Tag Using Distribute Lists." However, if the plan calls for route filtering only when redistributing, but none of the other functions supplied by a route map are needed, and you can match all the routes with a single ACL or prefix list, Cisco IOS supports a second style of route filtering configuration using the **distribute-list** command.

The **distribute-list** command can be configured to refer to the routing process from which routes are redistributed and cause the router to filter routes taken from that process. To do so, the command must use the **out** direction, and it must refer to the routing process from which routes are redistributed. For example, **distribute-list 1 out ospf 2**, configured under an EIGRP process, tells EIGRP to apply ACL 1 to routes redistributed from the OSPF 2 process. For another example, under an OSPF process, the **distribute-list prefix fred out eigrp 1** command tells OSPF to apply IP prefix list fred to routes redistributed from the EIGRP 1 process.

Finally, one note about internals of how this command works. The filtering takes place as the routes are redistributed. As a result, routes filtered by the **distribute-list** command prevent the routes from being added to the topology table of the destination routing protocol. So, the same verification commands seen in earlier examples, with a focus on the topology tables, can be used to show whether the filtering worked. Also, the counters in the **show ip access-list** and **show ip prefix-list detail** command output also increment to show whether the filtering worked.

Issues with Multiple Redistribution Points

The use of a single router to redistribute routes means that a single failure could cause hosts in different routing domains to fail. The redistributing router could simply fail, or interfaces or links on that router could fail. To avoid that single point of failure, many redistribution designs call for a minimum of two routers performing redistribution, particularly in cases where the redistribution function will be somewhat permanent.

The existence of two or more redistribution points between the same two routing domains introduces some complexity and caveats. The issues revolve around the concept that a route in one domain can be advertised into another domain, and then back into the original routing domain.

Figure 10-12 shows one of the issues when using multiple redistribution points. In this case, the arrowed lines show the best route from a router in domain 2 to reach a subnet also in domain 2. However, the route actually passes through domain 1.

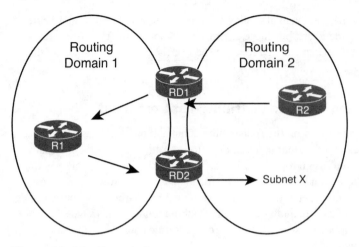

Figure 10-12   *Domain Loop*

Figure 10-12 shows the long route that goes from R2, through RD1, to R1, and back into routing domain 2 through RD2. This long route occurs because of the routing advertisements that flow in the opposite direction: advertised by RD2 into routing domain 1 and then by RD1 back into routing domain 2. The problem occurs when the twice-redistributed route for subnet X is redistributed back into the original domain with a relatively low metric. The twice-redistributed route then has a better metric than the route that was advertised only internal to that routing domain.

This section examines how to prevent this "domain loop" problem when using multiple redistribution points. Interestingly, this problem does not occur, at least with default settings, when EIGRP is one of the two routing protocols. So this section begins with examples of RIP and OSPF redistribution, showing how to prevent this domain-looping problem and then showing why EIGRP accomplishes this same feat with default settings.

> **Note**   I know of no industry-standard name for the problem shown in Figure 10-12. For the duration of this chapter, I refer to it simply as the *domain loop problem*.

Preventing Routing Domain Loops with Higher Metrics

One easy method of preventing the domain loop problem is to assign purposefully high metric values when redistributing routes. For example, consider the case shown in Figure 10-13, with a RIP domain on the left and OSPF on the right. In this case, the two routers doing the redistribution (RD1 and RD2) assign an OSPF metric of 500 when redistributing routes into OSPF and a metric value of 5 when redistributing routes into RIP.

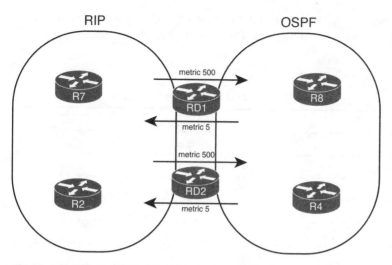

Figure 10-13 *Defeating Domain Loops by Using Very Large Metrics*

First, focus on routes inside the RIP domain. This design prevents the domain loop problem—routes that send packets from the RIP domain, into OSPF, and back again—if the normal intra-domain RIP routes never exceed a hop count of 4. Then, all routes redistributed from RIP into OSPF, and then back into RIP, will at least have a metric of 5. As a result, the route advertisements that looped back into the RIP domain will always have less desirable metrics than the RIP advertisements from within the RIP domain.

The same concept applies to OSPF. For routes completely internal to the OSPF domain, if the highest cost is 499, the redistribution of external routes with a metric of 500 prevents the domain loop. For example, a subnet that exists in the OSPF domain could be advertised into RIP by RD1 and then re-advertised by RD2 back into the OSPF domain—but with a metric value that begins at 500. Again, assuming that all the normal OSPF routes that were not reintroduced as external routes have a cost of less than 500, the domain loop problem is defeated.

Note that OSPF actually defeats the domain loop problem without using the higher metrics. OSPF always prefers internal routes over E1 routes, and E1 routes over E2 routes, before even considering the metrics.

Preventing Routing Domain Loops with Administrative Distance

Each router associates an *administrative distance (AD)* with every route it considers to be added to the routing table. When a router must consider multiple routes from different sources for the exact same prefix/length, the first item considered by the router is not the metric, but rather the AD. The lower the AD, the better the route.

Note that the AD is a local setting on a router and cannot be advertised to neighboring routers.

Each routing source has a default AD according to Cisco IOS. In some cases, a given routing source has different defaults for different types of routes inside that routing source. For example, EIGRP has different AD values for EIGRP internal routes (AD 90) and EIGRP external routes (AD 170). Table 10-10 lists the default settings.

Key Topic

Table 10-10 *Default Administrative Distances*

Route Type	Administrative Distance
Connected	0
Static	1
EIGRP summary route	5
eBGP	20
EIGRP (internal)	90
IGRP	100
OSPF	110
IS-IS	115
RIP	120
On-Demand Routing (ODR)	160
EIGRP (external)	170
iBGP	200
Unreachable	255

EIGRP Default AD Defeats Loop from EIGRP to OSPF to EIGRP

The default AD settings for EIGRP take care of the domain loop problem when redistributing between EIGRP and OSPF. First, consider an EIGRP and OSPF domain with two redistribution points (Routers RD1 and RD2), as shown in Figure 10-14. The figure shows a general idea of route advertisements for subnet X, which exists in the EIGRP domain. (Note: To reduce clutter, the figure shows only route advertisements that affect Router RD2's logic; the same issue exists on both redistributing routers.)

Router RD2 hears about a route for subnet X as an internal EIGRP route (default AD 90) on the left. RD2 also hears about the subnet as an external OSPF route on the right (default AD 110). As a result, RD2 will do a couple of things that are important to this discussion:

■ RD2 considers the internal EIGRP route as the best route, because of the lower AD, and places that route in its own IP routing table.

■ RD2 does not redistribute a route for subnet X from OSPF back to EIGRP, because RD2 does not have an OSPF route for subnet X.

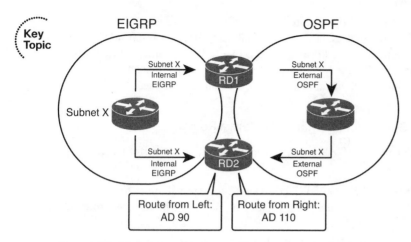

Figure 10-14 *Subnet X: Internal EIGRP, External OSPF, on Router RD2*

The second point is particularly important but easily missed. Remember that routers use the IP routing table as the basis for route redistribution. Both RD1 and RD2 redistribute routes in both directions between both domains. However, a route must be in the routing table before it can be redistributed. Because RD2's route for subnet X will list its EIGRP route, RD2's redistribution from OSPF into EIGRP will not redistribute a route for subnet X. Because RD2 will not advertise a route for subnet X from OSPF back into EIGRP, the domain loop has been prevented.

EIGRP Default AD Defeats Loop from OSPF to EIGRP to OSPF

The reverse case—routes taken from OSPF, advertised into EIGRP, and then advertised back into OSPF—is the more interesting possible domain loop case. However, the default EIGRP AD settings still defeat the domain loop issue. Figure 10-15 shows an example similar to Figure 10-14, but this time with subnet Y in the OSPF domain. As before, the focus of the figure is on the routing advertisements that reach Router RD2, with other details omitted to reduce clutter.

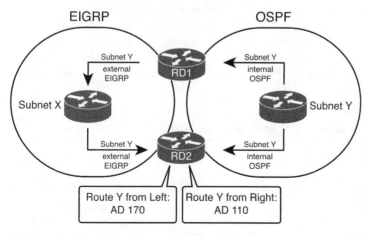

Figure 10-15 *IDS and IPS Operational Differences*

In this case, Router RD2 hears about a route for subnet Y as an external EIGRP route (default AD 170) and as an internal OSPF route (default AD 110). As a result, RD2 chooses the OSPF internal route as the best route and adds that to RD2's routing table. Because RD2 does not have an EIGRP route for subnet Y, RD2 will not redistribute a route for subnet Y from EIGRP into OSPF, again defeating the domain loop problem.

Setting AD per Route Source for Internal and External Routes

The reason that the default EIGRP AD settings work well can be summarized generically as follows:

> For each of the two routing protocols, the AD used for internal routes for one routing protocol is better than the AD used for external routes by the other routing protocol.

When comparing EIGRP's and OSPF's defaults, both of the generic criteria are met:

- EIGRP internal AD 90 < OSPF external AD 110

- OSPF internal AD 110 < EIGRP external AD 170

Likewise, when redistributing between EIGRP and RIP:

- EIGRP internal AD 90 < RIP external AD 120

- RIP internal AD 120 < EIGRP external AD 170

Note RIP does not have a concept of internal and external routes. The preceding references refer to internal routes as routes that exist inside the RIP domain and external as routes that exist outside the RIP domain.

When redistributing between OSPF and RIP, the default AD settings do not defeat the domain loop problem. However, Cisco IOS supports the definition of different AD settings for all routing protocols. With EIGRP, the internal and external AD settings can be overridden, although the defaults work well for the prevention of domain loops. OSPF can be configured to use a different AD for external routes, intra-area routes, and inter-area routes. RIP, which does not have a concept of internal and external routes, can only be set with a single AD value. Table 10-11 shows the router subcommands to set the AD values, per route category.

Table 10-11 *Setting AD Values with the* distance *Command*

Routing Protocol	Command
RIP	distance *ad-value*
EIGRP	distance eigrp *internal-ad external-ad*
OSPF	distance ospf {external *ad-value*} {intra-area *ad-value*} {inter-area *ad-value*}

To defeat the OSPF-RIP domain loop problem by setting AD, just configure the AD for OSPF external routes using the **distance ospf external** *ad-value* command in OSPF configuration mode. The actual AD value does not matter much, but it should be higher than RIP's AD on that same router. For example, the **distance ospf external 130** command in OSPF configuration mode results in the following, assuming that all other AD values are set to their defaults:

- RIP internal AD 120 < OSPF external AD 130

- OSPF internal AD 110 < RIP external AD 120

Domain Loop Problems with More Than Two Routing Domains

With only two routing domains, the solutions seen so far—setting higher metrics and AD values—can deal with domain loop problems. However, with three or more routing domains, setting metrics and AD values does not always solve the domain loop problem. Specifically, problems can occur when three or more routing domains connect in sequence, as shown in Figure 10-16. Such a situation might exist in the real world where a large company has multiple mergers and acquisitions with smaller companies (running a variety of routing protocols).

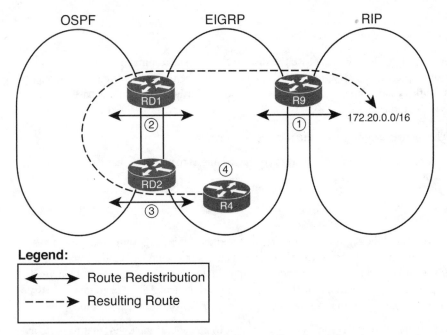

Figure 10-16 *Inefficient Routing with Looped Routing Advertisements*

The steps noted in the figure are as follows:

Step 1.   Router R9 advertises a route for network 172.20.0.0/16 from the RIP domain into the EIGRP domain, where the route is treated with (default) AD 170 as an external route.

Step 2. Router RD1 redistributes this EIGRP external route into OSPF, where it is treated as an E2 route, AD 110, by default.

Step 3. Router RD2 uses the AD 110 E2 route, rather than the AD 170 EIGRP external route, as its best route for 172.20.0.0/16. As a result, RD2 can then redistribute that OSPF route back into EIGRP as an external route.

Step 4. Router R4 learns of two external routes for 172.20.0.0/16, and the routes tie based on AD (170). R4 might have a better EIGRP metric through RD2, depending on the metrics used at redistribution, preferring this long route through the OSPF domain as shown.

This is just one example case for such problems, but the problem exists, because the obviously better route and the longer domain loop route are both external routes. The two competing routes tie on AD as a result. In the earlier cases, with only two routing domains, this problem does not occur.

Several solutions exist for such problems. None of the solutions require a lot of extra configuration, other than that some of the solutions require ACLs or prefix lists that match the prefixes from the various routing domains. The next three sections address each option, namely, using per-route AD settings, filtering routes based on prefix/length, and using route tags.

Using Per-Route Administrative Distance Settings

As seen in Table 10-11, you can use the **distance** router subcommand to set the AD value per routing protocol, per type (internal and external). The **distance** command also supports another syntax in which the router sets the AD for individual routes based on the following criteria:

■ The router that advertised the routing information

■ Optionally, for the prefixes/lengths of the routes as matched by a referenced ACL

The syntax of the command in this case is

```
distance distance ip-adv-router wc-mask [acl-number-or-name]
```

In this command, the required parameters match the neighboring router that advertises a route. The router with the **distance** command configured compares the advertising router's IP address to the range of addresses implied by the *ip-adv-router* and *wc-mask* parameters of the command, as if these were parameters in an ACL. For routes advertised by a matching neighbor, that router then applies the AD listed in the command.

Optionally, the **distance** command can also refer to an ACL. If included, that router compares the ACL to the prefix/length of each route learned from any matched neighbors and uses the listed AD only for routes permitted by the ACL.

For example, consider the problem shown in Figure 10-16. Assuming that the design calls for all hosts to have reachability to 172.20.0.0/16, the route must be redistributed by R9 into the EIGRP domain. For the best availability, this route should be redistributed from

EIGRP into OSPF at both redistribution points (RD1 and RD2). The unfortunate long-route choice by Router R4 in the figure occurs at what is listed as Step 3 in that figure, with Router RD2 using AD to determine that its external OSPF route for 172.20.0.0/16 (AD 110) is better than its EIGRP external route (AD 170) for that same prefix.

One solution would be to cause RD2 to use a higher AD—specifically higher than the 170 AD used for EIGRP external routes—for prefix 172.20.0.0/16 as learned with OSPF. A **distance** command on RD2 could solve the problem.

Upcoming Examples 10-21 and 10-22, plus Figure 10-17, demonstrate both the domain loop problem in this same case, along with the solution. First, Figure 10-17 shows a more detailed topology for reference. Then, Example 10-21 shows the relevant configuration and a few related **show** commands on Router RD2 before using the **distance** command to prevent the problem. This example shows Router R4 using the longer path through the OSPF domain on the left. Finally, Example 10-22 shows the configuration of the **distance** command and resulting solution.

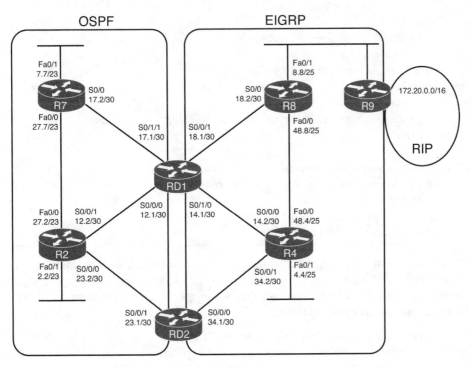

Figure 10-17   *Detailed View of Internetwork*

Example 10-21   *Long Route from RD2, into OSPF, for 172.20.0.0/16*

```
! The following is the routing protocol configuration on RD2
router eigrp 1
 redistribute ospf 2 metric 1000 200 255 1 1500
 network 172.16.0.0
 no auto-summary
```

```
!
router ospf 2
 router-id 3.3.3.3
 log-adjacency-changes
 redistribute eigrp 1 subnets
 network 172.30.0.0 0.0.255.255 area 0

! Next, the long route for 172.20.0.0/16 is listed. This route goes from
! RD2 back into the OSPF domain; interface S0/0/1 connects to router R2.
RD2# show ip route | include 172.20.0.0
O E2 172.20.0.0/16 [110/20] via 172.30.23.2, 00:06:57, Serial0/0/1


! Next, the source of this routing information is listed under the
! text "Known via". RD2's current route is learned by OSPF.
RD2# show ip route 172.20.0.0
Routing entry for 172.20.0.0/16
  Known via "ospf 2", distance 110, metric 20, type extern 2, forward metric 128
  Redistributing via eigrp 1
  Advertised by eigrp 1 metric 1000 200 255 1 1500
  Last update from 172.30.23.2 on Serial0/0/1, 00:07:04 ago
  Routing Descriptor Blocks:
  * 172.30.23.2, from 1.1.1.1, 00:07:04 ago, via Serial0/0/1
      Route metric is 20, traffic share count is 1


! RD2 does know a working (successor) route for the same prefix,
! but prefers the lower-AD route (110) through OSPF.
RD2#show ip eigrp topology | section 172.20.0.0
P 172.20.0.0/16, 1 successors, FD is 2611200
        via Redistributed (2611200/0)
```

The comments inside Example 10-21 detail the current state, with the longer route, as shown in Figure 10-16. Most importantly, note the "Known via..." text in the output of the **show ip route 172.20.0.0** command. This output specifically states the source of the route that is currently in the routing table.

Next, Example 10-22 shows the configuration on RD2 to solve this problem by setting RD2's AD for that specific route and additional **show** commands.

Example 10-22   *Configuring Per-Route AD on Router RD2*

```
RD2# conf t
Enter configuration commands, one per line.  End with CNTL/Z.
RD2(config)# router ospf 2
RD2(config-router)# distance 171 1.1.1.1 0.0.0.0 match-172-20
RD2(config-router)# ip access-list standard match-172-20
RD2(config-std-nacl)# permit host 172.20.0.0
```

```
RD2(config-std-nacl)# end
RD2#


! Now the best route for 172.20.0.0 is known from EIGRP 1.
RD2# show ip route 172.20.0.0
Routing entry for 172.20.0.0/16
  Known via "eigrp 1", distance 170, metric 3635200, type external
  Redistributing via ospf 2, eigrp 1
  Advertised by ospf 2 subnets
  Last update from 172.16.34.2 on Serial0/0/0, 00:08:01 ago
! lines omitted for brevity


! The next command lists the matching logic of the distance command.
RD2# show ip protocols | section ospf
Routing Protocol is "ospf 2"
  Outgoing update filter list for all interfaces is not set
  Incoming update filter list for all interfaces is not set
  Router ID 172.30.23.1
  It is an autonomous system boundary router
  Redistributing External Routes from,
    eigrp 1, includes subnets in redistribution
  Number of areas in this router is 1. 1 normal 0 stub 0 nssa
  Maximum path: 4
  Routing for Networks:
    172.30.0.0 0.0.255.255 area 0
  Reference bandwidth unit is 100 mbps
  Routing Information Sources:
    Gateway         Distance      Last Update
    1.1.1.1              171      00:00:35
    2.2.2.2              110      00:00:35
    7.7.7.7              110      00:00:35
  Distance: (default is 110)
    Address         Wild mask     Distance  List
    1.1.1.1         0.0.0.0          171    match-172-20
  Redistributing: ospf 2, eigrp 1
```

The configuration, although short, has one possibly counterintuitive twist. The IP address of the neighboring router, referenced in the **distance** command in OSPF configuration mode, will be compared to the OSPF RID of the OSPF router that owns the LSA. In this case, Router RD1 creates the Type 5 LSA for 172.20.0.0, and RD1's RID happens to be 1.1.1.1. RD2's **distance 171 1.1.1.1 0.0.0.0 match-172-20** command tells OSPF to look for LSAs owned by exactly RID 1.1.1.1, and if the prefix is permitted by the match-172-20 ACL, apply AD 171 to this route.

The **show ip route 172.20.0.0** command verifies that Router RD1 now prefers its AD 170 EIGRP route for 172.20.0.0/16. The highlighted portions of this command now refer to routing source EIGRP 1, with the outgoing interface of S0/0/0, which connects RD2 into the EIGRP domain. Because RD2 no longer has an OSPF route for 172.20.0.0/16, RD2 will not redistribute such an OSPF route back into EIGRP, defeating the domain loop problem.

Note A complete solution requires all redistributing routers to perform this kind of configuration, for all such routes from the third routing domain.

Although this example shows the OSPF version of the **distance** command, one notable difference exists between the OSPF version and the RIP and EIGRP **distance** commands. When used as a RIP or EIGRP subcommand, the **distance** command matches the interface IP address of the neighboring router that advertises the route.

Preventing Domain Loops by Filtering on Subnet While Redistributing

The next tool prevents domain loops by filtering the routes based on prefix. Figure 10-18 shows the idea from a redistribution design perspective.

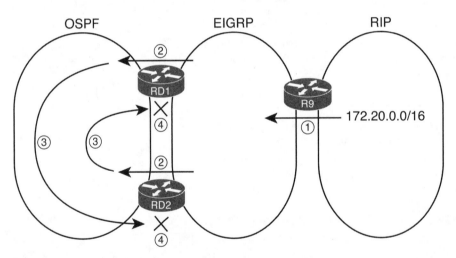

Figure 10-18 *Preventing Domain Loops with Route Filtering*

Following are the steps as listed in the figure:

Step 1. Router R9 advertises a route for network 172.20.0.0/16 from the RIP domain into the EIGRP domain.

Step 2. Routers RD1 and RD2 both redistribute this EIGRP external route into OSPF.

Step 3. Both RD1 and RD2 flood the route advertisement for the OSPF external route throughout the OSPF domain.

Step 4. Both RD1 and RD2 apply a route map to their redistribution from OSPF into EIGRP, filtering routes with prefix 172.20.0.0.

The configuration itself uses the same methods and commands as included earlier in the section "Filtering Redistributed Routes with Route Maps."

Interestingly, this design does prevent the long routes, as shown earlier in Figure 10-16, but it does leave the possibility of a long route on a redistributing router. For example, if using all default AD settings, RD2 still learns an OSPF (default AD 110) route for 172.20.0.0 from RD1, so it might choose as best route the OSPF route through RD1. Setting the AD for OSPF external routes to something larger than EIGRP's external AD of 170 would prevent this particular problem as well.

Preventing Domain Loops by Filtering on Route Tag Using Distribute Lists

Route tags, the last tool shown in this chapter for preventing the domain loop problem, have a much broader use than just preventing redistribution problems.

A route tag is a unitless 32-bit integer that most routing protocols can assign to any given route. The assignment of a tag occurs when some Cisco IOS function adds the tag—for example, it can be assigned by a route map referenced by a routing protocol **distribute-list** or **redistribute** command. That tag follows the route advertisement, even through the redistribution process. At some later point in the flooding of routing information, other Cisco IOS tools, typically other route maps, can match routes with a given route tag to make a decision.

In some cases, the idea of a route tag creates a mental block, because it has no one specific purpose. The network engineer chooses the purpose of a route tag; the purpose has not been predetermined by a particular protocol. The folks that created the routing protocol provided us all with a nice, convenient place to add the equivalent of a sticky note to each route. It's up to us to decide what the note means.

Figure 10-19 shows one common use of route tags other than for solving the domain loop problem. In the figure, one large company that uses EIGRP (the middle of the figure) bought two smaller companies, both of whom use OSPF. The larger company wants to connect both small companies into the larger network, but it wants to prevent hosts in the two smaller companies from knowing routes to the other smaller company. The figure shows only left-to-right advertisements of routes to reduce the clutter.

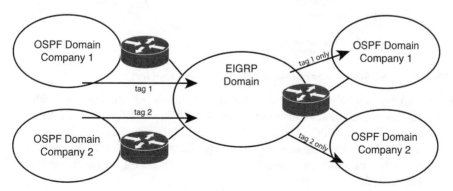

Figure 10-19 *Using Route Tags to Determine Routing Domain Origin*

The two routers on the left each redistribute routes from the smaller companies into the EIGRP. The routers apply a route tag of 1 to each route from OSPF domain 1 and a tag of 2 to routes redistributed from OSPF domain 2. The actual numbers do not matter, as long as they are unique. On the right, the routers know that the routes from OSPF domain 1 have route tag 1, and only these routes should be redistributed into the other part of OSPF domain 1. So, when redistributing into OSPF domain 1, the route map makes a comparison of the route tag (command **match tag 1**) and allows only those routes. Similarly, when redistributing into OSPF domain 2, the **match tag 2** command would be used, redistributing only routes with tag 2.

To use route tags to prevent domain loop problems, you can use the following strategy:

- Choose and set a tag value that identifies routes taken from domain X and advertised into domain Y.

- When redistributing in the opposite direction (from domain Y into domain X), match the tag value and filter routes with that tag.

For example, consider the case shown in Figure 10-20. The figure shows the usual RD1 and RD2 between two routing domains, with EIGRP on the right in this case and OSPF on the left. The engineer planned to use route tag 11 to mean "routes taken from EIGRP and redistributed into OSPF." The figure shows one direction of potential loops: from EIGRP through RD1, through OSPF, and back to EIGRP through RD2. However, the same concept would also apply to the other direction.

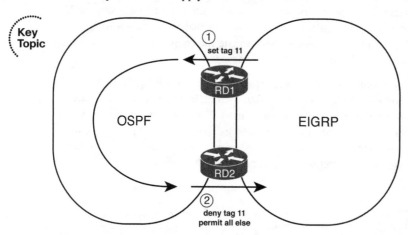

Figure 10-20 *Using Route Tags to Prevent Domain Loop Problems*

The first step (noted with a circled 1 in the figure) is the usual redistribution, but with a route map that tags all routes redistributed from EIGRP into OSPF with tag 11. RD2 learns these routes with OSPF. At Step 2, RD2 tries to redistribute the routes but chooses to filter all routes that have a tag value of 11. As a result, none of the routes learned from EIGRP are re-advertised back into EIGRP. Example 10-23 shows the configuration that matches Figure 10-20.

Example 10-23 *RD1 and RD2 Configuration with Route Tags to Prevent Domain Loops*

```
! The following is the routing protocol configuration on RD1
router ospf 2
 router-id 3.3.3.3
 log-adjacency-changes
 redistribute eigrp 1 subnets route-map set-tag-11
 network 172.30.0.0 0.0.255.255 area 0
!
route-map set-tag-11 permit 10
 set tag 11

! The following is the routing protocol configuration on RD2
router eigrp 1
 redistribute ospf 2 metric 1000 200 255 1 1500 route-map stop-tag-11
 network 172.16.0.0
 no auto-summary
!
route-map stop-tag-11 deny 10
 match tag 11
!
route-map stop-tag-11 permit 20
```

First, note that the configuration does rely on a couple of default route map actions that bear some review. In the set-tag-11 route map on RD1, only one route map clause exists, and that clause has no **match** commands. A route map clause with no **match** commands matches all routes, so all routes are assigned tag 11. In the stop-tag-11 route map on RD2, the first clause lists a **deny** action, meaning that all routes matched by that clause (all with tag 11) are filtered. All other routes, for example those routes for subnets native to the OSPF domain, match the second, because that second clause does not have a **match** command.

Example 10-23 shows the configuration that tags routes coming from EIGRP into OSPF and then filters routes with that same tag as they go from OSPF into EIGRP. For a complete solution, the reverse case would also need to be configured, using a different route tag value.

Exam Preparation Tasks

Planning Practice

The CCNP ROUTE exam expects test takers to review design documents, create implementation plans, and create verification plans. This section provides some exercises that can help you to take a step back from the minute details of the topics in this chapter so that you can think about the same technical topics from the planning perspective.

For each planning practice table, simply complete the table. Note that any numbers in parentheses represent the number of options listed for each item in the solutions in Appendix F, "Completed Planning Practice Tables."

Design Review Table

Table 10-12 lists several design goals related to this chapter. If these design goals were listed in a design document, and you had to take that document and develop an implementation plan, what implementation options come to mind? For any configuration items, a general description can be used, without concern about the specific parameters.

Table 10-12 *Design Review*

Design Goal	Possible Implementation Choices Covered in This Chapter
A design shows Router R1 as being connected to both an EIGRP and OSPF routing domain, with all external EIGRP routes using a particular set of component EIGRP metrics. How can these metrics be set? (3)	
A design shows Router R1 as being connected to two different EIGRP domains, with redistribution planned. Can the design cause the routers to calculate metrics based on both the metric assigned when redistributing and the internal EIGRP topology?	
The same design as in the previous row is shown, except describe whether the design can cause the routers to calculate metrics based solely on the metric components assigned when redistributing.	
A design shows Router R1 as being connected to two different OSPF domains, with redistribution planned, and all routes calculated by including internal and external OSPF distance.	

Design Goal	Possible Implementation Choices Covered in This Chapter
The same design as in the previous row is shown, except that all external route metrics are based solely on external metrics.	
Filter routes when redistributing. (2)	
Set different metrics for different routes redistributed from one routing source.	
Set some OSPF routes as E1 and some as E2, when redistributed from one routing source.	
The design shows multiple redistribution points with two routing domains, with a need to prevent domain loops. (3)	
The design shows multiple redistribution points with more than two routing domains and a need to prevent domain loops. (2)	

Implementation Plan Peer Review Table

Table 10-13 shows a list of questions that others might ask, or that you might think about, during a peer review of another network engineer's implementation plan. Complete the table by answering the questions.

Table 10-13 *Notable Questions from This Chapter to Consider During an Implementation Plan Peer Review*

Question	Answer
A design shows Router R1 as being connected to both an EIGRP and OSPF routing domain. What default metrics will be used by the **redistribute** command for each routing protocol, if not set in R1's configuration?	
A plan shows redistribution between two EIGRP domains. What must be done to use the source route's original component metrics?	
A plan shows redistribution between two OSPF domains. What must be done to use the source route's original metric?	

Question	Answer
The plan shows the **redistribute eigrp 2** command to redistribute from EIGRP 2 into OSPF. What other optional parameters are required to ensure redistribution of 10.1.1.0/24 from EIGRP?	
R1 has two connected interfaces in the EIGRP 2 domain and knows dozens of EIGRP routes. The plan shows the **redistribute eigrp 2 subnets** command under an OSPF process. What else must be done to redistribute the two connected subnets inside the EIGRP domain?	
A design shows an OSPF and EIGRP routing domain, with multiple redistributing routers, with no obvious configuration to prevent routing domain loops. What default AD values exist, and do they prevent any problems?	
The same question as the previous row, except with RIP and OSPF domains.	
The same question as the previous row, except with RIP and EIGRP domains.	
A plan shows redistribution between EIGRP and OSPF on two routers. The configuration for OSPF on one router lists **redistribute eigrp 1 subnets and distribute-list 1 out**. Will this configuration attempt to filter routes? Is a route map option required to filter when redistributing?	
A partially complete plan shows three different routing domains, with multiple redistribution points between each pair of routing domains. The configuration shows large ACLs matching various subnets and setting AD per-route using the **distance** command. What alternative method might be easier to maintain as the network changes?	
The plan shows an EIGRP for IPv6 and OSPFv3 domain with mutual redistribution. The configuration shows a **redistribute eigrp 1** command under the OSPF process. What kinds of routes should be redistributed? Which kinds will not?	

Create an Implementation Plan Table

To practice skills useful when creating your own implementation plan, list in Table 10-14 configuration commands related to the configuration of the following features. You might want to record your answers outside the book and set a goal to complete this table (and others like it) from memory during your final reviews before taking the exam.

Table 10-14 *Implementation Plan Configuration Memory Drill*

Feature	Configuration Commands/Notes
Configuring redistribution into EIGRP from OSPF (List all parameters that you can recall.)	
Configuring redistribution into OSPF from EIGRP (List all parameters that you can recall.)	
Setting default metrics for all **redistribute** commands, redistributing into EIGRP	
Setting default metrics for all **redistribute** commands, redistributing into OSPF	
Filtering routes on redistribution from OSPF into EIGRP	
Filtering routes on redistribution from EIGRP into OSPF	
Configuring a route map that will set metric components to 1000, 200, 255, 1, and 1500, for routes permitted by ACL 1, and filter all other routes	
Setting OSPF's administrative distance for all internal routes to 110 and all external routes to 180	
Setting EIGRP's administrative distance for routes learned from neighbor 1.1.1.1 to 190, only for subnets in the range 10.1.0.0–10.1.255.255	
Configuring RIPng to redistribute routes from OSPF process 1, including subnets and connected routes	

Choose Commands for a Verification Plan Table

To practice skills useful when creating your own verification plan, list in Table 10-15 all commands that supply the requested information. You might want to record your answers outside the book and set a goal to complete this table (and others like it) from memory during your final reviews before taking the exam.

Table 10-15   *Verification Plan Memory Drill*

Information Needed	Command(s)
Display a brief version of the EIGRP topology table, listing external routes.	
Display the EIGRP topology table, including notations identifying external routes.	
For external EIGRP routes, display the source of the route, external metric, and IP address of the router that redistributed the route.	
Identify external EIGRP-learned IP routes.	
Display a brief version of the OSPF topology table, listing Type 5 external LSAs.	
Display all OSPF Type 4 LSAs.	
Display all OSPF Type 5 LSAs.	
Display all OSPF Type 7 LSAs.	
Display the external route type for an OSPF external route.	
Display OSPF cost for each interface, briefly.	
On an internal router, display any same-area ABRs' costs to reach any ASBRs.	
On an internal router, display that router's best cost to reach an ASBR.	
Display the metric for all currently best external OSPF routes.	
Confirm that OSPF routes were redistributed from the IP routing table into that same router's EIGRP topology table.	
Display the number of matches in an ACL used for redistribution filtering.	
Display the number of matches in an IP prefix list used for redistribution filtering.	
Display the configuration of a route map.	
Display the component metrics of a route redistributed into EIGRP.	
Confirm the absence or presence of a route that could have been redistributed from OSPF into EIGRP.	

Information Needed	Command(s)
Confirm the absence or presence of a route that could have been redistributed from EIGRP into OSPF.	
Display an IP route's administrative distance.	
Display the administrative distance settings for EIGRP.	
Display the administrative distance settings for OSPF.	

Note Some of the entries in this table might not have been specifically mentioned in this chapter but are listed in this table for review and reference.

Review All the Key Topics

Review the most important topics from inside the chapter, noted with the Key Topic icon in the outer margin of the page. Table 10-16 lists a reference of these key topics and the page numbers on which each is found.

Table 10-16 *Key Topics for Chapter 10*

Key Topic Element	Description	Page Number
List	Requirements for redistribution in a router	408
Table 10-2	Parameters of the EIGRP **redistribute** Command	410
Table 10-3	Methods of Setting EIGRP Metrics When Redistributing into EIGRP	414
List	Rules from what is redistributed from an IGP	416
Table 10-4	Parameters on the OSPF **redistribute** Command	418
List	Defaults of the OSPF **redistribute** command	419
Table 10-5	Summary of Metric Values When Redistributing into OSPF	423
List	Tiebreaker rules for choosing the best E2 routes	425
List	Rules for calculating the metric of an interarea E1 route	432
List	A summary of functions that can be performed by a route map referenced by a **redistribute** command	436
Table 10-6	**match** Command Options for Redistribution	437

Key Topic Element	Description	Page Number
Table 10-7	set Command Options for Redistribution into IGPs	438
Table 10-10	Default Administrative Distances	450
Figure 10-14	Subnet X: Internal EIGRP, External OSPF, on Router RD2	451
List	Recommendations for how to use route tags to prevent the domain loop problems	460
Figure 10-20	Using Route Tags to Prevent Domain Loop Problems	460

Complete the Tables and Lists from Memory

Print a copy of Appendix D, "Memory Tables," (found on the CD) or at least the section for this chapter, and complete the tables and lists from memory. Appendix E, "Memory Tables Answer Key," also on the CD, includes completed tables and lists to check your work.

Define Key Terms

Define the following key terms from this chapter, and check your answers in the glossary.

redistribution, external route, Type 4 Summary ASBR LSA, Type 5 External LSA, Type 7 AS External LSA, External Type 1, External Type 2, domain loop, administrative distance, route tag

This chapter covers the following subjects:

- **Cisco Express Forwarding:** This section discusses how a router performs packet switching, primarily focusing on Cisco Express Forwarding (CEF).

- **Policy-Based Routing:** This section describes the Cisco IOS Policy-Based Routing (PBR) feature, which allows a router to make packet-forwarding decisions based on criteria other than the packet's destination address as matched with the IP routing table.

- **IP Service-Level Agreement:** This section gives a general description of the IP Service-Level Agreement (IP SLA) feature, with particular attention to how it can be used to influence when a router uses a static route and when a router uses PBR.

- **VRF-Lite:** This section demonstrates a basic configuration of VRF-Lite, which allows a single physical router to run multiple virtual router instances, thereby providing network segmentation.

CHAPTER 11

Route Selection

The term *path control* can mean a variety of things, depending on the context. The typical use of the term refers to any and every function that influences where a router forwards a packet. With that definition, path control includes practically every topic in this book. In other cases, the term *path control* refers to tools that influence the contents of a routing table, usually referring to routing protocols.

This chapter examines three path control topics that fit only into the broader definition of the term. The first, *Cisco Express Forwarding (CEF)*, is a feature that allows a router to very quickly and efficiently make a route lookup. This chapter contrasts CEF with a couple of its predecessors, *Process Switching* and *Fast Switching*.

The second major topic in this chapter is *Policy-Based Routing (PBR)*, sometimes called *Policy Routing*. PBR influences the IP data plane, changing the forwarding decision a router makes, but without first changing the IP routing table.

Then, this chapter turns its attention to the *IP Service-Level Agreement (IP SLA)* feature. IP SLA monitors network health and reachability. A router can then choose when to use routes, and when to ignore routes, based on the status determined by IP SLA.

Also, a physical router can be logically segmented into multiple virtual routers, each of which performs its own route selection. That is the focus of the final major topic in this chapter, which covers a basic *VRF-Lite* configuration. Specifically, *Virtual Routing and Forwarding (VRF)* enables you to have multiple virtual router instances running on a single physical router, and VRF-Lite is one approach to configuring VRF support on a router.

"Do I Know This Already?" Quiz

The "Do I Know This Already?" quiz allows you to assess whether you should read the entire chapter. If you miss no more than one of these nine self-assessment questions, you might want to move ahead to the "Exam Preparation Tasks" section. Table 11-1 lists the major headings in this chapter and the "Do I Know This Already?" quiz questions covering the material in those headings so that you can assess your knowledge of these specific areas. The answers to the "Do I Know This Already?" quiz appear in Appendix A.

Table 11-1 *"Do I Know This Already?" Foundation Topics Section-to-Question Mapping*

Foundation Topics Section	Questions
Cisco Express Forwarding	1, 2
Policy-Based Routing	3–5
IP Service-Level Agreement	6–8
VRF-Lite	9

1. Identify the architectural components of Cisco Express Forwarding (CEF). (Choose two.)

   a. Routing Information Base (RIB)

   b. Adjacency Table

   c. Forwarding Information Base (FIB)

   d. ARP Cache

2. What command can be used to globally enable CEF on a router?

   a. ip flow egress

   b. ip route-cache cef

   c. no ip route-cache

   d. ip cef

3. Policy-Based Routing (PBR) has been enabled on Router R1's Fa 0/0 interface. Which of the following are true regarding how PBR works? (Choose two.)

   a. Packets entering Fa 0/0 will be compared based on the PBR route map.

   b. Packets exiting Fa 0/0 will be compared based on the PBR route map.

   c. Cisco IOS ignores the PBR forwarding directions when a packet matches a route map **deny** clause.

   d. Cisco IOS ignores the PBR forwarding directions when a packet matches a route map **permit** clause.

4. Examine the following configuration on Router R1. R1's **show ip route 172.16.4.1** command lists a route with outgoing interface S0/1/1. Host 172.16.3.3 uses Telnet to connect to host 172.16.4.1. What will Router R1 do with the packets generated by host 172.16.3.3 because of the Telnet session, assuming that the packets enter R1's Fa0/0 interface? (Choose two.)

```
interface Fastethernet 0/0
 ip address 172.16.1.1 255.255.255.0
 ip policy route-map Q2
!
route-map Q2 permit
 match ip address 101
 set interface s0/0/1
!
access-list 101 permit tcp host 172.16.3.3 172.16.4.0 0.0.0.255
```

   a. The packets will be forwarded out S0/0/1, or not at all.

   b. The packets will be forwarded out S0/0/1 if it is up.

   c. The packets will be forwarded out S0/1/1 if it is up.

   d. The packets will be forwarded out S0/1/1 if it is up, or if it is not up, out S0/0/1.

   e. The packets will be forwarded out S0/0/1 if it is up, or if it is not up, out S0/1/1.

5. The following output occurs on Router R2. Which of the following statements can be confirmed as true based on the output?

```
R2# show ip policy
Interface      Route map
Fa0/0          RM1
Fa0/1          RM2
S0/0/0         RM3
```

   a. R2 will forward all packets that enter Fa0/0 per the PBR configuration.

   b. R2 will use route map RM2 when determining how to forward packets that exit interface Fa0/1.

   c. R2 will consider using PBR for all packets exiting S0/0/0 per route map RM3.

   d. R2 will consider using PBR for all packets entering S0/0/0 per route map RM3.

6. Which of the following are examples of traffic that can be created as part of an IP Service-Level Agreement operation? (Choose two.)

   a. ICMP Echo

   b. VoIP (RTP)

   c. IPX

   d. SNMP

7. The following configuration commands exist only in an implementation plan document. An engineer does a copy/paste of these commands into Router R1's configuration. Which of the following answers is most accurate regarding the results?

```
ip sla 1
icmp-echo 1.1.1.1 source-ip 2.2.2.2
ip sla schedule 1 start-time now life forever
```

   a. The SLA operation will be configured but will not start until additional commands are used.

   b. The SLA operation is not completely configured, so it will not collect any data.

   c. The SLA operation is complete and working, collecting data into the RTTMON MIB.

   d. The SLA operation is complete and working but will not store the data in the RTTMON MIB without more configuration.

8. The following output occurs on Router R1. IP SLA operation 1 uses an ICMP echo operation type, with a default frequency of 60 seconds. The operation pings from address 1.1.1.1 to address 2.2.2.2. Which of the following answers is true regarding IP SLA and object tracking on R1?

```
R1# show track
Track 2
  IP SLA 1 state
  State is Up
    3 changes, last change 00:00:03
  Delay up 45 secs, down 55 secs
  Latest operation return code: OK
  Latest RTT (millisecs) 6
  Tracked by:
    STATIC-IP-ROUTING 0
```

   a. The tracking return code fails immediately after the SLA operation results in an ICMP echo failure three times.

   b. The tracking return code fails immediately after the SLA operation results in an ICMP echo failure one time.

   c. After the tracking object fails, the tracking object moves back to an up state 45 seconds later in all cases.

   d. After moving to a down state, the tracking object moves back to an OK state 45 seconds after the SLA operation moves to an OK state.

9. Which of the following is a benefit of Cisco EVN as compared to VRF-Lite?

   a. Cisco EVN allows a single physical router to run multiple virtual router instances.

   b. Cisco EVN allows two routers to be interconnected through an 802.1Q trunk, and traffic for different VRFs is sent over the trunk, using router subinterfaces.

   c. Cisco EVN allows routes from one VRF to be selectively leaked to other VRFs.

   d. Cisco EVN allows two routers to be interconnected through a VNET trunk, and traffic for different VRFs is sent over the trunk, without the need to configure router subinterfaces.

Foundation Topics

Cisco Express Forwarding

Much of the literature on router architecture divides router functions into three operational planes:

- **Management plane:** The management plane is concerned with the management of the device. For example, an administrator connecting to a router through a Secure Shell (SSH) connection through one of the router's VTY lines would be a management plane operation.

- **Control plane:** The control plane is concerned with making packet-forwarding decisions. For example, routing protocol operation would be a control plane function.

- **Data plane:** The data plane is concerned with the forwarding of data through a router. For example, end-user traffic traveling from a user's PC to a web server on a different network would go across the data plane.

Of these three planes, the two planes that most directly impact how quickly packets can flow through a router are the control plane and the data plane. Therefore, we will consider these two planes of operation and examine three different approaches that Cisco routers can take to forward packets arriving on an ingress interface and being sent out an appropriate egress interface, a process called *packet switching*.

Note   Many learners have a challenge with the term *packet switching*, because they are accustomed to *switching* being a Layer 2 operation, while *routing* is a Layer 3 operation. The key to understanding this term is to think of *frame switching* being a Layer 2 operation, while *packet switching* (the same thing as *routing*) is a Layer 3 operation.

In general, Cisco routers support the following three primary modes of packet switching:

- Process switching
- Fast switching
- Cisco Express Forwarding (CEF)

The following subsections discuss each of these approaches.

Operation of Process Switching

When a router routes a packet (that is, performs packet switching), the router removes the packet's Layer 2 header, examines the Layer 3 addressing, and decides how to forward the packet. The Layer 2 header is then rewritten (which might involve changing the source and destination MAC addresses and computing a new cyclic redundancy check [CRC]), and the packet is forwarded out an appropriate interface. With process switching, as illustrated in Figure 11-1, a router's CPU becomes directly involved with packet-switching decisions. As a result, the performance of a router configured for process switching can suffer significantly.

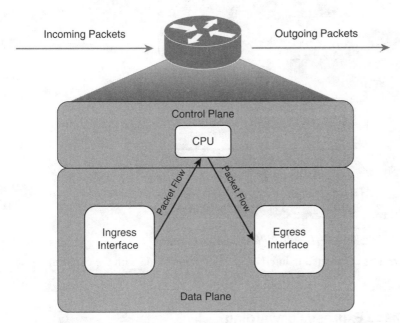

Figure 11-1 *Data Flow with Process Switching*

An interface can be configured for process switching by disabling fast switching on that interface. The interface configuration mode command used to disable fast switching is **no ip route-cache.**

Operation of Fast Switching

Fast switching uses *a fast cache* maintained in a router's data plane. The fast cache contains information about how traffic from different data flows should be forwarded. As seen in Figure 11-2, the first packet in a data flow is process switched by a router's CPU. After the router determines how to forward the first frame of a data flow, the forwarding information is stored in the fast cache. Subsequent packets in that same data flow are forwarded based on information in the fast cache, as opposed to being process switched. As a result, fast switching dramatically reduces a router's CPU utilization, as compared to process switching.

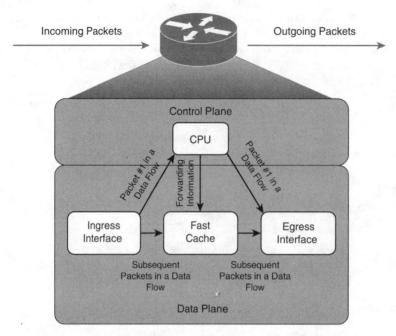

Figure 11-2   *Data Flow with Fast Switching*

Fast switching can be configured in interface configuration mode with the command **ip route-cache**.

Operation of Cisco Express Forwarding

Cisco Express Forwarding (CEF) maintains two tables in the data plane. Specifically, the *Forwarding Information Base (FIB)* maintains Layer 3 forwarding information, whereas the *adjacency table* maintains Layer 2 information for next hops listed in the FIB.

Using these tables, populated from a router's IP routing table and ARP cache, CEF can efficiently make forwarding decisions. Unlike fast switching, CEF does not require the first packet of a data flow to be process switched. Rather, an entire data flow can be forwarded at the data plane, as seen in Figure 11-3.

On many router platforms, CEF is enabled by default. If it is not, you can globally enable it with the **ip cef** command. Alternately, if CEF is enabled globally but is not enabled on a specific interface, you can enable it on that interface with the interface configuration mode command **ip route-cache cef**.

Table 11-2 lists and describes the configuration and verification commands for CEF.

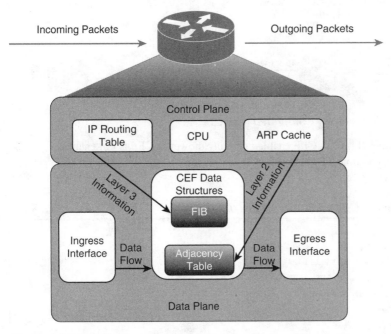

Figure 11-3   *Data Flow with Cisco Express Forwarding*

Table 11-2   *CEF Configuration and Verification Commands*

Command	Description
ip cef	Globally enables CEF, in global configuration mode.
ip route-cache cef	Enables CEF on an interface (if CEF is globally enabled), in interface configuration mode.
show ip interface *interface-id*	Displays multiple interface statistics, including information about an interface's packet-switching mode.
show ip cef	Displays the contents of a router's FIB.
show adjacency [detail]	Provides information contained in the adjacency table of a router, including protocol and timer information.

To illustrate the configuration and operation of CEF, the remainder of this section presents a series of CEF configuration and verification examples. Each of these examples is based on the topology shown in Figure 11-4. The routers in this topology have already been configured to exchange routes through Enhanced Interior Gateway Routing Protocol (EIGRP).

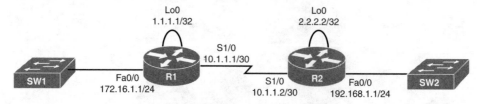

Figure 11-4 *Sample Topology Configured with CEF*

Router R1 in Figure 11-4 has CEF enabled globally; however, CEF is not enabled on interface Fa 0/0. Example 11-1 shows how to enable CEF on an interface if CEF is already enabled globally.

Example 11-1 *Enable CEF on Router R1's Fa 0/0 Interface*

```
R1# show ip int fa 0/0
FastEthernet0/0 is up, line protocol is up
  Internet address is 172.16.1.1/24
  Broadcast address is 255.255.255.255
  Address determined by non-volatile memory
  MTU is 1500 bytes
  Helper address is not set
  Directed broadcast forwarding is disabled
  Multicast reserved groups joined: 224.0.0.10
  Outgoing access list is not set
  Inbound  access list is not set
  Proxy ARP is enabled
  Local Proxy ARP is disabled
  Security level is default
  Split horizon is enabled
  ICMP redirects are always sent
  ICMP unreachables are always sent
  ICMP mask replies are never sent
  IP fast switching is enabled
  IP Flow switching is disabled
  IP CEF switching is disabled
... OUTPUT OMITTED ...


R1# conf term
R1(config)# int fa 0/0
R1(config-if)# ip route-cache cef
R1(config-if)# end


R1# show ip int fa 0/0
FastEthernet0/0 is up, line protocol is up
  Internet address is 172.16.1.1/24
  Broadcast address is 255.255.255.255
```

Key Topic

```
    Address determined by non-volatile memory
    MTU is 1500 bytes
    Helper address is not set
    Directed broadcast forwarding is disabled
    Multicast reserved groups joined: 224.0.0.10
    Outgoing access list is not set
    Inbound  access list is not set
    Proxy ARP is enabled
    Local Proxy ARP is disabled
    Security level is default
    Split horizon is enabled
    ICMP redirects are always sent
    ICMP unreachables are always sent
    ICMP mask replies are never sent
    IP fast switching is enabled
    IP Flow switching is disabled
    IP CEF switching is enabled
... OUTPUT OMITTED ...
```

Router R2 in Figure 11-4 has CEF disabled globally. Example 11-2 shows how to globally enable CEF.

Example 11-2 *Enable CEF on Router R2*

```
R2# show ip int fa 0/0
FastEthernet0/0 is up, line protocol is up
  Internet address is 192.168.1.1/24
  Broadcast address is 255.255.255.255
  Address determined by non-volatile memory
  MTU is 1500 bytes
  Helper address is not set
  Directed broadcast forwarding is disabled
  Multicast reserved groups joined: 224.0.0.10
  Outgoing access list is not set
  Inbound  access list is not set
  Proxy ARP is enabled
  Local Proxy ARP is disabled
  Security level is default
  Split horizon is enabled
  ICMP redirects are always sent
  ICMP unreachables are always sent
  ICMP mask replies are never sent
  IP fast switching is disabled
  IP Flow switching is disabled
  IP CEF switching is disabled
... OUTPUT OMITTED ...
```

```
R2# conf term
R2(config)# ip cef
R2(config)# end


R2# show ip int fa 0/0
FastEthernet0/0 is up, line protocol is up
  Internet address is 192.168.1.1/24
  Broadcast address is 255.255.255.255
  Address determined by non-volatile memory
  MTU is 1500 bytes
  Helper address is not set
  Directed broadcast forwarding is disabled
  Multicast reserved groups joined: 224.0.0.10
  Outgoing access list is not set
  Inbound  access list is not set
  Proxy ARP is enabled
  Local Proxy ARP is disabled
  Security level is default
  Split horizon is enabled
  ICMP redirects are always sent
  ICMP unreachables are always sent
  ICMP mask replies are never sent
  IP fast switching is enabled
  IP Flow switching is disabled
  IP CEF switching is enabled
... OUTPUT OMITTED ...
```

Example 11-3 shows the output of the **show ip cef** and **show adjacency detail** commands issued on Router R1.

Example 11-3   *Output from the* **show ip cef** *and* **show adjacency detail** *Commands*

```
R1# show ip cef
Prefix              Next Hop          Interface
0.0.0.0/0           no route
0.0.0.0/8           drop
0.0.0.0/32          receive
1.1.1.1/32          receive           Loopback0
2.2.2.2/32          10.1.1.2          Serial1/0
10.1.1.0/30         attached          Serial1/0
10.1.1.0/32         receive           Serial1/0
10.1.1.1/32         receive           Serial1/0
10.1.1.3/32         receive           Serial1/0
127.0.0.0/8         drop
172.16.1.0/24       attached          FastEthernet0/0
172.16.1.0/32       receive           FastEthernet0/0
172.16.1.1/32       receive           FastEthernet0/0
```

```
172.16.1.255/32        receive              FastEthernet0/0
192.168.1.0/24         10.1.1.2             Serial1/0
224.0.0.0/4            drop
224.0.0.0/24           receive
240.0.0.0/4            drop
255.255.255.255/32     receive


R1# show adjacency detail
Protocol Interface                  Address
IP       Serial1/0                  point2point (11)
                                    0 packets, 0 bytes
                                    epoch 0
                                    sourced in sev-epoch 1
                                    Encap length 4
                                    0F000800
                                    P2P-ADJ
```

Output from the **show ip cef** command, as seen in Example 11-3, contains the contents of the FIB for Router R1. Note that if the next hop of a network prefix is set to *attached*, the entry represents a *network* to which the router is directly attached. However, if the next hop of a network prefix is set to *receive*, the entry represents an *IP address* on one of the router's interfaces.

For example, the network prefix 10.1.1.0/30, with a next hop of *attached*, is a network (as indicated by the 30-bit subnet mask) directly attached to Router R1's Serial 1/0 interface. However, the network prefix of 10.1.1.1/32 with a next hop of *receive* is a specific IP address (as indicated by the 32-bit subnet mask). Note that the all-0s host addresses for directly attached networks (for example, 10.1.1.0/30) and the all-1s host addresses for directly attached networks (for example, 172.16.1.255/32) also show up as *receive* entries.

Output from the **show adjacency detail** command displays information about how to reach a specific adjacency shown in the FIB. For example, Example 11-3 indicates that network 192.168.1.0 /24 is reachable by going out of interface Serial 1/0. The adjacency table also shows interface Serial 1/0 uses a point-to-point connection. Therefore, the adjacent router is on the other side of the point-to-point link. If an interface in the adjacency table is an Ethernet interface, source and destination MAC address information is contained in the entry for the interface.

Policy-Based Routing

When a packet arrives at the incoming interface of a router, the router's data plane processing logic takes several steps to process the packet. The incoming packet actually arrives encapsulated inside a data link layer frame, so the router must check the incoming frame's Frame Check Sequence (FCS) and discard the frame if errors occurred in transmission. If the FCS check passes, the router discards the incoming frame's data-link header and trailer, leaving the Layer 3 packet. Finally, the router does the equivalent of comparing the destination IP address of the packet with the IP routing table, matching the longest-prefix route that matches the destination IP address.

Policy-Based Routing (PBR) overrides a router's natural destination-based forwarding logic. PBR intercepts the packet after deencapsulation on the incoming interface, before the router performs the CEF table lookup. PBR then chooses how to forward the packet using criteria other than the usual matching of the packet's destination address with the CEF table.

PBR chooses how to forward the packet by using matching logic defined through a route map, which in turn typically refers to an IP access control list (ACL). That same route map also defines the forwarding instructions—the next-hop IP address or outgoing interface—for packets matched by the route map. Figure 11-5 shows the general concept, with PBR on interface Fa0/0 overriding the usual routing logic, forwarding packets out three different outgoing interfaces.

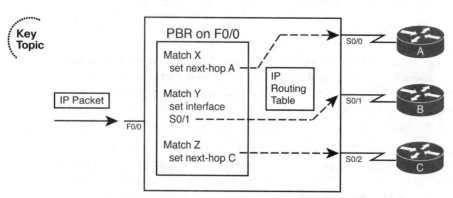

Figure 11-5 *PBR Concepts*

To perform the actions shown in Figure 11-5, the engineer configures two general steps:

Step 1.   Create a route map with the logic to match packets, and choose the route, as shown on the left side of the figure.

Step 2.   Enable the route map for use with PBR, on an interface, for packets entering the interface.

The rest of this section focuses on the configuration and verification of PBR.

Matching the Packet and Setting the Route

To match packets with a route map enabled for PBR, you use the familiar **route-map match** command. However, you have two **match** command options to use:

- **match ip address**
- **match length** *min max*

The **match ip address** command can reference standard and extended ACLs. Any item matchable by an ACL can be matched in the route map. The **match length** command allows you to specify a range of lengths, in bytes.

When a route map clause (with a **permit** action) matches a packet, the **set** command defines the action to take regarding how to forward the packet. The four **set** command options define either the outgoing interface or the next-hop IP address, just like routes in the IP routing table. Table 11-3 lists the options, with some explanations.

Table 11-3 *Choosing Routes Using the PBR set Command*

Command	Comments
set ip next-hop *ip-address* [*...ip-address*]	Next-hop addresses must be in a connected subnet; PBR forwards to the first address in the list for which the associated interface is up.
set ip default next-hop *ip-address* [*...ip-address*]	Same logic as previous command, except PBR first attempts to route based on the routing table.
set interface *interface-type interface-number* [*...interface-type interface-number*]	PBR forwards packets using the first interface in the list that is up.
set default interface *interface-type interface- number* [*...interface-type interface-number*]	Same logic as previous command, except PBR first attempts to route based on the routing table.

Note that two of the commands allow the definition of a next-hop router, and two allow the definition of an outgoing interface. The other difference in the commands relates to whether the command includes the **default** keyword. The section "How the default Keyword Impacts PBR Logic Ordering," later in this chapter, describes the meaning of the **default** keyword.

After the route map has been configured with all the clauses to match packets and to set an outgoing interface or next-hop address, the only remaining step requires the **ip policy route-map** *name* command to enable PBR for packets entering an interface.

PBR Configuration Example

To tie the concepts together, Figure 11-6 shows a sample internetwork to use in a PBR example. In this case, EIGRP on R1 chooses the upper route to reach the subnets on the right, because of the higher bandwidth on the upper link (T1) as compared with the lower link (64 kbps).

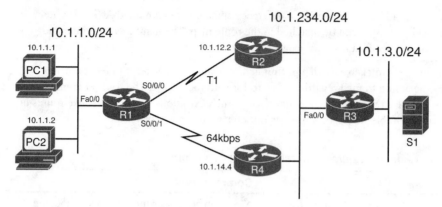

Figure 11-6 *Network Used in PBR Example*

For this example, the PBR configuration matches packets sent from PC2 on the left to server S1 in subnet 10.1.3.0/24 on the right. PBR on R1 routes these packets out S0/0/1 to R4. These packets will be routed over the lower path—out R1's S0/0/1 to R4—instead of through the current through R2, as listed in R1's IP routing table. The PBR configuration on Router R1 is shown in Example 11-4.

Example 11-4 *R1 PBR Configuration*

```
interface Fastethernet 0/0
 ip address 10.1.1.9 255.255.255.0
 ip policy route-map PC2-over-low-route
!
route-map PC2-over-low-route permit
 match ip address 101
 set ip next-hop 10.1.14.4
!
access-list 101 permit ip host 10.1.1.2 10.1.3.0 0.0.0.255
```

The configuration enables PBR with Fa0/0's **ip policy route-map PC2-over-low-route** command. The referenced route map matches packets that match ACL 101; ACL 101 matches packets from PC2 only, going to subnet 10.1.3.0/24. The **route-map** clause uses a **permit** action, which tells Cisco IOS to indeed apply PBR logic to these matched packets. (Had the **route-map** command listed a **deny** action, Cisco IOS would simply route the packet as normal—it would not filter the packet.) Finally, for packets matched with a **permit** action, the router forwards the packets based on the **set ip next-hop 10.1.14.4** command, which tells R1 to forward the packet to R4 next.

Note that for each packet entering Fa0/0, PBR either matches a packet with a **route map permit** clause or matches a packet with a **route map deny** clause. All route maps have an implicit deny clause at the end that matches all packets not already matched by the route map. PBR processes packets that match a **permit** clause using the defined **set** command. For packets matched by a **deny** clause, PBR lets the packet go through to the normal IP routing process.

To verify the results of the policy routing, Example 11-5 shows two **traceroute** commands: one from PC1 and one from PC2. Each shows the different paths. (Note that the output actually comes from a couple of routers configured to act as hosts PC1 and PC2 for this example.)

Example 11-5   *Confirming PBR Results Using* traceroute

```
! First, from PC1 (actually, a router acting as PC1):
PC1# trace 10.1.3.99
Type escape sequence to abort.
Tracing the route to 10.1.3.99

  1 10.1.1.9 4 msec 0 msec 4 msec
  2 10.1.12.2 0 msec 4 msec 4 msec
  3 10.1.234.3 0 msec 4 msec 4 msec
  4 10.1.3.99 0 msec *  0 msec

! Next, from PC2
PC2# trace 10.1.3.99

Type escape sequence to abort.
Tracing the route to 10.1.3.99

  1 10.1.1.9 4 msec 0 msec 4 msec
  2 10.1.14.4 8 msec 4 msec 8 msec
  3 10.1.234.3 8 msec 8 msec 4 msec
  4 10.1.3.99 4 msec *  4 msec
```

The output differs only in the second router in the end-to-end path—R2's 10.1.12.2 address as seen for PC1's packet and 10.1.14.4 as seen for PC2's packet.

The verification commands on the router doing the PBR function list relatively sparse information. The **show ip policy** command just shows the interfaces on which PBR is enabled and the route map used. The **show route-map** command shows overall statistics for the number of packets matching the route map for PBR purposes. The only way to verify the types of packets that are policy routed is to use the **debug ip policy** command, which can produce excessive overhead on production routers, given its multiple lines of output per packet, or to use **traceroute**. Example 11-6 lists the output of the **show** and **debug** commands on Router R1, with the debug output being for a single policy-routed packet.

Example 11-6   *Verifying PBR on Router R1*

```
R1# show ip policy
Interface      Route map
Fa0/0          PC2-over-low-route

R1# show route-map
```

```
    route-map PC2-over-low-route, permit, sequence 10
      Match clauses:
        ip address (access-lists): 101
      Set clauses:
        ip next-hop 10.1.14.4
      Policy routing matches: 12 packets, 720 bytes
R1# debug ip policy
*Sep 14 16:57:51.675: IP: s=10.1.1.2 (FastEthernet0/0), d=10.1.3.99, len 28,
policy match
*Sep 14 16:57:51.675: IP: route map PC2-over-low-route, item 10, permit
*Sep 14 16:57:51.675: IP: s=10.1.1.2 (FastEthernet0/0), d=10.1.3.99 (Serial0/0/1),
len 28, policy routed
*Sep 14 16:57:51.675: IP: FastEthernet0/0 to Serial0/0/1 10.1.14.4
```

How the default Keyword Impacts PBR Logic Ordering

The example in the previous section showed a **set** command that did not use the **default** keyword. However, the inclusion or omission of this keyword significantly impacts how PBR works. This parameter in effect tells Cisco IOS whether to apply PBR logic before trying to use normal destination-based routing, or whether to first try to use the normal destination-based routing, relying on PBR's logic only if the destination-based routing logic fails to match a nondefault route.

First, consider the case in which the **set** command omits the **default** parameter. When Cisco IOS matches the associated PBR route map **permit** clause, Cisco IOS applies the PBR logic first. If the **set** command identifies an outgoing interface that is up, or a next-hop router that is reachable, Cisco IOS uses the PBR-defined route. However, if the PBR route (as defined in the **set** command) is not working—because the outgoing interface is down or the next hop is unreachable using a connected route—Cisco IOS next tries to route the packet using the normal destination-based IP routing process.

Next, consider the case in which the **set** command includes the **default** parameter. When Cisco IOS matches the associated PBR route map **permit** clause, Cisco IOS applies the normal destination-based routing logic first, with one small exception: It ignores any default routes. Therefore, the router first tries to route the packet as normal, but if no nondefault route matches the packet's destination address, the router forwards the packet as directed in the **set** command.

For example, for the configuration shown in Example 11-4, by changing the **set** command to **set ip default next-hop 10.1.14.4**, R1 would have first looked for (and found) a working route through R2, and forwarded packets sent by PC2 over the link to R2. Summarizing:

Key Topic

- Omitting the **default** parameter gives you logic like this: "Try PBR first, and if PBR's route does not work, try to route as usual."

- Including the **default** parameter gives you logic like this: "Try to route as usual while ignoring any default routes, but if normal routing fails, use PBR."

Additional PBR Functions

Primarily, PBR routes packets received on an interface, but using logic other than matching the destination IP address and the CEF table. This section briefly examines three additional PBR functions.

Applying PBR to Locally Created Packets

In some cases, it might be useful to use PBR to process packets generated by the router itself. However, PBR normally processes packets that enter the interface(s) on which the **ip policy route-map** command has been configured, and packets generated by the router itself do not actually enter the router through some interface. To make Cisco IOS process locally created packets using PBR logic, configure the **ip local policy route-map** *name* global command, referring to the PBR route map at the end of the command.

The section "Configuring and Verifying IP SLA," later in this chapter, shows an example use of this command. IP SLA causes a router to create packets, so applying PBR to such packets can influence the path taken by the packets.

Setting IP Precedence

Quality of service (QoS) refers to the entire process of how a network infrastructure can choose to apply different levels of service to different packets. For example, a router might need to keep delay and jitter (delay variation) low for VoIP and Video over IP packets, because these interactive voice and video calls only work well when the delay and jitter are held very low. As a result, the router might let VoIP packets bypass a long queue of data packets waiting to exit an interface, giving the voice packet better (lower) delay and jitter.

Most QoS designs mark each packet with a different value inside the IP header, for the purpose of identifying groups of packets—a service class—that should get a particular QoS treatment. For example, all VoIP packets could be marked with a particular value so that the router can then find those marked bits, know that the packets are VoIP packets because of that marking, and apply QoS accordingly.

Although the most commonly used QoS marking tool today is Class-Based Marking, in the past, PBR was one of the few tools that could be used for this important QoS function of marking packets. PBR still supports marking. However, most modern QoS designs ignore PBR's marking capabilities.

Before discussing PBR's marking features, a little background about the historical view of the IP header's *type of service (ToS)* byte is needed. The IP header originally defined a ToS byte whose individual bits have been defined in a couple of ways over the years. One such definition used the three leftmost bits in the ToS byte as a 3-bit *IP Precedence (IPP)* field, which could be used for generic QoS marking, with higher values generally implying a better QoS treatment. Back in the 1990s, the ToS byte was redefined as the *Differentiated Services (DS)* byte, with the six leftmost bits defined as the *Differentiated Service Code Point (DSCP)* marking. Most QoS implementations today revolve around setting the DSCP value.

PBR supports setting the older QoS marking fields—the IP Precedence (IPP) and the entire ToS byte—using the commands **set ip precedence** *value* and **set ip tos** *value*, respectively, in a route map. To configure packet marking, configure PBR as normal, but add a **set** command that defines the field to be marked and the value.

PBR with IP SLA

Besides matching a packet's length, or matching a packet with an ACL, PBR can also react to some dynamic measurements of the health of an IP network. To do so, PBR relies on the IP Service-Level Agreement (IP SLA) tool. In short, if the IP SLA tool measures the network's current performance, and the performance does not meet the defined threshold, PBR chooses to not use a particular route. The last major section of this chapter discusses IP SLA, with the section "Configuring and Verifying IP SLA" demonstrating how PBR works with IP SLA.

IP Service-Level Agreement

The Cisco IOS IP Service-Level Agreement (IP SLA) feature measures the ongoing behavior of the network. The measurement can be as simple as using the equivalent of a ping to determine whether an IP address responds, or as sophisticated as measuring the jitter (delay variation) of VoIP packets that flow over a particular path. To use IP SLA, an engineer configures IP SLA operations on various routers, and the routers will then send packets, receive responses, and gather data about whether a response was received, and the specific characteristics of the results, such as delay and jitter measurements.

IP SLA primarily acts as a tool to test and gather data about a network. Network management tools can then collect that data and report whether the network reached SLAs for the network. Many network management tools support the ability to configure IP SLA from the management tools' graphical interfaces. When configured, the routers gather the results of the operations, storing the statistics in the CISCO-RTTMON-MIB. Management applications can later gather the statistics from this management information base (MIB) on various routers and report on whether the business SLAs were met based on the gathered statistics.

Why bother with a pure network management feature in this book focused on IP routing? Well, you can configure static routes and PBR to use IP SLA operations, such that if an operation shows a failure of a particular measurement or a reduced performance of the measurement below a configured threshold, the router stops using either the static route or PBR logic. This combination of features provides a means to control when the static and PBR paths are used and when they are ignored.

This section begins with a discussion of IP SLA as an end to itself. Following that, the topic of SLA object tracking is added, along with how to configure static routes and PBR to track IP SLA operations, so that Cisco IOS knows when to use, and when to ignore, these routes.

Understanding IP SLA Concepts

IP SLA uses the concept of an *operation*. Each operation defines a type of packet that the router will generate, the destination and source address, and other characteristics of the packet. The configuration includes settings about the time of day when the router should be sending the packets in a particular operation, the types of statistics that should be gathered, and how often the router should send the packets. Also, you can configure a router with multiple operations of different types.

For example, a single IP SLA operation could define the following:

- Use Internet Control Message Protocol (ICMP) echo packets.

- Measure the end-to-end round-trip response time (ICMP echo).

- Send the packets every 5 minutes, all day long.

> **Note**   For those of you who have been around Cisco IOS for a while, the function of IP SLA might sound familiar. Cisco IP SLA has origins in earlier Cisco IOS features, including the *Response Time Reporter (RTR)* feature. The RTR feature is configured with the **rtr** command and uses the term *probe* to refer to what IP SLA refers to as an *operation*.

All the SLA operations rely on the router sending packets and some other device sending packets back. Figure 11-7 shows the general idea and provides a good backdrop to discuss some related issues.

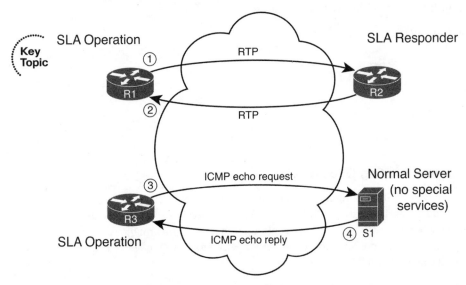

Figure 11-7   *Sending and Receiving Packets with IP SLA*

An IP SLA operation can cause the router to send packets to any IP address, whether on a router or a host. When sending to a host, as seen in the bottom part of the figure, the host does not need any special software or configuration—instead, the host just acts as normal. That means that if an SLA operation sends packets to a host, the router can only use operation types that send packets that the host understands. For example, the router could use ICMP echo requests (as seen in Steps 3 and 4), TCP connection requests, or even HTTP GET requests to a web server, because the server should try to respond to these requests.

The operation can also send packets to another router, which gives IP SLA a wider range of possible operation types. If the operation sends packets to which the remote router would normally respond, like ICMP echo requests, the other router needs no special configuration. However, IP SLA supports the concept of the IP SLA responder, as noted in Figure 11-7 for R2. By configuring R2 as an IP SLA responder, it responds to packets that a router would not normally respond to, giving the network engineer a way to monitor network behavior without having to place devices around the network just to test the network.

For example, the operation could send *Real-time Transport Protocol (RTP)* packets—packets that have the same characteristics as VoIP packets—as shown in Figure 11-7 as Step 1. Then the IP SLA responder function on R2 can reply as if a voice call exists between the two routers, as shown in Step 2 of that figure.

A wide range of IP SLA operations exist. The following list summarizes the majority of the available operation types, just for perspective:

- ICMP (echo, jitter)
- RTP (VoIP)
- TCP connection (establishes TCP connections)
- UDP (echo, jitter)
- DNS
- DHCP
- HTTP
- FTP

Configuring and Verifying IP SLA

This book describes IP SLA configuration in enough depth to get a sense for how it can be used to influence static routes and PBR. To that end, this section examines the use of an ICMP echo operation, which requires configuration only on one router, with no IP SLA responder. The remote host, router, or other device replies to the ICMP echo requests just like any other ICMP echo requests.

The general steps to configure an ICMP-based IP SLA operation are as follows:

Step 1. Create the IP SLA operation and assign it an integer operation number, using the **ip sla** *sla-ops-number* global configuration command.

Step 2.   Define the operation type and the parameters for that operation type. For ICMP echo, you define the destination IP address or host name, and optionally, the source IP address or host name, using the **icmp-echo** {*destination-ip-address* | *destination-hostname*} [**source-ip** {*ip-address* | *hostname*} | **source-interface** *interface-name*] SLA operation subcommand.

Step 3.   (Optional) Define a (nondefault) frequency at which the operation should send the packets, in seconds, using the **frequency** *seconds* IP SLA subcommand.

Step 4.   Schedule when the SLA will run, using the **ip sla schedule** *sla-ops-number* [**life** {**forever** | *seconds*}] [**start-time** {*hh:mm*[*:ss*] [*month day* | *day month*] | **pending** | **now** | **after** *hh:mm:ss*}] [**ageout** *seconds*] [**recurring**] global command.

Example 11-7 shows the process of configuring an ICMP echo operation on Router R1 from Figure 11-6. The purpose of the operation is to test the PBR route through R4. In this case, the operation will be configured as shown in Figure 11-8, with the following criteria:

■   Send ICMP echo requests to server S1 (10.1.3.99).

■   Use source address 10.1.1.9 (R1's F0/0 IP address).

■   Send these packets every 60 seconds.

■   Start the operation immediately, and run it forever.

■   Enable PBR for locally generated packets, matching the IP SLA operation with the PBR configuration so that the SLA operation's packets flow over the lower route.

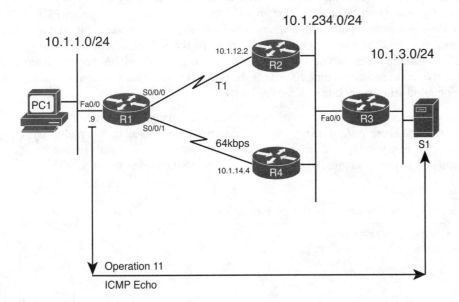

Figure 11-8   *Concept of IP SLA Operation on R1*

Example 11-7 *Configuring an ICMP Echo Operation on Router R1*

```
R1# conf t
Enter configuration commands, one per line.  End with CNTL/Z.
R1(config)# ip sla 11
R1(config-ip-sla)# icmp?
icmp-echo  icmp-jitter

R1(config-ip-sla)# icmp-echo 10.1.3.99 source-ip 10.1.1.9
R1(config-ip-sla)# frequency 60
R1(config-ip-sla)# exit
R1(config)# ip sla schedule 11 start-time now life forever

! Changes to the PBR configuration below
R1(config)# access-list 101 permit ip host 10.1.1.9 host 10.1.3.99
R1(config)# ip local policy route-map PC2-over-low-route
R1(config)# end
```

First, focus on the pure IP SLA configuration, located from the beginning of the example through command **ip sla schedule**. The configuration creates IP SLA operation 11. The parameters on the **icmp-echo** command act as if you used an extended ping from the command line, specifying both the source and destination IP address. The last command directly relates to IP SLA. The **ip sla schedule** command enables the operation now, and runs the operation until the network engineer takes some action to disable it, in some cases by removing the operation with the **no ip sla** *sla-ops-number* command.

The last two commands in the example show a change to the earlier PBR configuration so that the SLA operation's packets flow over the lower route. The **ip local policy PC2-over-low-route** global configuration command tells R1 to process packets generated by R1, including the IP SLA operation packets, using PBR. The addition of the **access-list 101** command to the configuration shown earlier in Example 11-4 makes the route map match the source and destination address of the SLA operation. That former route map's **set** command sent the packets over the link to R4.

IP SLA supports a couple of particularly useful verification commands: **show ip sla configuration** and **show ip sla statistics**. The first command confirms all the configuration settings for the operation, and the second lists the current statistics for the operation. Example 11-8 shows examples of each on R1, after the configuration shown in Example 11-7.

Example 11-8 *Verification of an IP SLA Operation*

```
R1# show ip sla configuration
IP SLAs Infrastructure Engine-II
Entry number: 11
Owner:
Tag:
Type of operation to perform: echo
Target address/Source address: 10.1.3.99/10.1.1.9
```

```
Type Of Service parameter: 0x0
Request size (ARR data portion): 28
Operation timeout (milliseconds): 5000
Verify data: No
Vrf Name:
Schedule:
   Operation frequency (seconds): 60   (not considered if randomly scheduled)
   Next Scheduled Start Time: Start Time already passed
   Group Scheduled : FALSE
   Randomly Scheduled : FALSE
   Life (seconds): Forever
   Entry Ageout (seconds): never
   Recurring (Starting Everyday): FALSE
   Status of entry (SNMP RowStatus): Active
Threshold (milliseconds): 5000 (not considered if react RTT is configured)
Distribution Statistics:
   Number of statistic hours kept: 2
   Number of statistic distribution buckets kept: 1
   Statistic distribution interval (milliseconds): 20
History Statistics:
   Number of history Lives kept: 0
   Number of history Buckets kept: 15
   History Filter Type: None
Enhanced History:


R1# show ip sla statistics 11
IPSLAs Latest Operation Statistics

IPSLA operation id: 11
        Latest RTT: 8 milliseconds
Latest operation start time: *19:58:08.395 UTC Mon Sep 14 2009
Latest operation return code: OK
Number of successes: 22
Number of failures: 0
Operation time to live: Forever
```

The highlighted lines in the output of the **show ip sla configuration** command corre-
spond to the values explicitly configured in Example 11-7. The more interesting output
exists in the output of the **show ip sla statistics 11** command, which lists the statistics
only for operation 11. In this case, 22 intervals have passed, showing 22 ICMP echo
requests as successful with no failures. The output also lists the latest round-trip time
(RTT). Finally, it lists the return code of the most recent operation (OK in this case)—a
key value used by SLA tracking.

Tracking SLA Operations to Influence Routing

As previously mentioned, you can configure both static routes and PBR to be used only when an SLA operation remains successful. The configuration to achieve this logic requires the configuration of a tracking object and cross-references between the static route, PBR, and IP SLA, as shown in Figure 11-9.

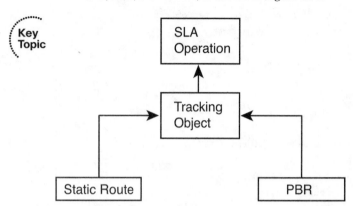

Figure 11-9 *Configuration Relationships for Path Control Using IP SLA*

The tracking object looks at the IP SLA operation's most recent return code to then determine the tracking state as either "up" or "down." Depending on the type of SLA operation, the return code can be a simple toggle, with "OK" meaning that the last operation worked. The tracking object would then result in an "up" state if the SLA operation resulted in an "OK" return code. Other SLA operations that define thresholds have more possible return codes. The tracking operation results in an "up" state if the IP SLA operation is within the configured threshold.

One of the main reasons that Cisco IOS requires the use of this tracking object is to prevent flapping routes. Route flapping occurs when a router adds a route to its routing table then quickly removes it, conditions change causing the route to be added back to the table again, and so on. If a static route tracked an IP SLA object directly, the SLA object's return code could change each time the operation ran, causing a route flap. The tracking object concept provides the ability to set a delay of how soon after a tracking state change the tracking object should change state. This feature gives the engineer a tool to control route flaps.

This section shows how to configure a tracking object for use with both a static route and with PBR.

Configuring a Static Route to Track an IP SLA Operation

To configure a static route to track an IP SLA, you need to configure the tracking object and then configure the static route with the **track** keyword. To do so, use these steps:

Step 1.   Use the **track** *object-number* **ip sla** *sla-ops-number* [**state** | **reachability**] global command.

Step 2. (Optional) Configure the delay to regulate flapping of the tracking state by using the **delay** {**down** *seconds* | **up** *seconds*} command in tracking configuration mode.

Step 3. Configure the static route with the **ip route** *destination mask* {*interface* | *next-hop*} **track** *object-number* command in global configuration mode.

Example 11-9 shows the configuration of tracking object 2, using the same design shown in Figures 11-6 and 11-8. In this case, the configuration adds a static route for subnet 10.1.234.0/24, the LAN subnet to which R2, R3, and R4 all connect. EIGRP chooses a route over R1's S0/0/0 interface as its best route, but this static route uses S0/0/1 as the outgoing interface.

Example 11-9 *Configuring a Static Route with Tracking IP SLA*

```
R1# conf t
Enter configuration commands, one per line.  End with CNTL/Z.
R1(config)# track 2 ip sla 11 state
R1(config-track)# delay up 90 down 90
R1(config-track)# exit
R1(config)# ip route 10.1.234.0 255.255.255.0 s0/0/1 track 2
R1(config)# end
```

The configuration begins with the creation of the tracking object number 2. As with IP SLA operation numbers, the number itself is unimportant, other than that the **ip route** command refers to this same number with the **track 2** option at the end of the command. The tracking object's delay settings have been made at 90 seconds.

The **show track** command lists the tracking object's configuration plus many other details. It lists the current tracking state, the time in this state, the number of state transitions, and the other entities that track the object (in this case, a static route).

Example 11-10 shows what happens when the IP SLA operation fails, causing the static route to be removed. The example starts with the configuration shown in Example 11-9, along with the SLA operation 11 as configured in Example 11-7. The following list details the current operation and what happens sequentially in the example:

Step 1. Before the text seen in Example 11-10, the current IP SLA operation already sends packets using PBR, over R1's link to R4, using source IP address 10.1.1.9 and destination 10.1.3.99 (server S1).

Step 2. At the beginning of the next example, because the IP SLA operation is working, the static route is in R1's IP routing table.

Step 3. An ACL is configured on R4 (not shown) so that the IP SLA operation fails.

Step 4. A few minutes later, R1 issues a log message stating that the tracking object changed state from up to down.

Step 5. The example ends with several commands that confirm the change in state for the tracking object, and confirmation that R1 now uses the EIGRP-learned route through R2.

Note This example uses the **show ip route ... longer-prefixes** command, because this command lists only the route for 10.1.234.0/24, which is the route that fails over in the example.

Example 11-10 *Verifying Tracking of Static Routes*

```
! Next - Step 2
R1# show ip route 10.1.234.0 255.255.255.0 longer-prefixes
! Legend omitted for brevity


     10.0.0.0/8 is variably subnetted, 7 subnets, 2 masks
S       10.1.234.0/24 is directly connected, Serial0/0/1
R1# show track
Track 2
  IP SLA 11 state
  State is Up
    1 change, last change 01:24:14
  Delay up 90 secs, down 90 secs
  Latest operation return code: OK
  Latest RTT (millisecs) 7
  Tracked by:
    STATIC-IP-ROUTING 0


! Next, Step 3
! Not shown - SLA Operations packets are now filtered by an ACL on R4
! Sometime later...
!


! Next - Step 4
R1#
*Sep 14 22:55:43.362: %TRACKING-5-STATE: 2 ip sla 11 state Up->Down


! Final Step - Step 5
R1# show track
Track 2
  IP SLA 11 state
  State is Down
  2 changes, last change 00:00:15
  Delay up 90 secs, down 90 secs
  Latest operation return code: No connection
  Tracked by:
    STATIC-IP-ROUTING 0
R1# show ip route 10.1.234.0 255.255.255.0 longer-prefixes
! Legend omitted for brevity
```

```
        10.0.0.0/8 is variably subnetted, 7 subnets, 2 masks
D       10.1.234.0/24 [90/2172416] via 10.1.12.2, 00:00:25, Serial0/0/0
```

Configuring PBR to Track an IP SLA

To configure PBR to use object tracking, use a modified version of the **set** command in the route map. For example, the earlier PBR configuration used the following set command:

>   **set ip next-hop 10.1.14.4**

Instead, use the **verify-availability** keyword, as shown in this command:

>   **set ip next-hop verify-availability 10.1.14.4 1 track 2**

When the tracking object is up, PBR works as configured. When the tracking object is down, PBR acts as if the **set** command does not exist. That means that the router will still attempt to route the packet per the normal destination-based routing process.

The output of the related verification commands does not differ significantly when comparing the configuration of tracking for static routes versus PBR. The **show track** command lists "ROUTE-MAP" instead of "STATIC-IP-ROUTING," but the details of the **show track**, **show ip sla statistics**, and object tracking log message seen in Example 11-10 remain the same.

VRF-Lite

Service providers often need to allow their customers' traffic to pass through their cloud without one customer's traffic (and corresponding routes) exposed to another customer. Similarly, enterprise networks might need to segregate various application types, such as keeping voice and video traffic separate from data. These are just a couple of scenarios that could benefit from the Cisco *Virtual Routing and Forwarding (VRF)* feature. VRF allows a single physical router to host multiple virtual routers, with those virtual routers logically isolated from one another, each with its own IP routing table.

Note   Some Cisco literature states that VRF is an acronym for *Virtual Routing and Forwarding*, while other Cisco literature states that VRF is an acronym for *VPN Routing/Forwarding* (because of its common use in Virtual Private Networks [VPN]). This book uses the more generic *Virtual Routing and Forwarding* definition.

Cisco *Easy Virtual Network (EVN)*, as described in Chapter 1, "Characteristics of Routing Protocols," is a newer approach to VRF configuration, as compared to VRF-Lite. With VRF-Lite, if you want to send traffic for multiple virtual networks (that is, multiple VRFs) between two routers, you need to create a subinterface for each VRF on each router. However, with Cisco EVN, you instead create a trunk (called a *Virtual Network (VNET) trunk*) between the routers. Then, traffic for multiple virtual networks can travel over that single trunk interface, which uses tags to identify the virtual networks to which packets belong.

Even though Cisco EVN can help reduce the amount of configuration required for a VRF solution, VRF-Lite configuration is still often used in VRF networks. This section covers the basics of setting up and verifying a VRF configuration, for VRFs using Open Shortest Path First (OSPF) as their interior gateway protocol (IGP).

VRF-Lite Configuration

Table 11-4 lists the steps to perform a basic VRF-Lite configuration for VRF instances running OSPF.

Note VRF-Lite has several other options, beyond the scope of this book. For example, you can allow VRF to selectively "leak" routes between VRF instances.

Table 11-4 *Steps for a Basic OSPF VRF-Lite Configuration*

Command	Description
ip vrf *vrf-name*	A global configuration mode command that creates a VRF and enters VRF configuration mode.
ip vrf forwarding *vrf-name*	An interface or subinterface configuration mode command that assigns an interface or a subinterface to a VRF instance. (Note: If the interface or subinterface already had an IP address assigned, this command will remove that address, and you will need to add it back.)
router ospf *process-id* **vrf** *vrf-name*	A global configuration mode command that associates a unique process ID with a VRF instance and enters OSPF router configuration mode for a specific VRF instance. (Note: When in OSPF router configuration mode, you can enter the OSPF commands that you would normally enter in this mode.)

To illustrate a basic VRF-Lite configuration, consider Figure 11-10. A goal of the network topology shown is to isolate the voice, data, and video networks into separate VRF instances. Notice that the Fa 0/0 interface on the COMMON router is divided into three subinterfaces (Fa 0/0.2, Fa 0/0.3, and Fa 0/0.4). The COMMON router then connects to switch SW1 over an 802.1Q trunk. Switch SW1 then connects out to the VOICE, DATA, and VIDEO routers, where the switch port connecting to each router belongs to a different VLAN (that is, VOICE VLAN = 2, DATA VLAN = 3, VIDEO VLAN = 4).

Example 11-11 illustrates the configuration of the three VRFs (VOICE, DATA, and VIDEO) shown in Figure 11-10.

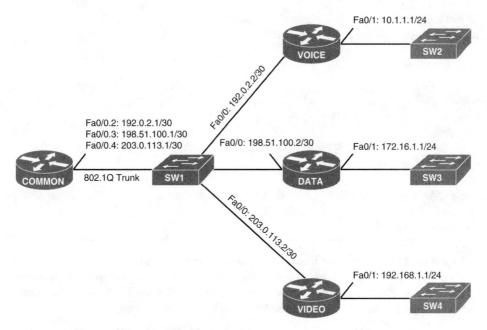

Figure 11-10 *VRF-Lite Sample Topology*

Example 11-11 *VRF-Lite Sample Configuration Using OSPF as the Routing Protocol*

Key Topic

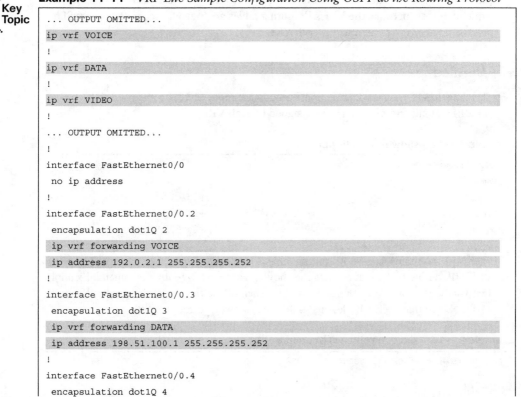

```
... OUTPUT OMITTED...
ip vrf VOICE
!
ip vrf DATA
!
ip vrf VIDEO
!
... OUTPUT OMITTED...
!
interface FastEthernet0/0
 no ip address
!
interface FastEthernet0/0.2
 encapsulation dot1Q 2
 ip vrf forwarding VOICE
 ip address 192.0.2.1 255.255.255.252
!
interface FastEthernet0/0.3
 encapsulation dot1Q 3
 ip vrf forwarding DATA
 ip address 198.51.100.1 255.255.255.252
!
interface FastEthernet0/0.4
 encapsulation dot1Q 4
```

```
ip vrf forwarding VIDEO
ip address 203.0.113.1 255.255.255.252
!
... OUTPUT OMITTED...
!
router ospf 1 vrf VOICE
 network 0.0.0.0 255.255.255.255 area 0
!
router ospf 2 vrf DATA
 network 0.0.0.0 255.255.255.255 area 0
!
router ospf 3 vrf VIDEO
 network 0.0.0.0 255.255.255.255 area 0
... OUTPUT OMITTED...
```

In Example 11-11, notice that the **ip vrf** *vrf-name* command is used to create each of the VRFs. Then each subinterface is assigned to one of the VRFs, using the **ip vrf forwarding** *vrf-name* command. If the subinterface previously had an IP address, the **ip vrf forwarding** *vrf-name* command removes the address, and it has to be reentered.

This example used OSPF as the routing protocol for the different VRFs, and the **router ospf** *process-id* **vrf** *vrf-name* command was used to enter OSPF configuration mode for each VRF. Also, keep in mind that even though different VRFs can have overlapping network addresses (because the VRF's IP routing tables are logically separated), the OSPF process ID needs to be unique for each VRF.

VRF Verification

The **show ip vrf** command, as demonstrated in Example 11-12, can be used to list a router's VRFs, along with the interfaces assigned to each VRF.

Example 11-12 show ip vrf *Output*

```
COMMON# show ip vrf
  Name                  Default RD           Interfaces
  DATA                  <not set>            Fa0/0.3
  VIDEO                 <not set>            Fa0/0.4
  VOICE                 <not set>            Fa0/0.2
```

Each VRF maintains its own IP routing table. Therefore, to view the contents of a specific VRF's IP routing table, you can use the **show ip route vrf** *vrf-name* command. Example 11-13 shows the output of this command for each of the three VRFs created in Example 11-11. Notice that each VRF learned a different network through OSPF.

Example 11-13 show ip route vrf vrf-name *Output*

```
COMMON# show ip route vrf VOICE

...OUTPUT OMITTED...
```

```
Gateway of last resort is not set


      10.0.0.0/24 is subnetted, 1 subnets
O        10.1.1.0 [110/2] via 192.0.2.2, 00:00:46, FastEthernet0/0.2
      192.0.2.0/24 is variably subnetted, 2 subnets, 2 masks
C        192.0.2.0/30 is directly connected, FastEthernet0/0.2
L        192.0.2.1/32 is directly connected, FastEthernet0/0.2
COMMON# show ip route vrf DATA


...OUTPUT OMITTED...


Gateway of last resort is not set


      172.16.0.0/24 is subnetted, 1 subnets
O        172.16.1.0 [110/2] via 198.51.100.2, 00:00:42, FastEthernet0/0.3
      198.51.100.0/24 is variably subnetted, 2 subnets, 2 masks
C        198.51.100.0/30 is directly connected, FastEthernet0/0.3
L        198.51.100.1/32 is directly connected, FastEthernet0/0.3
COMMON# show ip route vrf VIDEO


...OUTPUT OMITTED...


Gateway of last resort is not set


O     192.168.1.0/24 [110/2] via 203.0.113.2, 00:00:20, FastEthernet0/0.4
      203.0.113.0/24 is variably subnetted, 2 subnets, 2 masks
C        203.0.113.0/30 is directly connected, FastEthernet0/0.4
L        203.0.113.1/32 is directly connected, FastEthernet0/0.4
```

The **ping** command is commonly used to check connectivity with a remote IP address. However, on a router configured with multiple VRFs, you might need to specify the VRF in which the destination address resides. Example 11-14 shows a series of **ping vrf** *vrf-name destination-ip* commands. The destination IP addresses specified are IP addresses assigned to the Fa 0/1 interfaces on the VOICE, DATA, and VIDEO routers. Notice that for the VOICE VRF, only the 10.1.1.1 IP address is reachable, because the VOICE VRF is logically isolated from the DATA and VIDEO VLANs. Subsequent **ping** commands in the example demonstrate similar results for the DATA and VIDEO VRFs.

Example 11-14 *Pinging an IP Address in a VRF*

```
! Pinging from VRF VOICE
COMMON# ping vrf VOICE 10.1.1.1
Type escape sequence to abort.
Sending 5, 100-byte ICMP Echos to 10.1.1.1, timeout is 2 seconds:
!!!!!
Success rate is 100 percent (5/5), round-trip min/avg/max = 32/40/48 ms
COMMON# ping vrf VOICE 172.16.1.1
```

```
Type escape sequence to abort.
Sending 5, 100-byte ICMP Echos to 172.16.1.1, timeout is 2 seconds:
.....
Success rate is 0 percent (0/5)
COMMON# ping vrf VOICE 192.168.1.1
Type escape sequence to abort.
Sending 5, 100-byte ICMP Echos to 192.168.1.1, timeout is 2 seconds:
.....

! Pinging from VRF DATA
COMMON# ping vrf DATA 10.1.1.1
Type escape sequence to abort.
Sending 5, 100-byte ICMP Echos to 10.1.1.1, timeout is 2 seconds:
.....
Success rate is 0 percent (0/5)
COMMON# ping vrf DATA 172.16.1.1
Type escape sequence to abort.
Sending 5, 100-byte ICMP Echos to 172.16.1.1, timeout is 2 seconds:
!!!!!
COMMON# ping vrf DATA 192.168.1.1
Type escape sequence to abort.
Sending 5, 100-byte ICMP Echos to 192.168.1.1, timeout is 2 seconds:
.....

! Pinging from VRF VIDEO
COMMON# ping vrf VIDEO 10.1.1.1
Type escape sequence to abort.
Sending 5, 100-byte ICMP Echos to 10.1.1.1, timeout is 2 seconds:
.....
Success rate is 0 percent (0/5)
COMMON# ping vrf VIDEO 172.16.1.1
Type escape sequence to abort.
Sending 5, 100-byte ICMP Echos to 172.16.1.1, timeout is 2 seconds:
.....
Success rate is 0 percent (0/5)
COMMON# ping vrf VIDEO 192.168.1.1
Type escape sequence to abort.
Sending 5, 100-byte ICMP Echos to 192.168.1.1, timeout is 2 seconds:
!!!!!
Success rate is 80 percent (4/5), round-trip min/avg/max = 24/36/52 ms
COMMON#
```

Exam Preparation Tasks

Planning Practice

The CCNP ROUTE exam expects test takers to review design documents, create implementation plans, and create verification plans. This section provides some exercises that can help you to take a step back from the minute details of the topics in this chapter so that you can think about the same technical topics from the planning perspective.

For each planning practice table, simply complete the table. Note that any numbers in parentheses represent the number of options listed for each item in the solutions in Appendix F, "Completed Planning Practice Tables."

Design Review Table

Table 11-5 lists several design goals related to this chapter. If these design goals were listed in a design document, and you had to take that document and develop an implementation plan, what implementation options come to mind? You should write a general description; specific configuration commands are not required.

Table 11-5 *Design Review*

Design Goal	Possible Implementation Choices Covered in This Chapter
The design requires that the routers use the most efficient method of packet switching available.	
The design calls for traffic destined for one server in subnet 10.1.1.0/24 to be sent over a different route than the IGP-learned route for 10.1.1.0/24. (2)	
Same requirement as the previous row, except that only a subset of the source hosts should have their packets take a different route than the IGP-learned route.	
The design requires that a static route be used, but only when a particular database server is reachable.	
A design requires that a service provider router connect to and be able to communicate with three customer routers. (2)	

Implementation Plan Peer Review Table

Table 11-6 shows a list of questions that others might ask, or that you might think about, during a peer review of another network engineer's implementation plan. Complete the table by answering the questions.

Table 11-6 *Notable Questions from This Chapter to Consider During an Implementation Plan Peer Review*

Question	Answers
The plan shows an upgrade from an older router using Fast Switching to a new router using CEF. What is the fundamental difference in those packet-switching technologies?	
A plan lists two PBR route maps—one that uses the **default** keyword in its set command and the other that does not. What is the fundamental difference?	
A plan shows a route map enabled for policy routing, and the route map matches some packets with a **deny** route-map clause. What does Cisco IOS do with those packets?	
The plan document shows a PBR route map with the command **set ip dscp ef**. Does PBR support marking? And can it mark DSCP?	
The plan shows an IP SLA operation number 5, with a static route configured with the **track 5** parameter. What issues might exist with the linkages between these commands?	
The IP SLA configuration shows an IP SLA operation that uses ICMP Echo, with the destination IP address of a server. What must be done on the server to support this operation?	
Same scenario as the previous row, except the destination address is on a router.	
Same scenario as the previous row, except the operation generates RTP packets to measure voice jitter.	
How will a VRF-Lite configuration on a router (configured with a subinterface for each VRF) connect to a Cisco Catalyst switch while keeping traffic from each VRF isolated?	

Create an Implementation Plan Table

To practice skills useful when creating your own implementation plan, list in Table 11-7 all configuration commands related to the configuration of the following features. You might want to record your answers outside the book and set a goal to complete this table (and others like it) from memory during your final reviews before taking the exam.

Table 11-7 *Implementation Plan Configuration Memory Drill*

Feature	Configuration Commands/Notes
Globally enabled CEF.	
Enable CEF on an interface (if CEF is globally enabled).	
Configure the matching logic in a PBR route map (2).	
Configure the next-hop IP address in a PBR route map (2).	
Configure the outgoing interface in a PBR route map (2).	
Enable PBR on an interface.	
Enable PBR for packets created by a router.	
Create a VRF.	
Assign an interface or subinterface to a VRF.	
Enter OSPF router configuration mode for a specific VRF instance.	

Choose Commands for a Verification Plan Table

To practice skills useful when creating your own verification plan, list in Table 11-8 all commands that supply the requested information. You might want to record your answers outside the book and set a goal to complete this table (and others like it) from memory during your final reviews before taking the exam.

Table 11-8 *Verification Plan Memory Drill*

Information Needed	Command
Display multiple interface statistics, including information about an interface's packet-switching mode.	
Display the contents of a router's FIB.	

Information Needed	Command
Show information contained in the adjacency table of a router, including protocol and timer information.	
List interfaces on which PBR is enabled and the route map used.	
Display the configuration of a route map.	
Generate debug messages for each packet that matches PBR.	
Display the configuration of an SLA operation.	
Show the measurements from an SLA operation.	
Display the status of a tracking object.	
Display a listing of configured VRFs.	
Show the IP routing table for a specific VRF.	
Ping an IP address residing in a specific VRF.	

Note   Some of the entries in this table might not have been specifically mentioned in this chapter, but are listed in the table for review and reference.

Review All the Key Topics

Review the most important topics from inside the chapter, noted with the Key Topic icon in the outer margin of the page. Table 11-9 lists a reference of these key topics and the page numbers on which each is found.

Table 11-9   *Key Topics for Chapter 11*

Key Topic Element	Description	Page Number
Table 11-2	CEF Configuration and Verification Commands	479
Example 11-1	Enable CEF on Router R1's Fa 0/0 Interface	480
Figure 11-5	PBR Concepts	484
Table 11-3	Choosing Routes Using the PBR **set** Command	485
List	Comparisons of PBR logic when including/omitting the **set** command's **default** keyword	488
Figure 11-7	Sending and Receiving Packets with IP SLA	491

Key Topic Element	Description	Page Number
List	Configuration checklist for IP SLA	492
Figure 11-9	Configuration Relationships for Path Control Using IP SLA	496
List	Configuration checklist for object tracking	496
Example 11-11	VRF-Lite Sample Configuration Using OSPF as the Routing Protocol	501

Complete the Tables and Lists from Memory

Print a copy of Appendix D, "Memory Tables," (found on the CD) or at least the section for this chapter, and complete the tables and lists from memory. Appendix E, "Memory Tables Answer Key," also on the CD, includes completed tables and lists to check your work.

Definitions of Key Terms

Define the following key terms from this chapter, and check your answers in the glossary.

Cisco Express Forwarding, Policy-Based Routing, IP Service-Level Agreement, tracking object, path control, ToS, IP Precedence, SLA Operation, Virtual Routing and Forwarding (VRF), VRF-Lite

This chapter covers the following subjects:

- **Provider Assigned IPv4 Addresses:** This section contrasts a couple of ways that an Internet service provider (ISP) can assign IPv4 addresses to their customers' routers. Specifically, the ISP could give a customer an IP address to statically assign to his router, or the customer could use *Dynamic Host Configuration Protocol (DHCP)* to dynamically assign an IPv4 address from a pool of available addresses.

- **NAT:** This section discusses how the *Network Address Translation (NAT)* service allows an enterprise network to use private IPv4 addresses (that is, RFC 1918 addresses) internally, and have those private IP addresses translated into one or more publicly routable IPv4 addresses.

CHAPTER 12

Fundamentals of Internet Connectivity

The movie *Field of Dreams* said it best, "If you build it, they will come." That has happened with the Internet. Over the past couple of decades, Internet access speeds have gone up as prices have come down, resulting in an increasing dependence on the Internet. For example, companies with multiple locations frequently securely interconnect those locations by creating a *Virtual Private Network (VPN)* tunnel across the Internet. Cloud storage services allow computers to back up and synchronize files over the Internet. The Internet is increasingly being used for voice and video communication, not to mention its traditional web browsing and email uses.

With such a reliance on the Internet, most network designs need to include Internet connectivity. This module begins with a look at how a router connecting to an *Internet service provider (ISP)* obtains an IP address. One option is for the ISP to statically assign one or more publicly routable IP address(es) to a customer. Another approach is to use *Dynamic Host Configuration Protocol (DHCP)*, which allows an ISP to dynamically assign IP addresses to customer routers.

If an enterprise network is primarily using IPv4 addresses, as opposed to IPv6 addresses, it probably uses *Network Address Translation (NAT)* when connecting to the Internet. The issue necessitating the use of NAT is the depletion of IPv4 addresses, as discussed in Chapter 3, "IPv6 Review and RIPng." Because there are not enough IPv4 addresses to give every networked device in the world a unique IPv4 address, NAT allows networks to use private IP addresses (that is, IPv4 addresses defined by RFC 1918, which are not routable on the public Internet). Those internally used private IP addresses are then translated, using NAT, into one or more publicly routable IPv4 addresses. This chapter concludes with a discussion of NAT theory and configuration.

"Do I Know This Already?" Quiz

The "Do I Know This Already?" quiz allows you to assess whether you should read the entire chapter. If you miss no more than one of these seven self-assessment questions, you might want to move ahead to the "Exam Preparation Tasks" section. Table 12-1 lists the major headings in this chapter and the "Do I Know This Already?" quiz questions covering the material in those headings so that you can assess your knowledge of these specific areas. The answers to the "Do I Know This Already?" quiz appear in Appendix A.

Table 12-1 *"Do I Know This Already?" Foundation Topics Section-to-Question Mapping*

Foundation Topics Section	Questions
Provider-Assigned IPv4 Addresses	1–4
NAT	5–7

1. You are configuring a default route that should direct traffic for unknown networks out of interface Fa 0/0 to a next-hop IP address of 192.168.1.100. Which of the following commands should you use to configure the default route?

   a. ip route 255.255.255.255 255.255.255.255 fa 0/0

   b. ip route 255.255.255.255 255.255.255.255 192.168.1.100

   c. ip route 0.0.0.0 0.0.0.0 fa 0/0

   d. ip route 0.0.0.0 0.0.0.0 192.168.1.100

2. What interface configuration mode command instructs an interface to dynamically obtain its IP address from a DHCP server?

   a. ip address 255.255.255.255

   b. ip address dynamic

   c. ip address dhcp

   d. ip address bootp

3. Interface Fa 0/0 on your router has obtained an IP address through DHCP. You notice that in addition to an IP address assigned to interface Fa 0/0, your router now has a default static route configured. What command can you issue to prevent a router from automatically installing a default static route based on default gateway information learned through DHCP?

   a. no ip dhcp client request router

   b. ip dhcp suppress gateway

   c. ip dhcp route local

   d. no ip dhcp server response router

4. Interface Fa 0/0 on your router has obtained an IP address through DHCP. You notice that in addition to an IP address assigned to interface Fa 0/0, your router now has a default static route configured. What is the administrative distance (AD) of that route?

   a. 0

   b. 1

   c. 254

   d. 255

5. What type of Network Address Translation (NAT) allows a collection of inside local addresses to share a single inside global address, for use when communicating on the Internet?

    a. DNAT

    b. SNAT

    c. PAT

    d. MAT

6. A laptop inside your network has an IP address of 10.1.1.241. Using NAT, a router translates the 10.1.1.241 private IP address into 198.51.100.54, a public IP address, as the laptop is connecting to a web server on the Internet. The web server has an IP address of 203.0.113.10. What type of address is 10.1.1.241 in this scenario?

    a. Outside global

    b. Inside local

    c. Inside global

    d. Outside local

7. A laptop inside your network has an IP address of 10.1.1.241. Using NAT, a router translates the 10.1.1.241 private IP address into 198.51.100.54, a public IP address, as the laptop is connecting to a web server on the Internet. The web server has an IP address of 203.0.113.10. What type of address is 203.0.113.10 in this scenario?

    a. Outside global

    b. Inside local

    c. Inside global

    d. Outside local

Foundation Topics

Provider-Assigned IPv4 Addresses

ISPs have collections of publicly routable IPv4 addresses that they can distribute to their customers, thus allowing devices in the customer networks to communicate over the Internet. The IPv4 address assignments to customers could be either static assignments or dynamic assignments.

Static assignments might be useful to customers that have servers needing to be accessed from the Internet. For example, a company might have a web server as part of its network. If there is a static IP address assignment for that server, a Domain Name System (DNS) name could be associated with that IP address, allowing users on the Internet to access the web server by specifying the DNS name of the server (as opposed to its IP address) in their web browser.

However, if a company does not have any on-site servers needing to be accessed from the public Internet, it might not need a static IP address. In such situations, an ISP might dynamically assign one or more IP addresses to the company.

Note If an ISP does not offer static IP address assignment to its customers, or if there is an extra charge associated with a static IP address, the customers might be able to use *Dynamic DNS (DDNS)*, which dynamically updates DNS records to reflect current IP address assignments.

Static IP Address Assignment

Configuring an Internet-facing router with a statically assigned IP address involves two configuration steps:

Step 1.   Assign an IP address to the router interface connecting to the ISP, using the **ip address** *ip_address subnet_mask* command, in interface configuration mode.

Step 2.   Configure a default route pointing to the ISP, with the **ip route 0.0.0.0 0.0.0.0** *ip_address_of_isp_router* command, in global configuration mode.

Note Even though a default route can reference an egress router interface, rather than a next-hop IP address, specifying the next-hop IP address is considered a best practice. This is because, if you specify an Ethernet interface as the egress interface in a default route command, the router might generate an excessive number of ARP requests, resulting in poor router performance.

To illustrate the configuration of an Internet-facing router with a static IP address, consider Figure 12-1 and Example 12-1.

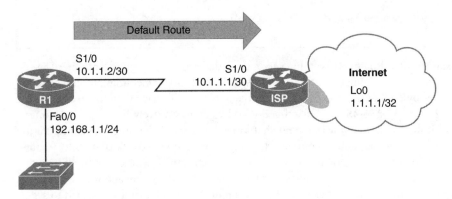

Figure 12-1   *Topology with Static IP Address Assignment*

Example 12-1   *Static IP Address and Default Route Configuration*

```
R1# conf term
Enter configuration commands, one per line.  End with CNTL/Z.
R1(config)# int s 1/0
R1(config-if)# ip address 10.1.1.2 255.255.255.252
R1(config-if)# no shutdown
R1(config-if)# exit
R1(config)# ip route 0.0.0.0 0.0.0.0 10.1.1.1
R1(config)# end
R1# show ip route
Codes: L - local, C - connected, S - static, R - RIP, M - mobile, B - BGP
       D - EIGRP, EX - EIGRP external, O - OSPF, IA - OSPF inter area
       N1 - OSPF NSSA external type 1, N2 - OSPF NSSA external type 2
       E1 - OSPF external type 1, E2 - OSPF external type 2
       i - IS-IS, su - IS-IS summary, L1 - IS-IS level-1, L2 - IS-IS level-2
       ia - IS-IS inter area, * - candidate default, U - per-user static route
       o - ODR, P - periodic downloaded static route, H - NHRP, l - LISP
       + - replicated route, % - next hop override


Gateway of last resort is 10.1.1.1 to network 0.0.0.0

S*     0.0.0.0/0 [1/0] via 10.1.1.1
       10.0.0.0/8 is variably subnetted, 2 subnets, 2 masks
C         10.1.1.0/30 is directly connected, Serial1/0
L         10.1.1.2/32 is directly connected, Serial1/0
       192.168.1.0/24 is variably subnetted, 2 subnets, 2 masks
C         192.168.1.0/24 is directly connected, FastEthernet0/0
L         192.168.1.1/32 is directly connected, FastEthernet0/0
R1# ping 1.1.1.1
```

```
Type escape sequence to abort.
Sending 5, 100-byte ICMP Echos to 1.1.1.1, timeout is 2 seconds:
!!!!!
Success rate is 100 percent (5/5), round-trip min/avg/max = 36/37/44 ms
R1#
```

In Example 12-1, Router R1 is an Internet-facing router located at a customer site. The ISP assigned the customer a static IP address of 10.1.1.2 /30. The configuration on Router R1 begins by configuring the IP address of the Serial 1/0 interface with the **ip address 10.1.1.2 255.255.255.252** command, followed by administratively bringing up the interface (if it were shut down) with the **no shutdown** command. Next, in global configuration mode, a default static route is configured, using the **ip route 0.0.0.0 0.0.0.0 10.1.1.1** command, to point to a next-hop address of 10.1.1.1, which is the IP address of the ISP router interface connecting to the customer. Then, the **show ip route** command was issued to verify the creation of the static route. Finally, a **ping 1.1.1.1** command was issued to see whether Router R1 had connectivity to an address residing in the Internet, and the ping was successful.

Dynamic IP Address Assignment

Dynamic IP address assignment, which is commonly used in residential and small-business environments, allows an Internet-facing interface on a customer router to learn IP address information from an ISP's *Dynamic Host Configuration Protocol (DHCP)* server.

Interestingly, there is no need to configure a static default route (as was configured in Example 12-1), because the DHCP server informs the customer router of an IP address of the default gateway (that is, the ISP router). Therefore, the customer router needs only a single command, issued in interface configuration mode: **ip address dhcp** (in addition to administratively bringing up the interface, if it were shut down).

To illustrate the configuration and verification of dynamic IP address assignment, consider Figure 12-2 and Example 12-2.

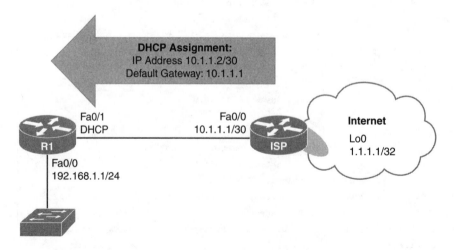

Figure 12-2 *Topology with Dynamic IP Address Assignment*

Key
Topic

Example 12-2   *Dynamic IP Address Configuration*

```
R1# conf term
R1(config)# interface fa 0/1
R1(config-if)# ip address dhcp
R1(config-if)# end
R1#
*Jun  3 10:56:42.111: %DHCP-6-ADDRESS_ASSIGN: Interface FastEthernet0/1 assigned
DHCP address
10.1.1.2, mask 255.255.255.252, hostname R1

R1# show ip interface brief
Interface              IP-Address      OK? Method Status                 Protocol
FastEthernet0/0        192.168.1.1     YES NVRAM  up                     up
FastEthernet0/1        10.1.1.2        YES DHCP   up                     up
Serial1/0              unassigned      YES NVRAM  administratively down down
Serial1/1              unassigned      YES NVRAM  administratively down down
Serial1/2              unassigned      YES NVRAM  administratively down down
Serial1/3              unassigned      YES NVRAM  administratively down down
R1# show ip route
Codes: L - local, C - connected, S - static, R - RIP, M - mobile, B - BGP
       D - EIGRP, EX - EIGRP external, O - OSPF, IA - OSPF inter area
       N1 - OSPF NSSA external type 1, N2 - OSPF NSSA external type 2
       E1 - OSPF external type 1, E2 - OSPF external type 2
       i - IS-IS, su - IS-IS summary, L1 - IS-IS level-1, L2 - IS-IS level-2
       ia - IS-IS inter area, * - candidate default, U - per-user static route
       o - ODR, P - periodic downloaded static route, H - NHRP, l - LISP
       + - replicated route, % - next hop override

Gateway of last resort is 10.1.1.1 to network 0.0.0.0

S*    0.0.0.0/0 [254/0] via 10.1.1.1
      10.0.0.0/8 is variably subnetted, 2 subnets, 2 masks
C        10.1.1.0/30 is directly connected, FastEthernet0/1
L        10.1.1.2/32 is directly connected, FastEthernet0/1
      192.168.1.0/24 is variably subnetted, 2 subnets, 2 masks
C        192.168.1.0/24 is directly connected, FastEthernet0/0
L        192.168.1.1/32 is directly connected, FastEthernet0/0
R1# ping 1.1.1.1
Type escape sequence to abort.
Sending 5, 100-byte ICMP Echos to 1.1.1.1, timeout is 2 seconds:
!!!!!
Success rate is 100 percent (5/5), round-trip min/avg/max = 24/30/56 ms
R1#
```

In Example 12-2, the **ip address dhcp** command is issued for interface Fa 0/1, which instructs the interface to obtain IP address information through DHCP. A syslog message is then displayed, stating that an IP address of 10.1.1.2, with a subnet mask of 255.255.255.252, has been assigned to Fa 0/1.

Output from the **show ip interface brief** command indicates that the Fa 0/1 interface obtained an IP address of 10.1.1.2 through DHCP. The **show ip route** command output shows a default static route pointing to a next-hop IP address of 10.1.1.1, which was learned through DHCP. Note that the administrative distance for the route is 254. This high value makes the route a *floating static route*, meaning that the route will only be used if a default route is not already known to another routing process (with a lower administrative distance). Finally, the **ping 1.1.1.1** output verifies that Router R1 has connectivity to an address on the Internet.

Note   You can prevent a router from installing a static default route, based on the default gateway information learned from a DHCP server, by issuing the **no ip dhcp client request router** command in interface configuration mode.

NAT

While IP addresses are routable through the public Internet, other IP addresses (as defined by RFC 1918) are considered private and are intended for use within an organization. *Network Address Translation (NAT)* allows private IP addresses to be translated into Internet-routable IP addresses (that is, public IP addresses). This section examines the operation of basic NAT and a variant called *Port Address Translation (PAT)*. Then, this section reviews a collection of NAT design considerations and a fairly recent enhancement to NAT configuration, called *NAT Virtual Interface (NVI)*.

Basic NAT

Consider Figure 12-3, which shows a basic NAT topology.

In the topology, two clients, with private IP addresses of 10.1.1.1 and 10.1.1.2, want to communicate with a web server on the public Internet. The server's IP address is 203.0.113.2. Router R1 is configured for NAT. As an example, Router R1 takes packets coming from 10.1.1.1 destined for 203.0.113.2 and changes the source IP address in the packets' headers to 198.51.100.3. When the server at IP address 203.0.113.2 receives traffic from the client, the server's return traffic is sent to a destination address of 198.51.100.3. When Router R1 receives traffic from the outside network destined for 198.51.100.3, the router translates the destination IP address to 10.1.1.1 and forwards the traffic to the inside network where Client 1 receives the traffic. Similarly, Client 2's IP address of 10.1.1.2 is translated into an IP address of 198.51.100.4.

Table 12-2 introduces you to the terminology used when describing the various IP addresses involved in a translation.

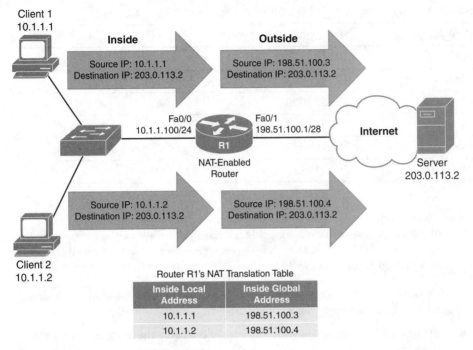

Figure 12-3 *Basic NAT Topology*

Key
Topic

Table 12-2 *Names of NAT IP Addresses*

NAT IP Address	Definition
Inside local	A private IP address referencing an inside device
Inside global	A public IP address referencing an inside device
Outside local	A private IP address referencing an outside device (seen when NAT is used at the destination location)
Outside global	A public IP address referencing an outside device

As a memory aid, remember that *inside* always refers to an inside device, while *outside* always refers to an outside device. Also, think of the word *local* being similar to the Spanish word *loco*, meaning crazy. That is what a local address could be considered. It is a crazy, made-up address (that is, a private IP address that is not routable on the Internet). Finally, let the *g* in *global* remind you of the *g* in *good*, because a global address is a good IP address (that is, routable on the Internet).

Based on these definitions, Table 12-3 categorizes the IP addresses previously shown in Figure 12-3.

Table 12-3 *Classifying the NAT IP Addresses Shown in Figure 12-3*

NAT IP Address	NAT IP Address Type
Inside local	10.1.1.1
Inside local	10.1.1.2
Inside global	198.51.100.3
Inside global	198.51.100.4
Outside local	N/A (There is no outside device using private IP addressing.)
Outside global	203.0.113.2

Whether an inside local address is randomly assigned an inside global address from a pool of available addresses or is assigned an address from a static configuration determines the type of NAT you are using. These two approaches to NAT are called *Dynamic NAT (DNAT)* and *Static NAT (SNAT)*:

■ **DNAT:** Dynamic NAT occurs when inside local addresses are automatically assigned an inside global address from a pool of available addresses.

■ **SNAT:** Sometimes you might want to statically configure the inside global address assigned to a specific device inside your network. For example, you might have an email server inside your company, and you want other email servers on the Internet to send email messages to your server. Those email servers on the Internet need to point to a specific IP address, not one that was randomly picked from a pool of available IP addresses. In such a case, you could statically configure the mapping of an inside local address (that is, the IP address of your internal email server) to an inside global address (that is, the IP address to which email servers on the Internet will send email for your company). This approach to NAT is referred to as static NAT (SNAT).

Dynamic NAT Configuration and Verification

You can configure dynamic NAT (where inside local addresses are translated into an inside global address by dynamically being assigned an address from a pool of available addresses) with the following steps:

Step 1. Create an access control list (ACL) to match the inside local addresses to be translated. While you could use either a named or numbered ACL and either a standard or an extended ACL, the command to create a standard numbered ACL (in global configuration mode) is **access-list** {1 – 99} **permit** *network_address wildcard_mask*.

Step 2. Define a NAT pool containing the available inside global addresses by issuing the **ip nat pool** *pool_name starting_ip ending_ip* **netmask** *subnet_mask* command in global configuration mode.

Step 3. Specify that an interface is an inside interface with the **ip nat inside** command (in interface configuration mode).

Step 4. Specify that an interface is an outside interface, with the **ip nat outside** command (in interface configuration mode).

Step 5. Associate the ACL (identifying the inside local addresses) with the NAT pool (identifying the inside global addresses) using the **ip nat inside source list** *acl* **pool** *nat_pool* command (in global configuration mode).

Example 12-3, based on the topology illustrated in Figure 12-4, shows a dynamic NAT configuration example.

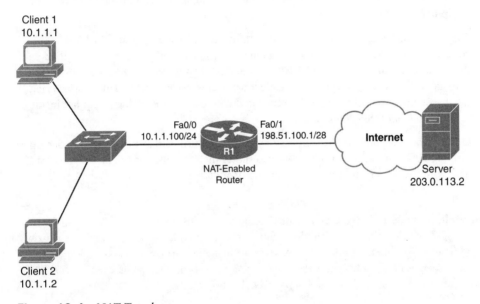

Figure 12-4 *NAT Topology*

Example 12-3 *Dynamic NAT Configuration*

```
R1# show run
... OUTPUT OMITTED ...
interface FastEthernet0/0
 ip address 10.1.1.100 255.255.255.0
 ip nat inside
!
interface FastEthernet0/1
 ip address 198.51.100.1 255.255.255.240
 ip nat outside
... OUTPUT OMITTED ...
ip nat pool ISP-POOL 198.51.100.3 198.51.100.14 netmask 255.255.255.240
ip nat inside source list 1 pool ISP-POOL
!
```

```
access-list 1 permit 10.1.1.0 0.0.0.255

R1# show ip nat translations
Pro Inside global      Inside local      Outside local      Outside global
icmp 198.51.100.3:6    10.1.1.1:6        203.0.113.2:6      203.0.113.2:6
--- 198.51.100.3       10.1.1.1          ---                ---
icmp 198.51.100.4:1    10.1.1.2:1        203.0.113.2:1      203.0.113.2:1
--- 198.51.100.4       10.1.1.2          ---                ---
```

In Example 12-3, the Fa 0/0 interface is designated as an inside interface with the **ip nat inside** command. Similarly, the Fa 0/1 interface is designated as an outside interface with the **ip nat outside** command.

The inside local addresses are identified with the **access-list 1 permit 10.1.1.0 0.0.0.255** command, and a NAT pool containing a range of inside global addresses is specified with the **ip nat pool ISP-POOL 198.51.100.3 198.51.100.14 netmask 255.255.255.240** command. The ACL specifying the inside local addresses and the NAT pool specifying the inside global addresses are then associated with one another using the **ip nat inside source list 1 pool ISP-POOL** command.

Output from the **show ip nat translations** command verifies that Router R1 is indeed performing NAT translations. The output also shows the sessions that Client 1 and Client 2 have with the Server, and the corresponding IP addresses being used.

> **Note**   In Example 12-3, the *Outside local* column contains the server's IP address of 203.0.113.2, which is the same IP address shown in the *Outside global* column. The reason these IP addresses are the same is that NAT is not being performed at the server's location. Because there is no private IP address representing the server, you can ignore the *Outside local* column for this topology (and in most NAT topologies).

Static NAT Configuration and Verification

Unlike a dynamic NAT configuration, a static NAT configuration requires no ACL or NAT pool. Instead, a series of **ip nat inside source static** *inside_local_address inside_global_address* commands can be issued (in global configuration mode) to instruct NAT how to perform its translations. The steps to perform a static NAT configuration are as follows:

Key Topic

Step 1.   Create one or more inside local address to inside global address mappings with the **ip nat inside source static** *inside_local_address inside_global_address* command in global configuration mode.

Step 2.   Specify that an interface is an inside interface with the **ip nat inside** command (in interface configuration mode).

Step 3.   Specify that an interface is an outside interface with the **ip nat outside** command (in interface configuration mode).

Example 12-4 shows a static NAT configuration performed on Router R1 from the topology in Figure 12-4.

Example 12-4 *Static NAT Configuration*

```
R1# show run
... OUTPUT OMITTED ...
interface FastEthernet0/0
 ip address 10.1.1.100 255.255.255.0
 ip nat inside
!
interface FastEthernet0/1
 ip address 198.51.100.1 255.255.255.240
 ip nat outside
... OUTPUT OMITTED ...
ip nat inside source static 10.1.1.1 198.51.100.3
ip nat inside source static 10.1.1.2 198.51.100.4

R1# show ip nat translations
Pro Inside global    Inside local     Outside local    Outside global
--- 198.51.100.3     10.1.1.1         ---              ---
--- 198.51.100.4     10.1.1.2         ---              ---
```

As you saw in Example 12-3, in Example 12-4, the Fa 0/0 interface is designated as an inside interface with the **ip nat inside** command. Also, the Fa 0/1 interface is designated as an outside interface with the **ip nat outside** command.

The **ip nat inside source static 10.1.1.1 198.51.100.3** command instructs the router to translate an inside local address of 10.1.1.1 into an inside global address of 198.51.100.3. Similarly, the **ip nat inside source static 10.1.1.2 198.51.100.4** command instructs the router to translate an inside local address of 10.1.1.2 into an inside global address of 198.51.100.4.

Also, notice that the output of the **show ip nat translations** command only shows the inside local and inside global addresses specified in the static assignments. There is no dynamic session information to show information about active sessions (such as an outside global address).

PAT

A challenge with basic NAT, however, is that there is a one-to-one mapping of inside local addresses to inside global addresses, meaning that a company would need as many publicly routable IP addresses as it had internal devices needing IP addresses. This does not scale well, because a service provider will often only provide a customer with a single IP address or a small block of IP addresses.

Fortunately, Cisco routers support *Port Address Translation (PAT)*, which allows multiple inside local addresses to share a single inside global address (that is, a single publicly routable IP address). Recall that when a client sends an IP packet, not only does that packet have a source and a destination IP address, but it also has a source and destination port number. PAT leverages these port numbers to keep track of separate communication flows.

As an example, consider Figure 12-5. Unlike the example shown in Figure 12-3, in which each inside local address was translated to its own inside global address, the example shown in Figure 12-5 only has one inside global address (198.51.100.1). This single inside global address is shared among all the devices inside a network. The different communication flows are kept separate in Router R1's NAT translation table by considering port numbers.

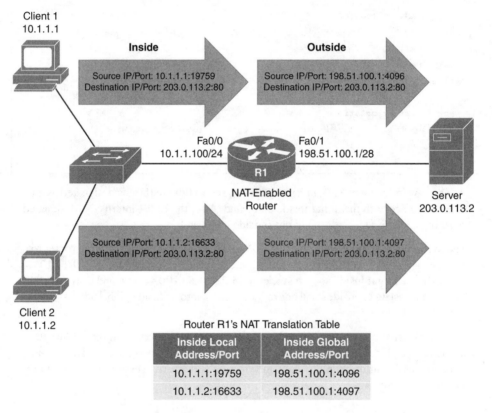

Figure 12-5 *PAT Topology*

When Client 1 (with an IP address of 10.1.1.1) sends a packet to the web server (with an IP address of 203.0.113.2), the client's ephemeral port number (that is, its source port, which is greater than 1023) is 19759. Router R1 notes that port number, and translates the inside local address of 10.1.1.1 with a port number of 19759 to an inside global address of 198.51.100.1 with a port number of 4096.

When Client 2 sends a packet to the same web server, its inside local address of 10.1.1.2 with a port number of 16633 is translated into an outside local address of 198.51.100.1 with a port number of 4097.

Notice that both Client 1 and Client 2 had their inside local addresses translated into the same inside global address of 198.51.100.1. Therefore, when the web server is sending packets back to Client 1 and Client 2, those packets are destined for the same IP address (that is, 198.51.100.1). However, when Router R1 receives those packets, it knows to which client each packet should be forwarded, based on the destination port number. For example, if a packet from the web server (203.0.113.2) arrived at Router R1 with a destination IP address of 198.51.100.1 and a destination port number of 4097, Router R1 would translate the destination IP address to 10.1.1.2 with a port number of 16633, and they forward the packet off to Client 2. The steps to configure PAT are as follows:

Key Topic

Step 1.   Create an access control list (ACL) to match the inside local addresses to be translated. While you could use either a named or numbered ACL and either a standard or an extended ACL, the command to create a standard numbered ACL (in global configuration mode) is **access-list {1 - 99} permit** *network_ address wildcard_mask*.

Step 2.   Specify that an interface is an inside interface with the **ip nat inside** command (in interface configuration mode).

Step 3.   Specify that an interface is an outside interface with the **ip nat outside** command (in interface configuration mode).

Step 4.   Associate the ACL (identifying the inside local addresses) with the router's outside interface, and enable overloading with the **ip nat inside source list** *acl* **interface** *outside_interface* **overload** command (in global configuration mode).

Example 12-5 shows a sample PAT configuration, based on the topology shown in Figure 12-5.

Example 12-5 *PAT Configuration*

```
R1# show run
... OUTPUT OMITTED ...
interface FastEthernet0/0
 ip address 10.1.1.100 255.255.255.0
 ip nat inside
!
interface FastEthernet0/1
 ip address 198.51.100.1 255.255.255.240
 ip nat outside
... OUTPUT OMITTED ...
ip nat inside source list 1 interface FastEthernet0/1 overload
!
access-list 1 permit 10.1.1.0 0.0.0.255

R1# show ip nat translations
Pro Inside global      Inside local      Outside local      Outside global
tcp 198.51.100.1:4096  10.1.1.1:19759    203.0.113.2:80     203.0.113.2:80
tcp 198.51.100.1:4097  10.1.1.2:16633    203.0.113.2:80     203.0.113.2:80
```

As in Examples 12-3 and 12-4, in Example 12-5, the Fa 0/0 interface is designated as an inside interface with the **ip nat inside** command. Also, the Fa 0/1 interface is designated as an outside interface with the **ip nat outside** command.

The **access-list 1 permit 10.1.1.0 0.0.0.255** command is used to identify inside local addresses. Then, the **ip nat inside source list 1 interface FastEthernet0/1 overload** command is used to associate the ACL defining the inside local addresses with the IP address of the Fa 0/1 interface. The **overload** parameter given in the command enables the PAT feature, allowing multiple inside local addresses to share an inside global address (specifically, the IP address of the Fa 0/1 interface).

Output from the **show ip nat translations** command shows that the same inside global address (the IP address of the Fa 0/1 interface) is being used by both Client 1 (10.1.1.1) and Client 2 (10.1.1.2). However, PAT is able to distinguish between these clients, because they have unique port numbers (4096 for Client 1 and 4097 for Client 2).

NAT Design Considerations

While NAT has done much to extend the life of IPv4, it does have limitations you should consider in your design. Consider the following:

- Applications requiring end-to-end connectivity, where source and destination IP addresses are not modified at any point on the data path, could fail because of NAT's modification of source and destination IP addresses.

- NAT might have compatibility issues with IPsec, because IPsec performs message integrity checks, which could fail because of NAT's manipulation of header contents.

- In a Public Key Infrastructure (PKI) environment, digital certificates can be used for authentication and encryption. However, the digital signature on a digital certificate could be incorrect, based on a device's IP being changed by NAT.

NVI

Cisco IOS Release 12.3(14)T introduced a feature called *NAT Virtual Interface (NVI)*, which allows you to do a NAT configuration without the need to specify an interface as being an inside or an outside interface. Specifically, instead of issuing the **ip nat inside** or **ip nat outside** command in interface configuration mode, you can issue the **ip nat enable** command. Not only does this feature make configuration easier, but it also allows traffic to flow between two interfaces that would both be considered *inside* interfaces, from a classic NAT perspective.

Note Not all platforms and Cisco IOS versions since Cisco IOS Release 12.3(14)T support the NAT Virtual Interface feature. Therefore, the **ip nat enable** command might not be accepted on your device, even though you are running Cisco IOS Release 12.3(14)T or later.

This feature is made possible by performing an additional routing operation. To better understand this change, consider how classic NAT operated. It would make a routing decision prior to performing the address translation. However, an NVI makes an initial routing decision, then performs address translation, and finally performs another routing decision (based on the translated addresses).

Example 12-6 illustrates an NVI configuration, based on the Figure 12-4 topology.

Example 12-6 *NVI Configuration*

```
R1# show run
... OUTPUT OMITTED ...
interface FastEthernet0/0
 ip address 10.1.1.100 255.255.255.0
 ip nat enable
!
interface FastEthernet0/1
 ip address 198.51.100.1 255.255.255.240
 ip nat enable
... OUTPUT OMITTED ...
ip nat inside source list 1 interface FastEthernet0/1 overload
!
access-list 1 permit 10.1.1.0 0.0.0.255
```

The only difference in the NVI configuration shown in Example 12-6 and the PAT configuration shown in Example 12-5 is the use of the **ip nat enable** command (in global configuration mode), as opposed to either the **ip nat inside** or **ip nat outside** command.

Note The NAT Virtual Interface feature can be used with a Dynamic NAT configuration or a PAT configuration, but it is not supported with a Static NAT configuration.

Exam Preparation Tasks

Planning Practice

The CCNP ROUTE exam expects test takers to review design documents, create implementation plans, and create verification plans. This section provides some exercises that can help you to take a step back from the minute details of the topics in this chapter so that you can think about the same technical topics from the planning perspective.

For each planning practice table, simply complete the table. Note that any numbers in parentheses represent the number of options listed for each item in the solutions in Appendix F, "Completed Planning Practice Tables."

Design Review Table

Table 12-4 lists several design goals related to this chapter. If these design goals were listed in a design document, and you had to take that document and develop an implementation plan, what implementation options come to mind? For any configuration items, a general description can be used, without concern about the specific parameters.

Table 12-4 *Design Review*

Design Goal	Possible Implementation Choices Covered in This Chapter
The design specifies that a router interface connecting to an ISP be assigned an IP address determined by the ISP. (2)	
The design specifies that private IP addresses be assigned to devices inside an office and that those private IP addresses be translated into publicly routable IP addresses, available from a pool of addresses provided by an ISP. (2)	
The design specifies that private IP addresses be assigned to devices inside an office and that those private IP addresses be translated into a single publicly routable IP address provided by an ISP.	

Implementation Plan Peer Review Table

Table 12-5 shows a list of questions that others might ask, or that you might think about, during a peer review of another network engineer's implementation plan. Complete the table by answering the questions.

Table 12-5 *Notable Questions from This Chapter to Consider During an Implementation Plan Peer Review*

Question	Answer
The plan requires that a remote site's Internet-facing router automatically be configured with a default static route pointing to the ISP's router. What addressing approach would support that requirement?	
NAT has a variety of descriptions for different types of IP addresses. What term is used to describe the private IP addresses assigned to devices inside a network?	
A network using NAT is configured with multiple inside interfaces. However, the plan requires that NAT be performed on traffic being routed between inside NAT interfaces. What NAT feature would make this possible?	

Create an Implementation Plan Table

To practice skills useful when creating your own OSPF implementation plan, list in Table 12-6 configuration commands related to the configuration of the following features. You might want to record your answers outside the book, and set a goal to complete this table (and others like it) from memory during your final reviews before taking the exam.

Table 12-6 *Implementation Plan Configuration Memory Drill*

Feature	Configuration Commands/Notes
Assign an IP address to a router interface connecting to an ISP (in interface configuration mode).	
Configure a default route pointing to an ISP (in global configuration mode).	
Instruct an Ethernet router interface to obtain its IP address through DHCP (in interface configuration mode).	
Instruct a router not to install a default static route based on default gateway information learned through DHCP.	
Create one or more inside local address to inside global address mappings (in global configuration mode).	

Feature	Configuration Commands/Notes
Designate an interface as an inside NAT interface (in interface configuration mode).	
Designate an interface as an outside NAT interface (in interface configuration mode).	
Create an ACL to match inside local addresses to be translated through NAT (in global configuration mode).	
Define a NAT pool containing a collection of inside global addresses (in global configuration mode).	
Associate an ACL identifying NAT inside local addresses with a NAT pool identifying NAT inside global addresses (in global configuration mode).	
Associate an ACL identifying NAT inside local addresses with a router's outside interface, and enable overloading (in global configuration mode).	
Configure an interface to use the NAT Virtual Interface (NVI) feature (in interface configuration mode).	

Choose Commands for a Verification Plan Table

To practice skills useful when creating your own OSPF verification plan, list in Table 12-7 all commands that supply the requested information. You might want to record your answers outside the book, and set a goal to complete this table (and others like it) from memory during your final reviews before taking the exam.

Table 12-7 *Verification Plan Memory Drill*

Information Needed	Command(s)
List a router's interfaces and their IP addresses, along with an indication of whether the IP address assigned to an interface was assigned through DHCP.	
Display active NAT translations.	

Review All the Key Topics

Review the most important topics from inside the chapter, noted with the Key Topic icon in the outer margin of the page. Table 12-8 lists a reference of these key topics and the page numbers on which each is found.

Key Topic

Table 12-8   *Key Topics for Chapter 12*

Key Topic Element	Description	Page Number
List	Steps to configure static IP addresses	514
Example 12-2	Dynamic IP Address Configuration	517
Table 12-2	Names of NAT IP Addresses	519
List	Steps to configure dynamic NAT	520
List	Steps to configure static NAT	522
List	Steps to configure PAT	525
Example 12-6	NVI Configuration	527

Complete the Tables and Lists from Memory

Print a copy of Appendix D, "Memory Tables," (found on the CD) or at least the section for this chapter, and complete the tables and lists from memory. Appendix E, "Memory Tables Answer Key," also on the CD, includes completed tables and lists to check your work.

Define Key Terms

Define the following key terms from this chapter, and check your answers in the glossary.

NAT, DNAT, SNAT, PAT, NVI

This chapter covers the following subjects:

- **The Basics of Internet Routing and Addressing:** This section reviews the use of public and private IP addresses in the Internet, both in theory and practice.

- **Introduction to BGP:** This section introduces several basic concepts about BGP, including the concept of autonomous system numbers (ASN), path attributes (PA), and both internal and external BGP.

- **Outbound Routing Toward the Internet:** This section examines the options and tradeoffs for how to influence outbound routes from an enterprise toward the Internet.

- **External BGP for Enterprises:** This section examines the required configuration for external BGP connections, plus a few optional but commonly used configuration settings. It also examines the commands used to verify that eBGP works.

- **Verifying the BGP Table:** This section discusses the contents of the BGP table, particularly the routes learned using eBGP connections.

- **Injecting Routes into BGP for Advertisement to the ISPs:** This section shows how you can configure an eBGP router to advertise the public IP address range used by an enterprise.

CHAPTER 13

Fundamental BGP Concepts

Enterprises almost always use some *interior gateway protocol (IGP)*. Sure, enterprises could instead choose to exclusively use static routes throughout their internetworks, but they typically do not. Using an IGP requires much less planning, configuration, and ongoing effort compared to using static routes. Routing protocols take advantage of new links without requiring more static route configuration, and the routing protocols avoid the misconfiguration issues likely to occur when using a large number of static routes.

Similarly, when connecting to the Internet, enterprises can use either static routes or a routing protocol; namely, *Border Gateway Protocol (BGP)*. However, the decision to use BGP instead of static routes does not usually follow the same logic that leads engineers to almost always use an IGP inside the enterprise. BGP might not be necessary or even useful in some cases. To quote Jeff Doyle, author of two of the most respected books on the subject of IP routing, "Not as many internetworks need BGP as you might think" (from his book *Routing TCP/IP*, Volume II).

This chapter examines the facts, rules, design options, and some perspectives on Internet connectivity for enterprises. Along the way, the text examines when static routes might work fine, how BGP might be useful in some cases, and the cases for which BGP can be of the most use.

The chapter then discusses the configuration and verification of BGP for basic operation, but with no overt attempt to influence BGP's choice of best paths. Chapter 14, "Advanced BGP Concepts," discusses the need for internal BGP (iBGP), along with BGP route filtering. Chapter 14 also examines the tools by which BGP can be made to choose different routes, and some basic configuration to manipulate the choices of best route.

"Do I Know This Already?" Quiz

The "Do I Know This Already?" quiz allows you to assess whether you should read the entire chapter. If you miss no more than two of these 15 self-assessment questions, you might want to move ahead to the "Exam Preparation Tasks" section. Table 13-1 lists the major headings in this chapter and the "Do I Know This Already?" quiz questions covering the material in those headings so that you can assess your knowledge of these specific areas. The answers to the "Do I Know This Already?" quiz appear in Appendix A.

Table 13-1   *"Do I Know This Already?" Foundation Topics Section-to-Question Mapping*

Foundation Topics Section	Questions
The Basics of Internet Routing and Addressing	1, 2
Introduction to BGP	3–5
Outbound Routing Toward the Internet	6, 7
External BGP for Enterprises	8–11
Verifying the BGP Table	12–14
Injecting Routes into BGP for Advertisement to the ISPs	15

1. Which of the following are considered private IPv4 addresses? (Choose two.)

   a. 192.16.1.1

   b. 172.30.1.1

   c. 225.0.0.1

   d. 127.0.0.1

   e. 10.1.1.1

2. Class C network 200.1.1.0/24 was allocated to an ISP that operated primarily in Asia. That ISP then assigned this entire Class C network to one of its Asian customers. Network 200.1.2.0/24 has yet to be assigned to any ISP. Which of the following is most likely to be true?

   a. 200.1.2.0/24 could be assigned to any registrar or ISP in the world.

   b. 200.1.2.0/24 will be assigned in the same geography (Asia) as 200.1.1.0/24.

   c. 200.1.2.0/24 cannot be assigned as public address space.

   d. Routers inside North American ISPs increase their routing table size by 1 as a result of the customer with 200.1.1.0/24 connecting to the Internet.

3. Router R1, in ASN 11, learns a BGP route from BGP peer R22 in ASN 22. R1 and then uses BGP to advertise the route to R2, also in ASN 11. What ASNs would you see in the BGP table on R2 for this route?

   a. 22

   b. 11

   c. 1

   d. None

4. Which of the following are most likely to be used as an ASN by a company that has a registered public 16-bit ASN? (Choose two.)

  a. 1

  b. 65,000

  c. 64,000

  d. 64,550

5. Which of the following statements is true about a router's eBGP peers that is not also true about that same router's iBGP peers?

  a. The eBGP peer neighborship uses TCP.

  b. The eBGP peer uses port 180 (default).

  c. The eBGP peer uses the same ASN as the local router.

  d. The eBGP peer updates its AS_PATH PA before sending updates to this router.

6. Which of the following is the primary motivation for using BGP between an enterprise and its ISPs?

  a. To influence the choice of best path (best route) for at least some routes

  b. To avoid having to configure static routes

  c. To allow redistribution of BGP routes into the IGP routing protocol

  d. To monitor the size of the Internet BGP table

7. The following terms describe various design options for enterprise connectivity to the Internet. Which of the following imply that the enterprise connects to two or more ISPs? (Choose two.)

  a. Single-homed

  b. Dual-homed

  c. Single-multihomed

  d. Dual-multihomed

8. Enterprise Router R1, in ASN 1, connects to ISP Router I1, ASN 2, using eBGP. The single serial link between the two routers uses IP addresses 10.1.1.1 and 10.1.1.2, respectively. Both routers use their S0/0 interfaces for this link. Which of the following commands would be needed on R1 to configure eBGP? (Choose two.)

  a. router bgp 2

  b. router bgp 1

  c. neighbor 10.1.1.2 remote-as 2

  d. neighbor 10.1.1.2 update-source 10.1.1.1

  e. neighbor 10.1.1.2 update-source S0/0

9. Enterprise Router R1, in ASN 1, connects to ISP Router I1, ASN 2, using eBGP. There are two parallel serial links between the two routers. The implementation plan calls for each router to base its BGP TCP connection on its respective loopback1 interfaces, with IP addresses 1.1.1.1 and 2.2.2.2, respectively. Which of the following commands would not be part of a working eBGP configuration on Router R1?

   a. router bgp 1

   b. neighbor 2.2.2.2 remote-as 2

   c. neighbor 2.2.2.2 update-source loopback1

   d. neighbor 2.2.2.2 multihop 2

10. The following output, taken from a **show ip bgp summary** command on Router R1, lists two neighbors. In what BGP neighbor state is neighbor 1.1.1.1?

```
...
Neighbor   V   AS   MsgRcvd   MsgSent   TblVer   InQ   OutQ   Up/Down    State/PfxRcd
1.1.1.1    4   1    60        61        26       0     0      00:45:01   0
2.2.2.2    4   3    153       159       26       0     0      00:38:13   1
```

   a. Idle

   b. Opensent

   c. Active

   d. Established

11. The following output was taken from the **show ip bgp summary** command on Router R2. In this case, which of the following commands are most likely to already be configured on R2? (Choose two.)

```
...
BGP router identifier 11.11.11.11, local AS number 11
Neighbor   V   AS   MsgRcvd   MsgSent   TblVer   InQ   OutQ   Up/Down    State/PfxRcd
1.1.1.1    4   1    87        87        0        0     0      00:00:06   Idle (Admin)
2.2.2.2    4   3    173       183       41       0     0      00:58:47   2
```

   a. router bgp 11

   b. neighbor 1.1.1.1 remote-as 11

   c. neighbor 2.2.2.2 prefix-limit 1

   d. neighbor 1.1.1.1 shutdown

12. Which of the following answers is most true about the BGP Update message?

    a. It lists a set of path attributes, along with a list of prefixes that use those PAs.

    b. It lists a prefix/length, plus the PA settings for that prefix.

    c. It lists withdrawn routes, but never in the same Update message as newly advertised routes.

    d. A single Update message lists at most a single prefix/length.

13. The following output occurs on Router R1. Which of the following cannot be determined from this output?

```
R1# show ip route 180.1.1.0 255.255.255.240
Routing entry for 180.1.1.0/28
  Known via "bgp 2", distance 20, metric 0
  Tag 3, type external
  Last update from 192.168.1.2 00:10:27 ago
  Routing Descriptor Blocks:
  * 192.168.1.2, from 192.168.1.2, 00:10:27 ago
      Route metric is 0, traffic share count is 1
      AS Hops 2
      Route tag 3
```

    a. The type of BGP peer (iBGP or eBGP) that advertised this route to R1

    b. R1's ASN

    c. The next-hop router's ASN

    d. The AS_PATH length

14. The following line of output was extracted from the output of the **show ip bgp** command on Router R1. Which of the following can be determined from this output?

```
   ...
   Network          Next Hop         Metric LocPrf Weight Path
*  130.1.1.0/28     1.1.1.1                        0 1 2 3 4 i
```

    a. The route is learned from an eBGP peer.

    b. The route has no more than three ASNs in the AS_PATH.

    c. The route is the best route for this prefix.

    d. None of these facts can be positively determined by this output.

15. Router R1 has eBGP connections to I1 and I2, routers at the same ISP. The company that owns R1 can use public address range 130.1.16.0/20. The following output lists all the IP routes in R1's routing table within this range. Which of the following answers would cause R1 to advertise the 130.1.16.0/20 prefix to its eBGP peers? (You should assume default settings for any parameters not mentioned in this question.)

```
R1# show ip route 130.1.16.0 255.255.240.0 longer-prefixes
...
O        130.1.16.0/24 [110/3] via 10.5.1.1, 00:14:36, FastEthernet0/1
O        130.1.17.0/24 [110/3] via 10.5.1.1, 00:14:36, FastEthernet0/1
O        130.1.18.0/24 [110/3] via 10.5.1.1, 00:14:36, FastEthernet0/1
```

a. Configure R1 with the **network 130.1.16.0 mask 255.255.240.0** command.

b. Configure R1 with the **network 130.1.16.0 mask 255.255.240.0 summary-only** command.

c. Redistribute from OSPF into BGP, filtering so that only routes in the 130.1.16.0/20 range are redistributed.

d. Redistribute from OSPF into BGP, filtering so that only routes in the 130.1.16.0/20 range are redistributed, and create a BGP summary for 130.1.16.0/20.

Foundation Topics

The Basics of Internet Routing and Addressing

The original design for the Internet called for the assignment of globally unique IPv4 addresses for all hosts connected to the Internet. The idea is much like the global telephone network, with a unique phone number, worldwide, for all phone lines, cell phones, and so on.

To achieve this goal, the design called for all organizations to register and be assigned one or more public IP networks (Class A, B, or C). Then, inside that organization, each address would be assigned to a single host. By using only the addresses in their assigned network number, each company's IP addresses would not overlap with other companies. As a result, all hosts in the world would have globally unique IP addresses.

The assignment of a single classful network to each organization actually helped keep Internet routers' routing tables small. The Internet routers could ignore all subnets used inside each company, and instead just have a route for each classful network. For example, if a company registered and was assigned Class B network 128.107.0.0/16, and had 500 subnets, the Internet routers just needed one route for that entire Class B network.

Over time, the Internet grew tremendously. It became clear by the early 1990s that something had to be done, or the growth of the Internet would grind to a halt. At the then-current rate of assigning new networks, all public IP networks would soon be assigned and growth would be stifled. Additionally, even with routers ignoring the specific subnets, the routing tables in Internet routers were becoming too large for the router technology of that day. (For perspective, more than 2 million public Class C networks exist, and 2 million IP routes in a single IP routing table would be considered quite large—maybe even too large—for core routers in the Internet even today.)

To deal with these issues, the Internet community worked together to come up with both some short-term and long-term solutions to two problems: the shortage of public addresses and the size of the routing tables. The short-term solutions to these problems included

- Reduce the number of wasted public IP addresses by using classless IP addressing when assigning prefixes, assigning prefixes/lengths instead of being restricted to assigning only Class A, B, and C network numbers.

- Reduce the need for public IP addresses by using *Port Address Translation* (PAT, also called NAT overload) to multiplex more than 65,000 concurrent flows using a single public IPv4 address.

- Reduce the size of IP routing tables by making good choices for how address blocks are allocated to ISPs and end users, allowing for route summarization on a global scale.

This section examines some of the details related to these three points, but this information is not an end to itself for the purposes of this book. The true goal is to understand outbound routing (from the enterprise to the Internet), and the reasons why you might or might not need to use a dynamic routing protocol, such as Border Gateway Protocol (BGP), between the enterprise and the Internet.

Public IP Address Assignment

The *Internet Corporation for Assigned Names and Numbers* (ICANN, www.icann.org) owns the processes by which public IPv4 (and IPv6) addresses are allocated and assigned. A related organization, the *Internet Assigned Numbers Authority* (IANA, www.iana.org) carries out many of ICANN's policies. These organizations define which IPv4 addresses can be allocated to different geographic regions, in addition to managing the development of the *Domain Name System (DNS)* naming structure and new *Top Level Domains (TLD)*, such as domains ending in *.com*.

ICANN works with several other groups to administer a public IPv4 address assignment strategy that can be roughly summarized as follows:

Step 1.   ICANN and IANA group public IPv4 addresses by major geographic region.

Step 2.   IANA allocates those address ranges to *Regional Internet Registries (RIR)*.

Step 3.   Each RIR further subdivides the address space by allocating public address ranges to *National Internet Registries (NIR)* or *Local Internet Registries (LIR)*. (ISPs are typically LIRs.)

Step 4.   Each type of *Internet Registry (IR)* can assign a further subdivided range of addresses to the end-user organization to use.

Figure 13-1 shows an example that follows the same preceding four-step sequence. In this example, a company in North America needs a subnet with six hosts, so the ISP assigns a /29 prefix (198.133.219.16/29). Before that happens, however, the process gave this company's ISP (NA-ISP1, an ISP in North America) the right to assign that particular prefix.

The process starts with ICANN and IANA. These organizations maintain a set of currently unallocated public IPv4 addresses. (See www.iana.org/numbers, and look for the IPv4 addresses link to see the current list.) When the American Registry for Internet Numbers (ARIN), the RIR for North America, notices that it is running out of IPv4 address space, ARIN requests a new public address block. IANA examines the request, finds a currently unallocated public address block (Step 1 in the figure), and allocates the block to ARIN (Step 2 in the figure).

Next, an ISP named NA-ISP1 (shorthand for North American ISP number 1) asks ARIN for a prefix assignment for a /16-sized address block. After ARIN ensures that NA-ISP1 meets some requirements, ARIN assigns a prefix of 198.133.0.0/16 (Step 3 in the figure). Then, when Company1 becomes a customer of NA-ISP1, NA-ISP1 can assign a prefix to Company 1 (198.133.219.16/29 in this example, Step 4).

Although the figure shows the process, the big savings for public addresses occur because the user of the IP addresses can be assigned a group much smaller than a single Class C network. In some cases, companies only need one public IP address; in other cases, they might need only a few, as with Company1 in Figure 13-1. This practice allows IRs to assign the right-sized address block to each customer, reducing waste.

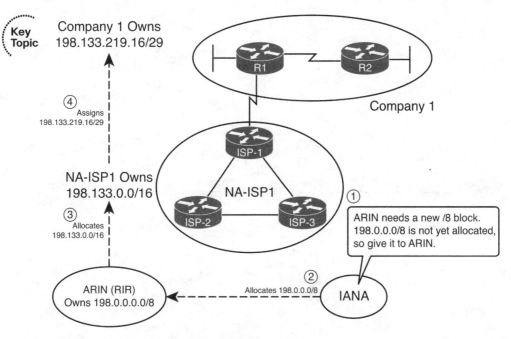

Figure 13-1 *Conceptual View of Public IPv4 Address Assignment*

Note On January 31, 2011, ICANN gave out its last two blocks of IPv4 addresses meant for general usage. This left only five blocks of usable addresses. ICANN's "Global Policy for the Allocation of the Remaining IPv4 Address Space" policy dictates how those remaining blocks (one for each Regional Internet Registry) will be given out as we approach the exhaustion of IPv4 addresses.

Internet Route Aggregation

Although the capability to assign small blocks of addresses helped extend the IPv4 public address space, this practice also introduced many more public subnets into the Internet, driving up the number of routes in Internet routing tables. At the same time, the number of hosts connected to the Internet, back in the 1990s, was increasing at a double-digit rate per month. Internet core routers could not have kept up with the rate of increase in the size of the IP routing tables.

The solution was, and still is today, to allocate numerically consecutive addresses—addresses that can be combined into a single route prefix/length—by geography and by ISP. These allocations significantly aid route summarization.

For example, continuing the same example shown in Figure 13-1, Figure 13-2 shows some of the routes that can be used in ISPs around the globe based on the address assignment shown in Figure 13-1.

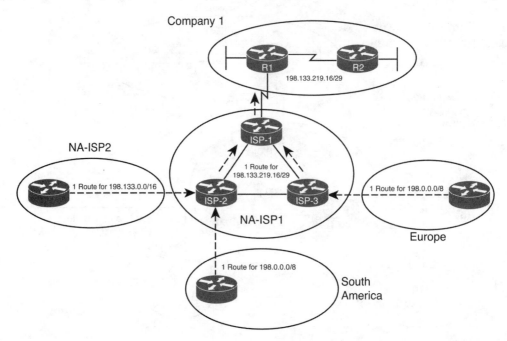

Figure 13-2 *IPv4 Global Route Aggregation Concepts*

First, focus on the routers shown in Europe and South America. Routers outside North America can use a route for prefix 198.0.0.0/8, knowing that IANA assigned this prefix to be used only by ARIN, which manages IP addresses in North America. The underlying logic is that if the routers outside North America can forward a packet into North America, the North American routers will have more specific routes. The single route for 198.0.0.0/8 shown in Europe and South America can be used instead of literally millions of subnets deployed to companies in North America, such as Company1.

Next, consider routers in North America, specifically those outside the NA-ISP1 network. Figure 13-2 shows one such ISP, named NA-ISP2 (North American ISP number 2), on the left. This router can learn one route for 198.133.0.0/16, the portion of the 198.0.0.0/8 block assigned to NA-ISP1 by IANA. Routers in NA-ISP2 can forward all packets for destinations inside this prefix to NA-ISP1, rather than needing a route for all small address blocks assigned to individual enterprises such as Company1. This significantly reduces the number of routes required on NA-ISP2 routers.

Finally, inside NA-ISP1, its routers need to know to which NA-ISP1 router to forward packets for that particular customer. So, the routes listed on NA-ISP1's routers lists a prefix of 198.133.219.16/29. As a result, packets are forwarded toward Router ISP-1 (located inside ISP NA-ISP1), and finally into Company 1.

The result of the summarization inside the Internet allows Internet core routers to have a much smaller routing table—on the order of a few hundred thousand routes instead of a few tens of millions of routes. For perspective, the website www.potaroo.net, a website maintained by Geoff Huston, who has tracked Internet growth for many years, lists a statistic showing approximately 480,000 BGP routes in Internet routers back in February 2014.

The Impact of NAT/PAT

Although classless public IP address assignment does help extend the life of the IPv4 address space, NAT probably has a bigger positive impact, because it enables an enterprise to use such a small number of public addresses. NAT allows an enterprise to use private IP addresses for each host, plus a small number of public addresses. As packets pass through a device performing NAT—often a firewall, but it could be a router—the NAT function translates the IP address from the private address (called an *inside local address* by NAT) into a public address (called an *inside global address*).

Note For the purposes of this book, the terms NAT, PAT, and NAT overload are used synonymously. There is no need to distinguish between static NAT, dynamic NAT without overload, and dynamic NAT with overload (also called PAT).

NAT reduces the need for public IPv4 addresses to only a few addresses per enterprise because of how NAT can multiplex flows using different TCP or UDP port numbers. Figure 13-3 shows a sample that focuses on a router performing NAT. The figure shows an enterprise network on the left, with the enterprise using private Class A network 10.0.0.0/8. The Internet sits on the right, with the NAT router using public IP address 200.1.1.2.

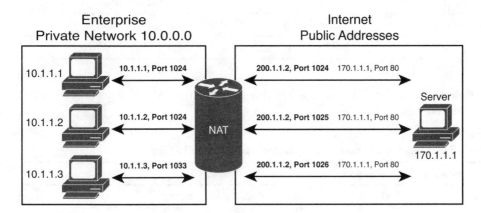

Dynamic NAT Table, With Overloading

Inside Local	Inside Global
10.1.1.1:1024	200.1.1.2:1024
10.1.1.2:1024	200.1.1.2:1025
10.1.1.3:1033	200.1.1.2:1026

Figure 13-3 *IPv4 Global Route Aggregation Concepts*

The figure shows how the enterprise, on the left, can support three flows with a single public IP address (200.1.1.2). The NAT feature dynamically builds its translation table, which tells the router what address/port number pairs to translate. The router reacts when a new flow occurs between two hosts, noting the source IP address and port number of the enterprise host on the left, and translating those values to use the public IP address (200.1.1.2) and an unused port number in the Internet. Note that if you collected the traffic using a network analyzer on the right side of the NAT router, the IP addresses would include 200.1.1.2 but not any of the network 10.0.0.0/8 addresses. Because the combination of the IP address (200.1.1.2 in this case) and port number must be unique, this one IP address can support 216 different concurrent flows.

Private IPv4 Addresses and Other Special Addresses

When allocating the public IPv4 address space, IANA/ICANN restricts themselves in several ways. Of course, the private IP address ranges cannot be assigned to any group for use in the public Internet. Additionally, several other number ranges inside the IPv4 address space, as summarized in RFC 3330, are reserved for various reasons. Tables 13-2 and 13-3 list the private addresses and other reserved values, respectively, for your reference.

Table 13-2 *Private IP Address Reference*

Number of Classful Networks	Range of Classful Networks	Prefix for Entire Range
(1) Class A	10.0.0.0	10.0.0.0/8
(16) Class B	172.16.0.0 through 172.31.0.0	172.16.0.0/12
(256) Class C	192.168.0.0 through 192.168.255.0	192.168.0.0/16

Table 13-3 lists other reserved ranges of IPv4 addresses that IANA will not allocate in the public Internet.

Table 13-3 *Reserved Values in IPv4 Address Range (RFC 3330)*

Value or Range	Reason
0.0.0.0/8	Used for self-identification on a local subnet
127.0.0.0/8	Loopback testing
169.254.0.0/16	This "link-local" block is used for default IPv4 address assignment when the DHCP process fails
192.0.2.0/24	Reserved for use in documentation and example code
192.88.99.0/24	Used for IPv6-to-IPv4 relay (6to4 relay) (RFC 3068)
198.18.0.0/15	Benchmark testing for Internet devices (RFC 2544)

In summary, every enterprise that connects to the Internet must use at least one public IP address and often several public IP addresses. Although some companies do have a large public IPv4 address block—often obtained before the shortage of public IPv4 addresses in the early to mid-1990s—most companies have a small address block, which then requires the use of NAT/PAT. These details have some impact on whether BGP is useful in a given case.

Introduction to BGP

Border Gateway Protocol (BGP) advertises, learns, and chooses the best paths inside the global Internet. When two ISPs connect, they typically use BGP to exchange routing information. Collectively, the ISPs of the world exchange the Internet's routing table using BGP. And enterprises sometimes use BGP to exchange routing information with one or more ISPs, allowing the enterprise routers to learn Internet routes.

One key difference when comparing BGP to the usual IGP routing protocols is BGP's robust best-path algorithm. BGP uses this algorithm to choose the best BGP path (route) using rules that extend far beyond just choosing the route with the lowest metric. This more complex best-path algorithm gives BGP the power to let engineers configure many different settings that influence BGP best-path selection, allowing great flexibility in how routers choose the best BGP routes.

BGP Basics

BGP, specifically BGP version 4 (BGPv4), is the one routing protocol in popular use today that was designed as an *exterior gateway protocol (EGP)* instead of as an interior gateway protocol (IGP). As such, some of the goals of BGP differ from those of an IGP, such as Open Shortest Path First (OSPF) or Enhanced Interior Gateway Routing Protocol (EIGRP), but some of the goals remain the same.

First, consider the similarities between BGP and various IGPs. BGP does need to advertise IPv4 prefixes, just like IGPs. BGP needs to advertise some information, so that routers can choose one of many routes for a given prefix as the currently best route. As for the mechanics of the protocol, BGP does establish a neighbor relationship before exchanging topology information with a neighboring router.

Next, consider the differences. BGP does not require neighbors to be attached to the same subnet. Instead, BGP routers use a TCP connection (port 179) between the routers to pass BGP messages, allowing neighboring routers to be on the same subnet or to be separated by several routers. (It is relatively common to see BGP neighbors who do not connect to the same subnet.) Another difference lies in how the routing protocols choose the best route. Instead of choosing the best route just by using an integer metric, BGP uses a more complex process, using a variety of information, called BGP path attributes (PAs), which are exchanged in BGP routing updates much like IGP metric information.

Table 13-4 summarizes some of these key comparison points.

Key
Topic

Table 13-4 *Comparing OSPF and EIGRP Logic to BGP*

OSPF/EIGRP	BGP
Forms neighbor relationship before sending routing information	Same
Neighbors typically discovered using multicast packets on the connected subnets	Neighbor IP address is explicitly configured and may not be on common subnet
Does not use TCP	Uses a TCP connection between neighbors (port 179)
Advertises prefix/length	Advertises prefix/length, called *Network Layer Reachability Information (NLRI)*
Advertises metric information	Advertises a variety of path attributes (PA) that BGP uses instead of a metric to choose the best path
Emphasis on fast convergence to the truly most efficient route	Emphasis on scalability; might not always choose the most efficient route
Link-state (OSPF) or distance-vector (EIGRP) logic	Path-vector logic (similar to distance-vector)

Note BGP also uses the term *Network Layer Reachability Information (NLRI)* to describe the IP prefix and length. This book uses the more familiar term *prefix*.

BGP ASNs and the AS_SEQ Path Attribute

BGP uses BGP path attributes for several purposes. PAs define information about a path, or route, through a network. Some BGP PAs describe information that can be useful in choosing the best BGP route, using the best-path algorithm. BGP also uses some PAs for purposes other than choosing the best path.

By default, if no BGP PAs have been explicitly set, BGP routers use the BGP AS_PATH (autonomous system path) PA when choosing the best route among many competing routes. The AS_PATH PA itself has many subcomponents, only some of which matter to the depth of the CCNP coverage of the topic. However, the most obvious component of AS_PATH, the AS_SEQ (AS_SEQUENCE), can be easily explained with an example when the concept of an *autonomous system number (ASN)* has been explained.

The integer BGP ASN uniquely identifies one organization that considers itself autonomous from other organizations. Each company whose enterprise network connects to the Internet can be considered to be an autonomous system and can be assigned a BGP ASN. (IANA/ICANN also assigns globally unique ASNs.) Additionally, each ISP has an ASN, or possibly several, depending on the size of the ISP.

When a router uses BGP to advertise a route, the prefix/length is associated with a set of PAs, including the AS_PATH. The AS_PATH PA associated with a prefix/length lists the ASNs that would be part of an end-to-end route for that prefix as learned using BGP. In a way, the AS_PATH implies information like this: "If you use this path (route), the path will go through this list of ASNs."

BGP uses the AS_PATH to perform two key functions:

■ Choose the best route for a prefix based on the shortest AS_PATH (fewest number of ASNs listed).

■ Prevent routing loops.

An example can help demonstrate the concept. This example, and some others in this chapter, uses the design shown in Figure 13-4. This network has five ASNs: three ISPs and two customers.

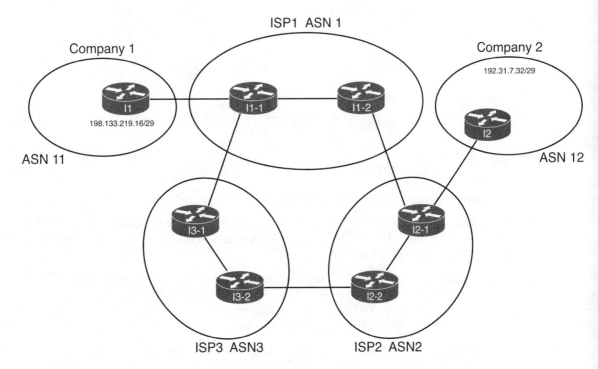

Figure 13-4 *Sample Portion of the Internet*

Figure 13-4 shows only a couple of routers in each ISP, and it also does not bother to show much of the enterprise networks for the two companies. However, the diagram does show enough detail to demonstrate some key BGP concepts. For the sake of discussion, assume that each line between routers represents some physical medium that is working. Each router will use BGP, and each router will form BGP neighbor relationships with the routers on the other end of each link. For example, ISP1's I1-2 router will have a BGP neighbor relationship with Routers I1-1 and I2-1.

With that in mind, consider Figure 13-5, which shows the advertisement of BGP updates for prefix 192.31.7.32/29 to the other ASNs. The figure shows four steps, as follows:

Step 1. I2, in ASN 12, advertises the route outside ASN 12. So, I2 adds its own ASN (12) to the AS_PATH PA when advertising the route.

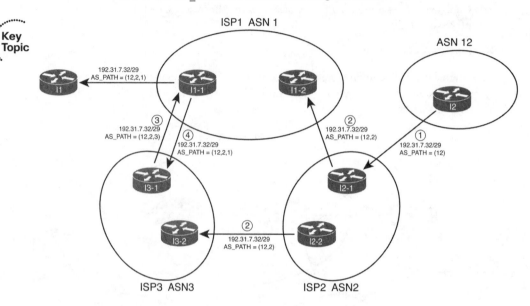

Figure 13-5 *Advertisement of NLRI to Demonstrate AS_PATH*

Step 2. The routers inside ASN 2, when advertising the route outside ASN 2, add their own ASN (2) to the AS_PATH PA when advertising the route. Their advertised AS_PATH is then (12,2).

Step 3. Router I3-1, inside ASN 3, had previously learned about the route for 192.31.7.32/29 from ASN 2, with AS_PATH (12,2). So, I3-1 advertises the route to ASN 1, after adding its own ASN (3) to the AS_PATH so that the AS_PATH is (12,2,3).

Step 4. Similarly, Router I1-1, inside ASN 1, advertises the route to ASN3. Because ASN 3 is a different ASN, I1-1 adds its own ASN (1) to the AS_PATH PA so that the AS_PATH lists ASNs 12, 2, and 1.

Now, step back from the details, and consider the two alternative routes learned collectively by the routers in ASN 1:

■ 192.31.7.32/29, AS_PATH (12,2)

■ 192.31.7.32/29, AS_PATH (12,2,3)

Because the BGP path selection algorithm uses the shortest AS_PATH, assuming that no other PAs have been manipulated, the routers in ASN 1 use the first of the two paths, sending packets to ASN 2 next, and not using the path through ASN 3. Also, as a result, note that the advertisement from ASN 1 into ASN 11 lists an AS_PATH that reflects the best-path selection of the routers inside ASN 1, with the addition of ASN 1 to the end of the AS_PATH of the best route (12,2,1).

BGP routers also prevent routing loops using the ASNs listed in the AS_PATH. When a BGP router receives an update, and a route advertisement lists an AS_PATH with its own ASN, the router ignores that route. This is because the route has already been advertised through the local ASN; to believe the route and then advertise it further might cause routing loops.

Internal and External BGP

BGP defines two classes of neighbors (peers): *internal BGP (iBGP)* and *external BGP (eBGP)*. These terms use the perspective of a single router, with the terms referring to whether a BGP neighbor is in the same ASN (iBGP) or a different ASN (eBGP).

A BGP router behaves differently in several ways depending on whether the peer (neighbor) is an iBGP or eBGP peer. The differences include different rules about what must be true before the two routers can become neighbors, different rules about which routes the BGP best-path algorithm chooses as best, and even some different rules about how the routers update the BGP AS_PATH PA.

When advertising to an eBGP peer, a BGP router updates the AS_PATH PA, but it does not do so when advertising to an iBGP peer. For example, Figure 13-6 shows the same design, with the same route advertisement, as in Figure 13-5. However, in this case, all the BGP connections have been listed as either iBGP or eBGP.

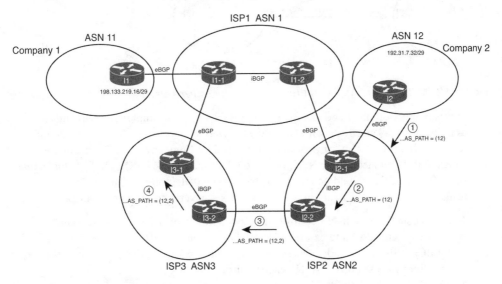

Figure 13-6 *iBGP, eBGP, and Updating AS_PATH for eBGP Peers*

The figure highlights the route advertisement from ASN 12, over the lower path through ASN 2 and 3. Note that at Step 1, Router I2, advertising to an eBGP peer, adds its own ASN to the AS_PATH. At Step 2, Router I2-1 is advertising to an iBGP peer (I2-2), so it does not add its own ASN (2) to the AS_PATH. Then, at Step 3, Router I2-2 adds its own ASN (2) to the AS_PATH before sending an update to eBGP peer I3-2, and so on.

Public and Private ASNs

For the Internet to work well using BGP, IANA administers the assignment of ASNs much like it does with IP address prefixes. One key reason why ASNs must be assigned as unique values is that if ASNs are duplicated, the BGP loop-prevention process can actually prevent parts of the Internet from learning about a route. For example, consider Figure 13-7, with the same design as in the last few figures—but this time with a duplicate ASN.

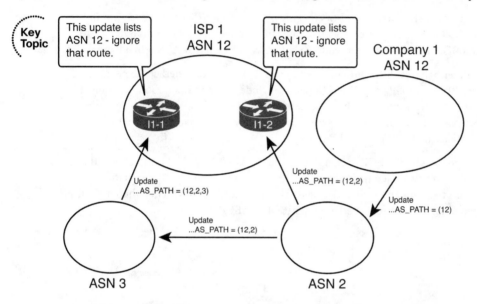

Figure 13-7 *Duplicate ASN (12) Preventing Route Advertisement*

In this figure, both ISP1 and Company 1 use ASN 12. The example's BGP updates begin as in Figures 13-5 and 13-6, with Company 1 advertising its prefix. Routers inside ISP1 receive BGP updates that list the same prefix used by Company 1, but both Updates list an AS_PATH that includes ASN 12. Because ISP1 thinks it uses ASN 12, ISP1 thinks that these BGP Updates should be ignored as part of the BGP loop-prevention process. As a result, customers of ISP1 cannot reach the prefixes advertised by routers in Company 1.

To prevent such issues, IANA controls the ASN numbering space. Using the same general process as for IPv4 addresses, ASNs can be assigned to different organizations. The 16-bit BGP ASN implies a decimal range of 0 through 65,535. Table 13-5 shows some of the details of IANA's current ASN assignment conventions.

Key Topic

Table 13-5   *16-Bit ASN Assignment Categories from IANA*

Value or Range	Purpose
0	Reserved
1 through 64,495	Assignable by IANA for public use
64,496 through 64,511	Reserved for use in documentation
64,512 through 65,534	Private use
65,535	Reserved

Like the public IPv4 address space has suffered with the potential for complete deple-tion of available addresses, the public BGP ASN space has similar issues. To help over-come this issue, the ASN assignment process requires that each AS justify whether it truly needs a publicly unique ASN or whether it can just as easily use a private ASN. Additionally, RFC 5398 reserves a small range of ASNs for use in documentation, so that the documents can avoid the use of ASNs assigned to specific organizations.

Private ASNs allow the routers inside an AS to participate with BGP, while using the same ASN as many other organizations. Most often, an AS can use a private AS in cases where the AS connects to only one other ASN. (Private ASNs can be used in some cases of connecting to multiple ASNs as well.) The reason is that with only one connection point to another ASN, loops cannot occur at that point in the BGP topology, so the need for unique ASNs in that part of the network no longer exists. (The loops cannot occur because of the logic behind the BGP best-path algorithm, coupled with the fact that BGP only advertises the best path for a given prefix.)

Outbound Routing Toward the Internet

The single biggest reason to consider using BGP between an enterprise and an ISP is to influence the choice of best path (best route). The idea of choosing the best path sounds appealing at first. However, because the majority of the end-to-end route exists inside the Internet, particularly if the destination is 12 routers and a continent away, it can be a challenge to determine which exit point from the enterprise is actually a better route.

As a result, enterprises typically have two major classes of options for outbound routing toward the Internet: default routing and BGP. Using default routes is perfectly reasonable, depending on the objectives. This section examines the use of default routes toward the Internet, and describes some of the typical enterprise BGP designs and how they can be used to influence outbound routes toward the Internet.

Comparing BGP and Default Routing for Enterprises

A *default static route* is a statically configured route that can be used by a router if a more specific route to a destination network is not found in the router's IP routing table. Oftentimes, a branch office router uses a default static route pointing toward the core of a network. The WAN edge routers then needed static routes for the subnets at each branch, with the WAN edge routers advertising these branch subnets into the core using an IGP.

The branch office default routing design results in less processing on the routers, less memory consumption, and no IGP overhead on the link between the branch and WAN distribution routers. Specifically, the branch routers can have a single or a few default routes, instead of potentially hundreds of routes for specific prefixes, all with the same next-hop information.

The same general concept of using defaults and static routes at enterprise branches can be applied to the enterprise network and its connections to one or a few ISPs. Similar to a branch router, an entire enterprise often has only a few connections to the Internet. If one of those connections is considered better than the others, all packets sent from the enterprise toward the Internet would normally follow that one Internet link, for all Internet destinations. Likewise, the ISPs, similar to WAN distribution routers in this analogy, could configure static routes for the enterprise's public IP address prefix and then use BGP in the Internet to advertise those routes. Figure 13-8 illustrates this idea.

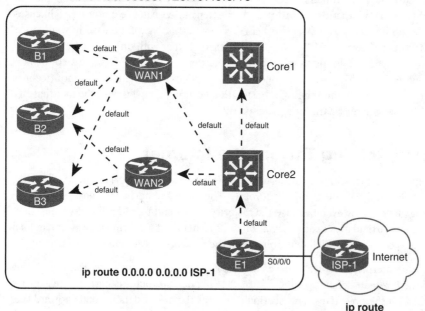

Figure 13-8 *Use of Static Default into the Internet*

Although the enterprise could choose to use BGP in this case, such a decision is not automatic. First, the alternative of using static routes, as shown in the figure, does not require a lot of work. The enterprise network engineer just needs to configure a default route and advertise it throughout the enterprise; the dashed lines in the figure represent the advertisement of the default route with the enterprise's IGP.

In addition to the configuration on the enterprise router (E1), the ISP network engineer has to configure static routes for that enterprise's public IP address range, and redistribute those routes into BGP to advertise them throughout the Internet. The figure shows a static route for Company 1's 128.107.0.0/16 public address range. Additionally, this prefix would need to be injected into BGP for advertising into the rest of the Internet.

Instead of using static default routes, you could enable BGP between E1 and ISP-1. Running BGP could mean that the enterprise router requires significant memory and more processing power on the router. The design might also require other enterprise routers besides the Internet-connected routers to know the BGP routes, requiring additional routers to have significant CPU and memory resources. Finally, although you can configure BGP to choose one route over another using PAs, the advantage of choosing one path over another might not be significant. Alternatively, you could ask the ISP to advertise only a default route with BGP.

Now that you have seen a few of the reasons why you might be fine using static routes instead of BGP, consider why you might want to use BGP. First, it makes the most sense to use BGP when you have at least two Internet connections. Second, BGP becomes most useful when you want to choose one outbound path over another path for particular destinations in the Internet. In short, when you have multiple Internet connections, and you want to influence some packets to take one path and some packets to take another, consider BGP.

This chapter next examines different cases of Internet connectivity and weighs the reasons why you might choose to use BGP. For this discussion, the perspective of the enterprise network engineer will be used. As such, outbound routing is considered to be routing that direct packets from the enterprise network toward the Internet, and inbound routing refers to routing that direct packets into the enterprise network from the Internet.

To aid in the discussion, this section examines four separate cases:

- Single-homed (1 link per ISP, 1 ISP)

- Dual-homed (2+ links per ISP, 1 ISP)

- Single-multihomed (1 link per ISP, 2+ ISPs)

- Dual-multihomed (2+ links per ISP, 2+ ISPs)

Note   The terms in the preceding list can be used differently depending on what book or document you read. For consistency, this book uses these terms in the same way as the Cisco authorized ROUTE course associated with the ROUTE exam.

Single-Homed

The *single-homed* Internet design uses a single ISP, with a single link between the enterprise and the ISP. With single-homed designs, only one possible next-hop router exists for any and all routes for destinations in the Internet. As a result, no matter what you do with BGP, all learned routes would list the same outgoing interface for every route, which minimizes the benefits of using BGP.

Single-homed designs often use one of two options for routing to and from the Internet:

- Use static routes (default in the enterprise, and a static route for the enterprise's public address range at the ISP).

- Use BGP, but only to exchange a default route (ISP to enterprise) and a route for the enterprise's public prefix (enterprise to ISP).

The previous section already showed the main concepts for the first option. For the second option, the concept still uses the IGP's mechanisms to flood a default route throughout the enterprise, causing all packets to go toward the Internet-facing router. Instead of using static routes, however, the following must happen:

- The ISP router uses BGP to advertise a default route to the enterprise.

- You must configure the IGP on the enterprise's Internet-facing router to flood a default route (typically only if the default route exists in that router's routing table).

- You must configure BGP on the enterprise router and advertise the enterprise's public prefix toward the ISP.

Both options—using static default routes and BGP-learned default routes—have some negatives. Some packets for truly nonexistent destinations flow through the enterprise to the Internet-facing router (E1 in the example of Figure 13-8) and over the link to the Internet, before being discarded for lack of a matching route. For example, if the enterprise used private network 10.0.0.0/8 internally, packets destined for addresses in network 10.0.0.0/8 that have not yet been deployed will match the default route and be routed to the Internet.

To avoid wasting this bandwidth by sending packets unnecessarily, a static route for 10.0.0.0/8, destination null0, could be added to the Internet-facing router but not advertised into the rest of the enterprise. (This type of route is sometimes called a *discard route*.) This route would prevent the Internet-facing router from forwarding packets destined for network 10.0.0.0/8 into the Internet.

Dual-Homed

The *dual-homed* design has two (or more) links to the Internet, but with all links connecting to a single ISP. This type of design can use a pair of routers, two pairs, or a combination, as shown in the three cases in Figure 13-9.

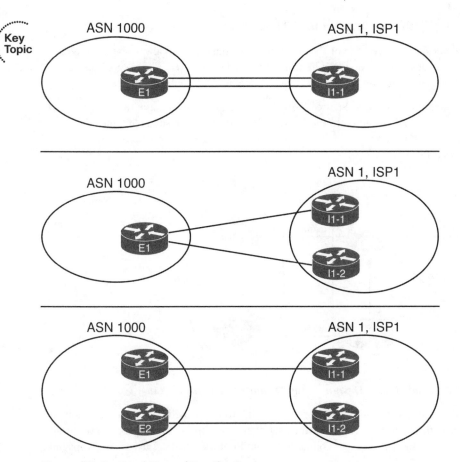

Figure 13-9 *Dual-Homed Design Options*

Comparing the dual-homed case to the single-homed design, the second link gives the enterprise a choice. The enterprise router(s) could choose between one of two links, and in the case with two enterprise routers, the choice of a different link also means the choice of sending packets to a different router.

Each of the cases shown in Figure 13-9 is interesting, but the case with two enterprise routers provides the most ideas to consider. When considering whether to use BGP in this case, and if so, how to use it, first think about whether you want to influence the choice of outbound route. The common cases when using defaults works well, ignoring BGP, are

■   To prefer one Internet connection over another for all destinations, but when the bet-ter ISP connection fails, all traffic reroutes over the secondary connection.

■   To treat both Internet connections as equal, sending packets for some destinations out each path. However, when one fails, all traffic reroutes over the one still-working path.

The text now examines each option, in order, including a discussion of how to choose the best outbound routing using both partial and full BGP updates.

Preferring One Path over Another for All Destinations

When the design calls for one of the two Internet connections to always be preferred, regardless of destination, BGP can be used, but it is not required. With a goal of preferring one path over another, the routers can use default routes into the Internet.

To demonstrate the concept, Figure 13-10 shows a dual-homed design, this time with two routers (E1 and E2) connected to the Internet. Each router has a single link into the single ISP. Figure 13-10 shows the routes that result from using default routes to forward all traffic toward Router E1.

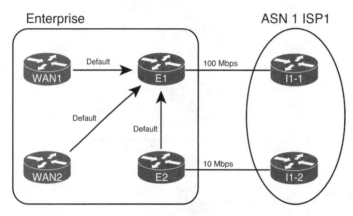

Figure 13-10 *Dual-Homed Design, Using Defaults to Favor One Link*

Figure 13-10 shows that all routers forward the Internet-destined packets toward Router E1, because this router has the faster Internet connection to ISP1 (100 Mbps in this case). Again in this example, the other connection from Router E2 to ISP1 uses a 10-Mbps link.

To make this design work, with failover, both E1 and E2 need to advertise a default route into the enterprise, but the route advertised by the primary router (E1) needs to have metrics set so that it is always the better of the two routes. For example, with EIGRP, E1 can configure a static default route with Router I1-1 as the next hop, but with very high bandwidth and very low delay upon redistribution into EIGRP. Conversely, E2 can create a default for Router I1-2 as the next-hop router, but with a low bandwidth but high delay. Example 13-1 shows the configuration of the static default route on both E1 and E2, with the **redistribute** command setting the metrics.

Note With EIGRP as the IGP, remember that the delay setting must be set higher to avoid cases where some routers forward packets toward the secondary Internet router (E2). The reason is that EIGRP uses constraining bandwidth, so a high setting of bandwidth at the redistribution point on E1 might or might not cause more remote routers to use that route.

Example 13-1 *Default Routing on Router E1*

```
! Configuration on router E1 - note that the configuration uses
! a hostname instead of I1-1's IP address
ip route 0.0.0.0 0.0.0.0 I1-1
router eigrp 1
 redistribute static metric 100000 1 255 1 1500
```

```
! Configuration on router E2 - note that the configuration uses
! a hostname instead of I1-2's IP address
ip route 0.0.0.0 0.0.0.0 I1-2
router eigrp 1
 redistribute static metric 10000 100000 255 1 1500
```

A slightly different approach can be taken in other variations of the dual-homed design, as seen back in Figure 13-9. The first two example topologies in that figure show a single router with two links to the same ISP. If the design called for using one link as the preferred link, and the engineer decided to use default routes, that one router would need two default routes. To make one route be preferred, that static default route would be assigned a better administrative distance (AD) than the other route. For example, the commands **ip route 0.0.0.0 0.0.0.0 I1-1 3** and **ip route 0.0.0.0 0.0.0.0 I1-2 4** could be used on Router E1 in Figure 13-9, giving the route through I1-1 a lower AD (3), preferring that route. If the link to I1-1 failed, the other static default route, through I1-2, would be used.

Choosing One Path over Another Using BGP

The big motivation to use BGP occurs when you want to influence which link is used for certain destinations in the Internet. To see such a case, consider Figure 13-11, which adds Company 3 to the design. In this case, Company 3 uses prefix 192.135.250.0/28 as its public address range. Company 3 might be located closer to I1-2 inside ISP1 than to Router I1-1, and in such cases, the BGP design calls for making the packets flow over the route as shown.

Two notable actions must take place for this design to work, beyond the basic configuration of the eBGP peers as shown. First, the engineers at the enterprise and ISP must agree on to how to make BGP specify a prefix as being best reached through a particular link. In this case, the routes advertised by I1-2 for prefix for 192.135.250.0/28 must have BGP PA settings that appear better than those learned from I1-1. In this case, you cannot just rely on the default of checking the AS_PATH length, because the AS_PATH length should tie, because I1-1 and I1-2 are in the same ASN. So when planning with the engineers of ISP1, the enterprise network engineer must discuss what kinds of prefixes that might work better through I1-1, which would be better through I1-2, and how the ISP might set PA values to which the enterprise routers (E1 and E2) can react.

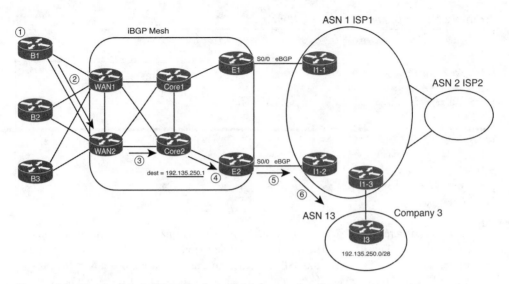

Figure 13-11 *Preferring One Outbound Link over Another*

The second big consideration occurs inside the enterprise network with a need to run BGP between multiple routers. So far in this chapter, the enterprise routers all used default routes to send packets to the Internet-facing routers, and only those routers knew Internet routes. However, for the design of Figure 13-11 to work, E1 and E2 must communicate BGP routes using an iBGP connection. And because packet forwarding between E1 and E2 goes through other routers (such as Core1 and Core2), those routers typically also need to run BGP. You might even decide to run BGP on the WAN routers as well. By doing so, the core routers know the best BGP routes. For example, they all know that the better route for Company 3's 192.135.250.0/28 public address space is through E2, so the packet is forwarded to E2. The following list outlines the logic matching Figure 13-11:

Step 1. A host at Branch B1 sends a packet to 192.135.250.1.

Step 2. Router B1 matches its default route, forwarding the packet to Router WAN2.

Step 3. WAN2 matches its iBGP-learned route for 192.135.250.0/28, forwarding to Core2.

Step 4. Core2 matches its iBGP-learned route for 192.135.250.0/28, forwarding to E2.

Step 5. E2 matches its eBGP-learned route for 192.135.250.0/28, forwarding to I1-2.

Step 6. The routers in ISP1 forward the packet to Router I3, in Company 3.

The routers in the core of the enterprise need to run BGP, because without it, routing loops can occur. For example, if WAN1, WAN2, Core1, and Core2 did not use BGP, and relied on default routes, their default would drive packets to either E1 or E2. Then, E1 or E2 might send the packets right back to Core1 or Core2. (Note that there is no direct link between E1 and E2.) Figure 13-12 shows just such a case.

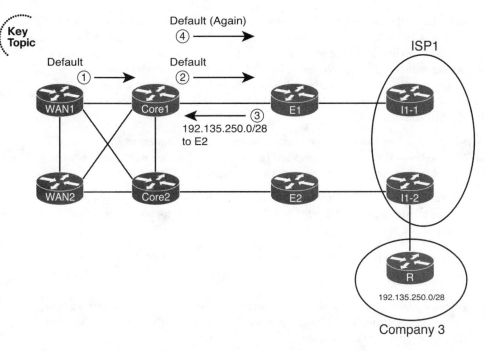

Figure 13-12 *Routing Loop Without BGP in the Enterprise Core*

In this case, both E1 and E2 know that E2 is the best exit point for packets destined to 192.135.250.0/28 (from Figure 13-11). However, the core routers use default routes, with WAN1 and Core1 using defaults that send packets to E1. Following the numbers in the figure:

Step 1.   WAN1 gets a packet destined for 192.135.250.1 and forwards the packet to Core1 based on its default route.

Step 2.   Core1 gets the packet and has no specific route, so it forwards the packet to E1 based on its default route.

Step 3.   E1's BGP route tells it that E2 is the better exit point for this destination. To send the packet to E2, E1 forwards the packet to Core1.

Step 4.   Core1, with no knowledge of the BGP route for 192.135.250.0/28, uses its default route to forward the packet to E1, so the packet is now looping.

A mesh of iBGP peerings between at least E1, E2, Core1, and Core2 would prevent this problem.

Partial and Full BGP Updates

Unfortunately, enterprise routers must pay a relatively large price for the ability to choose between competing BGP routes to reach Internet destinations. As previously mentioned, the BGP table in the Internet core is at approximately 480,000 routes as of the writing of this chapter in 2014. To make a decision to use one path instead of another, an enterprise router must know about at least some of those routes. Exchanging BGP information for such a large number of routes consumes bandwidth. It also consumes memory in the routers and requires some processing to choose the best routes. Some samples at Cisco.com show BGP using approximately 70 MB of RAM for the BGP table on a router with 100,000 BGP-learned routes.

To make matters a bit worse, in some cases, several enterprise routers might also need to use BGP, as shown in the previous section. Those routers also need more memory to hold the BGP table, and they consume bandwidth exchanging the BGP table.

To help reduce the memory requirements of receiving full BGP updates (BGP updates that include all routes), some ISPs give you three basic options for what routes the ISP advertises:

- **Default route only:** The ISP advertises a default route with BGP, but no other routes.

- **Full updates:** The ISP sends you the entire BGP table.

- **Partial updates:** The ISP sends you routes for prefixes that might be better reached through that ISP, but not all routes, plus a default route (to use as needed instead of the purposefully omitted routes).

If all you want to do with a BGP connection is use it by default, you can have the ISP send just a default route. If you are willing to take on the overhead of getting all BGP routes, asking for full updates is reasonable. However, if you want something in between, the partial updates option is useful.

BGP partial updates give you the benefit of choosing the best routes for some destinations, while limiting the bandwidth and memory consumption. With partial updates, the ISP advertises routes for prefixes that truly are better reached through a particular link. However, for prefixes that might not be any better through that link, the ISP does not advertise those prefixes with BGP. Then the enterprise routers can use the better path based on the routes learned with BGP, and use a default route for the prefixes not learned with BGP. For example, previously in Figure 13-11, Router I1-2 could be configured to only advertise routes for those such as 192.135.250.0/28 from Company 3 in that figure—in other words, only routes for which Router I1-2 had a clearly better route than the other ISP1 routers.

Single-Multihomed

A *single-multihomed* topology means a single link per ISP, but multiple (at least two) ISPs. Figure 13-13 shows a couple of single-multihomed designs, each with two ISPs.

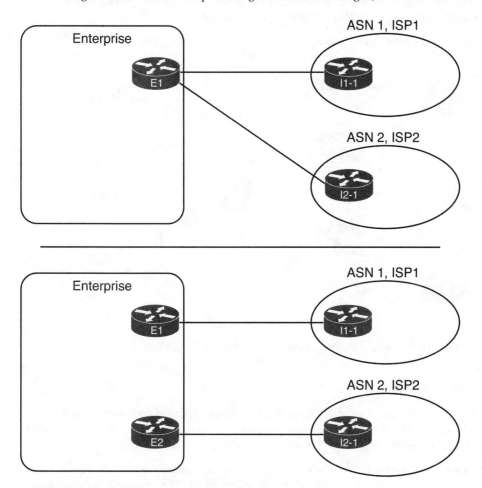

Figure 13-13 *Single-Multihomed Designs*

The single-multihomed design has some similarities with both the single-homed and dual-homed designs previously seen in this section. The single-multihomed design on the top of the figure, which uses a single router, acts like the single-homed design for default routes in the enterprise. This design can flood a default route throughout the enterprise, drawing traffic to that one router, because only one router connects to the Internet. With the two-router design on the lower half of Figure 13-13, default routes can still be used in the enterprise to draw traffic to the preferred Internet connection (if one is preferred) or to balance traffic across both.

The single-multihomed design works like the dual-homed design in some ways, because two (or more) links connect the enterprise to the Internet. With two links, the Internet design might call for the use of defaults, always preferring one of the links. The design engineer might also choose to use BGP, learn either full or partial updates, and then favor one connection over another for some of the routes.

Figure 13-14 shows these concepts with a single-multihomed design, with default routes in the enterprise to the one Internet router (E1).

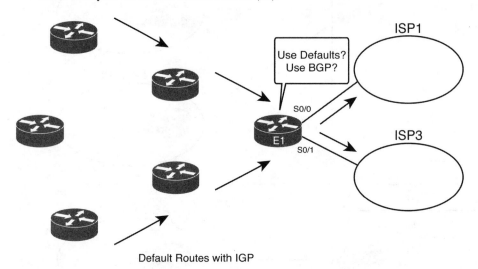

Figure 13-14   *Outbound Routing with a Single-Multihomed Design*

Dual-Multihomed

The last general category of Internet access topologies is called *dual-multihomed*. With this design, two or more ISPs are used, with two or more connections to each. A number of different routers can be used. Figure 13-15 shows several examples.

Figure 13-15 does not show all design options, but because at least two ISPs exist, with at least two connections per ISP, much redundancy exists. That redundancy can be used for backup, but most often, BGP is used to make some decisions about the best path to reach various destinations.

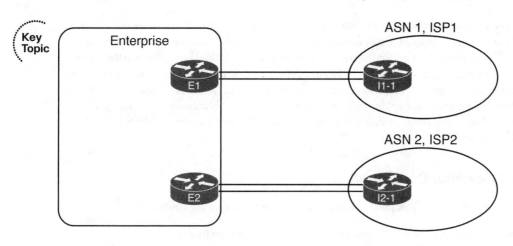

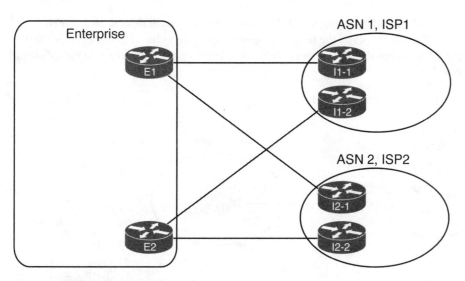

Figure 13-15   *Dual-Multihomed Options*

External BGP for Enterprises

Some of the core operational concepts of BGP mirror those of EIGRP and OSPF. BGP first forms a neighbor relationship with peers. BGP then learns information from its neighbors, placing that information in a table—the *BGP table*. Finally, BGP analyzes the BGP table to choose the best working route for each prefix in the BGP table, placing those routes into the IP routing table.

This section discusses *external BGP (eBGP)*, focusing on two of the three aspects of how a routing protocol learns routes: forming neighborships and exchanging the reachability or topology information that is stored in the BGP table. First, this section examines the baseline configuration of *eBGP peers* (also called *neighbors*), along with several optional settings that might be needed specifically for eBGP connections. This configuration should result in working BGP neighborships. Then, this section examines the BGP table, listing the prefix/length and path attributes (PA) learned from the Internet, and the IP routing table.

eBGP Neighbor Configuration

At a minimum, a router participating in BGP must configure the following settings:

- The router's own ASN (**router bgp** *asn* global command)

- The IP address of each neighbor and that neighbor's ASN (**neighbor** *ip-address* **remote-as** *remote-asn* BGP subcommand)

For example, consider a typical multihomed enterprise Internet design, as shown in Figure 13-16. In this case, the following design requirements have already been decided, but you must then determine the configuration, knowing the information in the following list and the figure:

- The enterprise uses ASN 11.

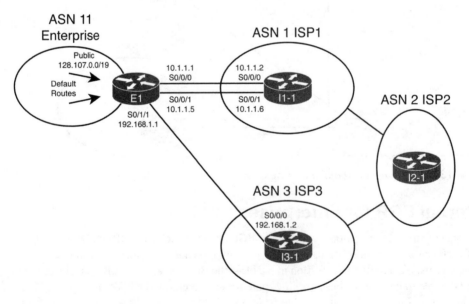

Figure 13-16   *Sample Single-Multihomed Design*

- The connection to ISP1 (two T-1s) is considered the primary connection, with the connection to ISP3 (one T-1) being secondary.

- ISP1 advertises a default route, plus full updates.

- ISP1 uses ASN 1.

- ISP3 advertises a default route, plus partial updates that include only ISP3's local customers.

- ISP3 uses ASN 3.

- Each ISP uses the IP address of its lowest-numbered interface for its peer relationships.

For Router E1, as shown in Example 13-2, the BGP configuration requires only three commands, at least to configure BGP to the point where E1 will form neighborships with the two other routers. (Note that this chapter continues to change and add to this configuration when introducing new concepts.) The example also shows the configuration on Routers I1-1 and I3-1 added solely to support the neighbor connections to E1; other BGP configuration on these routers is not shown.

Example 13-2 *BGP Configuration on E1: Neighborships Configured*

```
! Configuration on router E1
router bgp 11
 neighbor 10.1.1.2 remote-as 1
 neighbor 192.168.1.2 remote-as 3
```

```
! Next commands are on I1-1
router bgp 1
 neighbor 10.1.1.1 remote-as 11
```

```
! Next commands are on I3-1
router bgp 3
 neighbor 192.168.1.1 remote-as 11
```

The gray portions of the output highlight the configuration of the local ASN and the neighbors' ASNs—parameters that must match for the neighborships to form. First, E1 configures its own ASN as 11 by using the **router bgp 11** command. The other routers must refer to ASN 11 on the neighbor commands that refer to E1; in this case, I1-1 refers to ASN 11 with its **neighbor 10.1.1.1 remote-as 11** command. Conversely, I1-1's local ASN (1) on its **router bgp 1** global command must match what E1 configures in a **neighbor** command—in this case, with E1's **neighbor 10.1.1.2 remote-as 1** command.

Requirements for Forming eBGP Neighborships

Routers must meet several requirements to become BGP neighbors:

- A local router's ASN (on the **router bgp** *asn* command) must match the neighboring router's reference to that ASN with its **neighbor remote-as** *asn* command.

- The BGP router IDs of the two routers must not be the same.

■ If configured, authentication must pass.

■ Each router must be part of a TCP connection with the other router, with the remote router's IP address used in that TCP connection matching what the local router configures in a BGP **neighbor remote-as** command.

Consider the first two items in this list. First, the highlights in Example 13-2 demonstrate the first of the four requirements. Next, the second requirement in the list requires only a little thought if you recall the similar details about router IDs (RID) with EIGRP and OSPF. Like EIGRP and OSPF, BGP defines a 32-bit router ID, written in dotted-decimal notation. And like EIGRP and OSPF, BGP on a router chooses its RID the same general way, by using the following steps, in order, until a BGP RID has been chosen:

■ **Configured:** Use the setting of the **bgp router-id** *rid* router subcommand.

■ **Highest loopback:** Choose the highest numeric IP address of any up loopback interface, at the time the BGP process initializes.

■ **Highest other interface:** Choose the highest numeric IP address of any up nonloopback interface, at the time the BGP process initializes.

The third requirement in the list, the authentication check, occurs only if authentication has been configured on at least one of the two routers, using the **neighbor** *neighbor-ip* **password** *key* command. If two BGP neighbors configure this command, referring to the other routers' IP address, while configuring a matching authentication key value, the authentication passes. If both omit this command, no authentication occurs. However, the neighborship can still form. If the keys do not match, or if only one router configures authentication, authentication fails, resulting in no neighborship forming.

The fourth neighbor requirement—that the IP addresses used for the neighbor TCP connection match—requires a more detailed discussion. BGP neighbors first form a TCP connection. Later, BGP messages flow over that connection, which allows BGP routers to know when the messages arrived at the neighbor and when they did not.

A BGP router creates the TCP connection by trying to establish a TCP connection to the address configured in the **neighbor** *neighbor-ip* **remote-as** command. However, Cisco IOS does not require the BGP configuration to explicitly state the source address that router uses when establishing this TCP connection, and if not explicitly configured, Cisco IOS picks an IP address on the local router. By default, Cisco IOS chooses its BGP source IP address for a given neighbor as the interface IP address of the outgoing interface of the route used to forward packets to that neighbor. That's a lot of words to fight through, and much more easily seen with a figure, such as Figure 13-17, which focuses on the eBGP connection between E1 and I1-1 shown in Figure 13-16.

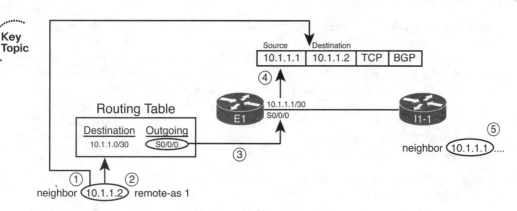

Figure 13-17 *Default Choice for Update Source*

A description of the steps in the logic shown in the figure follows:

Step 1. E1 finds the **neighbor 10.1.1.2** command, so E1 sends the BGP messages for this neighbor inside packets with destination IP address 10.1.1.2.

Step 2. E1 looks in the IP routing table for the route that matches destination 10.1.1.2.

Step 3. The route matched in Step 2 lists S0/0/0 as the outgoing interface.

Step 4. E1's interface IP address for S0/0/0 is 10.1.1.1, so E1 uses 10.1.1.1 as its source IP address for this BGP peer.

Step 5. The **neighbor** command on the other router, I1-1, must refer to E1's source IP address (10.1.1.1 in this case).

Now, consider again the last of the four requirements to become neighbors. Restated, for proper operation, the BGP update source on one router must match the IP address configured on the other router's **neighbor** command, and vice versa. As shown in Figure 13-16, E1 uses update source 10.1.1.1, with I1-1 configuring the **neighbor 10.1.1.1** command. Conversely, I1-1 uses 10.1.1.2 as its update source for this neighbor relationship, with E1 configuring a matching **neighbor 10.1.1.2** command.

Note The update source concept applies per neighbor.

Issues When Redundancy Exists Between eBGP Neighbors

In many cases, a single Layer 3 path exists between eBGP neighbors. For example, a single T1, or single T3, or maybe a single MetroE Virtual Private Wire Service (VPWS) path exists between the two routers. In such cases, the eBGP configuration can simply use the interface IP addresses on that particular link. For example, in Figure 13-16, a single serial link exists between Routers E1 and I3-1, and they can reasonably use the serial link's IP addresses, as shown in Example 13-2.

However, when redundant Layer 3 paths exist between two eBGP neighbors, the use of interface IP addresses for the underlying TCP connection can result in an outage when only one of the two links fails. BGP neighborships fail when the underlying TCP connection fails. TCP uses a concept called a *socket*, which consists of a local TCP port number and an IP address. That IP address must be associated with a working interface (an interface whose state is line status up, line protocol up, per the **show interfaces** command). If the interface whose IP address is used by BGP were to fail, the TCP socket would fail, closing the TCP connection. As a result, the BGP neighborship can only be up when the associated interface also happens to be up.

Two alternative solutions exist in this case. One option would be to configure two **neighbor** commands on each router, one for each of the neighbor's interface IP addresses. This solves the availability issue, because if one link fails, the other neighborship can remain up and working. However, in this case, both neighborships exchange BGP routes, consuming bandwidth and more memory in the BGP table.

The preferred option, which uses loopback interfaces as the TCP connection endpoints, solves the availability problem while avoiding the extra overhead. The two routers each configure a loopback interface and IP address, and use those loopback IP addresses as the source of their single BGP TCP connection. If one of the multiple links fails, the loopback interface does not fail. As long as the two routers have working routes to reach each other's loopback IP addresses, the TCP connection does not fail.

Configuring eBGP peers to use a loopback interface IP address with BGP requires several steps, as follows:

Step 1.   Configure an IP address on a loopback interface on each router.

Step 2.   Tell BGP on each router to use the loopback IP address as the source IP address using the **neighbor** *neighbor-ip* update-source *interface-id* command.

Step 3.   Configure the BGP **neighbor** command on each router to refer to the other router's loopback IP address at the neighbor IP address in the **neighbor** *neighbor-ip* **remote-as** command.

Step 4.   Make sure that each router has IP routes so that they can forward packets to the loopback interface IP address of the other router.

Step 5.   Configure eBGP multihop using the **neighbor** *neighbor-ip* ebgp-multihop *hops* command.

The first three steps in the list require configuration on both the routers. Figure 13-18 shows the details related to the first three steps, focusing on Router E1's use of its Loopback1 interface (based on Figure 13-16).

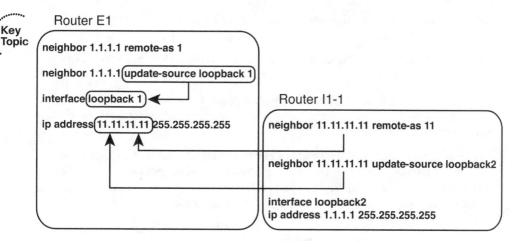

Figure 13-18 *Using Loopbacks with Update Source for eBGP*

The fourth step in the list is an overt reminder that for TCP to work, both routers must be able to deliver packets to the IP address listed in the **neighbor** commands. Because the **neighbor** commands now refer to loopback IP addresses, the routers cannot rely on connected routes for forwarding the packets. To give each router a route to the other router's loopback, you can run an instance of an IGP to learn the routes, or just configure static routes. If using static routes, make sure to configure the routes so that all redundant paths would be used (as seen in the upcoming Example 13-3). If using an IGP, make sure that the configuration allows the two routers to become IGP neighbors over all redundant links as well.

eBGP Multihop Concepts

The fifth configuration step for using loopback IP addresses with eBGP peers refers to a feature called *eBGP multihop*. By default, when building packets to send to an eBGP peer, Cisco IOS sets the IP Time-To-Live (TTL) field in the IP header to a value of 1. With this default action, the eBGP neighborship fails to complete when using loopback interface IP addresses. The reason is that when the packet with TTL=1 arrives at the neighbor, the neighbor decrements the TTL value to 0 and discards the packet.

The logic of discarding the BGP packets can be a bit surprising, so an example can help. For this example, assume that the default action of TTL=1 is used and that eBGP multihop is not configured yet. Router E1 from Figure 13-16 is trying to establish a BGP connection to I1-1, using I1-1's loopback IP address 1.1.1.1, as shown in Figure 13-18. The following occurs with the IP packets sent by E1 when attempting to form a TCP connection for BGP to use:

Step 1.   E1 sends a packet to destination address 1.1.1.1, TTL=1.

Step 2.   I1-1 receives the packet. Seeing that the packet is not destined for the receiving interface's IP address, I1-1 passes the packet off to its own IP forwarding (IP routing) logic.

Step 3.   I1-1's IP routing logic matches the destination (1.1.1.1) with the routing table and finds interface loopback 2 as the outgoing interface.

Step 4.   I1-1's IP forwarding logic decrements the TTL by 1, decreasing the TTL to 0, and as a result, I1-1 discards the packet.

In short, the internal Cisco IOS packet-forwarding logic decrements the TTL before giving the packet to the loopback interface, meaning that the normal IP forwarding logic discards the packet.

Configuring the routers with the **neighbor ebgp-multihop 2** command, as seen in the upcoming Example 13-3, solves the problem. This command defines the TTL that the router will use when creating the BGP packets (two in this case). As a result, the receiving router will decrement the TTL to 1, so the packet will not be discarded.

BGP Internals and Verifying eBGP Neighbors

Similar to OSPF, the BGP neighbor relationship goes through a series of states over time. Although the Finite State Machine (FSM) for BGP neighbor states has many twists and turns, particularly for handling exceptions, retries, and failures, the overall process works as follows:

Step 1.   A router tries to establish a TCP connection with the IP address listed on a **neighbor** command, using well-known destination port 179.

Step 2.   When the three-way TCP connection completes, the router sends its first BGP message, the BGP Open message, which generally performs the same function as the EIGRP and OSPF Hello messages. The Open message contains several BGP parameters, including those that must be verified before allowing the routers to become neighbors.

Step 3.   After an Open message has been sent and received and the neighbor parameters match, the neighbor relationship is formed and the neighbors reach the Established state.

Table 13-6 lists the various BGP states. If all works well, the neighborship reaches the final state: Established. When the neighbor relationship (also called a *BGP peer* or *BGP peer connection*) reaches the Established state, the neighbors can send BGP Update messages, which list PAs and prefixes. However, if neighbor relationship fails for any reason, the neighbor relationship can cycle through all the states listed in Table 13-6 while the routers periodically attempt to bring up the neighborship.

Key Topic

Table 13-6   *BGP Neighbor States*

State	Typical Reasons
Idle	The BGP process is either administratively down or awaiting the next retry attempt.
Connect	The BGP process is waiting for the TCP connection to be completed. You cannot determine from this state information whether the TCP connection can complete.

State	Typical Reasons
Active	The TCP connection has been completed, but no BGP messages have yet been sent to the peer.
Opensent	The TCP connection exists, and a BGP Open message has been sent to the peer, but the matching Open message has not yet been received from the other router.
Openconfirm	An Open message has been both sent to and received from the other router. The next step is to receive a BGP Keepalive message (to confirm that all neighbor-related parameters match) or a BGP Notification message (to learn that there is some mismatch in neighbor parameters).
Established	All neighbor parameters match, the neighbor relationship works, and the peers can now exchange Update messages.

Verifying eBGP Neighbor Status

The two most common commands to display a BGP neighbor's status are **show ip bgp summary** and **show ip bgp neighbors** [*neighbor-id*]. Interestingly, most people use the first of these commands, because it supplies a similar amount of information, one line per neighbor, as do the familiar **show ip eigrp neighbors** and **show ip ospf neighbor** commands. The **show ip bgp neighbors** command lists a large volume of output per neighbor, which, although useful, usually contains far too much information for the verification of the current neighbor state. Examples 13-3 and 13-4 show samples of the output of each of these two commands on Router E1, respectively, based on the configuration shown in Example 13-2, with some description following each example.

Example 13-3 *Summary Information with the* **show ip bgp summary** *Command*

```
E1# show ip bgp summary
BGP router identifier 11.11.11.11, local AS number 11
BGP table version is 26, main routing table version 26
6 network entries using 792 bytes of memory
7 path entries using 364 bytes of memory
6/4 BGP path/bestpath attribute entries using 888 bytes of memory
5 BGP AS-PATH entries using 120 bytes of memory
0 BGP route-map cache entries using 0 bytes of memory
0 BGP filter-list cache entries using 0 bytes of memory
Bitfield cache entries: current 1 (at peak 2) using 32 bytes of memory
BGP using 2196 total bytes of memory
BGP activity 12/6 prefixes, 38/31 paths, scan interval 60 secs

Neighbor        V    AS  MsgRcvd  MsgSent  TblVer  InQ OutQ  Up/Down   State/PfxRcd
1.1.1.1         4    1        60       61      26    0    0  00:45:01             6
192.168.1.2     4    3       153      159      26    0    0  00:38:13             1
```

The first line in the summary lists the local router's BGP RID (11.11.11.11), along with the local router's ASN (11). The rest of the summary focuses on statistics for the BGP table entries. The bottom of the output lists a heading line (highlighted in the output), plus one line per neighbor, with two neighbors in this case. The Neighbor column lists the IP address as defined on the local router's **neighbor** command and not the neighbor's BGP RID. Other notable information includes the neighbor's ASN (as configured on the local router's **neighbor remote-as** command), the time spent in the current state, and an interesting heading: State/PfxRcd.

This State/PfxRcd heading either lists the BGP neighbor state, as summarized in Table 13-6, or the number of prefixes received (PfxRcd) from that neighbor. A numeric value under this heading implies a neighbor state of Established, because the peers must be in the Established state before Updates can be sent. If the peer is not in an Established state, the value in this heading lists the text name of the current BGP state.

Example 13-4 shows a sample of the **show ip bgp neighbors 1.1.1.1** command on Router E1, which displays information about the connection to Router I1-1 in Figure 13-16. This command lists several facts not seen in the shorter **show ip bgp summary** command output in Example 13-3. The example highlights some of those key items, with the following comments referring to those highlighted items, in order:

- The neighbor is an eBGP neighbor (external link).

- The neighbor's BGP RID (1.1.1.1).

- The current state (Established) is explicitly listed.

- Route refresh is enabled.

- The eBGP multihop setting (two hops).

- Local and remote TCP socket information (IP addresses and port numbers).

Example 13-4 *Detailed Information with the* **show ip bgp neighbors** *Command*

```
E1# show ip bgp neighbors 1.1.1.1
BGP neighbor is 1.1.1.1,  remote AS 1, external link
  BGP version 4, remote router ID 1.1.1.1
  BGP state = Established, up for 00:45:08
  Last read 00:00:02, last write 00:00:38, hold time is 180, keepalive interval is
    60 seconds
  Neighbor capabilities:
    Route refresh: advertised and received(new)
    Address family IPv4 Unicast: advertised and received
  Message statistics:
    InQ depth is 0
    OutQ depth is 0
                       Sent        Rcvd
    Opens:              2           2
    Notifications:      0           0
```

```
    Updates:                16          12
    Keepalives:             43          47
    Route Refresh:           0           0
    Total:                  61          61
  Default minimum time between advertisement runs is 30 seconds


 For address family: IPv4 Unicast
  BGP table version 26, neighbor version 26/0
  Output queue size : 0
  Index 1, Offset 0, Mask 0x2
  1 update-group member
                              Sent       Rcvd
  Prefix activity:            ----       ----
    Prefixes Current:            6          6 (Consumes 312 bytes)
    Prefixes Total:             19          7
    Implicit Withdraw:          11          0
    Explicit Withdraw:           2          1
    Used as bestpath:          n/a          5
    Used as multipath:         n/a          0

                            Outbound   Inbound
  Local Policy Denied Prefixes:   ----       ----
    AS_PATH loop:              n/a          2
    Total:                       0          2
  Number of NLRIs in the update sent: max 3, min 1


  Address tracking is enabled, the RIB does have a route to 1.1.1.1
  Connections established 2; dropped 1
  Last reset 00:45:10, due to Peer closed the session
  External BGP neighbor may be up to 2 hops away.
  Transport(tcp) path-mtu-discovery is enabled
Connection state is ESTAB, I/O status: 1, unread input bytes: 0
Connection is ECN Disabled, Minimum incoming TTL 0, Outgoing TTL 2
Local host: 11.11.11.11, Local port: 179
Foreign host: 1.1.1.1, Foreign port: 28995
Connection tableid (VRF): 0


Enqueued packets for retransmit: 0, input: 0  mis-ordered: 0 (0 bytes)
Event Timers (current time is 0x8217A0):
Timer          Starts    Wakeups          Next
Retrans           49         0            0x0
TimeWait           0         0            0x0
AckHold           49        46            0x0
SendWnd            0         0            0x0
KeepAlive          0         0            0x0
GiveUp             0         0            0x0
```

```
PmtuAger            0           0           0x0
DeadWait            0           0           0x0
Linger              0           0           0x0
ProcessQ            0           0           0x0


iss: 2070882650  snduna: 2070884280  sndnxt: 2070884280    sndwnd:   15890
irs: 3327995414  rcvnxt: 3327996693  rcvwnd:       16156  delrcvwnd:    228


SRTT: 300 ms, RTTO: 306 ms, RTV: 6 ms, KRTT: 0 ms
minRTT: 0 ms, maxRTT: 300 ms, ACK hold: 200 ms
Status Flags: passive open, gen tcbs
Option Flags: nagle, path mtu capable, md5
IP Precedence value : 6


Datagrams (max data segment is 516 bytes):
Rcvd: 98 (out of order: 0), with data: 50, total data bytes: 1278
Sent: 99 (retransmit: 0, fastretransmit: 0, partialack: 0, Second Congestion: 0),
with data: 50, total data bytes: 1629
 Packets received in fast path: 0, fast processed: 0, slow path: 0
 fast lock acquisition failures: 0, slow path: 0
E1# show tcp brief
TCB         Local Address         Foreign Address        (state)
66D27FE0    192.168.1.1.179       192.168.1.2.16489       ESTAB
66D27378    11.11.11.11.179       1.1.1.1.28995           ESTAB
```

Note that the end of the example shows another command that you can use to confirm the TCP socket details of the underlying TCP connection: **show tcp brief**.

Administratively Controlling Neighbor Status

Interestingly, Cisco IOS provides a means by which network operations personnel can administratively disable any BGP neighbor. To do so, the operator would enter BGP configuration mode and issue the **neighbor** *neighbor-ip* **shutdown** command. This command brings down the current neighbor to an idle state. Later, when the BGP connection should be brought up, the operator should repeat the process, but with the **no** version of the command (**no neighbor** *neighbor-ip* **shutdown**).

These commands can be particularly useful to try in a lab when learning BGP. Teamed with the **debug ip bgp** command, you can bring down neighbors and see the somewhat-readable BGP messages. These messages list the BGP states from Table 13-6. They also show the information inside the Open messages. Example 13-5 shows a sample, with the debug messages that note a state transition highlighted. The output also lists the **show ip bgp summary** command output, with the administratively idle state created by the **neighbor 1.1.1.1 shutdown** BGP configuration command on Router E1.

Example 13-5 *BGP Shutdown and BGP Neighbor State Transitions*

```
E1# debug ip bgp
BGP debugging is on for address family: IPv4 Unicast
E1# conf t
Enter configuration commands, one per line.  End with CNTL/Z.
E1(config)# router bgp 11
E1(config-router)# neighbor 1.1.1.1 shutdown
E1(config-router)#

*Aug 11 20:23:01.335: BGPNSF state: 1.1.1.1 went from nsf_not_active to nsf_not_
  active
*Aug 11 20:23:01.335: BGP: 1.1.1.1 went from Established to Idle
*Aug 11 20:23:01.335: %BGP-5-ADJCHANGE: neighbor 1.1.1.1 Down Admin. Shutdown

E1(config-router)# do show ip bgp summary
! lines omitted for brevity

Neighbor        V  AS  MsgRcvd   MsgSent   TblVer  InQ   OutQ   Up/Down    State/PfxRcd
1.1.1.1         4  1    87        87        0       0     0      00:00:06   Idle (Admin)
192.168.1.2     4  3    173       183       41      0     0      00:58:47   1

E1(config-router)# no neighbor 1.1.1.1 shutdown
E1(config-router)#
*Aug 11 20:23:26.571: BGP: 1.1.1.1 went from Idle to Active
*Aug 11 20:23:26.571: BGP: 1.1.1.1 open active, local address 11.11.11.11
*Aug 11 20:23:26.575: BGP: 1.1.1.1 read request no-op
*Aug 11 20:23:26.575: BGP: 1.1.1.1 went from Active to OpenSent
*Aug 11 20:23:26.575: BGP: 1.1.1.1 sending OPEN, version 4, my as: 11, holdtime 180
  seconds
*Aug 11 20:23:26.579: BGP: 1.1.1.1 send message type 1, length (incl. header) 45
*Aug 11 20:23:26.583: BGP: 1.1.1.1 rcv message type 1, length (excl. header) 26
*Aug 11 20:23:26.587: BGP: 1.1.1.1 rcv OPEN, version 4, holdtime 180 seconds
*Aug 11 20:23:26.587: BGP: 1.1.1.1 rcv OPEN w/ OPTION parameter len: 16
*Aug 11 20:23:26.587: BGP: 1.1.1.1 rcvd OPEN w/ optional parameter type 2
  (Capability) len 6
*Aug 11 20:23:26.587: BGP: 1.1.1.1 OPEN has CAPABILITY code: 1, length 4
*Aug 11 20:23:26.587: BGP: 1.1.1.1 OPEN has MP_EXT CAP for afi/safi: 1/1
*Aug 11 20:23:26.587: BGP: 1.1.1.1 rcvd OPEN w/ optional parameter type 2
  (Capability) len 2
*Aug 11 20:23:26.587: BGP: 1.1.1.1 OPEN has CAPABILITY code: 128, length 0
*Aug 11 20:23:26.587: BGP: 1.1.1.1 OPEN has ROUTE-REFRESH capability(old) for all
address-families
*Aug 11 20:23:26.587: BGP: 1.1.1.1 rcvd OPEN w/ optional parameter type 2
  (Capability) len 2
*Aug 11 20:23:26.587: BGP: 1.1.1.1 OPEN has CAPABILITY code: 2, length 0
*Aug 11 20:23:26.587: BGP: 1.1.1.1 OPEN has ROUTE-REFRESH capability(new) for all
  address-families
```

```
BGP: 1.1.1.1 rcvd OPEN w/ remote AS 1
*Aug 11 20:23:26.587: BGP: 1.1.1.1 went from OpenSent to OpenConfirm
*Aug 11 20:23:26.591: BGP: 1.1.1.1 went from OpenConfirm to Established
*Aug 11 20:23:26.591: %BGP-5-ADJCHANGE: neighbor 1.1.1.1 Up
*Aug 11 20:23:26.603: BGP_Router: unhandled major event code 128, minor 0
```

BGP Message Summary

So far, this chapter has mentioned three of the four BGP messages. For reference, Table 13-7 lists the four BGP messages, with comparisons to EIGRP messages for perspective.

Table 13-7   *BGP Message Types*

Message	Purpose	Similarity with EIGRP
Open	Used to establish a neighbor relationship and exchange basic parameters, including ASN and authentication values.	Hello
Keepalive	Sent on a periodic basis to maintain the neighbor relationship. The lack of receipt of a Keepalive message within the negotiated Hold timer causes BGP to bring down the neighbor connection.	Hello
Update	Used to exchange PAs and the associated prefix/length (NLRI) that use those attributes.	Update
Notification	Used to signal a BGP error; typically results in a reset to the neighbor relationship.	No direct equivalent

Verifying the BGP Table

When an enterprise router has established its eBGP neighbor relationships, that router can advertise and learn routes using BGP. To learn routes, an enterprise BGP router does not need additional configuration beyond the configuration of eBGP neighbors, as discussed earlier. To advertise routes to eBGP peers, particularly the public IP address prefix(es) used by that enterprise, the enterprise BGP router needs some additional configuration, as discussed in the upcoming section "Injecting Routes into BGP for Advertisement to the ISPs."

The BGP table plays a key role in the process of learning and using routing information with BGP. A router stores all learned BGP prefixes and PAs in its BGP table. The router will later choose which route for each prefix is the best BGP route. The router can then advertise its BGP table to its neighbors, advertising only the best route for each prefix.

This section begins with a brief examination of the BGP Update process by which BGP neighbors exchange routing information. Next, the text looks at the various **show** commands that can be used to examine and confirm the contents of the BGP table.

The BGP Update Message

When a BGP neighborship reaches the Established state, those neighbors begin sending BGP Update messages to each other. The router receiving an Update places those learned prefixes into its BGP table, regardless of whether the route appears to be the best route. Like EIGRP and OSPF, BGP puts all learned routing information into its table, and then BGP processes all such potential routes to choose the best route for each prefix.

The BGP Update message itself can be revealing about the motivations behind BGP. Figure 13-19 shows the format of the Update message.

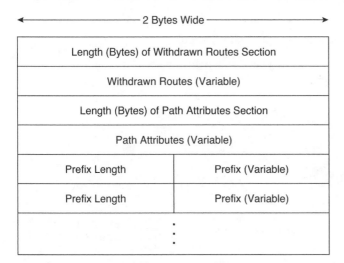

Figure 13-19 *Format of the BGP Update Message*

Interestingly, the format of the Update message tells us something about the nature of BGP as a Path Vector algorithm. The message lists a set of PAs and then a potentially long list of prefixes that use that set of PAs. So, you might view the BGP Update message as focusing on advertising paths, or a set of PAs, along with the associated list of prefixes that use the advertised path. Because BGP uses the information in the combined set of PAs to make a decision of which path is best, its underlying logic is called *path vector*.

BGP uses the Update message to both announce and withdraw routes. For example, when a router realizes that a route in the router's BGP table has failed, that router withdraws that route by sending a BGP Update to its neighbors, listing the prefix in the list of withdrawn routes. When a router receives an Update that lists a prefix as withdrawn, that router knows that the route has failed. (Note the field near the top of the Update message that lists withdrawn routes.) That same Update message might contain other announced prefixes later in the Update message.

Examining the BGP Table

One of the key tasks in a BGP verification plan should be to examine the prefixes in the BGP table and confirm that the right prefixes have been learned from the expected neighbors. The BGP table should hold all learned prefixes, from each neighbor, except for any prefixes filtered by an inbound BGP filter. For example, in a router configured with a **neighbor route-map in** command, the local router would first filter the routes and then add the allowed routes into the BGP table.

As an example, consider Figure 13-20, which shows the same basic topology as Figure 13-16 but with only the information pertinent to the upcoming discussions listed in the figure. In this case, five prefixes exist somewhere in the Internet, with ISP1 and ISP3 learning these prefixes from ISP2. An additional prefix exists at the site of a customer of ISP3. The design calls for the following actions by ISP1 and ISP3 in their eBGP advertisements to the enterprise:

■ ISP1 should supply a default route plus full BGP updates.

■ ISP3 should supply a default route plus partial BGP updates that include only ISP3's customers' prefixes (for example, 192.135.250.0/28).

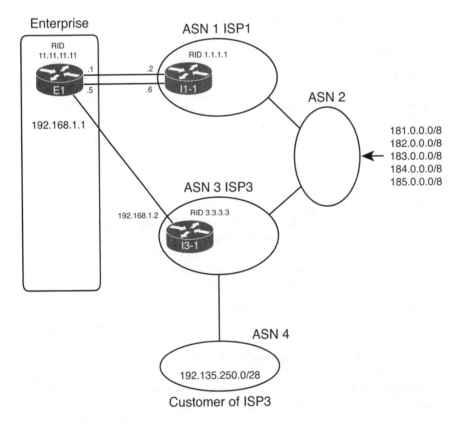

Figure 13-20 *Three Prefixes to Be Advertised to E1*

The **show ip bgp** output lists the entirety of the BGP routing table. Example 13-6 shows a sample from Router E1. Note that the configuration of this network is based on Example 13-2, with Routers E1 and I1-1 still using their loopback interfaces in their **neighbor** commands.

Example 13-6 *E1's BGP Table with Routes Learned from the ISPs*

```
E1# show ip bgp
BGP table version is 78, local router ID is 11.11.11.11
Status codes: s suppressed, d damped, h history, * valid, > best, i - internal,
              r RIB-failure, S Stale
Origin codes: i - IGP, e - EGP, ? - incomplete

   Network          Next Hop          Metric LocPrf Weight Path
*  0.0.0.0          192.168.1.2            0           0 3 i
*>                  1.1.1.1                0           0 1 i
*> 181.0.0.0/8      1.1.1.1                            0 1 2 111 111 i
*> 182.0.0.0/8      1.1.1.1                            0 1 2 222 i
*> 183.0.0.0/8      1.1.1.1                            0 1 2 i
*> 184.0.0.0/8      1.1.1.1                            0 1 2 i
*> 185.0.0.0/8      1.1.1.1                            0 1 2 i
*  192.135.250.0/28 1.1.1.1                            0 1 2 3 4 i
*>                  192.168.1.2                        0 3 4 i
```

First, examine the overall format and the headings in the output of the **show ip bgp** command. The Network column lists the prefix/length (NLRI). The Next Hop heading lists the next-hop IP address that would be used for the route. Then, skipping over to the far right, the Path heading lists the AS_PATH PA. (Note that it is difficult to see the beginning of the AS_PATH, but the weight [another PA] for each route is 0 in this case. So, the next number after the 0, in this case, is the beginning of the AS_PATH.)

Next, focus on the last two lines of output from the **show ip bgp** command. Each of the last two lines describes a different route to reach 192.135.250.0/28—one with next-hop 1.1.1.1 (Router I1-1) and one with next-hop 192.168.1.2 (Router I3-1). Because the second of these two lines does not list a prefix (under the heading "Network"), the output implies that this line is just another route for the prefix listed on the previous line. Next, examine the highlighted AS_PATH values at the end of each of these lines. For the route through I1-1 (1.1.1.1), the AS_PATH lists ASNs 1, 2, 3, and 4. Similarly, the AS_PATH for the other route lists only ASNs 3 and 4.

Note The **show ip bgp** command lists the AS_PATH with the first-added ASN on the right and the last-added ASN on the left. BGP uses this convention, because when BGP adds an ASN to the AS_PATH, BGP prepends the ASN to the list, causing the new ASN to show up as the leftmost ASN in the AS_PATH.

Continuing to focus on the final two lines of the **show ip bgp** output, examine the far left part of the output and note that the second of these two lines has a **>** highlighted. Per the legend at the top of the command output, the **>** denotes the chosen best route. In this case, none of the routers inside the various ISPs set PAs for the purpose of influencing the best-path choice, so the first-used BGP best-path decision is the shortest

AS_PATH. As a result, the path through ISP3, ASN 3, is best, having only two ASNs, compared to the path through ISP1, ASN 1, with four ASNs.

You can confirm that all of E1's BGP table entries were learned using eBGP, rather than iBGP, by the absence of the letter "i" in the third column. Immediately after the *>, a space appears in the output. If a route were learned with iBGP, an "i" would appear in this third character position. By implication, all the routes in Example 13-6 are eBGP routes because of the absence of the letter "i" in the third character of possible output.

Finally, taking a broader view of the output of the **show ip bgp** command, consider which prefixes have two known routes and which have only one. Then, consider the design requirements listed before Example 13-6: I1-1 would advertise all prefixes, plus a default, but I3-1 would advertise only partial updates plus a default. As such, I3-1 did not advertise the prefixes that begin 181 through 185, by design, resulting in Router E1 only learning one route for each of these prefixes.

E1 chose the route through I3-1 as the best route for prefix 192.135.250.0/28. Example 13-7 shows the details of the IP routing table entry for this route.

Example 13-7   *E1's IP Route for 192.135.250.0/28*

```
E1# show ip route 192.135.250.0 255.255.255.240
Routing entry for 192.135.250.0/28
  Known via "bgp 11", distance 20, metric 0
  Tag 3, type external
  Last update from 192.168.1.2 00:10:27 ago
  Routing Descriptor Blocks:
  * 192.168.1.2, from 192.168.1.2, 00:10:27 ago
      Route metric is 0, traffic share count is 1
      AS Hops 2
      Route tag 3
```

The output of the **show ip route 192.135.250.0 255.255.255.240** command lists the source of the route (BGP process 11), the next-hop router (192.168.1.2), and the AS Path length (AS Hops 2). The output also confirms that the route is an external (eBGP) route.

Viewing Subsets of the BGP Table

When accepting full or partial BGP updates, the sheer number of BGP table entries can be much too large for the **show ip bgp** command to be useful. The command could list thousands, or even hundreds of thousands, of prefixes. In practice, you need to be comfortable with a variety of options on the **show ip bgp** command, each listing a different part of the BGP table.

For example, you will likely want to look at BGP table entries for specific prefixes, including the default route prefix of 0.0.0.0/0. Additionally, you might want to see routes per neighbor, and see which routes were heard from that neighbor—and which of those routes passed through any inbound route filters to make it into the BGP table. Finally, to verify whether neighboring ISPs sent full or partial updates, you can look at counters for the number of prefixes learned from each neighbor. Although you probably will never know the exact number of prefixes to expect, you should see a significant difference in the number of prefixes learned from a neighbor sending full updates as compared to a neighbor sending partial updates.

Table 13-8 summarizes some of the key command options that can supply these subsets of information.

Table 13-8   *Verification Commands for eBGP-Learned Routes*

Verification Step	Command
List possible default routes	**show ip bgp 0.0.0.0 0.0.0.0**
List possible routes, per prefix	**show ip bgp** *prefix* [*subnet-mask*]
List routes learned from one neighbor, before any inbound filtering is applied	**show ip bgp neighbors** *ip-address* **received-routes**
List routes learned from a specific neighbor that passed any inbound filters	**show ip bgp neighbors** *ip-address* **routes**
Lists routes advertised to a neighbor after applying outbound filtering	**show ip bgp neighbors** *ip-address* **advertised-routes**
List the number of prefixes learned per neighbor	**show ip bgp summary**

Example 13-8 shows a few samples of these commands on Router E1 from Figures 13-16 and 13-20.

Example 13-8   *Command Samples from Table 13-8*

```
E1# show ip bgp 0.0.0.0 0.0.0.0
BGP routing table entry for 0.0.0.0/0, version 75
Paths: (2 available, best #2, table Default-IP-Routing-Table)
  Advertised to update-groups:
        1
  3
    192.168.1.2 from 192.168.1.2 (3.3.3.3)
      Origin IGP, metric 0, localpref 100, valid, external
  1
    1.1.1.1 from 1.1.1.1 (1.1.1.1)
      Origin IGP, metric 0, localpref 100, valid, external, best

E1# show ip bgp 192.135.250.0
BGP routing table entry for 192.135.250.0/28, version 78
Paths: (2 available, best #2, table Default-IP-Routing-Table)
  Advertised to update-groups:
     1
```

```
  1 2 3 4
    1.1.1.1 from 1.1.1.1 (1.1.1.1)
      Origin IGP, localpref 100, valid, external
  3 4
    192.168.1.2 from 192.168.1.2 (3.3.3.3)
      Origin IGP, localpref 100, valid, external, best

E1# show ip bgp summary
BGP router identifier 11.11.11.11, local AS number 11
BGP table version is 78, main routing table version 78
7 network entries using 924 bytes of memory
9 path entries using 468 bytes of memory
8/5 BGP path/bestpath attribute entries using 1184 bytes of memory
7 BGP AS-PATH entries using 168 bytes of memory
0 BGP route-map cache entries using 0 bytes of memory
0 BGP filter-list cache entries using 0 bytes of memory
Bitfield cache entries: current 1 (at peak 2) using 32 bytes of memory
BGP using 2776 total bytes of memory
BGP activity 7/0 prefixes, 53/44 paths, scan interval 60 secs


Neighbor        V    AS MsgRcvd MsgSent   TblVer  InQ OutQ Up/Down  State/PfxRcd
1.1.1.1         4     1     186     189       78    0    0 00:53:33     7
192.168.1.2     4     3     161     199       78    0    0 00:51:48     2
```

The first command, **show ip bgp 0.0.0.0 0.0.0.0**, displays details about the default routes in the BGP table. The output lists three lines per route, with the AS_PATH on the first line. Working through the highlighted portions of the output, in this case, the AS_PATH is either 3 or 1, because the ISP routers each originated the route, and those neighboring ASNs are ASN 1 and ASN 3. The output also lists the next-hop address of the route (192.168.1.2 and 1.1.1.1) and the neighbor's BGP RID (I1-1's is 1.1.1.1 and I3-1's is 3.3.3.3). Finally, instead of the **>** seen in the output of **show ip bgp**, this command simply lists the term "**best**" for the best route.

The next command, **show ip bgp 192.135.250.0**, looks much like the first. In this case, with no subnet mask listed in the command, Cisco IOS displays information for any prefix 192.135.250.0 regardless of prefix length. The output again lists three lines per route beginning with the AS_PATH values (as highlighted).

The final command, listed earlier in Table 13-8, **show ip bgp summary**, lists the number of prefixes received from each neighbor on the far right side. Also, you can see the amount of memory used for the prefixes (listed as network entries) and for different PAs.

The rest of the commands from Table 13-8 focus on displaying information relative to whether BGP filtering has yet occurred. The first, **show ip bgp neighbors** *ip-address* **received-routes**, lists routes received from the neighbor before inbound BGP filtering. The second, **show ip bgp neighbors** *ip-address* **routes**, lists routes received from that neighbor that passed through any inbound filtering. These commands are particularly useful when verifying the results of any configured BGP filters or route maps.

Injecting Routes into BGP for Advertisement to the ISPs

So far, this chapter has focused on configuring eBGP peers and the routes learned by enterprise routers from eBGP peers at ISPs. These outbound routes let the enterprise routers forward packets toward the Internet.

At the same time, the ISPs need to learn routes for the enterprise's public IP address space. This chapter assumes that the choice to use BGP has already been made, so using BGP to advertise the enterprise's public IP address range makes good sense. This short final major section of this chapter examines the options for advertising these routes. Specifically, this section looks at two options:

- BGP **network** command

- Redistribution from an IGP

Injecting Routes Using the network Command

The BGP **network** router subcommand differs significantly from the **network** command used by IGPs. For OSPF and EIGRP, the **network** command lists parameters that the router then compares to all its interface IP addresses. If matched, the router enables the IGP routing protocol on those interfaces. BGP does not use the **network** command to enable BGP on interfaces—in fact, BGP has no concept of being enabled on interfaces. For a point of comparison, note that the **show ip ospf interface** and **show ip eigrp interfaces** commands identify the enabled interfaces for OSPF and EIGRP, respectively, but no such equivalent BGP command even exists.

The BGP **network** command does cause a comparison to occur, but the comparison occurs between the **network** command's parameters and the contents of that router's IP routing table, as follows:

> Look for a route in the router's current IP routing table that exactly matches the parameters of the **network** command; if a route for that exact prefix/length exists, put the equivalent prefix/length into the local BGP table.

Note   The preceding statement, and the remaining logic in this section, assumes a BGP default setting of **no auto-summary**. The effect of reversing this setting to **auto-summary** is described in the next section.

For example, the enterprise shown earlier on the left side of Figure 13-16 might use a private address range and use NAT to translate to usable public addresses. For example, the enterprise might use private Class A network 10.0.0.0 for all private address needs and public address block 128.107.0.0/19 for public addresses. Enterprise Router E1 would then need to advertise the public prefix (128.107.0.0/19) to its ISPs, but not the private address range. Example 13-9 shows an example.

Example 13-9 *E1's Configuration of a* **network** *Command to Advertise Prefixes with eBGP*

```
router bgp 11
 network 128.107.0.0 mask 255.255.224.0
E1# sh ip bgp
BGP table version is 9, local router ID is 11.11.11.11
Status codes: s suppressed, d damped, h history, * valid, > best, i - internal,
              r RIB-failure, S Stale
Origin codes: i - IGP, e - EGP, ? - incomplete

   Network            Next Hop          Metric LocPrf Weight Path
*  0.0.0.0            192.168.1.2            0             0 3 i
*>                    1.1.1.1                0             0 1 i
*> 128.107.0.0/19     10.1.1.66              3         32768 i
*> 181.0.0.0/8        1.1.1.1                              0 1 2 111 111 i
*> 182.0.0.0/8        1.1.1.1                              0 1 2 222 i
*> 183.0.0.0/8        1.1.1.1                              0 1 2 i
*> 184.0.0.0/8        1.1.1.1                              0 1 2 i
*> 185.0.0.0/8        1.1.1.1                              0 1 2 i
*  192.135.250.0/28 1.1.1.1                                0 1 2 3 4 i
*>                    192.168.1.2                          0 3 4 i
```

The **network 128.107.0.0 mask 255.255.224.0** command lists both the subnet number and mask. It adds this prefix to the BGP table only if the exact prefix with that same mask exists in Router E1's routing table. In this case, such a route existed, so the **show ip bgp** command output that follows now lists 128.107.0.0/19 in the BGP table.

In some cases, the Internet-connected router might not have a single route for the entire public prefix. For example, with such a large range of public addresses as 128.107.0.0/19, the enterprise will most likely have broken that range into subnets, and the enterprise router might not have a route for the entire range. For example, Router E1 might see routes for 128.107.1.0/24, 128.107.2.0/24, and so on but no route for 128.107.0.0/19.

When a router knows routes only for subsets of the prefix that needs to be advertised, an additional step is needed when using the **network** command. For example, the **network 128.107.0.0 mask 255.255.224.0** command will not add this prefix to the BGP table even if routes for subsets of this range exist, such as 128.107.1.0/24. So, either configure a static route for the entire range, with outgoing interface null0, on the Internet-facing router, or use IGP route summarization to create a summary route for the entire prefix with IGP.

Note   The static route for 128.107.0.0/19 to null0—a discard route—is not meant to be advertised to other routers. Its only purpose is to enable the operation of the **network** command. This discard route should not cause routing problems on the local router, because of the more specific routes for subnets inside the same range of addresses.

Finally, the **network** command examples in this section use the mask parameter, but if omitted, Cisco IOS assumes a classful network mask. For example, a **network 9.0.0.0** command assumes a Class A default mask of 255.0.0.0, and the **network 128.1.0.0** command assumes a Class B default mask of 255.255.0.0.

The Effect of auto-summary on the BGP network Command

As of Cisco IOS Release 15.1 mainline, BGP defaults to a setting of **no auto-summary**, and the previous section's discussion of the **network** command assumed this default setting. However, if the configuration is changed to **auto-summary**, Cisco IOS makes a small change in how it interprets the **network** command.

The change in logic occurs only when the **network** command omits its **mask** parameter; there is no difference in logic if the **mask** parameter is explicitly configured. When the **network** command refers to a Class A, B, or C network, with no **mask** parameter configured and with **auto-summary** configured, the router adds a route for that classful network to the BGP table under one of the following conditions:

■ If the exact classful route is in the IP routing table

■ If any subset routes of that classful network are in the routing table

In summary, of the two actions in the list, the first occurs regardless of the **auto-summary** setting and the second occurs only if **auto-summary** is configured.

For example, with **network 9.0.0.0** configured, regardless of the **auto-summary** setting, if a route to 9.0.0.0/8 exists, the router adds 9.0.0.0/8 to the BGP table. However, if the **network 9.0.0.0** (without the mask parameter) and the **auto-summary** commands were both configured, and if only a subset route exists (for example, 9.1.1.0/24), but no route for exactly 9.0.0.0/8 exists, the router still adds a route for the classful network (9.0.0.0/8) to the BGP table. This second example demonstrates the additional logic that occurs with the **auto-summary** command configured.

Injecting Routes Using Redistribution

Instead of using a BGP **network** command to add routes to the BGP table, the enterprise BGP routers can instead redistribute routes from an IGP into BGP. The end goals are the same:

■ Inject the public address range, but not the private IP address range, into the BGP table.

■ Advertise one route for the public address range, instead of any individual subnets of the range.

The enterprise routers that run BGP often already run the IGP as well and have learned routes for either the entire public range as one route or with subset routes. If a single route exists for the entire public range, for example, the 128.107.0.0/19 range used in the last several examples, the engineer simply needs to add a **redistribute** command to the

BGP configuration to redistribute that route, and only that route, into BGP. If only subset routes exist, one of several additional steps needs to be taken to meet the design goal to inject one route for the entire public address range.

Example 13-10 shows the majority of the work in a case for which Router E1 has three subset routes in the 128.107.0.0/19 range: 128.107.1.0/24, 128.107.2.0/24, and 128.107.3.0/24. However, E1 does not have a single route for the entire 128.107.0.0/19 public prefix. The configuration matches prefixes in the public range and redistributes them into BGP.

Example 13-10   *Redistributing OSPF into BGP, but for Public Range Only*

```
router bgp 11
 redistribute ospf 1 route-map only-128-107
!
route-map only-128-107 permit
 match ip address prefix 128-107
!
ip prefix-list 128-107 permit 128.107.0.0/19 le 32

E1# show ip route 128.107.0.0 255.255.224.0 longer-prefixes
! Legend omitted for brevity

Gateway of last resort is 1.1.1.1 to network 0.0.0.0

     128.107.0.0/24 is subnetted, 3 subnets
O       128.107.3.0 [110/3] via 10.1.1.66, 00:05:26, FastEthernet0/0
O       128.107.2.0 [110/3] via 10.1.1.66, 00:05:26, FastEthernet0/0
O       128.107.1.0 [110/3] via 10.1.1.66, 00:05:36, FastEthernet0/0


E1# show ip bgp 128.107.0.0/19 longer-prefixes
BGP table version is 11, local router ID is 11.11.11.11
Status codes: s suppressed, d damped, h history, * valid, > best, i - internal,
              r RIB-failure, S Stale
Origin codes: i - IGP, e - EGP, ? - incomplete

   Network          Next Hop          Metric LocPrf Weight Path
*> 128.107.1.0/24   10.1.1.66              3         32768 ?
*> 128.107.2.0/24   10.1.1.66              3         32768 ?
*> 128.107.3.0/24   10.1.1.66              3         32768 ?
```

The two **show** commands following the configuration list the IP routes that should match the redistribution configuration, and the resulting BGP table entries. The **show ip route 128.107.0.0 255.255.224.0 longer-prefixes** command lists all three IP routes in the public address range in this case. The **show ip bgp 128.107.0.0/19 longer-prefixes** command shows the same range, listing the three BGP table entries created by the **redistribute ospf** command. These BGP table entries list the same next-hop IP addresses listed in the OSPF routes in the IP routing table, with the same metrics.

Left as is, this configuration results in Router E1 advertising all three BGP routes to the ISPs. However, to reach the goal of advertising only a single route for the entire public prefix 128.107.0.0/19, another step must be taken, typically one of the following:

■ Use IGP route summarization to create the route for the entire prefix.

■ Configure a null static route (a discard route) for the entire prefix on the Internet-connected router.

■ Configure BGP route summarization to make BGP advertise only the entire prefix.

The first two would cause Router E1 to list a route for the entire public prefix—128.107.0.0/19 in this case—in its IP routing table. The redistribution configuration could then be changed so that only that exact prefix would be redistributed. (For example, removing the **le 32** parameter from the **ip prefix-list 128-107 permit 128.107.0.0/19 le 32** command would make this command match only the exact route.)

The third option would be to use BGP route summarization, telling Router E1 that when any subset routes of 128.107.0.0/19 exist in the BGP table, advertise only 128.107.0.0/19 but none of the subset routes. Example 13-11 shows this last option.

Example 13-11 *BGP* **aggregate-address** *Command to Advertise the Entire Public IP Address Prefix*

```
E1# conf t
Enter configuration commands, one per line.  End with CNTL/Z.
E1(config)# router bgp 11
E1(config-router)# aggregate-address 128.107.0.0 255.255.224.0 summary-only
E1(config-router)# ^Z


E1# show ip bgp 128.107.0.0/19 longer-prefixes
BGP table version is 15, local router ID is 11.11.11.11
Status codes: s suppressed, d damped, h history, * valid, > best, i - internal,
              r RIB-failure, S Stale
Origin codes: i - IGP, e - EGP, ? - incomplete


   Network          Next Hop            Metric LocPrf Weight Path
*> 128.107.0.0/19   0.0.0.0                            32768 i
s> 128.107.1.0/24   10.1.1.66                3         32768 ?
s> 128.107.2.0/24   10.1.1.66                3         32768 ?
s> 128.107.3.0/24   10.1.1.66                3         32768 ?
```

Note that with the addition of the **aggregate-address** command, the BGP table now also has a route for 128.107.0.0/19, which will be advertised to E1's neighbors at the two ISPs. Also, the **summary-only** keyword in the **aggregate-address** command tells Cisco IOS to suppress the advertisement of the subset routes, as noted by the code "s" beside the other three routes listed at the end of the example.

Exam Preparation Tasks

Planning Practice

The CCNP ROUTE exam expects test takers to review design documents, create implementation plans, and create verification plans. This section provides some exercises that can help you to take a step back from the minute details of the topics in this chapter so that you can think about the same technical topics from the planning perspective.

For each planning practice table, simply complete the table. Note that any numbers in parentheses represent the number of options listed for each item in the solutions in Appendix F, "Completed Planning Practice Tables."

Design Review Table

Table 13-9 lists several design goals related to this chapter. If these design goals were listed in a design document, and you had to take that document and develop an implementation plan, what implementation options come to mind? You should write a general description; specific configuration commands are not required.

Table 13-9   *Design Review*

Design Goal	Possible Implementation Choices Covered in This Chapter
A design shows a single router connected to the Internet as part of a single-homed Internet design. It lists sections for enterprise routing toward the Internet-facing router(s) in the enterprise, and another section for choosing routes on the Internet-facing router into the Internet. List the reasonable options.	
Use the same criteria as the previous item in this table, except the single enterprise router connected to the Internet now has two links to the same ISP (dual-homed).	
Use the same criteria as the previous item, except use two routers with one link each to the same ISP (dual-homed).	
Use the same criteria as the previous row, but with a single-multihomed connection with two routers.	
The plan shows the use of public prefix 200.1.1.0/26 by an enterprise. What methods should you consider adding to your implementation plan for advertising that prefix to your ISPs using BGP? (2)	

Implementation Plan Peer Review Table

Table 13-10 shows a list of questions that others might ask, or that you might think about, during a peer review of another network engineer's implementation plan. Complete the table by answering the questions.

Table 13-10 *Notable Questions from This Chapter to Consider During an Implementation Plan Peer Review*

Question	Answer
The plan shows a single router in a dual-homed Internet design, with the router using BGP over each link to that same ISP. What criteria would impact your choice of accepting only default routes, or partial updates, or full updates, using BGP in this case? (3)	
The plan shows four enterprise routers with BGP configuration, with two of those routers with links to two different ISPs. Which connections are eBGP? iBGP?	
The plan shows enterprise Router R1, with two parallel Layer 3 paths to ISP Router R2, with a need for BGP. What options exist for high availability eBGP peering? (2) Which is better?	
The implementation plan shows an enterprise router with an eBGP connection to an ISP router, using a loopback interface as the Update source. What other feature must be configured to make the eBGP connection work?	
Router R1 connects through eBGP to Router I1 at ISP1. R1 has routes for 130.1.1.0/24 and 130.1.2.0/24 in its routing table. The design claims the company uses 130.1.0.0/21 as its public range. What methods can be used to advertise one route for the entire range to the eBGP peer? (2)	

Create an Implementation Plan Table

This chapter does not focus on implementation or verification, but it did review one concept about static routes, as listed in Table 13-11.

Table 13-11   *Implementation Plan Configuration Memory Drill*

Feature	Configuration Commands/Notes
Configure multiple static default routes, each with different administrative distance settings	
Configure an eBGP connection as follows: local AS 1, remote AS 2, remote router uses 1.1.1.1 for BGP peering, with 1.1.1.1 being an IP address on a common link between the routers.	
Configure an eBGP connection as follows: local AS 1, remote AS 2, local uses loopback1 (1.1.1.1), remote uses loopback2 (2.2.2.2).	
Administratively disable the neighbor configured in the previous two items in this table.	
Reenable the neighbor that was disabled in the previous row of this table.	
Cause the advertisement of IGP-learned prefix 130.1.1.0/24 to the neighbor configured in this table, without redistribution.	
Repeat the task in the previous row of this table, but this time with route redistribution, assuming that OSPF process 1 is used for the IGP.	

Choose Commands for a Verification Plan Table

To practice skills useful when creating your own verification plan, list in Table 13-12 all commands that supply the requested information. You might want to record your answers outside the book and set a goal to complete this table (and others like it) from memory during your final reviews before taking the exam.

Table 13-12   *Verification Plan Memory Drill*

Information Needed	Commands
Display a single-line neighbor status for each iBGP neighbor.	
Display the number of prefixes learned from a neighbor. (List where the information is located.)	

Information Needed	Commands
Display the number of prefixes advertised to a neighbor. (List where the information is located.)	
Display the local and neighbor ASN.	
Display the number of eBGP hops allowed.	
List the current TCP ports used for BGP connections.	
List all prefixes in the BGP table.	
List all the best routes in the BGP table.	
Find the AS_PATH for each BGP table entry. (Describe how.)	
Determine whether a particular BGP table entry is iBGP-learned. (Describe how.)	
Display one-line entries for all BGP table entries with a given prefix/length, plus any subnets inside that range.	
List possible default routes.	
List possible routes per prefix.	
List routes learned from one neighbor, which passed any inbound filters.	
List routes learned from one neighbor before any inbound filtering is applied.	
Display routes suppressed and added to the BGP table because of BGP route summarization (aggregation).	

Note   Some of the entries in this table might not have been specifically mentioned in this chapter but are listed in this table for review and reference.

Review All the Key Topics

Review the most important topics from inside the chapter, noted with the Key Topic icon in the outer margin of the page. Table 13-13 lists a reference of these key topics and the page numbers on which each is found.

Table 13-13 *Key Topics for Chapter 13*

Key Topic Element	Description	Page Number
Figure 13-1	Conceptual View of Public IPv4 Address Assignment	541
Table 13-4	Comparing OSPF and EIGRP Logic to BGP	546
List	Two key functions for BGP AS_PATH	547
Figure 13-5	Advertisement of NLRI to Demonstrate AS_PATH	548
Figure 13-7	Duplicate ASN (12) Preventing Route Advertisement	550
Table 13-5	16-Bit ASN Assignment Categories from IANA	551
List	Description of the terms single-homed, dual-homed, single-multihomed, and dual-multihomed	553
Figure 13-9	Dual-Homed Design Options	555
Figure 13-12	Routing Loop Without BGP in the Enterprise Core	559
List	Three options for the routes received from an ISP	560
Figure 13-15	Dual-Multihomed Options	563
List	Minimal eBGP configuration checklist	564
List	Required plus commonly used optional eBGP configuration command list	565
List	Rules for how a router chooses its BGP Router ID	566
Figure 13-17	Default Choice for Update Source	567
List	eBGP configuration checklist including use of loopbacks as Update source and eBGP Multihop	568
Figure 13-18	Using Loopbacks with Update Source for eBGP	569
Table 13-6	BGP Neighbor States	570
Table 13-7	BGP Message Types	576
Table 13-8	Verification Commands for eBGP-Learned Routes	581

Complete the Tables and Lists from Memory

Print a copy of Appendix D, "Memory Tables," (found on the CD) or at least the section for this chapter, and complete the tables and lists from memory. Appendix E, "Memory Tables Answer Key," also on the CD, includes completed tables and lists to check your work.

Define Key Terms

Define the following key terms from this chapter, and check your answers in the glossary.

public IP address, private IP address, Network Address Translation (NAT), Port Address Translation (PAT), AS_SEQUENCE, Path Attribute (PA), AS path, public ASN, private ASN, default route, single-homed, dual-homed, single-multihomed, dual-multihomed, autonomous system number (ASN), eBGP multihop, Update Source (BGP), Established (BGP state), Open, Update, Active (BGP state), BGP table

This chapter covers the following subjects:

- **Internal BGP Between Internet-Connected Routers:** This section examines the need for iBGP peering inside an enterprise, and both the required and the commonly used optional configuration settings.

- **Avoiding Routing Loops When Forwarding Toward the Internet:** This section discusses the issues that can occur when Internet-connected routers forward packets to each other through routers that do not use BGP, and how such a design requires some means to supply BGP-learned routes to the internal enterprise routers.

- **Route Filtering and Clearing BGP Peers:** This section gives a brief description of the options for filtering the contents of BGP Updates, along with explaining some operational issues related to the BGP **clear** command.

- **BGP Path Attributes and Best Path Algorithm:** This section describes the BGP *Path Attributes* (PA) that have an impact on the BGP best path algorithm–the algorithm BGP uses to choose the best BGP route for each destination prefix.

- **Influencing an Enterprise's Outbound Routes:** This section shows how to use the BGP features that influence the BGP best path algorithm.

- **Influencing an Enterprise's Inbound Routes with MED:** This section shows how to use the *Multi-Exit Discriminator* (MED) BGP feature that influences the BGP best path algorithm for inbound routes.

CHAPTER 14

Advanced BGP Concepts

Outbound routing is simple with a single Internet-connected router. An enterprise interior gateway protocol (IGP) could flood a default route throughout the enterprise, funneling all Internet traffic toward the one Internet-connected router. That router could then choose the best route to any and all Internet destinations it learned with external BGP (eBGP).

With two (or more) Internet-connected routers in a single enterprise, additional issues arise; in particular, issues related to outbound routing. These issues require the use of Border Gateway Protocol (BGP) between enterprise routers. In some cases, the design might require BGP even on enterprise routers that do not peer with routers at the various Internet service providers (ISP). This chapter examines the scenarios in which using internal BGP (iBGP) makes sense, and shows the related configuration and verification commands.

This chapter begins by focusing on the issues that can occur when an enterprise uses a pair of Internet-connected routers. Specifically, the examples use the sample network shown in Figure 14-1. This design uses the same ISPs and ISP routers as in Chapter 13, "Fundamental BGP Concepts," with familiar IP address ranges but with a few different links. The design now also shows two of the core routers (actually Layer 3 switches) inside the enterprise—routers that do not directly connect to any ISP. Figure 14-1 shows the design that will be referenced in the first few sections of this chapter.

Note Figure 14-1 shows the IP addresses as just the last octet of the address; in these cases, the first three octets are 10.1.1.

The first section of this chapter focuses on concepts, configuration, and verification of the iBGP connection between E1 and E2 in the figure. The second major section of this chapter, "Avoiding Routing Loops When Forwarding Toward the Internet," examines the need for iBGP on routers internal to the enterprise, such as Routers Core1 and Core2 in the figure. The third section of this chapter examines the process of filtering both iBGP and eBGP routing updates.

IGPs choose the best route based on some very straightforward concepts. Routing Information Protocol (RIP) uses the least number of router hops between a router and the destination subnet. Enhanced Interior Gateway Routing Protocol (EIGRP) uses a formula based on a combination of the constraining bandwidth and least delay, and Open Shortest Path First (OSPF) uses lowest cost with that cost based on bandwidth.

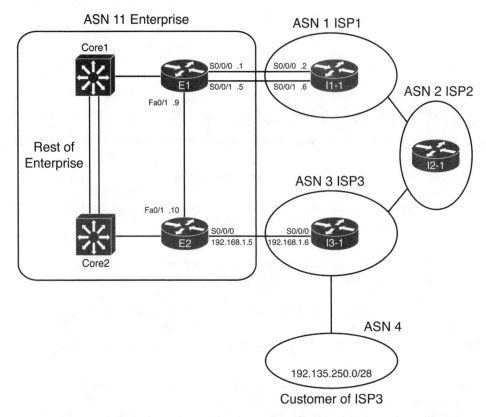

Figure 14-1   *Dual Internet Router Design Used in Chapter 14*

BGP uses a much more detailed process to choose the best BGP route. BGP does not consider router hops, bandwidth, or delay when choosing the best route to reach each subnet. Instead, BGP defines several items to compare about the competing routes, in a particular order. Some of these comparisons use BGP features that can be set based on the router configuration, allowing network engineers to then influence which path BGP chooses as the best path.

BGP's broader set of tools allows much more flexibility when influencing the choice of best route. This BGP best-path process also requires only simple comparisons by the router to choose the best route for a prefix. Although the detail of the BGP best-path selection process requires more work to understand, that complexity gives engineers additional design and implementation options, and gives engineers many options to achieve their goals when working with the large interconnected networks that comprise the Internet.

This chapter completes the BGP coverage in this book by examining the topic of BGP Path Control, including BGP Path Attributes, the BGP Best Path selection process, along with a discussion of how to use four different features to influence the choice of best path by setting BGP Path Attribute (PA) values.

"Do I Know This Already?" Quiz

The "Do I Know This Already?" quiz allows you to assess whether you should read the entire chapter. If you miss no more than two of these 14 self-assessment questions, you might want to move ahead to the "Exam Preparation Tasks" section. Table 14-1 lists the major headings in this chapter and the "Do I Know This Already?" quiz questions covering the material in those headings so that you can assess your knowledge of these specific areas. The answers to the "Do I Know This Already?" quiz appear in Appendix A.

Table 14-1   *"Do I Know This Already?" Foundation Topics Section-to-Question Mapping*

Foundation Topics Section	Questions
Internal BGP Between Internet-Connected Routers	1–4
BGP Synchronization and iBGP Meshes	5
Route Filtering and Clearing BGP Peers	6–8
BGP Path Attributes and Best-Path Algorithm	9–11
Influencing an Enterprise's Outbound Routes	12, 13
Influencing an Enterprise's Inbound Routes with MED	14

1. R1 in ASN 1 with loopback1 address 1.1.1.1 needs to be configured with an iBGP connection to R2 with loopback2 IP address 2.2.2.2. The connection should use the loopbacks. Which of the following commands is required on R1?

   a. neighbor 1.1.1.1 remote-as 1

   b. neighbor 2.2.2.2 remote-as 2

   c. neighbor 2.2.2.2 update-source loopback1

   d. neighbor 2.2.2.2 ibgp-multihop 2

   e. neighbor 2.2.2.2 ibgp-mode

2. The following output occurred as a result of the **show ip bgp** command on Router R1. The output shows all BGP table entries on R1. How many iBGP-learned routes exist on this router?

   ```
   *>i181.0.0.0/8      10.100.1.1            0    100    0 1 2 111 112 i
   *>i182.0.0.0/8      10.100.1.1            0    100    0 1 2 222 i
   *>i183.0.0.0/8      10.100.1.1            0    100    0 1 2 i
   *>i184.0.0.0/8      10.100.1.1            0    100    0 1 2 i
   *> 192.135.250.0/28 192.168.1.6                        0 3 4 i
   ```

   a. 1

   b. 2

   c. 3

   d. 4

   e. 5

3. The following output on Router R1 lists details of a BGP route for 190.1.0.0/16. Which of the following are true based on this output? (Choose two.)

```
R1# show ip bgp 190.1.0.0/16
BGP routing table entry for 190.1.0.0/16, version 121
Paths: (1 available, best #1, table Default-IP-Routing-Table)
  Advertised to update-groups:
      1
  1 2 3 4
    1.1.1.1 from 2.2.2.2 (3.3.3.3)
      Origin IGP, metric 0, localpref 100, valid, internal, best
```

    a. R1 has a **neighbor 1.1.1.1** command configured.

    b. R1 has a **neighbor 2.2.2.2** command configured.

    c. The **show ip bgp** command lists a line for 190.1.0.0/16 with both an **>** and an **i** on the left.

    d. R1 is in ASN 1.

4. A company uses Routers R1 and R2 to connect to ISP1 and ISP2, respectively, with Routers I1 and I2 used at the ISPs. R1 peers with I1 and R2. R2 peers with I2 and R1. Assuming that as many default settings as possible are used on all four routers, which of the following is true about the next-hop IP address for routes R1 learns over its iBGP connection to R2?

    a. The next hop is I2's BGP RID.

    b. The next hop is I2's IP address used on the R2-I2 neighbor relationship.

    c. The next hop is R2's BGP RID.

    d. The next hop is R2's IP address used on the R1-R2 neighbor relationship.

5. A company uses Routers R1 and R2 to connect to ISP1 and ISP2, respectively, with Routers I1 and I2 used at the ISPs. R1 peers with I1 and R2. R2 peers with I2 and R1. R1 and R2 do not share a common subnet, relying on other routers internal to the enterprise for IP connectivity between the two routers. Which of the following could be used to prevent potential routing loops in this design? (Choose two.)

    a. Using an iBGP mesh inside the enterprise core

    b. Configuring default routes in the enterprise pointing to both R1 and R2

    c. Redistributing BGP routes into the enterprise IGP

    d. Tunneling the packets for the iBGP connection between R1 and R2

6. R1 is currently advertising prefixes 1.0.0.0/8, 2.0.0.0/8, and 3.0.0.0/8 over its eBGP connection to neighbor 2.2.2.2 (R2). An engineer configures a prefix list (fred) on R1 that permits only 2.0.0.0/8 and then enables the filter with the **neighbor R2 prefix-list fred out** command. Upon exiting configuration mode, the engineer uses some **show** commands on R1, but no other commands. Which of the following is true in this case?

   a. The **show ip bgp neighbor 2.2.2.2 received-routes** command lists the three original prefixes.

   b. The **show ip bgp neighbor 2.2.2.2 advertised-routes** command lists the three original prefixes.

   c. The **show ip bgp neighbor 2.2.2.2 routes** command lists the three original prefixes.

   d. The **show ip bgp neighbor 2.2.2.2 routes** command lists only 2.0.0.0/8.

   e. The **show ip bgp neighbor 2.2.2.2 advertised-routes** command lists only 2.0.0.0/8.

7. Which of the following BGP filtering methods enabled with the **neighbor** command will filter BGP prefixes based on the prefix and prefix length? (Choose three.)

   a. A **neighbor distribute-list out** command, referencing a standard ACL

   b. A **neighbor prefix-list out** command

   c. A **neighbor filter-list out** command

   d. A **neighbor distribute-list out** command, referencing an extended ACL

   e. A **neighbor route-map out** command

8. Which of the following commands cause a router to bring down BGP neighbor relationships? (Choose two.)

   a. clear ip bgp *

   b. clear ip bgp 1.1.1.1

   c. clear ip bgp * soft

   d. clear ip bgp 1.1.1.1 out

9. An engineer is preparing an implementation plan in which the configuration needs to influence BGP's choice of best path. Which of the following is least likely to be used by the configuration in this implementation plan?

   a. Weight

   b. Origin code

   c. AS_Path

   d. Local_Pref

10. Router R1 learns two routes with BGP for prefix 200.1.0.0/16. Comparing the two routes, route 1 has a longer AS_Path Length, bigger MED, bigger Weight, and smaller Local Preference. Which of the following is true about Router R1's choice of best path for this prefix?

   a. Route 1 is the best route.

   b. Route 2 is the best route.

   c. The routes tie as best, but one will be picked to be placed in the routing table based on tiebreakers.

   d. Neither route is considered best.

11. Router R1 learns two routes with BGP for prefix 200.1.0.0/16. Comparing the two routes, route 1 has a shorter AS_Path Length, smaller MED, the same Weight, and smaller Local Preference. Which of the following is true about Router R1's choice of best path for this prefix?

   a. Route 1 is the best route.

   b. Route 2 is the best route.

   c. The routes tie as best, but one will be picked to be placed in the routing table based on tiebreakers.

   d. Neither route is considered best.

12. An engineer has been told to create an implementation plan to influence the choice of best BGP route on a single router using the Weight feature. The sole enterprise Internet-connected router, Ent1, has neighbor relationships with Routers ISP1 and ISP2, which reside inside two different ISPs. The goal is to prefer all routes learned from ISP1 over ISP2 using Weight. Which of the following answers list a configuration step that would not be useful for achieving these goals? (Choose two.)

   a. Configuring the **neighbor weight** command on Ent1

   b. Having the ISPs configure the **neighbor route-map out** command on ISP1 and ISP2, with the route map setting the Weight

   c. Configuring the **set weight** command inside a route map on Router Ent1

   d. Configuring a prefix list to match all Class C networks

13. An enterprise router, Ent1, displays the following excerpt from the **show ip bgp** command. Ent1 has an eBGP connection to an ISP router with address 3.3.3.3 and an iBGP connection to a router with address 4.4.4.4. Which of the following is most likely to be true?

```
    Network          Next Hop          Metric LocPrf Weight Path
*>                   3.3.3.3               0           0 1 1 1 1 2 18 i
```

   a. The enterprise likely uses ASN 1.

   b. The neighboring ISP likely uses ASN 1.

   c. The route has been advertised through ASN 1 multiple times.

   d. Router Ent1 will add another ASN to the AS_Path before advertising this route to its iBGP peer (4.4.4.4).

14. The following line of output was gathered on enterprise Router Ent1 using the command **show ip route**. Which of the following answers is most likely to be true, based on this output?

```
B     128.107.0.0 [20/10] via 11.11.11.11, 00:02:18
```

   a. This router has set the Weight of this route to 10.

   b. This router's BGP table lists this route as an iBGP route.

   c. This router's MED has been set to 10.

   d. This router's BGP table lists an AS_Path length of 10 for this route.

Foundation Topics

Internal BGP Between Internet-Connected Routers

When an enterprise uses more than one router to connect to the Internet, and those routers use BGP to exchange routing information with their ISPs, those same routers need to exchange BGP routes with each other as well. The BGP neighbor relationships occur inside that enterprise—inside a single AS—making these routers iBGP peers.

This first major section of this chapter begins with a look at why two Internet-connected routers need to have an iBGP neighbor relationship. Then, the text looks at various iBGP configuration and verification commands. Finally, the discussion turns to a common issue that occurs with next-hop reachability between iBGP peers, with an examination of the options to overcome the problem.

Establishing the Need for iBGP with Two Internet-Connected Routers

Two Internet-connected routers in an enterprise need to communicate BGP routes to each other, because these routers might want to forward IP packets to the other Internet-connected router, which in turn would forward the packet to the Internet. With an iBGP peer connection, each Internet-connected router can learn routes from the other router and decide whether that other router has a better route to reach some destinations in the Internet. Without that iBGP connection, the routers have no way to know whether the other router has a better BGP path.

For example, consider Figure 14-2, which shows two such cases.

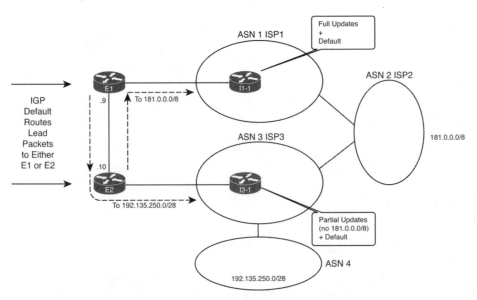

Figure 14-2 *Choosing the Best Routes from ASN 11 to 181.0.0.0/8 and 192.135.250.0/28*

The figure shows a topology that uses the following design options, as agreed upon with ISP1 and ISP3:

■ ISP1 sends full routing updates and a default route.

■ ISP3 sends partial updates and a default route.

First, consider the eBGP routing updates, particularly for the two prefixes highlighted in the figure. Both ISP1 and ISP3 know routes for 181.0.0.0/8, but ISP3's agreement with the enterprise is that ISP3 sends partial updates. This usually means that ISP3 sends updates for prefixes in its own autonomous system number (ASN) plus prefixes for customers attached to its ASN, such as 192.135.250.0/28 in this case. ISP1, however, sends full updates. So, E1 learns an eBGP route for both 181.0.0.0/8 and 192.135.250.0/28, but Router E2 only learns an eBGP route for 192.135.250.0/28.

Next, take a closer look at the routes for 181.0.0.0/8, both on E1 and E2. Only E1 learns an eBGP route for 181.0.0.0/8; E2 does not, because of ISP3's partial updates. If E1 and E2 did not use iBGP between each other, E2 would never know that E1 had a good route for 181.0.0.0/8. Without an iBGP connection, packets destined to hosts in 181.0.0.0/8, if they arrived at E2, would be sent to ISP3 because of E2's default route learned from ISP3. However, if E1 and E2 form an iBGP neighbor relationship, E2 would know a route for 181.0.0.0/8 through E1 and would choose this route as its best route and would forward such packets to E1. Then E1 would forward the packets to ISP1, as shown in the figure.

Finally, take a closer look at the routes for 192.135.250.0/28 on both E1 and E2. If none of the ISPs changed the default PA settings for these routes, both E1 and E2 would choose the route through E2 as the better route, because of the shorter AS_Path length (two ASNs away through ISP3 versus four ASNs away through ISP1). Without iBGP between E1 and E2, E1 would not learn of this better route through E2. So, any packets destined to 192.135.250.0/28 that reach E1 would be forwarded to ISP1. With iBGP, E1 would know of E2's better route and forward the packets toward E2, as shown in the figure.

For both prefixes, iBGP allowed both routers in the same ASN to reach the same conclusion about the better router through which to send packets for each Internet destination.

Configuring iBGP

The most basic iBGP configuration differs only slightly compared to eBGP configuration. The configuration does not explicitly identify an eBGP versus an iBGP peer. Instead, for iBGP, the neighbor's ASN listed on the **neighbor** *neighbor-ip* **remote-as** *neighbor-asn* command lists the same ASN as the local router's **router bgp** command. eBGP **neighbor remote-as** commands list a different ASN.

When two iBGP peers share a common physical link, such as E1 and E2 in Figure 14-2, the iBGP configuration simply requires a single **neighbor** *remote-as* command on each router. Example 14-1 shows the BGP configuration on both Router E1 and E2 with this single **neighbor** command highlighted. The rest of the configuration lists the commands used to configure other BGP settings (as described after the example). Note that Figure 14-1 in the introduction to this chapter shows more detail about the eBGP peers.

Example 14-1 *BGP Configuration on E1: Neighborships Configured*

```
! Configuration on router E1
router bgp 11
 no synchronization
 bgp log-neighbor-changes
 aggregate-address 128.107.0.0 255.255.224.0 summary-only
 redistribute ospf 1 route-map only-128-107
 neighbor 1.1.1.1 remote-as 1
 neighbor 1.1.1.1 password fred
 neighbor 1.1.1.1 ebgp-multihop 2
 neighbor 1.1.1.1 update-source Loopback1
 neighbor 10.1.1.10 remote-as 11
 no auto-summary
!
! Next, static routes so that the eBGP neighbor packets can reach
! I1-1's loopback interface address 1.1.1.1
ip route 1.1.1.1 255.255.255.255 Serial0/0/0
ip route 1.1.1.1 255.255.255.255 Serial0/0/1
!
ip prefix-list 128-107 seq 5 permit 128.107.0.0/19 le 32
!
route-map only-128-107 permit 10
 match ip address prefix-list 128-107

! Now, on router E2
router bgp 11
 no synchronization
 bgp log-neighbor-changes
 network 128.107.32.0
 aggregate-address 128.107.0.0 255.255.224.0 summary-only
 redistribute ospf 1 route-map only-128-107
 neighbor 10.1.1.9 remote-as 11
 neighbor 192.168.1.6 remote-as 3
 neighbor 192.168.1.6 password barney
 no auto-summary
!
ip prefix-list 128-107 seq 5 permit 128.107.0.0/19 le 32
!
route-map only-128-107 permit 10
 match ip address prefix-list 128-107
```

Only the four highlighted configuration commands are required for the E1-E2 iBGP peering. Both refer to the other router's IP address on the FastEthernet link between the two routers, and both refer to ASN 11. The two routers then realize that the neighbor is an iBGP neighbor, because the neighbor's ASN (11) matches the local router's ASN, as seen on the **router bgp 11** command.

The example also lists the rest of the BGP configuration. Focusing on Router E1, the configuration basically matches the configuration of Router E1 from the end of Chapter 13, except that E1 has only one eBGP peer (I1-1) in this case, instead of two eBGP peers. The configuration includes the eBGP peer connection to I1-1, using loopback interfaces (1.1.1.1 on I1-1 and 11.11.11.11 on E1). The eBGP peers need to use eBGP multihop because of the use of the loopbacks, and they use message digest algorithm 5 (MD5) authentication as well. Finally, the configuration shows the redistribution of the enterprise's public address range of 128.107.0.0/19 by redistributing from OSPF and summarizing with the **aggregate-address** BGP subcommand.

E2's configuration lists the same basic parameters, but with a few differences. E2 does not use a loopback for its peer connection to I3-1, because only a single link exists between the two routers. As a result, E2 also does not need to use eBGP multihop.

Refocusing on the iBGP configuration, Example 14-1 uses the interface IP addresses of the links between Routers E1 and E2. However, often the Internet-connected routers in an enterprise do not share a common subnet. For example, the two routers might be in separate buildings in a campus for the sake of redundancy. The two routers might actually be in different cities, or even different continents. In such cases, it makes sense to configure the iBGP peers using a loopback IP address for the TCP connection so that a single link failure does not cause the iBGP peer connection to fail. For example, in Figure 14-1, if the FastEthernet link between E1 and E2 fails, the iBGP connection defined in Example 14-1, which uses the interface IP addresses of that link, would fail even though a redundant IP path exists between E1 and E2.

The configuration to use loopback interfaces as the update source mirrors that same configuration for eBGP peers, except that iBGP peers do not need to configure the **neighbor** *neighbor-ip* **ebgp-multihop** command. One difference between iBGP and eBGP is that Cisco IOS uses the low TTL of 1 for eBGP connections by default but does not for iBGP connections. So, for iBGP connections, only the following steps are required to make two iBGP peers use a loopback interface:

Key Topic

Step 1.   Configure an IP address on a loopback interface on each router.

Step 2.   Configure each router to use the loopback IP address as the source IP address, for the neighborship with the other router, using the **neighbor** *neighbor-ip* **update-source** *interface-id* command.

Step 3.   Configure the BGP neighbor command on each router to refer to the other router's loopback IP address as the neighbor IP address in the **neighbor** *neighbor-ip* **remote-as** command.

Step 4.   Make sure that each router has IP routes so that they can forward packets to the loopback interface IP address of the other router.

Example 14-2 shows an updated iBGP configuration for Routers E1 and E2 to migrate to use a loopback interface. In this case, E1 uses loopback IP address 10.100.1.1/32 and E2 uses 10.100.1.2/32. OSPF on each router has already been configured with a **network 10.0.0.0 0.255.255.255 area 0** command (not shown), which causes OSPF to advertise routes to reach the respective loopback interface IP addresses.

Example 14-2 *iBGP Configuration to Use Loopbacks as the Update Source*

```
! Configuration on router E1
interface loopback 0
 ip address 10.100.1.1 255.255.255.255
router bgp 11
 neighbor 10.100.1.2 remote-as 11
 neighbor 10.100.1.2 update-source loopback0

! Configuration on router E2
interface loopback 1
 ip address 10.100.1.2 255.255.255.255
router bgp 11
 neighbor 10.100.1.1 remote-as 11
 neighbor 10.100.1.1 update-source loopback1
```

The highlighted portions of the output link the key values together for the E1's definition of its loopback as the update source and E2's reference of that same IP address on its
neighbor command. The **neighbor 10.100.1.2 update-source loopback0** command on E1
tells E1 to look to interface loopback0 for its update source IP address. Loopback0's IP
address on E1 has IP address 10.100.1.1. Then, E2's **neighbor** commands for Router E1 all
refer to that same 10.100.1.1 IP address, meeting the requirement that the update source
on one router matches the IP address listed on the other router's **neighbor** command.

Verifying iBGP

iBGP neighbors use the same messages and neighbor states as eBGP peers. As a result,
the same commands in Chapter 13 for BGP neighbor verification can be used for iBGP
peers. Example 14-3 shows a couple of examples, using Router E1's iBGP neighbor relationship with E2 (10.100.1.2) based on the configuration in Example 14-2.

Example 14-3 *Verifying iBGP Neighbors*

```
E1# show ip bgp summary
BGP router identifier 11.11.11.11, local AS number 11
BGP table version is 190, main routing table version 190
11 network entries using 1452 bytes of memory
14 path entries using 728 bytes of memory
11/7 BGP path/bestpath attribute entries using 1628 bytes of memory
7 BGP AS-PATH entries using 168 bytes of memory
0 BGP route-map cache entries using 0 bytes of memory
0 BGP filter-list cache entries using 0 bytes of memory
Bitfield cache entries: current 3 (at peak 4) using 96 bytes of memory
BGP using 4072 total bytes of memory
BGP activity 31/20 prefixes, 100/86 paths, scan interval 60 secs
```

```
Neighbor        V     AS MsgRcvd MsgSent   TblVer  InQ OutQ Up/Down  State/PfxRcd
1.1.1.1         4      1     339     344      190    0    0 00:28:41           7
10.100.1.2      4     11      92     132      190    0    0 01:02:04           3

E1# show ip bgp neighbors 10.100.1.2
BGP neighbor is 10.100.1.2,  remote AS 11, internal link
  BGP version 4, remote router ID 10.100.1.2
  BGP state = Established, up for 01:02:10
  Last read 00:00:37, last write 00:00:59, hold time is 180, keepalive interval is
    60 seconds
  Neighbor capabilities:
    Route refresh: advertised and received(new)
    Address family IPv4 Unicast: advertised and received
! lines omitted for brevity
```

The **show ip bgp summary** command lists E1's two neighbors. As with eBGP peers, if the last column (the State/PfxRcd column) lists a number, the neighbor has reached the established state, and BGP Update messages can be sent. The output can distinguish between an iBGP or eBGP neighbor but only by comparing the local router's ASN (in the first line of output) to the ASN listed in each line at the bottom of the output.

The **show ip bgp neighbors 10.100.1.2** command lists many details specifically for the neighbor. Specifically, it states that the neighbor is an iBGP neighbor with the phrase "internal link," as highlighted in the output.

Examining iBGP BGP Table Entries

To better understand the BGP table with two (or more) Internet-connected routers inside the same company, start with one prefix and compare the BGP table entries on the two routers for that one prefix. By examining several such examples, you can appreciate more about the benefits and effects of these iBGP neighborships.

This section examines the BGP tables on Routers E1 and E2, focusing on the prefixes highlighted in Figure 14-2—namely, prefixes 181.0.0.0/8 and 192.135.250.0/28. To make reading the output of the **show** commands a little more obvious, Figure 14-3 collects some key pieces of information into a single figure. This figure shows the two BGP neighbor relationships on each router, showing the update source and neighbor IP address of each BGP neighbor relationship. It also lists the BGP router ID (RID) of the routers.

Examples 14-4 and 14-5 compare the output on Routers E2 and E1 for prefix 181.0.0.0/8. Example 14-4 lists output on Router E2, listing the BGP table entries for prefix 181.0.0.0/8. Remember, the design calls for ISP3 to only send partial updates, so E2 has not received an eBGP route for 181.0.0.0/8 from I3-1. However, E1 has indeed learned of that prefix from I1-1 (ISP1), and E1 has already advertised prefix 181.0.0.0/8 to E2.

Note   Several BGP routes seen in the examples in this chapter originate in ASNs not shown in the figure. The figure shows enough of the topology to understand the first few ASNs in the AS_Path for these routes.

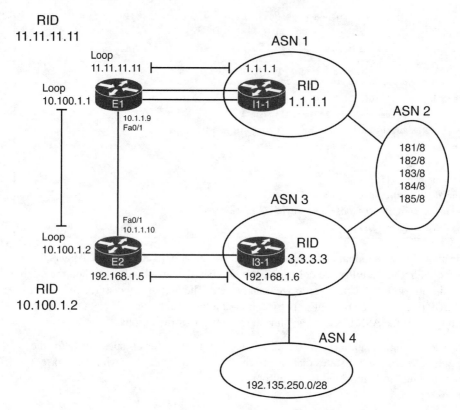

Figure 14-3 *Reference Information for BGP Table Verification*

Example 14-4 *Notations of iBGP-Learned Routes in the* **show ip bgp** *Command*

```
E2# show ip bgp 181.0.0.0/8 longer-prefixes
BGP table version is 125, local router ID is 10.100.1.2
Status codes: s suppressed, d damped, h history, * valid, > best, i - internal,
              r RIB-failure, S Stale
Origin codes: i - IGP, e - EGP, ? - incomplete


   Network          Next Hop            Metric LocPrf Weight Path
*>i181.0.0.0/8      1.1.1.1                  0    100      0 1 2 111 112 i

E2# show ip bgp 181.0.0.0/8
BGP routing table entry for 181.0.0.0/8, version 121
Paths: (1 available, best #1, table Default-IP-Routing-Table)
  Advertised to update-groups:
        1
  1 2 111 111
    1.1.1.1 from 10.100.1.1 (11.11.11.11)
      Origin IGP, metric 0, localpref 100, valid, internal, best
```

The first command, **show ip bgp 181.0.0.0/8 longer-prefixes**, lists output with the same general format as the **show ip bgp** command, but it limits the output to the prefixes in the listed range. Only one such route exists in this case. The legend information at the top of the output, plus the headings and meanings of the different fields, is the same as with the **show ip bgp** command.

Next, the first command's output denotes this route as an iBGP-learned route with code "i" in the third character. The second command in the example, **show ip bgp 181.0.0.0/8**, displays a more detailed view of the BGP table entry and denotes this route as iBGP-learned with the word "internal." Similarly, the briefer **show ip bgp 181.0.0.0/8** command output lists this one route as E2's best route by displaying a ">" in the second column, whereas the more verbose output in the second command simply lists this route as "best."

Next, consider these same commands on Router E1, as shown in Example 14-5. Comparing the highlighted fields as matched in each of the examples:

■ Both list the same AS_Path (1, 2, 111, 112), because iBGP peers do not add ASNs to the AS_Path when advertising to each other. So, both E1 and E2 have the same perspective on the AS_Path and AS_Path length.

■ Both list the one route for 181.0.0.0/8 as the best path, in part because each has learned only one such path.

■ Both list a Next_Hop (a BGP PA) as 1.1.1.1, which is I1-1's loopback interface used in the E1–to–I1-1 BGP neighbor relationship (also called the *BGP neighbor ID*).

■ E2 lists the route as an internal (iBGP-learned) route, whereas E1 lists it as an external route.

Example 14-5   *Router E1's* show *Commands for BGP Routes for 181.0.0.0/8*

```
E1# show ip bgp 181.0.0.0/8 longer-prefixes
BGP table version is 190, local router ID is 11.11.11.11
Status codes: s suppressed, d damped, h history, * valid, > best, i - internal,
              r RIB-failure, S Stale
Origin codes: i - IGP, e - EGP, ? - incomplete


   Network          Next Hop            Metric LocPrf Weight Path
*> 181.0.0.0/8      1.1.1.1                            0 1 2 111 112 i


E1# show ip bgp 181.0.0.0/8
BGP routing table entry for 181.0.0.0/8, version 181
Paths: (1 available, best #1, table Default-IP-Routing-Table)
  Advertised to update-groups:
        2
  1 2 111 111, (received & used)
    1.1.1.1 from 1.1.1.1 (1.1.1.1)
      Origin IGP, localpref 100, valid, external, best
```

The output from these examples confirms that E1 learned the eBGP route for 181.0.0.0/8 and advertised it to E2, and E2 chose to use that iBGP-learned route as its best route to reach 181.0.0.0/8.

Next, consider the route for 192.135.250.0/28, a route learned in the full BGP updates from ISP1's Router I1-1 and in the partial BGP updates from ISP3's Router I3-1. After exchanging this route using their iBGP peering, both E1 and E2 should see two possible routes: an eBGP route learned from their one connected ISP and the iBGP route learned from each other. Again assuming that the ISPs have not made any attempt to set PA values to influence the best-path choice, and knowing that neither E1 nor E2 have configured BGP to influence the best-path choice, the route through E2 should be best because of the shorter AS_Path.

Example 14-6 shows the output of the **show ip bgp** command on both E1 and E2, again for comparison. Note that the command used in the examples, **show ip bgp 192.135.250.0/28 longer-prefixes**, is used, because it lists only the routes for that prefix, rather than the full BGP table displayed by **show ip bgp**. However, the format of the output is almost identical.

Example 14-6 *Comparing BGP Routes for 192.135.250.0/28 on E1 and E2*

```
! First, on E1:
E1# show ip bgp 192.135.250.0/28 longer-prefixes
BGP table version is 26, local router ID is 128.107.9.1
Status codes: s suppressed, d damped, h history, * valid, > best, i - internal,
              r RIB-failure, S Stale
Origin codes: i - IGP, e - EGP, ? - incomplete


   Network          Next Hop            Metric LocPrf Weight Path
*  192.135.250.0/28 1.1.1.1                           0 1 2 3 4 i
*>i                 192.168.1.6              0    100  0 3 4 i
```

```
! Next, on E2:
E2# show ip bgp 192.135.250.0/28 longer-prefixes
BGP table version is 25, local router ID is 10.100.1.2
Status codes: s suppressed, d damped, h history, * valid, > best, i - internal,
              r RIB-failure, S Stale
Origin codes: i - IGP, e - EGP, ? - incomplete


   Network          Next Hop          Metric LocPrf Weight Path
*> 192.135.250.0/28 192.168.1.6                     0 3 4 i
```

First, E1 lists two routes for this prefix, one external and one internal. The output identifies external routes by the absence of an "i" in the third character, whereas the output lists an "i" in the third character for internal routes. In this case, E1's internal route, with Next_Hop 192.168.1.6, is E1's best route, as was shown back in Figure 14-2. E1 chose this iBGP route because of the shorter AS_Path length; the AS_Path is highlighted at the end of each line.

E2's output in the second half of Example 14-6 lists only a single route—its eBGP route for 192.135.250.0/28. That only one route appears, rather than two, is a good example of the effect of two rules about how BGP operates:

■ Only advertise the best route in any BGP Update.

■ Do not advertise iBGP-learned routes to iBGP peers.

E2's output lists a single route for 192.135.250.0/28—its external route learned from ISP3—because E1 chooses not to advertise a route for 192.135.250.0/28 over the iBGP connection. If you look back at E1's output, E1's best route for this prefix is its internal route. So, if E1 were to advertise any route for this prefix to E2, E1 would advertise this internal route, because it is E1's best BGP route for that prefix. However, the second rule—do not advertise iBGP-learned routes to iBGP peers—prevents E1 from advertising this route back to E2. (Logically speaking, it makes no sense for E1 to tell E2 about a route when E2 is the router that originally advertised the route to E1 in the first place—a concept much like Split Horizon, although technically the term does not apply to BGP.) As a result, E2 lists a single route for 192.135.250.0/28.

Note that if the route for 192.135.250.0/28 through ISP3 failed, E1 would start using the route through ISP1 as its best route. E1 would then advertise that best route to E2 that could then forward traffic through E1 for destinations in 192.135.250.0/28.

Understanding Next-Hop Reachability Issues with iBGP

With IGPs, the IP routes added to the IP routing table list a next-hop IP address. With few exceptions, the next-hop IP address exists in a connected subnet. For example, the E1-E2 iBGP connection uses loopback interfaces 10.100.1.1 (E1) and 10.100.1.2 (E2). E1's OSPF-learned route to reach 10.100.1.2 lists outgoing interface Fa0/1, next-hop 10.1.1.10—an address in the LAN subnet that connects E1 and E2. (See Figure 14-3 a few pages back for reference.)

Examples 14-5 and 14-6 also happened to show two examples of iBGP-learned routes and their next-hop addresses. The next-hop addresses were not in connected subnets; the next-hop addresses were not even IP addresses on a neighboring router. The two examples were as follows; again, it might be helpful to refer to the notations in Figure 14-3:

■ **Example 14-5:** E2's route for 181.0.0.0/8 lists next-hop address 1.1.1.1, a loopback interface IP address on I1-1.

■ **Example 14-6:** E1's route for 192.135.250.0/28 lists next-hop address 192.168.1.6, which is I3-1's interface IP address on the link between E2 and I3-1.

In fact, in the case of Example 14-5, the output of the **show ip bgp 181.0.0.0/8** command on E2 listed the phrase "1.1.1.1 from 10.100.1.1 (11.11.11.11)." This phrase lists the next hop (1.1.1.1) of the route, the neighbor from which the route was learned (10.100.1.1 or E1), and the neighbor's BGP RID (11.11.11.11, as listed in Figure 14-3).

BGP advertises these particular IP addresses as the next-hop IP addresses because of a default behavior for BGP. By default, when a router advertises a route using eBGP, the advertising router lists its own update-source IP address as the next-hop address of the route. In other words, the next-hop IP address is the IP address of the eBGP neighbor, as listed on the **neighbor remote-as** command. However, when advertising a route to an iBGP peer, the advertising router (by default) does not change the next-hop address. For example, when I1-1 advertises 181.0.0.0/8 to E1, because it is an eBGP connection, I1-1 sets its own IP address (1.1.1.1)—specifically the IP address I1-1 uses on its eBGP peer connection to E1—as the next hop. When E1 advertises that same route to iBGP peer E2, E1 does not change the next-hop address of 1.1.1.1. So, Router E2's iBGP-learned route lists 1.1.1.1 as the next-hop address.

The IP routing process can use routes whose next-hop addresses are not in connected subnets as long as each router has an IP route that matches the next-hop IP address. Therefore, engineers must understand these rules about how BGP sets the next-hop address and ensure that each router can reach the next-hop address listed in the BGP routes. Two main options exist to ensure reachability to these next-hop addresses:

■ Create IP routes so that each router can reach these next-hop addresses that exist in other ASNs.

■ Change the default iBGP behavior with the **neighbor** *neighbor-ip* **next-hop-self** command.

The text now examines each of these two options in more detail.

Ensuring That Routes Exist to the Next-Hop Address

Routers can still forward packets using routes whose next-hop addresses are not in connected subnets. To do so, when forwarding packets, the router performs a recursive route table lookup. For example, for packets arriving at E2 with a destination of 181.0.0.1, the following would occur:

Step 1. E2 would match the routing table for destination address 181.0.0.1, matching the route for 181.0.0.0/8, with next hop 1.1.1.1.

Step 2. E2 would next look for its route matching destination 1.1.1.1—the next hop of the first route—and forward the packet based on that route.

So, regardless of the next-hop IP address listed in the routing table, as long as a working route exists to reach that next-hop IP address, the packet can be forwarded. Figure 14-4 shows the necessary routes in diagram form using two examples. E1 has a route to 192.135.250.0/28 with next hop 192.168.1.6; two arrowed lines show the required routes on Routers E1 and E2 for forwarding packets to this next-hop address. Similarly, the dashed lines show the necessary routes on E2 and E1 for next-hop address 1.1.1.1, the next-hop IP address for their routes to reach 181.0.0.0/8.

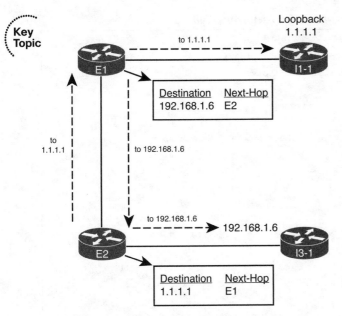

Figure 14-4 *Ensuring That Routes Exist for Next-Hop Addresses in Other ASNs*

Two easily implemented solutions exist to add routes for these nonconnected next-hop IP addresses: Either add static routes or use an IGP between the enterprise and the ISPs for the sole purpose of advertising these next-hop addresses.

Using neighbor *neighbor-ip* next-hop-self to Change the Next-Hop Address

The second option for dealing with these nonconnected next-hop IP addresses changes the iBGP configuration so that a router changes the next-hop IP address on iBGP-advertised routes. This option simply requires the **neighbor** *neighbor-ip* **next-hop-self** command to be configured for the iBGP neighbor relationship. A router with this command configured advertises iBGP routes with its own update source IP address as the next-hop IP address. And because the iBGP neighborship already relies on a working route for these update source IP addresses, if the neighborship is up, IP routes already exist for these next-hop addresses.

For example, on the iBGP connection from E1 to E2, E1 would add the **neighbor 10.100.1.2 next-hop-self** command, and E2 would add the **neighbor 10.100.1.1 next-hop-self** command. When configured, E1 advertises iBGP routes with its update source IP address (10.100.1.1) as the next-hop address. E2 likewise advertises routes with a next-hop address of 10.100.1.2. Example 14-7 shows E2's BGP table, with a few such examples highlighted, after the addition of these two configuration commands on the respective routers.

Example 14-7 *Seeing the Effects of* **next-hop-self** *from Router E2*

```
E2# show ip bgp
BGP table version is 76, local router ID is 10.100.1.2
Status codes: s suppressed, d damped, h history, * valid, > best, i - internal,
              r RIB-failure, S Stale
Origin codes: i - IGP, e - EGP, ? - incomplete

   Network          Next Hop         Metric LocPrf Weight Path
*> 0.0.0.0          192.168.1.6           0             0 3 i
*  i                10.100.1.1            0    100      0 1 i
*  i128.107.0.0/19  10.100.1.1            0    100      0 i
*>                  0.0.0.0                           32768 i
s> 128.107.1.0/24   10.1.1.77             2           32768 ?
s> 128.107.2.0/24   10.1.1.77             2           32768 ?
s> 128.107.3.0/24   10.1.1.77             2           32768 ?
*>i181.0.0.0/8      10.100.1.1            0    100      0 1 2 111 112 i
*>i182.0.0.0/8      10.100.1.1            0    100      0 1 2 222 i
*>i183.0.0.0/8      10.100.1.1            0    100      0 1 2 i
*>i184.0.0.0/8      10.100.1.1            0    100      0 1 2 i
*>i185.0.0.0/8      10.100.1.1            0    100      0 1 2 i
*> 192.135.250.0/28 192.168.1.6                        0 3 4 i
```

This completes the discussion of iBGP configuration and operation as related to the routers actually connected to the Internet. The next section continues the discussion of iBGP but with a focus on some particular issues with routing that might require iBGP on routers other than the Internet-connected routers.

Avoiding Routing Loops When Forwarding Toward the Internet

A typical enterprise network design uses default routes inside an enterprise, as advertised by an IGP, to draw all Internet traffic toward one or more Internet-connected routers. The Internet-connected routers then forward the traffic into the Internet.

However, as discussed in Chapter 13, in the section "Choosing One Path over Another Using BGP," routing loops can occur when the Internet-connected routers do not have a direct connection to each other. For example, if the Internet-connected routers sit on opposite sides of the country, the two routers might be separated by several routers internal to the enterprise, because they do not have a direct link.

To show a simple example, the same enterprise network design shown in all previous figures in this chapter can be changed slightly by just disabling the FastEthernet link between the two routers, as shown in Figure 14-5.

Figure 14-5 shows an example of the looping problem.

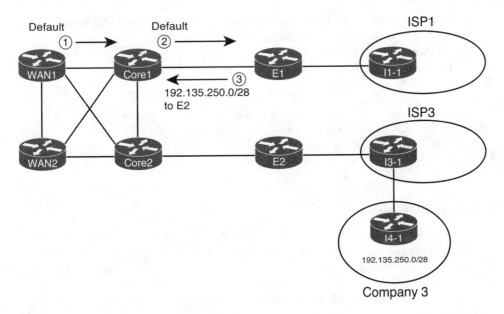

Figure 14-5   *Routing Loop for Packets Destined to 192.135.250.1*

The figure uses the same general criteria as the other examples in this chapter, such that E1's best route for 192.135.250.0/28 points to Router E2 as the next hop. E1's best route for the next-hop IP address for its route to 192.135.250.0/28—regardless of whether using the **next-hop-self** option or not—sends the packet back toward the enterprise core. However, some of (or possibly all) the enterprise routers internal to the enterprise, such as WAN1 and Core1, use a default that sends all packets toward Router E1. Per the steps in the figure, the following happens for a packet destined to 192.135.250.1:

Step 1.   WAN1 sends the packet using its default route to Core1.

Step 2.   Core1 sends the packet using its default route to E1.

Step 3.   E1 matches its BGP route for 192.135.250.0/28, with next-hop E2 (10.100.1.2). The recursive lookup on E1 matches a route for 10.100.1.2 with a next hop of Core1, so E1 sends the packet back to Core1.

At this point, Steps 2 and 3 repeat until the packet's TTL mechanism causes one of the routers to discard the packet.

The lack of knowledge about the best route for subnet 192.135.250.0/28, particularly on the routers internal to the enterprise, causes this routing loop. To avoid this problem, internal routers, such as Core1 and Core2, need to know the best BGP routes. Two solutions exist to help these internal routers learn the routes:

■   Run BGP on at least some of the routers internal to the enterprise (such as Core1 and Core2 in Figure 14-5).

■   Redistribute BGP routes into the IGP (not recommended).

Both solutions solve the problem by giving some of the internal routers the same best-path information already known to the Internet-connected routers. For example, if Core1 knew a route for 192.135.250.0/28, and that route caused the packets to go to Core2 next and then on to Router E2, the loop could be avoided. This section examines both solutions briefly.

> **Note** BGP Confederations and BGP Route Reflector features, which are outside the scope of this book, can be used instead of a full mesh of iBGP peers.

Using an iBGP Mesh

To let the internal routers in the enterprise learn the best BGP routes, one obvious solution is to just run BGP on these routers as well. The not-so-obvious part relates to the implementation choice of what routers need to be iBGP peers with each other. Based on the topology shown in Figure 14-5, at first glance, the temptation might be to run BGP on E1, E2, Core1, and Core2, but use iBGP peers as shown in Figure 14-6.

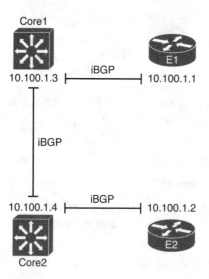

Figure 14-6 *Partial Mesh of iBGP Peers*

The iBGP peers shown in the figure actually match the kinds of IGP neighbor relationships you might expect to see with a similar design. With an IGP routing protocol, each router would learn routes and tell its neighbor so that all routers would learn all routes. Unfortunately, with this design, not all the routers learn all the routes because of the following feature of iBGP:

When a router learns routes from an iBGP peer, that router does not advertise the same routes to another iBGP peer.

> **Note**   This particular iBGP behavior helps prevent BGP routing loops.

Because of this feature, to ensure that all four routers in ASN 11 learn the same BGP routes, a full mesh of iBGP peers must be created. By creating an iBGP peering between all routers inside ASN 11, they can all exchange routes directly and overcome the restriction. In this case, six such neighborships exist: one between each pair of routers.

The configuration itself does not require any new commands that have not already been explained in this book. However, for completeness, Example 14-8 shows the configuration on both E1 and Core1. Note that all configuration related to iBGP has been included, and the routers use the loopback interfaces shown in Figure 14-6.

Example 14-8   *iBGP Configuration for the Full Mesh Between E1, E2, Core, and Core2—E1 and Core1 Only*

```
! First, E1's configuration
router bgp 11
 neighbor 10.100.1.2 remote-as 11
 neighbor 10.100.1.2 update-source loopback0
 neighbor 10.100.1.2 next-hop-self
!
 neighbor 10.100.1.3 remote-as 11
 neighbor 10.100.1.3 update-source loopback0
 neighbor 10.100.1.3 next-hop-self
!
 neighbor 10.100.1.4 remote-as 11
 neighbor 10.100.1.4 update-source loopback0
 neighbor 10.100.1.4 next-hop-self

! Next, Core1's configuration
interface loopback0
 ip address 10.100.1.3 255.255.255.255
!
router bgp 11
 neighbor 10.100.1.1 remote-as 11
 neighbor 10.100.1.1 update-source loopback0
!
 neighbor 10.100.1.2 remote-as 11
 neighbor 10.100.1.2 update-source loopback0
!
 neighbor 10.100.1.4 remote-as 11
 neighbor 10.100.1.4 update-source loopback0
```

The configurations on E1 and Core1 mostly match. The commonly used commands simply define the neighbor's ASN (**neighbor** *neighbor-ip* **remote-as**) and list the local router's BGP update source interface (**neighbor** *neighbor-ip* **update-source**). However, note that the engineer also configured E1—the Internet-connected router—with the **neighbor** *neighbor-ip* **next-hop-self** command. In this case, the Internet-connected routers want to set their own update source IP addresses as the next hop for any routes. However, the engineer purposefully chose not to use this command on the two internal routers (Core1 and Core2), because the eventual destination of these packets will be to make it to either E1 or E2 and then out to the Internet. By making the next-hop router for all iBGP-learned routes an address on one of the Internet-connected routers, the packets will be correctly forwarded.

For perspective, Example 14-9 shows Core1's BGP table after adding the configuration shown in Example 14-8, plus the equivalent configuration in E2 and Core2. Focusing on the routes for 181.0.0.0/8 and 192.135.250.0/28 again, note that E1 and E2 had already agreed that E1's route for 181.0.0.0/8 was best and that E2's route for 192.135.250.0/28 was best. As a result, Core1 knows only one route for each of these destinations, as shown in the example. Also, the next-hop addresses for each route refer to the correct router of the two Internet-connected routers: 10.100.1.1 (E1) for the route to 181.0.0.0/8 and 10.100.1.2 (E2) for the route to 192.135.250.0/28.

Example 14-9   *BGP Table on Router Core1*

```
Core-1# show ip bgp
BGP table version is 10, local router ID is 10.100.1.3
Status codes: s suppressed, d damped, h history, * valid, > best, i - internal,
              r RIB-failure, S Stale
Origin codes: i - IGP, e - EGP, ? - incomplete

   Network          Next Hop        Metric LocPrf Weight Path
r i0.0.0.0          10.100.1.2           0    100      0 3 i
r>i                 10.100.1.1           0    100      0 1 i
* i128.107.0.0/19   10.100.1.2           0    100      0 i
*>i                 10.100.1.1           0    100      0 i
*>i181.0.0.0/8      10.100.1.1           0    100      0 1 2 111 112 i
*>i182.0.0.0/8      10.100.1.1           0    100      0 1 2 222 i
*>i183.0.0.0/8      10.100.1.1           0    100      0 1 2 i
*>i184.0.0.0/8      10.100.1.1           0    100      0 1 2 i
*>i185.0.0.0/8      10.100.1.1           0    100      0 1 2 i
*>i192.135.250.0/28 10.100.1.2           0    100      0 3 4 i
```

IGP Redistribution and BGP Synchronization

You can also redistribute BGP routes into the IGP to solve the routing loop problem. This solution prevents the routing loop by giving the internal enterprise routers knowledge of the best exit point for each known Internet destination.

Although this solves the problem, particularly when just learning with lab gear at home, redistribution of BGP routes into an IGP is generally not recommended. This redistribution requires a relatively large amount of memory and a relatively large amount of processing by an IGP with the much larger number of routes to process. Redistributing all the routes in the full Internet BGP table could crash the IGP routing protocols.

Note BGP consumes less memory and uses less CPU resources for a large number of routes as compared to the equivalent number of routes advertised by an IGP, particularly when compared to OSPF. So, using the iBGP mesh can cause internal routers to learn all the same routes but without risk to the IGP.

Although not recommended, the idea of redistributing eBGP-learned Internet routes into the enterprise IGP needs to be discussed as a backdrop to discuss a related BGP feature called *synchronization*, or *sync*. The term refers to the idea that the iBGP-learned routes must be synchronized with IGP-learned routes for the same prefix before they can be used. In other words, if an iBGP-learned route is to be considered to be a usable route, that same prefix must be in the IP routing table and learned using some IGP protocol such as EIGRP or OSPF. More formally, the synchronization features tells a BGP router the following:

> Do not consider an iBGP-learned route as "best" unless the exact prefix was learned through an IGP and is currently in the IP routing table.

For companies, such as the enterprise shown in Figure 14-5, the combination of redistributing eBGP routes into an IGP, and configuring synchronization on the two routers that run BGP (E1 and E2), prevents the routing loop shown in that figure. Again using prefix 192.135.250.0/28 as an example (see Figure 14-5), E2 learns this prefix with eBGP. E1 learns this same prefix through its iBGP neighborship with E2, and both agree that E2's BGP route is best.

When E2 has successfully redistributed prefix 192.135.250.0/28 into the enterprise's IGP (OSPF in the examples in this chapter), E1, with sync enabled, thinks like this:

> I see an IGP route for 192.135.250.0/28 in my IP routing table, so my iBGP route for that same prefix is safe to use.

However, if for some reason the redistribution does not result in an IGP route for 192.135.250.0/28, E1 thinks as follows:

> I do not see an IGP-learned route for 192.135.250.0/28 in my IP routing table, so I will not consider the iBGP route through E2 to be usable.

In this second case, E1 uses its eBGP route learned through I1-1, which defeats the routing loop caused at Step 3 of Figure 14-5.

Later Cisco IOS versions default to disable synchronization, because most sites avoid redistributing routes from BGP into an IGP when using BGP for Internet routes, instead preferring iBGP meshes (or alternatives) to avoid these routing black holes. The setting is applied to the entire BGP process, with the **synchronization** command enabling synchronization and the **no synchronization** command (default) disabling it.

Note The suggestion to avoid redistribution from BGP into an IGP generally applies to cases in which BGP is used to exchange Internet routes. However, BGP can be used for other purposes as well, including the implementation of Multiprotocol Label Switching (MPLS). Redistribution from BGP into an IGP when using BGP for MPLS is reasonable and commonly done.

Route Filtering and Clearing BGP Peers

BGP allows the filtering of BGP Update messages on any BGP router. The router can filter updates per neighbor for both inbound and outbound Updates on any BGP router.

After adding a new BGP filter to a router's configuration, the BGP neighbor relationships must be reset or cleared to cause the filter to take effect. The Cisco IOS BGP **clear** command tells the router specifically how to reset the neighborship. This section also examines the variations on the BGP **clear** command, including the more disruptive hard reset options and the less disruptive soft reset options.

BGP Filtering Overview

BGP filtering works generally like IGP filtering, particularly like EIGRP. Similar to EIGRP, BGP Updates can be filtered on any router, without the restrictions that exist for OSPF with various area design issues. The filtering can examine the prefix information about each router and both the prefix and prefix length information, in either direction (in or out), on any BGP router.

The biggest conceptual differences between BGP and IGP filtering relate to what BGP can match about a prefix to make a choice of whether to filter the route. EIGRP focuses on matching the prefix/length. Not only can BGP also match the prefix/length, but it can also match a large set of BGP Path Attributes (PA). For example, a filter could compare a BGP route's AS_Path PA and check to see whether the first ASN is 4, that at least three ASNs exist, and that the AS_Path does not end with 567. The matching of routes based on their PA settings has no equivalent with any of the IGPs.

The biggest configuration difference between BGP and IGP filtering, besides the details of matching BGP PAs, has to do with the fact that the filters must apply to specific neighbors with BGP. With EIGRP, the filters can be applied to all outbound updates from EIGRP, or all inbound updates into EIGRP, using a single EIGRP **distribute-list** command. BGP configuration does not allow filtering of all inbound or outbound updates. Instead, the BGP filtering configuration enables filters per neighbor (using a **neighbor** command), referencing the type of BGP filter, the filter number or name, and the direction (in or out). So, a router could literally use the same filter for all BGP Updates sent by a router, but the configuration would require a **neighbor** command for each neighbor that enabled the same filter.

The ROUTE course and exam focus on enterprise routing topics, whereas BGP filtering—especially the more detailed filtering with BGP PAs—is used most frequently by ISP network engineers. As a result, CCNP ROUTE covers BGP filtering very lightly, at least compared to IGP filtering.

This section briefly describes the BGP filtering commands, showing a few samples just for perspective. Table 14-2 summarizes the BGP filtering options and commands, along with the fields in the BGP Update message that can be matched with each type. Following the table, the text shows an example of how an enterprise might apply an outbound and inbound filter based on prefix/length.

Table 14-2 *BGP Filtering Tools*

BGP Subcommand	Commands Referenced by the neighbor Command	What Can Be Matched
neighbor distribute-list (standard ACL)	access-list, ip access-list	Prefix, with WC mask
neighbor distribute-list (extended ACL)	access-list, ip access-list	Prefix and prefix length, with WC mask for each
neighbor prefix-list	ip prefix-list	Exact or "first N" bits of prefix, plus range of prefix lengths
neighbor filter-list	ip as-path access-list	AS_Path contents; all NLRI whose AS_Paths are matched considered to be a match
neighbor route-map	route-map	Prefix, prefix length, AS_Path, and/or any other PA matchable within a BGP route map

Inbound and Outbound BGP Filtering on Prefix/Length

Enterprises that choose to use BGP benefit from both learning routes from the connected ISPs and advertising the enterprise's public prefix to the same ISPs. However, when the eBGP connections to the various ISPs come up, the enterprise BGP routers advertise all the best routes in each router's BGP table over the eBGP connection. As a result, the ISPs could learn a best route that causes one ISP to send packets to the enterprise, with the enterprise then forwarding the packet out to another ISP. In such a case, the enterprise AS would be acting as a transit AS.

Enterprise engineers can, and probably should, make an effort to filter inappropriate routes sent to the ISP over the eBGP peer connections with the goal of preventing their enterprise AS from becoming a transit AS. Additionally, the enterprise can filter all private IP address ranges, in case any such address ranges get into the enterprise BGP router's BGP table.

As an example, consider Figure 14-7, with the now-familiar prefix 192.135.250.0/28. As seen in earlier examples, both E1 and E2 learn this prefix, and both agree that the best route from ASN 11 (the enterprise) toward this prefix is through E2. The figure shows the BGP routing updates as dashed lines.

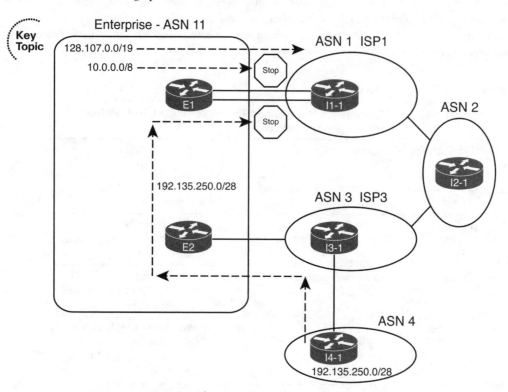

Figure 14-7 *Need for Enterprise BGP Filtering*

E1's best route for 192.135.250.0/28 lists E2 as the next-hop router. So, without any filtering in place, E1 then advertises prefix 192.135.250.0/28 to Router I1-1 in ISP1. I1-1 can be configured to filter this prefix. (In the Chapter 13 examples, Router I1-1 was indeed configured to filter such prefixes.) However, if the enterprise did not filter this prefix when advertising to ISP1, and ISP1 did not filter it, ISP1 might choose the route through ASN 11 as its best route, making ASN 11 a transit AS for this prefix and consuming the enterprise's Internet bandwidth.

Typically, an enterprise would use outbound filtering on its eBGP neighborships, filtering all routes except for the known public prefixes that need to be advertised into the Internet. Example 14-10 shows just such a case, using the **neighbor prefix-list** command. The example also highlights a particularly useful command, **show ip bgp neighbor** *neighbor-ip* **advertised-routes**, which shows the post-filter BGP update sent to the listed neighbor. The example shows the BGP Update before adding the filter, after adding the filter, and then after clearing the peer connection to router I1-1.

Example 14-10   *Filtering to Allow Only Public Prefix 128.107.0.0/19 Outbound*

```
! The next command occurs before filtering is added.
E1# show ip bgp neighbor 1.1.1.1 advertised-routes
BGP table version is 16, local router ID is 128.107.9.1
Status codes: s suppressed, d damped, h history, * valid, > best, i - internal,
              r RIB-failure, S Stale
Origin codes: i - IGP, e - EGP, ? - incomplete


   Network          Next Hop          Metric LocPrf Weight Path
*> 128.107.0.0/19   0.0.0.0                         32768 i
*>i192.135.250.0/28 10.100.1.2             0    100     0 3 4 i


Total number of prefixes 2


! Next, the filtering is configured.
E1# configure terminal
Enter configuration commands, one per line.  End with CNTL/Z.

E1(config)# ip prefix-list only-public permit 128.107.0.0/19
E1(config)# router bgp 11
E1(config-router)# neighbor 1.1.1.1 prefix-list only-public out
E1(config-router)# end
E1#


! Next, the Update sent to I1-1 is displayed.
E1# show ip bgp neighbor 1.1.1.1 advertised-routes
BGP table version is 16, local router ID is 128.107.9.1
Status codes: s suppressed, d damped, h history, * valid, > best, i - internal,
              r RIB-failure, S Stale
Origin codes: i - IGP, e - EGP, ? - incomplete


   Network          Next Hop          Metric LocPrf Weight Path
*> 128.107.0.0/19   0.0.0.0                         32768 i
*>i192.135.250.0/28 10.100.1.2             0    100     0 3 4 i


Total number of prefixes 2


! Next, the peer connection is cleared, causing the filter to take effect.
E1# clear ip bgp 1.1.1.1
E1#
*Aug 17 20:19:51.763: %BGP-5-ADJCHANGE: neighbor 1.1.1.1 Down User reset
*Aug 17 20:19:52.763: %BGP-5-ADJCHANGE: neighbor 1.1.1.1 Up


! Finally, the Update is displayed with the filter now working.
E1# show ip bgp neighbor 1.1.1.1 advertised-routes
```

```
BGP table version is 31, local router ID is 128.107.9.1
Status codes: s suppressed, d damped, h history, * valid, > best, i - internal,
              r RIB-failure, S Stale
Origin codes: i - IGP, e - EGP, ? - incomplete


   Network          Next Hop            Metric LocPrf Weight Path
*> 128.107.0.0/19    0.0.0.0                          32768 i

Total number of prefixes 1
```

Example 14-10 shows an interesting progression if you just read through the example from start to finish. To begin, the **show ip bgp 1.1.1.1 advertised-routes** command lists the routes that E1 has advertised to neighbor 1.1.1.1 (Router I1-1) in the past. Then, the configuration shows a prefix list that matches only 128.107.0.0/19, with a permit action; all other prefixes will be denied by the implied deny all at the end of each prefix list. Then, the **neighbor 1.1.1.1 prefix-list only-public out** BGP subcommand tells BGP to apply the prefix list to filter outbound routes sent to I1-1.

The second part of the output shows an example of how BGP operates on a Cisco router, particularly how BGP requires that the neighbor be cleared before the newly config-ured filter takes effect. Router E1 has already advertised two prefixes to this neighbor: 128.107.0.0/19 and 192.135.250.0/28, as seen at the beginning of the example. To make the filtering action take effect, the router must be told to clear the neighborship with Router I1-1. The **clear ip bgp 1.1.1.1** command tells E1 to perform a hard reset of that neighbor connection, which brings down the TCP connection and removes all BGP table entries associated with that neighbor. The neighbor (I1-1, using address 1.1.1.1) also removes its BGP table entries associated with Router E1. After the neighborship recovers, E1 resends its BGP Update to Router I1-1—but this time with one less prefix, as noted at the end of the example with the output of the **show ip bgp neighbor 1.1.1.1 advertised-routes** command.

This same filtering action could have been performed with several other configuration options: using the **neighbor distribute-list** or **neighbor route-map** commands. The **neighbor distribute-list** command refers to an IP ACL, which tells Cisco IOS to filter routes based on matching the prefix (standard ACL) or prefix/length (extended ACL). The **neighbor route-map** command refers to a route map that can use several matching options to filter routes, keeping routes matched with a route map permit clause and filtering routes matched with a route map deny clause. Example 14-11 shows two such options just for comparison's sake.

Example 14-11   *Alternatives to the Configuration in Example 14-10*

```
! First option - ACL 101 as a distribute-list
access-list 101 permit ip host 128.107.0.0 host 255.255.224.0
router bgp 11
 neighbor 1.1.1.1 distribute-list 101 out


! Second option: Same prefix list as Example 14-10, referenced by a route map
```

```
ip prefix-list only-public seq 5 permit 128.107.0.0/19
!
route-map only-public-rmap permit 10
 match ip address prefix-list only-public
!
router bgp 11
 neighbor 1.1.1.1 route-map only-public-rmap out
```

Clearing BGP Neighbors

As noted in Example 14-10 and the related explanations, Cisco IOS does not cause a newly configured BGP filter to take effect until the neighbor relationship is cleared. The neighborship can be cleared in several ways, including reloading the router and by administratively disabling and reenabling the BGP neighborship using the **neighbor shutdown** and **no neighbor shutdown** configuration commands. However, Cisco IOS supports several options on the **clear ip bgp** EXEC command for the specific purpose of resetting BGP connections. This section examines the differences in these options.

Each variation on the **clear ip bgp...** command either performs a hard reset or soft reset of one or more BGP neighborships. When a hard reset occurs, the local router brings down the neighborship, brings down the underlying TCP connection, and removes all BGP table entries learned from that neighbor. Both the local and neighboring router react just like they do for any failed BGP neighborship by removing their BGP table entries learned over that neighborship. With a soft reset, the router does not bring down the BGP neighborship or the underlying TCP connection. However, the local router resends outgoing Updates, adjusted per the outbound filter, and reprocesses incoming Updates per the inbound filter, which adjusts the BGP tables based on the then-current configuration.

Table 14-3 lists many of the variations on the **clear ip bgp** command, with a reference as to whether it uses hard or soft reset.

Key Topic

Table 14-3 *BGP* clear *Command Options*

Command	Hard or Soft	One or All Neighbors	Direction (In or Out)
clear ip bgp *	Hard	All	Both
clear ip bgp *neighbor-id*	Hard	One	Both
clear ip bgp *neighbor-id* out	Soft	One	Out
clear ip bgp *neighbor-id* soft out	Soft	One	Out
clear ip bgp *neighbor-id* in	Soft	One	In
clear ip bgp *neighbor-id* soft in	Soft	One	In
clear ip bgp * soft	Soft	All	Both
clear ip bgp *neighbor-id* soft	Soft	One	Both

The commands listed in the table should be considered as pairs. In the first pair, both commands perform a hard reset. The first command uses a * instead of the neighbor IP address, causing a hard reset of all BGP neighbors, while the second command resets that particular neighbor.

The second pair of commands performs soft resets for a particular neighbor but only for outgoing updates, making these commands useful when a router changes its outbound BGP filters. Both commands do the same function; two such commands exist in part because of the history of BGP's implementation in Cisco IOS. When issued, these two commands cause the router to reevaluate its existing BGP table and create a new BGP Update for that neighbor. The router builds that new Update based on the existing configuration, so any new or changed outbound filters affect the contents of the Update. The router sends the new BGP Update, and the neighboring router receives the new Update and adjusts its BGP table as a result.

The third pair of commands performs soft resets for a particular neighbor, but only for incoming updates, making these commands useful when a router changes its inbound BGP filters. However, unlike the two previous commands in the table, these two commands do have slightly different behavior and need a little more description.

The **clear ip bgp** *neighbor-id* **soft in** command, the older command of the two, works only if the configuration includes the **neighbor** *neighbor-id* **soft-reconfiguration inbound** BGP configuration command for this same neighbor. This configuration command causes the router to retain the received BGP Updates from that neighbor. This consumes extra memory on the router, but it gives the router a copy of the original pre-filter Update received from that neighbor. Using that information, the **clear ip bgp** *neighbor-id* **soft in** command tells Cisco IOS to reapply the inbound filter to the cached received Update, updating the local router's BGP table.

The newer version of the **clear ip bgp** command, namely, the **clear ip bgp** *neighbor-id* **in** command (without the **soft** keyword), removes the requirement for the **neighbor** *neighbor-id* **soft-reconfiguration inbound** configuration command. Instead, the router uses a newer BGP feature, the route refresh feature, which essentially allows a BGP router to ask its neighbor to resend its full BGP Update. The **clear ip bgp** *neighbor-id* **in** command tells the local router to use the route refresh feature to ask the neighbor to resend its BGP Update, and then the local router can apply its current inbound BGP filters, updating its BGP table.

Example 14-12 shows a sample of how to confirm whether a router has the route refresh capability. In this case, both the local router (E1 from Figure 14-5) and the neighbor (I1-1 from Figure 14-5) have route refresh capability. As a result, E1 can perform a soft reset inbound without the need to consume the extra memory with the **neighbor soft-reconfiguration inbound** configuration command.

Example 14-12   *Alternatives to the Configuration in Example 14-10*

```
E1# show ip bgp neighbor 1.1.1.1
BGP neighbor is 1.1.1.1,  remote AS 1, external link
  BGP version 4, remote router ID 1.1.1.1
```

```
 BGP state = Established, up for 00:04:21
 Last read 00:00:20, last write 00:00:48, hold time is 180, keepalive interval is
  60 seconds
 Neighbor capabilities:
   Route refresh: advertised and received(new)
! Lines omitted for brevity
```

The last pair of commands in Table 14-3 do a soft reset both inbound and outbound at the same time, either for all neighbors (the * option) or for the single neighbor listed in the **clear** command.

Displaying the Results of BGP Filtering

To verify and troubleshoot filtering configurations, you need to see both the results before and after the filter. Cisco IOS provides several **show** commands that allow you to do exactly that. For example, Example 14-10 shows several cases of the **show ip bgp neighbor advertised-routes** command that shows the post-filter BGP Updates sent by a router. Figure 14-8 summarizes these commands, showing how they can be used to display the pre- and post-filter BGP table contents. The figure shows Router E1, with inbound filtering for Updates received from Router I3-1 and outbound filtering of BGP Updates sent to Router I1-1.

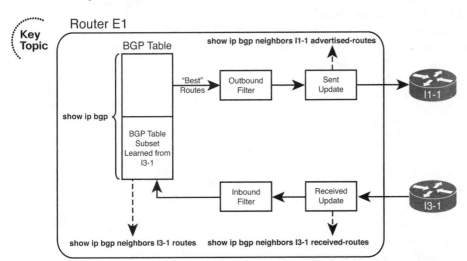

Figure 14-8   show *Commands Related to BGP Filtering*

The commands for displaying inbound updates, at the bottom of the figure, display output in the same format as the **show ip bgp** command. These commands restrict the contents to either exactly what has been received from that one neighbor (the **show ip bgp neighbors received-routes** command) or what has been received and passed through any inbound filter (the **show ip bgp neighbors routes** command).

One of the two commands helpful for the inbound direction, namely, the **show ip bgp neighbor received-routes** command, requires the configuration of the BGP subcommand

neighbor soft-reconfiguration inbound. As a result, to see the pre-filter BGP Update received from a neighbor, a router must configure this extra command, which causes the router to use more memory to store the inbound Update. However, when learning in a lab, the extra memory should not pose a problem.

Of the two commands for outbound filtering, the post-filter command is somewhat obvious, but there is no command to specifically display a pre-filter view of the BGP Update sent to a neighbor. However, BGP advertises the best route for each prefix in the BGP table, within certain restrictions. Those restrictions state that BGP will not advertise iBGP-learned routes to an iBGP peer, and a router will not advertise the best route back to the same neighbor that advertised that route. So, to see the pre-filter BGP table entries, use the **show ip bgp** command, look for all the best routes, and then consider the additional rules. Use the **show ip bgp neighbor advertised-routes** command to display the post-filter BGP Update for a given neighbor.

Example 14-13 shows the output of these commands on E1. In this case, E1 has already been configured with an inbound filter that filters inbound prefixes 184.0.0.0/8 and 185.0.0.0/8. (The filter configuration is not shown.) As a result, the post-filter output lists five prefixes, and the pre-filter output lists seven prefixes. The example also shows the error message when soft reconfiguration is not configured.

Example 14-13 *Displaying the BGP Table Pre- and Post-Inbound Filter*

```
E1# show ip bgp neighbors 1.1.1.1 routes
BGP table version is 78, local router ID is 11.11.11.11
Status codes: s suppressed, d damped, h history, * valid, > best, i - internal,
              r RIB-failure, S Stale
Origin codes: i - IGP, e - EGP, ? - incomplete

   Network          Next Hop          Metric LocPrf Weight Path
*> 0.0.0.0          1.1.1.1                0         0 1 i
*> 181.0.0.0/8      1.1.1.1                          0 1 2 111 111 i
*> 182.0.0.0/8      1.1.1.1                          0 1 2 222 i
*> 183.0.0.0/8      1.1.1.1                          0 1 2 i
*  192.135.250.0/28 1.1.1.1                          0 1 2 3 4 i

Total number of prefixes 5
E1# show ip bgp neighbors 1.1.1.1 received-routes
% Inbound soft reconfiguration not enabled on 1.1.1.1

E1# configure terminal
Enter configuration commands, one per line.  End with CNTL/Z.
E1(config)# router bgp 11
E1(config-router)# neighbor 1.1.1.1 soft-reconfiguration inbound
E1(config-router)# end
E1#
E1# show ip bgp neighbors 1.1.1.1 received-routes
BGP table version is 78, local router ID is 11.11.11.11
```

```
Status codes: s suppressed, d damped, h history, * valid, > best, i - internal,
              r RIB-failure, S Stale
Origin codes: i - IGP, e - EGP, ? - incomplete

   Network          Next Hop         Metric LocPrf Weight Path
*> 0.0.0.0          1.1.1.1              0            0 1 i
*> 181.0.0.0/8      1.1.1.1                           0 1 2 111 111 i
*> 182.0.0.0/8      1.1.1.1                           0 1 2 222 i
*> 183.0.0.0/8      1.1.1.1                           0 1 2 i
*> 184.0.0.0/8      1.1.1.1                           0 1 2 i
*> 185.0.0.0/8      1.1.1.1                           0 1 2 i
*  192.135.250.0/28 1.1.1.1                           0 1 2 3 4 i

Total number of prefixes 7
```

Peer Groups

Cisco IOS creates BGP updates, by default, on a neighbor-by-neighbor basis. As a result, more neighbors result in more CPU resources being used. Also, by applying nondefault settings (for example, performing filtering using prefix lists, route maps, or filter lists) to those neighbors, even more CPU resources are required.

However, many neighbors might have similarly configured parameters. Cisco IOS allows you to logically group those similar neighbors into a BGP *peer group*. Then, you can apply your nondefault BGP configuration to the peer group, as opposed to applying those parameters to each neighbor individually. In fact, a single router can have multiple peer groups, each representing a separate set of parameters. The result can be a dramatic decrease in required CPU resources.

Note   Even though the filtering operations are performed for a peer group, rather than the individual members of the peer group, a Cisco IOS router still sends out individual BGP Updates to each of its neighbors. This is a requirement, based on BGP's characteristic of establishing a TCP session with each neighbor.

To illustrate the configuration of a peer group, consider Figure 14-9. In the figure, the HQ router has connections to two ISPs. Because the same IP prefix list needs to be applied to each peer, a BGP peer group is used in the configuration, as shown in Example 14-14.

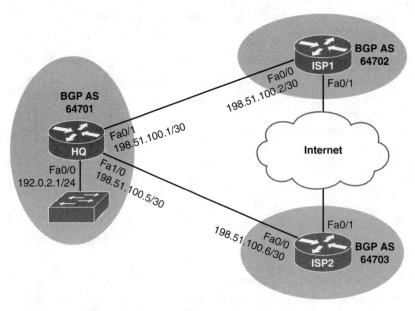

Figure 14-9 *Topology Using a BGP Peer Group*

Example 14-14 *BGP Peer Group Configuration*

```
router bgp 64701
 bgp log-neighbor-changes
 network 192.0.2.0
 network 198.51.100.0 mask 255.255.255.252
 network 198.51.100.4 mask 255.255.255.252
 neighbor ROUTE-PG peer-group
 neighbor ROUTE-PG prefix-list ROUTE-DEMO in
 neighbor 198.51.100.2 remote-as 64702
 neighbor 198.51.100.2 peer-group ROUTE-PG
 neighbor 198.51.100.6 remote-as 64703
 neighbor 198.51.100.6 peer-group ROUTE-PG
!
ip prefix-list ROUTE-DEMO seq 5 deny 10.0.0.0/8 le 32
ip prefix-list ROUTE-DEMO seq 10 deny 172.16.0.0/12 le 32
ip prefix-list ROUTE-DEMO seq 15 deny 192.168.0.0/16 le 32
ip prefix-list ROUTE-DEMO seq 20 permit 0.0.0.0/0
ip prefix-list ROUTE-DEMO seq 25 permit 0.0.0.0/0 ge 8
```

The purpose of Example 14-14 is to prevent RFC 1918 private IP addresses from being learned by Router HQ. The **neighbor ROUTE-PG peer-group** command creates a BGP peer group named **ROUTE-PG**. The **neighbor ROUTE-PG prefix-list ROUTE-DEMO in** command applies the **ROUTE-DEMO** IP prefix list, in the inbound direction, to the peer group. Also, the commands **neighbor 198.51.100.2 peer-group ROUTE-PG** and **neighbor 198.51.100.6 peer-group ROUTE-PG** make ISP1 (198.51.100.2) and ISP2 (198.51.100.6) members of the peer group.

BGP Path Attributes and Best-Path Algorithm

BGP supports a wide variety of *Path Attributes (PA)*. Some of the PAs exist solely to be used as part of the litany of options in the BGP best-path algorithm, some have nothing to do with the BGP best-path algorithm, and some impact the best-path algorithm as well as being used for other purposes. For example, the Local Preference PA exists to give control to a single AS regarding its outbound routes from an AS-wide perspective. Conversely, the BGP Next_Hop PA provides BGP with a place to list the next-hop IP address for a path, but it does not provide a useful means for engineers to set different values for the purpose of influencing the best-path choice.

The term *BGP best-path algorithm* refers to the process by which BGP on a single router examines the competing BGP paths (routes) in its BGP table, for a single prefix, choosing one route as the best route. The best path algorithm has many steps, but it eventually results in the choice of a single route for each prefix as that router's best BGP path.

This section of the chapter examines the BGP PAs used by the BGP best-path algorithm, the BGP best-path algorithm itself, and some related topics.

BGP Path Attributes

BGP Path Attributes define facts about a particular route or path through a network. Each PA defines something different about the path, so to truly understand BGP PAs, you need to examine each PA. This section begins by reviewing a few PAs that should now be familiar, and then this section introduces a few new PAs.

BGP uses the *Autonomous System Path (AS_Path)* PA for several purposes. This particular PA lists the ASNs in the end-to-end path. BGP uses the AS_Path PA as its primary loop-prevention tool. Specifically, when an eBGP peer receives an Update, if its own ASN is already in the received AS_Path, that route has already been advertised into the local ASN and should be ignored. In addition to loop prevention, the BGP best-path algorithm uses the AS_Path PA to calculate the AS_Path length, which the algorithm considers as one of its many steps.

BGP also defines the *next-hop IP address (Next_Hop)* of a route as a PA. BGP can advertise one of several different IP addresses as a route's Next_Hop, depending on several factors. To support such features, BGP needs to list the Next_Hop IP address for each path (route), and BGP defines this concept in the Next_Hop PA. The best-path algorithm includes a check related to the Next_Hop IP address of the route.

Table 14-4 lists these two PAs, plus a few more PAs, and a related BGP feature (Weight) that is not a PA but is used by Cisco BGP best-path implementation. The table lists the PAs in the same order that the BGP best-path algorithm will consider them. The table also describes each feature listed in the table, relative to whether it is most useful to influence outbound routes (away from the enterprise) and inbound routes (toward the enterprise).

**Key
Topic**

Table 14-4 *BGP Path Attributes That Affect the BGP Best-Path Algorithm*

PA	Description	Enterprise Route Direction (Typical)
Next_Hop	Lists the next-hop IP address used to reach a prefix.	—
Weight[1]	A numeric value, range 0 through $2^{16} - 1$, set by a router when receiving Updates, influencing that one router's route for a prefix. Not advertised to any BGP peers.	Outbound
Local Preference (Local_Pref)	A numeric value, range 0 through $2^{32} - 1$, set and communicated throughout a single AS for the purpose of influencing the choice of best route for all routers in that AS.	Outbound
AS_Path (length)	The number of ASNs in the AS_Path PA.	Outbound, Inbound
Origin	Value implying that the route was injected into BGP; I (IGP), E (EGP), or ? (incomplete information).	Outbound
Multi-Exit Discriminator (MED)	Set and advertised by routers in one AS, impacting the BGP decision of routers in the other AS. Smaller is better.	Inbound

[1] Weight is not a BGP PA; it is a Cisco-proprietary feature that acts somewhat like a PA.

The short descriptions in the table can be helpful for review when doing your final preparation study, but the table does not hold enough information to truly appreciate how an engineer might use these PAs effectively. The next two major sections of this chapter examine most of these PAs and describe how to influence the best-path choice with each.

To find the current settings of the features in Table 14-4, you can use commands like **show ip bgp** and **show ip bgp** *prefix/length*. However, picking the values out of the clutter in the output of the **show ip bgp** command can be a challenge. Figure 14-10 shows a sample of this command's output and some notations on where to find the various PA settings.

The examples throughout the rest this chapter include examples of these commands, along with the PA settings as changed by various route maps.

Key Topic

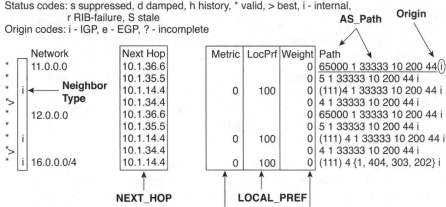

R3 #**show ip bgp**
BGP table version is 12, local router ID is 3.3.3.3
Status codes: s suppressed, d damped, h history, * valid, > best, i - internal,
            r RIB-failure, S stale
Origin codes: i - IGP, e - EGP, ? - incomplete

Figure 14-10 *Finding PA Settings in the Output of the* show ip bgp *Command*

Overview of the BGP Best-Path Algorithm

The BGP best-path algorithm follows the steps shown in shorthand form in Table 14-5. The table lists steps 0 through 8, a short descriptive phrase, and a notation about the criteria for one value to be better than another.

Key Topic

Table 14-5 *BGP Decision Process Plus Mnemonic: N WLLA OMNI*

Step	Mnemonic Letter	Short Phrase	Which Is Better?
0	N	Next hop: reachable?	If no route to reach Next_Hop, router cannot use this route.
1	W	Weight	Bigger.
2	L	Local_Pref	Bigger.
3	L	Locally injected routes	Locally injected is better than iBGP/ eBGP learned.
4	A	AS_Path length	Smaller.
5	O	Origin	Prefer I over E. Prefer E over ?
6	M	MED	Smaller.
7	N	Neighbor type	Prefer eBGP over iBGP.
8	I	IGP metric to Next_Hop	Smaller.

Note The step numbering of the BGP best-path steps does not exist in the BGP RFCs. The steps are numbered in this book for easier reference. Because the RFCs do not dictate a particular step numbering, other references likely use different step numbers. Therefore, do not be concerned about memorizing the step numbers.

Starting with a Step 0 might seem odd, but it helps make an important point about the logic listed at this step. Some BGP best-path references include the logic in this step as a best-path step, and some just list this same information as a side note. Regardless, the Step 0 concept is important. For Step 0, a router looks at the BGP route and compares the Next_Hop IP address to the IP routing table.

If that router does not have a matching IP route for the BGP route's Next_Hop IP address, that router will not know how to forward packets for that particular prefix, using that particular route. To avoid using such a route, at Step 0, the BGP best-path algorithm removes such routes from consideration. BGP then uses the following eight steps, in order, until one best route is chosen for a given prefix.

If a router still did not determine a best route when finishing Step 8, the router takes several other small steps to break the tie. At this point, the competing routes are considered to be just as good as each other. However, unlike IGPs, BGP needs to choose one and only one route as best, in part because BGP advertises only the best routes to its neighbors. In such cases, BGP breaks the tie with these additional steps, which would be considered Steps 9–11:

Step 9. Oldest (longest-known) eBGP route

Step 10. Lowest neighbor BGP RID

Step 11. Lowest neighbor IP address

Taking a more detailed view of the entire best-path algorithm, BGP begins by choosing the oldest known route for a given prefix as the best route. It then takes the next longest-known route for that same prefix and compares the two routes using the best-path algorithm. The router eventually chooses one of the two BGP routes as the best path (route). If another route exists for the same prefix, the router repeats the process, using the winner of the previous comparisons and the new route, choosing one of those as the better route. The process continues until all routes have been considered, with one route being listed as best in the BGP table.

For example, if Router R1 were considering two routes for prefix 181.0.0.0/8, it would first make sure that both routes had reachable Next_Hop IP addresses. The router would then compare the Weight settings, choosing the route with the bigger Weight. If they tied on Weight, the router would prefer the route with a bigger Local_Pref. If again a tie, the router would prefer the one route that was injected into BGP locally (using the **network** command or using route redistribution). If neither or both routes were locally injected, the router moves on to AS_Path length, and so on, until the router chooses one of the two as the better route.

As soon as one of the steps determines a best route, the comparison of those two routes stops.

Perspectives on the Core Eight Best-Path Steps

Some of the BGP best-path steps purposefully give the engineer a tool for influencing the choice of best path, whereas other steps have a different purpose, often simply being a side effect of some BGP feature. So, when an engineer starts building a BGP implementation plan, only a subset of the core eight BGP best-path steps need be considered, as follows:

Key Topic

- Weight (Step 1)

- Local_Pref (Step 2)

- AS_Path Length (Step 4)

- MED (often called metric) (Step 6)

Because the ROUTE exam focuses on the more practical aspects of BGP for enterprises, it gives much more attention to these four features and less attention to the other BGP best-path steps. This chapter describes each of these four features in some depth in the context of best-path selection. However, before focusing on these four items, it can be helpful to see a small glimpse into the meaning of the other steps, which can be helpful as you work to memorize the steps in the BGP best-path algorithm.

Step 3 compares the source from which the routes were added to the BGP table. When the BGP best-path algorithm compares two routes at this step, if one were injected into BGP locally and the other were not (it was learned from a BGP peer), the router chooses the route that was injected locally. The Chapter 13 section "Injecting Routes into BGP for Advertisement to the ISPs" describes the two ways to locally inject these routes, the **network** command, and redistribution from an IGP.

Step 5 refers to the BGP Origin PA. The Origin PA attempts to identify the source from outside BGP from which the route was injected into BGP. The three Origin code values are

- **i:** Injected from an IGP (using a **network** command)

- **e:** Injected from exterior gateway protocol (EGP)

- **?:** Undetermined

Although the original intent of the Origin PA is to identify the source from which BGP learned the route, routers can also set the Origin PA as part of a strategy to influence the BGP best path.

Step 7 refers to the Neighbor type: iBGP or eBGP. Remembering that BGP compares two routes at a time, if one is learned with eBGP and the other with iBGP, the router chooses the eBGP route as best. Using this feature to influence the best-path choice would be difficult, because the ASN in which a router resides is fixed by the BGP design.

Finally, Step 8 refers to the IGP metric to the Next_Hop address. At this step, the router compares the metrics of the IP routes for each Next_Hop IP address and chooses the BGP route with the lower IGP metric to its Next_Hop. (If an IGP-learned route is not used—for example, if both use connected routes—BGP considers the metrics to tie.) It is conceivable that an engineer might tune the IGP to manipulate BGP's best-path choice, but this step is so far into the algorithm that the earlier and more flexible settings would be much better options.

Memorization Tips for BGP Best Path

This short section suggests a mnemonic tool to help you memorize Steps 0 through 8 of the BGP best-path algorithm. Feel free to skim this section for now, or ignore it entirely—there is no requirement that you memorize the best-path algorithm using the mnemonics in this section. (However, you might want to at least review upcoming Figure 14-11, which gives a good visual reference for some of the information summarized in Table 14-5.) But you should plan on memorizing the list at some point before the exam, even if you ignore the mnemonic device.

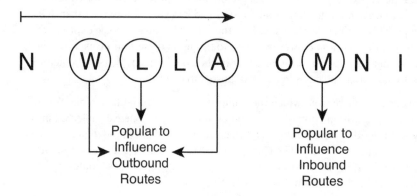

Figure 14-11 *BGP Best-Path Mnemonics*

First, if you refer back to the BGP best-path algorithm as listed in Table 14-5, you see that the second column lists a single-letter mnemonic letter. These letters match the first letter of the description in the third column of that table. Then, take these initial letters and group them as follows:

- N

- WLLA

- OMNI

The N is listed separately, because it represents the "Is the next-hop reachable?" logic of Step 0 and is somewhat separate from the other steps.

The mnemonic groups the eight main steps as two sets of four letters for a couple of reasons. Both sets can be pronounced, even if they don't spell words. It should be easier to memorize as two sets of four. And maybe most importantly, the first set of four letters, representing Steps 1 through 4, include all the features that engineers typically use to influence outbound routes from the enterprise:

- **WLLA:** Refers to the three steps that an engineer might use to influence outbound routes: Weight, Local_Pref, and AS_Path length. (Additionally, the second L, in WLLA for Step 3, represents the "Locally injected routes" choice.)

- **OMNI:** As listed in Table 14-5, the letters represent Origin (i, e, or ?), MED, neighbor type (eBGP over iBGP), and IGP metric to Next_Hop.

So, if you can memorize N WLLA OMNI, by the time you've read this chapter, you can probably pick out which of those correlate to the four bigger topics later in this chapter: Weight, Local_Pref, AS_Path length, and MED. Hopefully with a little more study, you can memorize the rest of the list.

Figure 14-11 shows the mnemonic letters in graphical form just as another aid in memorizing the steps. It also shows a reminder of which features are most likely to be used to influence outbound routes from the enterprise, and the one setting (MED) most likely to be used to influence inbound routes into the enterprise.

The rest of this chapter focuses on a deeper explanation of the four best-path steps that engineers typically use to influence the choice of best path.

Influencing an Enterprise's Outbound Routes

This section examines three different features that can influence the outbound routes from an enterprise: Weight, the Local_Pref PA, and AS_Path length. The topics are listed in the order used by the BGP best-path algorithm (Steps 1, 2, and 4). It also introduces the concept of a *Routing Table Manager (RTM)* function on a router.

Influencing BGP Weight

A Cisco router can use the BGP Weight, on that single router, to influence that one router's choice of outbound route. To do so, when a router receives a BGP Update, that router can set the Weight either selectively, per route, using a route map, or for all routes learned from a single neighbor. The router's best-path algorithm then examines the Weight of competing routes, choosing the route with the bigger Weight.

The Cisco-proprietary Weight settings configured on a single router can influence only that one router, because the Weight cannot be communicated to other neighboring BGP routers. So, to use the Weight, a router must be configured to examine incoming Updates to set the Weight. The Weight cannot simply be learned in a received Update, because that Update message does not support a field in which to communicate the Weight setting.

Table 14-6 summarizes some of the key facts about BGP administrative Weight. Following the table, the text first explains a sample internetwork and its existing configuration, a configuration that begins with configurations that do not set any values that influence the choice of best paths. The next section shows how to set the Weight using the **neighbor route-map in** command, which allows a router to set different Weights for different routes. The second example shows how to set the Weight for all routes learned from a neighbor, using the **neighbor weight** command.

Table 14-6 *Key Features of Administrative Weight*

Feature	Description
Is it a PA?	No; Cisco-proprietary feature
Purpose	Identifies a single router's best route
Scope	Set on inbound route Updates; influences only that one router's choice
Range	0 through 65,535 (2^{16} − 1)
Which is better?	Bigger values are better
Default	0 for learned routes, 32,768 for locally injected routes
Defining a new default	Not supported
Configuration	**neighbor route-map** (per prefix) **neighbor weight** (all routes learned from this neighbor)

Note For those of you memorizing using the N WLLA OMNI mnemonic, Weight is the W in WLLA.

Sample Internetwork Used in the Weight Examples

Figure 14-12 shows a sample internetwork used to demonstrate setting the Weight. The figure shows a single enterprise and a single enterprise router. The following design requirements have already been met by the configuration in Router E1 and in the ISP routers:

- E1 and I1-1 use loopback IP addresses (11.11.11.11 and 1.1.1.1) for their neighborship.

- E1 and I3-1 use interface IP addresses for their neighborship.

- None of the routers have attempted to change any settings that can impact the choice of best path.

Next, to have some routes to manipulate with the upcoming examples, the ISP routers each advertise BGP routes for the same five prefixes. Figure 14-13 shows five such prefixes that both ISPs advertise to E1.

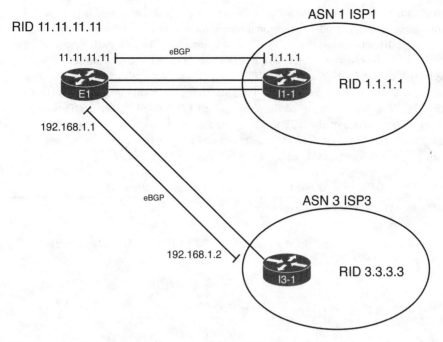

Figure 14-12   *Sample Internetwork for BGP Weight Examples*

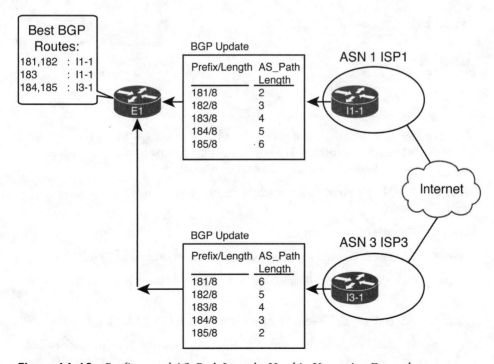

Figure 14-13   *Prefixes and AS_Path Lengths Used in Upcoming Examples*

Just to get a little deeper understanding of the best-path algorithm before getting into the Weight configuration, consider the original configuration state of the sample internetwork, with no attempt to influence E1's choice of best path. The best path for four of the five prefixes will be obvious. Prefixes 181.0.0.0/8 and 182.0.0.0/8 have a shorter AS_Path through ISP1, and 184.0.0.0/8 and 185.0.0.08 have a shorter AS_Path through ISP3. Only 183.0.0.0/8 is in question, because its AS_Path length for the competing routes is equal. Example 14-15 shows the output of the **show ip bgp 176.0.0.0/4 longer-prefixes** command, which lists all five of the BGP prefixes listed in Figure 14-13, confirming the results. (Prefix 176.0.0.0/4 implies a range of values whose first octets are in the range 176 through 191, which includes the routes listed in Example 14-15.)

Example 14-15   *BGP Configuration on E1: Neighborships Configured*

```
E1# show ip bgp 176.0.0.0/4 longer-prefixes
BGP table version is 41, local router ID is 128.107.9.1
Status codes: s suppressed, d damped, h history, * valid, > best, i - internal,
              r RIB-failure, S Stale
Origin codes: i - IGP, e - EGP, ? - incomplete


   Network          Next Hop          Metric LocPrf Weight Path
*  181.0.0.0/8      192.168.1.2            0             0 3 2 50 51 52 1811 i
*>                  1.1.1.1                0             0 1 1811 i
*  182.0.0.0/8      192.168.1.2            0             0 3 2 50 51 1822 i
*>                  1.1.1.1                0             0 1 2 1822 i
*  183.0.0.0/8      192.168.1.2            0             0 3 2 50 1833 i
*>                  1.1.1.1                0             0 1 2 50 1833 i
*> 184.0.0.0/8      192.168.1.2            0             0 3 2 1844 i
*                   1.1.1.1                0             0 1 2 50 51 1844 i
*> 185.0.0.0/8      192.168.1.2            0             0 3 1855 i
*                   1.1.1.1                0             0 1 2 50 51 52 1855 i
```

First, consider the best-path algorithm on Router E1 for 181.0.0.0/8. E1 knows two BGP routes for 181.0.0.0/8, as expected. The one listed as the best path has 1.1.1.1 (I1-1) as Next_Hop. The following list outlines the best-path logic:

Step 0.   The Next_Hop of each is reachable. (Otherwise the neighbors would not be up.)

Step 1.   The Weight ties (both 0).

Step 2.   The Local_Pref ties (unset, so no value is listed; defaults to 100).

Step 3.   Neither route is locally injected; both are learned using BGP, so neither is better at this step.

Step 4.   AS_Path length is shorter for the route through I1-1 (1.1.1.1).

Next, consider the example of the route to 183.0.0.0/8. E1 currently lists the path through I1-1 (1.1.1.1) as best, but the best-path decision actually falls all the way to Step 9. For completeness' sake, E1's best-path logic runs as follows:

Step 0.   The Next_Hop of each is reachable. (Otherwise the neighbors would not be up.)

Step 1.   The Weight ties (both 0).

Step 2.   The Local_Pref ties (unset, defaults to 100).

Step 3.   Neither route is locally injected.

Step 4.   AS_Path length is 4 in both cases.

Step 5.   Both Origin codes are **i**.

Step 6.   MED, listed under the Metric column, ties (0).

Step 7.   Neighbor type for each neighbor is eBGP.

Step 8.   IGP metric does not apply, because neither uses IGP routes. (The routes from E1 to 1.1.1.1 are static routes.)

Step 9.   The route learned from 1.1.1.1 is the oldest route.

Although you might believe the claims at Step 9, the output in Example 14-15 does not explicitly state that fact. However, when Cisco IOS lists output in the variations of the **show ip bgp** command, the oldest route for each prefix is listed last, and the newest (most recently learned) is listed first. Example 14-16 confirms this logic, and confirms how Step 9 works in this case. Example 14-16 clears peer 1.1.1.1 (I1-1), making E1's route through 192.168.1.2 (I3-1) become the oldest known route for 183.0.0.0/8.

Example 14-16   *Clearing Neighbors to Force a New Route*

```
E1# clear ip bgp 1.1.1.1
E1#
*Aug 24 11:30:41.775: %BGP-5-ADJCHANGE: neighbor 1.1.1.1 Down User reset
*Aug 24 11:30:43.231: %BGP-5-ADJCHANGE: neighbor 1.1.1.1 Up
E1# show ip bgp 176.0.0.0/4 longer-prefixes
BGP table version is 47, local router ID is 128.107.9.1
Status codes: s suppressed, d damped, h history, * valid, > best, i - internal,
              -r RIB-failure, S Stale
Origin codes: i - IGP, e - EGP, ? - incomplete

   Network          Next Hop          Metric LocPrf Weight Path
*> 181.0.0.0/8      1.1.1.1                0             0 1 1811 i
*                   192.168.1.2            0             0 3 2 50 51 52 1811 i
*> 182.0.0.0/8      1.1.1.1                0             0 1 2 1822 i
*                   192.168.1.2            0             0 3 2 50 51 1822 i
*  183.0.0.0/8      1.1.1.1                0             0 1 2 50 1833 i
*>                  192.168.1.2            0             0 3 2 50 1833 i
*  184.0.0.0/8      1.1.1.1                0             0 1 2 50 51 1844 i
*>                  192.168.1.2            0             0 3 2 1844 i
*  185.0.0.0/8      1.1.1.1                0             0 1 2 50 51 52 1855 i
*>                  192.168.1.2            0             0 3 1855 i
```

After the hard reset of peer 1.1.1.1, E1's oldest-known route for 183.0.0.0/8 is the route through 192.168.1.2, listed second (last). That E1 now chooses this route as best is another confirmation that E1's best-path decision fell to Step 9.

Setting the BGP Administrative Weight Using a Route Map

The **neighbor** *neighbor-ip* **route-map in** BGP subcommand tells a router to apply the route map to all BGP Updates received from the listed neighbor. Such route maps always attempt to filter routes. The router allows routes first matched in a permit clause and filters (discards) routes first matched with a deny clause.

BGP route maps can also be used to change the PAs of routes by using the **set** command. For example, a router could use a **neighbor 1.1.1.1 route-map fred in** command. The route map could contain permit clauses that cause some routes to not be filtered. In those same route map clauses, the inclusion of commands such as **set weight 100 and set local-preference 200** can be used to set items such as the Weight or Local_Pref of a route. (Although you can configure a **set** command in a route map deny clause, the **set** command has no effect, because the deny clause filters the route.)

Example 14-17 shows a sample configuration that sets the Weight for prefix 181.0.0.0/8 as learned from I3-1 (neighbor ID 192.168.1.2). As shown in Example 14-15, E1's original best route for this prefix is through I1-1 (1.1.1.1), because of the shorter AS_Path length at Step 4 of the best-path algorithm. By setting the Weight higher on the route learned from I3-1, E1 now chooses the route through I3-1.

Example 14-17 *Setting the Weight to 50 for 181/8, as Learned from I3-1*

```
E1# conf t
Enter configuration commands, one per line.  End with CNTL/Z.
E1(config)# ip prefix-list match-181 permit 181.0.0.0/8
E1(config)# route-map set-weight-50 permit 10
E1(config-route-map)# match ip address prefix-list match-181
E1(config-route-map)# set weight 50
E1(config-route-map)# route-map set-weight-50 permit 20
E1(config-route-map)# router bgp 11
E1(config-router)# neighbor 192.168.1.2 route-map set-weight-50 in
E1(config-router)# end
E1#
E1# clear ip bgp 192.168.1.2 soft
E1# show ip bgp 176.0.0.0/4 longer-prefixes
BGP table version is 48, local router ID is 128.107.9.1
Status codes: s suppressed, d damped, h history, * valid, > best, i - internal,
              r RIB-failure, S Stale
Origin codes: i - IGP, e - EGP, ? - incomplete

   Network          Next Hop            Metric LocPrf Weight Path
*  181.0.0.0/8      1.1.1.1                  0             0 1 1811 i
*>                  192.168.1.2              0            50 3 2 50 51 52 1811 i
```

```
*> 182.0.0.0/8        1.1.1.1                 0          0 1 2 1822 i
*                     192.168.1.2             0          0 3 2 50 51 1822 i
*  183.0.0.0/8        1.1.1.1                 0          0 1 2 50 1833 i
*>                    192.168.1.2             0          0 3 2 50 1833 i
*  184.0.0.0/8        1.1.1.1                 0          0 1 2 50 51 1844 i
*>                    192.168.1.2             0          0 3 2 1844 i
*  185.0.0.0/8        1.1.1.1                 0          0 1 2 50 51 52 1855 i
*>                    192.168.1.2             0          0 3 1855 i


! The next command lists the pre-route-map received Update
E1# show ip bgp neigh 192.168.1.2 received-routes | include 181
*  181.0.0.0/8        192.168.1.2             0          0 3 2 50 51 52 1811 i


! The next command shows the post-route-map received Update
E1# show ip bgp neigh 192.168.1.2 routes | incl 181
*> 181.0.0.0/8        192.168.1.2             0          50 3 2 50 51 52 1811 i
```

The configuration uses a single-line IP prefix list that matches exactly prefix 181.0.0.0/8, and a two-clause route map. The first route map clause, a permit clause, matches 181.0.0.0/8. The permit action allows the route through the filter. The **set weight 50** command then sets the Weight.

The second route map clause, also with a permit action, matches the rest of the prefixes in the Update, because there is no **match** command. The permit action allows these routes through the filter. Without clause 20, this route map would have matched all other routes with the route map's implied deny clause at the end of every route map, filtering all other routes learned from 192.168.1.2 except 181.0.0.0/8.

The configuration also includes a **neighbor 192.168.1.2 route-map set-weight-50 in** command to enable the route map for incoming updates from Router I3-1. The example also shows that the neighbor must be cleared, in this case with a soft reset command of **clear ip bgp 192.168.1.2 soft**, which causes the route map logic to take effect.

Examining the results of this change, note that E1 now thinks the better route is through I3-1 (192.168.1.2). The output lists the new Weight of 50, with the route through I1-1 (1.1.1.1) using the default Weight of 0. With Weight, bigger is better.

Finally, the last two commands in the example show the pre-route map received update (with the **received-routes** option) and the post-route map results of the received update (with the **routes** option). The received Update does not include Weight, because it is Cisco-proprietary. So, E1 initially assigned the Weight to its default value (0). After applying the route map, E1 now lists a Weight of 50.

Setting Weight Using the neighbor weight Command

Alternatively, the Weight can be set for all routes learned from a neighbor using the **neighbor weight** command. Example 14-18 shows this configuration added to E1, setting the Weight for all routes learned from I1-1 (1.1.1.1) to 60. As a result, E1's route for 181.0.0.0/8 switches back to using the route through 1.1.1.1 (I1-1).

Example 14-18 *Setting the Weight to 60 for All Routes Learned from I1-1*

```
E1# conf t
Enter configuration commands, one per line.  End with CNTL/Z.
E1(config)# router bgp 11
E1(config-router)# neighbor 1.1.1.1 weight 60
E1(config-router)# end
E1# clear ip bgp 1.1.1.1 soft

E1# show ip bgp 176.0.0.0/4 longer-prefixes
BGP table version is 54, local router ID is 128.107.9.1
Status codes: s suppressed, d damped, h history, * valid, > best, i - internal,
              r RIB-failure, S Stale
Origin codes: i - IGP, e - EGP, ? - incomplete

    Network          Next Hop          Metric LocPrf Weight Path
*>  181.0.0.0/8      1.1.1.1                0           60 1 1811 i
*                    192.168.1.2            0           50 3 2 50 51 52 1811 i
*>  182.0.0.0/8      1.1.1.1                0           60 1 2 1822 i
*                    192.168.1.2            0            0 3 2 50 51 1822 i
*>  183.0.0.0/8      1.1.1.1                0           60 1 2 50 1833 i
*                    192.168.1.2            0            0 3 2 50 1833 i
*>  184.0.0.0/8      1.1.1.1                0           60 1 2 50 51 1844 i
*                    192.168.1.2            0            0 3 2 1844 i
*>  185.0.0.0/8      1.1.1.1                0           60 1 2 50 51 52 1855 i
*                    192.168.1.2            0            0 3 1855 i
```

The **neighbor weight** command does not use an in or out direction, because Weight can only be set on input. The configuration results in all routes learned from 1.1.1.1 (I1-1) having a Weight of 60, as noted in the Weight column of the **show ip bgp** output.

Setting the Local Preference

The BGP Local Preference (Local_Pref) PA gives the routers inside a single AS a value that they can set per-route and advertise to all iBGP routers inside the AS, so that all routers in the AS agree about which router is the best exit point for packets destined for that prefix. By design, Local_Pref can be set by routers as they receive eBGP routes by using an inbound route map. The routers then advertise the Local_Pref in iBGP updates. As a result, all the routers in the same AS can then make the same choice of which route is best, agreeing as to which router to use to exit the AS for each prefix.

As with the discussion of Weight, this section begins with a description of a sample scenario. Following that, a sample Local_Pref configuration is shown, using a route map to set Local_Pref for routes advertised into an enterprise. Table 14-7 summarizes some of the key features of Local_Pref as demonstrated in the upcoming pages.

Key Topic

Table 14-7   *Key Features of Local_Pref*

Feature	Description
PA?	Yes
Purpose	Identifies the best exit point from the AS to reach a given prefix
Scope	Throughout the AS in which it was set; not advertised to eBGP peers
Range	0 through 4,294,967,295 ($2^{32} - 1$)
Which is better?	Higher values are better
Default	100
Changing the default	Using the **bgp default local-preference <0-4294967295>** BGP subcommand
Configuration	Through the **neighbor route-map** command; **in** option is required for updates from an eBGP peer

Note   For those of you memorizing using the N WLLA OMNI mnemonic, Local_Pref is the first L in WLLA.

Sample Internetwork Used in the Local_Pref and AS_Path Length Examples

Figure 14-14 shows a sample internetwork used to demonstrate setting both Local_Pref, and later, AS_Path length. The figure shows a single enterprise with two Internet-connected routers. A full iBGP mesh exists with these two routers plus two routers internal to the enterprise. Two eBGP neighborships exist, one with ISP1 and one with ISP3. (Note in particular that unlike Figure 14-12, E1 does not have a neighborship with Router I3-1 in this case.) The following design requirements have already been met by the initial configuration in all routers shown in the figure:

■ E1 and I1-1 use loopback IP addresses (11.11.11.11 and 1.1.1.1) for their neighborship.

■ E2 and I3-1 use interface IP addresses for their neighborship.

■ None of the routers have attempted to change any settings that can impact the choice of best path, and Weight settings in the previous examples have been removed.

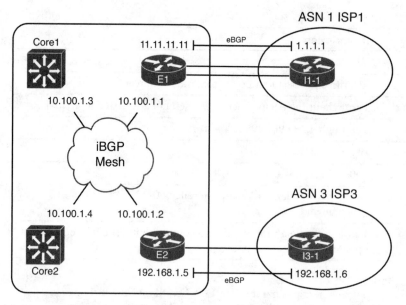

Figure 14-14   *Sample Internetwork for BGP Local_Pref and AS_Path Length Examples*

As with the Weight example, both ISPs advertise the same five prefixes, with different AS_Paths, so that the routers have some prefixes to manipulate. Figure 14-15 shows five such prefixes that both ISPs advertise to E1 and E2. Note that this example network uses the same five prefixes, prefix lengths, and AS_Path values as the previous Weight examples in this chapter.

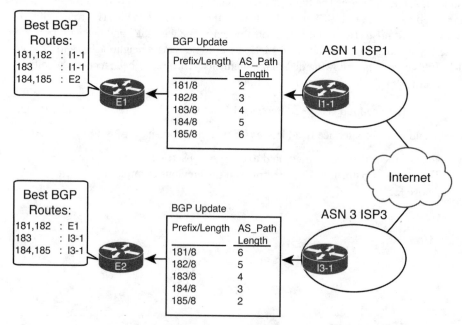

Figure 14-15   *Prefixes and AS_Path Lengths Used in Upcoming Examples*

Before showing the example of how to set the Local_Pref and how it impacts the routes, it is helpful to look at the best BGP routes on the enterprise routers before any PAs have been changed. Example 14-19 shows the relevant BGP table entries on E1, E2, and Core1 with no attempt to influence E1's choice of best path. The best path for four of the five prefixes will be obvious, but the output listed in the commands requires some review. Prefixes 181.0.0.0/8 and 182.0.0.0/8 have a shorter AS_Path through ISP1, so E1 and E2 will agree that E1's path, through ISP1, is best. Similarly, 184.0.0.0/8 and 185.0.0.08 have a shorter AS_Path through ISP3, so both E1 and E2 agree that E2's path is best for these prefixes. Again, 183.0.0.0/8 ties on AS_Path length.

Example 14-19 *BGP Tables on E1, E2, and Core1, with No Changes to Settings That Affect Best Path*

```
! First, on router E1

E1# show ip bgp 176.0.0.0/4 longer-prefixes
BGP table version is 15, local router ID is 128.107.9.1
Status codes: s suppressed, d damped, h history, * valid, > best, i - internal,
              r RIB-failure, S Stale
Origin codes: i - IGP, e - EGP, ? - incomplete


   Network          Next Hop          Metric LocPrf Weight Path
*> 181.0.0.0/8      1.1.1.1              0              0 1 1811 i
*> 182.0.0.0/8      1.1.1.1              0              0 1 2 1822 i
*  i183.0.0.0/8     10.100.1.2           0    100       0 3 2 50 1833 i
*>                  1.1.1.1              0              0 1 2 50 1833 i
*>i184.0.0.0/8      10.100.1.2           0    100       0 3 2 1844 i
*                   1.1.1.1              0              0 1 2 50 51 1844 i
*>i185.0.0.0/8      10.100.1.2           0    100       0 3 1855 i
*                   1.1.1.1              0              0 1 2 50 51 52 1855 i


! Next, on router E2

E2# show ip bgp 176.0.0.0/4 longer-prefixes
! legend omitted for brevity


   Network          Next Hop          Metric LocPrf Weight Path
*>i181.0.0.0/8      10.100.1.1           0    100       0 1 1811 i
*                   192.168.1.6          0              0 3 2 50 51 52 1811 i
*>i182.0.0.0/8      10.100.1.1           0    100       0 1 2 1822 i
*                   192.168.1.6          0              0 3 2 50 51 1822 i
*  i183.0.0.0/8     10.100.1.1           0    100       0 1 2 50 1833 i
*>                  192.168.1.6          0              0 3 2 50 1833 i
*> 184.0.0.0/8      192.168.1.6          0              0 3 2 1844 i
*> 185.0.0.0/8      192.168.1.6          0              0 3 1855 i


! Next, on router Core1

Core1# show ip bgp 176.0.0.0/4 longer-prefixes
! legend omitted for brevity
```

```
Network            Next Hop                Metric LocPrf Weight Path
*>i181.0.0.0/8     10.100.1.1                  0    100      0 1 1811 i
*>i182.0.0.0/8     10.100.1.1                  0    100      0 1 2 1822 i
*>i183.0.0.0/8     10.100.1.1                  0    100      0 1 2 50 1833 i
* i                10.100.1.2                  0    100      0 3 2 50 1833 i
*>i184.0.0.0/8     10.100.1.2                  0    100      0 3 2 1844 i
*>i185.0.0.0/8     10.100.1.2                  0    100      0 3 1855 i
```

First, pay close attention to the LocPrf column of output in the example. This column lists the Local_Pref settings of each route. Some list a (default) value of 100, and some list nothing. As it turns out, because Updates received from eBGP peers do not include the Local_Pref PA, Cisco IOS lists a null value for Local_Pref for eBGP-learned routes by default. However, Updates from iBGP peers do include the Local_Pref. Because this network does not have any configuration that attempts to set Local_Pref yet, the routers advertise their default Local_Pref value of 100 over the iBGP connections.

Also note that when comparing the output on both E1 and E2, the output lists a single eBGP route, but not the alternative iBGP route through the other Internet-connected router in the enterprise. For example, E2 lists a single route for 184.0.0.0/8 and 185.0.0.0/8, through I3-1 (192.168.1.6). The reason that E2 does not list an alternative route through E1 is that E1's best route for these prefixes, as seen near the top of the example, is E1's iBGP-learned route through E2 (10.100.1.2). BGP does not allow a router to advertise iBGP-learned routes to iBGP peers, so E1 will not advertise routes for 184.0.0.0/8 or 185.0.0.0/8 to Router E2.

Finally, for prefix 183.0.0.0/8, both E1 and E2 tie on the AS_Path length. In this case, all best-path choices tie until Step 7, which prefers eBGP routes over iBGP routes. E1 prefers its eBGP route for 183.0.0.0/8 through ISP1's Router I1-1, and E2 prefers its eBGP route through ISP3's Router I3-1.

Setting the BGP Local_Pref Using a Route Map

To set the Local_Pref, a router can use the **neighbor** *neighbor-ip* **route-map in** BGP sub-command. Typically, a router uses this command with the inbound direction for routes received from eBGP peers. Then, with no additional configuration required, the router then advertises the Local_Pref to any iBGP peers.

To show the Local_Pref configuration and results, start with the sample network shown in the previous section. The configuration will now be changed to set the Local_Pref for two different prefixes for Updates received on E1 from I1-1, as shown in Figure 14-16. Note that the figure reinforces the idea that BGP does not include the Local_Pref PA in eBGP Updates but will in iBGP Updates.

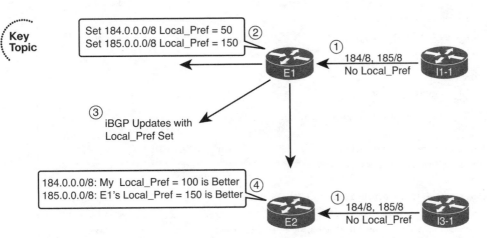

Figure 14-16 *Example Local_Pref Settings for the Upcoming Example*

The figure shows a series of steps, as follows:

Step 1.   I1-1 and I3-1 advertise the prefixes into the enterprise but with no Local_Pref set, because the connections are eBGP peers.

Step 2.   E1 sets the Local_Pref for routes learned from I1-1: 184.0.0.0/8 (50) and 185.0.0.0/8 (150).

Step 3.   E1 includes the Local_Pref settings in its iBGP Updates to Core1, Core2, and E2.

Step 4.   E2 realizes that E1's route for 185.0.0.0/8, Local_Pref 150, is better than E2's eB-GP route for this prefix, which E2 assigned default Local_Pref 100. Conversely, E1's advertised route for 184.0.0.0/8, Local_Pref 50, is worse than E2's eBGP route for that same prefix, with the assigned default Local_Pref of 100.

Example 14-20 shows the configuration on Router E1 to assign the Local_Pref values shown in Figure 14-16. The example also shows the results on E1 and E2. Note that the configuration differs only slightly as compared with the configuration for administrative Weight as shown in Example 14-17, the only substantive difference being the **set local-preference route map** command rather than the **set weight** command.

Example 14-20 *Configuring Local_Pref on Router E1 (Step 2 per Figure 14-16)*

```
E1# show running-config
! only pertinent portions shown
ip prefix-list match-184 seq 5 permit 184.0.0.0/8
!
ip prefix-list match-185 seq 5 permit 185.0.0.0/8
!
route-map set-LP-150 permit 10
 match ip address prefix-list match-185
 set local-preference 150
!
route-map set-LP-150 permit 15
```

```
   match ip address prefix-list match-184
   set local-preference 50
 !
 route-map set-LP-150 permit 20
 !
 router bgp 11
   neighbor 1.1.1.1 route-map set-LP-150 in

 ! The clearing of BGP neighbor I1-1 is done next, but not shown.
 ! Next, E1's Updated BGP Table

 E1# show ip bgp 176.0.0.0/4 longer-prefixes
 BGP table version is 29, local router ID is 128.107.9.1
 Status codes: s suppressed, d damped, h history, * valid, > best, i - internal,
               r RIB-failure, S Stale
 Origin codes: i - IGP, e - EGP, ? - incomplete


    Network          Next Hop          Metric LocPrf Weight Path
 *> 181.0.0.0/8      1.1.1.1                0              0 1 1811 i
 *> 182.0.0.0/8      1.1.1.1                0              0 1 2 1822 i
 *  i183.0.0.0/8     10.100.1.2             0    100       0 3 2 50 1833 i
 *>                  1.1.1.1                0              0 1 2 50 1833 i
 *>i184.0.0.0/8      10.100.1.2             0    100       0 3 2 1844 i
 *                   1.1.1.1                0    50        0 1 2 50 51 1844 i
 *> 185.0.0.0/8      1.1.1.1                0    150       0 1 2 50 51 52 1855 i


 E1# show ip bgp 185.0.0.0/8
 BGP routing table entry for 185.0.0.0/8, version 7
 Paths: (1 available, best #1, table Default-IP-Routing-Table)
   Advertised to update-groups:
        1
 1 2 50 51 52 1855, (received & used)
    1.1.1.1 from 1.1.1.1 (1.1.1.1)
      Origin IGP, metric 0, localpref 150, valid, external, best

 ! The next output occurs on router E2
 E2# show ip bgp 185.0.0.0/8 longer-prefixes
 ! heading lines omitted


    Network          Next Hop          Metric LocPrf Weight Path
 *>i185.0.0.0/8      10.100.1.1             0    150       0 1 2 50 51 52 1855 i
 *                   192.168.1.6            0              0 3 1855 i
```

Example 14-20's output shows E1's BGP table entries, now with updated Local_Pref values as compared with Example 14-19. E1 now uses its eBGP route, Next_Hop 1.1.1.1, for prefix 185.0.0.0/8 because of the higher Local_Pref.

The end of the example shows E2 with two possible routes for 185.0.0.0/8. The following list outlines E2's BGP best-path logic in this case:

Step 0. The two routes both have reachable Next_Hop IP addresses.

Step 1. Both have Weight 0 (tie).

Step 2. The iBGP route through 10.100.1.1 (E1) has a bigger (better) Local_Pref (150 versus 100) than the route through 192.168.1.6 (I3-1), so it is the better route.

Also, note that both the **show ip bgp longer-prefixes** command's briefer output, and the **show ip bgp 185.0.0.0/8** commands more verbose output, both identify the Local_Pref value. However, the longer command output does not list the Weight value.

IP Routes Based on BGP Best Paths

Some of the complexity related to BGP occurs around the BGP functions created by BGP PAs, including their use by the best-path algorithm. When the BGP best-path algorithm has gotten through this complexity and chosen a best route for a prefix, the router then tries to add that route to the IP routing table. However, rather than add the BGP route to the IP routing table directly, BGP actually gives that best BGP route to another process for consideration: the Cisco IOS Routing Table Manager (RTM).

The Cisco IOS RTM chooses the best route among many competing sources. For example, routes can be learned by an IGP, BGP, or even as connected or static routes. Cisco IOS collects the best such route for each prefix and feeds those into the RTM function. The RTM then chooses the best route. Figure 14-17 shows the general idea.

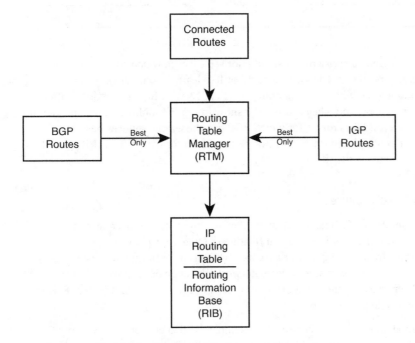

Figure 14-17 *Routing Table Manager Concept*

Among its tasks, RTM uses the concept of administrative distance (AD) to choose the best route among these different sources. Table 14-8 provides a reminder (and a reference) for the default AD of various route information sources. However, focus on the eBGP and iBGP AD values.

Table 14-8 *Default Administrative Distances*

Route Type	Administrative Distance
Connected	0
Static	1
EIGRP summary route	5
eBGP	20
EIGRP (internal)	90
IGRP	100
OSPF	110
IS-IS	115
RIP	120
On-Demand Routing (ODR)	160
EIGRP (external)	170
iBGP	200
Unreachable	255

For the most part, an enterprise router should not see cases in which a prefix learned with BGP has also been learned as a connected or IGP-learned route. (Conversely, these issues occur more often when implementing MPLS VPNs with BGP/IGP redistribution.) However, it can happen, and when it does, the **show ip bgp rib-failures** command can be helpful. This command lists routes for which BGP has chosen the route as best, but the RTM function has not placed the route into the Routing Information Base (RIB), which is simply another name for the IP routing table.

Example of a BGP RIB Failure

To show an example of a RIB failure, imagine that an enterprise engineer needs to do some testing, so the engineer just picks an IP address range to use. The engineer tries to avoid problems by not using network 10.0.0.0, which is used throughout the enterprise. Rather than choosing another private network, the engineer chooses public range 185.0.0.0/8. After changing the lab configuration repeatedly, a route for 185.0.0.0/8 leaks into the OSPF topology database.

Keep in mind that at the end of the previous example, E1 had chosen its eBGP route for 185.0.0.0/8 as its best route, and E2 had chosen its iBGP route as its best route for

185.0.0.0/8. Example 14-21 shows the results, based on RTM's comparisons of the AD values.

Example 14-21 *Example with the RTM and RIB Failures*

```
! First, E1's IP Routing table for 185.0.0.0/8
E1# show ip route 185.0.0.0 255.0.0.0 longer-prefixes
Codes: C - connected, S - static, R - RIP, M - mobile, B - BGP
          D - EIGRP, EX - EIGRP external, O - OSPF, IA - OSPF inter area
          N1 - OSPF NSSA external type 1, N2 - OSPF NSSA external type 2
          E1 - OSPF external type 1, E2 - OSPF external type 2
          i - IS-IS, su - IS-IS summary, L1 - IS-IS level-1, L2 - IS-IS level-2
          ia - IS-IS inter area, * - candidate default, U - per-user static route
          o - ODR, P - periodic downloaded static route

Gateway of last resort is 1.1.1.1 to network 0.0.0.0


B     185.0.0.0/8 [20/0] via 1.1.1.1, 00:25:11
```

```
! Next, E2's IP Routing table
E2# show ip route 185.0.0.0 255.0.0.0 longer-prefixes
! Legend omitted for brevity


Gateway of last resort is 192.168.1.6 to network 0.0.0.0


O     185.0.0.0/8 [110/2] via 10.1.1.77, 00:15:44, FastEthernet0/0


E2# show ip bgp rib-failure
Network          Next Hop                   RIB-failure    RIB-NH Matches
185.0.0.0/8      10.100.1.1          Higher admin distance         n/a
```

The first command shows that E1, with an eBGP route, actually adds its route to the IP routing table. The route lists a code of **B**, meaning BGP. The output lists the eBGP default AD of 20, which is a better default AD than OSPF's 110. RTM added this BGP route to the IP routing table on E1 because of eBGP's better AD.

E2 currently lists its iBGP route through E1 as its current best BGP route for 185.0.0.0/8 because of the higher Local_Pref configured in Example 14-20. However, after giving this route to the RTM, RTM instead chose the lower-AD OSPF route (AD 110) rather than the higher-AD iBGP route (AD 200).

Finally, the **show ip bgp rib-failure** command lists one line for each best BGP route that the RTM does not place into the IP routing table. In this case, this command on Router E2 lists the route for 185.0.0.0/8, with the reason listed.

BGP and the maximum-paths Command

Like the IGP protocols, BGP supports the **maximum-paths** *number-of-paths* subcommand, but BGP uses significantly different logic than the IGPs. Unlike the IGP routing protocols, BGP truly needs to pick one route, and only one route, as the best path for a given prefix/length. In effect, the BGP best-path algorithm already breaks the ties for "best" route for each prefix. Therefore, from BGP's perspective, one route for each prefix is always best.

BGP does allow multiple BGP routes for a prefix to be considered to tie, at least for the purpose of adding multiple routes to the IP routing table. The conditions are as follows:

If the BGP best-path algorithm does not choose a best path by Step 8 (per the numbering in this book), the routes which still tie for being best path will be allowed into the IP routing table, up to and including the number defined by the BGP **maximum-paths** *number-of-paths* router subcommand.

The section "Overview of the BGP Best-Path Algorithm," earlier in this chapter, lists the best-path steps, including the tiebreaker steps that allow routes to be considered by the **maximum-paths** command.

Increasing the Length of the AS_Path Using AS_Path Prepend

Step 4 of the BGP best-path algorithm examines the length of the AS_Path PA. The length of the AS_Path might appear to be obvious: Just add the number of ASNs listed in the AS_Path. However, some BGP features outside the scope of this book actually impact the AS_Path length calculation as well. However, for the purposes of this book, AS_Path length is simply the number of ASNs listed in the AS_Path.

The AS_Path prepend tool gives engineers a means to increase the length of an AS_Path by adding ASNs to the AS_Path, while not impacting the loop-prevention role of the AS_Path PA. By increasing the length of an AS_Path, a route is less likely to become the best route. By adding ASNs that already exist inside a particular route's AS_Path, the feature does not inadvertently prevent a route from being ignored because of AS_Path loop prevention.

For example, using the design shown most recently in Figures 14-13, 14-14, and 14-15, imagine that the enterprise considers ISP1 to be the better ISP, but it does not want to send all traffic through ISP1. So, the enterprise network engineers could make the following type of implementation choice:

Make the AS_Paths received from ISP3 be two ASNs longer.

By making such a choice, when an AS_Path through ISP1 is better, or when it's a tie on AS_Path length between ISP1 and ISP3, or when the AS_Path through ISP1 is even slightly longer than through ISP3, the routers can still choose their routes through ISP1. Only when the AS_Path (before prepending) is at least two ASNs shorter through ISP3 can the ISP3 path be chosen.

Note   For those of you memorizing using the N WLLA OMNI mnemonic, AS_Path Length is the A in WLLA.

Figure 14-18 shows the mechanics of how an enterprise router would prepend the AS_Path for routes received by Router E2 from ISP3, namely, Router I3-1. Looking specifically at the route for 185.0.0.0/8, in this case, I3-1 has not changed the AS_Path and advertised the route with AS_Path (3, 1855). At Step 2, Router E2 prepends ASN 3—twice—making the AS_Path length 4. At Step 3, E2 advertises the route to its iBGP peers—peers that might now prefer the other route for this prefix through Router E1.

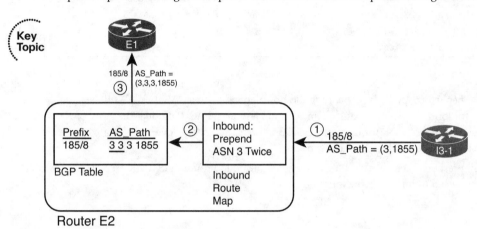

Figure 14-18   *Prepending Two ASNs to an AS_Path*

The configuration itself requires only a little additional work compared to the other examples. As shown in Figure 14-18, Router E2 could use an inbound route map, using the **set as-path prepend 3 3** command to add the two ASN instances. (The router sending the Update, ISP3's Router I3-1 in this case, could instead use an outbound route map.) Example 14-22 shows the configuration on E2 to add the ASNs at ingress into E2. (Note that all configuration for changing the Weight and Local_Pref, and the extra OSPF route for 185.0.0.0/8 shown in Example 14-20, has been removed before gathering the output in this example.)

Example 14-22   *Prepending Additional ASNs to the AS_Path*

```
! First, E2's new configuration
route-map add-two-asns permit 10
 set as-path prepend 3 3
router bgp 11
 neighbor 192.168.1.6 route-map add-two-asns in
!
! Next, note the AS_Path values all start with 3, 3, 3
E2# show ip bgp 176.0.0.0/4 longer-prefixes
BGP table version is 41, local router ID is 10.100.1.2
```

```
Status codes: s suppressed, d damped, h history, * valid, > best, i - internal,
             r RIB-failure, S Stale
Origin codes: i - IGP, e - EGP, ? - incomplete

   Network          Next Hop        Metric LocPrf Weight Path
*>i181.0.0.0/8      10.100.1.1          0    100     0 1 1811 i
*                   192.168.1.6         0            0 3 3 3 2 50 51 52 1811 i
*>i182.0.0.0/8      10.100.1.1          0    100     0 1 2 1822 i
*                   192.168.1.6         0            0 3 3 3 2 50 51 1822 i
*>i183.0.0.0/8      10.100.1.1          0    100     0 1 2 50 1833 i
*                   192.168.1.6         0            0 3 3 3 2 50 1833 i
* i184.0.0.0/8      10.100.1.1          0    100     0 1 2 50 51 1844 i
*>                  192.168.1.6         0            0 3 3 3 2 1844 i
*> 185.0.0.0/8      192.168.1.6         0            0 3 3 3 1855 i
```

Note When using AS_Path prepending, do not prepend just any ASN. BGP still uses the AS_Path for loop avoidance. So, using an ASN already in the AS_Path, like the ASN of the most recently added ASN (for example, ASN 3 in this case), or the local ASN (for example, ASN 11 in this case), makes the most sense.

Although presented here as a tool for influencing outbound routes, AS_Path prepending can also be used to influence the inbound routes.

Influencing an Enterprise's Inbound Routes with MED

An enterprise has reasonably good control over its outbound IP routes. The engineers can configure BGP to set and react to Weight, Local_Pref, and AS_Path length, manipulating each to choose a different outgoing link or different router through which to forward packets to the Internet.

An enterprise has much less control over inbound routes: routes for packets coming back toward the enterprise. First, these inbound routes exist on routers that the enterprise does not own. Even if an ISP or set of ISPs can be convinced by engineers at the enterprise to make their routes toward an enterprise take a particular path, technical issues can prevent the design from being implemented. In particular, if the enterprise's public IP address range is summarized, the companies that use addresses in that range might have competing goals. As a result, no policy can be applied to influence the best route.

However, several tools exist that allow some control over the last ASN hop between an ISP and its enterprise customer. This book examines one such tool, called *Multi-Exit Discriminator (MED)*, which originally worked for a dual-homed design—that is, with a single ISP but with multiple links to that ISP. MED was later expanded to support dual-multihomed designs (2+ ASNs, 2+ links), relying on the concept that ISPs would work together. This section examines the dual-homed case, with a single ISP.

MED Concepts

The name *Multi-Exit Discriminator* actually describes its function to a great degree. With a dual-homed design, at least two links exist between an enterprise and its ISP. The enterprise can announce to the ISP a value (MED) that tells the ISP which path into the enterprise is best. As a result, the ISP can discriminate between the multiple exit points from that ISP to the enterprise.

Because MED lets the enterprise ASN tell just the neighboring ASN which link into the enterprise to use, engineers typically use MED when advertising an enterprise's public IP address space. Those inbound routes into the enterprise from the ISP typically consist of either one, or a few, public IP address ranges.

For example, consider a new network design as shown in Figure 14-19. In this case, the enterprise uses the same 128.107.0.0/19 public address range used in Chapter 13 and in this chapter. The enterprise connects only to ASN 1 with a total of four physical links and three BGP neighbors.

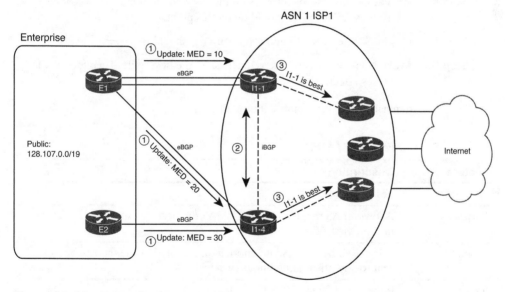

Figure 14-19   *Example of Using MED*

MED uses smallest-is-best logic. As a result, the figure shows a design in which the enterprise engineer prefers the top BGP neighborship as the best path to use for inbound routes (MED 10), the middle link next (MED 20), and the bottom connection last (MED 30). Following the steps in the figure:

Step 1.   E1 and E2 advertise 128.107.0.0/19, setting MED with an outbound route map, to various settings: MED 10 sent by E1 to I1-1, MED 20 sent by E1 to I1-4, and MED 30 sent by E2 to I1-4.

Step 2.   I1-1 and I1-4 have an iBGP connection, so they learn each other's routes and agree as to which route wins based on MED.

Step 3.   I1-1 and I1-4 also tell the other routers inside ISP1, causing all inbound traffic to funnel toward Router I1-1.

Note that Routers I1-1 and I1-4 in this example could have chosen a better route based on all the earlier best-path steps. However, a brief analysis of the steps tells us that unless someone makes an effort to override the effects of MED, these routers' best-path algorithms will use MED. Assuming that the enterprise and ISP agree to rely on MED, the earlier best-path steps should not matter. Here's why:

Step 1.   **Weight:** Needs to be set locally. Therefore, if relying on MED, the ISP simply chooses to not set the Weight for received Updates from the enterprise.

Step 2.   **Local_Pref:** Again, this takes overt effort to match and set the Local_Pref. If relying on MED, the ISP simply chooses to not set the Local_Pref.

Step 3.   **Locally injected?** All these public routes from the enterprise will be learned with eBGP and not locally injected.

Step 4.   **AS_Path length:** All such routes on the ISP routers should list one ASN—the enterprise's ASN—so all should tie on this point.

Step 5.   **Origin:** Whatever the Origin is (i, e, or ?), it should tie.

Step 6.   **MED:** None of the other steps determined the best route. Therefore, MED now takes effect.

Table 14-9 summarizes the key points about MED.

Key Topic

Table 14-9   *Key Features of MED*

Feature	Description
Is it a PA?	Yes.
Purpose	Allows an AS to tell a neighboring AS the best way to forward packets into the first AS.
Scope	Advertised by one AS into another, propagated inside the AS, but not sent to any other autonomous systems.
Range	0 through 4,294,967,295 ($2^{32} - 1$).
Which is better?	Smaller is better.
Default	0
Configuration	Through **neighbor** *neighbor-ip* **route-map** *route-map-name* **out** command, using the **set metric** command inside the route map.

Note   For those of you memorizing using the N WLLA OMNI mnemonic, MED is the M in OMNI.

MED Configuration

MED configuration usually occurs on the routers in the AS that want to control inbound routes from the neighboring AS. As such, in the example design shown in Figure 14-19, Routers E1 and E2 would configure MED. Example 14-23 shows E1's configuration.

Example 14-23 *MED Configuration on Router E1*

```
route-map set-med-to-I1-1 permit 10
 match ip address prefix-list only-public
 set metric 10
!
route-map set-med-to-I1-4 permit 10
 match ip address prefix-list only-public
 set metric 20
!
ip prefix-list only-public permit 128.107.0.0/19
!
router bgp 11
 neighbor 1.1.1.1 route-map set-med-I1-1 out
 neighbor 192.168.1.2 route-map set-med-I1-4 out
```

Both the configuration and the **show ip bgp** command output refer to MED as *metric*. Note that the route map in Example 14-23 uses the **set metric** command, rather than **set med** (which does not exist). And as shown in I1-1's output for the **show ip bgp** command in Example 14-24, the output lists MED under the heading *metric*. Specifically, note that even the **show ip route** command lists the MED value in brackets as the metric for the BGP route.

Example 14-24 *BGP Table and IP Routing Table on Router I1-1*

```
I1-1# show ip bgp 128.107.0.0/19
BGP routing table entry for 128.107.0.0/19, version 13
Paths: (1 available, best #1, table Default-IP-Routing-Table)
Flag: 0x820
  Not advertised to any peer
  11, (aggregated by 11 128.107.9.1), (received & used)
    11.11.11.11 from 11.11.11.11 (128.107.9.1)
      Origin IGP, metric 10, localpref 100, valid, external, atomic-aggregate, best

I1-1# sh ip bgp 128.107.0.0/19 longer-prefixes
BGP table version is 13, local router ID is 1.1.1.1
Status codes: s suppressed, d damped, h history, * valid, > best, i - internal,
            r RIB-failure, S Stale
Origin codes: i - IGP, e - EGP, ? - incomplete

   Network          Next Hop            Metric LocPrf Weight Path
```

```
*> 128.107.0.0/19     11.11.11.11              10              0 11 i

I1-1# show ip route 128.107.0.0 255.255.224.0 longer-prefixes
! Legend omitted for brevity

Gateway of last resort is not set

     128.107.0.0/19 is subnetted, 1 subnets
B        128.107.0.0 [20/10] via 11.11.11.11, 00:02:18
```

Exam Preparation Tasks

Planning Practice

The CCNP ROUTE exam expects test takers to review design documents, create implementation plans, and create verification plans. This section provides some exercises that can help you to take a step back from the minute details of the topics in this chapter so that you can think about the same technical topics from the planning perspective.

For each planning practice table, simply complete the table. Note that any numbers in parentheses represent the number of options listed for each item in the solutions in Appendix F, "Completed Planning Practice Tables."

Design Review Table

Table 14-10 lists several design goals related to this chapter. If these design goals were listed in a design document, and you had to take that document and develop an implementation plan, what implementation options come to mind? You should write a general description; specific configuration commands are not required.

Table 14-10   *Design Review*

Design Goal	Possible Implementation Choices Covered in This Chapter
The plan shows a typical single-multihomed design with two routers connected to two ISPs. How will you ensure next-hop reachability? (2)	
The plan shows the same design as the last item. The two enterprise Internet-connected routers do not have a direct link between each other. What methods discussed in this chapter can be used to prevent packet loops in the enterprise core? (2)	
The plan shows the same design as the previous items but with public range 200.1.1.0/24 being the only public address range used by the enterprise. How can the enterprise avoid becoming a transit AS?	
Influence the outbound route from an enterprise toward prefixes in the Internet (3).	

Design Goal	Possible Implementation Choices Covered in This Chapter
Influence the outbound route from an enterprise toward prefixes in the Internet so that multiple Internet-connected enterprise routers make the same choice based on the same information (2).	
Influence inbound routes into an enterprise from a neighboring AS (2).	

Implementation Plan Peer Review Table

Table 14-11 shows a list of questions that others might ask, or that you might think about, during a peer review of another network engineer's implementation plan. Complete the table by answering the questions.

Table 14-11 *Notable Questions from This Chapter to Consider During an Implementation Plan Peer Review*

Question	Answers
The plan shows a typical single-multihomed design with two routers (R1 and R2) connected to two ISPs. Will R1 and R2 be BGP neighbors? Why?	
The plan shows the same design as the previous item. What configuration setting must be used to ensure that the routers are iBGP rather than eBGP peers?	
The plan calls for filtering all prefixes except the 200.1.1.0/24 public address range when advertising any eBGP peers. Which **neighbor** command options exist for filtering based on the prefix/length? (3)	
A plan shows two enterprise routers, R1 and R2, connected to two different ISPs, with iBGP between R1 and R2. The plan shows R1 setting Weight for routes learned from an ISP. Will R2 react to those settings? Why or why not?	

Question	Answers
A plan shows two enterprise routers, R1 and R2, connected to two different ISPs, with iBGP between R1 and R2. The plan shows R1 setting Local_Pref for routes learned from an ISP. Will R2 react to those settings? Why or why not?	
The plan calls for the use of BGP Weight, but the incomplete plan lists no configuration yet. What configuration alternatives exist? (2)	
The plan calls for the use of BGP Local Preference, but the incomplete plan lists no configuration yet. What configuration alternatives exist?	
A plan shows two enterprise routers, R1 and R2, connected to different ISPs. The plan calls for using MED to influence inbound routes. Which configuration options exist?	
A plan shows the use of BGP Weight, Local Preference, AS_Path prepending, and MED to influence the best-path algorithm. Which of these can be set and advertised to eBGP peers?	

Create an Implementation Plan Table

To practice skills useful when creating your own implementation plan, list in Table 14-12 all configuration commands related to the configuration of the following features. You might want to record your answers outside the book and set a goal to complete this table (and others like it) from memory during your final reviews before taking the exam.

Table 14-12 *Implementation Plan Configuration Memory Drill*

Feature	Configuration Commands/Notes
Configure an iBGP peer.	
Advertise the local router's Update source IP address as the next-hop address to iBGP peers.	
Configure an iBGP mesh with peers 1.1.1.1, 2.2.2.2, and 3.3.3.3.	
Enable BGP synchronization.	

Feature	Configuration Commands/Notes
Configure filtering of routes sent to eBGP peer 9.9.9.9, using a prefix list to allow only 200.1.1.0/24.	
Configure filtering of routes sent to eBGP peer 9.9.9.9, using an ACL to allow only 200.1.1.0/24.	
Configure a route map that sets Weight.	
Enable a route map to set BGP Weight.	
Enable a router to set BGP Weight for all routes received from a neighbor.	
Configure a route map that sets BGP Local Preference.	
Enable a route map to set BGP Local Preference.	
Configure a route map that prepends ASNs to an AS_Path.	
Enable a route map to perform AS_Path prepending.	
Configure a route map that sets MED.	
Enable a route map to set MED.	

Choosing Commands for a Verification Plan Table

To practice skills useful when creating your own verification plan, list in Table 14-13 all commands that supply the requested information. You might want to record your answers outside the book and set a goal to complete this table (and others like it) from memory during your final reviews before taking the exam.

Table 14-13 *Verification Plan Memory Drill*

Information Needed	Commands
Display a single-line neighbor status for all iBGP neighbors.	
Determine whether a particular BGP table entry is iBGP-learned.	
Determine the next-hop IP address of an iBGP-learned route.	

Information Needed	Commands
Identify the neighbor from which a BGP route was learned.	
Display one-line entries for all BGP table entries with a given prefix/length, plus any subnets inside that range.	
Display BGP routes learned from a neighbor, before being processed by an inbound filter.	
The same as the previous item, but after applying the inbound filter.	
Display BGP routes sent to a neighbor but after applying the outbound filter.	
Display whether a neighbor can perform BGP route refresh.	
Display the BGP table, including the chosen best path for each prefix. (State how to identify the best paths.)	
List one line per BGP route but for the prefixes within a range.	
Identify a BGP table entry's BGP Weight. (Specify where to find the output.)	
Identify a BGP table entry's BGP Local Preference. (Specify where to find the output.)	
Identify a BGP table entry's AS_Path length. (Specify where to find the output.)	
Identify a BGP table entry's MED. (Specify where to find the output.) (4 methods)	
Display routes received from a neighbor before being processed by an inbound filter.	
The same as the previous item but after applying the outbound filter.	
Display BGP routes sent to a neighbor but after applying the outbound filter.	
Display BGP best paths that were not added to the IP routing table.	

Note   Some of the entries in this table may not have been specifically mentioned in this chapter but are listed in this table for review and reference.

Review All the Key Topics

Review the most important topics from inside the chapter, noted with the Key Topic icon in the outer margin of the page. Table 14-14 lists a reference of these key topics and the page numbers on which each is found.

Table 14-14   *Key Topics for Chapter 14*

Key Topic Element	Description	Page Number
List	Configuration steps for iBGP peer using a loopback as the Update source	605
Figure 14-4	Ensuring That Routes Exist for Next-Hop Addresses in Other ASNs	613
Text	iBGP behavior regarding not forwarding iBGP-learned routes	616
Figure 14-7	Need for Enterprise BGP Filtering	622
Table 14-3	BGP **clear** Command Options	625
Figure 14-8	**show** Commands Related to BGP Filtering	627
Table 14-4	BGP Path Attributes That Affect the BGP Best-Path Algorithm	632
Figure 14-10	Finding PA Settings in the Output of the **show ip bgp** Command	633
Table 14-5	BGP Decision Process Plus Mnemonic: N WLLA OMNI	633
List	Four items commonly set for the purpose of influencing the BGP best-path decision	635
Table 14-6	Key Features of Administrative Weight	638
Table 14-7	Key Features of Local_Pref	645
Figure 14-16	Example Local_Pref Settings for the Upcoming Example	649
Figure 14-18	Prepending Two ASNs to an AS_Path	655
Table 14-9	Key Features of MED	658

Complete the Tables and Lists from Memory

Print a copy of Appendix D, "Memory Tables," (found on the CD) or at least the section for this chapter, and complete the tables and lists from memory. Appendix E, "Memory Tables Answer Key," also on the CD, includes completed tables and lists to check your work.

Define Key Terms

Define the following key terms from this chapter, and check your answers in the glossary.

BGP synchronization, iBGP Mesh, next-hop self, BGP soft reset, BGP hard reset, BGP Weight, Local Preference, AS_Path Prepending, Multi-Exit Discriminator, best-path algorithm, Routing Table Manager, RIB failure, path attribute

This chapter covers the following subjects:

■ **IPv6 Internet Connections:** This section examines how to configure a single-homed connection to an Internet service provider (ISP) using IPv6 on your Internet-facing router.

■ **BGP Support for IPv6:** This section discusses how Multiprotocol BGP (MP-BGP) can be used to support the routing of both IPv4 and IPv6 networks. Two configuration approaches are demonstrated, followed by a look at route filtering and influencing outbound path selection.

CHAPTER 15

IPv6 Internet Connectivity

For decades, enterprise networks have connected to the Internet through IPv4 connections. However, with IPv6's growing popularity, those IPv4 Internet connections are being joined by (and in some cases, replaced by) IPv6 Internet connections.

This chapter begins its look at IPv6 Internet connectivity by considering a single-homed Internet connection. With a single-homed connection, an enterprise's Internet-facing router probably does not need to learn IPv6 routes through BGP from its ISP. Instead, that enterprise router could be configured with an IPv6 address and point to the IPv6 address of the ISP's router, using a default static route. This chapter begins by discussing how that IPv6 address could be assigned to the enterprise's Internet-facing router.

When an enterprise has more than one connection to the Internet, the use of default static routes might not be sufficient. Fortunately, an update to Border Gateway Protocol version 4 (BGP-4), called *Multiprotocol BGP (MP-BGP)*, allows the advertisement of both IPv4 and IPv6 networks. This chapter demonstrates two approaches to MP-BGP configuration. Specifically, you will see how both IPv4 and IPv6 routes can be advertised over a single IPv4 BGP session. Then, you will see how IPv6 routes can use their own IPv6 BGP session, while IPv4 routes use their own IPv4 BGP session. Finally, this chapter looks at how to perform route filtering with MP-BGP and how to influence outbound path selection using the Local Preference attribute.

"Do I Know This Already?" Quiz

The "Do I Know This Already?" quiz allows you to assess whether you should read the entire chapter. If you miss no more than one of these seven self-assessment questions, you might want to move ahead to the "Exam Preparation Tasks" section. Table 15-1 lists the major headings in this chapter and the "Do I Know This Already?" quiz questions covering the material in those headings so that you can assess your knowledge of these specific areas. The answers to the "Do I Know This Already?" quiz appear in Appendix A.

Table 15-1 *"Do I Know This Already?" Foundation Topics Section-to-Question Mapping*

Foundation Topics Section	Questions
IPv6 Internet Connections	1–3
BGP Support for IPv6	4–7

1. Which of the following methods of address assignment can assign a collection of IPv6 networks to a router, which could then assign those IPv6 networks to its various interfaces?

   a. Stateful DHCPv6

   b. DHCPv6-PD

   c. SLAAC

   d. Stateless SLAAC

2. Identify the command used to create an IPv6 default static route.

   a. **ipv6 route ::0** *next_hop_ipv6_address*

   b. **ipv6 route 0/128** *next_hop_ipv6_address*

   c. **ipv6 route 0/0** *next_hop_ipv6_address*

   d. **ipv6 route ::/0** *next_hop_ipv6_address*

3. Select the implicit instructions that reside at the bottom of an IPv6 ACL. (Choose all that apply.)

   a. **permit icmp any any nd-na**

   b. **deny ipv6 any any**

   c. **permit icmp any any na-ns**

   d. **permit icmp any any nd-ns**

4. You are configuring IPv6 routing over an IPv4 BGP session. Your initial configuration on Router R1 is the following:

   ```
   router bgp 64702
    neighbor 198.51.100.1 remote-as 64701
    !
    address-family ipv4
     network 203.0.113.0
     neighbor 198.51.100.1 activate
    exit-address-family
    !
    address-family ipv6
     network 2000:3::/64
     neighbor 198.51.100.1 activate
   ```

   Your BGP neighbor has a similar configuration. You notice that IPv4 routes are being successful exchanged, but IPv6 routes are not being exchanged. What is missing from the above configuration?

   a. You need an IPv6 ACL to match the routes to be advertised.

   b. You need a route map that specifies a local next-hop IPv6 address to advertise to a neighbor.

   c. You need a **neighbor** statement that references an IPv6 address.

   d. You need an additional BGP AS for IPv6.

5. What information can be obtained by issuing the **show bgp ipv6 unicast summary** command? (Choose all that apply.)

    a. The local router's BGP router ID

    b. A list of IPv6 routes known to the BGP table

    c. A list of configured BGP neighbors

    d. The AS of configured BGP neighbors

6. Identify the valid IPv6 prefix list commands. (Choose two.)

    a. **ipv6 prefix-list LIST1 seq 10 permit 2000::/16 ge 64**

    b. **ipv6 prefix-list LIST1 seq 10 permit 2000::/16 le 64**

    c. **ipv6 prefix-list LIST1 seq 10 permit 2000::/16 eq 64**

    d. **ipv6 prefix-list LIST1 seq 10 permit 2000::/16 ne 64**

7. Given the following output, determine why BGP chose 2000:3::2 as the best next hop to reach the 2000:4::/64 network.

```
R1# show bgp ipv6 unicast
BGP table version is 7, local router ID is 198.51.100.5
Status codes: s suppressed, d damped, h history, * valid, > best, i - inter-
nal,
              r RIB-failure, S Stale, m multipath, b backup-path, f
                RT-Filter,
              x best-external, a additional-path, c RIB-compressed,
Origin codes: i - IGP, e - EGP, ? - incomplete
RPKI validation codes: V valid, I invalid, N Not found


        Network          Next Hop       Metric LocPrf Weight Path
  *>    2000:1::/64       ::                  0         32768 i
  *     2000:2::/64       2000:2::2           0     50     0 64702 i
  *>                      ::                  0         32768 i
  *     2000:3::/64       2000:3::2           0    150     0 64703 i
  *>                      ::                  0         32768 i
  *>    2000:4::/64       2000:3::2           0    150     0 64703 i
  *                       2000:2::2           0     50     0 64702 i
```

    a. Lower router ID

    b. Shorter AS path

    c. Higher Local Preference

    d. Lower Weight

Foundation Topics

IPv6 Internet Connections

Not only is IPv6 rapidly being adopted inside enterprise networks, but it is also increasingly being used for connecting enterprises out to the public Internet. Interestingly, connecting to an Internet service provider (ISP) using IPv6 (as opposed to IPv4) comes with some new security concerns, and network engineers need to be aware of these new threats and have strategies to mitigate them.

Therefore, this section begins with a look at how an ISP might assign an IPv6 address to one of its customer's Internet-facing routers. Then, a configuration example is presented, showing how to assign an IPv6 address to an Internet-facing router, and how to configure that router with a default gateway that points to the IPv6 address of an ISP router. Next, IPv6 access control lists (ACL) are introduced, and their configuration is contrasted with the configuration of IPv4 ACLs. Finally in this section, you are introduced to IPv6-specific security threats and methods for defending against these threats.

Methods of Assigning an IPv6 Address to a Customer Router

A router residing at a customer's location (often referred to as *customer premises equipment [CPE]*) needing to connect with an ISP using IPv6 can obtain an IPv6 address in a variety of ways:

- **Manual configuration:** An ISP could provide an IPv6 address to its customer and instruct the customer to manually configure that IPv6 address on its router's Internet-facing interface.

- **Stateless Address Autoconfiguration (SLAAC):** With SLAAC, an ISP router could send Router Advertisements (RA), which advertise an IPv6 prefix, on the link connecting to a customer router. The customer router could then take the advertised prefix and fill in the remainder of the IPv6 address by either randomly selecting those bits or by using the EUI-64 process.

- **Stateless DHCPv6:** If a router needs more IPv6 information than just an IPv6 address, it might benefit from a stateless DHCPv6 configuration. With this approach, a router obtains an IPv6 address using SLAAC. However, the RA has an *other-config-flag* set, which tells the router to check with a DHCP server to obtain additional IPv6 information (for example, the address of a Domain Name System [DNS] server). However, because the router's IPv6 address was obtained through SLAAC, the DHCPv6 server does not keep track of IPv6 address assignment.

- **Stateful DHCPv6:** While stateless DHCPv6 allowed a router (or other device) to obtain an IPv6 address through SLAAC and set the *other-config-flag* instructing the router to learn additional IPv6 configuration information from a DHCPv6 server, stateful DHCPv6 sets the *managed-config-flag* to instruct the router to obtain its IPv6 address (along with other IPv6 configuration information) from a DHCPv6 server. Therefore, with stateful DHCPv6, a DHCPv6 server does keep track of IPv6 address assignment.

■ **DHCPv6 Prefix Delegation (DHCPv6-PD):** Rather than assigning a single IPv6 address to a router, DHCPv6-PD allows a DHCPv6 server to assign a collection of IPv6 networks to the router (or other DHCPv6 client). A router could then assign those different IPv6 networks to its various interfaces.

Manual Configuration of IPv6 Address and Default Route

Manually configuring a CPE router to point to an IPv6-speaking ISP router is a fairly simple process, involving only two steps:

Step 1. Configure the ISP-provided IPv6 address on a CPE router's Internet-facing interface with the **ipv6 address** *ipv6_address/prefix_length* command in interface configuration mode.

Step 2. Statically configure a default route pointing to the IPv6 address of the next-hop ISP router, using the **ipv6 route ::/0** *next_hop_ipv6_address* command in global configuration mode.

To illustrate this configuration, consider Figure 15-1. Router R1 needs to point to the ISP router to allow devices at its site to reach the Internet. The ISP has told the network engineer responsible for Router R1's configuration to assign an IPv6 address of 2000:1::2/64 to Router R1's Internet-facing interface (that is, Fa 0/0). Also, for other devices at Router R1's site to reach the Internet, Router R1 should be statically configured with a default routing pointing to the ISP router's IPv6 address of 2000:1::1. Example 15-1 shows the required configuration on router R1, along with **ping** command output from R1, CLIENT1, and TFTP_SERVER, verifying that all three of those devices can reach the web server (with an IPv6 address of 2000:A::1/64) located on the Internet.

Note The type of connection seen in Figure 15-1 is called a *single-homed* Internet connection, because there is a single connection to the Internet from the customer's location.

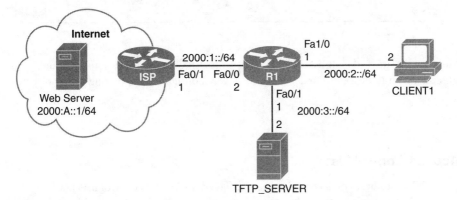

Figure 15-1 *IPv6 Router with a Single-Homed Internet Connection*

Key Topic

Example 15-1 *Manual IPv6 Address Assignment and Static Default Route Configuration*

```
*** CONFIGURATION AND VERIFICATION ON ROUTER R1 ***


R1# conf term
R1(config)# interface fa 0/0
R1(config-if)# ipv6 address 2000:1::2/64
R1(config-if)# exit
R1(config)# ipv6 route ::/0 2000:1::1
R1(config)# end
R1# ping 2000:a::1
Type escape sequence to abort.
Sending 5, 100-byte ICMP Echos to 2000:A::1, timeout is 2 seconds:
!!!!!
Success rate is 100 percent (5/5), round-trip min/avg/max = 44/62/88 ms
R1#


*** VERIFICATION ON CLIENT1 ***


CLIENT1# ping 2000:a::1
Type escape sequence to abort.
Sending 5, 100-byte ICMP Echos to 2000:A::1, timeout is 2 seconds:
!!!!!
Success rate is 100 percent (5/5), round-trip min/avg/max = 60/87/96 ms
Client1#


*** VERIFICATION ON TFTP_SERVER ***


TFTP_SERVER# ping 2000:a::1
Type escape sequence to abort.
Sending 5, 100-byte ICMP Echos to 2000:A::1, timeout is 2 seconds:
!!!!!
Success rate is 100 percent (5/5), round-trip min/avg/max = 60/82/120 ms
TFTP_SERVER#
```

Note In Example 15-1, the CLIENT1 and TFTP_SERVER computers are actually routers (configured with an IPv6 address and a default gateway configuration pointing to Router R1).

IPv6 Access Control Lists

In your CCNA studies, you learned how to configure IPv4 access control lists (ACL). Recall that ACLs are not exclusively used to permit or deny traffic. You could also use an ACL to match traffic (for example, to identify traffic to be forwarded using Policy-Based Routing or to match inside local addresses to be translated with Network Address Translation).

Cisco IOS also supports IPv6 ACLs; however, a few differences exist with IPv6 ACLs as compared with IPv4 ACLs:

- While IPv4 ACLs could be either standard or extended, and either numbered or named, IPv6 ACLs are always extended and named.

- IPv4 ACLs have an implicit *deny all* instruction as the last instruction in all ACLs, whereas IPv6 ACLs have three implicit instructions residing at the bottom of all ACLs:

```
permit icmp any any nd-na
permit icmp any any nd-ns
deny ipv6 any any
```

The **permit icmp any any nd-na** command permits Neighbor Discovery – Neighbor Advertisements, and the **permit icmp any any nd-ns** command permits Neighbor Discovery – Neighbor Solicitations. These Neighbor Discovery commands are required for IPv6 to function correctly, because they serve a purpose, similar to Address Resolution Protocol (ARP) in an IPv4 network. Therefore, be aware that these messages will be denied if you enter a **deny ipv6 any any** command in an IPv6 ACL.

Example 15-2 illustrates an IPv6 ACL, based on the topology previously seen in Figure 15-1. The goal of the configuration is to allow HTTP and HTTPS connections to the Internet, while blocking other connection types.

Example 15-2 *IPv6 ACL Configuration and Verification*

Key Topic

```
*** TESTING ON CLIENT 1 ***
Client1# telnet 2000:a::1 80
Trying 2000:A::1, 80 ... Open     *** SUCCESSFUL HTTP CONNECTION ***
exit
HTTP/1.1 400 Bad Request
Date: Tue, 10 Jun 2014 14:34:55 GMT
Server: cisco-IOS
Accept-Ranges: none

400 Bad Request
[Connection to 2000:a::1 closed by foreign host]
Client1# telnet 2000:a::1
Trying 2000:A::1 ... Open         *** SUCCESSFUL TELNET CONNECTION ***

User Access Verification

Password:
WEB_SERVER> exit
```

```
[Connection to 2000:a::1 closed by foreign host]
Client1#


*** IPv6 ACL CONFIGURATION AND VERIFICATION ON R1 ***
R1# conf term
Enter configuration commands, one per line.  End with CNTL/Z.
R1(config)# ipv6 access-list ALLOW_WEB
R1(config-ipv6-acl)# permit tcp any any eq www
R1(config-ipv6-acl)# permit tcp any any eq 443
R1(config-ipv6-acl)# exit
R1(config)# interface fa 0/0
R1(config-if)# ipv6 traffic-filter ALLOW_WEB out
R1(config-if)# end
R1# show access-lists
IPv6 access list ALLOW_WEB
    permit tcp any any  eq www (23 matches) sequence 10
    permit tcp any any  eq 443 sequence 20


*** TESTING ON CLIENT 1 ***
Client1# telnet 2000:a::1 80
Trying 2000:A::1, 80 ... Open     *** SUCCESSFUL HTTP CONNECTION ***
exit
HTTP/1.1 400 Bad Request
Date: Tue, 10 Jun 2014 14:37:55 GMT
Server: cisco-IOS
Accept-Ranges: none


400 Bad Request
[Connection to 2000:a::1 closed by foreign host]
Client1# telnet 2000:a::1
Trying 2000:A::1 ...
% Destination unreachable; gateway or host down    *** UNSUCCESSFUL TELNET
  CONNECTION ***
```

Example 15-2 begins on Client 1, where the **telnet 2000:a::1 80** command is used to telnet to the Internet-based web server, using port 80 (that is, the HTTP port). The connection was successful as evidenced by the *Open* response. Similarly, Client 1 successfully
established a Telnet session with the Internet-based server (using the default Telnet port
of 23), as seen with the *Open* response.

Next, an extended-named ACL was created on Router R1 with the **ipv6 access-list
ALLOW_WEB** command. In IPv6 ACL configuration mode, the **permit tcp any any eq
www** and **permit tcp any any eq 443** commands instruct the ACL to permit HTTP and
HTTPS (that is, port 443) traffic. Then, in interface configuration mode, the **ALLOW_
WEB** IPv6 ACL was applied to interface Fa 0/0 in the outbound direction with the **ipv6
traffic-filter ALLOW_WEB out** command. Notice the use of the **traffic-filter** command
option, as opposed to **access-group** used with IPv4 ACLs. Finally on Router R1, the

show access-lists command was issued, showing the configuration of the **ALLOW_WEB** IPv6 ACL.

Finally, to test the operation of the IPv6 ACL, two connection attempts are once again made, one using a permitted protocol (HTTP) and one using a denied protocol (Telnet). This time, with the IPv6 ACL in place, the HTTP session succeeds while the Telnet session fails.

IPv6 Internet Connection Security

Connecting an enterprise network to the Internet through IPv6 introduces some security risks. A couple of examples are as follows:

- The Neighbor Discovery process used by IPv6 might be leveraged by a malicious user to launch a man-in-the-middle attack, similar to a gratuitous ARP attack in an IPv4 network.

- If an IPv4 network used NAT, the inside local addresses assigned to network devices would not be visible to devices on the Internet, because of NAT's translation of inside local addresses to inside global addresses. However, because NAT is not typically used in IPv6 networks, IPv6 addresses of network devices are no longer concealed.

To mitigate such threats, Cisco recommends protecting an enterprise network with a stateful firewall. Additionally, IPv6 protocols should be hardened by disabling any unnecessary functions or services and tweaking any suboptimal default settings.

BGP Support for IPv6

The predominant routing protocol found on the Internet is Border Gateway Protocol (BGP), as discussed in Chapter 13, "Fundamental BGP Concepts," and Chapter 14, "Advanced BGP Concepts." A challenge with traditional BGP version 4 (BGP-4) is that it only supported the routing of IPv4 networks. Fortunately, an update to BGP, called *Multiprotocol BGP (MP-BGP)*, allows BGP to support multiple address types. This update consists of a set of multiprotocol extensions added to BGP-4.

This section begins by introducing MP-BGP and discussing its new components. Then, you will see how IPv6 networks can be routed across an IPv4 BGP session, in addition to an IPv6 session. Next, from a design perspective, this section contrasts the benefits and drawbacks of routing IPv4 and IPv6 networks over a single IPv4 BGP session versus using separate BGP sessions for IPv4 and IPv6 networks. Finally, this section discusses the filtering of IPv6 networks and describes how to perform IPv6 path selection using the Local Preference attribute.

Multiprotocol BGP Fundamentals

MP-BGP allows you to consolidate a variety of protocol types under a single BGP configuration. These protocol types are called *address families* and include (as just a few examples):

- Unicast IPv4

- Multicast IPv4

- Unicast IPv6

- Multicast IPv6

Note   MP-BGP supports several additional address families, largely used to support virtualization technologies, such as Virtual Private LAN Service (VPLS) and Layer 2 VPN (L2VPN). However, the ROUTE curriculum focuses on IPv4 and IPv6 address families.

MP-BGP contains several new elements and features not found in BGP-4, including

- **Address Family Identifier (AFI):** Specifies the type of address being used by an Address Family.

- **Subsequent Address Family Identifier (SAFI):** Provides additional address family information for some address families.

- **Multiprotocol Reachable Network Layer Reachability Information (MP_REACH_NLRI):** An attribute that transports a collection of reachable networks, along with next-hop information.

- **Multiprotocol Unreachable Network Layer Reachability Information (MP_UNREACH_NLRI):** An attribute that transports a collection of unreachable networks (used to indicate that specific previously reachable networks are no longer reachable).

- **BGP Capabilities Advertisement:** Used by a router to tell a neighboring router its BGP capabilities—used during BGP session negotiation.

Note that the multiprotocol extensions making up MP-BGP are backward compatible with traditional BGP-4. As a result, a traditional BGP-4 router can form a neighborship with an MP-BGP router, and simply ignore any received BGP messages containing unrecognized extensions.

IPv6 Routing over an IPv4 BGP Session

MP-BGP routers can exchange updates for a variety of address families over an IPv4 BGP session. The steps to configure IPv6 routing over an IPv4 BGP session are as follows:

Step 1. Enable IPv6 routing with the **ipv6 unicast-routing** command, in global configuration mode.

Step 2. Create a route map by issuing the **route-map** *route_map_name* command, in global configuration mode.

Step 3. Specify the IPv6 address of the router's interface connecting to a neighbor as a next-hop IPv6 address, using the **set ipv6 next-hop** *ipv6_address*, in route map configuration mode.

Step 4. Define the BGP autonomous system with the **router bgp** *as-number* command, in global configuration mode.

Step 5. Define an IPv4 BGP neighbor with the **neighbor** *neighbor's_ipv4_address* **remote-as** command, in router configuration mode.

Step 6. Enter address family configuration mode for the IPv4 address family with the **address-family ipv4** command, in router configuration mode.

Step 7. Specify which interfaces will participate in the IPv4 address family by issuing one or more **network** *ip4_network_address* [**mask** *subnet_mask*] commands, in IPv4 address family configuration mode. (Note: The **neighbor** *neighbor's_ ipv4_address* **activate** command is automatically entered for you in IPv4 address family configuration mode.)

Step 8. Exit IPv4 address family configuration mode with the **exit-address-family** command, in IPv4 address family configuration mode.

Step 9. Enter address family configuration mode for the IPv6 address family with the **address-family ipv6** command, in router configuration mode.

Step 10. Specify which interfaces will participate in the IPv6 address family by issuing one or more **network** *ipv6_network_address/prefix-length* commands, in IPv6 address family configuration mode.

Step 11. Activate the BGP neighbor for the IPv6 address family with the **neighbor** *neighbor's_ipv4_address* **activate** command, in IPv6 address family configuration mode.

Step 12. Associate the previously configured route map (which specifies the next-hop IPv6 address to advertise to a neighbor) with the neighbor using the **neighbor** *neighbor_ipv4_address* **route-map** *route_map_name* **out** command, in IPv6 address family configuration mode.

As an example, consider Figure 15-2.

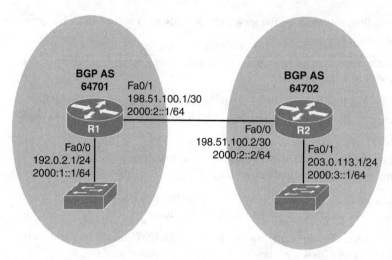

Figure 15-2 *BGP Routing for IPv4 and IPv6 Networks*

In Figure 15-2, two BGP autonomous systems are configured with both IPv4 and IPv6 networks. The BGP session between Routers R1 and R2 is an IPv4 BGP session. However, both IPv4 and IPv6 route updates are exchanged over the IPv4 BGP session. Example 15-3 shows the configuration on Router R1.

Example 15-3 *IPv6 over IPv4 BGP Session—R1 Configuration*

```
ipv6 unicast-routing
! *** OUTPUT OMITTED ***
router bgp 64701
 neighbor 198.51.100.2 remote-as 64702
 !
 address-family ipv4
  network 192.0.2.0
  neighbor 198.51.100.2 activate
 exit-address-family
 !
 address-family ipv6
  network 2000:1::/64
  neighbor 198.51.100.2 activate
  neighbor 198.51.100.2 route-map IPV6-NEXT-HOP out
 exit-address-family
! *** OUTPUT OMITTED ***
route-map IPV6-NEXT-HOP permit 10
 set ipv6 next-hop 2000:2::1
```

In Example 15-3, Router R1 belongs to AS 64701 and is forming a neighborship with Router R2, which has an IPv4 address of 198.51.100.2 and resides in AS 64702. Then, in IPv4 address family configuration mode, the **network 192.0.2.0** command was issued to make Router R1's Fa 0/0 interface participate in the IPv4 address family. The **neighbor**

198.51.100.2 activate command is automatically entered in IPv4 address family configuration mode, to activate the previously configured neighbor for the IPv4 address family.

In IPv6 address family configuration mode, the **network 2000:1::/64** command is issued to make Router R1's Fa 0/0 interface participate in the IPv6 address family. Also, unlike the IPv4 address family, the BGP neighbor (198.51.100.2) configuration has to be manually activated to associate the preconfigured neighbor with the IPv6 address family. This is done with the **neighbor 198.51.100.2 activate** command. Finally, in IPv6 address family configuration mode, the **neighbor 198.51.100.2 route-map IPV6-NEXT-HOP out** command is issued. This command causes BGP route advertisements sent to Router R2 to specify Router R1's Fa 0/1 IPv6 address as an IPv6 next-hop address, as specified in the **IPV6-NEXT-HOP** route map.

The previously mentioned route map is created with the **route-map IPV6-NEXT-HOP permit 10** command. Then, in route map configuration mode, the **set ipv6 next-hop 2000:2::1** command was entered to specify the IPv6 address of Router R1's Fa 0/1 interface as the next-hop IPv6 address that Router R2 should use when attempting to reach IPv6 networks advertised by Router R1. Without this route map instruction, Router R2 will receive IPv6 route advertisements, but those advertisements will not have a reachable next-hop address and therefore will not be injected into Router R2's IPv6 routing table.

Example 15-4 shows the complementary configuration on Router R2.

Example 15-4 *IPv6 over IPv4 BGP Session—R2 Configuration*

```
ipv6 unicast-routing
! *** OUTPUT OMITTED ***
router bgp 64702
 neighbor 198.51.100.1 remote-as 64701
 !
 address-family ipv4
  network 203.0.113.0
  neighbor 198.51.100.1 activate
 exit-address-family
 !
 address-family ipv6
  network 2000:3::/64
  neighbor 198.51.100.1 activate
  neighbor 198.51.100.1 route-map IPV6-NEXT-HOP out
 exit-address-family
! *** OUTPUT OMITTED ***
route-map IPV6-NEXT-HOP permit 10
 set ipv6 next-hop 2000:2::2
```

The **show ipv6 route** command issued on both Routers R1 and R2, as seen in Example 15-5, confirms that Routers R1 and R2 are exchanging IPv6 routing information.

Example 15-5 show ipv6 route *Output on Routers R1 and R2*

```
*** ROUTER R1 ***
R1# show ipv6 route
IPv6 Routing Table - default - 6 entries
Codes: C - Connected, L - Local, S - Static, U - Per-user Static route
       B - BGP, R - RIP, H - NHRP, I1 - ISIS L1
       I2 - ISIS L2, IA - ISIS interarea, IS - ISIS summary, D - EIGRP
       EX - EIGRP external, ND - ND Default, NDp - ND Prefix, DCE - Destination
       NDr - Redirect, O - OSPF Intra, OI - OSPF Inter, OE1 - OSPF ext 1
       OE2 - OSPF ext 2, ON1 - OSPF NSSA ext 1, ON2 - OSPF NSSA ext 2, l - LISP
C   2000:1::/64 [0/0]
     via FastEthernet0/0, directly connected
L   2000:1::1/128 [0/0]
     via FastEthernet0/0, receive
C   2000:2::/64 [0/0]
     via FastEthernet0/1, directly connected
L   2000:2::1/128 [0/0]
     via FastEthernet0/1, receive
B   2000:3::/64 [20/0]
     via FE80::C801:13FF:FE74:8, FastEthernet0/1
L   FF00::/8 [0/0]
     via Null0, receive

*** ROUTER R2 ***
R2# show ipv6 route
IPv6 Routing Table - default - 6 entries
Codes: C - Connected, L - Local, S - Static, U - Per-user Static route
       B - BGP, R - RIP, H - NHRP, I1 - ISIS L1
       I2 - ISIS L2, IA - ISIS interarea, IS - ISIS summary, D - EIGRP
       EX - EIGRP external, ND - ND Default, NDp - ND Prefix, DCE - Destination
       NDr - Redirect, O - OSPF Intra, OI - OSPF Inter, OE1 - OSPF ext 1
       OE2 - OSPF ext 2, ON1 - OSPF NSSA ext 1, ON2 - OSPF NSSA ext 2, l - LISP
B   2000:1::/64 [20/0]
     via FE80::C800:13FF:FE74:6, FastEthernet0/0
C   2000:2::/64 [0/0]
     via FastEthernet0/0, directly connected
L   2000:2::2/128 [0/0]
     via FastEthernet0/0, receive
C   2000:3::/64 [0/0]
     via FastEthernet0/1, directly connected
L   2000:3::1/128 [0/0]
     via FastEthernet0/1, receive
L   FF00::/8 [0/0]
     via Null0, receive
```

The **show bgp ipv6 unicast** command, as seen in Example 15-6, displays IPv6 networks known to BGP, along with next-hop information to reach those networks. Note that a next-hop address of :: indicates that the network is local to the router.

Example 15-6 **show bgp ipv6 unicast** *Output on Routers R1 and R2*

```
*** ROUTER R1 ***

R1# show bgp ipv6 unicast
BGP table version is 3, local router ID is 198.51.100.1
Status codes: s suppressed, d damped, h history, * valid, > best, i - internal,
              r RIB-failure, S Stale, m multipath, b backup-path, f RT-Filter,
              x best-external, a additional-path, c RIB-compressed,
Origin codes: i - IGP, e - EGP, ? - incomplete
RPKI validation codes: V valid, I invalid, N Not found

     Network          Next Hop          Metric LocPrf Weight Path
 *>  2000:1::/64      ::                     0            32768 i
 *>  2000:3::/64      2000:2::2              0                0 64702 i


*** ROUTER R2 ***

R2# show bgp ipv6 unicast
BGP table version is 3, local router ID is 203.0.113.1
Status codes: s suppressed, d damped, h history, * valid, > best, i - internal,
              r RIB-failure, S Stale, m multipath, b backup-path, f RT-Filter,
              x best-external, a additional-path, c RIB-compressed,
Origin codes: i - IGP, e - EGP, ? - incomplete
RPKI validation codes: V valid, I invalid, N Not found

     Network          Next Hop          Metric LocPrf Weight Path
 *>  2000:1::/64      2000:2::1              0                0 64701 i
 *>  2000:3::/64      ::                     0            32768 i
```

The **show bgp ipv6 unicast summary** command, as demonstrated in Example 15-7, provides a collection of valuable output, including a router's BGP router ID, the local autonomous system (AS) number, and a listing of neighbors and their AS numbers.

Example 15-7 **show bgp ipv6 unicast summary** *Output on Routers R1 and R2*

```
*** ROUTER R1 ***

R1# show bgp ipv6 unicast summary
BGP router identifier 198.51.100.1, local AS number 64701
BGP table version is 3, main routing table version 3
2 network entries using 336 bytes of memory
2 path entries using 208 bytes of memory
2/2 BGP path/bestpath attribute entries using 272 bytes of memory
1 BGP AS-PATH entries using 24 bytes of memory
0 BGP route-map cache entries using 0 bytes of memory
```

```
   0 BGP filter-list cache entries using 0 bytes of memory
   BGP using 840 total bytes of memory
   BGP activity 4/0 prefixes, 4/0 paths, scan interval 60 secs


   Neighbor          V       AS MsgRcvd MsgSent   TblVer  InQ OutQ Up/Down   State/PfxRcd
   198.51.100.2      4    64702      8       8        3    0    0 00:02:10          1
```

```
*** ROUTER R2 ***
R2# show bgp ipv6 unicast summary
BGP router identifier 203.0.113.1, local AS number 64702
BGP table version is 3, main routing table version 3
2 network entries using 336 bytes of memory
2 path entries using 208 bytes of memory
2/2 BGP path/bestpath attribute entries using 272 bytes of memory
1 BGP AS-PATH entries using 24 bytes of memory
0 BGP route-map cache entries using 0 bytes of memory
0 BGP filter-list cache entries using 0 bytes of memory
BGP using 840 total bytes of memory
BGP activity 4/0 prefixes, 4/0 paths, scan interval 60 secs


Neighbor          V       AS MsgRcvd MsgSent   TblVer  InQ OutQ Up/Down   State/PfxRcd
198.51.100.1      4    64701     11      10        3    0    0 00:04:28          1
```

IPv6 Routing over an IPv6 BGP Session

While you could configure an IPv4 BGP session and advertise IPv6 networks over that session (as seen in the previous discussion), an alternative is to create an IPv6 BGP session between two routers and then advertise IPv6 networks over that session. If you also needed to advertise IPv4 networks, you could do so by creating an additional BGP routing process, using an IPv4 BGP session, just for the handling of IPv4 networks.

The steps to configure IPv6 routing over an IPv6 BGP session are as follows:

Step 1. Enable IPv6 routing with the **ipv6 unicast-routing** command, in global configuration mode.

Step 2. Define the BGP autonomous system with the **router bgp** *as-number* command, in global configuration mode.

Step 3. Define an IPv6 BGP neighbor with the **neighbor** *neighbor's_ipv6_address* **remote-as** command, in router configuration mode.

Step 4. Enter address family configuration mode for the IPv6 address family with the **address-family ipv6** command, in router configuration mode.

Step 5. Specify which interfaces will participate in the IPv6 address family by issuing one or more **network** *ipv6_network_address/prefix-length* commands, in IPv6 address family configuration mode.

Step 6. Activate the BGP neighbor for the IPv6 address family with the **neighbor** *neighbor's_ipv4_address* **activate** command, in IPv6 address family configuration mode.

> **Note** Unlike the configuration for IPv6 routing over an IPv4 BGP session, the configuration for IPv6 routing over an IPv6 session does not require the configuration of a route map to specify a next-hop IPv6 address. This step is not required, because the neighbors are configured with one another's IPv6 addresses. Therefore, they know the appropriate next-hop IPv6 address to associate with IPv6 route updates received from a neighbor.

To illustrate this configuration, consider Example 15-8, which is using the topology previously seen in Figure 15-2.

Example 15-8 *IPv6 over IPv6 BGP Session—R1 Configuration*

```
ipv6 unicast-routing
! *** OUTPUT OMITTED ***
router bgp 64701
neighbor 2000:2::2 remote-as 64702
 !
address-family ipv4
 no neighbor 2000:2::2 activate
exit-address-family
 !
address-family ipv6
 network 2000:1::/64
 neighbor 2000:2::2 activate
exit-address-family
```

In Example 15-8, note that the **neighbor 2000:2::2 remote-as 64702** command points to the IPv6 address of Router R2, as opposed to the IPv4 address of Router R2, as seen in Example 15-3. Also, be aware that you do not have to go into IPv4 address family configuration mode and issue the **no neighbor neighbor's_ipv6_address activate** command, because that is done automatically. Another difference that you will notice from the configuration in Example 15-3 is the absence of a route map, which is no longer needed, because the **neighbor** commands on both routers point to one another's IPv6 addresses, instead of one another's IPv4 addresses.

Example 15-9 shows the complementary configuration on Router R2.

Example 15-9   *IPv6 over IPv6 BGP Session—R2 Configuration*

```
ipv6 unicast-routing
! *** OUTPUT OMITTED ***
router bgp 64702
 bgp log-neighbor-changes
 neighbor 2000:2::1 remote-as 64701
 !
 address-family ipv4
  no neighbor 2000:2::1 activate
 exit-address-family
 !
 address-family ipv6
  network 2000:3::/64
  neighbor 2000:2::1 activate
 exit-address-family
```

The **show ipv6 route** command issued on both Routers R1 and R2, as seen in Example 15-10, confirms that Routers R1 and R2 are exchanging IPv6 routing information.

Example 15-10   **show ipv6 route** *Output on Routers R1 and R2*

```
*** ROUTER R1 ***
R1# show ipv6 route
IPv6 Routing Table - default - 6 entries
Codes: C - Connected, L - Local, S - Static, U - Per-user Static route
       B - BGP, R - RIP, H - NHRP, I1 - ISIS L1
       I2 - ISIS L2, IA - ISIS interarea, IS - ISIS summary, D - EIGRP
       EX - EIGRP external, ND - ND Default, NDp - ND Prefix, DCE - Destination
       NDr - Redirect, O - OSPF Intra, OI - OSPF Inter, OE1 - OSPF ext 1
       OE2 - OSPF ext 2, ON1 - OSPF NSSA ext 1, ON2 - OSPF NSSA ext 2, l - LISP
C   2000:1::/64 [0/0]
     via FastEthernet0/0, directly connected
L   2000:1::1/128 [0/0]
     via FastEthernet0/0, receive
C   2000:2::/64 [0/0]
     via FastEthernet0/1, directly connected
L   2000:2::1/128 [0/0]
     via FastEthernet0/1, receive
B   2000:3::/64 [20/0]
     via FE80::C804:12FF:FEA8:8, FastEthernet0/1
L   FF00::/8 [0/0]
     via Null0, receive

*** ROUTER R2 ***
R2# show ipv6 route
IPv6 Routing Table - default - 6 entries
Codes: C - Connected, L - Local, S - Static, U - Per-user Static route
```

```
        B - BGP, R - RIP, H - NHRP, I1 - ISIS L1
        I2 - ISIS L2, IA - ISIS interarea, IS - ISIS summary, D - EIGRP
        EX - EIGRP external, ND - ND Default, NDp - ND Prefix, DCE - Destination
        NDr - Redirect, O - OSPF Intra, OI - OSPF Inter, OE1 - OSPF ext 1
        OE2 - OSPF ext 2, ON1 - OSPF NSSA ext 1, ON2 - OSPF NSSA ext 2, l - LISP
B   2000:1::/64 [20/0]
      via FE80::C803:12FF:FEA8:6, FastEthernet0/0
C   2000:2::/64 [0/0]
      via FastEthernet0/0, directly connected
L   2000:2::2/128 [0/0]
      via FastEthernet0/0, receive
C   2000:3::/64 [0/0]
      via FastEthernet0/1, directly connected
L   2000:3::1/128 [0/0]
      via FastEthernet0/1, receive
L   FF00::/8 [0/0]
      via Null0, receive
```

The **show bgp ipv6 unicast** command output, seen in Example 15-11, is similar to what was seen in Example 15-6.

Example 15-11   show bgp ipv6 unicast *Output on Routers R1 and R2*

```
*** ROUTER R1 ***

R1# show bgp ipv6 unicast
BGP table version is 3, local router ID is 198.51.100.1
Status codes: s suppressed, d damped, h history, * valid, > best, i - internal,
              r RIB-failure, S Stale, m multipath, b backup-path, f RT-Filter,
              x best-external, a additional-path, c RIB-compressed,
Origin codes: i - IGP, e - EGP, ? - incomplete
RPKI validation codes: V valid, I invalid, N Not found

     Network          Next Hop            Metric LocPrf Weight Path
 *>  2000:1::/64      ::                        0         32768 i
 *>  2000:3::/64      2000:2::2                 0             0 64702 i


*** ROUTER R2 ***

R2# show bgp ipv6 unicast
BGP table version is 3, local router ID is 203.0.113.1
Status codes: s suppressed, d damped, h history, * valid, > best, i - internal,
              r RIB-failure, S Stale, m multipath, b backup-path, f RT-Filter,
              x best-external, a additional-path, c RIB-compressed,
Origin codes: i - IGP, e - EGP, ? - incomplete
RPKI validation codes: V valid, I invalid, N Not found

     Network          Next Hop            Metric LocPrf Weight Path
 *>  2000:1::/64      2000:2::1                 0             0 64701 i
 *>  2000:3::/64      ::                        0         32768 i
```

Also, as previously seen in Example 15-7, the **show bgp ipv6 unicast summary** command, as shown in Example 15-12, provides information such as a router's BGP router ID, the local AS number, and a listing of neighbors and their AS numbers.

Example 15-12   show bgp ipv6 unicast summary *Output on Routers R1 and R2*

```
*** ROUTER R1 ***
R1# show bgp ipv6 unicast summary
BGP router identifier 198.51.100.1, local AS number 64701
BGP table version is 3, main routing table version 3
2 network entries using 336 bytes of memory
2 path entries using 208 bytes of memory
2/2 BGP path/bestpath attribute entries using 272 bytes of memory
1 BGP AS-PATH entries using 24 bytes of memory
0 BGP route-map cache entries using 0 bytes of memory
0 BGP filter-list cache entries using 0 bytes of memory
BGP using 840 total bytes of memory
BGP activity 2/0 prefixes, 2/0 paths, scan interval 60 secs


Neighbor        V       AS MsgRcvd MsgSent    TblVer   InQ OutQ Up/Down State/PfxRcd
2000:2::2       4    64702       8       9         3     0    0 00:03:52           1

*** ROUTER R2 ***
R2# show bgp ipv6 unicast summary
BGP router identifier 203.0.113.1, local AS number 64702
BGP table version is 3, main routing table version 3
2 network entries using 336 bytes of memory
2 path entries using 208 bytes of memory
2/2 BGP path/bestpath attribute entries using 272 bytes of memory
1 BGP AS-PATH entries using 24 bytes of memory
0 BGP route-map cache entries using 0 bytes of memory
0 BGP filter-list cache entries using 0 bytes of memory
BGP using 840 total bytes of memory
BGP activity 2/0 prefixes, 2/0 paths, scan interval 60 secs


Neighbor        V       AS MsgRcvd MsgSent    TblVer   InQ OutQ Up/Down State/PfxRcd
2000:2::1       4    64701      11      10         3     0    0 00:05:42           1
```

Single IPv4 BGP Session Versus Dual (IPv4 and IPv6) Sessions

At this point in this chapter, you have seen two approaches to support both the routing of IPv4 and IPv6 networks in a BGP environment. One option was to have a single IPv4 BGP session, and use that single session to carry IPv4 and IPv6 route information. The second option was to have an IPv4 BGP session, carrying just IPv4 network advertisements, and an IPv6 BGP session, carrying just IPv6 network advertisements.

While you can choose either approach to support IPv4 and IPv6 routing, from a design perspective, you should understand the benefits (and any drawbacks) of each approach. The following lists highlight the characteristics of each approach:

Key Topic

- Single IPv4 BGP session:

    - Fewer neighborships are formed.

    - When sending IPv6 route information over the IPv4 BGP session, you need to create a route map to modify the Next-Hop BGP attribute.

- Dual (IPv4/IPv6) BGP sessions:

    - More neighborships must be configured.

    - You do not need to configure a route map to modify the Next-Hop BGP attribute.

Filtering IPv6 Routes with Prefix Lists

The Cisco IOS implementation of MP-BGP allows you to filter IPv6 routes in much the same way that you filtered IPv4 routes. Specifically, you can filter IPv6 routes using prefix lists, filter lists, and route maps. However, you should understand the order of operations of these various filtering mechanisms. The following lists show the order in which these mechanisms are applied to IPv6 routes, for both incoming and outgoing route advertisements.

- Order of operations for ingress IPv6 BGP route filtering:

    - Inbound route map

    - Inbound filter list

    - Inbound prefix list

- Order of operations for egress IPv6 BGP route filtering:

    - Outbound prefix list

    - Outbound filter list

    - Outbound route map

As an example, consider the IPv6 prefix list filtering example presented in Examples 15-13, 15-14, 15-15, and 15-16. The topology is illustrated in Figure 15-3.

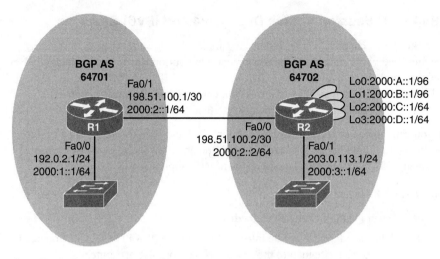

Figure 15-3 *Prefix List Filtering Sample Topology*

Example 15-13 *Starting Configuration on Router R2*

```
R2# show run
... OUTPUT OMITTED ...
router bgp 64702
 bgp log-neighbor-changes
 neighbor 198.51.100.1 remote-as 64701
 !
 address-family ipv4
  network 203.0.113.0
  neighbor 198.51.100.1 activate
 exit-address-family
 !
 address-family ipv6
  network 2000:3::/64
  network 2000:A::/96
  network 2000:B::/96
  network 2000:C::/64
  network 2000:D::/64
  neighbor 198.51.100.1 activate
  neighbor 198.51.100.1 route-map IPV6-NEXT-HOP out
 exit-address-family
 ... OUTPUT OMITTED ...
route-map IPV6-NEXT-HOP permit 10
 set ipv6 next-hop 2000:2::2
```

Example 15-13 shows the starting configuration on Router R2. Notice that Router R2 is configured to route both IPv4 and IPv6 networks over a single IPv4 BGP session.

Example 15-14 *Starting IPv6 Routing Table on Router R1*

```
R1# show ipv6 route
IPv6 Routing Table - default - 10 entries
Codes: C - Connected, L - Local, S - Static, U - Per-user Static route
       B - BGP, R - RIP, H - NHRP, I1 - ISIS L1
       I2 - ISIS L2, IA - ISIS interarea, IS - ISIS summary, D - EIGRP
       EX - EIGRP external, ND - ND Default, NDp - ND Prefix, DCE - Destination
       NDr - Redirect, O - OSPF Intra, OI - OSPF Inter, OE1 - OSPF ext 1
       OE2 - OSPF ext 2, ON1 - OSPF NSSA ext 1, ON2 - OSPF NSSA ext 2, l - LISP
C   2000:1::/64 [0/0]
     via FastEthernet0/0, directly connected
L   2000:1::1/128 [0/0]
     via FastEthernet0/0, receive
C   2000:2::/64 [0/0]
     via FastEthernet0/1, directly connected
L   2000:2::1/128 [0/0]
     via FastEthernet0/1, receive
B   2000:3::/64 [20/0]
     via FE80::C801:10FF:FED0:8, FastEthernet0/1
B   2000:A::/96 [20/0]
     via FE80::C801:10FF:FED0:8, FastEthernet0/1
B   2000:B::/96 [20/0]
     via FE80::C801:10FF:FED0:8, FastEthernet0/1
B   2000:C::/64 [20/0]
     via FE80::C801:10FF:FED0:8, FastEthernet0/1
B   2000:D::/64 [20/0]
     via FE80::C801:10FF:FED0:8, FastEthernet0/1
L   FF00::/8 [0/0]
     via Null0, receive
```

Example 15-15 shows that Router R1 has learned five IPv6 routes through BGP from Router R2. Notice that two of the IPv6 networks have a prefix length of 96 bits, while three of the IPv6 networks have a prefix length of 64 bits.

Key Topic

Example 15-15 *Prefix List Configuration on Router R2*

```
R2# conf term
R2(config)# ipv6 prefix-list SMALL_NETS seq 10 permit 2000::/16 ?
  ge  Minimum prefix length to be matched
  le  Maximum prefix length to be matched
  <cr>
R2(config)# ipv6 prefix-list SMALL_NETS seq 10 permit 2000::/16 le 64
R2(config)# router bgp 64702
R2(config-router)# address-family ipv6
R2(config-router-af)# neighbor 198.51.100.1 prefix-list SMALL_NETS out
R2(config-router-af)# end
R2# clear ip bgp * soft
```

In Example 15-15, an IPv6 prefix list (named **SMALL_NETS**) is configured to match IPv6 routes beginning with 2000 (as the first 16 bits in hexadecimal notation) and a prefix length less than or equal to 64 bits. This prefix list is then applied in the outbound direction to a neighbor with an IP address of 198.51.100.1 (which is Router R1). Therefore, the 2000:A::/96 and 2000:B::/96 networks known to Router R2 should not be advertised to Router R1, because their prefix length of 96 bits is not less than or equal to the 64-bit length specified by the prefix list.

Note   The **clear ip bgp * soft** command was used to trigger route changes to immediately be sent to Router R1, without tearing down the existing IPv4 BGP session.

Example 15-16   *Final IPv6 Routing Table on Router R1*

```
R1# show ipv6 route
IPv6 Routing Table - default - 8 entries
Codes: C - Connected, L - Local, S - Static, U - Per-user Static route
       B - BGP, R - RIP, H - NHRP, I1 - ISIS L1
       I2 - ISIS L2, IA - ISIS interarea, IS - ISIS summary, D - EIGRP
       EX - EIGRP external, ND - ND Default, NDp - ND Prefix, DCE - Destination
       NDr - Redirect, O - OSPF Intra, OI - OSPF Inter, OE1 - OSPF ext 1
       OE2 - OSPF ext 2, ON1 - OSPF NSSA ext 1, ON2 - OSPF NSSA ext 2, l - LISP
C    2000:1::/64 [0/0]
     via FastEthernet0/0, directly connected
L    2000:1::1/128 [0/0]
     via FastEthernet0/0, receive
C    2000:2::/64 [0/0]
     via FastEthernet0/1, directly connected
L    2000:2::1/128 [0/0]
     via FastEthernet0/1, receive
B    2000:3::/64 [20/0]
     via FE80::C801:10FF:FED0:8, FastEthernet0/1
B    2000:C::/64 [20/0]
     via FE80::C801:10FF:FED0:8, FastEthernet0/1
B    2000:D::/64 [20/0]
     via FE80::C801:10FF:FED0:8, FastEthernet0/1
L    FF00::/8 [0/0]
     via Null0, receive
```

In Example 15-16, notice that networks 2000:A::/96 and 2000:B::/96 no longer appear in Router R1's IPv6 routing table. This output confirms that Router R2 filtered those routes, using a prefix list.

Using Local Preference for IPv6 Path Selection

Frequent real-world BGP implementations require you to influence outbound path selection on your router. In Chapter 14, you saw how the Local Preference BGP attribute could be used to influence outbound IPv4 path selection decisions. Similarly, you can use the Local Preference attribute to influence outbound IPv6 path selection decisions.

Example 15-17, as illustrated in Figure 15-4, shows a sample Local Preference configuration.

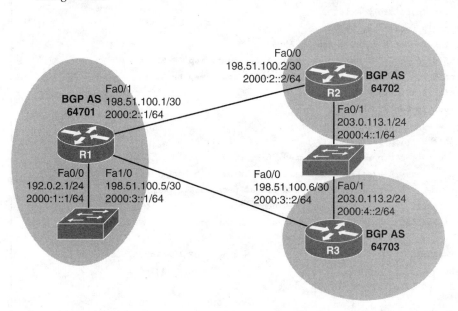

Figure 15-4 *Influencing Path Selection with Local Preference*

Example 15-17 *Local Preference Configuration*

```
R1# show bgp ipv6 unicast
BGP table version is 5, local router ID is 198.51.100.5
Status codes: s suppressed, d damped, h history, * valid, > best, i - internal,
              r RIB-failure, S Stale, m multipath, b backup-path, f RT-Filter,
              x best-external, a additional-path, c RIB-compressed,
Origin codes: i - IGP, e - EGP, ? - incomplete
RPKI validation codes: V valid, I invalid, N Not found

   Network          Next Hop          Metric LocPrf Weight Path
*> 2000:1::/64      ::                     0         32768 i
*  2000:2::/64      2000:2::2              0             0 64702 i
*>                  ::                     0         32768 i
*  2000:3::/64      2000:3::2              0             0 64703 i
*>                  ::                     0         32768 i
*  2000:4::/64      2000:3::2              0             0 64703 i
```

```
*>                     2000:2::2            0          0 64702 i
R1# conf term
Enter configuration commands, one per line.  End with CNTL/Z.
R1(config)# route-map LP-R2
R1(config-route-map)# set local-preference 50
R1(config-route-map)# exit
R1(config)# route-map LP-R3
R1(config-route-map)# set local-preference 150
R1(config-route-map)# exit
R1(config)# router bgp 64701
R1(config-router)# address-family ipv6
R1(config-router-af)# neighbor 198.51.100.2 route-map LP-R2 in
R1(config-router-af)# neighbor 198.51.100.6 route-map LP-R3 in
R1(config-router-af)# end
R1# clear ip bgp * soft
R1# show bgp ipv6 unicast
BGP table version is 7, local router ID is 198.51.100.5
Status codes: s suppressed, d damped, h history, * valid, > best, i - internal,
              r RIB-failure, S Stale, m multipath, b backup-path, f RT-Filter,
              x best-external, a additional-path, c RIB-compressed,
Origin codes: i - IGP, e - EGP, ? - incomplete
RPKI validation codes: V valid, I invalid, N Not found

   Network          Next Hop          Metric LocPrf Weight Path
*> 2000:1::/64      ::                     0          32768 i
*  2000:2::/64      2000:2::2              0     50       0 64702 i
*>                  ::                     0          32768 i
*  2000:3::/64      2000:3::2              0    150       0 64703 i
*>                  ::                     0          32768 i
*> 2000:4::/64      2000:3::2              0    150       0 64703 i
*                   2000:2::2              0     50       0 64702 i
R1#
```

The **show bgp ipv6 unicast** command output at the beginning of Example 15-17 shows that BGP initially prefers Router R2 as the next hop to reach the 2000:4::/64 network. The reason for this path selection is that Router R2 has the lowest router ID. The purpose of the example is to show how that outbound path selection decision can be altered through a Local Preference configuration.

Two route maps are then configured for Router R1. One route map sets the Local Preference attribute to a value of 50 and is associated with incoming routes from Router R2, while the other route map sets the Local Preference attribute to a value of 150 and is associated with incoming routes from Router R3. BGP prefers higher preference values. Therefore, after refreshing the BGP table with the **clear ip bgp * soft** command, the **show bgp ipv6 unicast** command output indicates that Router R1 now prefers Router R3 as the next-hop router to reach the 2000:4::/64 network.

Exam Preparation Tasks

Planning Practice

The CCNP ROUTE exam expects test takers to review design documents, create implementation plans, and create verification plans. This section provides some exercises that can help you to take a step back from the minute details of the topics in this chapter so that you can think about the same technical topics from the planning perspective.

For each planning practice table, simply complete the table. Note that any numbers in parentheses represent the number of options listed for each item in the solutions in Appendix F, "Completed Planning Practice Tables."

Design Review Table

Table 15-2 lists several design goals related to this chapter. If these design goals were listed in a design document, and you had to take that document and develop an implementation plan, what implementation options come to mind? For any configuration items, a general description can be used, without concern about the specific parameters.

Table 15-2 *Design Review*

Design Goal	Possible Implementation Choices Covered in This Chapter
The design specifies that a customer's Internet-facing router should dynamically obtain the IPv6 address for its Internet-facing interface from an ISP. (4)	
The design specifies that a customer's Internet-facing router exchange IPv4 and IPv6 routes with an ISP.	
The design requires that you filter specific IPv6 routes sent to or received from an ISP.	
The design has a dual-homed Internet connection running MP-BGP, with a requirement that you influence the outbound path selection.	

Implementation Plan Peer Review Table

Table 15-3 shows a list of questions that others might ask, or that you might think about, during a peer review of another network engineer's implementation plan. Complete the table by answering the questions.

Table 15-3 *Notable Questions from This Chapter to Consider During an Implementation Plan Peer Review*

Question	Answer
The plan requires a client's Internet-facing router to obtain an IPv6 address from the client's ISP. What approach to dynamically assigning IPv6 addresses allows an Internet-facing router to obtain a single IP address from an ISP's DHCP server?	
The plan requires the use of an IPv6 ACL. What two traffic types does an IPv6 ACL implicitly permit? (2)	
The plan calls for the use of MP-BGP. List at least three of the new elements introduced by MP-BGP. (3)	
The plan calls for the routing of both IPv4 and IPv6 networks with an ISP. What variant of BGP supports this requirement?	
The plan calls for the use of MP-BGP, configured such that both IPv4 and IPv6 routes can be advertised over a single IPv4 BGP session. What additional configuration element is required to support this type of design, as opposed to a design where IPv6 routes are advertised over an IPv6 BGP session?	
The plan calls for the use of the Local Preference attribute to influence outbound path selection for an MP-BGP network. Are higher or lower Local Preference values preferred?	

Create an Implementation Plan Table

To practice skills useful when creating your own OSPF implementation plan, list in Table 15-4 configuration commands related to the configuration of the following features. You might want to record your answers outside the book, and set a goal to complete this table (and others like it) from memory during your final reviews before taking the exam.

Table 15-4 *Implementation Plan Configuration Memory Drill*

Feature	Configuration Commands/Notes
Assign an IPv6 address to a router interface connecting to an ISP (in interface configuration mode).	
Configure a default route pointing to an ISP (in global configuration mode).	
Create an IPv6 ACL (in global configuration mode).	
Apply an IPv6 ACL to an interface (in interface configuration mode).	
Enable IPv6 unicast routing (in global configuration mode).	
Create a route map (in global configuration mode).	
Specify the IPv6 address of a router's interface connecting to a neighbor as a next-hop IPv6 address (in route map configuration mode).	
Define a BGP autonomous system (in global configuration mode).	
Define an IPv4 neighbor (in router configuration mode for BGP).	
Enter IPv4 address family configuration mode (in router configuration mode for BGP).	
Specify which interface(s) will participate in the IPv4 address family (in address family configuration mode).	
Enter IPv6 address family configuration mode (in router configuration mode for BGP).	
Specify which interface(s) will participate in the IPv6 address family (in address family configuration mode).	
Activate the BGP neighbor for the IPv6 address family (in address family configuration mode).	
Associate a route map with a neighbor, to advertise an appropriate next-hop IPv6 address to that neighbor (in address family configuration mode).	

Feature	Configuration Commands/Notes
Define an IPv6 BGP neighbor (in router configuration mode for BGP).	
Create an IPv6 prefix list (in global configuration mode).	
Apply an IPv6 prefix list (in address family configuration mode).	
Specify a Local Preference (in route map configuration mode).	

Choose Commands for a Verification Plan Table

To practice skills useful when creating your own OSPF verification plan, list in Table 15-5 all commands that supply the requested information. You might want to record your answers outside the book, and set a goal to complete this table (and others like it) from memory during your final reviews before taking the exam.

Table 15-5 *Verification Plan Memory Drill*

Information Needed	Command(s)
Display ACLs (both IPv4 and IPv6 ACLs).	
Display IPv6 routes.	
Display the IPv6 networks known to BGP.	
Display the BGP router ID, local AS number, and a listing of neighbors and their AS numbers in an MP-BGP configuration.	

Review All the Key Topics

Review the most important topics from inside the chapter, noted with the Key Topic icon in the outer margin of the page. Table 15-6 lists a reference of these key topics and the page numbers on which each is found.

Key Topic

Table 15-6 *Key Topics for Chapter 15*

Key Topic Element	Description	Page Number
List	Methods of assigning an IPv6 address to a router	672
List	Steps to configure an IPv6 address and a default static route	673

Key Topic Element	Description	Page Number
Example 15-1	Manual IPv6 Address Assignment and Static Default Route Configuration	674
Example 15-2	IPv6 ACL Configuration and Verification	675
List	Steps to configure IPv6 routing over an IPv4 BGP session	679
List	Steps to configure IPv6 routing over an IPv6 BGP session	684
List	Characteristics of single or dual BGP sessions	689
Example 15-15	Prefix List Configuration on Router R2	691
Example 15-17	Local Preference Configuration	693

Complete the Tables and Lists from Memory

Print a copy of Appendix D, "Memory Tables," (found on the CD) or at least the section for this chapter, and complete the tables and lists from memory. Appendix E, "Memory Tables Answer Key," also on the CD, includes completed tables and lists to check your work.

Define Key Terms

Define the following key terms from this chapter, and check your answers in the glossary.

SLAAC, Stateless DHCPv6, Stateful DHCPv6, DHCPv6-PD, MP-BGP

This chapter covers the following subjects:

- **Elements of a Router Security Policy:** This section defines a router security policy, explains why it is important to have one, and lists common elements comprising such a policy.

- **Access Control Lists:** This section builds on your CCNA-level knowledge of standard, extended, and named access control lists (ACL) by introducing time-based ACLs and the concept of infrastructure ACLs.

- **Management Plane Security:** This section discusses a collection of features and services available in Cisco IOS routers that can be used to better secure a router from attack.

CHAPTER 16

Fundamental Router Security Concepts

Cisco uses the term *defense-in-depth* to describe an approach to network security having multiple layers of overlapping security mechanisms. One such layer of protection is the *hardening* (that is, more strictly enforcing security) of Cisco IOS routers. This chapter focuses on some of the techniques used to better secure these critical infrastructure devices. The first section of this chapter begins with a look at the importance of having a router security policy and what a policy might contain.

Next, this chapter builds on your CCNA-level knowledge of access control lists (ACL) and introduces time-based ACLs that are only active at specified times. Also, the chapter presents a best-practice recommendation for creating infrastructure ACLs (that is, ACLs that sit at the edge of a network and help protect a network infrastructure from external attacks).

The remainder of the chapter examines a collection of features and services that you can use to better secure a router's management plane. These features and services include Secure Shell (SSH), password encryption, Unicast Reverse Path Forwarding (uRPF), AAA, SNMP security, and NTP authentication.

"Do I Know This Already?" Quiz

The "Do I Know This Already?" quiz allows you to assess whether you should read the entire chapter. If you miss no more than one of these eight self-assessment questions, you might want to move ahead to the "Exam Preparation Tasks" section. Table 16-1 lists the major headings in this chapter and the "Do I Know This Already?" quiz questions covering the material in those headings so that you can assess your knowledge of these specific areas. The answers to the "Do I Know This Already?" quiz appear in Appendix A.

Table 16-1 *"Do I Know This Already?" Foundation Topics Section-to-Question Mapping*

Foundation Topics Section	Questions
Elements of a Router Security Policy	1, 2
Access Control Lists	3, 4
Management Plane Security	5–8

1. What mechanisms can be used to defend against IP spoofing? (Choose two.)

    a. AAA

    b. uRPF

    c. CAR

    d. ACLs

2. Which of the following features can provide router redundancy?

    a. SNMP

    b. HSRP

    c. AAA

    d. TACACS+

3. Identify two types of time-based ACLs. (Choose two.)

    a. Reflexive

    b. Periodic

    c. Absolute

    d. Adaptive

4. What term is given to an ACL that typically resides on a network's boundary routers (that is, routers facing another autonomous system), which is designed to protect a network from malicious traffic?

    a. Time-based ACL

    b. Reflexive ACL

    c. Absolute ACL

    d. Infrastructure ACL

5. When configuring a router to support SSH connections, which of the following are used in generating an RSA key pair? (Choose two.)

    a. Host name

    b. Router ID

    c. Domain name

    d. Configuration revision number

6. Which type of Cisco IOS password encryption uses the Vigenere cipher?

   a. Type 0

   b. Type 4

   c. Type 5

   d. Type 7

7. Which mode of uRPF causes a router interface to accept a packet, if the network to which the packet's source IP address belongs is found in the router's FIB?

   a. Strict mode

   b. Loose mode

   c. Auto mode

   d. Desirable mode

8. Which of the following are characteristics of TACACS+? (Choose two.)

   a. Uses UDP

   b. Encrypts an entire packet

   c. Offers robust accounting

   d. Cisco-proprietary

Foundation Topics

Elements of a Router Security Policy

In today's enterprise networks, routers often sit at the edge of the network, connecting out to other sites. As a result, they often come under a multitude of attacks.

Because these precariously positioned devices reside at a critical line of defense, Cisco recommends that you have a documented plan detailing how your routers are secured. Having a formalized approach to router security helps ensure a consistent configuration across multiple devices and helps identify potential security weaknesses.

A document defining the security features deployed on a router is called a *router security policy*. While the elements of a router security policy can vary from network to network, the following list provides a collection of security topics commonly addressed in a router security policy:

- **Passwords:** Will passwords appear encrypted in the router's running configuration? How often should passwords be changed? How complex should passwords be?

- **Authentication:** Will users be authenticated by a router's local database or by an external authentication, authorization, and accounting (AAA) server (for example, a TACACS+ or RADIUS server)? Will a AAA server be used to log login and logout events? Will a banner be presented to someone logging in, letting him know that only authorized users should attempt to log in?

- **Access:** When administrators remotely connect to the router, what protocols are they allowed to use (for example, SSH, HTTPS, Telnet, HTTP)? If Simple Network Management Protocol (SNMP) is configured to use community strings for authentication, how often should those community strings be changed?

- **Services:** What services currently running on the router are unneeded and should be disabled?

- **Filtering:** Are private IP addresses (as defined in RFC 1918) being filtered? How is the router configured to defend against IP spoofing attacks, where a malicious user on a remote network makes his source IP address appear to be a trusted IP address? (Examples of antispoofing mechanisms include ACLs and uRPF.)

- **Routing protocols:** What kind of authentication (if any) is used by the router's routing protocol(s)?

- **Backups:** How is the router configuration backed up (for example, to a TFTP server)? How often does this backup occur?

- **Documentation:** What procedure is in place to ensure that all router configuration changes are documented?

- **Redundancy:** If a router fails, is there a backup router to take over? If there is a backup router, is it a hot standby router (for example, a router that is currently running and configured with a first-hop redundancy protocol such as Hot Standby Router Protocol [HSRP]) or a cold standby router (for example, a router that was on-site, but was not necessarily powered on or configured)?

- **Monitoring:** What parameters are being monitored and logged (for example, CPU utilization, memory utilization, and failed access attempts)?

- **Updates:** What procedure is in place to determine whether security vulnerabilities have been identified in the version of Cisco IOS running on the router? What procedure is in place to update the version of Cisco IOS running on the router?

Note This book lightly touches on router and network security topics; however, router and network security are much larger fields of study. If you are interested in learning more about router and network security, consider taking the courses or reading the books in the Cisco CCNA Security and CCNP Security tracks.

Access Control Lists

In your CCNA studies, you learned about access control lists (ACL). Specifically, you learned how standard ACLs could match traffic based on source IP addresses and how extended ACLs could match traffic based on source IP addresses, destination IP addresses, and a variety of other criteria such as port numbers. You also learned how to create numbered or named ACLs. These ACLs are frequently used to protect a router's data plane (that is, to filter traffic traveling through a router). However, ACLs can also be used to help protect the management plane and the control plane.

The ROUTE exam blueprint requires that you remember these fundamental ACL concepts. Additionally you need to know how to configure *time-based ACLs*. This section introduces you to time-based ACLs and illustrates how to create *infrastructure ACLs*, which are applied to routers sitting at the edge of an enterprise network.

Time-Based ACLs

You might want to allow specific protocols to come into your network during business hours, but not outside of business hours. For example, imagine that a company has an internal web server that it wants to be accessible to its remote employees during working hours (that is, Monday through Friday from 8:00 a.m. to 5:00 p.m.). You could accomplish such a design goal through the use of *time-based ACLs*, which are only in effect during a specified *time range*.

Note A time range configured on a router references a router's clock. Therefore, a best practice is to configure *Network Time Protocol (NTP)* on a router, which can help ensure that the router's internal clock has the correct time.

A time range can be *periodic*, where it becomes active or inactive at specific times of the day on specific days of the week. Alternately, a time range can be *absolute*, where there is a fixed starting and stopping date and time during which the ACL is active. Table 16-2 presents a list of commands used in creating a time-based ACL.

Table 16-2   *Time-Based ACL Commands*

Command	Description
time-range *name*	Create a named time range (in global configuration mode).
periodic *days-of-week bh:mm* **to** *bh:mm*	Define a periodic time range (in time range configuration mode).
absolute [**start** *bh:mm day_of_month month year*] **end** *bh:mm day_of_month month year*	Define an absolute time range (in time range configuration mode).
access-list *ACL_number* *<matching_parameters>* **time-range** *name_of_time_range*	Apply a time range to a numbered ACL (in global configuration mode).
<matching_parameters> **time-range** *name_of_ time_range*	Apply a time range to a named ACL (in named access list configuration mode).

Consider the topology presented in Figure 16-1, where an enterprise network needs remote employees to access an internal web server Monday through Friday from 8:00 a.m. to 5:00 p.m.

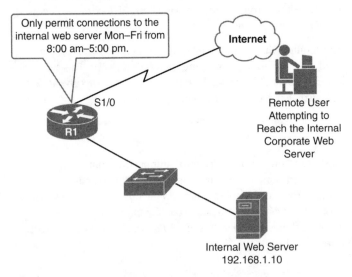

Figure 16-1   *Web Server with Time-Based Access Permissions*

Example 16-1 shows the configuration on Router R1 that supports time-based access to the internal web server for an external user.

Example 16-1 *Time-Based ACL Configuration Example*

```
R1# conf term
R1(config)# time-range WEEKDAYS
R1(config-time-range)# periodic ?
  Friday      Friday
  Monday      Monday
  Saturday    Saturday
  Sunday      Sunday
  Thursday    Thursday
  Tuesday     Tuesday
  Wednesday   Wednesday
  daily       Every day of the week
  weekdays    Monday thru Friday
  weekend     Saturday and Sunday

R1(config-time-range)# periodic weekdays 8:00 to 17:00
R1(config-time-range)# exit
R1(config)# access-list 100 permit tcp any host 192.168.1.10 eq 80 time-range
   WEEKDAYS

... OUTPUT OMITTED FOR OTHER PERMIT ACL STATEMENTS NOT RELEVANT TO THIS EXAMPLE ...

R1(config)# interface serial 1/0
R1(config-if)# ip access-group 100 in
R1(config-if)# end
```

In Example 16-1, a time range named **WEEKDAYS** was created. Context-sensitive help revealed that a keyword of **weekdays** could be used to specify the days Monday through Friday, without the need to list each day. An extended access list, numbered 100, was created to permit traffic to IP address 192.168.1.10 (that is, the internal web server) on TCP port 80, and the time range of WEEKDAYS was applied.

Infrastructure ACLs

An infrastructure ACL is typically an extended ACL that is applied to routers residing on the outer edges of an enterprise network. The primary purpose of this ACL is to prevent malicious traffic from entering the enterprise. As an example, an infrastructure ACL could be used to block packet fragments while permitting packets being exchanged with trusted Border Gateway Protocol (BGP) peers, management stations, and transit traffic (that is, traffic whose source and destination are both off-net).

Although the specific elements present in an infrastructure ACL can vary widely from network to network, Example 16-2 shows a sample infrastructure ACL configuration.

Example 16-2   *Sample Infrastructure ACL*

```
ip access-list extended INFRASTRUCTURE
!
! BLOCK PACKET FRAGMENTS
 deny   tcp any any fragments
 deny   udp any any fragments
 deny   icmp any any fragments
 deny   ip any any fragments
!
! ALLOW NECESSARY ROUTING PROTOCOL
! AND NETWORK MANAGMENT TRAFFIC
 permit tcp host <external-bgp-peer> host <internal-bgp-peer> eq bgp
 permit tcp host <external-bgp-peer> eq bgp host <internal-bgp-peer>
 permit tcp <address-of-management-stations> any eq 22
 permit tcp <address-of-management-stations> any eq 161
 permit icmp <address-of-management-stations> any echo
!
! BLOCK ALL OTHER TRAFFIC DESTINED FOR INTERNAL NETWORK
 deny   ip any <address-space-of-internal-network>
!
! PERMIT OFF-NET TO OFF-NET TRAFFIC
 permit ip any any
!
! APPLY ACL IN THE INBOUND DIRECTION TO AN INTERFACE
! CONNECTING TO AN EXTERNAL NETWORK
interface Serial1/0
 ip access-group INFRASTRUCTURE in
```

To make Example 16-2 simpler to understand, variables (which are in italics) representing IP addresses and network address spaces are used instead of actual IP addresses. In the example, an ACL named **INFRASTRUCTURE** was created. A collection of **deny** statements was then given to block packet fragments. Next, a series of **permit** statements was given to allow peering with an external BGP router (possibly a service provider's router), SSH and SNMP connections from trusted management stations, and pings from trusted management stations. All other traffic destined for internal IP addresses was denied, while traffic that originated off-net and was destined for an off-net IP address was permitted. The INFRASTRUCTURE ACL was then applied in the inbound direction to an Internet-facing interface (interface Serial 1/0 in this example).

Management Plane Security

As mentioned in Chapter 11, "Route Selection," a router's architecture can be categorized into three operational planes:

- **Management plane:** The management plane is concerned with the management of the device. For example, an administrator connecting to a router through a Secure Shell (SSH) connection through one of the router's VTY lines would be a management plane operation.

- **Control plane:** The control plane is concerned with making packet-forwarding decisions. For example, routing protocol operation would be a control plane function.

- **Data plane:** The data plane is concerned with the forwarding of data through a router. For example, end-user traffic traveling from a user's PC to a web server on a different network would go across the data plane.

The ROUTE exam blueprint requires that you know how to protect each of these planes. This chapter discusses approaches for protecting the management plane. Chapter 17, "Routing Protocol Authentication," covers control plane security, by performing authentication for a variety of routing protocols. Finally, you should be familiar with access control lists (ACL) to protect the data plane. ACLs were discussed in your CCNA studies.

Secure Shell Versus Telnet

Many network engineers commonly use Telnet to remotely connect to their routers; however, Cisco strongly recommends using Secure Shell (SSH) instead of Telnet.

The issue with Telnet is that it sends data (including passwords) across a network in clear text. This opens the door for a malicious user to launch a man-in-middle attack and use packet capture software to read the contents of the Telnet session's packets.

Fortunately, SSH encrypts this traffic. So, even if a malicious user did capture packets from the SSH session, the packets would be unreadable.

The steps to configure SSH on a router are as follows:

Step 1. Specify a host name for the router, with the **hostname** *name* command in global configuration mode. (The host name is one of the elements used to create an RSA key pair.)

Step 2. Specify a domain name for the router with the **ip domain-name** *domain_name* command in global configuration mode. (The domain name is one of the elements used to create an RSA key pair.)

Step 3. Create a username and password for a user with a privilege level of 15 using the **username** *username* **privilege 15 secret** *password* global configuration mode command.

Step 4. Generate an RSA key pair with the **crypto key generate rsa modulus** *size_of_modulus* command in global configuration mode.

Step 5. Use the **transport input ssh** command in VTY line configuration mode to make SSH the only supported VTY transport protocol.

Step 6. Issue the **login local** command in VTY line configuration mode to tell SSH to use a router's local user database for authentication.

Step 7. (Optional) Use the **access-class** *acl* **in** command in VTY line configuration mode to limit VTY access to IP addresses matched by the specified ACL.

Example 16-3 illustrates a sample SSH configuration on Router R1, as shown in Figure 16-2.

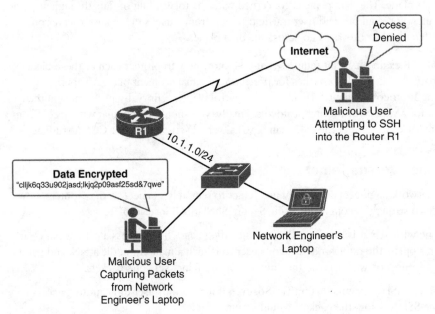

Figure 16-2 *Defending Against Unauthorized VTY Access*

Example 16-3 *Enabling SSH for VTY Access*

```
hostname R1
ip domain-name 1ExamAMonth.com
!
crypto key generate rsa modulus 2014
!
username kevin privilege 15 secret cisco
!
access-list 1 permit 10.1.1.0 0.0.0.255
access-list 1 deny   any log
!
line vty 0 15
 access-class 1 in
 login local
 transport input ssh
```

Figure 16-2 shows a network engineer's laptop on subnet 10.1.1.0 /24 that currently has an SSH session open to Router R1; however, a malicious user located on the same subnet is capturing packets from the SSH session (possibly after a man-in-the-middle attack). Fortunately, the network engineer used SSH to connect to the router, causing the packets captured by the malicious user to be unreadable.

Another malicious user, located somewhere on the Internet, is attempting to set up an SSH session with Router R1, possibly using a program that does a brute-force attack (that is, repeatedly trying different passwords until the correct password is determined). Fortunately, this user is not even presented with a login prompt, because an access class has been configured for the router's VTY lines that does not permit connections from any source IP address not on the 10.1.1.0 /24 subnet.

Example 16-3 shows Router R1's configuration that allows it to defend against the malicious users pictured in Figure 16-1. First, the host name is set to **R1** and the domain name is set to **1ExamAMonth.com**. These values are used in the calculation of the RSA key pair, which is initiated with the **crypto key generate rsa modulus 2014** command. Note that you can use different modulus lengths in the range 260–4096. However, longer lengths are considered more secure.

A username of **kevin** with a password of **cisco** was created, and that user account was given a privilege level of **15**, which is the highest privilege level. An access list was then created to match IP addresses in the 10.1.1.0 /24 subnet.

In VTY line configuration mode, the **transport input ssh** command causes the VTY lines to accept only SSH connections. The **access-class 1 in** command tells the VTY lines to accept only those connections coming from IP addresses matched by ACL 1. Finally, the **login local** command tells SSH to use the router's local database (as populated with the **username** command) for authentication.

Password Encryption

Ideally, all passwords associated with your routers would be stored on an external AAA server; however, it is often necessary to locally store passwords on a router. If someone were to see that router's running configuration, she would be able to see any of those passwords, if they were in clear text. Therefore, a best-practice security recommendation is to encrypt any passwords appearing in a router's configuration.

Cisco IOS has a few different passwords that you might want to encrypt (or represent as a hash value), including the enable secret password, line password, and username password.

Enable Secret Password

The enable secret password can be used to give a network engineer full privileges on a router. This password is configured with the **enable secret** *password* global configuration mode command. The password then appears in a router's running configuration as a Secure Hash Algorithm–256 (SHA-256) hash value, which is very difficult to reverse, even if it did fall into the hands of a malicious user.

Example 16-4 shows the configuration and verification of an enable secret password.

Example 16-4 *Enable Secret Password Configuration and Verification*

```
R1# conf term
R1(config)# enable secret cisco
R1(config)# end

R1# show run
...OUTPUT OMITTED...
enable secret 4 tnhtc92DXBhelxjYk8LWJrPV36S2i4ntXrpb4RFmfqY
```

In Example 16-4, an enable secret password of **cisco** is configured on Router R1. The running configuration then shows the SHA-256 hash of the password. The **4** indicates that the string is an SHA-256 hash. On some older versions of Cisco IOS, you will see a **5** there instead of a **4**. A **5** indicates that the hash is a Message Digest 5 (MD5) hash, which is not considered as secure as SHA-256.

Note If you happen to know the MD5 or SHA-256 hash of the password you want to use, you can specify the actual hash as part of the **enable secret** command. Specifically, you could use the **enable secret 5** *md5-hash* command to specify an MD5 hash for a password. Alternately, you could use the **enable secret 4** *sha-256-hash* command to specify an SHA-256 hash for a password.

Line Password

A line password is used to authenticate a user attempting to log in to one of the router's lines; for example, a VTY (virtual TTY) line, the console line, or the auxiliary line. You can define a line password in line configuration mode with the **password** *password* command; however, at that point, the password still shows up in the router's running configuration in clear text. To encrypt that password, you can issue the **service password-encryption** command in global configuration mode. Unfortunately, this type of encryption is not very strong. It uses the *Vigenere cipher* and is also known as *Type 7* encryption. While this type of encryption can protect passwords from a casual observer who happens to catch a glimpse of the password, it can easily be deciphered (using freely available utilities on the Internet) if someone were to come into possession of a router's running configuration. Therefore, Cisco recommends configuring username/password combinations (discussed in the next section) and requiring those credentials to be entered before accessing one of the router's lines.

Example 16-5 shows the configuration and verification of a line password for the console line. The example continues to show the configuration and verification of Type 7 encryption.

Key Topic

Example 16-5 *Line Password Configuration and Verification*

```
R1# conf term
R1(config)# line con 0
R1(config-line)# password cisco
R1(config-line)# login
R1(config-line)# end
R1# show run | s line
line con 0
 password cisco
 login
... OUTPUT OMITTED ...


R1# conf term
R1(config)# service password-encryption
R1(config)# end
R1# show run | s line
line con 0
 password 7 1511021F0725
... OUTPUT OMITTED ...
```

In Example 16-5, a line password of **cisco** is configured for the console 0 line. The **login** command enables the ability for someone to log in to the console port, supplying the configured password as his only authentication credential. However, as seen in the running configuration, the password was not encrypted. Therefore, the example then shows the **service password-encryption** command being entered, which does encrypt the password. Unfortunately, the type of encryption used is Type 7 encryption, which is very weak encryption. A more preferable approach (as demonstrated in the next section) is to authenticate users based on a username/password combination, where the password appears in the running configuration as an SHA-256 hash value.

Username Password

Instead of just requiring a password to log in to a router, you can create a username/password combination that a network engineer must enter to gain access to the router. Usernames can also be configured with various privilege levels (where a privilege level of 15 indicates a full set of privileges). These privilege levels can be used to control what Cisco IOS commands a user can execute.

You can populate a locally stored user database with the command **username** *username* **privilege** *privilege* **secret** *password*. This causes an SHA-256 hash of the password to appear in the router's running configuration, which is vastly more secure than Type 7 encryption.

Example 16-6 shows the configuration and verification of creating a local user and allowing that user account to access a router's VTY lines.

Example 16-6 *Local User Account Creation and Verification*

```
R1# conf term
R1(config)# username kevin privilege 15 secret cisco
R1(config)# line vty 0 15
R1(config-line)# login local
R1(config-line)# end

R1# show run
... OUTPUT OMITTED ...
!
username kevin privilege 15 secret 4 tnhtc92DXBhelxjYk8LWJrPV36S2i4ntXrpb4RFmfqY
!
... OUTPUT OMITTED ...
!
line vty 0 15
 login local
... OUTPUT OMITTED ...
```

Example 16-6 shows the configuration of a username of **kevin** with a password of **cisco**. The **login local** command issued in line configuration mode tells the VTY lines to use the router's local user account database for authentication. This is as opposed to only using a password configured in line configuration mode for authentication, as was seen in Example 16-5. Notice that the password appears in the running config as an SHA-256 hash of the password, as evidenced by the **4** preceding the hash. On some older versions of Cisco IOS, you might instead see a **5** preceding the hash, indicating an MD5 hash.

Unicast Reverse Path Forwarding

One approach to preventing malicious traffic from entering a network is to use *Unicast Reverse Path Forwarding (uRPF)*. Specifically, uRPF can help block packets having a spoofed IP address. The way that uRPF works is to check the source IP address of a packet arriving on an interface and determine whether that IP address is reachable, based on the router's Forwarding Information Base (FIB) used by Cisco Express Forwarding (CEF). Optionally, the router can also check to see whether the packet is arriving on the interface the router would use to send traffic back to that IP address.

Note CEF must be enabled on a router to use uRPF.

You can choose between three modes of operation for uRPF:

- **Strict mode:** With strict mode operation, a router not only checks to make sure that the source IP address of an arriving packet is reachable, based on the router's FIB, but the packet must also be arriving on the same interface the router would use to send traffic back to that IP address.

■ **Loose mode:** With loose mode operation, a router only verifies that the source IP address of a packet is reachable, based on the router's FIB.

■ **VRF mode:** *Virtual Routing and Forwarding (VRF)* is a technology that allows a router to have multiple IP routing table instances, thus allowing overlapping IP addresses to be used. uRPF operating in VRF mode (also known as *uRPF version 3* or *uRPFv3*) is similar to loose mode operation in that source IP addresses are checked against the FIB for a specific VRF.

Note   Based on the scope of the ROUTE exam blueprint, this book covers the configuration and verification of strict mode and loose mode.

From a design perspective, strict mode could cause traffic to be dropped if an asynchronous routing situation exists (that is, traffic from a network address space might be received on one router interface, but traffic to that same network address space might be transmitted out of a different router interface). Therefore, strict mode should typically be used where there is no chance of asynchronous routing (for example, a branch office with only one connection going back to a corporate headquarters).

Some IP routing tables (and therefore, the associated FIBs) might not have explicit entries for individual networks with which they communicate. Instead, a default route might be used. In such a situation, would a router configured with uRPF drop an arriving packet if the network for that packet's source IP address was not present in the router's FIB?

By default, a router with uRPF configured would drop a packet whose source IP address was only reachable by a default route; however, uRPF supports an **allow-default** option that accepts a default route as a valid way to get back to a source IP address.

To further fine-tune uRPF operation, you can configure an ACL and reference that ACL in the uRPF configuration command. If you do reference an ACL, it is checked only when a uRPF check fails. After a uRPF check failure, if a packet is matched and permitted by the associated ACL, it is transmitted. If a packet fails the uRPF check and is denied by the associated ACL, however, the packet is dropped.

The command used to configure uRPF in interface configuration mode is as follows:

```
ip verify unicast source reachable-via {rx | any} [allow-default] [allow-self-
   ping] [acl]
```

Table 16-3 describes the parameters of this command.

Key Topic

Table 16-3   *uRPF Configuration Parameters*

Parameter	Description
rx	Enables uRPF in strict mode
any	Enables uRPF in loose mode

Parameter	Description
allow-default	Allows uRPF to use a default route if a network is not found in a router's FIB (Note: The **allow-default** option can be used with either strict or loose mode.)
allow-self-ping	Allows a router to ping itself when checking the reachability of an IP address (Note: Cisco recommends against using the **allow-self-ping** option in most cases, because it introduces a security risk.)
acl	Identifies an optional access control list that can either permit or deny traffic that fails the uRPF check

To illustrate the configuration of uRPF, consider Figure 16-3 and Examples 16-7 and 16-8.

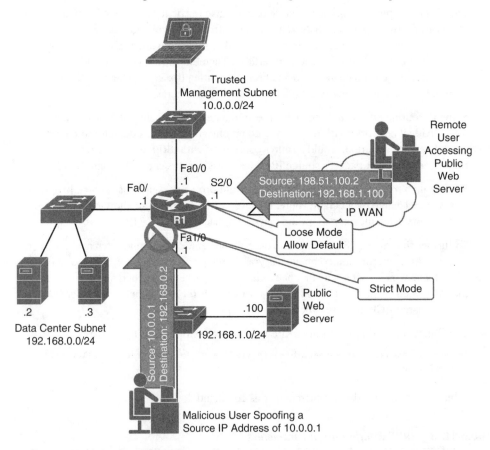

Figure 16-3   *uRPF Sample Topology*

Example 16-7 *uRPF Sample Configuration*

```
interface FastEthernet1/0
 ip address 192.168.1.1 255.255.255.0
 ip verify unicast source reachable-via rx
!
... OUTPUT OMITTED ...
!
interface Serial2/0
 ip address 172.16.0.1 255.255.255.252
 ip verify unicast source reachable-via any allow-default
```

Example 16-8 *Router R1's FIB*

```
R1# show ip cef
Prefix              Next Hop          Interface
0.0.0.0/0           172.16.0.2        Serial2/0
0.0.0.0/8           drop
0.0.0.0/32          receive
10.0.0.0/24         attached          FastEthernet0/0
10.0.0.0/32         receive           FastEthernet0/0
10.0.0.1/32         receive           FastEthernet0/0
10.0.0.255/32       receive           FastEthernet0/0
127.0.0.0/8         drop
172.16.0.0/30       attached          Serial2/0
172.16.0.0/32       receive           Serial2/0
172.16.0.1/32       receive           Serial2/0
172.16.0.2/32       attached          Serial2/0
172.16.0.3/32       receive           Serial2/0
192.168.0.0/24      attached          FastEthernet0/1
192.168.0.0/32      receive           FastEthernet0/1
192.168.0.1/32      receive           FastEthernet0/1
192.168.0.255/32    receive           FastEthernet0/1
192.168.1.0/24      attached          FastEthernet1/0
192.168.1.0/32      receive           FastEthernet1/0
192.168.1.1/32      receive           FastEthernet1/0
192.168.1.255/32    receive           FastEthernet1/0
Prefix              Next Hop          Interface
224.0.0.0/4         drop
224.0.0.0/24        receive
240.0.0.0/4         drop
255.255.255.255/32  receive
```

In the preceding example, a malicious user on the 192.168.1.0 /24 network is spoofing his IP address. Specifically, he is sending packets to a server (with an IP address of
192.168.0.2) in the data center subnet, and he is altering his source IP address to 10.0.0.1.
The reason for this IP spoofing is so that the user's traffic will appear to come from the

trusted management subnet of 10.0.0.0 /24 (which has permission to access the data center servers). However, as his traffic enters interface Fa 1/0 on Router R1, uRPF (configured for strict mode) checks to see what interface would be used to send traffic back to an IP address of 10.0.0.1. As seen in Example 16-8, Router R1's FIB indicates that traffic destined for 10.0.0.1 would go out of interface Fa 0/0. Because the received traffic is being received on interface Fa 1/0, the uRPF check fails and the traffic is dropped.

Also, a remote user with an IP address of 198.51.100.2 is attempting to access a public web server with an IP address of 192.168.1.100. Traffic from the remote user enters Router R1 on interface Serial 2/0. This interface has been configured with uRPF in loose mode, along with the **allow-default** option. As seen in Example 16-8, Router R1's FIB does not have a specific entry for this user's network. However, there is a default route in the FIB (that is, the 0.0.0.0/0 route). Because uRPF configured on interface Serial 2/0 is using the **allow-default** option, the default route is considered to be a route that matches the source IP address. Therefore, the traffic from this remote user is permitted into Router R1.

You can use the **show cef interface** *interface_id* command to determine whether uRPF is enabled on an interface. Example 16-9 shows the output of this command for both interface Fa 1/0 and Serial 2/0.

Example 16-9   *uRPF Verification*

```
R1# show cef interface fa 1/0
FastEthernet1/0 is up (if_number 4)
  Corresponding hwidb fast_if_number 4
  Corresponding hwidb firstsw->if_number 4
  Internet address is 192.168.1.1/24
  ICMP redirects are always sent
  Per packet load-sharing is disabled
  IP unicast RPF check is enabled
  Input features: uRPF
  IP policy routing is disabled
  BGP based policy accounting on input is disabled
  BGP based policy accounting on output is disabled
  Hardware idb is FastEthernet1/0
  Fast switching type 1, interface type 18
  IP CEF switching enabled
  IP CEF switching turbo vector
  IP CEF turbo switching turbo vector
  IP prefix lookup IPv4 mtrie 8-8-8-8 optimized
  Input fast flags 0x4000, Output fast flags 0x0
  ifindex 4(4)
  Slot  Slot unit 0 VC -1
  IP MTU 1500
R1# show cef interface s 2/0
Serial2/0 is up (if_number 6)
  Corresponding hwidb fast_if_number 6
```

```
Corresponding hwidb firstsw->if_number 6
Internet address is 172.16.0.1/30
ICMP redirects are never sent
Per packet load-sharing is disabled
IP unicast RPF check is enabled
Input features: uRPF, iEdge
Output features: iEdge
IP policy routing is disabled
BGP based policy accounting on input is disabled
BGP based policy accounting on output is disabled
Interface is marked as point to point interface
Hardware idb is Serial2/0
Fast switching type 7, interface type 70
IP CEF switching enabled
IP CEF switching turbo vector
IP CEF turbo switching turbo vector
IP prefix lookup IPv4 mtrie 8-8-8-8 optimized
Input fast flags 0x10004000, Output fast flags 0x100000
ifindex 6(6)
Slot  Slot unit 0 VC -1
IP MTU 1500
```

Authentication, Authorization, and Accounting

Enforcing router login security in larger networks can be challenging if you have to manage multiple user databases (for example, having a separate user database locally configured on each router of your network). Fortunately, with AAA (authentication, authorization, and accounting) services, you can have a single repository for user credentials. Then, when a network engineer attempts to log in to, for example, a router, the credentials that she supplies can be authenticated against a centralized AAA database.

Another advantage of giving different network administrators their own login credentials, as opposed to an enable secret password used on all routers, is that users can quickly be added and deleted from the database without the need to reconfigure each router. Not only can AAA service administrative logins connecting to a router, but AAA can also control connections passing through a router to, for example, resources inside a network.

Three services are offered by a AAA server, as follows:

- **Authentication:** The authentication service can check a user's credentials to confirm he is who he claims to be.

- **Authorization:** After being authenticated, the authorization service determines what that user is allowed to do.

- **Accounting:** The accounting service can collect and store information about a user's login. This information can be used, for example, to keep an audit trail of what a user did on the network.

Figure 16-4 shows a AAA topology where only authentication is being performed. The user at an IP address of 192.168.1.50 is attempting to establish a Telnet session with a router at an IP address of 10.3.3.2. The router's configuration, shown in Example 16-10, causes Router R1 to prompt a user for username and password credentials and to check those credentials against a AAA server (a TACACS+ server in this example, as opposed to a RADIUS server). If the provided credentials match the database being referenced by the AAA configuration, the user is permitted to log in to the router.

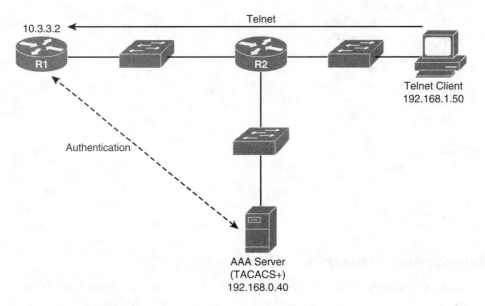

Figure 16-4 *AAA Sample Topology*

Example 16-10 *AAA Configuration for Authenticating Remote Logins*

```
aaa new-model
aaa authentication login ADMIN group tacacs+ local
!
username kevin secret cisco
!
tacacs server CISCO-ACS
 address ipv4 192.168.0.40
 key cisco
!
line vty 0 4
 login authentication ADMIN
```

In the previous example, the **aaa new-model** command is used to enable AAA services on the router. The **aaa authentication login ADMIN group tacacs+ local** command defines a *method list* named **ADMIN**, which attempts to perform authentication through a TACACS+ server. However, if the TACACS+ is unavailable, the **local** key work instructs the router to perform authentication using the local user database (which includes the user **kevin** with a password of **cisco** in this example).

The TACACS+ server is defined as having an IP address of 192.168.0.40 with a shared secret key of **cisco**. The method list of ADMIN is then applied as the authentication method list for connections coming into the router over VTY lines 0 through 4. Therefore, when someone attempts to Telnet into this router, she is challenged to provide valid username and password credentials, which are then validated by the TACACS+ server or the router's local user database if the TACACS+ server is not available.

Note The Cisco IOS implementation of AAA services includes multiple configuration options, and a comprehensive discussion of AAA is beyond the scope of the ROUTE exam blueprint. For more information on AAA configuration, consult the Cisco "Authentication, Authorization, and Accounting Configuration Guide" available at the following URL: http://bit.ly/aaaconfig.

While Example 16-10 used a TACACS+ server as an external AAA server, another option is to use a RADIUS server. Table 16-4 compares these two authentication protocols.

Key
Topic

Table 16-4 *Contrasting the TACACS+ and RADIUS Protocols*

Characteristic	TACACS+	RADIUS
Transport layer protocol	TCP	UDP
Modularity	Provides separate services for authentication, authorization, and accounting	Combines authentication and authorization functions
Encryption	Encrypts entire packet	Only encrypts the password
Accounting functionality	Offers basic accounting features	Offers robust accounting features
Standards-based	No (Cisco-proprietary)	Yes

SNMP Security

The first *Request for Comments (RFC)* for SNMP came out in 1988. Since then, SNMP has become the de facto standard for network management protocols. The original intent for SNMP was for SNMP to manage network nodes, such as network servers, routers, switches, and hubs. SNMP version 1 (SNMPv1) and SNMP version 2c (SNMPv2c) specify three major components of an SNMP solution, as detailed in Table 16-5.

Table 16-5 *Components of an SNMPv1 and SNMPv2c Network Management Solution*

Component	Description
SNMP manager	An SNMP manager runs a network management application. This SNMP manager is sometimes referred to as a Network Management Server (NMS).
SNMP agent	An SNMP agent is a piece of software that runs on a managed device (for example, a server, router, or switch).
Management Information Base (MIB)	Information about a managed device's resources and activity is defined by a series of objects. The structure of these management objects is defined by a managed device's Management Information Base (MIB).

As depicted in Figure 16-5, an SNMP manager (an NMS) can send information to, request information from, or receive unsolicited information from a managed device (a managed router in this example). The managed device runs an SNMP agent and contains a MIB.

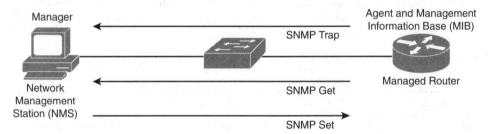

Figure 16-5 *SNMPv1 and SNMPv2c Network Management Components and Messages*

Even though multiple SNMP messages might be sent between an SNMP manager and a managed device, consider the three broad categories of SNMP message types:

- **GET:** An SNMP GET message retrieves information from a managed device.

- **SET:** An SNMP SET message sets a variable in a managed device or triggers an action on a managed device.

- **Trap:** An SNMP Trap message is an unsolicited message sent from a managed device to an SNMP manager, which can notify the SNMP manager about a significant event that occurred on the managed device.

SNMP offers security against malicious users attempting to collect information from a managed device, changing the configuration of a managed device, or intercepting information being sent to an NMS. However, the security integrated with SNMPv1 and SNMPv2c is considered weak. Specifically, SNMPv1 and SNMPv2c use *community strings* to gain read-only or read-write access to a managed device. You can think of a community string as being much like a password. Also, be aware that multiple SNMP-compliant devices on the market today have a default read-only community string of *public* and a default read-write community string of *private*. As a result, such devices, left at their default SNMP settings, might be compromised.

Note   This section refers to SNMPv2c as opposed to SNMPv2. SNMPv2 contained security enhancements in addition to other performance enhancements. However, few network administrators adopted SNMPv2 because of the complexity of the newly proposed security system. Instead, *Community-Based Simple Network Management Protocol (SNMPv2c)* gained widespread acceptance, because SNMPv2c included the feature enhancements of SNMPv2 without using SNMPv2's complex security solution. Instead, SNMPv2c kept the SNMPv1 concept of community strings.

If you do need to secure an SNMPv1 or SNMPv2c environment, you should change the community strings to nondefault values and possibly reference an ACL. The ACL could match a trusted subnet of management stations or a specific IP address of a management station. To illustrate how to better secure SNMPv1 and SNMPv2c router configurations, consider Example 16-11.

Example 16-11   *Securing SNMPv1 and SNMPv2c*

```
R1(config)# snmp-server community $3cr3T ro 10
R1(config)# snmp-server community c1$c0 rw 10
R1(config)# access-list 10 permit host 10.1.1.1
```

In Example 16-11, the read-only and read-write community strings (as specified with the **ro** and **rw** options) are being set to nondefault values, and the **snmp-server community** commands are referencing ACL 10, which is matching a trusted network management station with an IP address of 10.1.1.1. With this configuration, even if the community strings were compromised, an attacker would still have to appear to have an IP address of 10.1.1.1.

Fortunately, the security weakness of SNMPv1 and SNMPv2c are addressed in SNMPv3. To better understand these security enhancements, consider the concept of a security model and a security level:

■ **Security model:** Defines an approach for user and group authentications (for example, SNMPv1, SNMPv2c, and SNMPv3).

■ **Security level:** Defines the type of security algorithm performed on SNMP packets. The three available security levels are

   ■ **noAuthNoPriv:** The *noAuthNoPriv* (no authentication, no privacy) security level uses a username for authentication and does not use encryption to provide privacy.

   ■ **authNoPriv:** The *authNoPriv* (authentication, no privacy) security level provides authentication using Hash Message Authentication Code (HMAC) with MD5 or SHA-1. However, no encryption is used.

   ■ **authPriv:** The *authPriv* (authentication, privacy) security level offers HMAC MD5 or SHA-1 authentication and provides privacy through encryption. Specifically, the encryption uses the Data Encryption Standard (DES), Triple DES (3DES), or Advanced Encryption Standard (AES) algorithm.

As summarized in Table 16-6, SNMPv3 supports all three security levels. Notice that SNMPv1 and SNMPv2c only support the noAuthNoPriv security level.

Key Topic

Table 16-6 *Security Models and Security Levels Supported by Cisco IOS*

Security Model	Security Level	Authentication Strategy	Encryption Type
SNMPv1	noAuthNoPriv	Community string	None
SNMPv2c	noAuthNoPriv	Community string	None
SNMPv3	noAuthNoPriv	Username	None
SNMPv3	authNoPriv	MD5 or SHA-1	None
SNMPv3	authPriv	MD5 or SHA-1	DES, 3DES, or AES

Through the use of security algorithms, as shown in Table 16-6, SNMPv3 dramatically increases the security of network-management traffic, as compared to SNMPv1 and SNMPv2c. Specifically, SNMPv3 offers three primary security enhancements:

■ **Integrity:** Using hashing algorithms, SNMPv3 ensures that an SNMP message was not modified in transit.

■ **Authentication:** Hashing allows SNMPv3 to validate the source of an SNMP message.

■ **Encryption:** Using the DES, 3DES, or AES encryption algorithm, SNMPv3 provides privacy for SNMP messages, making them unreadable by an attacker who might capture SNMP packets.

NTP Authentication

Imagine that you are reviewing device logs collected in a router's buffer and are attempting to correlate the events in the device logs with an issue that you are troubleshooting. To make that correlation, the logged events need to have accurate timestamps.

Although you could individually set the clock on each of your routers, those clocks might drift over time and not agree. You might have heard the saying that a man with one watch always knows what time it is, but a man with two watches is never quite sure. This implies that devices need to have a common point of reference for their time. Such a reference point is made possible by Network Time Protocol (NTP), which allows routers to point to a device acting as an NTP server. Because devices in different time zones might reference the same NTP server, each device has its own time zone configuration, which indicates how many hours its time zone differs from Greenwich Mean Time (GMT).

NTP uses a value, called a *stratum value*, to indicate the believability of a time source. Valid stratum values are in the range 0–15, with a value of 16 being used to indicate that a device does not have its time synchronized. However, Cisco IOS only permits you to set stratum values in the range 1–15. Lower stratum values are considered more authoritative than higher stratum values, with a stratum value of 0 being the most authoritative.

Stratum calculations work much like a hop count. For example, an Internet-based time source using a cesium clock might have a stratum value of a 0. If one of your routers learns time from this stratum 0 time source, your router will have a stratum level of 1. If other devices (for example, servers, switches, and other routers) in your network get their time from your stratum 1 router, they will each have a stratum level of 2.

> **Note**   NTP represents time as a 64-bit value, 32 bits for seconds and 32 bits for a fractional second. At the time of this writing, the current version of NTP is NTP version 4 (NTPv4), as defined in RFC 5905. NTPv4 is backward compatible with NTPv3.

From a security perspective, consider how an attacker might use NTP as part of an attack. She might introduce her own NTP device into a network and advertise false time to network devices. This could not only result in misleading timestamp information appearing in logs (which might be reviewed by a network engineer after an attack), but routers with time-based ACLs might also be convinced to permit traffic that should currently be denied.

To mitigate the risk of having a rogue NTP device advertise false time to your network routers, you can configure NTP authentication. This authentication should be configured on your router that is providing NTP information and on your routers receiving NTP information.

The steps to configure an NTP server (that is, the router providing time, also known as an *NTP master*) and an NTP client (that is, the router receiving time) are as follows:

NTP server configuration steps:

Step 1.   Enter the **ntp authentication-key** *key-id* **md5** *key* command to specify both the secret key and a key ID, which can be used to reference the secret key.

Step 2.   Enter the **ntp authenticate** command to instruct the router to authenticate time sources.

Step 3.   Enter the **ntp trusted-key** *key-id* command to indicate which previously configured key should be trusted for NTP authentication.

Step 4.   (Optional) If the router is not receiving time from an external time source, enter the **ntp master** *stratum-number* command to tell a router to use its local clock as its time source and to specify the stratum level of the router.

NTP client configuration steps:

Step 1.   Enter the **ntp authentication-key** *key-id* **md5** *key* command to specify both the secret key and a key ID, which can be used to reference the secret key.

Step 2.   Enter the **ntp authenticate** command to instruct the router to authenticate time sources.

Step 3.   Enter the **ntp trusted-key** *key-id* command to indicate which previously configured key should be trusted for NTP authentication.

Step 4.   Enter the **ntp server** *ip-address-of-ntp-server* **key** *key-id* command to tell the router to receive time from an NTP server at the specified IP address and to use the specified key ID for authentication.

Example 16-12 shows a sample NTP authentication example for Routers R1 and R2 depicted in Figure 16-6. The configurations are identical with two exceptions. Only the NTP server has the **ntp master** *stratum-number* command, which says that the router is getting time from its local clock. If, however, Router R1 were getting time from a different NTP server, this command would not be required. The other difference in the configurations is the **ntp server** *ip-address-of-ntp-server* **key** *key-id* command on Router R2, which tells Router R2 to receive time from Router R1.

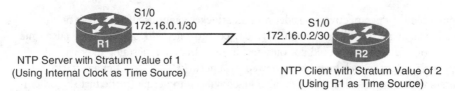

Figure 16-6   *NTP Server and NTP Client Sample Topology*

Example 16-12   *NTP Authentication Configuration*

```
ROUTER R1 CONFIGURATION


R1# conf term
Enter configuration commands, one per line.  End with CNTL/Z.
R1(config)# ntp authentication-key 1 md5 $3cretKEY
R1(config)# ntp authenticate
R1(config)# ntp trusted-key 1
R1(config)# ntp master 1
ROUTER R2 CONFIGURATION

R2# conf term
Enter configuration commands, one per line.  End with CNTL/Z.
R2(config)# ntp authentication-key 1 md5 $3cretKEY
R2(config)# ntp authenticate
R2(config)# ntp trusted-key 1
R2(config)# ntp server 172.16.0.1 key 1
```

A router's current NTP status can be checked with the **show ntp status** and **show ntp associations detail** commands. Example 16-13 shows output from these commands issued on Routers R1 and R2 in Figure 16-6.

Example 16-13   *Verification of Current NTP Status*

```
ROUTER R1


R1# show ntp status
```

```
Clock is synchronized, stratum 1, reference is .LOCL.
nominal freq is 250.0000 Hz, actual freq is 250.0000 Hz, precision is 2**18
ntp uptime is 333900 (1/100 of seconds), resolution is 4000
reference time is D729D7CC.5CEC43FD (14:21:00.362 UTC Fri May 23 2014)
clock offset is 0.0000 msec, root delay is 0.00 msec
root dispersion is 0.44 msec, peer dispersion is 0.23 msec
loopfilter state is 'CTRL' (Normal Controlled Loop), drift is 0.000000000 s/s
system poll interval is 16, last update was 14 sec ago.

R1# show ntp associations detail
127.127.1.1 configured, ipv4, our_master, sane, valid, stratum 0
ref ID .LOCL., time D729D7DC.5CEBD803 (14:21:16.362 UTC Fri May 23 2014)
our mode active, peer mode passive, our poll intvl 16, peer poll intvl 16
root delay 0.00 msec, root disp 0.00, reach 377, sync dist 1.00
delay 0.00 msec, offset 0.0000 msec, dispersion 0.23, jitter 0.00 msec
precision 2**18, version 4
assoc id 30001, assoc name 127.127.1.1
assoc in packets 21, assoc out packets 21, assoc error packets 0
org time D729D7DC.5CEBD803 (14:21:16.362 UTC Fri May 23 2014)
rec time 00000000.00000000 (00:00:00.000 UTC Mon Jan 1 1900)
xmt time D729D7DC.5CEBA253 (14:21:16.362 UTC Fri May 23 2014)
filtdelay =     0.00    0.00    0.00    0.00    0.00    0.00    0.00    0.00
filtoffset =    0.00    0.00    0.00    0.00    0.00    0.00    0.00    0.00
filterror =     0.00    0.24    0.48    0.72    0.96    1.20    1.44    1.68
minpoll = 4, maxpoll = 4
```

```
ROUTER R2

R2# show ntp status
Clock is synchronized, stratum 2, reference is 172.16.0.1
nominal freq is 250.0000 Hz, actual freq is 250.0006 Hz, precision is 2**18
ntp uptime is 313800 (1/100 of seconds), resolution is 4000
reference time is D729D70A.90E382F6 (14:17:46.565 UTC Fri May 23 2014)
clock offset is -34.9053 msec, root delay is 31.96 msec
root dispersion is 4035.10 msec, peer dispersion is 1.40 msec
loopfilter state is 'CTRL' (Normal Controlled Loop), drift is -0.000002539 s/s
system poll interval is 128, last update was 243 sec ago.
R2# show ntp associations detail
172.16.0.1 configured, ipv4, authenticated, our_master, sane, valid, stratum 1
ref ID .LOCL., time D729D78C.5CEB7981 (14:19:56.362 UTC Fri May 23 2014)
our mode client, peer mode server, our poll intvl 128, peer poll intvl 128
root delay 0.00 msec, root disp 0.24, reach 3, sync dist 30.29
delay 23.91 msec, offset -34.9053 msec, dispersion 1.40, jitter 14.95 msec
precision 2**18, version 4
assoc id 54223, assoc name 172.16.0.1
assoc in packets 8, assoc out packets 8, assoc error packets 0
org time 00000000.00000000 (00:00:00.000 UTC Mon Jan 1 1900)
```

```
rec time D729D78D.85E1EDAD (14:19:57.522 UTC Fri May 23 2014)
xmt time D729D78D.85E1EDAD (14:19:57.522 UTC Fri May 23 2014)
filtdelay =    23.93   40.04   36.09   40.09   23.91   28.08   31.96   63.89
filtoffset =  -20.95  -12.96  -16.83  -18.82  -34.90  -24.91  -26.99  -22.98
filterror =     0.00    0.03    1.85    1.88    1.91    1.94    1.97    2.00
minpoll = 6, maxpoll = 10
```

In Example 16-13, notice that Router R1 is synchronized with itself. This is evidenced by the **.LOCL** reference in the output of the **show ntp status** command and the **127.127.1.1** IP address in the output of the **show ntp associations detail** command. The **127.127.1.1** IP address is a well-known IP address used to communicate with a local NTP source.

Similarly, you can see that Router R2 is synchronized with Router R1's IP address and has a stratum level of 2. Also, Router R2 is configured to receive time from 172.16.0.1 (Router R1's IP address), which is shown to have a stratum value of 1.

Exam Preparation Tasks

Planning Practice

The CCNP ROUTE exam expects test takers to review design documents, create implementation plans, and create verification plans. This section provides some exercises that can help you to take a step back from the minute details of the topics in this chapter so that you can think about the same technical topics from the planning perspective.

For each planning practice table, simply complete the table. Note that any numbers in parentheses represent the number of options listed for each item in the solutions in Appendix F, "Completed Planning Practice Tables."

Design Review Table

Table 16-7 lists several design goals related to this chapter. If these design goals were listed in a design document, and you had to take that document and develop an implementation plan, what implementation options come to mind? For any configuration items, a general description can be used, without concern about the specific parameters.

Table 16-7   *Design Review*

Design Goal	Possible Implementation Choices Covered in This Chapter
The design requires a documented router security policy. (List five or more security topics commonly addressed in a router security policy.) (11)	
The design requires that an accounting server (located in a data center subnet) only be accessible during business hours.	
The design requires that router management traffic be encrypted.	
The design requires that a router's line passwords be encrypted, so that someone catching a glimpse of the router's running configuration would not be able to read any of the passwords.	

Design Goal	Possible Implementation Choices Covered in This Chapter
The design requires that a router's Internet-facing interface check the source IP address of an incoming packet and only permit that packet if a route back to the packet's IP source address is found in the router's FIB and if the FIB indicates that the egress interface to get back to that source IP address is the same interface on which the packet arrived.	
The design requires that router authentication requests be handled by an external server. However, if that external server is not available, router authentication requests should be handled by the router's local user database.	
You want to prevent an attacker from influencing a router's time, in an effort to pass traffic through a time-based ACL.	

Implementation Plan Peer Review Table

Table 16-8 shows a list of questions that others might ask, or that you might think about, during a peer review of another network engineer's implementation plan. Complete the table by answering the questions.

Table 16-8 *Notable Questions from This Chapter to Consider During an Implementation Plan Peer Review*

Question	Answer
The plan is using a time-based ACL to protect specific servers. What types of time-based ACLs can be configured in Cisco IOS? (2)	
The plan calls for the use of SSH as opposed to Telnet. What two configurable router parameters are used in the generation of the RSA key pair used by SSH?	
The plan shows a variety of password types to be used, including Type 0, Type 4, Type 5, and Type 7. What is the difference in these password types?	

Question	Answer
The plan calls for the configuration of uRPF. What are uRPF's three modes of operation?	
The plan calls for the use of AAA with an external server running an open standard protocol. What AAA protocol should you choose?	
Even though you know that SNMPv3 is more secure than SNMPv2c, the plan requires the use of SNMPv2c on your routers. What can you do to better secure this network management protocol? (2)	
The plan calls for one enterprise router to receive time from an Internet-based cesium clock. That router will then provide time to all other routers inside the enterprise. Will that router need to have the **ntp master** command configured?	

Create an Implementation Plan Table

To practice skills useful when creating your own OSPF implementation plan, list in Table 16-9 configuration commands related to the configuration of the following features. You might want to record your answers outside the book, and set a goal to complete this table (and others like it) from memory during your final reviews before taking the exam.

Table 16-9   *Implementation Plan Configuration Memory Drill*

Feature	Configuration Commands/Notes
Create a named time range for an ACL (in global configuration mode).	
Define a periodic time range (in time range configuration mode).	
Define an absolute time range (in time range configuration mode).	
Apply a time range to a numbered ACL (in global configuration mode).	
Apply a time range to a named ACL (in named access list configuration mode).	
Specify a router's host name.	
Specify a router's domain name.	

Feature	Configuration Commands/Notes
Create a user with a privilege level of 15 and a hashed password.	
Generate an RSA key pair.	
In VTY line configuration mode, only permit SSH connections.	
In VTY configuration skills mode, instruct SSH to use a router's local user database for authentication.	
Enable the password encryption service to encrypt line passwords.	
Enable uRPF in interface configuration mode.	
Enable AAA services on a router.	
Create a AAA method list named TEST that attempts to use a TACACS+ server for authentication, but will fall back to a local user database if the TACACS+ server is unavailable.	
Configure the read-only or read-write community string on a router, and specify an ACL that defines trusted IP addresses.	
Specify an NTP authentication key, along with a key ID.	
Instruct a router to authenticate time sources.	
Specify a trusted NTP key ID.	
Instruct a router to provide time to other NTP-speaking devices, using its internal clock as the time source, and specify the router's stratum value.	
Specify the IP address of an NTP server from which a router should receive time, along with the key ID that should be used to authenticate with that NTP server.	

Choose Commands for a Verification Plan Table

To practice skills useful when creating your own OSPF verification plan, list in Table 16-10 all commands that supply the requested information. You might want to record your answers outside the book, and set a goal to complete this table (and others like it) from memory during your final reviews before taking the exam.

Table 16-10 *Verification Plan Memory Drill*

Information Needed	Command(s)
Display the contents of a router's FIB.	
Determine whether an interface has uRPF enabled.	
Display a router's NTP stratum value.	
Display the stratum value of a router's NTP reference.	

Review All the Key Topics

Review the most important topics from inside the chapter, noted with the Key Topic icon in the outer margin of the page. Table 16-11 lists a reference of these key topics and the page numbers on which each is found.

Key
Topic

Table 16-11 *Key Topics for Chapter 16*

Key Topic Element	Description	Page Number
List	Topics commonly addressed in a router security policy	704
Table 16-2	Time-Based ACL Commands	706
Example 16-1	Time-Based ACL Configuration Example	707
Example 16-2	Sample Infrastructure ACL	708
List	A router's architectural planes of operation	709
List	Steps to configure SSH on a router	709
Example 16-3	Enabling SSH for VTY Access	710
Example 16-5	Line Password Configuration and Verification	713
Table 16-3	uRPF Configuration Parameters	715
Example 16-7	uRPF Sample Configuration	717
Example 16-10	AAA Configuration for Authenticating Remote Logins	720
Table 16-4	Contrasting the TACACS+ and RADIUS Protocols	721
Table 16-5	Components of an SNMPv1 and SNMPv2c Network Management Solution	722
Table 16-6	Security Models and Security Levels Supported by Cisco IOS	724

Key Topic Element	Description	Page Number
List	Steps to configure an NTP server and an NTP client	725
Example 16-12	NTP Authentication Configuration	726

Complete the Tables and Lists from Memory

Print a copy of Appendix D, "Memory Tables," (found on the CD) or at least the section for this chapter, and complete the tables and lists from memory. Appendix E, "Memory Tables Answer Key," also on the CD, includes completed tables and lists to check your work.

Define Key Terms

Define the following key terms from this chapter, and check your answers in the glossary.

router security policy, time-based ACL, infrastructure ACL, NTP, uRPF, AAA, SNMP

This chapter covers the following subjects:

- **Authentication Methods:** This section contrasts different approaches to routing protocol authentication, including simple password authentication and hashing authentication. Routing protocol authentication can be used to prevent a malicious user from forming a neighborship between his router and a production router.

- **EIGRP Authentication:** This section examines the operation and configuration of EIGRP authentication, including EIGRP for IPv4, EIGRP for IPv6, and Named EIGRP.

- **OSPF Authentication:** Similar to the concepts presented in the preceding "EIGRP Authentication" section, this section demonstrates how to authenticate OSPF neighbor relationships, using a variety of approaches.

- **BGP Authentication:** This section explains the threat of session hijacking in a BGP environment and demonstrates how to configure authentication between BGP peers.

CHAPTER 17

Routing Protocol Authentication

Protocols such as Enhanced Interior Gateway Routing Protocol (EIGRP) and Open Shortest Path First (OPSF), using multicasts, can dynamically form neighborships with adjacent routers. The ease with which neighborships can be formed is a concern from a security perspective.

For example, consider a malicious user that introduces his router into a network. If that router successfully forms one or more neighborships, that rogue router could inject false routing information into a corporate network, perhaps causing corporate data traffic to flow through the rogue router, thus allowing the malicious user to capture that traffic. To help mitigate such a situation, this short chapter begins with a comparison of authentication methods followed by a discussion of the operation and configuration of EIGRP and OSPF authentication.

Unlike the dynamic neighbor formation of EIGRP and OSPF, Border Gateway Protocol (BGP) requires neighbors to be statically configured. Therefore, the previous scenario of injecting a rogue router with the intent of manipulating routing tables is less likely with BGP. However, session hijacking can still occur, where a router takes over an existing TCP session between two routers that have already formed a BGP neighborship. Therefore, this chapter concludes with examples of BGP authentication, including IPv4 and IPv6 environments.

"Do I Know This Already?" Quiz

The "Do I Know This Already?" quiz allows you to assess whether you should read the entire chapter. If you miss no more than one of these eight self-assessment questions, you might want to move ahead to the "Exam Preparation Tasks" section. Table 17-1 lists the major headings in this chapter and the "Do I Know This Already?" quiz questions covering the material in those headings so that you can assess your knowledge of these specific areas. The answers to the "Do I Know This Already?" quiz appear in Appendix A.

Table 17-1 *"Do I Know This Already?" Foundation Topics Section-to-Question Mapping*

Foundation Topics Section	Questions
Authentication Methods	1, 2
EIGRP Authentication	3, 4
OSPF Authentication	5, 6
BGP Authentication	7, 8

1. Identify possible approaches that Cisco IOS uses to authenticate neighboring routers. (Choose two.)

   a. Plain text authentication

   b. Two-factor authentication

   c. Hashing authentication

   d. Biometric authentication

2. Two neighboring routers are each configured with a key chain. What element(s) of the key chain must match for the two routers to mutually authenticate? (Choose all that apply.)

   a. Key chain name

   b. Key number

   c. Key string

   d. Accept-lifetime

   e. Send-lifetime

3. What types of neighbor authentication does Named EIGRP support? (Choose all that apply.)

   a. Plain text authentication

   b. MD5 hashing authentication

   c. SHA hashing authentication

   d. PAP authentication

4. What command can be used to view the configuration of a key chain used by EIGRP?

   a. show key chain

   b. show key-chain

   c. show authentication key chain

   d. show eigrp key chain

5. Routers R1 and R2 are both running OSPFv2, and they are currently authenticated with one another, using MD5, over their Fa 0/0 interfaces. Interface Fa 0/0 on Router R1 is participating in area 0. However, you notice that the OSPF router configuration on Router R1 does not contain the **area 0 authentication message-digest** command. What command must have been configured under Router R1's Fa 0/0 interface?

   a. area 0 authentication md5

   b. ip ospf authentication message-digest

   c. ip ospf authentication 0 md5

   d. area 1 authentication message-digest

6. Identify the valid types of OSPFv3 authentication supported in Cisco IOS. (Choose all that apply.)

   a. SHA

   b. MD5

   c. PAP

   d. Clear text

7. BGP can use what type of authentication?

   a. SHA

   b. Clear text

   c. MD5

   d. DH Group 1

8. Because BGP neighborships require neighbors to be statically configured, what is the most likely approach that an attacker would take to inject a rogue router into a network and have that rogue router form a BGP neighborship with a production router?

   a. Man-in-the-middle attack

   b. Denial of service (DoS) attack

   c. Session hijacking

   d. Distributed DoS (DDoS) attack

Foundation Topics

Authentication Methods

Cisco routers support a couple of different approaches to authenticating route advertisements received from a neighboring router:

- Plain text authentication

- Hashing authentication

Both of these approaches require routers to have matching passwords (also referred to as *keys*); however, Cisco recommends the use of hashing authentication.

Plain text authentication, as the name suggests, simply sends a password from one router to another in clear text. This leads to the security concern of having a malicious user capture authentication traffic containing a password and then injecting her own router, which could use the compromised password to authenticate with one of the network's production routers.

Hashing authentication is preferred over plain text authentication, because it never sends the password over the network. Instead, a mathematical algorithm is run on the password, and the result of that algorithm (called a *hash digest*) is sent from one router to its neighbor. That neighboring router also runs the hashing algorithm on its configured password, and if its hash digest matches the hash digest it receives from the first router, it can conclude that the passwords match.

The two hashing algorithms that you can select from (depending on the routing protocol) include *Message Digest 5 (MD5)* and *Secure Hash Algorithm (SHA)*. SHA is generally considered to be somewhat more secure than MD5; however, either algorithm is vastly superior to using plain text authentication.

Plain Text Authentication

The plain text authentication process follows a procedure that can generally be summarized as follows:

Step 1. A routing update is sent from one router to another. That routing update includes a key (that is, a password) and a key number, because some routing protocols support the configuration of multiple keys. Note that if a routing protocol does not support multiple keys, the key number associated with a routing update is 0.

Step 2. A neighboring router receives the routing update. That router determines whether the received key matches its configured key (with a matching key number).

Step 3. If the neighboring router determines that the keys match, it accepts the routing update. However, the routing update is rejected if the keys do not match.

The only routing protocols supported in Cisco IOS that you can configure with plain text authentication are

- Routing Information Protocol version 2 (RIPv2)

- Open Shortest Path First version 2 (OSPFv2)

- Intermediate System–to–Intermediate System (IS-IS)

Hashing Authentication

The basic operation of hashing authentication bears some similarity to plain text authentication. Notably different, however, is how hashing authentication never transmits a key across a network, instead sending the hash digest (that is, the result of running a hashing algorithm on a router's configured password).

The hashing authentication process follows a procedure that can generally be summarized as follows:

Key Topic

Step 1.   A hashing algorithm is run on a routing update along with a router's configured key. The result of the hashing algorithm (that is, the hash digest) is added to the end of the routing update, which is then sent to a neighboring router.

Step 2.   The neighboring router receives the update and runs a hashing algorithm on the routing update combined with its locally configured key, which results in a hash digest.

Step 3.   If the locally configured hash digest matches the received hash digest, the receiving router accepts the packet. If the independently calculated hash digest values do not match, the update is rejected.

Hashing authentication using MD5 can be configured for the following protocols within Cisco IOS:

- RIPv2

- EIGRP

- OSPFv2

- OSPFv3

- IS-IS

- BGP

SHA authentication is supported by the following protocols:

- RIP next generation (RIPng)

- Named EIGRP

- OSPFv2 (see note)

- OSPFv3

- IS-IS (see note)

> **Note**   While RFC 5709 states that OSPFv2 can support SHA authentication, this feature is not widely deployed in Cisco IOS. Therefore, depending on your version of Cisco IOS, you might not have the option of configuring SHA authentication for OSPFv2. The same holds true for IS-IS (as described in RFC 5310).
>
> Also note that RIPng and OSPFv3, used for routing in IPv6 networks, do not have any native authentication features. Instead, they rely on IPsec to handle their authentication.

Key Chains

Having two routers each configured with an identical key (called a *shared secret key*) is a basic requirement for routing protocol authentication. However, if that shared secret key were learned, that might permit a malicious user to introduce a rogue router into a network and have that router form one or more neighborships with existing routers. The probability that a shared secret key will be learned increases with time. Therefore, Cisco recommends that you frequently change your keys.

Fortunately, you can configure *time-based key chains*. A *key chain* is a collection of keys, each identified with a *key ID*, that is associated with an interface. A time-based key chain not only includes a collection of keys and key IDs, but it also includes *key lifetimes*. These lifetimes dictate the periods of time when a router will send a specific key and when a router will accept a specific key. The period of time during which a router will accept a specific key is called the *accept lifetime*, while the period of time during which a router will send a specific key is called the *send lifetime*.

> **Note**   To make sure that there is never a period of time when no key is active, you should configure your key lifetimes to overlap. If a router sends an update at a time when multiple keys are active, the router uses the key with the lowest key ID.

To better understand the concept and configuration of time-based key chains, consider Example 17-1. This example shows the configuration for the two routers pictured in Figure 17-1.

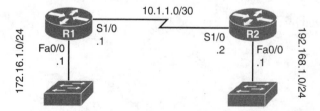

Figure 17-1   *Two Routers Configured with Time-Based Key Chains*

Example 17-1 *Time-Based Key Chain Configuration*

```
!Configuration on Router R1
R1# conf term
R1(config)# key chain R1KEYCHAIN
R1(config-keychain)# key 1
R1(config-keychain-key)# key-string PRIMARY_KEY
R1(config-keychain-key)# accept-lifetime 01:00:00 April 1 2014 01:00:00 May 2 2014
R1(config-keychain-key)# send-lifetime 01:00:00 April 1 2014 01:00:00 May 2 2014
R1(config-keychain-key)# exit
R1(config-keychain)# key 2
R1(config-keychain-key)# key-string SECONDARY_KEY
R1(config-keychain-key)# accept-lifetime 01:00:00 May 1 2014 infinite
R1(config-keychain-key)# send-lifetime 01:00:00 May 1 2014 infinite
R1(config-keychain-key)# end
R1#


!Configuration on Router R2
R2# conf term
R2(config)# key chain R2KEYCHAIN
R2(config-keychain)# key 1
R2(config-keychain-key)# key-string PRIMARY_KEY
R2(config-keychain-key)# accept-lifetime 01:00:00 April 1 2014 01:00:00 May 2 2014
R2(config-keychain-key)# send-lifetime 01:00:00 April 1 2014 01:00:00 May 2 2014
R2(config-keychain-key)# exit
R2(config-keychain)# key 2
R2(config-keychain-key)# key-string SECONDARY_KEY
R2(config-keychain-key)# accept-lifetime 01:00:00 May 1 2014 infinite
R2(config-keychain-key)# send-lifetime 01:00:00 May 1 2014 infinite
R2(config-keychain-key)# end
R2#
```

In Example 17-1, a key chain with a name of **R1KEYCHAIN** is created on Router R1. This key chain is then configured with two keys, **key 1** and **key 2**. The value of the first key was set to **PRIMARY_KEY**, and the value of the second key was set to **SECONDARY_KEY**.

The configuration also specifies that the first key is valid, for both sending and receiving, for a time period beginning at 1:00 a.m. on April 1, 2014, and ending at 1:00 a.m. on May 2, 2014. The second key becomes valid, for both sending and receiving, at 1:00 a.m. on May 1, 2014, but the **infinite** keyword in the **accept-lifetime** and **send-lifetime** commands means that when the second key becomes valid, it will stay valid indefinitely.

A nearly identical key chain configuration is then created for Router R2, with the only difference being the name of the key chain. On R2, the key chain name is **R2KEYCHAIN**.

In the example, key 1 stays valid for one day after key 2 becomes valid. Using overlapping time periods for key lifetimes helps ensure that there will not be a period of time when no key is valid.

Note   This key chain configuration will be used in the next section of this chapter.

EIGRP Authentication

EIGRP authentication causes routers to authenticate every EIGRP message. To do so, the routers should use the same preshared key (PSK) and generate an MD5 digest for each EIGRP message based on that PSK. If a router configured for EIGRP authentication receives an EIGRP message, and the message's MD5 digest does not pass the authentication checking based on the local copy of the key, the router silently discards the message. As a result, when authentication fails, two routers cannot become EIGRP neighbors, because they ignore each other's EIGRP Hello messages.

From a design perspective, EIGRP authentication helps prevent denial of service (DoS) attacks, but it does not provide any privacy. The device that physically receives the bits can read the EIGRP messages. Note that on LANs, the updates flow to the 224.0.0.10 multicast IP address, so any attacker could join the 224.0.0.10 multicast group and read the packets. However, authentication prevents attackers from forming neighborships with legitimate routers, thus preventing the advertisement of incorrect routing information.

This section examines EIGRP authentication configuration generically, followed by examples of authentication configurations for EIGRP for IPv4, EIGRP for IPv6, and Named EIGRP.

EIGRP for IPv4 Authentication

The EIGRP for IPv4 authentication configuration process requires a few steps, which are summarized as follows:

Step 1.   Create a key chain. (This procedure was discussed in the earlier section "Authentication Methods.")

Step 2.   Enable EIGRP MD5 authentication on an interface, for a particular EIGRP autonomous system number (ASN), using the **ip authentication mode eigrp** *asn* **md5** interface subcommand.

Step 3.   Refer to the correct key chain to be used on an interface using the **ip authentication key-chain eigrp** *asn name-of-chain* interface subcommand.

The configuration in Step 1 is fairly detailed, but Steps 2 and 3 are relatively simple. Essentially, Cisco IOS configures the key values separately (Step 1) and then requires an interface subcommand to refer to those key values. To support the capability to have multiple keys, and even multiple sets of keys, the configuration includes the concept of a key chain and multiple keys on each key chain.

To illustrate this configuration further, consider Example 17-2, which shows the configuration of the routers in Figure 17-2.

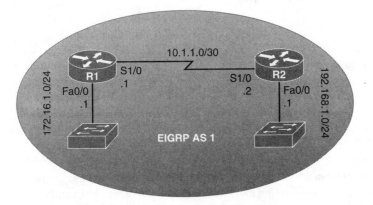

Figure 17-2 *Two Routers Configured with EIGRP for IPv4 Authentication*

Example 17-2 *EIGRP for IPv4 Authentication Configuration*

Key
Topic

```
!Configuration on Router R1
key chain R1KEYCHAIN
 key 1
   key-string PRIMARY_KEY
   accept-lifetime 01:00:00 Apr 1 2014 01:00:00 May 2 2014
   send-lifetime 01:00:00 Apr 1 2014 01:00:00 May 2 2014
 key 2
   key-string SECONDARY_KEY
   accept-lifetime 01:00:00 May 1 2014 infinite
   send-lifetime 01:00:00 May 1 2014 infinite
!
interface Serial1/0
 ip address 10.1.1.1 255.255.255.252
 ip authentication mode eigrp 1 md5
 ip authentication key-chain eigrp 1 R1KEYCHAIN
!
router eigrp 1
 network 0.0.0.0


!Configuration on Router R2
key chain R2KEYCHAIN
 key 1
   key-string PRIMARY_KEY
   accept-lifetime 01:00:00 Apr 1 2014 01:00:00 May 2 2014
   send-lifetime 01:00:00 Apr 1 2014 01:00:00 May 2 2014
 key 2
```

```
     key-string SECONDARY_KEY
     accept-lifetime 01:00:00 May 1 2014 infinite
     send-lifetime 01:00:00 May 1 2014 infinite
 !
interface Serial1/0
 ip address 10.1.1.2 255.255.255.252
 ip authentication mode eigrp 1 md5
 ip authentication key-chain eigrp 1 R2KEYCHAIN
 !
router eigrp 1
 network 0.0.0.0
```

Example 17-2 builds on the key chain configuration shown in Example 17-1. Specifically, Router R1 has a key chain named **R1KEYCHAIN**, and Router R2 has a key chain named **R2KEYCHAIN**. In interface configuration mode for each of the routers, the **ip authentication mode eigrp** *asn* **md5** command was issued for EIGRP autonomous system **1**. Then, the **ip authentication key-chain eigrp** *asn name-of-chain* command was issued in interface configuration mode to specify which key chain the interface would use for its MD5 authentication.

The **show key chain** command can be used to view the details of any configured key chains. Also, you can issue the **show ip eigrp neighbors** command to confirm that expected EIGRP neighborships have been formed. Example 17-3 shows sample output from Router R1 and confirms that key 1 is currently valid.

Example 17-3 *Verifying EIGRP for IPv4 Authentication*

```
R1# show key chain
Key-chain R1KEYCHAIN:
    key 1 -- text "PRIMARY_KEY"
        accept lifetime (01:00:00 UTC Apr 1 2014) - (01:00:00 UTC May 2 2014) [valid
          now]
        send lifetime (01:00:00 UTC Apr 1 2014) - (01:00:00 UTC May 2 2014) [valid
          now]
    key 2 -- text "SECONDARY_KEY"
        accept lifetime (01:00:00 UTC May 1 2014) - (infinite)
        send lifetime (01:00:00 UTC May 1 2014) - (infinite)
R1# show ip eigrp neighbors
EIGRP-IPv4 Neighbors for AS(1)
H   Address              Interface          Hold Uptime   SRTT   RTO  Q   Seq
                                            (sec)         (ms)        Cnt Num
0   10.1.1.2             Se1/0              12  01:01:05   79    474   0   7
```

EIGRP for IPv6 Authentication

Configuring authentication for EIGRP for IPv6 is nearly identical to configuring authentication for EIGRP for IPv4. The only difference is the **ip authentication mode eigrp** *asn* **md5** and **ip authentication key-chain eigrp** *asn name-of-chain* commands have **ip** replaced with **ipv6**. These steps can be summarized as follows:

Step 1.   Create a key chain. (This procedure was discussed in the earlier section "Authentication Methods.")

Step 2.   Enable EIGRP MD5 authentication on an interface, for a particular EIGRP ASN, using the **ipv6 authentication mode eigrp** *asn* **md5** interface subcommand.

Step 3.   Refer to the correct key chain to be used on an interface using the **ipv6 authentication key-chain eigrp** *asn name-of-chain* interface subcommand.

Consider Example 17-4, based on the topology in Figure 17-3. Note how the configuration closely mirrors Example 17-2, which showed how to configure authentication for EIGRP for IPv4.

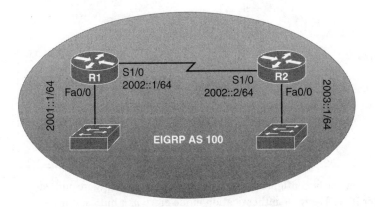

Figure 17-3   *Two Routers Configured with EIGRP for IPv6 Authentication*

Example 17-4   *EIGRP for IPv6 Authentication Configuration*

```
!Configuration on Router R1
key chain R1KEYCHAIN
 key 1
  key-string PRIMARY_KEY
  accept-lifetime 01:00:00 Apr 1 2014 01:00:00 May 2 2014
  send-lifetime 01:00:00 Apr 1 2014 01:00:00 May 2 2014
 key 2
  key-string SECONDARY_KEY
  accept-lifetime 01:00:00 May 1 2014 infinite
  send-lifetime 01:00:00 May 1 2014 infinite
!
interface Serial1/0
 ipv6 address 2002::1/64
 ipv6 eigrp 100
 ipv6 authentication mode eigrp 100 md5
```

```
 ipv6 authentication key-chain eigrp 100 R1KEYCHAIN
 !
ipv6 router eigrp 100
 eigrp router-id 1.1.1.1


!Configuration on Router R2
key chain R2KEYCHAIN
 key 1
   key-string PRIMARY_KEY
   accept-lifetime 01:00:00 Apr 1 2014 01:00:00 May 2 2014
   send-lifetime 01:00:00 Apr 1 2014 01:00:00 May 2 2014
 key 2
   key-string SECONDARY_KEY
   accept-lifetime 01:00:00 May 1 2014 infinite
   send-lifetime 01:00:00 May 1 2014 infinite
 !
interface Serial1/0
 ipv6 address 2002::2/64
 ipv6 eigrp 100
 ipv6 authentication mode eigrp 100 md5
 ipv6 authentication key-chain eigrp 100 R2KEYCHAIN
 !
ipv6 router eigrp 100
 eigrp router-id 2.2.2.2
```

In Example 17-4, the previously configured key chains were used to configure authentication for EIGRP for IPv6. The **ipv6 authentication mode eigrp** *asn* **md5** and **ipv6 authentication key-chain eigrp** *asn name-of-chain* commands were issued in interface configuration mode, to make the interface authenticate any received EIGRP messages using the specified key chain for EIGRP autonomous system **100**.

Example 17-5 shows how to verify your configuration. The **show key chain** command displays the details of the key chain, while the **show ipv6 eigrp neighbors** command confirms that a neighborship has formed.

Example 17-5 *Verifying EIGRP for IPv6 Authentication*

```
R1# show key chain
Key-chain R1KEYCHAIN:
    key 1 -- text "PRIMARY_KEY"
        accept lifetime (01:00:00 UTC Apr 1 2014) - (01:00:00 UTC May 2 2014) [valid
        now]
        send lifetime (01:00:00 UTC Apr 1 2014) - (01:00:00 UTC May 2 2014) [valid
        now]
    key 2 -- text "SECONDARY_KEY"
        accept lifetime (01:00:00 UTC May 1 2014) - (infinite)
        send lifetime (01:00:00 UTC May 1 2014) - (infinite)
```

```
R1# show ipv6 eigrp neighbors
EIGRP-IPv6 Neighbors for AS(100)
H   Address                 Interface        Hold Uptime    SRTT   RTO   Q  Seq
                                             (sec)          (ms)        Cnt Num
0   Link-local address:     Se1/0            11  00:35:12   38    228   0  3
    FE80::C801:17FF:FE94:0
```

Named EIGRP Authentication

The configuration of Named EIGRP authentication is very similar to the authentication configuration of EIGRP for IPv4. After configuring a key chain, you enter the **authentication mode {md5 | hmac-sha-256}** command in address family interface configuration mode. Finally, still in address family interface configuration mode, you enter the **authentication key-chain** *name-of-chain* command. Following are the steps:

Step 1.   Create a key chain.

Step 2.   Enable authentication for Named EIGRP in address family interface configuration mode, using the command **authentication mode {md5 | hmac-sha-256}**.

Step 3.   Refer to the correct key chain to be used, while still in address family interface configuration mode, with the command **authentication key-chain** *name-of-chain*.

Example 17-6 demonstrates the configuration of Named EIGRP authentication for the topology shown in Figure 17-4.

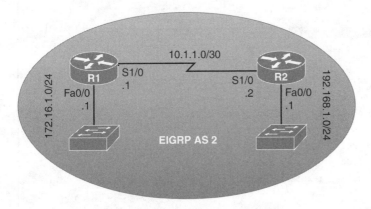

Figure 17-4 *Two Routers Configured with EIGRP for IPv6 Authentication*

Example 17-6 *Named EIGRP Authentication Configuration*

```
!Configuration on Router R1
key chain R1KEYCHAIN
 key 1
  key-string PRIMARY_KEY
  accept-lifetime 01:00:00 Apr 1 2014 01:00:00 May 2 2014
```

```
    send-lifetime 01:00:00 Apr 1 2014 01:00:00 May 2 2014
  key 2
    key-string SECONDARY_KEY
    accept-lifetime 01:00:00 May 1 2014 infinite
    send-lifetime 01:00:00 May 1 2014 infinite
!
interface FastEthernet0/0
 ip address 172.16.1.1 255.255.255.0
!
interface Serial1/0
 ip address 10.1.1.1 255.255.255.252
!
router eigrp AUTH_DEMO
 !
 address-family ipv4 unicast autonomous-system 2
  !
  af-interface Serial1/0
   authentication mode md5
   authentication key-chain R1KEYCHAIN
  exit-af-interface
  !
  topology base
  exit-af-topology
  network 0.0.0.0
 exit-address-family


!Configuration on Router R2
key chain R2KEYCHAIN
 key 1
   key-string PRIMARY_KEY
   accept-lifetime 01:00:00 Apr 1 2014 01:00:00 May 2 2014
   send-lifetime 01:00:00 Apr 1 2014 01:00:00 May 2 2014
 key 2
   key-string SECONDARY_KEY
   accept-lifetime 01:00:00 May 1 2014 infinite
   send-lifetime 01:00:00 May 1 2014 infinite
!
interface FastEthernet0/0
 ip address 192.168.1.1 255.255.255.0
!
interface Serial1/0
 ip address 10.1.1.2 255.255.255.252
!
router eigrp AUTH_DEMO
 !
 address-family ipv4 unicast autonomous-system 2
```

```
!
af-interface Serial1/0
  authentication mode md5
  authentication key-chain R2KEYCHAIN
  exit-af-interface
!
topology base
exit-af-topology
network 0.0.0.0
exit-address-family
```

Verification can be performed with the same **show key chain** and **show ip eigrp neighbors** command used for verifying a classic EIGRP for IPv4 configuration. Note that the authentication mode specified in Example 17-6 is **md5**. However, **hmac-sha-256** is another supported authentication mode.

OSPF Authentication

OSPF authentication causes routers to authenticate every OSPF message. To do so, the routers use the same preshared key value. This key might be in plain text, or it might be a hash digest from either the MD5 hashing algorithms (although SHA might also be supported depending on the type and version of Cisco IOS you are running). Table 17-2 lists the authentication types supported by OSPF.

Table 17-2 *OSPF Authentication Types*

OSPF Authentication Type	Description
Type 0	Does not provide any authentication
Type 1	Provides plain text authentication
Type 2	Provides hashing authentication

On a router, OSPF authentication can be enabled on individual interfaces or an entire area. This section begins by examining plain text and hashing authentication for OSPFv2. Then, the section concludes with a look at hashing authentication for OSPFv3. Interestingly, OSPFv3 relies on the authentication features provided by IPsec, rather than any authentication function natively built into OSPFv3.

Plain Text OSPFv2 Authentication

Plain text authentication (also known as *clear text authentication* or *simple password authentication*) for OSPFv2 requires neighboring OSPF routers to be preconfigured with the same authentication key (that is, a shared secret password). The steps to configure plain text OSPFv2 authentication are as follows:

Step 1. Plain text authentication must be enabled for either an interface or an OSPF area:

- Enable per interface using the **ip ospf authentication** interface subcommand.

- Enable on all interfaces in an area by changing the area-wide authentication setting using the **area** *area-number* **authentication** subcommand under OSPF router configuration mode.

Step 2. The authentication keys must be configured per interface, using the **ip ospf authentication-key** *name-of-key* interface subcommand.

Note OSPFv3 does not support the plain text authentication supported by OSPFv2.

Example 17-7 illustrates the configuration of OSPFv2 plain text authentication for the topology shown in Figure 17-5.

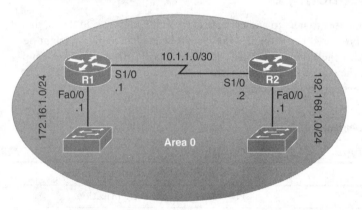

Figure 17-5 *Two Routers Configured with OSPFv2 Plain Text Authentication*

Example 17-7 *OSPFv2 Plain Text Authentication Configuration*

```
!Configuration on Router R1
interface Serial1/0
 ip address 10.1.1.1 255.255.255.252
 ip ospf authentication-key KEYLIME
!
router ospf 1
 area 0 authentication
 network 0.0.0.0 255.255.255.255 area 0

!Configuration on Router R2
interface Serial1/0
 ip address 10.1.1.2 255.255.255.252
```

```
ip ospf authentication
ip ospf authentication-key KEYLIME
!
router ospf 1
 network 0.0.0.0 255.255.255.255 area 0
```

Note   The maximum length of the authentication key is eight characters. If you enter a longer key, it will automatically be truncated to eight characters.

Example 17-7 shows two approaches for configuring plain text authentication for OSPF. The **ip ospf authentication-key** *key-string* command is issued in interface configuration mode on both Routers R1 and R2. However, Router R1 uses the **area** *area_number* **authentication** command in router configuration mode to enable authentication for all its interfaces participating in area 0, while Router R2 uses the **ip ospf authentication** command in interface configuration mode to enable authentication for an individual interface. These two approaches are compatible with one another, and a neighborship successfully forms.

The **show ip ospf interface** *interface_identifier* command can be used to confirm that plain text authentication (referred to as *simple password authentication* in Cisco IOS command output) is enabled on an interface. Of course, you could also use the **show ip ospf neighbor** command to confirm that a neighborship exists between two routers. Example 17-8 offers sample output from these commands issued on Router R1.

Example 17-8   *Verifying OSPFv2 Plain Text Authentication*

```
R1# show ip ospf interface s 1/0
Serial1/0 is up, line protocol is up
  Internet Address 10.1.1.1/30, Area 0, Attached via Network Statement
  Process ID 1, Router ID 172.16.1.1, Network Type POINT_TO_POINT, Cost: 64
  Topology-MTID    Cost    Disabled    Shutdown      Topology Name
        0           64        no          no             Base
  Transmit Delay is 1 sec, State POINT_TO_POINT
  Timer intervals configured, Hello 10, Dead 40, Wait 40, Retransmit 5
    oob-resync timeout 40
    Hello due in 00:00:00
  Supports Link-local Signaling (LLS)
  Cisco NSF helper support enabled
  IETF NSF helper support enabled
  Index 2/2, flood queue length 0
  Next 0x0(0)/0x0(0)
  Last flood scan length is 1, maximum is 1
  Last flood scan time is 4 msec, maximum is 4 msec
  Neighbor Count is 1, Adjacent neighbor count is 1
    Adjacent with neighbor 192.168.1.1
```

```
    Suppress hello for 0 neighbor(s)
    Simple password authentication enabled
R1# show ip ospf neighbor


Neighbor ID     Pri   State          Dead Time     Address       Interface
192.168.1.1       0   FULL/   -      00:00:32      10.1.1.2      Serial1/0
```

OSPFv2 MD5 Authentication

Unlike EIGRP for IPv4 MD5 authentication, OSPFv2 MD5 authentication does not allow the configuration of a key chain with time-based authentication keys. However, multiple keys can be configured on an interface, each with a different key number, called a *key ID*. To migrate to a new key, you would first configure a new key value on all routers in a subnet and then delete the configuration of the old keys. To avoid having network failures during this cutover, OSPF actually sends and accepts messages that use all the currently configured authentication keys on an interface.

Unlike OSPFv2 plain text authentication (which has a maximum key length of eight characters), OSPFv2 MD5 authentication allows a key length of 16 characters. This key, along with the key ID, is used to calculate the MD5 hash for each OSPF packet. As with OSPFv2 plain text authentication, you can enable OSPFv2 MD5 authentication on a per-interface basis or on an area-wide basis (which applies to all router interfaces belonging to the specific area). Also, you could (but are not required to) have a separate key string for each interface. The configuration steps can be summarized as follows:

Step 1.   Plain text authentication must be enabled for either an interface or an OSPF area:

   ■   Enable per interface using the **ip ospf authentication message-digest** interface subcommand.

   ■   Enable on all interfaces in an area by changing the area-wide authentication setting using the **area** *area-number* **authentication message-digest** subcommand under OSPF router configuration mode.

Step 2.   The authentication keys must be configured per interface, using the **ip ospf message-digest-key** *key-id* **md5** *name-of-key* interface subcommand.

Example 17-9 illustrates the configuration of OSPFv2 MD5 authentication between Routers R1 and R2 pictured in Figure 17-6.

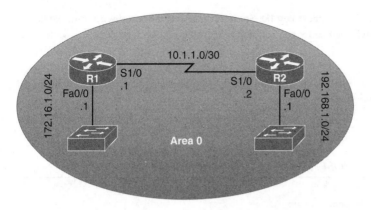

Figure 17-6 *Two Routers Configured with OSPFv2 MD5 Authentication*

Example 17-9 *OSPFv2 MD5 Authentication Configuration*

```
!Configuration on Router R1
interface Serial1/0
 ip address 10.1.1.1 255.255.255.252
 ip ospf message-digest-key 1 md5 KEYLIME
!
router ospf 1
 area 0 authentication message-digest
 network 0.0.0.0 255.255.255.255 area 0
!

!Configuration on Router R2
interface Serial1/0
 ip address 10.1.1.2 255.255.255.252
 ip ospf authentication message-digest
 ip ospf message-digest-key 1 md5 KEYLIME
!
router ospf 1
 network 0.0.0.0 255.255.255.255 area 0
```

In Example 17-9, both Routers R1 and R2 have the **ip ospf message-digest-key** *key-id*
md5 *key-string* command entered in interface configuration mode. However, Router R1's
configuration enables authentication for all the router's interface participating in area 0,
using the **area** *area-number* **authentication message-digest** command in router configuration mode. Conversely, Router R2's configuration enables authentication at the interface
level, with the **ip ospf message-digest-key** *key-id* **md5** *key-string* command issued in
interface configuration mode.

The same verification commands used for OSPFv2 plain text authentication apply to
OSPFv2 MD5 configuration. However, the output of the **show ip ospf interface** *interface_
identifier* command, as shown in Example 17-10, shows that message digest authentication

is enabled, along with the youngest key ID. So, if a router is configured with multiple keys, the youngest key ID will be used when sending authenticated OSPF packets.

> **Note**   The youngest key ID appearing in the output of the **show ip ospf interface** *inter-face_identifier* command is not necessarily the lowest key ID. Rather it is the key that has been most recently configured, regardless of its key ID.

Example 17-10   *Verifying OSPFv2 MD5 Authentication*

```
R1# show ip ospf interface s 1/0
Serial1/0 is up, line protocol is up
  Internet Address 10.1.1.1/30, Area 0, Attached via Network Statement
  Process ID 1, Router ID 172.16.1.1, Network Type POINT_TO_POINT, Cost: 64
  Topology-MTID    Cost    Disabled    Shutdown      Topology Name
        0           64        no          no            Base
  Transmit Delay is 1 sec, State POINT_TO_POINT
  Timer intervals configured, Hello 10, Dead 40, Wait 40, Retransmit 5
    oob-resync timeout 40
    Hello due in 00:00:02
  Supports Link-local Signaling (LLS)
  Cisco NSF helper support enabled
  IETF NSF helper support enabled
  Index 2/2, flood queue length 0
  Next 0x0(0)/0x0(0)
  Last flood scan length is 1, maximum is 1
  Last flood scan time is 4 msec, maximum is 4 msec
  Neighbor Count is 1, Adjacent neighbor count is 1
    Adjacent with neighbor 192.168.1.1
  Suppress hello for 0 neighbor(s)
  Message digest authentication enabled
    Youngest key id is 1
```

OSPFv3 Authentication

OSPFv3 has no authentication field in its headers. So, rather than using any authentication mechanism natively built into OSPFv3, it relies on IPsec to provide authentication. Interestingly, IPsec is capable of encrypting messages in addition to authenticating them. The Authentication Header (AH) encapsulation type for IPsec provides authentication services, but no encryption, while Encapsulating Security Payload (ESP) provides both authentication and encryption services.

The **ipv6 ospf authentication** command enables the use of AH to provide authentication, while the **ipv6 ospf encryption** command enables authentication and encryption services through ESP.

In addition to specifying whether you want to just perform authentication or also perform encryption, you need to specify an identifier called the *security policy index (SPI)* and a *key string*. The combination of an SPI and a key string is called a *security policy*. As with OSPFv2 authentication, OSPFv3 authentication (and encryption) can be performed on a per-interface or per-area basis; however, Cisco recommends the per-interface approach for enhanced security.

Unlike configuring OSPFv2 authentication, OSPFv3 authentication can be accomplished with a single command, as illustrated in Example 17-11 for the topology in Figure 7-7.

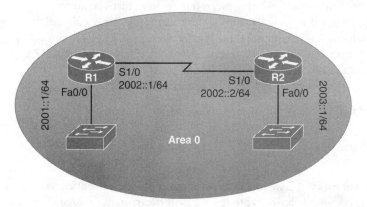

Figure 17-7   *Two Routers Configured for OSPFv3 SHA1 Authentication*

Example 17-11   *OSPFv3 Authentication Configuration*

```
!Configuration on Router R1
interface Serial1/0
 ipv6 address 2002::1/64
 ipv6 ospf 2 area 0
!
ipv6 router ospf 2
 router-id 1.1.1.1
 area 0 authentication ipsec spi 256 sha1 01234567890123456789012345678901234567890123456789
!

!Configuration on Router R2
interface Serial1/0
 ipv6 address 2002::2/64
 ipv6 ospf authentication ipsec spi 256 sha1
  01234567890123456789012345678901234567890123456789
 ipv6 ospf 2 area 0
!
ipv6 router ospf 2
 router-id 2.2.2.2
```

Note that OSPFv3 authentication can be configured on a router with a single command. In Example 17-11, Router R1 has OSPFv3 authentication configured for an area, while Router R2 has OSPFv3 authentication configured for an interface.

In router configuration mode, the command to enable authentication is

```
area area_number authentication ipsec spi security_policy_index [md5 | sha1]
  {0 | 7} key-string
```

Notice that you can specify either **md5** or **sha1** as your hashing algorithm. After specifying the algorithm you want to use, you can enter a **0** to indicate that you do not want your key string encrypted when it appears in your router's running configuration. Alternately, you can select a **7** if you do want it to appear encrypted. Finally in this command, you enter the key string, which is a hexadecimal number. If you are using MD5 as your hashing algorithm, the key string must be 32 hexadecimal digits. However, if you selected SHA1, the key string must be 40 hexadecimal characters.

If you are configuring OSPFv3 authentication in interface configuration mode, then the command you issue is

```
ipv6 ospf authentication ipsec spi security_policy_index [md5 | sha1] {0 | 7}
  key-string
```

Because OSPFv3 authentication is based on IPsec, you can verify the authentication configuration with the command **show crypto ipsec sa interface** *interface_identifier*. Example 17-12 illustrates sample output from this command from Router R1.

Example 17-12   *Verifying OSPFv3 Authentication*

```
R1# show crypto ipsec sa interface s 1/0

interface: Serial1/0

   IPsecv6 policy name: OSPFv3-256

   protected vrf: (none)
   local  ident (addr/mask/prot/port): (FE80::/10/89/0)
   remote ident (addr/mask/prot/port): (::/0/89/0)
   current_peer FF02::5 port 500
     PERMIT, flags={origin_is_acl,}
    #pkts encaps: 517, #pkts encrypt: 517, #pkts digest: 517
    #pkts decaps: 517, #pkts decrypt: 517, #pkts verify: 517
    #pkts compressed: 0, #pkts decompressed: 0
    #pkts not compressed: 0, #pkts compr. failed: 0
    #pkts not decompressed: 0, #pkts decompress failed: 0
    #send errors 0, #recv errors 0

     local crypto endpt.: FE80::C800:8FF:FEA4:0,
     remote crypto endpt.: FF02::5
     path mtu 1500, ipv6 mtu 1500, ipv6 mtu idb Serial1/0
     current outbound spi: 0x100(256)
```

```
     PFS (Y/N): N, DH group: none
     inbound esp sas:


     inbound ah sas:
      spi: 0x100(256)
        transform: ah-sha-hmac ,
        in use settings ={Transport, }
        conn id: 1, flow_id: 1, sibling_flags 80000011, crypto map:
          Serial1/0-OSPF-MAP
        sa timing: remaining key lifetime (sec): (0)
        Kilobyte Volume Rekey has been disabled
        replay detection support: N
        Status: ACTIVE(ACTIVE)


     inbound pcp sas:


     outbound esp sas:


     outbound ah sas:
      spi: 0x100(256)
        transform: ah-sha-hmac ,
        in use settings ={Transport, }
        conn id: 2, flow_id: 2, sibling_flags 80000011, crypto map:
          Serial1/0-OSPF-MAP
        sa timing: remaining key lifetime (sec): (0)
        Kilobyte Volume Rekey has been disabled
        replay detection support: N
        Status: ACTIVE(ACTIVE)


     outbound pcp sas:
 Crypto map tag: Serial1/0-OSPF-MAP, local addr FE80::C800:8FF:FEA4:0
```

Notice that the transform sets shown in the output use **ah-sha-hmac**. This indicates that
the configuration is using Authentication Header (AH) for authentication (as opposed
to Encapsulating Security Payload [ESP] for authentication and encryption). It also indicates that Secure Hash Algorithm (SHA) is the specific hashing algorithm being used for
authentication (as opposed to Message Digest 5 [MD5]).

BGP Authentication

Unlike EIGRP and OSPF, which can (in some configurations) dynamically form neighborships, BGP requires neighboring routers to be explicitly configured. Therefore, the threat
of someone maliciously forming a neighborhood with your BGP router is far less likely, as
compared to OSPF or EIGRP.

However, imagine that your BGP-speaking router had already established a TCP session
with a configured BGP peer. In such a scenario, an attacker could possibly hijack that

existing TCP session and proceed to corrupt the BGP table on your router. To help mitigate such a threat, you can configure authentication for BGP. This authentication is going
to be through MD5. There is no Cisco IOS support for plain text or SHA authentication
for BGP.

BGP does not require a series of configuration steps. Rather, BGP can be enabled on a
router with a single command, as demonstrated next.

IPv4 BGP Authentication

To configure BGP authentication between two neighboring BGP neighbors, enter the
neighbor *neighbor-ip* **password** *key* command in BGP router configuration mode on
each router.

Example 17-13 shows a BGP authentication configuration for an IPv4 network, the topology for which is provided in Figure 17-8.

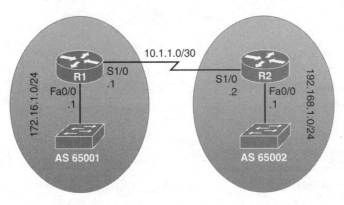

Figure 17-8 *Two Routers in an IPv4 Network Configured for BGP Authentication*

Example 17-13 *IPv4 BGP Authentication Configuration*

```
!Configuration on Router R1
router bgp 65001
 network 172.16.1.0 mask 255.255.255.0
 neighbor 10.1.1.2 remote-as 65002
 neighbor 10.1.1.2 password KEYNOTE


!Configuration on Router R2
router bgp 65002
 network 192.168.1.0
 neighbor 10.1.1.1 remote-as 65001
 neighbor 10.1.1.1 password KEYNOTE
```

There is no BGP command to specifically troubleshoot BGP authentication; however,
you can issue the **show ip bgp summary** command to determine whether a neighborship
is currently up, as demonstrated in Example 17-14. If the neighborship is not up, you

can check the keys on each neighbor to make sure that they match, just like the key of **KEYNOTE** matches on Routers R1 and R2 in Example 17-13.

Example 17-14   *Verification of IPv4 BGP Authentication*

```
R1# show ip bgp summary
BGP router identifier 172.16.1.1, local AS number 65001
BGP table version is 5, main routing table version 5
2 network entries using 288 bytes of memory
2 path entries using 160 bytes of memory
2/2 BGP path/bestpath attribute entries using 272 bytes of memory
1 BGP AS-PATH entries using 24 bytes of memory
0 BGP route-map cache entries using 0 bytes of memory
0 BGP filter-list cache entries using 0 bytes of memory
BGP using 744 total bytes of memory
BGP activity 7/5 prefixes, 7/5 paths, scan interval 60 secs

Neighbor        V           AS MsgRcvd MsgSent    TblVer  InQ OutQ Up/Down  State/PfxRcd
10.1.1.2        4        65002       9      10         5    0    0 00:05:21            1
```

IPv6 BGP Authentication

The procedure to configure BGP authentication on an IPv6 network is identical to the procedure previously seen for IPv4. Specifically, you issue the **neighbor** *neighbor-ip* **password** *key* command in BGP router configuration mode; however, the *neighbor-ip* value will be an IPv6 address, as opposed to an IPv4 address.

Example 17-15 shows a sample BGP authentication for the IPv6 network illustrated in Figure 17-9.

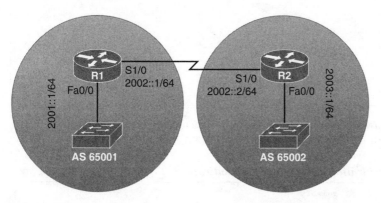

Figure 17-9   *Two Routers in an IPv6 Network Configured for BGP Authentication*

Example 17-15 *IPv6 BGP Authentication Configuration*

```
!Configuration on Router R1
router bgp 65001
 bgp router-id 1.1.1.1
 bgp log-neighbor-changes
 no bgp default ipv4-unicast
 neighbor 2002::2 remote-as 65002
 neighbor 2002::2 password KEYNOTE
 !
 address-family ipv4
 exit-address-family
 !
 address-family ipv6
  network 2001::/64
  network 2002::/64
  neighbor 2002::2 activate
 exit-address-family
```

```
!Configuration on Router R2
router bgp 65002
 bgp router-id 2.2.2.2
 bgp log-neighbor-changes
 no bgp default ipv4-unicast
 neighbor 2002::1 remote-as 65001
 neighbor 2002::1 password KEYNOTE
 !
 address-family ipv4
 exit-address-family
 !
 address-family ipv6
  network 2002::/64
  network 2003::/64
  neighbor 2002::1 activate
 exit-address-family
```

Example 17-16 shows output from the **show bgp ipv6 unicast summary** command, confirming that Router R1 has a BGP neighborship with Router R2.

Example 17-16 *Verification of IPv6 BGP Authentication*

```
R1# show bgp ipv6 unicast summary
BGP router identifier 1.1.1.1, local AS number 65001
BGP table version is 6, main routing table version 6
3 network entries using 504 bytes of memory
4 path entries using 416 bytes of memory
2/2 BGP path/bestpath attribute entries using 272 bytes of memory
```

```
1 BGP AS-PATH entries using 24 bytes of memory
0 BGP route-map cache entries using 0 bytes of memory
0 BGP filter-list cache entries using 0 bytes of memory
BGP using 1216 total bytes of memory
BGP activity 6/3 prefixes, 8/4 paths, scan interval 60 secs
```

Neighbor	V	AS	MsgRcvd	MsgSent	TblVer	InQ	OutQ	Up/Down	State/PfxRcd
2002::2	4	65002	10	10	6	0	0	00:04:56	2

Exam Preparation Tasks

Planning Practice

The CCNP ROUTE exam expects test takers to review design documents, create implementation plans, and create verification plans. This section provides some exercises that can help you to take a step back from the minute details of the topics in this chapter so that you can think about the same technical topics from the planning perspective.

For each planning practice table, simply complete the table. Note that any numbers in parentheses represent the number of options listed for each item in the solutions in Appendix F, "Completed Planning Practice Tables."

Design Review Table

Table 17-3 lists several design goals related to this chapter. If these design goals were listed in a design document, and you had to take that document and develop an implementation plan, what implementation options come to mind? For any configuration items, a general description can be used, without concern about the specific parameters.

Table 17-3 *Design Review*

Design Goal	Possible Implementation Choices Covered in This Chapter
Prevent a malicious user from injecting a rogue router into an EIGRP autonomous system and forming a neighborship.	
Configure OSPFv2 authentication such that a malicious user could not do a packet capture of the authentication traffic and determine the authentication key.	
Prevent a malicious user from causing a rogue router to hijack an existing BGP session.	

Implementation Plan Peer Review Table

Table 17-4 shows a list of questions that others might ask, or that you might think about, during a peer review of another network engineer's implementation plan. Complete the table by answering the questions.

Table 17-4 *Notable Questions from This Chapter to Consider During an Implementation Plan Peer Review*

Question	Answer
An EIGRP-speaking router is configured with a key chain containing multiple keys. Which key is going to be used?	
What authentication types are available for OSPFv3?	
Why would you want to authenticate BGP neighbors, because BGP requires a router to have a static configuration of its neighbors' IP addresses?	

Create an Implementation Plan Table

To practice skills useful when creating your own OSPF implementation plan, list in Table 17-5 configuration commands related to the configuration of the following features. You might want to record your answers outside the book, and set a goal to complete this table (and others like it) from memory during your final reviews before taking the exam.

Table 17-5 *Implementation Plan Configuration Memory Drill*

Feature	Configuration Commands/Notes
For EIGRP, create a key chain and give it a name.	
For EIGRP, create one or more key numbers.	
For EIGRP, define an authentication key's value.	
Enable EIGRP for IPv4 MD5 authentication on an interface for a particular EIGRP autonomous system.	
For EIGRP for IPv4, specify the key chain to be used on an interface.	
Enable EIGRP for IPv6 authentication on an interface for a particular EIGRP autonomous system.	
For EIGRP for IPv6, specify the key chain to be used on an interface.	
Enable Named EIGRP authentication for an interface.	
For Named EIGRP, specify the key chain to be used on an interface.	
Enable OSPFv2 authentication on an interface.	

Feature	Configuration Commands/Notes
Enable OSPFv2 authentication on all interfaces in an area by configuring area-wide authentication.	
Specify a key to use with OSPFv2 plain text authentication.	
Specify a key to use with OSPFv2 MD5 authentication.	
Enable OSPFv3 authentication on an interface.	
Enable OSPFv3 authentication on all interfaces in an area by configuring area-wide authentication.	
Specify an authentication key to use with a BGP neighbor.	

Choose Commands for a Verification Plan Table

To practice skills useful when creating your own OSPF verification plan, list in Table 17-6 all commands that supply the requested information. You might want to record your answers outside the book, and set a goal to complete this table (and others like it) from memory during your final reviews before taking the exam.

Table 17-6   *Verification Plan Memory Drill*

Information Needed	Command(s)
Verify that an EIGRP for IPv4 neighborship is up.	
Verify that an EIGRP for IPv6 neighborship is up.	
Collect information about a configured key chain.	
Verify that OSPFv2 authentication is enabled.	
Verify that OSPFv3 authentication is enabled.	
Verify that an OSPF neighborship is up.	
Verify that a BGP for IPv4 neighborship is up.	
Verify that a BGP for IPv6 neighborship is up.	

Note   Some of the entries in this table might not have been specifically mentioned in this chapter but are listed in this table for review and reference.

Review All the Key Topics

Review the most important topics from inside the chapter, noted with the Key Topic icon in the outer margin of the page. Table 17-7 lists a reference of these key topics and the page numbers on which each is found.

Table 17-7 *Key Topics for Chapter 17*

Key Topic Element	Description	Page Number
List	Hashing authentication process	741
Example 17-1	Time-Based Key Chain Configuration	743
List	EIGRP for IPv4 authentication configuration steps	744
Example 17-2	EIGRP for IPv4 Authentication Configuration	745
List	EIGRP for IPv6 authentication configuration steps	747
Example 17-4	EIGRP for IPv6 Authentication Configuration	747
List	Named EIGRP authentication configuration steps	749
Example 17-6	Named EIGRP Authentication Configuration	749
Table 17-2	OSPF Authentication Types	751
List	OSPF plain text authentication configuration steps	752
Example 17-7	OSPFv2 Plain Text Authentication Configuration	752
List	OSPFv2 MD5 configuration steps	754
Example 17-9	OSPFv2 MD5 Authentication Configuration	755
Example 17-11	OSPFv3 Authentication Configuration	757
Example 17-13	IPv4 BGP Authentication Configuration	760
Example 17-15	IPv6 BGP Authentication Configuration	762

Complete the Tables and Lists from Memory

Print a copy of Appendix D, "Memory Tables," (found on the CD) or at least the section for this chapter, and complete the tables and lists from memory. Appendix E, "Memory Tables Answer Key," also on the CD, includes completed tables and lists to check your work.

Define Key Terms

Define the following key terms from this chapter, and check your answers in the glossary.

authentication, key chain, Message Digest 5 authentication, Secure Hash Algorithm (SHA), shared key

CHAPTER 18

Final Preparation

The first 17 chapters of this book cover the technologies, protocols, commands, and features required to be prepared to pass the ROUTE exam. Although these chapters supply the detailed information, most people need more preparation than simply reading the first 17 chapters of this book. This chapter details a set of tools and a study plan to help you complete your preparation for the exams.

This short chapter has two main sections. The first section lists the exam preparation tools useful at this point in the study process. The second section details a suggested study plan now that you have completed all the preceding chapters in this book.

Note   Appendixes D, E, F, and G exist as soft-copy appendixes on the CD included in the back of this book.

Tools for Final Preparation

This section lists some information about exam preparation tools and how to access the tools.

Exam Engine and Questions on the CD

The CD in the back of the book includes the Pearson Cert Practice Test engine. This software presents you with a set of multiple-choice questions, covering the topics that you will be challenged with on the real exam. The Pearson Cert Practice Test engine lets you study the exam content (using study mode) or take a simulated exam (in practice exam mode).

The CD in the back of the book contains the exam engine. After it is installed, you can then activate and download the current ROUTE exam from Pearson's website. Installation of the exam engine takes place in two steps:

Step 1.   Install the exam engine from the CD.

Step 2.   Activate and download the ROUTE practice exam.

Install the Exam Engine

The software installation process is pretty routine as compared with other software installation processes. To be complete, the following steps outline the installation process:

Step 1. Insert the CD into your PC.

Step 2. The software that automatically runs is the Cisco Press software to access and use all CD-based features, including the exam engine and the CD-only appendixes. From the main menu, click the option to **Install the Exam Engine**.

Step 3. Respond to prompts as with any typical software installation process.

The installation process gives you the option to activate your exam with the activation code supplied on the paper in the CD sleeve. This process requires that you establish a Pearson website login. You will need this login to activate the exam. Therefore, please do register when prompted. If you already have a Pearson website login, there is no need to register again. Just use your existing login.

Activate and Download the Practice Exam

After the exam engine is installed, you should then activate the exam associated with this book (if you did not do so during the installation process) as follows:

Step 1. Start the Pearson Cert Practice Test (PCPT) software.

Step 2. To activate and download the exam associated with this book, from the **My Products** or **Tools** tab, click the **Activate** button.

Step 3. At the next screen, enter the activation key from the paper inside the cardboard CD holder in the back of the book. After it is entered, click the **Activate** button.

Step 4. The activation process will download the practice exam. Click **Next**; then click **Finish**.

When the activation process is completed, the **My Products** tab should list your new exam. If you do not see the exam, make sure that you selected the **My Products** tab on the menu. At this point, the software and practice exam are ready to use. Simply select the exam and click the **Use** button.

To update a particular exam you have already activated and downloaded, simply select the **Tools** tab and click the **Update Products** button. Updating your exams will ensure that you have the latest changes and updates to the exam data.

If you want to check for updates to the Pearson Cert Practice Test exam engine software, simply select the **Tools** tab and click the **Update Application** button. This will ensure that you are running the latest version of the software engine.

Activating Other Exams

The exam software installation process, and the registration process, only has to happen once. Then, for each new exam, only a few steps are required. For example, if you buy another new Cisco Press Official Cert Guide or Pearson IT Certification Cert Guide, remove the activation code from the CD sleeve in the back of that book; you don't even need the CD at this point. From there, all you have to do is start the exam engine (if not still up and running) and perform Steps 2 through 4 from the previous list.

Premium Edition

In addition to the free practice exam provided on the CD-ROM, you can purchase additional exams with expanded functionality directly from Pearson IT Certification. The Premium Edition of this title contains an additional two full practice exams as well as an eBook (in both PDF and ePub format). In addition, the Premium Edition title also has remediation for each question to the specific part of the eBook that relates to that question.

Because you have purchased the print version of this title, you can purchase the Premium Edition at a deep discount. There is a coupon code in the CD sleeve that contains a one-time use code, as well as instructions for where you can purchase the Premium Edition.

To view the Premium Edition product page, go to www.ciscopress.com/title/9780133149920.

The Cisco Learning Network

Cisco provides a wide variety of CCNP preparation tools at a Cisco website called the *Cisco Learning Network*. Resources found here include sample questions, forums on each Cisco exam, learning video games, and information about each exam.

To reach the Cisco Learning Network, go to http://learningnetwork.cisco.com or just search for "Cisco Learning Network." To access some of the features/resources, you need to use the login that you created at www.cisco.com. If you don't have such a login, you can register for free. To register, simply go to www.cisco.com, click **Register** at the top of the page, and supply some information.

Memory Tables

Like most Certification Guides from Cisco Press, this book purposefully organizes information into tables and lists for easier study and review. Rereading these tables can be very useful before the exam. However, it is easy to skim over the tables without paying attention to every detail, especially when you remember having seen the table's contents when reading the chapter.

Instead of simply reading the tables in the various chapters, this book's Appendixes D and E give you another review tool. Appendix D, "Memory Tables," lists partially completed versions of many of the tables from the book. You can open Appendix D (a PDF file on the CD that comes with this book) and print the appendix. For review, you can attempt to complete the tables. This exercise can help you focus during your review. It also exercises the memory connectors in your brain, plus it makes you think about the information without as much information, which forces a little more contemplation about the facts.

Appendix E, "Memory Tables Answer Key," also a PDF file located on the CD, lists the completed tables to check yourself. You can also just refer to the tables as printed in the book.

Chapter-Ending Review Tools

Chapters 1 through 17 each have several features in the "Exam Preparation Tasks" section at the end of the chapter. You might have used some or all of these tools at the end of each chapter. It can also be useful to use these tools again as you make your final preparations for the exam.

Suggested Plan for Final Review/Study

This section lists a suggested study plan from the point at which you finish reading through Chapter 17 until you take the ROUTE exam. Certainly, you can ignore this plan, use it as is, or just take suggestions from it.

The plan uses seven steps. If following the plan verbatim, you should proceed by part through the steps. That is, starting with Part I (Fundamental Routing Concepts), do the following seven steps. Then, for Part II (IGP Routing Protocols), do the following seven steps, and so on. The steps are as follows:

Step 1. **Review key topics and DIKTA questions:** You can use the table that lists the key topics in each chapter, or just flip the pages looking for the Key Topic icons. Also, reviewing the Do I Know This Already? (DIKTA) questions from the beginning of the chapter can be helpful for review.

Step 2. **Complete memory tables:** Open Appendix D on the CD and print the entire appendix, or print the tables by major part. Then complete the tables and check your answers in Appendix E, which also appears on the CD.

Step 3. **Hands-on practice:** Most people practice CCNP configuration and verification before the exam. Whether you use real gear, a simulator, or an emulator, practice the configuration and verification commands.

Step 4. **Build configuration checklists:** Glance through the Table of Contents, looking for major configuration tasks. Then from memory create your own configuration checklists for the various configuration commands.

Step 5. **Planning practice:** Even if you used the "Planning Practice" tables when you initially read each chapter, repeat the process, particularly for the tables related to interpreting a design and reviewing another engineer's implementation plan.

Step 6. **Subnetting practice:** If you can no longer do subnetting well and quickly without a subnetting calculator, take some time to get better and faster before going to take the ROUTE exam.

Step 7. **Use the exam engine to practice:** The exam engine on the CD can be used to study using a bank of unique exam-realistic, multiple-choice questions available only with this book.

The rest of this section describes Steps 1, 3, 6, and 7, for which a little more explanation might be helpful.

Step 1: Review Key Topics and DIKTA Questions

This review step focuses on the core facts related to the ROUTE exam. The exam certainly covers other topics as well, but the DIKTA questions and the key topics items attempt to focus attention on the more important topics in each chapter.

As a reminder, if you follow this plan after reading the first 17 chapters, working a major part at a time (Fundamental Routing Concepts in Chapters 1 and 2, for example) helps you pull each major topic together.

Step 3: Hands-On Practice

Although this book gives you many configuration checklists, specific configuration examples, examples of output, and explanations for the meaning of that output, there is no substitute for hands-on practice. This short section provides a few suggestions regarding your efforts to practice from the command-line interface (CLI).

First, most people use one or more of the following options for hands-on skills:

- **Real gear:** Either purchased (often used), borrowed, or rented
- **Simulators:** Software that acts like real gear
- **Emulators:** Software that emulates Cisco hardware and runs Cisco IOS

For real gear, the minimum recommended home lab configuration would have three ISR (or ISR2) routers running Cisco IOS Release 15.2 (or later). This would allow you to experiment with most of the technologies discussed in this book.

Pearson IT Certification offers an excellent simulator with nearly 400 structured labs to help you get hands-on experience. Even though the simulator targets the CCNA exam, many of its labs are appropriate for your ROUTE studies. You can learn more about the "CCNA Routing and Switching 200-120 Network Simulator" here:

http://kwtrain.com/netsim

As for emulators, you can purchase access to emulated routers from the Cisco Learning Network. What you are purchasing is a block of hours to access the emulated gear, along with structured labs to follow. The product is called *Cisco Learning Labs*, and more information can be found here:

http://kwtrain.com/route-emulator

Step 6: Subnetting Practice

This book assumes that you have mastered subnetting and the related math. However, many people who progress through CCNA, and move on to CCNP, follow a path like this:

Step 1.   Learn subnetting conceptually.

Step 2.   Get really good at doing the math quickly.

Step 3.   Pass CCNA.

Step 4.   Don't practice regularly and therefore become a lot slower at doing the subnetting math.

Step 5.   Study for CCNP ROUTE.

Although subnetting should not be assessed as an end to itself on CCNP ROUTE, many questions require that you understand subnetting math and do that math just as quickly as you did when you passed CCNA. If you are a little slow on doing subnetting math, before you go to the ROUTE exam, try some of the following exercises:

■   Practice finding the subnet number, broadcast address, and range of addresses in a subnet. To do so, pick a network address and mask, calculate the values, and use your favorite subnet calculator to check your work.

■   Use the Cisco Subnetting Game, also at the Cisco Learning Network. You can find it here:http://kwtrain.com/subnet-game

■   Practice choosing the best summary route for a range of subnets. Pick three or four addresses/masks. Calculate the subnet number and range. Then, try to choose the summary (subnet number/mask) that includes those three or four subnets, without including any more subnets than what is required. You can check your math with a subnet calculator.

If you like performing binary/decimal conversions when you work through these problems, but just need to go faster, check out the Cisco Binary Game, also at the Cisco Learning Network. You can find it here:

http://kwtrain.com/binary-game

Step 7: Use the Exam Engine

The Pearson Cert Practice Test engine on the CD lets you access a database of questions created specifically for this book. The Pearson Cert Practice Test engine can be used either in *study mode* or *practice exam mode*, as follows:

■   **Study mode:** Study mode is most useful when you want to use the questions for learning and practicing. In study mode, you can select options like randomizing the order of the questions and answers, automatically viewing answers to the questions as you go, testing on specific topics, and many other options.

- **Practice exam mode:** This mode presents questions in a timed environment, providing you with a more exam-realistic experience. It also restricts your ability to see your score as you progress through the exam and view answers to questions as you are taking the exam. These timed exams not only allow you to study for the actual 300-101 ROUTE exam, but they also help you simulate the time pressure that can occur on the actual exam.

When doing your final preparation, you can use study mode, practice exam mode, or both. However, after you have seen each question a couple of times, you will likely start to remember the questions, and the usefulness of the exam database might go down. So, consider the following options when using the exam engine:

- Use the question database for review. Use study mode to study the questions by chapter, just as with the other final review steps listed in this chapter. Consider upgrading to the Premium Edition of this book if you want to take additional simulated exams.

- Save the question database, not using it for review during your review of each book part. Save it until the end so that you will not have seen the questions before. Then, use practice exam mode to simulate the exam.

Picking the correct mode from the exam engine's user interface is pretty obvious. The following steps show how to move to the screen from which you can select the study or practice exam mode:

Step 1.   Click the **My Products** tab if you are not already in that screen.

Step 2.   Select the exam that you want to use from the list of available exams.

Step 3.   Click the **Use** button.

By taking these actions, the engine should display a window from which you can choose **Study Mode** or **Practice Exam Mode**. When in study mode, you can further choose the book chapters, limiting the questions to those explained in the specified chapters of the book.

Note   Please revisit Table I-1, "Route Exam (300-101) Topics," in the Introduction. This table identifies the topic areas that you are responsible for on the ROUTE exam; note that several are topics you covered in your CCNA studies. Therefore, you might want to review those topics in your CCNA study materials. If you need current CCNA materials for your study, they can be purchased from Cisco Press:

- **CCNA Complete Video Course:** http://kwtrain.com/ccnacourse
- **CCNA Official Certification Library:** http://kwtrain.com/ccnabooks

Summary

The tools and suggestions listed in this chapter have been designed with one goal in mind: to help you develop the skills required to pass the ROUTE exam. This book has been developed from the beginning to not just tell you the facts but also to help you learn how to apply the facts. No matter what your experience level is leading up to when you take the exams, it is my hope that the broad range of preparation tools, and even the structure of the book, can help you pass the exams with ease. I wish you all the best in your studies and on your exam.

Keep in Touch with Kevin

Please take a few moments to follow me on one of (or all) the social media platforms listed here. You'll find that I periodically post technical tips, free training videos, announcements about my new training products, and random things that make me laugh:

Blog: http://kwtrain.com

Twitter: http://twitter.com/kwallaceccie

Facebook: http://facebook.com/kwallaceccie

YouTube: http://youtube.com/kwallaceccie

LinkedIn: http://linkedin.com/in/kwallaceccie

Google+: http://google.com/+KevinWallace

Answers to the "Do I Know This Already?" Quizzes

Chapter 1

1. C. The *Split Horizon* feature prevents a route learned on one interface from being advertised back out of that same interface.

    The *Summarization* feature allows multiple contiguous networks to be represented with a single route advertisement.

    The *Poison Reverse* feature causes a route received on one interface to be advertised back out of that same interface with a metric considered to be infinite.

    Convergence is the speed at which a backup route takes over for a failed preferred route.

2. B and C. Both RIP and EIGRP are distance-vector routing protocols, although EIGRP is considered an advanced distance-vector routing protocol.

    Both OSPF and IS-IS are link-state routing protocols, and BGP is a path-vector routing protocol.

3. D. A *unicast* network communication flow is considered a "one-to-one" flow, because there is one source and one destination.

    A *multicast* network communication flow is considered a "one-to-many" flow, because there is one source and potentially many destinations (specifically, destinations that have joined a multicast group).

    A *broadcast* network communication flow is considered a "one-to-all" flow, because there is one source, and the destinations include all devices in a subnet.

    An *anycast* network communication flow is considered as "one-to-nearest" flow, because there are multiple devices assigned the same IPv6 address, and traffic is routed from one source to the nearest device assigned the destination IPv6 address.

4. A and D. A nonbroadcast multiaccess (NBMA) network can have Split Horizon issues in a hub-and-spoke topology, because a route learned by the hub router from a spoke router might not be advertised back out to any other spoke routers, because of Split Horizon operation. Also, if the NBMA network is using OSPF, there can be designated router issues, because the spoke routers might not be able to communicate with one another through broadcasts.

5. B. The term *TCP Maximum Segment Size (MSS)* seems to imply the size of the entire Layer 4 segment (that is, including Layer 2, Layer 3, and Layer 4 headers). However, TCP MSS only refers to the amount of data in the segment (without the inclusion of any headers).

6. C. The bandwidth-delay product of a segment is the measure of the maximum number of bits that can be on the segment at any one time. The bandwidth-delay product is calculated by multiplying the segment's bandwidth (in bits/sec) by the latency that packets experience as they cross the segment (in sec).

In this question, the bandwidth-delay product can be calculated as follows:

bandwidth-delay product = 10,000,000 bits/sec * 0.1 sec = 1,000,000 bits.

7. A and C. When converting a Cisco Catalyst switch to Rapid-PVST+, you can remove the UplinkFast and BackboneFast features, because similar features are built into Rapid-PVST+. However, the following features can still be used with Rapid-PVST+: PortFast, BPDU Guard, BPDU Filter, Root Guard, and Loop Guard.

8. A. Cisco Easy Virtual Network (EVN) uses a Virtual Network Trunk (VNET Trunk) to carry traffic for each virtual network, and eliminates the need to manually configure a subinterface for each virtual network on all routers.

Inter-Switch Link (ISL) is a Cisco-proprietary trunking technology for Ethernet networks.

IEEE 802.1Q is an industry-standard trunking technology for Ethernet networks.

IEEE 802.10 is an industry-standard trunking technology for FDDI networks.

Chapter 2

1. C. A hybrid VPN uses more than one VPN technology. While you can encrypt a packet that has already been encapsulated by a VPN technology, and while you can encapsulate a packet that has already been encrypted, you might need to decrease the MTU for a frame on an interface configured for tunneling. The reason for the MTU decrease is that additional header information is added for each VPN technology you use. As a result, the maximum amount of data contained in a frame is reduced.

2. A. In a Layer 3 MPLS VPN, a customer edge (CE) router forms a neighborship with a provider edge (PE) router (or an edge label switch router [ELSR]) in an MPLS network. In a Layer 2 MPLS VPN, the MPLS network acts as a Layer 2 switch. IP multicast traffic can flow across an MPLS network with no issue.

3. C. A GRE tunnel can encapsulate any Layer 3 protocol, including IP unicast, multicast, and broadcast traffic. However, a GRE tunnel does not offer encryption. An IPsec tunnel does offer encryption, but it can only transmit unicast IP traffic. Therefore, to meet the design requirements in this question, you could encapsulate the IP unicast, multicast, and broadcast traffic inside of a GRE tunnel. Because a GRE packet is a unicast IP packet, you could encapsulate the GRE packets inside of an IPsec tunnel, thus providing the required encryption.

4. A, B, and D. A DMVPN network uses mGRE to dynamically form GRE tunnels between two sites needing a direct tunnel. NHRP is used by mGRE to discover the IP address of the device at the remote side of the tunnel. IPsec is used to secure the GRE packets. However, MPLS is not a requirement.

5. A and B. Like traditional GRE, mGRE can transport a wide variety of protocols (for example, IP unicast, multicast, and broadcast traffic). Also, a single mGRE interface can service multiple tunnels.

6. B and D. *NHRP (Next Hop Resolution Protocol)* spokes are configured with the IP address of an NHRP hub, but the hub is not configured with the IP addresses of the spokes. When the spokes come online, they inform the hub of both the physical IP address (assigned to a physical interface) and the logical IP address (assigned to a virtual tunnel interface) that are going to be used for their tunnels. With the hub's database populated, a spoke can query the hub to find out the IP address of a physical interface that corresponds to a specific tunnel interface's IP address.

7. B. Data confidentiality is provided by encrypting data. Data integrity ensures that data is not modified in transit. Data authentication allows parties involved in a conversation to verify that the other party is the party it claims to be. IPsec uses antireplay protection to ensure that packets being sent are not duplicate packets.

Chapter 3

1. D. Inside a quartet, any leading 0s can be omitted, and one sequence of one or more quartets of all 0s can be replaced with "::". The correct answer replaces the longer three-quartet sequence of 0s with ::.

2. C. The name of the prefix generally represents the group to which the prefix is given, with the exception of the term *global routing*. IANA assigns a prefix to a registry (registry prefix). The registry can assign a subset of that range as a prefix to an ISP (ISP prefix). That ISP then subdivides that range of addresses into prefixes and assigns a prefix to one of its customers (site prefix, also called global routing prefix). The enterprise network engineers then further subdivide the range, often with prefix length 64, into subnet prefixes.

3. A and C. IPv6 supports stateful DHCP, which works similarly to IPv4's DHCP to dynamically assign the entire IP address. Stateless autoconfiguration also allows for the assignment by finding the prefix from some nearby router and calculating the Interface ID using the EUI-64 format. Stateless DHCP simply supplies the DNS server IP addresses, and NDP supplies Layer 2 mapping information.

4. D. Stateless autoconfiguration only helps a host learn and form its own IP address, but it does not help the host learn a default gateway. Stateless RS is not a valid term or feature. Neighbor Discovery Protocol (NDP) is used for several purposes, including the same purpose as ARP in IPv4, plus to learn configuration parameters such as a default gateway IP address.

5.   D. Global unicast addresses begin with 2000::/3, meaning that the first 3 bits match the value in hex 2000. Similarly, unique local addresses match FD00::/8, and link-local addresses match FE80::/10 (values that begin with FE8, FE9, FEA, and FEB hex). Multicast IPv6 addresses begin FF00::/8, meaning that the first two hex digits are F.

6.   B. When created automatically, link-local addresses begin FE80::/64, because after the prefix of FE80::/10, the device builds the next 54 bits as binary 0s. Statically assigned link-local addresses simply need to conform to the FE80::/10 prefix. As a result, only two answers are candidates with a beginning quartet of FE80. Of these, only one has only hex 0s in the second, third, and fourth quartets, making answer B the only valid answer.

7.   A and C. The **ipv6 address** command does not list an **eui-64** parameter, so R1 does not form its global unicast address using the EUI-64 format. However, it does form its link-local address using EUI-64. The **show ipv6 interface brief** command lists both the global unicast and link-local addresses in its output.

8.   A. The group addresses listed in the output are the all IPv6 hosts address (FF02::1), the all IPv6 routers address (FF02::2), and the solicited node address that is based on R1's global unicast address (FF02::1:FF12:3456). Also, R1's global unicast address is listed correctly in answer B, but the "[EUI]" notation implies that R1 derived the interface ID portion using EUI-64 conventions.

9.   A, B, and D. RIPv2 and RIPng both use UDP, both use distance-vector logic, and both use the same metric, with the same maximum (15) and same metric that means infinity (16). RIPng does not perform automatic route summarization because IPv6 has no concept of a classful network. RIPng also uses the built-in IPv6 authentication mechanisms rather than a RIP-specific authentication such as RIPv2.

10. B. The fact that the configuration will be copied/pasted into a router means that the order of the commands matters. In this case, the fact that the **ipv6 rip one enable** command precedes the **ipv6 address** command on interface f0/0 means that Cisco IOS will reject the first of these commands, therefore not enabling RIPng on F0/0. The correct order listed under S0/0/0 means that RIPng will be enabled on S0/0/0. As a result, RIPng on R1 will advertise about S0/0/0's connected IPv6 prefixes, and send Updates on S0/0/0, but will do nothing related for F0/0.

Chapter 4

1.   B and C. The **network 172.16.1.0 0.0.0.255** command tells Cisco IOS to match the first three octets when comparing the interface IP addresses to the configured "172.16.1.0" value. Only two answers match in the first three octets. The other two answers have a 0 in the third octet, making the addresses not match the **network** command.

2.   D. The **show ip eigrp interfaces** command displays interfaces on which EIGRP has been enabled but omits passive interfaces. Making the interface passive would omit the interface from the output of this command.

3. D. The **show ip eigrp interfaces detail** command does display a router's EIGRP Hello timer setting for each enabled interface. The other listed commands do not display the timer. Also, EIGRP routers do not have to have matching Hello timers to become neighbors.

4. C. The **neighbor 172.16.2.20 fa0/0** command would only be rejected if the IP address (172.16.2.20) is not inside the range of addresses in the subnet (172.16.2.0/26, range 172.16.2.0–172.16.2.63). This command does not impact the interface state. The command does disable all EIGRP multicasts, and because the three dynamically discovered neighbors require the EIGRP multicasts, all three neighbors fail. Although 172.16.2.20 is a valid potential neighbor, both routers must be configured with static **neighbor** commands, and we know that 172.16.2.20 was not previously configured with a static **neighbor** command; otherwise, it could not have been a neighbor with R1.

5. A and D. Table 4-4 lists the issues. For EIGRP, Router IDs do not have to be unique for EIGRP routers to become neighbors, and the hold timer does not have to match between the two neighbors. However, making an interface passive disables the processing of all EIGRP messages on the interface, preventing all neighborships. Mismatched IP subnets also prevent neighborships from forming.

6. A. The configuration requires the **ip authentication mode eigrp** *asn* **md5** command, which is currently missing. This command enables MD5-style authentication, rather than the default of no authentication. Adding this one command completes the configuration. Any valid key numbers can be used. Also, the **9** in the **ip authentication key-chain eigrp 9 fred** command refers to the EIGRP ASN, not an authentication type.

7. A. EIGRP forms neighborships only when two routers can communicate directly over a data link. As a result, with Frame Relay, EIGRP neighborships occur only between routers on the ends of a PVC, so in this case, 100 neighborships exist.

Chapter 5

1. B and C. Other than the two listed correct answers, the local router also adds connected routes for which the **network** command matches the corresponding interfaces, so it might not add all connected routes. Also, EIGRP does not add static routes to the EIGRP topology table, unless those routes are redistributed.

2. B and D. EIGRP sends bandwidth, delay, reliability, load, MTU, and hop count in the message. The formula to calculate the metric includes bandwidth, delay, reliability, and load.

3. A. EIGRP performs WAN bandwidth control without any explicit configuration, using default settings. Because no **bandwidth** commands have been configured, each subinterface uses the default 1544-kbps setting. For S0/0.1, WAN bandwidth control divides the 1544 by 3 (515 kbps) and then takes the (default) WAN bandwidth of 50 percent, meaning about 250 kbps for each of the three DLCIs. For the two subinterfaces with one PVC, the default 1544 is multiplied by the 50 percent default WAN bandwidth, meaning that each could use about 750 kbps.

4. A. This command lists all successor and feasible successor routes. The output states that two successors exist, and only two routes (listed with the "via..." text) exist. So, no feasible successor routes exist.

5. A and C. By default, the metric weights cause EIGRP to consider bandwidth and delay in the metric calculation, so changing either bandwidth or delay impacts the calculation of the feasible distance and reported distance, and impacts the choice of feasible successor routes. Offset lists also change the metric, which in turn can change whether a route is an FS route. Link loading would impact the metrics, but not without changing the metric weights to nonrecommended values. Finally, variance impacts which routes end up in the IP routing table, but it is not considered by EIGRP when determining which routes are FS routes.

6. C and E. The EIGRP metric calculation treats bandwidth and delay differently. For bandwidth, EIGRP takes the lowest bandwidth, in kbps, which is in this case 500 kbps. For delay, EIGRP takes the cumulative delay, which is 20100 per the various **show interfaces** commands. However, the **show interfaces** command uses a unit of microseconds, and the interface **delay** command and the EIGRP metric formula use a unit of tens-of-microseconds, making the delay that feeds into the formula be 2010.

7. C and E. R1, as a stub router with the **connected** option, still advertises routes, but only routes for connected subnets. R1 announces its stub attribute to R2, so R2 chooses to not send Query messages to R1, knowing that R1 cannot be a transit router for other subnets anyway.

8. D. EIGRP considers only successor and feasible successor routes. Each of those routes must have metrics such that variance * metric is less than the best route's metric; the best route's metric is called the feasible distance (FD).

9. B. Of the five options, **show ip route eigrp all-links** and **show ip eigrp topology all-learned** are not valid commands. Both **show ip eigrp topology** and **show ip route eigrp** can show at most successor and feasible successor routes. However, **show ip eigrp topology all-links** shows also nonfeasible successor routes, making it more likely to show all possible neighbors.

10. D and E. The two listed commands correctly configure EIGRP route filtering such that prefixes matched by the ACL's permit clause will be allowed. All other prefixes will be filtered because of the implied **deny all** at the end of the ACL. The ACL permits numbers in the range 10.10.32.0–10.10.47.255, which leaves 10.10.48.0 and 10.10.60.0 unmatched by the permit clause.

11. B, C, and E. Sequence number 5 matches prefixes 10.1.2.0–10.1.2.255, with prefix lengths between 25 and 27, and denies (filters) those prefixes. This results in answer A being incorrect, because the prefix length (/24) is not in the correct range. Clause 15 matches prefixes 10.2.0.0–10.2.255.255, with prefix length exactly 30, matching answer C. Clause 20 matches only prefix 0.0.0.0 with length /0, so only a default route would match this entry. As a result, 10.0.0.0/8 does not match any of the three clauses.

12. C. When used for route filtering, the route map action (**permit** or **deny**) defines the filtering action, and any referenced **match** commands' **permit** or **deny** action just defines whether the prefix is matched. By not matching ACL 1 with a permit action, EIGRP does not consider a match to have occurred with clause **10**, so it moves to clause **20**. The prefix list referenced in clause **20** has a **permit** action, matching prefixes 10.10.10.0–10.10.11.255, with prefix lengths from 23 to 25. Both criteria match the prefix in question, making answer C correct.

13. B and C. Answer A is invalid. The **ge** value must be larger than /24 in this case, so the command is rejected. Answer B implies a prefix length range of 24–28, inclusive. Answer C implies a range of 25–32 inclusive, because no **le** parameter exists to limit the prefix length lower than the full length of an IPv4 subnet mask. The same logic applies with answer D, but with a range of 28–32, so this final list could not match prefix lengths of /27.

14. B. 10.1.0.0/18 implies a range of 10.1.0.0–10.1.63.255, which includes none of the four subnets. 10.1.64.0/18 implies a range of 10.1.64.0–10.1.127.255, which includes all subnets. 10.1.100.0/24 implies a range of 10.1.100.0–10.1.100.255, which leaves out two of the subnets. Finally, 10.1.98.0/22 does not actually represent a summary. Instead, 10.1.96.0/22 represents a range of 10.1.96.0–10.1.99.255, with 10.1.98.0 as listed in answer D being an IP address in that range. As such, Cisco IOS would actually accept the command, would change the parameter from 10.1.98.0 to 10.1.96.0, and would not include the four listed subnets.

15. B. The **ip summary-address** command does reset neighborships, but only on the interface under which it is configured. After those neighborships come up, R1 will advertise the summary route, but none of the subordinate routes inside that summary. The summary route will use a metric equal to the metric of the lowest metric subordinate route, approximately 1,000,000 in this case.

16. B and D. R2 has interfaces only in Class A network 10.0.0.0, so the **auto-summary** setting has no effect. R3 has interfaces in both Class A network 10.0.0.0 and Class B network 172.16.0.0, so **auto-summary** causes R3 to summarize all subnets of 172.16.0.0/16 as a summary route when advertising to R2.

17. D. The phrase quoted in the question means that R1 is using its route for Class A network 2.0.0.0 to decide where to send packets by default. R1's route for network 2.0.0.0 must have 1.1.1.1 as its next-hop router. This phrase occurs when EIGRP has learned a route for Class A network 2.0.0.0 that has been flagged as a candidate default route by another router. The router flagging a route as a candidate default route, using the **ip default-network** command, does not actually use the route as its default route.

18. C and E. With the suggested configuration style, the static route must first be configured statically, as shown in answer A. Then, either this route must be redistributed as a static route into EIGRP (answer B) or pulled into EIGRP by virtue of the **network 0.0.0.0** EIGRP subcommand (answer D). The other two options have no effect on default route creation and advertisement.

Chapter 6

1. A. By default, IPv6 routing is not enabled on a router. To enable it, you issue the **ipv6 unicast-routing** command in global configuration mode.

As a best practice, you should also enter **ipv6 cef** in global configuration mode (not router configuration mode) to enable Cisco Express Forwarding for IPv6.

However, **ipv6 eigrp** is not a valid command.

2. B. EIGRP uses the link-local address as the next hop for routing protocols. Based on R2's MAC address, R2's link-local address on Fa 0/0 will be FE80::1311:11FF:FE11:1111. This value is derived by splitting the MAC, inserting FFFE, and flipping bit 7, making the initial hex 11 become hex 13.

3. B. General EIGRP commands (for example, **metric**, **eigrp stub**, and **eigrp router-id**) are configured under address-family configuration mode.

Commands entered under interface configuration mode with a traditional EIGRP configuration (for example, **authentication, bandwidth-percent, hello-interval, hold-time, passive-interface,** and **split-horizon**) are entered under address-family-interface configuration mode with Named EIGRP.

Commands having a direct impact on a router's EIGRP topology (for example, **auto-summary, maximum-paths, redistribute,** and **variance**) are given under address-family-topology configuration mode.

There is no address-family-global configuration mode.

4. D. General EIGRP commands (for example, **metric**, **eigrp stub**, and **eigrp router-id**) are configured under address-family configuration mode.

Commands entered under interface configuration mode with a traditional EIGRP configuration (for example, **authentication, bandwidth-percent, hello-interval, hold-time, passive-interface,** and **split-horizon**) are entered under address-family-interface configuration mode with Named EIGRP.

Commands having a direct impact on a router's EIGRP topology (for example, **auto-summary, maximum-paths, redistribute,** and **variance**) are given under address-family-topology configuration mode.

There is no address-family-global configuration mode.

5. B. EIGRP parameters configured under interface configuration mode with a traditional EIGRP configuration can be configured under address-family-interface configuration mode with Named EIGRP. To enter address-family-interface configuration mode for a specific interface, you can enter the **af-interface** *interface_identifier* command.

However, if you want an interface setting to be applied to all interfaces, you can enter the **af-interface default** command. Although commands entered from this configuration mode are inherited by all router interfaces, you can go into address-family-interface configuration mode for specific interfaces to override any globally configured interface settings.

None of the commands given in the question, other than **af-interface default**, are valid.

6. B. Even though Named EIGRP is configured quite differently than a traditional EIGRP configuration, the verification commands remain the same. Therefore, to view a router's EIGRP for IPv4 topology table, you would issue the same **show ip eigrp topology** command that you would use with a traditional EIGRP for IPv4 configuration.

Chapter 7

1. A and D. The wildcard mask is used for matching the prefix only, and not the prefix length. As such, 172.16.1.0 0.0.0.255 matches all addresses that begin with 172.16.1, and 172.16.0.0 0.0.255.255 matches all addresses that begin 172.16. Also, OSPF reviews the **network** command with the most specific wildcard masks (wildcard masks with the most binary 0s) first, so an interface IP address beginning with 172.16.1 matches the command that references area 8.

2. D. ABRs, by definition, connect the backbone area to one or more nonbackbone areas. To perform this function, a router must have at least one interface assigned to the backbone area and at least one interface assigned to a nonbackbone area.

3. B and C. First, for the two correct answers: **show ip ospf interface brief** explicitly lists all OSPF-enabled interfaces that are not passive. **show ip protocols** lists either the details of the configured **network** commands, or if configured using the **ip ospf area** command, it lists the interfaces on which OSPF is enabled. This command also lists the passive interfaces, so armed with interface IP address information, the list of OSPF-enabled nonpassive interfaces could be derived. Of the three wrong answers, **show ip ospf database** does not list enough detail to show the OSPF-enabled interfaces. **show ip route ospf** lists only routes learned with OSPF, so if no routes use a particular OSPF-enabled interface as an outgoing interface, this command would not indirectly identify the interface. Finally, an interface might be OSPF-enabled but with no neighbors reachable on the interface, so the **show ip ospf neighbor** command might not identify all OSPF-enabled interfaces.

4. B and C. On a LAN, the non-DRs form fully adjacent neighborships with only the DR and BDR, giving R1 two neighbors in the FULL state. The other two neighbors settle into the 2-Way state.

5. C and D. The **show ip ospf interface** command displays a router's OSPF Hello Interval setting for each enabled interface. The other listed commands do not display the timer. Also, OSPF routers do need to have matching Hello timers to become neighbors, so the neighborship would fail.

6. E. Table 7-5 in Chapter 7 lists the issues. For OSPF, Router IDs must be unique, the interfaces must not be passive, the dead timers must match, and the primary IP addresses must be in the same subnet, with the same subnet mask. However, the process IDs, found in the **router ospf** *process-id* command, do not have to match.

7. A. Frame Relay is a Layer 2 service and as such does not participate in customer routing protocols. Because the design uses a separate subnet per PVC, and one point-to-point subinterface per PVC/subnet, OSPF will use a point-to-point network type. That means that the two routers on either end of a PVC will become neighbors, and become fully adjacent, meaning that the central-site router will have 100 fully adjacent neighborships.

8. D. The answer with **area 0 virtual-link 4.4.4.4 cost 3** is incorrect, because the **show** command output lists a transit area of 1, but the answer's area parameter refers to area 0 as the transit area. (There is also no cost parameter on the **area virtual-link** command.) The RID of the router on the other end of the virtual link, 4.4.4.4 per the **show** command output, does not have to be pingable for the virtual link to work. The cost of the virtual link is 3, but that cost is calculated as the cost to reach the other router through the transit area, so the command output listed with the question cannot be used to predict Fa0/1's OSPF interface cost alone. However, because the output lists area 1 as the transit area, and because the neighbor RID is listed as 4.4.4.4, R1 will use the area 1 LSDB entries to calculate the cost to reach 4.4.4, a process that will include the area 1 Type 1 LSA for RID 4.4.4.4.

9. B. The **area virtual-link** command defines the virtual link, with the transit area—the area through which the virtual link passes—listed as the first parameter. The other parameter is the RID of the other router. Two of the wrong answers are not Cisco IOS commands.

Chapter 8

1. D. As an ABR connected to areas 0 and 2, ABR2 will have LSDB entries for both area 0 and area 2. In area 0, ABR2 learns Type 1 LSAs from the four routers internal to area 0, plus ABR1, and plus 1 for the area 0 Type 1 LSA that ABR2 creates for itself. In area 2, ABR2 learns 1 each for the five routers internal to area 2, plus the 1 Type 1 LSA ABR2 created for itself inside area 2. The total is 12.

2. E. OSPF creates a Type 2 LSA for a subnet when the router interface connected to the subnet calls for the election of a designated router (DR) and at least two routers have discovered each other and elected a DR. Then, the DR creates and floods the Type 2 LSA. IOS by default does not elect a DR on point-to-point topologies. It does on router LAN interfaces. One answer states that one router only exists in the subnet, so it does not actually find a second router and elect a DR. In the other case, a DR and BDR have been elected, but the router described in the answer is the BDR, not the DR. So, none of the other answers is correct.

3. C. Each ABR, by definition, creates a single Type 3 LSA to represent a subnet known in one area to be advertised into another area. Assuming that 10.100.0.0 is a subnet in area 0, both ABR1 and ABR2 would advertise a Type 3 LSA into area 100. The **show ip ospf database summary** command specifically lists Type 3 network summary LSAs.

4. C. The Database Description (DD) packet lists a short LSA header but not the entire LSA. The Link State Request (LSR) packet asks the neighbors for a copy of an LSA. The Link State Update (LSU) holds the LSAs. LSAck simply acknowledges received LSAs, and Hello is used for neighbor discovery and neighbor state maintenance.

5. B and D. Because the subnet was stable before R5 arrived, the other routers will have elected a DR and BDR. OSPF does not preemptively elect a new DR or BDR, so R5 will be neither (DROther). As a result, R5's messages to the DR will be sent to the 224.0.0.6 all-DR-routers multicast address, and the DR's messages directed to R5 will be sent to the 224.0.0.5 all-SPF-router address.

6. E. R1, internal to area 1, can use LSAs only in the area 1 LSDB. R2's Type 1 LSA exists only in area 2's LSDB. The Type 2 LSA for subnet 10.1.1.0/24, if one exists, also only exists in area 2's LSDB. R1 will use ABR1's Type 1 LSA in area 1 to calculate the possible intra-area routes inside area 1, but R1 will use ABR1's Type 1 LSA in area 1. Finally, the Type 3 LSA, created for 10.1.1.0/24 and flooded into area 1, is also needed to calculate the metric.

7. A and B. OSPF builds the SPF tree based on the topology information in Type 1 and Type 2 LSAs. Changes therefore require another SPF run. Changes to the other LSA types do not require an SPF calculation.

8. A and B. Because none of the interfaces have a **bandwidth** command configured, the only commands that can influence the OSPF cost are the **auto-cost reference-bandwidth** router subcommand and the **ip ospf cost** interface subcommand. To give the output shown in the question, the interface cost could be set directly on all three interfaces listed. Alternatively, the reference bandwidth could be set (in router configuration mode) to cause one of the interface costs to be as shown in the output, with the other two interfaces having their costs set directly.

   For the wrong answers, the **ip ospf cost interface s0/0/0.1** router subcommand does not exist—instead, it is an interface subcommand. An auto-cost of 64700, used as the numerator in the ref-bw/bandwidth cost calculation, does not result in any of the three listed interface costs.

   For the two correct answers, with a default bandwidth of 1544 (kbps) on the serial subinterfaces, a reference bandwidth of 1000 (Mbps) implies the math 1,000,000 / 1544, for an interface cost of 647. With a default bandwidth of 100,000 kbps (100 Mbps) on Fa0/0, a reference bandwidth of 2000 (Mbps) implies math of 2000 / 100 = 20.

9. A, B, and C. OSPF uses Types 1, 2, and 3 for calculating routes internal to the OSPF domain. OSPF uses Types 4, 5, and 7 for external routes redistributed into the OSPF domain, as discussed in Chapter 10, "Route Redistribution."

Chapter 9

1. C. The output lists all of B1's routes for subnets within the range 10.1.0.0–10.1.255.255 whose prefix lengths are longer than /16. One answer lists subnet 10.2.2.0/24, which is not in this range, so the output cannot be used to confirm or deny whether the subnet was filtered. B1's route for 10.1.2.0/24 is an intra-area route by virtue of not listing an inter-area (IA) code by the route. Type 3 LSA filtering only filters Type 3 LSAs, which routers use to calculate interarea routes, so the output tells us nothing about any filtering of 10.1.2.0/24. The output shows a single interarea route for 10.1.3.0/24, so at least one ABR has flooded a Type 3 LSA for this route. Additionally, the output confirms that at least one ABR flooded a Type 3 LSA for 10.1.3.0/24, or the output would not show an IA route for 10.1.3.0/24. So, the Type 3 LSA for 10.1.3.0/24 was not filtered by both ABRs.

2. C. When referenced from a distribute list, OSPF filters routes from being added to that router's IP routing table but has no impact on the flow of LSAs. As such, neither A nor B is correct. An OSPF **distribute-list** command does attempt to filter routes from being added to the IP routing table by OSPF, so the two answers that mention the IP routing table might be correct. Sequence number 5 matches prefixes from 10.1.2.0 through 10.1.2.255, with prefix lengths in the range 25–27, and denies (filters) those prefixes. So, the prefix list will match 10.1.2.0/26 with the first line, with a deny action. The 10.1.2.0/24 subnet does not match the first line of the prefix list, but it does match the third line, the match all line, with a permit action. Because 10.1.2.0/26 is matched by a deny clause, this route is indeed filtered, so it is not added to R1's IP routing table. 10.1.2.0/24, matched with a permit clause, is allowed and would be in the IP routing table.

3. A. When referenced from an **area filter-list** command, OSPF filters Type 3 LSAs created on that router, preventing them from being flooded into area 1 (per the configuration command). As an ABR, R1 would calculate intra-area routes to these area 0 subnets, so this filtering will have no effect on R1's routes. Sequence number 5 matches prefixes from 10.1.2.0 through 10.1.2.255, with prefix lengths in the range 25–27, and denies (filters) those prefixes. So, the prefix list will match 10.1.2.0/26 with the first line, with a deny action. The 10.1.2.0/24 subnet does not match the first line of the prefix list, because the prefix length does not match. However, it does match the third line, the match all line, with a permit action. By matching subnet 10.1.2.0/26 with a deny action, the filter list does prevent R1 from flooding a Type 3 LSA for that subnet. By matching 10.1.2.0/24 with a permit action, R1 does not filter the Type 3 LSA for that subnet.

4. B and D. The **area range** command does not cause a failure in neighborships. Because at least one intra-area subordinate subnet of 10.1.0.0/16 exists in R1, R1 both creates a summary route for 10.1.0.0/16 and stops advertising LSAs for the (three) subordinate subnets. By default, the metric of the summary is the metric of the lowest-metric component subnet.

5. D. The **show ip ospf database summary** command lists only Type 3 LSAs. The **summary-address** command creates Type 5 LSAs on ASBRs, ruling out one answer. The output does not specify whether the LSA was created as a summary route; all references to the word "summary" refer to Type 3 Summary LSAs. If created by an **area range** command, the metric defaults to be the best metric of all subordinate subnets, but it can also be explicitly set, ruling out another of the possible answers. In short, this LSA can represent a route summarized by the **area range** command, but that fact cannot be proved or disproved by the output as shown.

6. B. Without the **always** parameter, the **default-information originate** command generates an LSA for a default route, with prefix 0.0.0.0/0, but only if its own IP routing table has a route for 0.0.0.0/0. It does not flag another LSA as being used as a candidate default route.

7. C and D. Both types of NSSA stubby areas allow the redistribution of external routes into an area, but these routes are advertised as Type 7 LSAs. As a totally NSSA, the ABR should flood no Type 5 LSAs into the area and flood no Type 3 LSAs into the area, except for the Type 3 LSAs used to advertise the default route into the area. As such, a router internal to a totally stubby area should see zero Type 5 LSAs and a small number of Type 3 LSAs for the default route(s) advertised by the ABR(s).

8. B. The **stub** keyword means either a stub area or a totally stubby area. The **no-summary** command means that the area is totally stubby.

9. B. When using OSPFv3's Address Family configuration to support both IPv4 and IPv6, LSAs for both IPv4 and IPv6 networks populate a single link-state database. The database can be viewed with the **show ospfv3 database** command.

10. D. With Named EIGRP, all EIGRP configuration can be done under a single EIGRP virtual instance. However, with an OSPFv3 Address Family configuration, you have to enter interface configuration mode to instruct an interface to participate in the routing process. The command (issued in interface configuration mode) is **ospfv3** *process_id* **ipv6 area** *area_number*.

11. C. OSPFv3 introduces two LSAs, Type 8 LSAs (called *Link LSAs*) and Type 9 LSAs (called *Intra-Area Prefix LSAs*).

    The Type 8 LSAs, called Link LSAs, only exist on a local link, where they are used by a router to advertise its link-local address to all other routers on the same link. Additionally, the Type 8 LSA provides a listing of all IPv6 addresses associated with a link to routers on that link. OSPFv3 also uses the Type 8 LSA to set option bits for a specific network's LSA.

    A Type 9 LSA can send information about IPv6 networks (including stub networks) attached to a router (similar to the Type 1 LSA for IPv4 networks). Additionally, a Type 9 LSA can send information about transit network segments within an area (similar to the Type 2 LSA for IPv4 networks).

Chapter 10

1. D. The three incorrect answers list typical reasons for using route redistribution. The correct answer—the least likely reason among the answers for using route redistribution—lists a problem for which an OSPF virtual link is often used. Route redistribution could be attempted to solve a problem with a discontiguous OSPF area, but the redistribution completely changes the LSAs that would have otherwise been known and could have negative impacts on route summaries and cause routing loops, and have other problems as well.

2. B and D. For a router to redistribute routes between two routing protocols, the router must have both routing protocols configured, have a working link into each routing domain, and configure **redistribute** commands under each routing process. The **redistribute** command, issued in routing protocol configuration mode, pulls routes into that routing process from another routing process as referenced on the **redistribute** command.

3. B and C. Because the metrics come from a different routing protocol than EIGRP, the metric must be set. The metric must be set with five components; EIGRP will then use those components as it would for an internal route. The metric components can be set as listed in the two correct answers, plus using a route map as referenced by the **redistribute** command.

4. C. This output is the external data section of a detailed view of an EIGRP topology table entry for an external route. This output confirms that this route was redistributed into EIGRP. If R1 were the redistributing router, the output would include the phrase "(this system)"; this example does not include that notation. The output means that on the router that did the redistribution, the route was redistributed from OSPF process 1, and the OSPF metric was 64. R1's metric is not based on the OSPF metric of the route.

5. B. The **redistribute ospf** command will attempt to redistribute OSPF routes and connected routes from interfaces on which OSPF is enabled. The metric components include 1000 kbps (or 1 Mbps), 100 tens-of-microseconds (or 1000 microseconds), 10 for the loading, 1 for the reliability, and 1500 for MTU. The EIGRP version of the **redistribute** command does not include a **subnets** option.

6. A and C. Because the routes come from OSPF and feed into OSPF, the metrics can be set with the usual tools or the metric can default. When taking routes from OSPF into another OSPF process, the default metric is taken from the source route's OSPF cost. Alternatively, the metric can be set for all routes, regardless of the route source, using the **default-metric** OSPF subcommand. The **metric transparent** keywords cannot be used for an OSPF **redistribute** command.

7. D. This command lists the output of Type 4 Summary ASBR LSAs. The LSID identifies the redistributing ASBR (9.9.9.9). The advertising router is the ABR that created and flooded the LSA (3.3.3.3), and the metric is the ABR's best metric route to reach the ASBR.

8. D. Routers add internal and external costs for E1 routes and use only external costs for E2 routes, so the cost for the route through R22 will always be lower. However, for a given prefix/length, OSPF always prefers intra-area routes first, then interarea, then E1, and finally, E2, all regardless of metric.

9. E. Because OSPF does not use hop count as a metric, the information about the number of hops is not available in OSPF routes in the IP routing table. The other answers list items that can be matched with the route map **match** subcommand.

10. A. The deny clauses in the route map mean that the route map will filter routes matched by that clause. The permit or deny action of the referenced ACLs just defines whether the route is matched. So, routes permitted by ACL "two" will be matched and then filtered because of the route map clause deny action. Routes denied by ACL "one" simply do not match the route map clause numbered 10; such routes might or might not be redistributed depending on the next two clauses. Clause number 100 does not have a **match** command, meaning that it matches all routes not otherwise matched, with a permit action, allowing these routes to be redistributed.

11. A and C. The problem states that R1 has learned OSPF intra-area routes for 10.1.1.0/24, so **show ip route** will display that subnet. As an intra-area route based on a Type 2 LSA, the **show ip ospf database** command lists the summary of the LSAs, including the 10.1.1.0 subnet number for that Type 2 LSA. However, because the redistribution filtering discards subnet 10.1.1.0/24, this value will not be included in the EIGRP topology table.

12. B. The **external 2** parameters on the **redistribute** command act as matching logic. Only routes from the source routing protocol (in this case OSPF 2) that match this extra logic will be considered for redistribution by this **redistribute** command. The **set metric-type type-1** route map subcommand sets the route type as it is injected into the destination routing protocol (in this case, OSPF 1); this logic is not used for matching the source routes. The routes permitted by ACL 1 will be redistributed, but only those that are also E2 routes from the (source) OSPF 2 domain. The redistribute function will not change the attributes of routes inside a single routing domain, but only in the destination routing domain (OSPF 1), so the configuration has no effect on the OSPF 2 routes that remain in OSPF 2.

13. C. EIGRP, by default, sets a different AD for internal (90) and external (170) routes. The rest of the answers are accurate regarding default settings.

14. A. All the answers list reasonable options in some cases, but the only feature listed that is useful with all three routing protocols is the route tag feature. RIPv2 does not support the concept of differentiating between internal and external routes, so the two answers that suggest setting administrative distance (AD) based on the route type (internal or external) could not be used in all three routing domains, as required by the question. All three routing protocols support setting route tags and setting the AD per route. However, because RIPv2 cannot match based on the route type (internal/external), the option to set the route tags is the only option that applies to all three routing domains.

15. D. AD can be used to prevent the domain loop problem with two routing domains by making each routing protocol's AD for internal routes be better (lower) than the other routing protocol's AD for external routes. RIP uses AD 120 for all routes, with no distinction of internal or external. As such, OSPF's internal default AD settings of 110 meet the requirement that OSPF's internal AD (110) is better than RIP's external (120). However, RIP's default of 120 is not better than OSPF's default for externals (110), so the **distance ospf external 180** command changes that setting to meet both requirements. The three wrong answers, while syntactically valid, do not help meet the requirements.

16. E. Route tags are unitless integers that can be given to a route and even passed between different routing protocols by routers that perform redistribution.

Chapter 11

1. B and C. Cisco Express Forwarding (CEF) maintains its information in two tables, the Adjacency Table (which contains information about Layer 2 adjacencies) and the Forwarding Information Base (FIB) (which contains Layer 3 information). The Routing Information Base (RIB) is a data structure used by a routing protocol such as OSPF. The ARP Cache contains IP address to MAC address mappings. Although information from the ARP Cache is used to help populate the Adjacency Table, the ARP Cache itself is not a CEF table.

2. D. To globally enable CEF on a router, use the **ip cef** command in global configuration mode. The **ip flow egress** interface configuration mode command is used to enable outbound NetFlow. The **ip route-cache cef** interface configuration mode command is used to enable CEF on an individual interface, if CEF has already been globally enabled on the router. The **no ip route-cache** interface configuration mode command is used to enable process switching on an interface.

3. A and C. PBR supports processing packets on an interface, for the inbound direction only. The referenced route map causes PBR to attempt policy routing of packets that match a **permit** clause in the route map.

4. B and E. Packets created by Telnet use TCP, so the packets will match ACL 101 with a **permit** action. PBR will match the only route map clause shown in the configuration, with the **permit** route map clause listing a **set** command. The **set** command lists S0/0/1 as the outgoing interface and without a default parameter. So, Router R1 will first attempt to forward the packet based on the **set** command (interface S0/0/1), but if the interface is down, R1 will then try to forward based on the IP routing table (interface S0/1/1).

5. D. The output from the **show ip policy** command shows the interfaces on which PBR has been enabled and the name of the route map enabled for PBR on each interface. For the purposes of this question, the output tells us the interfaces on which PBR has been enabled. Two answers mention packets exiting the interface. Therefore, these answers cannot be correct, because PBR applies to packets entering an interface. For the two interfaces that mention inbound packets, one suggests that all packets will be forwarded per the PBR configuration; some might not be forwarded per PBR, depending on the configuration of the route map. The correct answer specifically mentions that PBR will consider all packets with PBR, which is the more accurate statement about PBR operations.

6. **A and B.** The IP SLA feature focuses on IP traffic. Therefore, Cisco IOS does not include Novell's older IPX protocol as part of IP SLA. IP SLA uses SNMP MIBs to store statistics, but it does not use SNMP as an operation.

7. **C.** The three lines shown create the operation number (first command), define the operation (second command), and start the operation (third command). All commands are correct. After the operation is started, IP SLA stores the data in the RTTMON MIB; no additional configuration is necessary.

8. **D.** The up timer on the tracking object defines how long to wait, when in a down state, after seeing the IP SLA object transition to an OK state. Similarly, the down timer defines how long to wait, when in an OK state, after seeing the IP SLA object move to a down state, before moving the tracking object to a down state.

9. **D.** Both Cisco EVN and VRF-Lite allow a single physical router to run multiple virtual router instances, and both technologies allow routes from one VRF to be selectively leaked to other VRFs. However, a major difference is the way that two physical routers interconnect. With VRF-Lite, a router is configured with multiple subinterfaces, one for each VRF. However, with Cisco EVN, routers interconnect using a VNET trunk, which simplifies configuration.

Chapter 12

1. **D.** A default route is specified with an IP address/mask combination of **0.0.0.0 0.0.0.0**. As a best practice, you should point a default route to a next-hop IP address, rather than an Ethernet interface, because specifying an Ethernet interface can generate an excessive number of ARP requests and hurt router performance.

2. **C.** The command used to instruct an interface to obtain its IP address information from a DHCP server is **ip address dhcp**. All the other options are not valid commands.

3. **A.** The **no ip dhcp client request router** command can be used to prevent a router from automatically installing a static default route based on default gateway information learned from a DHCP server. None of the other options are valid commands.

4. **C.** The administrative distance (AD) of a static default route automatically installed in a router based on default gateway information provided by a DHCP server is 254. This makes the default static route a "floating static route," meaning that it will only be used if another routing source (with a lower AD) does not know of a default static route.

5. **C.** Dynamic NAT (DNAT) allows an inside local address to be dynamically associated with an inside global address specified in a pool of available inside global addresses. Static NAT (SNAT) specifies an inside global address to be associated with an inside local address. Port Address Translation (PAT) allows multiple inside local addresses to use a single inside global address, for use when communicating on the Internet. MAT is not a valid variant of NAT.

6. B. An outside global address represents a device outside of a network with a globally routable address. In this scenario, the web server's IP address of 203.0.113.10 would be an outside global address.

An inside local address represents a device inside of a network with an address that is not routable on the public Internet. In this scenario, the laptop's IP address of 10.1.1.241 would be an inside local address.

An inside global address represents a device on the inside of our network with an address that is a globally routable address. In this scenario, the laptop's translated address of 198.51.100.54 would be an inside global address.

An outside local address represents a device on the outside of a network that has an address that is not routable on the public Internet. For example, if NAT were being performed at a remote site, the destination device at the remote site would have an outside local address. In the scenario presented in this question, there is no outside local address.

7. A. An outside global address represents a device outside of a network with a globally routable address. In this scenario, the web server's IP address of 203.0.113.10 would be an outside global address.

An inside local address represents a device inside of a network with an address that is not routable on the public Internet. In this scenario, the laptop's IP address of 10.1.1.241 would be an inside local address.

An inside global address represents a device on the inside of our network with an address that is a globally routable address. In this scenario, the laptop's translated address of 198.51.100.54 would be an inside global address.

An outside local address represents a device on the outside of a network that has an address that is not routable on the public Internet. For example, if NAT were being performed at a remote site, the destination device at the remote site would have an outside local address. In the scenario presented in this question, there is no outside local address.

Chapter 13

1. B and E. The private IPv4 address space consists of Class A network 10.0.0.0, Class B networks 172.16.0.0–172.31.0.0, and the 256 Class C networks that begin 192.168.

2. B. ICANN and IANA manage the assignment of public IPv4 address space such that large address blocks (often called CIDR blocks) exist in a particular geography or are assigned to particular ISPs. As such, Internet routers can more easily create summary routes to help keep the routing table small in the Internet. 200.1.2.0/24 would likely also be allocated to some registrar, ISP, or customer in Asia. Because of the large route summaries, in this case possibly a summary for 200.0.0.0/8, routers in North America would not see an increase in the size of their routing tables.

3. A. The router in ASN 22, R22, advertises the BGP update with (at least) 22 in the AS_Path Path Attribute (PA). When R1 advertises the route to R2, also in ASN 11, R1 does not add an ASN. As a result, R2's AS_Path has at least ASN 22 and not ASN 11.

4. A and C. The public range of 16-bit BGP ASNs is 1 through 64,495.

5. D. The question asks which answers are true about the eBGP peer but also not true about an iBGP peer. Both iBGP and eBGP use TCP port 179. An eBGP peer uses a different ASN than the local router, by definition, making that answer incorrect. The correct answer refers to the fact that an eBGP peer adds its own ASN to the BGP AS_Path PA before sending routing information to another router, whereas iBGP peers do not.

6. A. Although using BGP does avoid some static configuration at the enterprise and the ISP, the primary reason to consider using BGP in the enterprise is to influence and react to Path Attributes for the purpose of choosing the best path. Typically, engineers do not redistribute BGP routes into the IGP because of scalability problems. And although it can be interesting to monitor the size of the Internet BGP table, it is not a primary motivation for choosing to use BGP on a router.

7. C and D. The term "homed" makes reference to a single-homed ISP, and "multi-homed" references multiple ISPs. The terms "single" and "dual" refer to the number of connections to each ISP.

8. B and C. The **router bgp** command lists the local ASN, and the **neighbor remote-as** command lists the neighbor's ASN. Because the neighbor relationship uses the IP addresses on the common link, the routers do not need to identify the update source interface, because each will default to use their S0/0 interfaces (in this case) as the update source.

9. D. Three of the commands list valid commands. The **neighbor 2.2.2.2 multihop 2** command is syntactically incorrect; it should be **neighbor 2.2.2.2 ebgp-multihop 2**.

10. D. The **show ip bgp** command lists the BGP neighbor state in the last column of output, listing the literal state, unless in an established state. In that state, the output lists the number of prefixes learned from the neighbor, so a numeric value implies an established state.

11. A and D. The output lists R2's local ASN as ASN 11, a value that is configured in the **router bgp** *asn* command. The line for neighbor 1.1.1.1 lists that router's ASN as 1, so a **neighbor 1.1.1.1 remote-as 1** command should exist on R2 instead of the **neighbor 1.1.1.1 remote-as 11** command. The state for neighbor 1.1.1.1 lists "Idle (Admin)," implying that the **neighbor 1.1.1.1 shutdown** command has been configured. The other answer lists a nonexistent command.

12. A. The BGP Update message lists a set of PAs, plus any prefixes/lengths that use those PAs. It can also list withdrawn routes in the same Update message as newly advertised routes. It can also list multiple prefixes in a single Update message.

13. C. The "Known via" text refers to the local router's (R1's) **router bgp** command, which identifies the local router's ASN. The rest of the output does not identify the neighboring ASN, nor the rest of the AS_Path details. It does list that the route is external, with the text "type external" and the AS Hops (which is the AS_Path length).

14. A. The third character in each line for each router is either blank, meaning that the route is an eBGP route, or an "i," meaning an iBGP-learned route. The contents of the AS_Path can be determined (1, 2, 3, 4), but the answer about AS_Path does not suggest four ASNs. The best route for each prefix has a ">" in the second character, and this route does not.

15. D. The **network** command will take the route from the IP routing table and put the equivalent into the BGP table, if that exact route exists. The output does not show a route for 130.1.16.0/20, so the **network 130.1.16.0 mask 255.255.240.0** command does not match a specific route. The other answer with a **network** command is syntactically incorrect. Redistribution without aggregation would redistribute the three routes, but all three subordinate routes would be advertised into eBGP. By also using BGP route summarization, a single route for 130.1.16.0/20 can be advertised.

Chapter 14

1. C. R1 needs to be configured with **router bgp 1, neighbor 2.2.2.2 remote-as 1**, and **neighbor 2.2.2.2 update-source loopback1**. The **neighbor 2.2.2.2 ibgp-multihop 2** and **neighbor 2.2.2.2 ibgp-mode** commands are simply unsupported commands. The **neighbor 1.1.1.1 remote-as 1** command has correct syntax and is used as a command in R2's configuration but not on R1. The **neighbor 2.2.2.2 remote-as 2** command has the correct syntax but with the wrong ASN (2 instead of 1).

2. D. The small letter "i" in the third character position implies that the route was learned with iBGP. Of the five lines, four have an "i" in the third column.

3. B and C. The line reading "1.1.1.1 from 2.2.2.2..." implies the BGP RID of the neighbor is 1.1.1.1, with neighbor ID—the IP address on the local router's **neighbor** command—of 2.2.2.2. The end of the output shows that the route is internal (iBGP learned) and is best, so both the > and i will be displayed for this route by the **show ip bgp** command. Finally, the output does not identify the local ASN, although it does list the AS_Path of the route (1, 2, 3, 4).

4. B. By default, when a router advertises an iBGP route, it leaves the Next-Hop PA unchanged. By default, R2's next hop for routes learned from I2 will be I2's IP address used on the R2-I2 neighbor relationship.

5. A and C. The enterprise core routers need to know which exit point (R1 or R2) is best; the correct answers supply those routes to the routers internal to the company. Note that redistribution from BGP into the IGP is not recommended, but it does defeat this particular problem.

6. B. The **show ip bgp neighbors 2.2.2.2 advertised-routes** command does list the post-outbound-filter BGP Update; however, the user did not issue a clear command, so the filter has not yet taken effect. As such, the output still lists the original three prefixes as if the filter had not yet been applied.

7. B, D, and E. The neighbor distribute-list out command refers to an ACL, but for the ACL to match on both prefix and prefix length, the ACL must be an extended ACL. The **neighbor filter-list** command refers to an AS-path filter and cannot match based on prefix/length.

8. A and B. The router resets the BGP neighborship when performing a hard reset of the peer. See Table 14-3 in the chapter for a list of several variations of the **clear** command and whether they perform a hard or soft reset.

9. B. Weight and Local_Pref were created for the purpose of giving engineers tools to influence the BGP best-path choice. AS_Path was created for loop avoidance, but AS_Path length can also be manipulated (for example, with AS_Path prepend) to influence the best-path choice. Although the Origin PA can be changed by configuration for the purpose of influencing the best-path decision, the intent of this PA is to identify the source from which the route was introduced into BGP. Additionally, the best-path algorithm considers the Origin PA after the other PAs listed in the answers, making Origin the least useful of these answers for influencing path choice.

10. A. Of the items listed in the question, Weight is the first one considered in the best-path algorithm, with a bigger Weight being better. As a result, Route 1 is the better route of the two.

11. B. Of the items listed in the question, Weight is the first one considered in the best-path algorithm, and it is a tie. The next item considered, Local Preference, uses bigger-is-better logic, so Route 2 will be considered best.

12. B and D. Weight, a Cisco-proprietary feature of BGP on Cisco routers, cannot be transmitted in a BGP Update, so setting Weight on an outbound route map at the ISPs will have no effect. Also, the goals call for setting Weight for all routes from an ISP to the same number, so creating a prefix list to match a subset of reachable prefixes, in this case all Class C networks, is not useful. However, two methods of configuring Weight do exist: the **neighbor weight** command and configuring an inbound route map with a **set weight** command in the route map.

13. B. The output shows the results of AS_Path prepending. The repetitive 1s cannot mean that the route has been advertised into and out of the same ASN repeatedly because loop prevention would have prevented such an advertisement. With AS_Path prepending, the neighboring ASN typically adds its own ASN to the end of the AS_Path (as listed on the left of the output).

14. C. The command lists the administrative distance as the first number inside the square brackets and the MED values as the second number in brackets. The AD of 20 implies an eBGP route instead of iBGP. The output says nothing about the Weight or AS_Path length.

Chapter 15

1. B. With Stateless Address Autoconfiguration (SLAAC), an ISP router could send Router Advertisements (RA), which advertise an IPv6 prefix, on the link connecting to a customer router. Stateless DHCPv6 uses SLAAC for IP address assignment and a DHCPv6 server to provide additional configuration options. Stateful DHCPv6 uses a DHCPv6 server for address assignment, as opposed to SLAAC. DHCPv6 Prefix Delegation (DHCPv6-PD) allows a DHCPv6 server to assign a collection of IPv6 networks to a DHCPv6 client (such as a router). However, stateless SLAAC is not a valid option.

2. D. The **ipv6 route ::/0** *next_hop_ipv6_address* command is used to create a default static IPv6 route.

3. A, B, and D. In addition to the **deny ipv6 any any** implicit command (which blocks all IPv6 traffic) at the very bottom of an IPv6 ACL, the **permit icmp any any nd-na** and **permit icmp any any nd-ns** commands are used to permit *Neighbor Discovery – Neighbor Advertisements* and *Neighbor Discovery – Neighbor Solicitations*. These Neighbor Discovery commands are required for IPv6 to function properly.

4. B. When configuring IPv6 routing over an IPv4 BGP session, you need to create a route map that specifies the local router interface's IPv6 address as the next-hop IPv6 address to advertise to its neighbor. However, this step is not a requirement when configuring IPv6 routing over an IPv6 BGP session.

5. A, C, and D. The **show bgp ipv6 unicast summary** command displays several valuable pieces of information, including the local router's BGP router ID, a list of configured BGP neighbors, and the AS of configured BGP neighbors. However, while the **show bgp ipv6 unicast summary** command does not list IPv6 routes known to the BGP table, the **show bgp ipv6 unicast** command does.

6. A and B. The only valid options after **ipv6 prefix-list LIST1 seq 10 permit 2000::/16** are **le** (meaning less than or equal to) and **ge** (meaning greater than or equal to). The number of bits in the prefix length then follows those options.

7. C. The AS path length and weights are the same for both next hops. However, the next-hop IPv6 address of 2000:3::2 has a higher Local Preference (150) than 2000:2::2 (50). Therefore, 2000:3::2 is chosen as the best next hop (as indicated with the ">" sign). Also, while having a lower router ID can cause BGP to select a best path, it is used as a tiebreaker, which is not needed in this example.

Chapter 16

1. B and D. Unicast Reverse Path Forwarding (uRPF) can help prevent IP spoofing attacks by checking the source IP address of received traffic and verifying that the traffic is arriving on the interface that would be used to send traffic to that IP address. ACLs can also be used to help prevent IP spoofing attacks by denying traffic coming in on an interface having a source address that lives off of a different interface. AAA is a technology that is used to authenticate users, authorize what they can do, and keep a log of what they did. However, AAA does not protect against IP spoofing attacks. CAR (Committed Access Rate) is a legacy quality of service (QoS) policing mechanism that does not protect against IP spoofing.

2. B. Hot Standby Router Protocol (HSRP) is a first-hop redundancy protocol that provides router redundancy. Specifically, HSRP can have two or more routers capable of servicing a single IP address, and that IP address can be used as the default gateway IP address for devices residing on a subnet connected to the HSRP routers. SNMP is a network management protocol. AAA is a technology that is used to authenticate users, authorize what they can do, and keep a log of what they did. TACACS+ is a type of server that can be used with AAA.

3. B and C. A periodic time-based ACL can specify a recurring time period during which the ACL will be active. An absolute time-based ACL can specify a specific starting and ending time and date (or just an ending time and date). A reflexive ACL contains temporary entries that are created when a session begins. There is no "adaptive" ACL.

4. D. An infrastructure ACL is typically an extended ACL that is applied to routers residing on the outer edges of an enterprise network. The primary purpose of this ACL is to prevent malicious traffic from entering the enterprise. A time-based ACL is an ACL that specifies a time period during which the ACL is active. A reflexive ACL contains temporary entries that are created when a session begins. "Absolute" is a type of time-based ACL.

5. A and C. Of the options listed, only *host name* and *domain name* are used by a router when generating an RSA key pair.

6. D. Type 7 password encryption is a very weak encryption, and it uses the Vigenere cipher. A Type 0 password has no encryption. A Type 4 password is represented by an SHA-256 hash value, and a Type 5 password is represented by an MD5 hash value.

7. B. Unicast Reverse Path Forwarding (uRPF) has three modes of operation: *strict mode*, *loose mode*, and *VRF mode*. In strict mode, a router not only checks to make sure that the source IP address of an arriving packet is reachable, based on the router's FIB, but the packet must also be arriving on the same interface that the router would use to send traffic back to that IP address. In loose mode, a router only verifies that the source IP address of the packet is reachable, based on the router's FIB. VRF mode is similar to loose mode, in that the source IP addresses are checked against the FIB of a specific VRF. There is no *auto* or *desirable* uRPF mode.

8. B and D. TACACS+ and RADIUS are each protocols that can be used by a AAA server. TACACS+ uses TCP, while RADIUS uses UDP. TACACS+ encrypts an entire packet, while RADIUS only encrypts a password. TACACS+ offers basic accounting functionality. However, RADIUS offers robust accounting. Also, TACACS+ is a Cisco-proprietary protocol, while RADIUS is an open standard protocol.

Chapter 17

1. A and C. Cisco IOS supports both plain text and hashing authentication for neighboring routers to authenticate themselves to one another. Plain text authentication sends a shared secret key across a network in clear text. However, hashing authentication sends the hash value of a key across a network, as opposed to the key itself. Therefore, hashing authentication is considered more secure. There is no support for two-factor or biometric authentication to authenticate neighboring routers.

2. C. A key string specifies a preshared key to be used between routers. Therefore, the key string must match on two routers for them to mutually authenticate. The key chain name and key number values are locally significant and do not have to match on a neighboring router. Also, as long as a matching key on each router is currently active, the specific send and receive lifetimes do not have to match on mutually authenticating routers.

3. B and C. Plain text authentication is not supported by Named EIGRP, nor is Password Authentication Protocol (PAP), which might be found on WAN connections using the Point-to-Point Protocol (PPP). Named EIGRP does support both MD5 and SHA hashing authentication. Traditional EIGRP does not support SHA hashing authentication, but does support MD5 hashing authentication.

4. A. A key chain, which consists of one or more key numbers each of which can be assigned a key string, can be viewed with the **show key chain** Cisco IOS command. None of the other options are valid Cisco IOS commands.

5. B. OSPF can have authentication enabled at the area level (in router configuration mode) or at the interface level (in interface configuration mode). The question states that authentication is functioning and is using MD5 hashing, but there is no **area 0 authentication message-digest** command in router configuration mode. Therefore, OSPF MD5 authentication must be enabled in interface configuration mode, which is done with the **ip ospf authentication message-digest** command.

6. A and B. Authentication is not a feature natively built into OSPFv3. However, OSPFv3 can leverage IPsec for authentication (and even encryption). As a result, both the MD5 and SHA hashing algorithms can be used. Plain text authentication is not supported by OSPFv3, nor is Password Authentication Protocol (PAP), which might be found on WAN connections using the Point-to-Point Protocol (PPP).

7. C. BGP only supports MD5 for neighbor authentication. Neither plain text nor SHA is supported, and Diffie Hellman Group 1 is an approach to exchanging shared secret keys over an untrusted network.

8. C. Unlike OSPF and EIGRP, which can dynamically find neighbors through multicast, BGP requires neighbors to be statically configured. Therefore, BGP is less susceptible to a malicious user adding a router to a network and using that router to corrupt the routing table of production routers. However, after a session (which is TCP-based) is established between two BGP neighbors, a malicious user could attempt to do session hijacking to take over the existing BGP neighborship.

ROUTE Exam Updates

Over time, reader feedback allows Cisco Press to gauge which topics give our readers the most problems when taking the exams. To assist readers with those topics, the authors create new materials clarifying and expanding upon those troublesome exam topics. As mentioned in the Introduction, the additional content about the exam is contained in a PDF document on this book's companion website, at www.ciscopress.com/title/9781587205590.

This appendix is intended to provide you with updated information if Cisco makes minor modifications to the exam upon which this book is based. When Cisco releases an entirely new exam, the changes are usually too extensive to provide in a simple update appendix. In those cases, you might need to consult the new edition of the book for the updated content.

This appendix attempts to fill the void that occurs with any print book. In particular, this appendix does the following:

- Mentions technical items that might not have been mentioned elsewhere in the book

- Covers new topics if Cisco adds new content to the exam over time

- Provides a way to get up-to-the-minute current information about content for the exam

Always Get the Latest at the Companion Website

You are reading the version of this appendix that was available when your book was printed. However, given that the main purpose of this appendix is to be a living, changing document, it is important that you look for the latest version online at the book's companion website. To do so, follow these steps:

Step 1. Browse to www.ciscopress.com/title/9781587205590.

Step 2. Select the Appendix option under the More Information box.

Step 3. Download the latest "Appendix B" document.

Note   Note that the downloaded document has a version number. Comparing the version of the print Appendix B (Version 1.0) with the latest online version of this appendix, you should do the following:

■   **Same version:** Ignore the PDF file that you downloaded from the companion website.

■   **Website has a later version:** Ignore this Appendix B in your book and read only the latest version that you downloaded from the companion website.

Technical Content

The current version of this appendix does not contain any additional technical coverage.

Conversion Tables

This appendix lists two conversion tables for reference when studying:

- Hex-to-decimal
- Decimal-to-binary

Use these tables for learning; however, such tables will not be available on the exam.

Table C-1 *Hex-to-Decimal Conversion Table*

Hex	Decimal
0	0
1	1
2	2
3	3
4	4
5	5
6	6
7	7
8	8
9	9
A	10
B	11
C	12
D	13
E	14
F	15

Table C-2   *Binary-to-Decimal Conversion Table*

Decimal Value	Binary Value	Decimal Value	Binary Value	Decimal Value	Binary Value	Decimal Value	Binary Value
0	00000000	32	00100000	64	01000000	96	01100000
1	00000001	33	00100001	65	01000001	97	01100001
2	00000010	34	00100010	66	01000010	98	01100010
3	00000011	35	00100011	67	01000011	99	01100011
4	00000100	36	00100100	68	01000100	100	01100100
5	00000101	37	00100101	69	01000101	101	01100101
6	00000110	38	00100110	70	01000110	102	01100110
7	00000111	39	00100111	71	01000111	103	01100111
8	00001000	40	00101000	72	01001000	104	01101000
9	00001001	41	00101001	73	01001001	105	01101001
10	00001010	42	00101010	74	01001010	106	01101010
11	00001011	43	00101011	75	01001011	107	01101011
12	00001100	44	00101100	76	01001100	108	01101100
13	00001101	45	00101101	77	01001101	109	01101101
14	00001110	46	00101110	78	01001110	110	01101110
15	00001111	47	00101111	79	01001111	111	01101111
16	00010000	48	00110000	80	01010000	112	01110000
17	00010001	49	00110001	81	01010001	113	01110001
18	00010010	50	00110010	82	01010010	114	01110010
19	00010011	51	00110011	83	01010011	115	01110011
20	00010100	52	00110100	84	01010100	116	01110100
21	00010101	53	00110101	85	01010101	117	01110101
22	00010110	54	00110110	86	01010110	118	01110110
23	00010111	55	00110111	87	01010111	119	01110111
24	00011000	56	00111000	88	01011000	120	01111000
25	00011001	57	00111001	89	01011001	121	01111001
26	00011010	58	00111010	90	01011010	122	01111010
27	00011011	59	00111011	91	01011011	123	01111011
28	00011100	60	00111100	92	01011100	124	01111100
29	00011101	61	00111101	93	01011101	125	01111101
30	00011110	62	00111110	94	01011110	126	01111110
31	00011111	63	00111111	95	01011111	127	01111111

Table C-2 *Binary-to-Decimal Conversion Table*

Decimal Value	Binary Value	Decimal Value	Binary Value	Decimal Value	Binary Value	Decimal Value	Binary Value
128	10000000	160	10100000	192	11000000	224	11100000
129	10000001	161	10100001	193	11000001	225	11100001
130	10000010	162	10100010	194	11000010	226	11100010
131	10000011	163	10100011	195	11000011	227	11100011
132	10000100	164	10100100	196	11000100	228	11100100
133	10000101	165	10100101	197	11000101	229	11100101
134	10000110	166	10100110	198	11000110	230	11100110
135	10000111	167	10100111	199	11000111	231	11100111
136	10001000	168	10101000	200	11001000	232	11101000
137	10001001	169	10101001	201	11001001	233	11101001
138	10001010	170	10101010	202	11001010	234	11101010
139	10001011	171	10101011	203	11001011	235	11101011
140	10001100	172	10101100	204	11001100	236	11101100
141	10001101	173	10101101	205	11001101	237	11101101
142	10001110	174	10101110	206	11001110	238	11101110
143	10001111	175	10101111	207	11001111	239	11101111
144	10010000	176	10110000	208	11010000	240	11110000
145	10010001	177	10110001	209	11010001	241	11110001
146	10010010	178	10110010	210	11010010	242	11110010
147	10010011	179	10110011	211	11010011	243	11110011
148	10010100	180	10110100	212	11010100	244	11110100
149	10010101	181	10110101	213	11010101	245	11110101
150	10010110	182	10110110	214	11010110	246	11110110
151	10010111	183	10110111	215	11010111	247	11110111
152	10011000	184	10111000	216	11011000	248	11111000
153	10011001	185	10111001	217	11011001	249	11111001
154	10011010	186	10111010	218	11011010	250	11111010
155	10011011	187	10111011	219	11011011	251	11111011
156	10011100	188	10111100	220	11011100	252	11111100
157	10011101	189	10111101	221	11011101	253	11111101
158	10011110	190	10111110	222	11011110	254	11111110
159	10011111	191	10111111	223	11011111	255	11111111

Index

B

E

P

T